CALIFORNIA

Goose Lake

MT. SHASTA

Klamath R.

Pitt R.

Trinity R.

Mad R.

Eel R.

LASSEN

Honey Lake

COAST

Russian R.

Marysville

Lake Tahoe

Sacramento

Santa Rosa

Napa

Vallejo

GREAT VALLEY

San Rafael

Oakland

San Joaquin R.

Stockton

Mono Lake

San Francisco

San Jose

SIERRA

Santa Cruz

KINGS

Pt. Cypress

CANYON

Salinas R.

RANGES

INYO MTS.

SANTA LUCIA RANGE

NEVADA

PANAMINT RANGE

Owens R.

DEATH VALLEY

Cuyama R.

MOJAVE DESERT

Santa Ynez R.

Pt. Conception

Santa Barbara

Santa Rosa I.

Santa Cruz I.

Santa Monica

Pasadena

Los Angeles

Pt. Vincente

Long Beach

Salton Sea

PACIFIC OCEAN

Pt. Loma

San Diego

IMPERIAL VALLEY

MEXICO

EVERYMAN'S EDEN

A History of California

BY

RALPH J. ROSKE

THE MACMILLAN COMPANY, New York

COLLIER-MACMILLAN LTD., London

The Macmillan Company, New York
Collier-Macmillan Canada Ltd., Toronto, Ontario
Printed in the United States of America

Acknowledgments

This attempt to write a general history of California which provides an introduction to the complicated history of America's most populous state has benefited from the help of many persons.

First, I should like to acknowledge the assistance of my editor at The Macmillan Company, Peter V. Ritner, who conceived the idea of this book.

The author gratefully acknowledges the assistance of his colleagues on the Humboldt State College faculty, Dr. James I. McNelis, Dr. Stuart Johnson and Claude G. Albright, who made valuable suggestions. Also, Dr. Sheilagh Brooks and Professor Robert W. Davenport of the Nevada Southern University faculty rendered valuable assistance. Thanks are also due to the staffs of the Humboldt State College Library, Nevada Southern University Library, the Bancroft Library of the University of California at Berkeley, the Henry E. Huntington Library at San Marino, California, and the History Room of the Wells Fargo Bank in San Francisco. Most particularly, I should like to thank Eric Simms and Mrs. Frances H. Purser of the Humboldt State College faculty, who aided me far above the routine call of duty. Richard H. Dillon, noted author and librarian, assisted me in obtaining photographs with which to illustrate this book.

I am indebted to the following persons who typed the manuscript, or who helped in many different ways: Miss Nancy Shirk, Mrs. Ann Pettit, Mrs. Jane Myers, Mr. Walter Savard, Mr. James Stamper, Miss Brenda Morgan, Mr. Leonard Brommers, Miss Angela Divicino, Miss Trina Hornefius and Mr. Fred Williams.

I gratefully acknowledge the help of my wife, Rosemary, and my two sons, Mark and Randall—all of whom helped when emergencies arose.

Finally, despite all this help, I fear that errors have crept into this work, and for them I alone am responsible.

Contents

List of Maps   *ix*

Preface   *xi*

CHAPTER ONE The Setting: California Geography   *1*

CHAPTER TWO The Native Californian (Indian)   *10*

CHAPTER THREE Spanish Background   *18*

CHAPTER FOUR The White Man Discovers California   *31*

CHAPTER FIVE The Exploration Continues   *46*

CHAPTER SIX The First Colonies   *62*

CHAPTER SEVEN California Begins to Grow   *82*

CHAPTER EIGHT Spanish California Flowers   *104*

CHAPTER NINE Foreign Visits and Explorations   *120*

CHAPTER TEN Mexico Takes a Shaky Control   *145*

CHAPTER ELEVEN The Outsiders Arrive in Numbers   *170*

CHAPTER TWELVE The Pioneers: The Vigil of American Rule   *193*

CHAPTER THIRTEEN The United States Hungrily Eyes California   *209*

CHAPTER FOURTEEN The Gold of Ophir   *237*

CHAPTER FIFTEEN California Founds a New Economy   *252*

CHAPTER SIXTEEN California Becomes a State   *261*

CHAPTER SEVENTEEN The New Society   *280*

CHAPTER EIGHTEEN California and the Civil War   *303*

CHAPTER NINETEEN California Land Titles and Frauds   *320*

CHAPTER TWENTY California Society in Post-Gold-Rush Days   *331*

CHAPTER TWENTY-ONE Links to the West   *354*

CHAPTER TWENTY-TWO California: Growing Pains and Social Unrest   *374*

CHAPTER TWENTY-THREE A New Agricultural California Arises   *391*

CHAPTER TWENTY-FOUR The Healthseekers, the Real Estate
    Promoters and the Land Boom   *413*

CHAPTER TWENTY-FIVE The Second-Generation Californians:
    1875–1920   *425*

CHAPTER TWENTY-SIX Political Uprisings: The Progressives   *445*

CHAPTER TWENTY-SEVEN The Ugly Shadows of Racism and
    Labor Unrest   *466*

CHAPTER TWENTY-EIGHT California Rides the Wave of Prosperity   *484*

CHAPTER TWENTY-NINE The Dark Era of the Great Depression   *502*

CHAPTER THIRTY California in World War II   *513*

CHAPTER THIRTY-ONE An Uneasy Peace and Its Problems   *527*

CHAPTER THIRTY-TWO Culture in Contemporary California   *540*

CHAPTER THIRTY-THREE Contemporary California and Its Problems   *560*

Bibliographical Note   *585*

A Note on Sources and Suggestions for Further Reading on
    California History   *587*

Index   *599*

List of Maps

Early Spanish Voyages / 32

Early Expedition Routes of California / 83

Missions, Pueblos, and Presidios of California / 105

Spanish and Mexican Period Land Grants / 168

Main Routes Across Western United States to California / 194

Gold-Rush Period / 238

Land Links from Eastern United States to California / 355

Counties and Cities of California / 528

Preface

CALIFORNIA, land of promise! For centuries California has beckoned to people who journey there to find gold, fame, health or adventure. The riches of California have been a siren song for many. Yet through the years so many immigrants have earned rich rewards that its promises carry the ring of conviction. As a result, all over the globe millions who do not know the name of any other American state regard California with wistful awe.

California is a modern land. In 1769 it was a *tabula rasa*—as yet untouched by European influences. The white man has brought about his vast changes upon the face of this once virgin wilderness in the last two hundred years. Actually, only in the last 120 years has much been done in the way of exploration and settlement. As late as 1940, the atmosphere of southern California was still clear and the smog problem unknown. In his rush to exploit this smiling land, modern man has wrought tremendous changes. Many have been beneficial and have made life in California easier and more pleasant; more have had the opposite effect. In any event, California has seen more immigrants arrive within its boundaries in many single months of the era of modern migration since 1940 than came in the entire Spanish period.

California is big in an age that prizes bigness. Its land area is greater than that of eighty-five individual nations; it houses more people than do 114 sovereign countries.

Yet the ideas of too many people about California are composed of clichés: it is a Spanish California with romantic dons and dedicated missionaries; a Mexican California in which contented rancheros reposed in a pastoral Eden; a gold-rush California with roaring '49ers. Modern California has its own clichés: it is the California of jokes about Anaheim, Azusa and Cucamonga; it is the familiar tale of Hollywood folk who call everybody "baby" and "darling"; it is hedonism rampant in the sun—a sensual paradise. All this has obscured the true California. This book is an attempt to describe California's true history and allure—its wonderful diversity and perpetual change.

EVERYMAN'S EDEN

ONE

The Setting: California Geography

KNOW *the geography* is a maxim applicable to any regional
study. However, in the study of California a knowledge of its
geography is necessary for a thorough understanding of that
state's history. Successive groups of migrants settled the area, and each
developed a culture closely integrated with its climate and land.

California's geography is so different from the eastern half of the
United States that most Americans are able to comprehend this difference
only through experience or study. The eastern portion of the United
States is characterized by a significant uniformity of elevation, nonsea-
sonal precipitation, and a temperature variation largely determined by
latitude. Most eastern states, moreover, are generally uniform in climate
and terrain, while California's geography reveals few uniformities and
fantastic differences.

California, the third largest of the fifty states, has a gross area of 158,-
693 square miles, or 101,563,520 acres, of which 100,313,600 is land
area. This makes California considerably larger than Japan, three times
the size of England, and four times the size of Virginia.

From Oregon to Mexico, in a straight line, California runs for 758
miles. A line from the Oregon coast to the southeastern border point at
the Colorado-Gila river confluence is 828 miles long. California's width
varies from 150 miles between San Francisco and Lake Tahoe, to 257
miles from Point Argüello to Nevada.

California's large land area gives it an advantage over the relatively
small states of the northeastern United States, which are largely incapable

I

of existing as viable geographical units. On the other hand, California's elongated shape is a handicap contrasted with the compact form of Colorado. The detrimental effects of California's outline are largely political, since the state has been divided historically into northern and southern factions. Marked differences in population and climate between northern and southern portions of the state also play their role in this political rivalry.

California's boundaries combine both natural and artificial features. Several are as regular and straight as a surveyor's eye could make them. The northern boundary which separates it from Oregon is the forty-second parallel, set in 1819 by the Adams-Onis Treaty as the farthest extent of Spanish possessions. For the eastern boundary, the Constitutional Convention of 1848 agreed upon 120° west longitude, from the forty-second to the thirty-ninth parallel. The junction of the 120th meridian of west longitude and the thirty-ninth parallel lies in Lake Tahoe. From these, the Constitutional Convention decreed the boundary should be a straight line drawn to that part of the Colorado River which transverses the thirty-fifth parallel. These boundaries proved difficult to trace on the ground. Surveyors until 1899 proved unable to determine accurately California's eastern boundary from Lake Tahoe to the Colorado.

The huge, wiggly gorge cut by the Colorado River has been a poor and often disputed marker between California and Arizona, because in the years since 1849, the river has shifted its bed along two-thirds of the boundary which separates the two states.

The Treaty of Guadalupe-Hidalgo, which established California's southern boundary with Mexico, set the international border from the confluence of the Gila and Colorado rivers to a point set at one marine league (3.45 miles) south of the end of San Diego Bay.

California has a seacoast extending 1,264 miles along the Pacific's shores and spanning nearly ten degrees of latitude. Transferred to the Atlantic seaboard, California's shoreline would extend from Boston to Charleston, South Carolina. The California Current and uncounted years of savage storms have battered the California coastline, which is primarily composed of long, white beaches, although the sand of the northern beaches is darker. Jagged capes, improbable harbors and wildly irregular sand bars complete California's unusual seafront, which is in a state of constant transformation. Each year some of the soft cliffs crumble into the ocean as the shoreline continues to change—wearing away here, building up there. The eastward curve of the southern coast is pronounced and misleading; San Diego lies to the east of more than 90 per cent of the land area of Oregon and Washington and almost half of Nevada. Nevertheless, Eureka in northwestern California is the westernmost city (but not point) of the first forty-eight states.

Lying next to the Pacific Ocean, California benefits from the tempering effect of the prevailing westerly winds and its ideal latitude, almost halfway between the North Pole and the equator, both of which give coastal California a climate enjoyed by only 1 per cent of the earth's land area. Despite California's latitude, the state's coastal temperatures are lower than might be expected because of the cooling effects of north winds and the cold California Current.

Further, California's position on the Pacific Ocean is commercially significant and may become more so as the emerging nations of the Pacific rim advance economically. For example, the Mediterranean, as the focus of the ancient world, gave commercial importance to all countries along its shores. Its importance was replaced by the Atlantic Ocean. If the last quarter of the twentieth century sees the Pacific nations realize their economic potential, California may reap additional benefits from its location.

There are many Californias. Within the state's boundaries are areas where the rainfall is tropical in intensity and white-hot deserts in which the rain rarely falls. Within California stands Mount Whitney, 14,496 feet—the highest point in the continental United States south of Canada. To the east lies Death Valley at Bad Water, 279.6 feet below sea level, the lowest and often the hottest place in the entire United States.

Although most Californians can boast that they have climate without weather, California has always lent itself to hyperbole as the land of the highest peaks, the lowest valleys, the driest deserts, the heaviest snowfalls (well over four hundred inches in the Sierras in some winters), and some of the wettest regions in the United States. In the winter, temperatures in the Sierra fall to thirty degrees below zero, while one of the highest shade temperatures ever recorded was 134°F. at Death Valley in 1913. In fact, California has almost all the physical diversity of the other forty-nine states combined. It contains samples of virtually all geologic processes, despite the fact that by most calculations California is considered to be 300,000,000 years younger than the American east coast. California contains Lassen Peak, 10,543 feet, an active volcano which has had hundreds of minor eruptions, the latest occuring between 1914 and 1917. The peak is best described as quiescent rather than extinct. Were it not for its summer drought, California would also approach the climatic diversity of all the other states. As it is, northwestern California is much like western Washington, while the Mojave is as dry as any desert in Arizona or Nevada, and the high Sierra can be as cold as arctic Alaska.

California's soils, a by-product of the state's botanic, climatic, and geologic diversity, amount to more than five hundred distinctive types. The variety of soils is so great that the state has become one of the world's great laboratories for the study of soil formation and reaction processes. During the nineteenth century, the soils of California were a matter of consternation to scientists, since they did not fit existing scientific classifications.

Relatively speaking, California contains excellent, deep, fertile soil. Yet its good arable soil equals only 15 per cent of the land area. Most of this highly productive land lies within the rainfall-deficient region. The steep slopes of the Sierra Nevada range area produce soils which are shallow and generally unfavorable for agriculture. Where the slopes are gentle and the land is flat, as in the Central Valley, soils are deeper and productivity generally greater.

California also possesses great mineral wealth. More than seven hundred different minerals have been identified in its soil—including some forty-six that are not known to occur anywhere else in the world. Over thirty useful minerals are mined in some quantity. California lacks only good deposits of iron ore and coal. The lack of coal today is not as vital as in earlier times because of the development of the state's petroleum industry.

Apart from its coastline, California's principal surface features are the two mountain chains that run nearly the length of the state and the vast Central Valley—really two valleys, the Sacramento and the San Joaquin —which lies between them. The Central Valley is the largest arable area west of the Sierra Nevada chain. It is a great oblong bowl stretching about 430 miles from Shasta Lake to its southern terminus near Bakersfield. This is equivalent to the distance it would take to travel in a straight line across eight eastern states from Portland, Maine, to Ocean City, Maryland. The Central Valley is almost fifty miles in width, bulging to its widest point just below the city of Fresno. As the heart of the most intensively cultivated and richest agricultural region in the world, the valley is literally a giant outdoor hothouse which raises a billion-dollar crop of fruit and vegetables which are sent throughout the year to every corner of America.

To the west of the Central Valley is the mountain complex rising from the sea which terminates the continent. The coast ranges extend from the area north of Eureka down into Santa Barbara County, while to the north and south of them are jumbled mountain masses which are not, strictly speaking, part of the coast ranges themselves. Although the coastal ranges rise in places to over eight thousand feet, most of the peaks are generally low, between three and four thousand feet in elevation.

To the east of the Central Valley, the Sierra Nevada range stands as a majestic rampart far taller than the coastal ranges. For miles the crest of this mountain chain seldom dips below seven thousand feet; over fifty peaks rise to at least 10,000 feet, while approximately a dozen mountain tops push skyward for more than 14,000 feet. As masses of air push eastward into California, they bump into the Sierra, where they must yield their precipitation before drifting over into Nevada. As a result, much of Nevada's share of precipitation is given as ransom to California before the former state can claim it. The Sierra is a snowy range; a snowfall as high as 884 inches has been recorded there. Thus the Sierra range performs the very necessary function of water-gatherer for California. Without this great granitic bastion, California's economic development would have been dramatically different.

California's rainfall presents a problem. The coast's weather begins generally in the Gulf of Alaska, sweeping down to the south and east across coastal Washington and Oregon. Only the larger storms lash the Pacific coast as far south as California. Thus from the north California gets only the leavings of rainstorms after Washington and Oregon have been drenched. If Colonel J. W. Powell's famous definition of an arid region is valid—one with less than twenty inches of annual rainfall—California as a whole is an arid state. Yet the rainfall varies widely. In the north, where the Hawaiian (Pacific) High Pressure Area exerts much less influence than it does farther south, the rainfall tends to be heavier and the wet season longer. Generally, precipitation decreases southeast of the California-Oregon coastal junction. Crescent City reports an average rainfall of seventy-four inches, Eureka, thirty-nine, and San Francisco, twenty-two. Rain falls on twice as many days in Eureka as it does in San Francisco. In the central California city of San Luis Obispo, the precipitation decreases to an annual total of nineteen inches. At Los Angeles it falls off to fifteen inches, and at San Diego, averages less than five inches annually.

Yet average figures fail to tell the complete story of California's weather, for there is tremendous annual variation. Honeydew, in the Mattole Valley of Humboldt County, recorded 174 inches of rain in the winter of 1957–58. In 1850 Sacramento received thirty-six inches of rain, but only 4.71 inches in 1851. Hence the rainfall in California has been known to vary sevenfold from year to year! In the approximately 110 years of recorded rainfall totals in the state, dry cycles appear every thirty years and last about seven years.

Although contemporary California is foremost in population and agricultural output among the fifty states, it is still often thought of as clad in its "natural" vegetation, since only 14 per cent of California is urbanized or tilled. Yet, in another sense, it is hard to locate land where the vegetation has not been altered. European immigrants, such as wild oats, alfilaria, mustard and bur clover, today give character to the California grasslands. And in truth, if one would discover what southern California's original plants and soil profiles looked like, he could see them more easily in Baja California than within the state.

In California there is a strong correlation between climate and plant distribution; green forests stand in the northwest, and desert shrubs grow in the southeast. Most of California is botanically and climatically inter-mediate and reveals a great mixture of trees, grasses and shrubs. The varied climate of the state supports almost every shrub, herb or tree that grows in the temperate zone, as well as many tropical forms of vegetation.

Wildlife in the state has been greatly depleted since 1848, when exten-sive immigration began. The Indians and Spaniards caused only minor changes in the state's wildlife, but the Americans killed recklessly, even purposelessly, so that by the beginning of the twentieth century, game was greatly reduced. Since then, under the control of an effective organi-zation which later became the state Department of Fish and Game, the slaughter of wild animals has been effectually diminished. Today there are rigid regulations concerning what may be hunted, and when and where. Consequently, some game species have increased, and hunters, game officials and conservationists frequently engage in controversies over more stringent laws for the preservation of wildlife. One theory reports that there are still about six hundred kinds of birds in the state and nearly four hundred species of mammals—from the horned toad to the coyote, elk and deer. Nevertheless, indiscriminate killing has taken its toll. The distinctive California grizzly bear, so much in evidence in the early history of the state, is now extinct, and there are few sea otter left. The California condor, perhaps the largest land bird in North America, which prospered during the Spanish-Mexican days when it feasted on abundant cattle carcasses, now has almost disappeared; only fifty-one were counted at the end of 1966, although it is strictly protected by game laws. Despite the fact that some species of wildlife have vanished, greatly upsetting the balance between the species, hunting and fishing are still popular sports, although they are under strict state supervision.

Contrary to its appearance, the earth's crust is not a stable platform. Throughout the world each year, there are approximately 56,000 earth tremors of all types, some of them noticeable only on seismographs. About 85 to 90 per cent of all earthquakes in the United States each year occur in California's restless earth. Since the coming of the Spaniard in 1769, it has been estimated that about five thousand earthquakes have shaken California and Nevada annually. The vast majority of these tremors are insignificant, but California does average one earthquake of destructive magnitude each year. In the famous earthquake of 1906, the average earth displacement was six to eight feet and in at least one case a twenty-two-foot displacement occurred in about one minute.

Why does the earth move? In any individual case, this is difficult to determine. In general, the following factors are present: forces in the earth's interior, redistribution of the earth's surface load, tidal forces of the sun and moon, and energy generated by the earth's rotation.

California's landscape is traversed by innumerable faults (crustal fractures) that vary in length from a few hundred feet to hundreds of miles. They also vary as to their depth in the earth. According to various computations, there are ten to thirteen major fault groups. The greatest of these is the San Andreas, so named for its passage over St. Andrews Lake, located near South San Francisco. This rift, over a thousand miles long, extends from Point Arena above San Francisco through that city's ocean front down into central California, and finally into the Salton Sink of southern California. Some scientists have speculated that it extends north of Point Arena into the Pacific Ocean and originates in the Mendocino Escarpment off Cape Mendocino.

In the historical period, California has experienced many damaging earthquakes. In 1812, a tremor destroyed the San Juan Capistrano Mission. Other quakes hit southern California in 1857, Owens Valley in 1870, San Francisco in 1906, Santa Barbara in 1925, Long Beach in 1933, and still another damaged Tehachapi in 1952. In 1957 San Francisco experienced a mild 5.3 Richter-scale shake. Only those of 1857, 1872 and 1906, however, rank as monster quakes. That of 1906 has been rated as an 8.3 tremblor on the Richter scale.

In January 1967 a rash of minor earthquakes jarred coastal areas southwest of Los Angeles. The tremors—at least thirteen in number—at their worst registered somewhat over 4 on the Richter scale. This was enough to alarm inhabitants in the Redondo Beach and Palos Verdes Estates region, but did not cause substantial property damage. Also in late April 1968 a rolling earthquake centered ten miles southeast of Santa Rosa, measuring 4.8 on the Richter scale (a moderate tremor), shook the Bay area. It caused little damage, but grimly reminded Californians of the continuing earthquake threat.

The most severe tremor that has been measured in California happened in 1872, when the Sierra Nevada showed an eight-foot uplift along a fault. A horizontal displacement of nearly twenty feet seemed to have occurred, as evidenced by broken fences. The shock of this massive earthquake was felt in the entire state. At the nearby town of Lone Pine, twenty-five of the 275 inhabitants were killed, and fifty-two of the town's fifty-nine structures destroyed.

The Golden State has suffered at intervals from so-called tidal waves, or more accurately, seismic sea waves, which are associated with earthquakes. These waves, often known by the Japanese term *tsunamis*, are actually unrelated to tidal action. Developing from earth tremors, they travel as unseen energy impulses through the water at 470 miles per hour. On December 21, 1812, the largest recorded seismic sea wave, estimated at fifty feet, struck the California coast near Gaviota. The most recent severe *tsunamis* struck the northwest California coast in the spring of 1964. On Good Friday afternoon of that year, an earthquake in Alaska, originating thirty to sixty miles beneath the surface of Prince William Sound, devastated Anchorage. The quake, which may have been more severe than the one which ravaged San Francisco in 1906, set in motion a tidal wave that dashed against the California coast at Crescent City. There a twelve-foot wave swept over four downtown blocks, shattering some one hundred fifty structures, killing at least ten inhabitants and causing fifty other people to be listed as missing. In addition, approximately ninety persons were injured severely enough to require medical treatment. In general, however, the state's relatively shallow coastline has prevented frequent damage from tidal waves.

Until very recently, California has been isolated. The high Sierra Nevada range, while a blessing to California in many ways, has blocked easy access from the east. From the west the mountain range is deceptive, sloping gently upward for many miles; but from the east, its 14,000-foot peaks, frowning, almost impenetrable, present a formidable barrier with only a few good passes, and even these are often blocked by snow. Not many years ago, an entire train was trapped in the Sierra's drifts, and in 1843, even the intrepid John C. Frémont and his group of hardy mountain men almost died of cold and starvation in the deep snows of this range. In southeast California there are two passes to the coastal plain, lower in elevation than those of the Sierra, but the parched desert which must be crossed on the passage west discouraged much traffic through these passes until the modern period. From the south, a land link with Mexico crosses rough arid regions, making this journey too difficult to be routine.

By sea, the approach to California from Mexico and Central America was greatly impeded by head winds which often drove Spanish ships miles off their course into the Pacific. Only by skillful, patient tacking and beating to windward could the small vessels of the sixteenth and seventeenth centuries bear northward. The rocky, foggy California coast made exploration hazardous. In addition, Alta California (as the Spaniards styled the area of the present state) had only three excellent natural harbors: San Diego Bay; San Francisco Bay, which the Spaniards discovered two hundred years after they had first sighted the state's coastline; and Humboldt Bay in the north, which the Spaniards never utilized because of geographic obstacles.

Alta California remained unoccupied for more than two hundred years after its first discovery. The Spaniards despaired of ever making much of this seemingly cold, inaccessible region. They seriously debated leaving the land to be occupied by the halting Russian advance down the Pacific coast from Alaska. Even after its settlement by the Spanish, California continued as a marginal colony, with no regular land link with Mexico. This isolation from the rest of the North American continent persisted until 1869, when the first transcontinental railroad was completed. Until then, Hawaii, or even China, was economically closer to California than New York City. The opening in 1914 of the Panama Canal made the sea route to the American east coast substantially shorter. Yet it remained for the automobile and finally jet aircraft to make a Californian's journey to the East Coast relatively quick and easy, although still not an inexpensive experience.

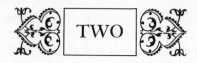

TWO

The Native Californian (Indian)

D ESPITE modern research techniques, uncertainty still persists about where and when prehistoric man first established himself in California. A British anthropologist, Dr. Louis B. Leakey, announced in July 1961 his discovery in East Africa of fossil remains of a man judged to be 1,750,000 years old. Later finds have pushed the possible date of early man back even further into the dark shadows of the past. Although scientists have long been reluctant to ascribe such antiquity to man in the New World, recent discoveries have verified man's presence earlier than was believed even a few years back. Some experts now theorize that man might have occupied the New World as long ago as 30,000 years. Although there is no concrete evidence that man has dwelt that long on the Pacific slope, Carbon 14 studies of some sandals found in an Oregon cave indicate that they are approximately 9,000 years old. It is now widely believed that man occupied California's area for thousands of years longer than we have any historical record.

There is general agreement that the prehistoric Californians were men of Asiatic origin who crossed into North America by way of the Bering Straits, probably during the last great Ice Age 15,000 to 30,000 years ago when a land bridge existed between the two continents. These migrations may have continued into relatively recent times. While the possibility of a few trans-Pacific crossings cannot be dismissed, they must have been few, late and unimportant.

By estimating the time necessary for languages to split off from their common ancestral tongue and become separate dialects—glottochronol-ogy—the noted anthropologist A. L. Kroeber, about forty years ago, suggested four periods of settlement by the California Indians. According to Kroeber's theory, in the first period, lasting for an indeterminate number of years until 500 B.C., a group of Hokan-speaking Indians lived undisturbed in their possession of California. The second period of set-tlement began about 500 B.C., with the migration of several tribes from the east. By A.D. 500, the different cultures of the California Indians had become pronounced. In the last period, which began about A.D. 1200, the Indians had established themselves in the various patterns of occupancy discovered by the Spaniards when they arrived. Unfortunately, this theory of Indian occupancy today has been placed in serious doubt by the recent discovery of archaeological evidence and no generally accepted theory has replaced it.

Within the area of California lived an unusually great number of In-dians, who varied among themselves to some extent in appearance, differed quite considerably in language, but possessed in common many fundamental cultural attributes. Favorable geographical environment al-lowed a sizable number of inhabitants, since California was a land well suited to primitive living. The climate was generally mild and native food occurred in both variety and abundance. In addition, raw material from which to make tools and equipment abounded. The number of Indians has been estimated from 133,000 to a high of 250,000 at the time of the beginning of white contact. Even if the lower figure is accepted, the number of native inhabitants of California would still contrast strongly with comparative thinness of population found in most other areas of Anglo-America. California, with about 5 per cent of the total land area, contained perhaps 13 per cent of the Indians, a density some three to four times that of the rest of North America north of the Rio Grande. The Indian population was not evenly distributed over the present area of the state. The coastal belt and the lower courses of the large rivers were thickly settled. Population tapered off markedly in arid or mountainous regions. Nonetheless, the California Indians may have had the greatest population density of any nonagricultural area in the world.

California Indians possessed a number of physical traits in common. They all had black, coarse straight hair, deep brown eyes, a brownish (not red) skin coloring, and heavy, broad faces. In features such as nose form, head structure and stature they displayed extreme variability. Cali-fornia Indians showed pronounced contrasts in nose form. Also, practi-cally all the variations in head form found among American aborigines were present within the state. California Indians had examples such as the tallest (Mohave) and the shortest (Yuki) people found among North American Indians.

Far more exceptional than the numbers of physical differences among the California Indians was the amazing diversity in language. Of the six North American linguistic "superstocks" classified by some anthropologists, five are represented in California. The Athabascan spoke a language much like that spoken in northwestern Canada and by the Navajo and Apache of southwestern United States. Penutian had several related tongues in Mexico. Shoshonean was similar to the languages of the Great Basin. In addition, there were two independent linguistic groups—the Yukian, probably found only in California, and the Lutuomian, native to California and Oregon. These seven basic tongues may be broken into at least twenty-one linguistic groups, which can be further subdivided into possibly 135 idioms and dialects. As a result, it seems unlikely that a native twenty miles from his group could converse with his neighbor. Some Indian tongues were as disparate as Chinese is from Greek. Only part of the Sudan and the island of New Guinea offer as much language diversity in an area of comparable size.

Indian civilization in the New World reached a high degree of development in Peru, Yucatán and highland Mexico. North and south of this general area there was a gradual shading off from this high civilization. Above the Rio Grande, the people of the north and west generally had a more simple culture than those of the south and east. The great exception to this rule of thumb was the northwest coastal culture area from British Columbia southward.

Some anthropologists have divided North American Indians into ten great cultural areas. Most of California is included in one of these divisions. While the California area is not synonymous with the political borders of the present state, it is reasonably close. Many experts feel that the area east of the Sierra Nevada is better included with the Great Basin culture area. A number of scientists would also exclude from the California culture complex the agricultural tribes of the Colorado River, classifying them with the agglomerations of the southwest culture area. Some anthropologists would also exclude the northwestern California coastal Indians, believing that they should more properly be lumped with the natives of the Pacific northwest area. On the other hand, other anthropologists would not only retain these northwest California Indians in the state's culture area, but would add those to southwest Oregon as well. Other experts would add at least the northern Baja California Indians to the California culture complex.

The California culture area, excluding the Colorado River Valley tribes, exhibited a basic uniformity in economy, material goods, religion and social organization. Most of the Indians' food was derived from the gathering of the products of wild plants. Only the Indians of the lower Colorado practiced agriculture. This absence of farming in a large region of gentle climate has been attributed by thoughtless observers to the sufficiency of wild food supplies and the cultural backwardness of the natives. It would seem that lack of contact with the agricultural peoples of the Colorado River area would not account for this condition since the southern California Indians did have some contact with them. Nor does it appear likely that the Indians of the California cultural area would have failed to experiment with the crops grown by the Colorado River groups.

Westward diffusion of agriculture, as the eminent geographer Carl Sauer suggests, was prevented more by environment than cultural forces. The available crops simply had small prospect of success in the winter-rain region. Indian corn and squash, in particular, were excluded by the seasonal character of the rain. Even beans were ruled out as a staple by the same conditions. California, as a land of essentially Mediterranean climate, had to wait for agricultural development until the transfer of European Mediterranean-type crops. Credence for this theory is gained from a look at the other great winter-rain region, southern and central Chile. There Indian agriculture only flourished with the cultivation of the potato, a crop unavailable to the California natives.

Minimizing the possibility of famine, the subsistence base of the California Indians was rather broad, resting as it did upon a wide variety of fauna and flora. Local emphasis shifted according to the available resources. The desert Indians found life more difficult, while the coastal Indians of northwestern California enjoyed a life of relative ease.

Since oak trees grew over a wide area in California, the acorn was the major staple in all nondesert areas. The Indians may not have been purely passive gatherers of the acorn, for Carl Sauer has intimated that the park-like stands of oak found in predominately grassy country were probably not climatically determined. Instead, the Indians could have engaged in a customary burning of the land that restricted the spread of the forests. The Indians *may* have actively protected their food supply, thus changing their environment.

Acorns contain oil, but little protein. One of the components of acorns is tannin, an astringent and glucoside, which has to be removed before eating by an elaborate grinding and leaching process. By the end of their preparation of the acorn, the Californians had reduced it to a flour or boiled it into a soup or mush.

In the desert areas, the Indians' subsistence base rested upon pine nuts, mesquite, other xerophytic plants and a variety of seeds. Other Indian foods included seasonal plants such as buckeye, manzanita berries, wild raspberries, plums, grapes, elderberries, huckleberries, barberries, thimbleberries, peppermint, sunflowers, wild oats, wild onions, spearmint, clover and cat's ears. Some of these foods were dried and stored. Using earth ovens, the Indians roasted the roots of the tiger lily, anise, camass and brodiaea.

In northwestern California, the Indians' diet depended almost as much upon salmon as upon acorns. Actually many California rivers carry salmon, but the really heavy runs occur only north of Cape Mendocino. As a result, there were many small villages in this area close to the fishing stations along the riverbanks. Some groups of Indians considered these fishing stations private property. Trespassers were distinctly unwelcome. Surprisingly, the catching of fish by poison, which would disable the fish and make them an easy prey, was practiced by the less advanced Indian groups, not the most advanced. The Chumash of coastal central California also gathered shellfish and hunted sea mammals from canoes. Around the interior lakes such as Clear Lake, the Indians lived principally upon the abundant waterfowl and fish. They literally lived off the land. With few exceptions, they caught and ate anything that crept, wriggled or crawled. Deer were universally hunted where the Indians' weapons—small bows and arrows and flint-tipped lances—could kill them. In addition, they burrowed for rodents, snared birds and shot them with specially designed arrows, and often hunted small game such as rabbits. The Californians ate earthworms, grasshoppers and caterpillars, while some captured locusts, which they parched and served as a delicacy. For some reason, the natives never ate snakes or frogs.

California Indians did not require much clothing. Most men and the children went naked as long as the weather permitted it. On their feet the men wore rude moccasins or sandals. Cold weather in the higher elevations sometimes forced the Californians to wear deerskin or rabbit capes, or other animal-skin blankets. Generally the women wore more concealing dress than did the men. In some areas they wore an apron of animal skin, from cottontails, jack rabbits or squirrels. Women often used Indian hemp to string the skins together. In other regions, the adult females made skirts of tule grass; in cold weather they often wore capes or cloaks similar to those worn by the men.

The California Indians' material culture was not elaborate. Generally the state's aborigines constructed single-family dwellings of rather simple design. In northwestern California, the Indians built gabled plank houses. Where trees were less common than in northwestern California, brush houses of varying ornateness were commonly built. Many groups in southern California lived in tule-thatched huts that resembled half an orange.

It was only in basket weaving that the California Indians displayed exceptional aptitude. Other types of handicraft were poorly developed. Art was expressed mostly in geometric designs applied to household articles.

Religious practices that were shared by nearly all California Indians were elaborate observances for girls arriving at puberty and ceremonial dances for war. Other nearly universal rituals included group ceremonies, which were often enactments of legendary events. The shamans or witch doctors were the foremost men of religion. Shamans attempted to cure disease and engaged in rain-making ceremonies. Witchcraft was widely accepted as a fact of life. Indeed, witchcraft troubled the California natives more than it did those who lived in other parts of the North American continent.

Since the California Indian was relatively isolated in his own language group, he tended to be provincial. The smallest cohesive unit in Indian life was the extended family. Two or more extended families related through the male line might constitute a small village, styled by the Spanish a *rancheria*. The next largest political unit, which was not universally present, was the tribelet. It consisted of one main settlement and several minor outlying hamlets. It has been estimated that there may have been 250 tribelets in California at the time of the coming of the white men. Larger tribes have been described by some observers, but they were really ethnolinguistic divisions, not political entities. The tribal organization common in other parts of North America was lacking.

Although the California Indians were among the most peace-loving Indians on the North American continent, this did not mean the total absence of conflict among them. Most hostilities occurred between small parties or villages. Tribelets occasionally clashed, however, and when they did, it may accurately be called war. They fought for diverse reasons: revenge of violence, revenge of witchcraft (in which the California Indians were strong believers) or disputes over the use of productive land areas. War leaders might be civil leaders, or temporary or permanent leaders particularly chosen for that purpose. Surprise attacks were the rule, but occasionally some prearranged contests occurred. The more formal contests usually stopped when a single prominent man on either side had been killed. Whole heads and sometimes other parts of the body were taken as trophies. Interestingly, in all of the California culture areas there were no special weapons other than the tools of everyday life. Only the Colorado River Indians (probably constituting part of another culture division) possessed a special weapon of war—the club.

Some Shoshonean Indians kept the custom of verbal wars. When individuals or even whole families could not get along, a feud might develop, expressed relatively harmlessly as a war of songs (generally insulting and obscene) composed and sung against the opposing party. Occasionally the chanting groups would stamp their feet on the ground to express the pleasure they would derive from trampling upon their enemies' graves. This war of song could last a week or even longer.

The Indian vitally affected the pattern of Spanish and American exploration and settlement of California. The white explorers reconnoitered an Indian country, using native guides between Indian settlements.

Routes of movement and places of settlement were determined in the main by the previous experience of the Indians. Spanish missionaries ordinarily went to places where there were Indians—customarily to the principal settlement of the tribelet. Although the influx of mission settlements greatly reduced the number of native communities, those chosen as mission sites were enlarged and developed. Rarely did the missions mean new foundations.

California Indians suffered much from the white man's diseases and violence during the historical period. The Spaniards arrived in relatively small numbers and did not traverse all the state. However, when the Americans, lured by the glint of gold, reached California they arrived by the hundreds of thousands, systematically searching every portion of the state in their quest for the precious metal. With the appearance of the first Europeans, the Indians, lacking an immunity to many of the white man's diseases and with only a primitive ability to combat them, suffered a dramatic increase in their death rate. In the barracks society of the Americans during the gold-rush era, Indian women were singled out for exploitation by the newcomers. As a result, in the first twenty years after the Marshall gold strike, venereal diseases accounted for from 40 to 80 per cent of all Indian deaths. Measles, smallpox, chicken pox, tuberculosis, malaria, typhoid, pneumonia, and dysentery also took their toll of a population that had no immunity to these common diseases.

Moreover, the Americans reduced the number of Indians by violence. To the Americans the natives were at best a nuisance, and at worst a menace. The Spaniards and Mexicans, it is true, were guilty of individual savage acts against the Indians, but the smallness of their numbers, combined with the fact that most of them were men rigidly subject to religious and civil authority, reduced the number of atrocities. To the Spanish and Mexican authorities there was an important place for the Indian in their California. There was no comparable role for the Indian in American California. Not that Indian labor was wholly undesired, for the demand for domestic servants during the gold rush was heavy; a law that remained on the statute books for years provided that an Indian could be indentured by a white man. Between 1852 and 1867, at least three thousand Indian children were legally so bound to service. Many more were simply impressed into servitude. Americans cleared the land, as they had need to, by direct violence. In the small but bloody wars of the 1860's and 1870's, the military power of the Indians was utterly broken.

By 1834, when the mission period ended, the population of the California Indians had probably declined by one-fifth. Cast upon their own resources after having been wards of the church, most mission Indians had difficulty making their way in the world. Their total count declined to 100,000 by 1849. In just seven more years, under the pressure of the exploding population of gold seekers, the Indians numbered only 50,000. This decline continued until the number of Indians enrolled in the census of 1900 reached a mere 15,500. By that time the Indian was more of a curiosity than a menace, and by active attempts to aid him, his numbers have gradually increased until the census of 1960 counted 39,000 Indians.

Today Los Angeles County ranks first in the enumeration of Indian residents. San Diego County to the south and Humboldt County in the northwest are next. The southern California counties have many non-California Indians such as the Hopi and Navajo who now make that area their home. The Humboldt County Indians are almost all indigenous—most notably the Hupa, Yurok and Karok.

THREE

Spanish Background

CALIFORNIA'S discovery by Europe occurred when Christopher Columbus sailed westward in August 1492, seeking a short cut to the Far East. His accidental discovery of what proved to be a New World quickly put Spain in a position to exploit the new territory. Other nations were left behind in the race to claim new possessions.

From 1492 to 1607—some 115 years—except for the Portugese presence in Brazil, Spain had the New World to herself so far as permanent settlements were concerned. As we shall see, the French, Dutch and English all harassed Spain before they themselves permanently settled the New World, but they could not prevent her from conquering where she willed during this period.

Spain did not permanently settle California until 1769, 277 years after her arrival in the New World. Thus a mature, even senile, colonial power finally occupied California. But Spain had well-developed colonial institutions and proven colonial techniques.

In 1492, Spain, although a major European power, lacked even the most basic characteristics of nationality, such as a common language, a literature of significance, and religious unity (the Moors and Jews were both present in some numbers). Another extremely serious deficiency from which Spain suffered was the absence of a seafaring tradition. The Spaniards, with the exception of the Barcelonese, had almost an aversion for nautical life. Furthermore, the Spanish lacked an adequate military or naval establishment for overseas adventure. All that Spain really possessed was the personal union between Ferdinand of Aragon and Isabella of Castile and the spirit of conquest whetted by the Spanish victory over the Moors at Granada in 1492.

Although Columbus' discovery was first considered an annoyance—a screen of land blocking off the rich countries of the East—the new lands soon sparked the curiosity and imagination of the Spaniards. The four voyages of Columbus, in addition to the explorations of several of his contemporaries in the service of Spain, pushed the boundary of the known lands to the shores of the Caribbean Sea. In the next thirty years, Spanish navigators mapped the eastern coastline of both North and South America. The Magellan expedition revealed how remote South America really was from the fabled Spice Islands—that group forming the eastern-most division of the Malay archipelago, also styled the Moluccas.

Actual colonization of the New World began with Columbus' genera-tion. The island of Haiti, called Española, was occupied during the years 1493–1508, and for a fifteen-year period was the only Spanish settlement in the New World. Haiti was the laboratory wherein the Spanish colonial institutions evolved, and it served as the base for further colonization. Hence it has been called the "Mother of America."

Among the colonial institutions developed by the Spanish were boards and councils. They also instituted the titles and powers of colonial administrators, the relationship between church and state in the New World, and the official Spanish policy toward the Indians. In theory the official attitude was kind, but in practice, the desire to exploit the Indians economically rendered it more merciless.

Between 1508 and 1511 the Spaniards established settlements on the is-lands of Jamaica, Cuba and Puerto Rico. Diego Columbus, son of the great navigator, was appointed governor of Haiti in 1508. When he de-cided to conquer Cuba, he picked as leader of the expedition Diego Velásquez, who had become one of the wealthiest and most esteemed old settlers in the New World. Velásquez's conquest of Cuba is important to the California story because his victories there ultimately led to the or-ganization of Hernando Cortés' expedition to Mexico.

As one of Cortés' followers has described him, the great conquistador was well proportioned and very athletic, although a bit bowlegged. He was proficient in the use of all known weapons, whether ahorse or on foot. As befitted a former university student, he knew some Latin. More sensitive than most conquistadors, he could write passable poetry. Greatly feared by his men, he was also trusted. He could be cruel, even brutal, but he still conducted himself with the high manners of old Spanish chivalry. Above all, he possessed the gift of making correct practical judgments, and he had the courage to carry out his decisions, despite all difficulties. Outwardly religious, Cortés always spoke and acted as if God were on his side. His dispatches to the King were written in vivid reportorial style.

Cortés was born in Medellín, Estremadura, in 1485. He studied law at the University of Salamanca, although he dropped out after two years. Cortés was always quarrelsome, mischievous, and haughty—traits that won him a legion of determined enemies. He migrated from Spain to the Caribbean islands in 1504, when he was about nineteen. There he turned to ranching and mining on the islands of Haiti and Cuba.

When he was thirty-three, stirred by reports of golden cities in the Mexican interior, he resolved to lead an expedition there. The governor of Cuba, Velásquez, had already sent his cousin Juan de Grijalba (Grijalva) on an expedition to Mexico, but Grijalba was extremely timid and accomplished little. Determined to try a bolder man, Velásquez turned to Cortés. Cortés quickly organized a private expedition of eleven vessels, perhaps 508 soldiers and 109 seamen, in addition to two hundred Cuban Indians and two previously captured Mayan Indians. Although both horses and cannon were scarce in Cuba, Cortés found at least sixteen horses, ten bronzed fieldpieces, and four falconets. Since the Mexican Indians were greatly intimidated by horses and cannon, he could have used more of both supplies.

As Cortés organized and equipped this force, he demonstrated sufficient ability so that Velásquez quickly became suspicious and jealous of him. As a result, Cortés shipped out of Santiago harbor in November 1518. Secretly he recruited additional men, obtained additional supplies in the western Cuban ports, and in February 1519 boldly sailed for Mexico.

Cortés journeyed up the Mexican coast where he founded the first Spanish city in Mexico, Villa Rica de la Vera Cruz, in June 1519. Here he secretly scuttled his ships to prevent desertion and to force his men to fight harder. Their ships gone, the Spanish soldiers were compelled to realize that the alternatives to victory would be death in battle or capture by the Aztecs, who practiced human sacrifice by stretching their victims on an altar and cutting out their beating hearts. Cortés was encouraged when he heard that the powerful but despotic Aztec confederacy was torn with dissension, and that several subject tribes seemed ready to rebel if Cortés appeared among them.

The war chief and emperor of the Aztec Federation, Montezuma, had heard of earlier Spanish explorations along his coast, and he learned quickly of Cortés' presence. He worried that Quetzalcoatl, the "Fair God" of the subject Nahua groups' legend, had returned in the white castles of the sea to reclaim his captive people. Montezuma sent messengers with rich gifts to Cortés in an attempt to persuade him to leave Mexico peacefully. Each gift only intensified the Spaniards' avarice. On August 31, 1519, leaving behind a garrison of 150 men to guard the port of Vera Cruz, Cortés and many Indian allies started the inland march to the Aztec capital of Tenochtitlán. This islandlike city was connected to the mainland by three long causeways and contained an estimated 270,000 people. Cortés and Montezuma met face to face on November 8, 1519, on the shores of Lake Texcoco, which surrounded the city. The two leaders of the forces of the Old and New Worlds met as equals. Then the Aztecs and Spaniards marched together over the great causeway into Tenochtitlán, an imposing city of gleaming towers and buildings of solid masonry. The Spaniards gaped at the wondrous treasures of the city, no less than at the "filthy" priests who offered the blood sacrifices of the Aztecs and stank "like sulphur" and smelled "like carrion."

Montezuma, whose uncertainty sapped the Aztec will to resist the intruders, welcomed the Spaniards and gave them his own castle as their quarters. Soon Cortés, feeling insecure since he had left most of his Indian allies outside the city, seized Montezuma and made him his hostage.

Soon danger approached from a new quarter. Choleric Governor Velásquez, back in Cuba, decided to send a force under the experienced leader Pánfilo de Narváez to arrest Cortés. In May 1520, the wily Cortés made a quick foray to the seacoast to neutralize this threatening force of approximately one thousand Spaniards. After a brief battle, Narváez lost his eye to a pike thrust and his army to Cortés, who had convinced most of Narváez's men to join him. The contumacious Cortés sent Narváez to Vera Cruz in irons.

Cortés marched back to Tenochtitlán, where he found the Aztecs ominously cool to him. He had left Pedro de Alvarado in charge, a handsome, athletic swashbuckler with curly red hair, who was called by the Indians "Sunlight" or "Child of the Sun." Alvarado was a stout and prudent soldier, but displayed a dark streak of vengeance when upset. Under the strain of the tense situation, Alvarado had by force dispersed the Aztecs while they were attempting to celebrate a dancing festival. In the wild melee, several hundred Indians lost their lives. As a result, an air of brooding hung over Tenochtitlán, and although Cortés rebuked Alvarado, he could not undo the damage. The Indians withheld food and water from the Spaniards. Although Montezuma still sulked as a captive in Spanish headquarters, the Aztecs had selected a new chief, who rallied them to rid the capital of the now-hated Spaniards. The hostile Indians had the Spaniards under a veritable siege. The Aztec warriors were formidable fighters. Although they had no iron, they were expert archers and fought skillfully with double-edged obsidian knives mounted on clubs. The luckless Montezuma was sent out on the palace roof by the Spaniards to calm his people, only to be greeted by a shower of stones. He fell, wounded in the forehead, and died several days later from injuries and mortification.

Cortés, now throughly alarmed, decided to steal out of the city under cover of night along the western causeway. This was the shortest route, being only two miles long; however, it was breached in several places and was only eight horses wide. To overcome these obstacles, Cortés had secretly built a portable bridge to help his men cross over the gaps in the causeway. On the dark, rainy night of June 30, 1520, a silent parade of Spaniards, led by Cortés, stole out of the palace and crept along the streets. Suddenly a woman's shriek pierced the darkness. Booming drums aroused the Aztecs, who swarmed down screaming war cries to attack the retreating Spaniards. The bridge proved to be useful in surmounting the first gap, but it stuck fast and could not be moved in the midst of the fierce attacks of the Aztecs. Many of the retreating Spaniards, especially the latecomers from Cuba, were heavily laden with Aztec loot, which fatally slowed their escape. It proved to be an even greater handicap when the Spaniards had to negotiate the gaps in the causeway. Many greedy soldiers fell heavily into the water, only to sink from sight, pulled down by the weight of their booty. Other fallen Spaniards were seized and carried off to the sacrifical altars. A small group of retreating Spaniards (Alvarado's men) were able to escape by passing over the bodies of their comrades, which seemed literally to bridge the gaps in the causeway. Along with the men, valuable equipment, cannons and horses all sank beneath the waves of the lake. According to some accounts, Cortés' impetuous lieutenant Alvarado escaped when he made a spectacular vault over a gap in the causeway, using his lance as a pole. This leap became famous as "El Salto de Alvarado." Fighting valiantly, the Spaniards did cut their way through the causeway, although it took them four hours to go the two miles.

The cost of "La Noche Triste," as this night became known, was heavy. In the morning when Cortés saw the tattered remnants of his force, he is said to have wept bitterly. Although he had saved most of his lieutenants, his two best interpreters, a ship's carpenter and some of his Indian allies, he had only twenty-three cavalrymen left and had lost many of his 1300 footsoldiers. No exact count was kept of the losses, but perhaps two-thirds of the Spaniards—some eight hundred men—were lost to Aztec weapons or sacrificial altars.

Cortés was not yet safe; he had to fight off other Aztec armies until he reached the safety of his Indian allies. If he had become discouraged at this point, the whole expedition would have been nothing but a costly failure. However, Cortés found his Indian allies willing to carry on the fight, and he quickly planned a new campaign. Additional men and supplies from Cuba, intended for Narváez's men, were diverted to him. Munitions and further reinforcements came directly from Haiti. Cortés' rescued ship's carpenter directed other craftsmen to build parts for thirteen brigantines. Each was built of thick planks about forty feet long, had mounted cannons, carried sails and boasted a double row of oarsmen. Indian porters carried these ships in sections to Lake Texcoco to besiege Tenochtitlán. Cortés, with his augmented Spanish forces plus many thousands of Indian allies, laid siege to the city on April 28, 1521. Small-pox, brought to Mexico from Cuba, had ravaged the Aztec defenders, weakening their powers of resistance. The number of casualties during this ten-week fight is unknown, but it is estimated to have been very large. The defenders lost an estimated 100,000 men. The Aztecs in Tenochtitlán, commanded by Montezuma's brother, Cuauhtémoc, put up a stout defense, even though the Spaniards were able to cut off their water supply. Their food supply soon failed, and they were forced to live on rats and mice. Finally the Spaniards landed from the brigantines onto the causeways and began a block-by-block devastation of the city. Only when five-sixths of the city had been destroyed did Cortés capture Cuauhtémoc and end Aztec resistance. On August 13, 1522, the survivors were allowed to flee, and the remainder of the city was destroyed.

The fall of Tenochtitlán was a prelude to a less spectacular, but even more important, series of conquests. Spreading out like an oil spot from the site of Tenochtitlán, "the men of Cortés" fanned out in all directions, coercing the countryside. At first the Spaniards had no plan other than to seize precious metals or stones from the Indians. When the living Indians had exhausted their wealth, the Spaniards turned to grave robbing. Such pillaging soon reduced the natives' wealth to almost nothing. As a priest with them observed, the conquistadors viewed the Indians as not quite human, and acted toward them "like the most cruel Tygres, Wolves, and Lions, enrag'd with a sharp and tedious hunger." Since mining had greatly declined, the Spaniards ultimately were forced for a livelihood to a dependence upon agriculture.

Using Indian labor, Cortés occupied himself for the next three years rebuilding the site of Tenochtitlán. He constructed a Spanish city, the municipality of Mexico City, complete with monasteries, churches and government buildings. As the Spaniards turned to agriculture and settled down to rule the conquered countryside, they imported European plants and animals, began the conversion of the natives to Christianity, and finally, set up the *encomienda* system. This system was one of the hall-marks of Spanish colonization, although it was never employed in California, Texas or Venezuela, and seemed to take root best among the more advanced Indian cultures. According to encomienda, an expedition's leader extended his power over a region and then received the right to rule it. In the King's name, he granted lands to his followers. These tracts of land were usually contiguous to Indian villages, whose inhabitants were forced to work for their lord—the *encomendero*—for purely nominal pay. In return, the lord was supposed to protect the natives and see to it that they were converted to Christianity.

Cortés' success called dramatic attention to this quarter of the New World, known as New Spain after 1518. The cautious explorer Grijalba gave it this name because of the supposed resemblance of the buildings along the southern Mexican coast to those of Spain. Charles V (Charles I of Spain) and his advisers soon considered this area too important to be left long in the control of Cortés. They were determined to assert royal control over it. During the next few years, Cortés' authority was gradually but steadily whittled away.

By 1524, a royal order had vested financial control of Mexico in the King's officials. In 1526, the court ministers summoned Cortés back to Spain for a hearing upon his official conduct. In 1527, during Cortés' absence from Mexico, the King instituted an *audencia*, a kind of administrative court unknown to Anglo-America, which in Spain was an important law court. As it evolved in Santo Domingo, the audencia was a device to check the conquistadors' power and assert royal control. In America, in addition to its judicial functions, it had a large place in administrative and legislative affairs prior to the rise of the office of viceroy. An audencia was composed of *oidores* (judges), and eventually Mexico had a bench of eight. The first audencia was headed by an inveterate foe of Cortés, Captain Nuño de Guzmán. Under Guzmán the audencia proved to be inefficient and possibly corrupt. As a result, Cortés and the Church were able to make a successful common campaign against it. In 1530, the King replaced the members of the audencia with new men, and in 1535 he abolished the audencia and sent a new official, the viceroy, to Mexico. This was the final action in the King's campaign to rivet royal control upon New Spain. The royal choice of a viceroy fell upon a member of one of the most distinguished noble families in Spain, a man with extensive diplomatic and military experience, Antonio de Mendoza. Mendoza came to Mexico with a large retinue and almost kingly power. Both Cortés and Guzmán tried the viceroy but did not find him wanting, and ultimately submitted to his power. Mendoza figured prominently in the history of California as the senior officer who sent out the Coronado and Cabrillo expeditions. He ruled successfully and well in New Spain, until he was transferred to Peru. Eight different viceroys served during the remainder of the sixteenth century, while New Spain grew in wealth and area.

In the last two-thirds of the sixteenth century, the Spanish occupied northern Mexico as part of their push into the interior of North America, during which they also occupied Florida and New Mexico. The reasons, methods, and especially the pace of the last part of the century of occupation were very different from the frenetic and romantic first phase.

After 1550, the Spanish, having overcome their first excitement, became more interested in mining silver, growing crops and raising cattle to feed the bustling new cities of the western hemisphere. They also began systematic missionary work among the Indians. By this time the French and English evinced some interest in the New World, and Spain found herself forced to act defensively against them. She planted outposts to check their encroachments. The tone of Spain's colonial activities became cautiously defensive. Spain had arrived as a colonial power and was most interested in seeing that her aggressive rivals were unable to loot her new-found wealth.

The advance of the Mexican frontier had as its main purposes the founding of permanent towns and the development of the mineral and agricultural potential of these new areas. The leaders of this advance were men of substance, more analogous to the English land proprietors of the North American colonies than to the daring Spanish scamps, such as Cortés and Balboa. These entrepreneurs of the latter part of the sixteenth century, dubbed *adelantados*, moved out from the settled towns of New Spain where the Indians were already docilely working. The adelantados transported these civilized Indians north and west, establishing them as the nucleus of the settlers for succeeding waves of colonization.

An early adelantado was Cortés' arch enemy, Nuño de Guzmán. He had amassed a fortune by illegally shipping slaves from the area of his governorship, Pánuco, to Cuba and the other Caribbean islands. Instead of being punished, he was promoted by being made head of the first Mexican audencia. He proved to be a conspicuous failure. Despite his many peccadillos and shortcomings, he was not disgraced, probably because of his fast friendship with the powerful governor of Cuba, Diego Velásquez, and the slavebuyers of that island. In December 1529, he was permitted to go to the northwestern frontier, where he soon carved out a personal empire. With his characteristic gnarled egotism, Guzmán named his conquest Mayor España, or Greater Spain. The astounded authorities in the mother country thought the name much too pretentious, and dubbed it instead Nueva Galicia. In a single campaign in 1530–31, Nuño de Guzmán conquered the country northwest of Mexico City, as far as Sinaloa. Guzmán was drawn to explore and claim this area by tales of an Amazon island and the fabled Seven Cities. His conquests were cheaply won. Often he met no resistance, being welcomed with open arms by the Indians. In return, he ravaged the countryside, leaving behind him a track of smoldering ruins and wreckage. The surviving Indians were driven out in gangs and parceled out as serfs with the land, which he granted lavishly to himself and his cronies. Although he destroyed the Indian villages and reduced the surviving inhabitants to serfdom, he could never make his empire pay. Labor was relatively scarce, markets were remote, and the produce wrung from the soil by the reluctant Indians proved expensive. When Guzmán failed to obtain the wealth his reports always promised, his official conduct was minutely scrutinized by the judge of his *residencia*, Diego Perez de la Torre. Perez suggested Guzmán's arrest, which occurred just before the rascal could flee to Genoa. Guzmán occupied a common jail cell in Mexico City until 1538, when he returned to Spain, a broken, discredited man. The explorer Francisco Vásquez de Coronado replaced him as governor of Nueva Galicia.

By 1540, while Coronado was leading his expedition far to the north across the sun-seared plateaus and plains of the American southwest, the tensions created by Spanish penetration into the northwestern frontier zone gave rise to the most formidable Indian outbreak in New Spain's history: the Mixton War. The Mixton country was the jagged promontory of high Indian culture jutting north from Guadalajara. There civilized Indians were neighbors to barbarians. These docile, civilized Indians had long been forced to hard, unremitting work by their Spanish lords. Simultaneously, these same encomenderos had irritated the highland nomadic tribes by their relentless slave-raiding. Yet no great revolt might have occurred without the stimulus of a new pagan religion introduced by the unconquered natives of the north. This new religion breathed defiance of Christianity and preached war against the Spaniards. At first the Spaniards underestimated the extent of the rebellion, and sent insufficient forces against the natives; the frontier region ran with blood. In the fighting, Pedro de Alvarado, one-time lieutenant of Cortés and later the Governor of Guatemala, was killed. He did not die a warrior's death in battle, a fate he had often courted. After his troops were repulsed in an attack upon the peñol of Nochistlán, June 1541, Alvarado saw that nothing could allay the flight of his men, so he attempted to escape by leading his horse and retreating on foot. His secretary Montoya, mad with fright, spurred his jaded nag up a slope, slipped and fell directly into the path of Alvarado, who was thrown into a ravine where his own horse landed upon him. He was rescued and carried from the field on a litter only to die July 4, 1541. Alvarado's defeat worsened the situation, until Mendoza himself led fresh troops to crush the revolt. By 1548, after strenuous exertions by the Spanish and their Indian allies, the rebels were pacified as much by an outbreak of smallpox as by the royal troops. The Nueva Galicia Indians found no rest, since a new prosperity came to their region following the war, and they were forced to labor in the fields and mines.

This prosperity was created by a frantic silver rush. The first silver deposits were discovered in 1546 by Juan de Tolosa near the present city of Zacatecas. Tolosa was a soldier sent to wipe out pockets of resistance which remained late in the Mixton War. A group of friendly Indians showed him a vein of silver ore; he took samples, which upon assay turned out to be very rich. Carefully, making no announcement of his find, he formed a partnership with three of his friends, also veterans of the Indian wars, Diego de Ibarra, Cristóbal de Oñate, and Baltasar Trevino de Bañuelos. The four had money to exploit the diggings and soon became the richest men in Mexico. Southern Nueva Galicia was almost depopulated as men rushed to the mines. The excitement raised by the silver boom was roughly analogous to that which was generated by the gold rush three centuries later in California. The region of Nueva Galicia, which had languished ever since its premature settlement by Guzmán, now became a center of cattle-raising and farming as well as mining.

Francisco de Ibarra, a nephew of one of the Nueva Galicia "big four," used his uncle's wealth to send mule teams, soldiers and Indians farther north into an area called Nueva Vizcaya (presently the states of Zacatecas, Durango and Sinaloa). For twenty years he worked to carve out this new province. In 1562 the royal government organized a provisional government headed by Francisco de Ibarra.

There were relatively few native laborers, so many civilized Indians had to be brought into the mining areas from the south to serve as the nucleus of a labor force in the new colonies. The working of the mines required even more men, and in their desperation for additional workers, the Spaniards raided as far away as Texas across the Rio Grande. Hoping for more tractable and civilized neighbors to serve as a source of labor, and urged on by the desire for new geographical knowledge, Ibarra himself explored Sinaloa and pushed on into Chihuahua.

Meanwhile, in 1579, on the northeastern Gulf Coast of the present-day state of Tamaulipas, a Portuguese Jew, Luís de Carbajal, founded another province, then called Nuevo León. Carbajal authorized many money-making slave raids to gain labor for the mines of his new frontier, and thereby ran afoul of the Inquisition, which took advantage of the situation to brand him a heretic. With its leader in trouble, this particular frontier thrust was blunted until 1596. At that time, the lieutenant governor of Nueva León, Montemayor, founded the city of Monterrey, which later became a center of Franciscan missionary activity.

One surge of the Spanish frontier had an adverse impact upon early Spanish colonization of the area to be known as California, since it diverted energy and attention away from the exploration of the Pacific coast. The Indians seized on slave raids north of the Rio Grande reported large pueblo towns in the region later to be called New Mexico. A Spanish foray north of the settlement line in Mexico and into Arizona found evidence of rich ores. Spanish officials, after due deliberation, righteously called for the christianization of the Indian pueblo dwellers of the north. If wealth could be discovered, they added, it would be the reward for good works. Another factor in their calculation was the belief that extending the frontier northward would make it more strategically defensible.

As a result, in 1595, Viceroy Velasco appointed Don Juan de Oñate, a wealthy relative of two of the Zacatecas silver kings, as *adelantado* and governor of this northern frontier region. One delay piled on another, and it was almost three years later, in January 1598, before Oñate, largely at his own expense, could set out with 130 soldiers, their families, and a retinue of Indian servants. Some eighty-three heavy wagons carried the gear of the party and slowed their progress. Oñate, a stubborn man, drove the heavily laden column northward into the Rio Grande valley and into New Mexico, where in the late summer he set up a temporary settlement called San Juan. That fall, the restless Oñate wandered into Arizona. Upon his return, he was confronted by an uprising of the powerfully fortified Indian pueblo of Acoma. In the winter of 1598–99, Oñate reduced this settlement completely. After reorganizing his affairs in New Mexico, in June 1601, he marched northeast on a great foray in which he may have reached the Arkansas River before returning to New Mexico in October of the same year. After three years of bickering with other Spanish officials, he cut loose from bureaucratic red tape by heading an expedition west from New Mexico in a new thrust that carried him over the deserts and mountains to the Gulf of California. He believed the Indian legends that this body of water separated the mainland of Mexico from an island. On the return trip, his men slaughtered and ate their horses in order to still the persistent pangs of hunger. Nevertheless, despite all perils, they safely reached New Mexico in April 1605.

Unable to make any money from his strife-ridden colony in New Mexico, even the persistent Oñate became discouraged. He resigned his governorship and returned to Zacatecas, and finally to Spain. The King then assumed direct control of the colony of New Mexico, which after study the royal officials had deemed too valuable to abandon. In 1609, a royal governor, Pedro de Peralta, founded Santa Fe, or San Francisco de la Santa Fe, which has endured to the present.

Although colonial activities in New Mexico drained off much of Spain's feeble efforts to expand further along the Pacific coast in the seventeenth century, the Spanish settlements in that area helped to unite California with the Great Basin area of North America.

The story of transplanting European culture to the English colonies along the North American coast may seem less spectacular, although more important than the activities of the gold-hungry conquistadors, yet before the settlement at Jamestown in 1607, Spain had already finished most of her cycle of discovery, exploration and settlement. Her civilization had been firmly planted in an area many times the size of the Spanish homeland. Over 160,000 Spaniards had migrated to the New World, and the Spanish empire there embraced a greater population than that of Spain. Mexico City was a sophisticated center of civilization before the settlement at Boston had been thought of. By 1600, there were over two hundred chartered towns in Spain's New World possessions. Wealth and culture flourished in many provincial towns. The Spanish religion and language had been transmitted to millions. In addition, the mineral wealth of the New World made Spain preeminent in Europe. The tax, the royal fifth, shrank to a tenth and even a twentieth, and yet the Spanish crown had ample resources throughout all the sixteenth century to hire armies and create navies that were the awe of Europe.

By the beginning of the seventeenth century, certain definite patterns had not only emerged, but had hardened in the Spanish empire. The pattern of colonial rule was established under Spain's sixteenth-century Hapsburg kings. Even in theory, the colonies did not belong to the Spanish nation, but to the crown of Castile. Emperor Charles V (Charles I of Spain) held the colonies as his personal estates. He and his son, Philip II, tried to rule the colonies for their own benefit, as well as to provide good government for them. Predictably, considering all the difficulties they encountered, they failed to a considerable extent. The distances were too vast, the differences between Spain and the Americas were too great, mercantile economic theory too outlandish, the bureaucracy too complicated, the sums handled too large to enable their administrators to be uncorruptible. Finally, the tremendously detailed laws and regulations were too cumbersome, complex and remote from the actual life of the people to accomplish their purpose.

In addition, native-born Spaniards dominated all the top administrative positions in the New World. The number of Creoles (colonials of Spanish descent) who held important civil or religious posts were few. One authority claims that of 166 viceroys and 588 captain-generals, governors and presidents in the colonies, only eighteen were Creoles. Only twelve of the first 369 bishops in America were Creoles. Of course colonials of mixed Spanish-Indian or Spanish-Negro blood were much less likely to receive official recognition.

Another characteristic of Spanish colonization was the stellar role played by the Roman Catholic Church, the official state religion of Spain. All Spanish kings were rigidly orthodox, and in the spirit of the times, banished all religious dissent. There was no barrier between church and state. The Church traditionally ran all charitable and religious institutions in Spain and in the colonies, and was the vehicle by which the Spanish governments tried to christianize and hispanicize the Indians.

This last condition was the great difference between the English and Spanish colonies. The English settlers, who considered their Indians unsuitable as laborers, felt they were just one more physical barrier to settlement. To the Spaniard, the Indian was a soul to be saved, as well as a source of labor. The English found it incongruous to both convert and exterminate the Indians, so they encouraged relatively little missionary work among them. On the other hand, the Spaniards did not consciously desire the extermination of the Indian. It is true that in Spanish possessions Indians could be killed by overwork, white man's diseases, or as a disciplinary measure, but their systematic elimination was not a matter of Spanish policy. Indeed, since single Spanish women could travel to the New World only with special permission of the King, intermarriage or extra-legal unions with the native women was an inevitability. The Anglo-Saxon disdain for this kind of "race mixing" was absent. In time, the size of the Indian population stabilized under Spanish rule, and even increased if the *mestizos*—descendants of Indian-white unions—are counted.

FOUR

The White Man Discovers California

THE historian Charles Edward Chapman has suggested that there might have been Oriental contact with California long before the advent of the Spaniards. He has speculated that Asiatic vessels, as a result of some navigational error or storm, could have sailed to the American west coast. Chapman has pointed out that it was quite possible for the Japanese Current to drive junks over the Pacific to California. He believed that there was much evidence of cultural transfer from the Orient to California. In addition, Chapman was impressed by the old legend concerning regular trade between China and California in the first century of the Christian era. Several nineteenth-century scholars of ancient Chinese literature have indicated that a certain Hwui Shan and a party of Buddhist monks discovered a land they called Fusang, whose description matches that of California. Certainly such a crossing would have required no extraordinary feat of navigation. In fact, the most clumsy Chinese junk could have sailed from the Orient to California, island-hopping along the land masses of Asia and the North Pacific. Reports of Asian visitations from the fifth century onward persisted in California into the late 1700's. One particularly detailed legend described an expedition of men with kinky hair and vessels with figureheads of golden peacocks. By signs, the strangers related that they had come from Asia.

If the Chinese evinced some interest in pre-Spanish California, it is strange that Japan did not display an even more active interest. In the late 1500's and early 1600's, Japan was a great maritime power, maintaining

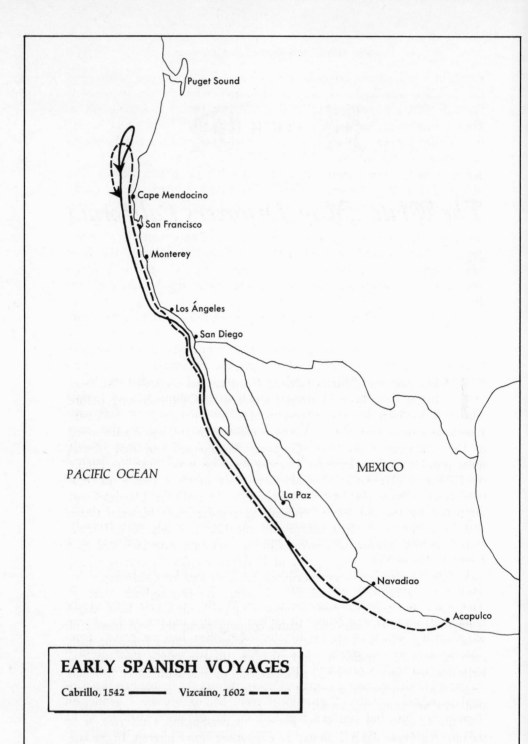

Puget Sound

Cape Mendocino

San Francisco

Monterey

Los Ángeles

San Diego

PACIFIC OCEAN

MEXICO

La Paz

Navadiao

Acapulco

EARLY SPANISH VOYAGES

Cabrillo, 1542 ——— Vizcaíno, 1602 ------

a careful watch on the Spanish occupation of the Philippines. Moreover, the Japanese manifested an interest in commercial contacts with New Spain. In 1610 a ship arrived in Mexico which had been constructed by an Englishman, Will Adams, a resident of Japan. The vessel was largely manned by Japanese sailors and carried a company of merchants and an ambassador to the viceroy of New Spain. In 1614 and again in 1616, a Japanese lord, Date Masamune, sent two other vessels to Mexico. The object of these Japanese overtures was direct trade between their country and New Spain. Commercial regulations and suspicions about Japanese intentions led the Spanish officials to spurn these proposals, whereupon the disgruntled Japanese gave up their attempts. There might have been a Japanese-Spanish confrontation in the Far East, but suddenly the Japanese, resenting attempts to christianize them, virtually ended all contacts and sealed themselves off from the outside world. By default, then, the Pacific became a Spanish lake.

Despite possible Oriental contacts in pre-Spanish California, the Spaniards made the first effective discoveries there. Any early Oriental contacts with California are analogous to the early voyages of the Vikings to pre-Columbian America. In the fall of 1965, the announcement that a pre-Columbian map had been found which depicted northeastern North America caused a flurry of speculation that Columbus did not in fact discover America. Even if the map is authentic, in a very real sense Columbus did find the New World. Despite some Viking voyages, they had no major impact upon either contemporary or later Europe. Columbus made the first *significant* discovery of America. Similarly, Oriental voyages to America in the pre-Spanish period possess only antiquarian interest. When Chapman wrote in the early twentieth century, there was a burst of interest in possible Oriental voyages, much in the way that the Viking explorations have excited the American imagination recently. Scientific history casts a cold light upon attempts to overemphasize these exotic expeditions.

Columbus' objective—a short cut to the riches of the Orient—was not entirely forgotten by the Spaniards, once it became clear that the Genoese had in truth discovered a New World. The discovery of the Pacific Ocean by Vasco Nuñez de Balboa rekindled interest in the Orient. A relatively young man in his thirties, Balboa had emigrated from Estremadura in western Spain. This area was the natal region of such intrepid fighters as Cortés and Pizarro. A poor, rocky region, whose sons migrated to other, more prosperous areas, it bred far more than the general population's share of prominent men. Balboa became a gentleman farmer in Haiti, but his luck was bad and his creditors insistent, so he left the island as a stowaway in an empty provision cask. On the Isthmus of Panama, he overcame his unsuccessful past and developed into a leader of men. He was an impressive figure, taller than the average Spaniard of that day, with a natural dignity and a gift for persuasive oratory. From his Indian friends, he heard whispers of a Western Ocean or a South Sea on the far side of the Isthmus. According to the rumors, wealthy Indians lavishly adorned with gold and pearls dwelt upon its shores. In 1513, Balboa formed a small expedition of Spaniards and Indian allies, and struck out boldly across the Isthmus of Panama to see this fabled land for himself. Among the Spaniards accompanying Balboa was the stouthearted Francisco Pizarro, who would later tame the mighty Incas of Peru, only to fall victim to the jealousy of his Spanish rivals.

With unflagging zeal, Balboa forced his expedition across the Isthmus and through a succession of streams, swamps and forests. He first saw the waters of the Pacific from a hilltop on September 25, 1513. Four days later, after beating his way through the brush and rough country, he waded into the waters of the Pacific and, in the name of the King of Spain, took possession of all lands it washed. A short four years later, he was executed by his Spanish rivals as a traitor. Still, his work of discovery had been well done. A few years later, the perilous circumnavigation of South America touched off an explosion of interest in a safe passage through America to the Pacific Ocean. Most navigators who sought this elusive waterway along the Atlantic Ocean dubbed it the Northwest Passage. The Spaniards of the Pacific knew it as the Strait of Anían, a name of unknown origin.

In addition to the Strait of Anían, there were other magnets drawing the Spaniards to explore to the north and west. Indian legends about rich cities and other marvels made the credulous Spaniards impatient for travel and exploration. After gazing upon the wonders of Peru and Mexico, the Spaniards became overtrustful and believed even the most extravagant tall tales.

One persistent fable concerned the Seven Cities of Cíbola. These cities, insofar as they existed in fact, were the dwelling place of the Zuni Indians. According to the legends, the cities were wondrously wealthy. Another popular fable concerned the kingdom of La Gran Quivira, a city so affluent that even ordinary kitchen utensils were composed of solid gold! Diligently, the Spaniards tracked down every rumored place in which these cities were supposed to exist, but with negative results.

Perhaps the most exciting legend concerned the golden lake of El Dorado, or El Hombre Dorado—the gilded man. The story was based upon the reputed existence of an Indian chief in the mountains of Bogotá. According to rumor, the attendants painted their chief every morning with gold dust and then ceremoniously washed the auriferous covering from him in the waters of a nearby lake. During the course of this ceremonial bath, the noble's followers excitedly cast gold objects into the lake. This soon became the favorite tall story of Spanish explorers.

These yarns may have been a result of the human tendency to exaggerate before an appreciative audience, for some of the stories had a slight basis in fact. The strong possibility cannot be overlooked that the Indians told the Spaniards what they knew the white men wanted to hear, in order to send them elsewhere.

After Cortés finished his conquest of the Aztec empire, his attention became riveted upon the newly discovered Pacific Ocean. Explorations by land to the north were blocked by his enemy, the governor of Nueva Galicia, Nuño de Guzmán; however, Cortés believed that the stories of wealth indicated that another treasure trove lay close at hand which could make his coffers bulge anew. Cortés had a faulty geographic knowledge of North America. To him the continent seemed nothing but a chain of islands off the Asian coast. He believed that Mexico was merely an extension of the Asian coast, separated from it by the Strait of Anían. This legendary strait, which the Portuguese navigator Corte Real claimed to have discovered between 1499 and 1501 while exploring Labrador, was believed by Cortés to connect the Atlantic and Pacific somewhere north of the North American land mass. Cortés even possessed a chart which showed North America extending from Newfoundland to the East Indies. Cortés also knew that Fernando de Magallanes (Magellan is the Anglicized version) in 1520 had discovered an opening—really the southern tip of South America—and had penetrated into the Pacific. Before Magellan died in a skirmish with the natives there, he had reached what he called Las Islas San Lázaro, soon known as Las Islas Ponientes, or the Westerly Islands. Eventually the Spaniards named the entire archipelago the Philippines.

To obtain ships for Pacific exploration, Cortés opened a shipbuilding station at Zacátula where carpenters and shipbuilders laboriously constructed four vessels at the explorer's own expense. This project illustrates the craggy determination of Cortés. All the way from Vera Cruz, Indian porters packed all the rigging, nails, and other ironwork needed for the ships.

When the vessels were finally finished, royal orders diverted at least three of them to the Molucca Islands to look for the survivors of the Loaysa expedition. In 1525, Charles V had sent Juan Garcia Jofre de Loaysa with six ships to the Spice Islands, as the Moluccas were sometimes called. Loaysa died at sea, and his expedition disintegrated. About 120 bedraggled survivors of the original crew of 450 men eventually established a post on Tidore, one of the mountainous islands of the Molucca chain. When no word came of the fate of Loaysa's excursion, Charles V ordered Cortés to search for them. Alvaro de Saavedra, a cousin of Cortés, led out the search party. In 1528 this band of men reached the Moluccas. Saavedra had arranged to obtain a cargo of cloves for the return trip to New Spain, but two attempts to return to Mexico were beaten back by fierce, adverse winds. Saavedra died, and his expedition also dissolved among the inlets of the Malay archipelago. The survivors, after some wandering, took refuge with Loaysa's remaining men. In time the Portuguese, who controlled the area, allowed them to be repatriated.

Despite the diversion of his planned expedition to the north, Cortés did not lose his desire to explore that area. His plans, however, received a setback when he was ordered back to Spain to defend his official conduct. The delay was only temporary; upon his return in 1532, Cortés sent out the two ships under the command of Diego Hurtado de Mendoza. This expedition never returned. Some garbled news of its achievements and fate drifted back by way of the Indians, who reported that Nuño de Guzmán had harassed the expedition by denying it needed supplies. A mutiny and a shipwreck on the east side of the Gulf of California completed the ruin of the expedition. The Indians probably murdered the survivors. Guzmán's rascally men arrived in time to loot what remained of the vessels and their cargoes.

On October 30, 1533, Cortés sent out two additional ships commanded by Captain Diego de Becerra, another of his relatives. On the first night at sea, the captain of one of the vessels deserted the expedition, sailing on to discover the Revilla Gigedo Islands, some 420 miles off the Mexican coast. The remaining vessel soon ran into difficulty. Becerra was a tyrant, and many of the crew, especially the Basque element, conspired against him. The leader of the plot was the pilot Fortún Jimenez, who stole upon the sleeping Becerra one dark night and killed him. Assuming command, Jimenez sailed the vessel to the shores of Baja California—the first European known to have accomplished this feat. There, late in 1533 or early in 1534 (the fog of accumulated centuries hangs heavily over this expedition), the mutineers landed on what they believed to be an island, but which in reality was the peninsula of Lower California. They anchored in the Bay of La Paz. Going ashore to replenish their water supply, they were suddenly startled by a surprise Indian attack which killed twenty-one of them, including Jimenez himself, it is believed. The few survivors escaped in the ship's boat and crossed the Gulf of California, only to fall into the hands of Guzmán's men. These captives told of their vicissitudes, but they also babbled about great pearl beds which lay near the island across the gulf. (If Jimenez did not die in the Indian ambush at La Paz, he was probably imprisoned and ultimately killed by Guzmán.) In any event Guzmán immediately sent his own followers across the gulf to salvage the expeditionary ship, the *Concepción.*

Cortés quickly appealed to the second audencia for redress against Guzmán. That body, having been secretly instructed to undermine Cortés' authority, refused to give the frustrated conquistador any satisfaction. Instead, they ordered Cortés to stop his exploring activities. Despite this opposition, Cortés felt that he had royal sanction for his schemes, and excited by the tales of great wealth in pearls, decided to lead the next expedition himself.

In the spring of 1535, after stopping off in Nueva Galicia to claim the *Concepción* (which had been stripped and gutted), he sailed his ships across the gulf to the Bay of La Paz. He promptly named the place La Tierra de Santa Cruz (Land of the Holy Cross), since he had arrived there on May 3, the feast day of the Holy Cross. He discovered mounds of oyster shells piled up by the Indians of the area, who were more interested in the oysters as food than as a source of pearls. Cortés and his men discovered at least thirty oyster beds off the cape—150 to 300 feet deep. To the Spaniards' dismay, the natives proved to be totally uninterested in diving for the Europeans. Consequently, Cortés had to be content with the shells torn loose by the storms and tossed up on the beach. The unpromising, arid land along the coast quickly indicated that Cortés would have trouble planting a colony there. To supply the colony from across the gulf proved to be uncommonly difficult, for heavy storms and strong currents could sweep in with little warning and turn the Gulf of California into a tempestuous waterway. During one storm-tossed passage from the Mexican mainland, Cortés' pilot was killed by a fall, and the great conquistador himself took the helm.

Eventually some twenty-three colonists died of starvation, and the remaining inhabitants became sullenly rebellious. In 1536, perhaps under pressure from Viceroy Mendoza of New Spain, Cortés unwillingly ordered the evacuation of the colony. Chafing under orders from the new viceroy, Cortés longed to free himself of official controls by finding a new land of riches to the north.

Consequently, on July 8, 1539, Cortés sent out a new expedition under the command of Francisco de Ulloa. Ulloa commanded three ships whose tonnage was listed by the old Italian liquid measure, called a *boute* or a "bottle," which equaled approximately half a ton in weight. The largest vessel, the *Santa Águeda*, weighed in at 240 bottles, the next largest, the *Trinidad*, at seventy-five bottles, and the smallest, the *Santo Tomás*, at sixty bottles. After a stop at the port of Manzanillo, the expedition proceeded north on August 27. On August 31, a fierce Gulf of California storm buffeted the little squadron and sank the *Santo Tomás*. The two remaining ships journeyed to La Paz, and from there they proceeded up the Gulf of California, then called the Sea of Cortés, or the Vermillion Sea. They sailed past the lush, verdant lands of tropical Mexico and then watched the shore gradually turn into the arid brown flatlands of the north. On and on Ulloa sailed, until he came to an impasse against the sandy delta of the Colorado River. He anchored his vessels and scanned the northwest horizon, where he could dimly perceive the San Diego mountains. The area seemed one vast emptiness. Ulloa snorted that the fabled gold cities could not be here, and after claiming all the land for Spain, he turned the prows of his vessels southward, following the eastern coast of Baja California, often landing and skirmishing with the hostile Indians, until he had returned to La Paz. All Ulloa had managed to prove was that Baja California was not an island. His report of this discovery would not be favorably accepted by the Spanish authorities.

Rounding Cabo San Lucas at the tip of the peninsula, Ulloa once more turned his vessels northward and sailed as far as Cedros Island, or perhaps even farther to Point San Antonio. Stormy northern winds and lack of provisions compelled him to turn about before he had reached Alta California.

The last part of Ulloa's voyage is heavily cloaked in mystery. Ulloa probably did not survive; perhaps he met with some disaster along the Baja California shore. According to one account, he returned to the port of Jalisco in Mexico, and while he was resting, a disgruntled soldier from his flagship ran him through with a sword.

In any event, his was the last expedition with which Cortés had an official tie. In 1540, Cortés, who felt his star waning, returned to Spain in a fresh attempt to win the honors to which he felt entitled by his services. Until his death in 1547, he was immersed in interminable legal bickering.

At this point, Francisco de Coronado took command of what may have been the most elaborate official Spanish expedition in North America. Antonio de Mendoza, the wily military man and diplomat, had long coveted a large role in exploration, so that he too might uncover an Aztec or Inca treasure. He commissioned Coronado, the governor of Neuva Galicia, to travel by land into the unknown territory of the north. Mendoza had also planned a companion thrust by sea, commanded by Hernando de Alarcón. Coronado's trip is not of direct concern to the history of California. He plodded north and east through New Mexico, and eventually reached the area which is today called Kansas. In the end he was reluctantly forced to conclude that the Zuni Indian pueblos of pale yellow adobe, when seen from a distance, had led credulous viewers to believe they were made of gold, and that wealthy cities simply did not exist in the region he had traversed.

As for the water prong of the exploratory fork which Viceroy Mendoza tentatively stuck into the wastes of the north, it sailed under the command of the Viceroy's chamberlain, Hernando de Alarcón, up the Gulf of California with additional supplies for Coronado. Since Coronado had been deflected toward the northeast, the two expeditions never met.

Alarcón had outfitted two ships at Acapulco, the *Santa Catalina* and the *San Pedro;* he later added the *San Gabriel* to his small fleet at a more northerly port. For this journey he was fortunate to obtain the services of the skilled cartographer who had sailed with Ulloa, Domingo Castillo. Intrepidly Alarcón sailed to the head of the Gulf of California. There his ships encountered a tidal clash—the result of the descending Colorado River's power crashing against the ascending tide which surged northward up the narrow gulf. These tides had once discouraged Ulloa from sailing farther north, and in the days before the September equinox, they were even more severe than usual. The waters rose and fell forty feet, terrifying the superstitious sailors. Alarcón's crews begged him to turn back, but he stubbornly refused. Giving the order to press on, he almost lost his vessels when they washed aground as a result of a sudden drop in the tidal bore, or flood. The deck of his flagship was actually under water several times, but somehow his terrified crews passed the shoal, and on August 26, 1540, journeyed into the mouth of the Colorado River. He eventually named this tributary the Rio de Buena Guía—River of Good Guidance. Since the river's current was too strong to sail against, Alarcón ordered twenty of his men into two small boats and proceeded up the river. His sailors eventually arrived in the country of the large, powerfully built Yuma Indians, who were overwhelmed by Alarcón's presence. He cut a dramatic figure as he strutted along in his shiny, resplendent uniform, followed by a fifer and a drummer who announced his entrances and exits. When he learned that the Indians were sun worshippers, he proclaimed that he was the "Son of the Sun." In all, he made two separate forays up the river in vain attempts to contact Coronado. How far he journeyed is uncertain. He may have gotten as far as present-day Yuma, although he claimed to have made a voyage to an area near that of the present Lake Meade and Boulder City. He could have been the first Spanish explorer to touch the present state of California, but his jumbled records make it impossible to know if he ever reached there or not. In any event, Alarcón found no more rich cities than Coronado had. On his return trip, he hugged the western Mexican coast and landed frequently, still hoping to find Coronado. According to various authorities, he completed his journey in November at one of the Mexican ports of Colima, Navidad or Santiago. He reported his experiences to representatives of Viceroy Mendoza, who was still interested in finding Coronado and who had organized another exploritory party according to instructions which he issued on May 31, 1541. The outbreak of the Mixton War diverted the viceroy's attention, and instead of launching Alarcón's search for Coronado, Mendoza ordered him to hold Autlán for the Spanish. At this point, Alarcón disappears from the history of California.

Meanwhile, Coronado had detached an expedition under Melchior Díaz to rendezvous with Alarcón. Díaz headed toward the coast with twenty-five mounted soldiers, a force of Indian allies, some live sheep for food, and a pet greyhound dog. This motley band painfully made its way over the harsh Sonora Desert, inadvertently blazing a trail for the overland route to California, which the Spaniards were later to call Camino del Diablo (Devil's Highway). They eventually emerged from the desert and reached the Colorado River. The Yuma Indians who had welcomed Alarcón not long before now looked askance when more white men arrived from a different direction. Soon the Indians began to harass Díaz, who fended them off and anxiously searched for traces of the viceroy's chamberlain. Finally, about fifteen leagues upstream, he found a tree carved with a message from Alarcón, which told him to dig at the base for hidden dispatches. Díaz uncovered the bitter news that Alarcón had already returned downstream. Ready now to do some exploring on his own, Díaz turned north and crossed the Colorado River on a raft, despite the danger of increasing Indian hostility. He sought a nearby seacoast which the natives had mentioned as being not too far away. Searching for this coast, Díaz and his men found themselves among the hot springs and mud volcanoes of Baja California. Here the party encountered a great misfortune when Díaz, while chasing his dog, accidentally impaled himself on his own lance. Although fatally wounded, the commander doctored himself and for twenty days, while carried on a litter, he encouraged his men in their retreat into the mainland of Mexico. As they fled southward, the small band was continually harassed by Indian attacks. On January 18, 1541, Díaz died from the effects of his wound, and was buried in an unmarked grave somewhere between the Sonoma Valley and the Gulf of California. The historical importance of Díaz' trip was largely vitiated when his personal papers were lost.

Since both Cortés and Guzmán had departed from the scene, there was now left in Mexico only one of the old-fashioned conquistadors for Mendoza to reckon with, if he wished to discover new lands. That man was Pedro de Alvarado, former lieutenant of Cortés, and later the conquerer of Guatemala. Alvarado had recently returned from Spain with many honors, bearing a contract dated April 16, 1538, which entitled him to discover and occupy new lands in the Pacific. At first these credentials seemed threatening to Mendoza, but after a closer inspection, the viceroy's alarm relaxed. First, Alvarado was limited to a sea voyage. Secondly, the viceroy, in exchange for whatever aid he might extend to Alvarado, was promised a one-third interest in the governor of Guatemala's project. When Alvarado arrived off the coast of Colima with his fleet in August 1540, his need for assistance and supplies put him at Mendoza's mercy. In November 1540, at Michoacán, the sober-minded viceroy and the aging conquistador met for an intense bargaining session. The result of this meeting was a partnership agreement. Alvarado would take only a one-fourth share in all of Mendoza's projects. In return, the viceroy's share of

Alvarado's expedition was raised from a third to a half. Furthermore, the two partners agreed to share all future expenses equally. The tragic death of Alvarado in July 1541, from an accident suffered during the Mixton War, left Mendoza in control of his fleet.

In September 1541, Mendoza dispatched a small squadron to the north under the command of Captain Francisco de Bolaños. The ships sailed from the port of Navidad and proceeded up the coast of Baja California, perhaps as far as two hundred miles north of Magdalena Bay. Bolaños achieved lasting fame, even though his expedition proved to be a minor one. He is generally credited with christening California, although he left no record that he had done so. In the journal of the next Spanish sea expedition (that of Cabrillo) California is used as a name already in general circulation. Since other place names given by Bolaños have remained fastened to the map, he is generally acknowledged as the first person to use California to describe the peninsula.

The origin of the name California was long shrouded in mystery. When the Americans arrived there, one of the most widely accepted explanations of its name was that the word had been coined from two Latin words, *calida fornax*, or hot furnace. To those who had been burned by the hot sun of California's desert area, this name seemed appropriate. In 1862 a better explanation appeared, and over the years it has won almost universal acceptance. A New England clergyman, Edward Everett Hale, discovered an old Spanish novel, *Las Sergas de Esplandían*, in which the word California appears as the name of a wonderful island. Following the Crusades, western Europe was swept by an interest in tales of chivalry (not unlike the science-fiction craze of today). Improbable heroes doing fantastic feats in impossible settings were the theme of countless writings. In the late fourteenth or early fifteenth century, a Portuguese writer, Vasco de Lobeira, wrote a famous work of this flavor called *Amadís de Gaula*. This novel became tremendously popular and was translated into many other languages, including Spanish. The editor of the Spanish edition, Ordóñez de Montalvo, took Lobeira's four volumes and added one of his own as a sequel. This sequel, *Las Sergas de Esplandían*, tells the story of Esplandían, the son of the fabulous Amadís of Gaul. A perfect knight, Esplandían had many wild adventures. One involved the siege of Constantinople by pagan forces, including a band of comely black Amazons and Calafía their queen, who was at once a Joan of Arc and a Cleopatra. Their island home, California, was said to be located "at the right hand of the Indies" and close to the "Terrestial Paradise." California was a wonderful land, populated exclusively by Amazons wearing golden garments and carrying golden weapons. They owned trained griffins which would attack any man who dared to enter their domain.

The process by which this name became attached to the California coast can easily be conjectured. This area previously had no fixed name, although some maps had called it Las Islas de Carolinas, after King Charles. Both Cortés in 1524 and Guzmán in 1530 had expressed their belief that an Amazon island lay close to the Mexican coast. Since the Spaniards still believed Baja California to be an island, a devotee of Montalvo's could easily have given the name California to the area. In any event, from the tip of Baja northward, the land was permanently christened California. California is the only state named for a mythical place in a fantastic novel.

Historians still know relatively little about Alta California's discoverer, Juan Rodríguez Cabrillo. Even the names he gave to places in Alta California have been largely obliterated by later explorers.

We know that he was a Portuguese soldier-sailor, described variously in old documents as a horseman, a navigator and a crossbowman. Cabrillo, or Cabrilho, was either an exile from his homeland or, more likely, an adventurer who had taken a foreign command. He signed himself as Juan Rodríguez or "Juan Rodz" and his contemporaries may have called him Rodríguez. Cabrillo probably indicates the village of his birth. Before he appeared in the New World in the service of Spain, he presumably had already taken part in several hazardous expeditions for Portugal. While a young man of twenty or thirty, he appeared as a soldier of Pánfilo de Narváez, in that Spanish officer's ill-starred attempt to punish the upstart Cortés in 1520. When Cortés defeated Narváez's army, Cabrillo, along with most of the survivors, was incorporated into the victor's army. Cabrillo experienced the horrors of La Noche Triste, and later served with distinction in Cortés' navy, which helped so greatly to reduce Tenochtitlán. Later Cabrillo fought in Alvarado's army when it subdued Guatemala. In this fighting, he may have been wounded.

After these battles Cabrillo established a home in Mexico with his wife, the sister of a fellow conquistador. He settled down to family life and fathered several children. Soon, however, he became restless for more adventure than the life of a planter in Mexico could offer, and he returned to Guatemala. Here he soon caught the eye of Governor Alvarado, as a leader of great energy. Therefore, when Alvarado considered backing further maritime exploration, he decided to make Cabrillo a sort of junior partner in his enterprise. After many delays, Alvarado and Cabrillo constructed a fleet of thirteen vessels of all types and recruited a crew of a thousand men, including a force of cavalry. Although Alvarado was described in contemporary documents as captain-general of this force, Cabrillo was listed as its admiral. The fleet sailed to Navidad, where the agreement between Alvarado and Viceroy Mendoza was reached. During this bargaining, Cabrillo and the fleet chafed at the inactivity they had to endure while the fleet tossed at anchor. Their lethargy was quickly dissipated when they heard that Alvarado had died of his injuries in an accident during the Mixton War. The uncertainty concerning the future of the fleet lifted when Mendoza, as the surviving major partner, claimed possession of the ships and confirmed Cabrillo's command of them. It was Cabrillo who actually dispatched Bolaños on his preliminary expedition in 1541.

The restless Mendoza decided that the entire fleet was not needed for the expedition along the California coast; therefore, he detached two ships and three smaller craft with some 370 men for a trans-Pacific voyage to the islands discovered by Magellan, the Philippines. The leader of this portion of the fleet was Ruy Gómez (or López) de Villalobos.

Cabrillo was thus left with only two small ships to penetrate the "northern mystery," as the area of California was called. These two vessels, the *Victoria* and the *San Salvador*, were probably caravels, round ships with a square stern, rather high bulwarks, narrow poops and wide bows. These vessels were commonly undecked between two castles, one fore and one aft. They possessed three or four masts carrying lateen sails, although the foremast may have been square-rigged. They had a crude, homemade look to them, and in truth had been rather badly constructed. Cabrillo's ships were manned by a motley assortment of rogues and drifters.

With this poorly built, badly supplied fleet, Cabrillo set sail from the port of Navidad on June 27, 1542, on what was to prove one of the most remarkable of all voyages in the history of California. The two ships proceeded up the coast of Mexico, crossed the mouth of the Gulf of California with its adverse currents and hostile winds, and rounded the tip of Baja California on July 3. Then they proceeded up the west coast of the peninsula. On August 5, the vessels reached Cedros Island, the probable outer limit of previous explorations. Cabrillo's party fought their way through violent seas, traveling fifteen to twenty miles each day, anchoring every night and making frequent stops to obtain food and water. Progress was even slower on those days when the seas were becalmed and his ships bobbed idly on the waves. On September 17, Cabrillo finally reached Ensenada, high on the Baja California peninsula. Cabrillo tarried here five days and then sailed northward along the shore to Alta California. There on September 28, 1542, somewhere along the beach where Ballast Point veers into the Point Loma bluffs, Cabrillo stepped ashore, claiming the land for Spain. The Indians of this area were drawn at first by the landing of the strangers, although they fled at the start of Cabrillo's landing ceremonies. Only three curious onlookers were left behind. In contrast to the history of earlier expeditions, the Indians of this region generally treated Cabrillo's expedition with kindness, since they regarded the Spaniards as ghosts.

This port, which the Spaniards described as "closed and very good," Cabrillo christened San Miguel (it was later renamed San Diego). After Cabrillo sailed from San Miguel, the real troubles of his expedition began. It now faced the autumnal storms along the Alta California coast. Cabrillo refused to be discouraged or to turn back. Traveling among the islands of the Santa Barbara Channel, the ships encountered stormy weather and adverse winds at Point Concepción, forcing them to make port at what is now known as Cuyler's Harbor, on San Miguel Island. During his stay on this island, Cabrillo fell on the rocky shore and broke his arm near the shoulder. There is some confusion about this accident. Some of Cabrillo's surviving crew members later testified that he had suffered a broken leg while on the island.

Despite his injury, he insisted that the expedition continue northward. In the midst of severe storms, the ships rounded Point Concepción on November 6. Still battling the seas, one of the ships sighted land on November 14, near the future site of Fort Ross, north of San Francisco. The expedition had missed both Monterey and San Francisco Bay because of heavy coastal fog. The rough winter waters of the Pacific were too violent for the Spanish sailors to navigate, so they put about, and in their drift southward discovered Drake's Bay just above San Francisco. Continuing storms drove the vessels south again to Cuyler's Harbor at San Miguel Island, where they dropped anchor for the winter.

During this last voyage, Cabrillo's health deteriorated as gangrene infested his injury. On January 3, 1543, he died and was buried in an unmarked grave beneath the shifting sands of San Miguel Island. The chief navigation officer, as second in command, took over the leadership of the expedition. He was Bartolomé Ferrelo, a native of the Levant. Since Cabrillo's dying wish had been that the expedition continue, Ferrelo decided to lead one more cruise to the north before returning to New Spain. After some preparations, he headed out to sea on February 8. Displaying courage and skill equal to Cabrillo's, he managed to sail as far north as the Rogue River in Oregon by March 1. At this point the health of his crew, suffering from that scourge of all early explorers, scurvy, and from the fatigue of interminable watches in raging seas, forced Ferrelo to issue the command for a return voyage. His storm-beaten ships became separated, but they reunited at Cedros Island on March 24, 1543. Together they sailed back into the port of Navidad, after an absence of nine and a half months. From the records of this party, nearly seventy places have been identified by modern researchers. This geographical treasure trove, however, did not greatly interest the Spanish officials, who labeled the report of the expedition "unimportant." No other treasures were brought back to compensate the viceroy for the expense of the trip. He promptly forgot it, and Cabrillo's name slipped into obscurity.

Mendoza then sent the surviving mariners to Peru with horses from his ranches. During this voyage their ships were seized by the viceroy's political rivals. This event helped to dim the memory of Cabrillo's and Ferrelo's efforts, for the only men who could have testified about their exploits were kept out of the way until there was no further interest in their exploring trip.

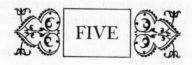

FIVE

The Exploration Continues

T H E Manila Galleon, or "China ship" as it was known to contemporaries in New Spain, played a prominent role in California history, for it both advanced and retarded Spanish interest
in California. Throughout the state's history, the Galleon expresses the
link between California and the Orient.

The Manila Galleon—so dubbed by English writers of the sixteenth
century—was not one ship but a commercial line of ships that sailed
between Mexico and Manila between 1565 and 1815, thus spanning two
epochs in the history of the New World. When this trade route began,
proud Philip II was absolute monarch of Spain and a tremendous colonial
empire. When the Philippine trade ended, royal rule in Spain had been
badly shaken by the Napoleonic invasion, and Mexico seethed in revolt
from the mother country. For 250 years, the galleons made the arduous
and lonely journey between Acapulco in Mexico and Manila in the
Philippines. They had to fight off marauding Dutch and English assail-
ants, and lost four galleons to the English raiders. The greatest danger to
the ships was not from political enemies, however, but from relentless
natural adversaries—poor visibility, storms and contrary winds. More
than thirty galleons fell victim to these natural foes.

The expedition which first traveled the Manila-Acapulco route left
Mexico in 1542, commanded by Ruy Gómez de Villalobos. Following
orders from Viceroy Mendoza, Villalobos took several vessels from the
Cabrillo fleet and sailed across the Pacific. His destination was vaguely
described on maps as the Western Islands, which were ultimately re-

named the Filipinas (Philippines) for Philip, then heir-apparent to the Spanish throne. The Villalobos expedition soon dissolved into the usual mélange of hardships, mutinies and Portuguese attacks, which plagued Spanish incursions into that part of the Pacific, the Portuguese-dominated East Indies. Nonetheless, the journey so excited Spanish interest in the western Pacific that Philip II, in 1559, ordered the second viceroy of Mexico, Luís de Velasco, to arrange for the occupation of the Philippines.

To execute this royal order, in November 1564, a fleet of five vessels with well over four hundred men aboard sailed under a Basque commander, Miguel López de Legaspi. To insure the success of this expedition, the royal authorities had plucked from an Augustinian monastery, where he had taken holy orders, the aging Andrés de Urdaneta to act as chief navigation officer for the undertaking. Nearly a quarter of a century before, Urdaneta had sailed with Loaysa, and so possessed vital navigational knowledge about the waters surrounding the East Indies. Spanish authorities hoped that with Urdaneta aboard this new expedition would be successful.

With remarkable ease, the Spanish vessels sailed to the Philippines, where Legaspi laid the groundwork for Spanish rule in that area. To their dismay, the Spanish found that the clove tree did not thrive in the Philippines. Even worse, from the Spanish standpoint, the natives possessed only minuscule quantities of gold, and that supply came from an unknown source. In the entire island chain, the only available commercial product was cinnamon, which was grown exclusively on the island of Mindanao. But the Spaniards forgot their disappointment when they saw native boats heavily laden with porcelain and silks from China.

Trade with New Spain began when the five-hundred-ton *San Pablo* sailed for Mexico under the nominal command of Legaspi's nephew, Felipe de Salcedo (the Spaniards, as was the almost universal European custom, practiced nepotism shamelessly). The vessel, which was really under the leadership of Andrés de Urdaneta, sailed up to the prevailing westerlies, and with the aid of these winds, the *San Pablo* reached Acapulco after a voyage of 129 days. Urdaneta's successful route was traveled a year later by another vessel, and soon trading ships were running on a regular basis between Mexico and the Philippines.

Acapulco became the eastern terminus of the Pacific trade route, while Manila preëmpted the western end. The westward passage from Acapulco was the easier voyage. According to this route, ships turned slightly south from Acapulco and then sailed almost due west for three months through the Marshall and Mariana Islands to the Philippines. The return trip was extremely difficult because these same prevailing winds which blew ships toward the Orient, now would beat them back if they steered directly toward Acapulco. To avoid them, the galleons sailed northeast from the Philippines for twenty degrees of latitude, almost to the shores of Japan (in the early years of the trade, many vessels actually stopped at Japan) and then headed eastward for the North American coast. During the early days of the line, the first landfall of this route was made on the coast north of San Francisco Bay. From here the ships sailed southeastward along the California coast to Acapulco. Lamentably, the several hundred voyages of the Galleon yielded little geographic information about California, since the ships generally avoided its rocky foggy coast.

At the time, this was the longest unbroken transocean voyage. Since the ships were always scandalously overloaded and sailed by improvised, inexperienced crews, and since the eastward voyage called for the most precise navigation, it is not surprising that the journey to Mexico often extended for six to eight months. During the eighth month, the normal supply of food and water would be exhausted, and the weary crews were forced to sail on short rations. Scurvy then broke out—the bane of navigators whose diet was deficient in greens. As the diseased crews limped on, their gums bled, their teeth loosened, their bones and joints ached and swelled. Scurvy could disable the strongest man; in its most acute stages it could kill.

Once the Manila-Acapulco trade became regular, some twenty to sixty Chinese junks annually visited Manila, the commercial entrepôt of the entire Far East. These junks brought Chinese silks in all stages of manufacture and in every variety of weave and pattern; silk usually formed the bulk of the Galleon's cargo on the eastward voyage. In addition, cotton goods from both India and China, Persian rugs by way of India, and considerable gold—either as bullion or manufactured jewelry—were also important imports in Spain's Pacific commerce. On occasion thousands of women's combs formed part of the cargo. These slow galleons returning from the islands were sometimes filled with European merchandise that had been carried three-quarters of the way around the world. Virtually any of the exotic products of the East that enjoyed popularity in Mexico were transported there.

The westward voyage was less heavily laden. Silver, copper and cocoa from Mexico and Peru were carried from Acapulco to be exchanged for Oriental goods. In addition, passengers from Spain bound for the Philippines traveled by way of this trade route, rather than journey around the Cape of Good Hope off the tip of Africa.

At first the traffic of the Manila Galleon was lightly regulated. Anyone who could survive the rough voyage was free to tap its rich profits. In the Spanish empire of that day, such a state of affairs was intolerable. Quickly the Spanish government directed its attention to the burgeoning competition of Chinese silks with those woven on Spanish looms, as well as the drain of New World silver to Asia. Between 1587 and 1593, restrictive laws began to shackle the trade. A royal decree in 1593 limited the value of the annual cargo to 250,000 pesos at Manila (at least twice that value in the New World). This limit remained in force until 1702, when it was raised to 300,000 pesos. In 1734 it was increased to 500,000 pesos, and finally in 1776, to 750,000 pesos. The decree of 1593 also limited to two the number of vessels which could cross the Pacific yearly, each ship being limited to three hundred tons. After 1593, only one or two galleons a year made the long voyage. As was generally the case in the overregulated Spanish empire, all these maritime restrictions were applied irregularly and half-heartedly. The Manila merchants refused to limit the size of their ships to three hundred tons, and as trade continued, the galleons gradually increased in size. In 1589, the Pacific galleons weighed seven hundred tons; in 1614 they totaled over one thousand tons. By the eighteenth century, the size of the galleons had actually increased to two thousand tons. The Philippine trade proved enormously valuable to Spain, particularly before her economic decline during the eighteenth century. To avoid taxation and regulation, the merchants hid the total value of the commerce from the prying eyes of royal officials. Consequently, any generalizations must be tentative; estimates have been made that profits ranged from 100 to 300 per cent in its heyday. The value of the trade decreased after 1763, when goods could go directly from the Philippines to Spain.

A traffic so valuable passing near California made a way station along its shores seem advisable to many Spanish officials. If enemy raiders were in the area, the station might forward a warning to Spanish vessels. When the Galleon groaned under the weight of its scurvy-sickened passengers and crew, a friendly station with provisions of green vegetables and fresh water might save many lives.

As Spanish officials began to ponder the advisibility of exploring the California coast to find a station site from which to revictual the Manila Galleon, Francis Drake plundered his way into the history of California. To the English-speaking world, Drake's one Pacific voyage has overshadowed the hundreds made by the Manila Galleon.

Francis Drake's standard was not the first English flag to fly in the Pacific breezes. The honor of first unfurling the English colors fell to John Oxenham, or as his contemporaries pronounced it, Oxnam. Oxenham, from a wealthy Devonshire family and Drake's senior by a few years, had commanded one of Drake's ships on the Caribbean in 1572–73. While raiding the Isthmus of Panama, both Drake and Oxenham conceived the idea of pillaging the Spaniards in the Pacific.

Oxenham, described as a man of "grave demeanour, much feared and respected and obeyed by his soldiers," was a skillful navigator—imaginative, courageous, short tempered and by some accounts wildly emotional.

Returning to England from the Drake raid, Oxenham fitted out a 140-ton ship with seventy men (some authorities say fifty) and sailed in 1575 for Panama. Arriving on the north coast of Panama in late 1575, he renewed his previous alliance with the Cimarrones (maroons), a cross-breed of Negro runaways and Indians, who lived in the jungle and carried on sporadic warfare against the hated Spaniards. Oxenham beached his ship and hid it among the mangroves. Then he and his men marched twelve leagues through jungle and rugged mountains to the Pacific side of the isthmus. There his men spent weeks building a pinnace and arming it with two small guns which they had painfully dragged from the Atlantic coast. Eventually the vessel was finished, and Oxenham boldly sailed it athwart the main shipping lane from the south to Panama. He quickly took two rich prizes. The Spanish ships which fell to him were unarmed, and their crews were astonished that English sailors were at large in what had been for fifty years a Spanish lake.

Aboard one of the ships captured by the English was a young lady whom Oxenham found fascinating, according to one account. As a result, although Oxenham had promised his Spanish prisoners to the Cimarrones, he could not bring himself to surrender the lady to them upon his return to Panama. Feeling betrayed, the disgruntled Cimarrones revealed Oxenham's hiding place to the Spanish authorities. Another story tells that Negro pearl divers who had been robbed of their treasure by Oxenham disclosed his lair to the Spaniards. It is more likely that the Spaniards stumbled upon his ship and cache of supplies while he was absent, or that his location was revealed by some of the prisoners he had previously released. Whatever the reason for his betrayal, soon overwhelming forces of Spanish troops systematically searched the isthmus for Oxenham. Once they had captured his party, the Spanish hanged the common English seamen and carried Oxenham and his officers to captivity in Lima. There the Spaniards paraded their captives about for a time, and then growing weary of this sport, ceremoniously executed them. The fate of Oxenham and his men was not known in England for years, and to this day we do not know the exact date of their execution.

The Spaniards were less lucky with Francis Drake—known to them at the height of his power as El Dragon (the Dragon). Drake was born in England about 1545. He went to sea as a boy, and became a skilled navigator and accomplished seaman by experience aboard the vessels which he served. As a young man, he accompanied his cousin John Hawkins on several voyages to America. These were part trading, part piratical ventures. When only twenty-four years old, he commanded his first ship on a Caribbean cruise, where he narrowly escaped capture by the Spanish. In 1572, with two small ships manned by seventy-three men and boys, he raided the Spanish Main and returned to England with enormous plunder. Contemporary opinions of Drake varied, even among professional seamen; many regarded him as the greatest of sea captains, others denounced him in England as a disloyal colleague and a bragging pirate.

In the fall of 1577, Drake set out with five ships and a total complement of 164 men on a mission ostensibly bound for Alexandria, Egypt, but with the Pacific as its real goal. Drake's flag flew aboard the *Pelican*, renamed the *Golden Hind* shortly after the voyage started. This ship weighed 120 tons, measured eighty feet from stem to stern post, and had a company of one hundred. There has been much controversy concerning Drake's motives for this undertaking. His financial backers (who possibly included Queen Elizabeth I) may have wanted to open a spice trade between England and the Orient. A secondary aim may have been the discovery of the elusive Northwest Passage. For Drake, the prospect of seizing Spanish loot could hardly have been unattractive.

Drake had a sense of the dramatic and practiced that kind of showmanship which is so necessary if a company of men is to preserve pride in its ship. He dined in state on silver plates and maintained trumpeteers for ceremonial occasions. He exacted the severest discipline from all ranks. Month after month, he imposed his will upon his men, inspiring in them the necessary courage to face the unknown coasts, disease and the Spaniards.

Leading his squadron through the Straits of Magellan, Drake entered the Pacific early in September 1578; the *Golden Hind* accomplished this difficult feat in just sixteen days, the shortest time recorded for this voyage in the sixteenth century. A series of storms buffeted his squadron. Disaster, desertion and abandonment cut his force to his flagship, a formidable fighting machine. She had a single row of gun ports, seven on either side, armed with twelve cast-iron and two brass cannon. In addition, she was equipped with several bow chasers of brass. By contrast, the Spanish ships in the Pacific were not armed with artillery except under extraordinary circumstances.

Undaunted by his losses, Drake pressed up the coast of South America. At Valparaiso, Chile, in December 1578, he captured his first Pacific prize, the *Grand Captain of the South*, bearing a valuable quantity of gold. Proceeding north toward Central America, Drake took several minor prizes and raided the harbor of Callao, the port of Lima. Catching word that a Spanish treasure ship was sailing to the north, he crowded sail to chase her. On March 1, 1579, he overtook the ship, nicknamed the *Cacafuego*, sluggishly creaking and heaving under the weight of gold, silver and jewels worth more than eight million dollars in today's currency. It became an easy prize.

Continuing north off Central America, Drake next captured a Spanish ship upon which he found two pilots of the Manila Galleon. In their luggage, the overjoyed Drake found Pacific charts called sea cards and sailing directions for the Manila Galleon. For these prizes, Drake was glad to pay fifty or one hundred reales. It is possible that before this capture, Drake had never heard of the valuable Galleon.

With these charts Drake hoped to get the silver-ballasted *Golden Hind* back to England without returning the same way he had come. It has sometimes been asserted that Drake was forced to circumnavigate the globe, since he feared that ships would be lying in wait for him at the Straits of Magellan. This is emphatically not so, since the befuddled Spaniards could not have blocked him. Setting his prisoners free, with the exception of the veteran Manila Galleon pilot, Sánchez Colchero, Drake continued north. When Colchero refused to lead the English in raids on coastal towns, Drake ducked him from the *Golden Hind*'s yardarm. Drake released the veteran pilot after the fearless Spaniard had refused a reward of 1,000 ducados to lead the Briton back home across the Pacific.

Meanwhile Spanish officials had spread the word of Drake's arrival as far as Acapulco, where a Manila galleon was waiting to clear for passage. At once the viceroy ordered the galleon and some smaller craft to chase Drake. The wily Englishman had already slipped by to the north, and to their great relief, the lightly armed Spaniards did not find him.

Drake pointed the prow of the *Golden Hind* northward, perhaps spurred by a desire to win further renown through exploration; perhaps he was looking for the elusive Northwest Passage as a short cut back to England. Whatever his reasons, he sailed past Alta California, probably skirting the Oregon coast and perhaps cruising as far as present-day British Columbia. Finally the weather turned cold and the seas became rough, compelling him to put in at a "fit harborough" on June 17, 1579. Some historians of the late nineteenth and early twentieth century have argued that he had discovered San Francisco Bay, but today's historians commonly agree that he did not. Drake could easily have missed seeing San Francisco Bay, as many later seamen did. Eye level for a man on deck of the *Golden Hind* was about twenty-five feet high which gave him about a six-mile vision to his horizon. The channel of San Francisco Bay is not ordinarily visible from six miles offshore. It may have been Drake's Bay in which he took refuge, or any number of ports, from Half Moon Bay to Trinidad, which have been suggested as the site of the "fit harborough." At any rate, he remained on the California coast until July 23. He built a rude fort of stone to store his considerable loot while the travel-weary, leaky *Golden Hind* was careened and overhauled. The coastal Indians proved friendly to Drake. They regarded the English as either ghosts or gods, and their worshipful adulation made the devoutly Protestant Drake uncomfortable. The Indians looked on happily, if uncomprehendingly, while Drake in a solemn ceremony claimed the land for Queen Elizabeth, calling it Nova Albion, or New England.

Finally, the *Golden Hind* again shipshape, Drake sailed toward the southwest, returning to England by way of Java and the Cape of Good Hope. From Java to Sierra Leone on the African coast, Drake sailed 9,700 miles without a port of call or a stop. Groaning with plunder, his vessel sailed into Plymouth harbor in September 1580. On board were fifty-six survivors of the original crew. Drake's losses from illness were small enough to suggest that he had roughly conjectured the causes of scurvy and so prevented a more disastrous outbreak of the disease among his crew. His men boasted that he had accomplished his extraordinary feats while wounding only two Spaniards and directly causing the death of none. A grateful Queen Elizabeth knighted Drake for his accomplishments, which included the first English circumnavigation of the globe. If Drake's exploits had stirred the English to entertain thoughts of colonizing Nova Albion, these aspirations soon dissolved into a tangle of personal rivalries and political intrigues in the Old World. Drake went on to play an important role in the defeat of the Spanish Armada. An incorrigible seadog and rover, he died in 1596 on a raid into the Caribbean.

The Spaniards in Mexico, perplexed by Drake's success, concluded that they had better find a Northwest Passage before their enemies did. Spanish officials began to finger the rough maps of the California coast, questioning where they might best plant a station to supply and, if necessary, to warn their precious Manila Galleon of English raiders.

Before a site could be chosen, a new intruder entered the Pacific—Thomas Cavendish. Cavendish was more bloodthirsty than Drake, killing as he looted. He was a small young man, who looked even more youthful than he was. He came from the gentry of Trimley in Suffolk, and before he took to the sea in earnest, he had spent much time at Queen Elizabeth's court. Stirring tales of adventure on the high seas fired his imagination, and through the favor of Lord Hunsdon, the Lord High Chamberlain, Cavendish obtained a commission. Thus he differed from Drake, who technically went on his voyage as a pirate, while the legal sanction given to Cavendish made him a privateer. By mortgaging his ancestral estates, Cavendish outfitted three small ships, manned by a crew of 128 men.

Leaving Plymouth on July 21, 1586, he boldly set his course for the Pacific by way of Cape Horn. Some seven months later, he entered the Pacific Ocean. Starting along the southern portion of South America, Cavendish looted, burned and killed his way up the coast of the New World. Hearing a report that the Manila Galleon was nearing the California coast, he took his two surviving vessels to Bernabé Bay, twenty miles east of Cape San Lucas at the tip of Baja California, to await the coming of the Spanish ship.

There were actually two Manila galleons making the trans-Pacific trip that year. The first, the *Nuesta Señora de Esperanza*, eluded Cavendish's lookout and reached Mexico safely. The second was the new, but lumbering and unwieldy *Santa Ana*. Aboard her were two men destined to play important roles in later California history: a pilot, Sebastián Rodríguez Cermeño, and a Basque soldier-merchant, Sebastián Vizcaíno, who had a heavy investment in the cargo of the *Santa Ana*. Suddenly, on November 4, 1587, the two English ships put out from their hiding place and intercepted the Spanish galleon. When the *Santa Ana* refused to surrender, the English vessels quickly and unceremoniously opened fire upon her. Although the seven-hundred-ton galleon was far larger than both her English opponents (the 120-ton *Desire* and the sixty-ton *Constant*), she could not outfight them. Both ships had mounted cannon (eighteen and ten cannon apiece), while the Spaniards had so loaded their vessel that they could carry no artillery. Yet the plucky Spaniards, refusing all appeals to surrender, defended themselves as well as possible with hand weapons. Although the Spaniards beat off several English attempts to board the *Santa Ana*, the contest was too unequal for the Spanish crew to defend itself for very long. The English abandoned their attempts to board, and when they began to disable the galleon with their cannon, the Spaniards reluctantly surrendered. The English buccaneers viewed with glee the rich prize they had taken; the *Santa Ana*'s cargo was valued at one million pesos in Manila. Cavendish removed the most valuable part of the freight to his own vessels, but to his dismay he could not find room for the remaining Spanish merchandise. He marooned his 190 Spanish prisoners on the Baja California coast after setting the *Santa Ana* afire. With a gesture of gentlemanly courtesy, Cavendish left several hand weapons with his prisoners so that they might defend themselves against the Indians. He gave them adequate provisions as well. However, he also hanged one of the galleon's passengers, a priest returning from the Philippines who had in some way angered him.

As the disgruntled Spaniards huddled on the shore cursing their luck after Cavendish had sailed away, they were surprised to see the hulk of the smoldering *Santa Ana* turn away from the open sea and drift toward them, eventually grinding to a halt against a sand bar off the coast. Vizcaíno at once organized a boarding party which extinguished the rather carelessly lit fires aboard the ship. He then supervised the salvage operations which patched the ship's leaky hull. With makeshift sails, the Spaniards somehow managed to steer the battered craft to the safety of the Mexican mainland.

Meanwhile, Cavendish had determined to circumnavigate the globe and return to England by way of the Cape of Good Hope. He expected to accomplish the trans-Pacific crossing easily, since he had retained the chief pilot of the *Santa Ana* and his precious sea charts as well. In addition, he had retained two Japanese and three Filipinos from the passengers and crew of the galleon. With the help of this skilled pilot, Cavendish, in the larger ship the *Desire*, had little difficulty in sailing to the Philippines. However, the *Constant* became separated from the lead ship and was never seen again. Having landed near Manila, Cavendish charged his pilot with plotting to betray the English vessel to the Spanish authorities. The English commander hanged the protesting Spaniard on the spot. From the Philippines, Cavendish was able to steer a course around the Cape of Good Hope, arriving at Plymouth on September 9, 1588. In his typical grand manner, Cavendish gave an elaborate banquet for his sovereign Queen Elizabeth I aboard his travel-stained ship—one of the many extravagances which quickly depleted the fortune he had acquired at sea. In three years he was penniless again. His debtors were demanding payment, so Cavendish put to sea on a new venture to America to recoup his fortune. One misfortune after another dogged this last undertaking, and Cavendish soon suffered an obvious attack of mental illness. Before the expedition could return to England, he died in 1592 at the age of thirty-seven.

Spanish interest in California was whetted by rumors that Drake had discovered the Straits of Anían and had returned to England by way of this passage. In 1584, a commander of a Manila galleon, Francisco de Gali, loudly proclaimed to all who would listen that he had seen evidence of the fabled strait while sailing from Manila to Acapulco. Although his report stimulated interest in the exploration of California's coastline, the Spanish moved slowly, and it was 1591 before the viceroy of New Spain wrote the king stressing the necessity of surveying California's ports. Two years passed before the Spanish authorities reluctantly ordered a survey, indicating, however, their unwillingness to spend any significant sums. Consequently, the viceroy of New Spain and his advisers decided that they could only proceed by making an arrangement with a private party who would agree to supply the necessary funds in return for personal profits from the mission.

In 1594 the Portuguese pilot Sebastián Rodríguez Cermeño, stepped forward to accept the viceroy's bargain. The navigator was to receive command of the Manila Galleon during the next year (with all the profit that assignment would allow) in return for conducting the required soundings and other explorations along the course of the California coastline. Cermeño was well qualified for this task, having been one of the pilots on the *Santa Ana*, which sailed the Manila Galleon route.

Sailing from Manila on July 5, 1595, Cermeño set the course of the *San Augustín* for the voyage to Acapulco. On November 4, his lookout caught a glimpse of the California coastline, a little north of forty-one degrees latitude. The stormy season had set in, with howling winds and mountainous seas which battered the Manila Galleon and her crew, who begged Cermeño to abandon any attempt to survey the California coast and return at once to Acapulco. Cermeño contemptuously refused their pleas and headed instead toward a sheltered anchorage, later called Drake's Bay, although it is not certain that the English buccaneer ever stopped there. Cermeño named this inlet San Francisco Bay, a name later applied to a much larger body of water in the same general vicinity.

From November 6 to December 8, Cermeño remained ashore. He ordered his men to assemble an open sailboat, the *San Buenaventura*, in which he could carry on a detailed exploration of the coast. When this launch was nearly finished, a storm drove the *San Augustín* against the shore, completely wrecking it.

Although only two men drowned in the disaster, the seventy drenched survivors soon became hungry, for seawater had destroyed almost all of their remaining provisions. The Spaniards bartered for a supply of acorns from the Indians, but found them bitter, disagreeable food. A new problem now plagued them: the natives began to carry away useful planking and other materials from the wreck of the *San Augustín*. Angered, Cermeño and an armed body of men tramped to the nearest Indian village to demand the return of the salvaged parts of their galleon. A shower of arrows greeted them. Led by Cermeño, the Spaniards drove the Indians from the village with small-arms fire and then plundered the rancheria. The Indians later suffered a change of heart and peacefully appeared at the Spanish camp to trade.

Salvaging as much as he dared from the freight of the galleon, Cermeño, on December 8, 1595, left the bay aboard the overloaded, small sailboat. Although Cermeño missed the Golden Gate in the poor visibility, he did sight Monterey Bay, naming it San Pedro. Although his crew suffered much from inadequate food and insufficient water, Cermeño continued to survey the coast until he had skirted most of Baja California. On January 7, 1596, the *San Buenaventure* sailed lamely into Navidad.

The Spanish authorities were decidedly chilly to Cermeño upon his return. No one congratulated him upon his feat of navigation; no one appeared interested in his geographical reports. All that concerned Spanish officials was the wreck of the Manila Galleon and the loss of most of its cargo. Cermeño's coastal-survey reports were labeled inadequate and pigeonholed. Cermeño received no credit for his navigation, nor were his coastal names inscribed on official maps. The only lesson which the Spanish officials derived from his experience was that valuable Manila galleons should not be risked in exploring ventures. That function, they concluded, should be turned over to specially built, smaller, and more maneuverable vessels. Orders were given to commanders of the Manila galleons, commanding them to eschew any temptation to land or explore along the foggy, storm-ridden California coast, and hasten as quickly as possible to their Mexican destination.

After a profitable Manila Galleon trip, Sebastián Vizcaíno recouped the losses he had suffered in the capture of the *Santa Ana*. With a group of several business associates, he sought permission to exploit California's fabled riches. The partners agreed that they would supply the Spanish government with geographical information in return for a license to seek pearls off the shores of Baja California. In 1594, Viceroy Luís de Velasco granted them this permission, but a squabble among the associates prevented them from sailing immediately. At this stage, a new viceroy, Conde de Monterey, appeared in Mexico. Monterey reinvestigated the terms of Vizcaíno's grant when he learned that the Basque merchant had been preparing to settle in California, as well as hunt pearls off its shores. Although Monterey evinced some distrust of Vizcaíno in his official report, he thought it best to allow the merchant's expedition to depart. Vizcaíno was eager to sail, but he had to raise additional funds for the journey since some of his partners had withdrawn from the venture. Reports say that Vizcaíno offered his seven-year-old son in pawn with the boy's mother as collateral.

He was successful in obtaining the needed financial backing, and in March 1596, he sailed from Acapulco with three small ships and at least two hundred men, including four Franciscan missionary priests, and some soldiers and their wives. As Vizcaíno's squadron made its way up the coast of Mexico, many of his personnel had second thoughts about the enterprise, and at least fifty of them deserted before he had crossed the Gulf of California. Vizcaíno journeyed to many of the sites visited by Cortés, designating them with names which have endured to the present. It was the Vizcaíno expedition which gave the Bay of La Paz its permanent name.

Since the natives seemed friendly, Vizcaíno left part of his force in La Paz, and with two vessels pressed northward up the Gulf of California. Storms and troubles followed the party. Upon one occasion, Vizcaíno sent a Spanish force ashore in small boats to reconnoiter the country. The Spanish scouts provoked a fight when one soldier jabbed his arquebus into the side of an Indian. Howling war cries, the Indians charged the Spanish, who used their firearms to disperse the attack. The Spanish retreated to their boats, and as they pulled away from shore, the emboldened Indians fired arrows at them. One shot hit a soldier in the nose, causing him to thrash wildly about, overturning his boat and drowning nineteen men.

Returning to La Paz, Vizcaíno found more trouble brewing. During his absence the unruly Spanish soldiers had repeatedly molested the Indian women, creating feelings of hostility among the natives. Attempts at pearl fishing had been frustrated by severe storms. In addition, food supplies had run low, and the arid country around the settlement offered little to supplement the Spaniards' diet. The morale of the Spanish quickly plummeted. Finally on October 28, Vizcaíno issued the order for two ships to return the hungry, grumbling colonists to Mexico. He and forty picked men made one last effort to explore the northern reaches of the Gulf. Storms and a broken rudder soon frustrated this expedition, forcing it to return to Mexico.

Upon his return Vizcaíno's official reception was unenthusiastic. Yet he was more successful than Cermeño at warming the chilly attitude of Spanish officials. The Basque merchant had a salesman's hyperbole, and he soon stimulated the interest of the Spaniards with his tales of California's plentiful pearls, rich salt deposits, and wealthy Indians clamoring for conversion to Christianity.

He pleaded for another chance and persuaded the viceroy to write to the King in his behalf. The notoriously deliberate Council of the Indies also sanctioned his plan. Nonetheless Vizcaíno's hopes for a speedy second chance faded with the alarm created by the appearance in the Pacific of a Dutch pirate, Oliver Van Noort.

Eventually Vizcaíno's determination was rewarded, for on March 18, 1602, he received formal instructions to make another California voyage. Specifically, he was to explore from Cape San Lucas at the tip of Baja to Cape Mendocino. He was to proceed as far north as Cape Blanco, and if the coastline veered westward, he was to follow it for only one hundred leagues. Furthermore, he was admonished not to waste time surveying large bays and not to change the names of landmarks already given. (Vizcaíno renamed everything in sight as he sailed along the California coast. His excuse for disobeying his instructions was that he could not identify the places named by earlier explorers because of imprecise longitudinal and latitudinal designations.) Finally, he was not to fight with the natives unnecessarily, and he was not to enter the Gulf of California or be distracted in that direction, unless he did so incidentally on the homeward voyage.

The penury of other years was forgotten, and Vizcaíno spared no expense to outfit the expedition. His crews consisted of two hundred specially selected men from Mexico City, and none from the tatterdemalion sailors available in the Mexican Pacific ports as had been the case in earlier expeditions. His fleet included a flagship, the twenty-ton *San Diego*, a small frigate, the *Tres Reyes*, an older vessel from the Peruvian coastal trade, the *Santo Tomás*, and finally a longboat which was left along the way.

On Sunday, May 5, 1602, the expedition sailed out of Acapulco, battling constant headwinds as it laboriously tacked to the north. As the

Spaniards sailed along the Baja California coast, they were frightened by giant fires, probably signal fires kindled by the Indians. It is also possible that the Indians, not always conservationists, as they have been pictured, had set the blazes to burn the vegetation and drive game into the open lands. In any event, a pall of smoke hung over the little fleet by day, and at night the skyline seemed ablaze.

On November 10, 1602, the expedition sailed into San Diego Bay. Two days later, on the feast of Saint Diego de Alcalá, the appellation San Diego was firmly fixed to the map to designate that body of water. The Indians of this area proved friendly, offering the explorers roasted sardines and fruit. After staying ashore for ten days to allow the scurvy-ridden crews to recover, on Wednesday, November 20, the squadron sailed north and sighted Santa Catalina Island. Landing, the explorers were impressed by the beauty of the Indian women and thievery of the Indian men who dwelt there. A genuinely religious man, Vizcaíno was shocked to find that the Indians practiced idolatry, and he tried at once to substitute a cross for the Indians' idol. Vizcaíno had a missionary with him, Father Fray Antionio de la Ascension, who looked forward to the conversion of the Indians. This priest, who served as cosmographer, also ministered to the spiritual needs of the explorers.

On Sunday, December 1, Vizcaíno sailed northward. Three days later, on the feast day of Santa Barbara, Vizcaíno named the channel between the mainland and the Santa Barbara Islands in her honor. On December 16, he reached a great bay which he named Monterey in honor of the viceroy. In his relief at finding this feature, he gave a glowing description of it, misleading later Spanish explorers who found that Monterey was not the closed harbor that he had described, but merely an open anchorage. He described the harbor as an excellent site for establishing a relief station for the Manila Galleon, ignoring the superior claims of San Diego Bay for this purpose.

At Monterey, Vizcaíno took stock of his situation. The trip had lasted over seven months, nearly exhausting the supplies brought from Mexico. At least forty-five of the party exhibited symptoms of scurvy, and perhaps as many as sixteen had died of it or other illnesses. As a result, a council of his captains urged Vizcaíno to allow the *Santo Tomás* to return to Mexico with most of the ill men and such reports as had been written to date. Vizcaíno agreed, and the vessel departed on December 29. After riding out storms and other mishaps, the *Santo Tomás*, with twenty-five of her original thirty-four men aboard, made port in Mexico.

Having provided for the return of the most seriously ill, Vizcaíno determined to complete his original plans, and ordered his vessels northward for additional exploration. On January 5, 1603, the two remaining vessels parted in rough seas, not to be reunited again. Aboard the *San*

Diego, Vizcaíno touched Drake's Bay and then journeyed north as far as Cape Mendocino. Here he encountered unusually severe storms. As his flagship pitched and tossed upon the waves, a box broke loose and struck Vizcaíno, fracturing several of his ribs. Nevertheless, the *San Diego* probably ventured slightly further north, rounding the Cape before Vizcaíno reluctantly ordered the helmsman to put about. The same winds that had previously hindered the advance of the vessel now blew it southward at an unusually fast speed. Now began a race with death, for many of the crew had fallen ill with scurvy, and it was necessary to find a safe harbor quickly to insure the survival of the crew. Finally, on March 21, 1603, Vizcaíno's vessel entered a port on the west coast of Mexico.

Buffeted by the same generally bad weather which had hampered the flagship, the *Tres Reyes* was driven northward as far as Cape Blanco. Both the captain and the pilot died. The fate of the small ship seemed doomed until a resourceful boatswain, Esteban López, stepped forward and won acceptance as the commander. Although relatively inexperienced, he guided the craft on its return trip with both skill and luck. The ship reached the port of Navidad on February 26, 1603.

Although all three of Vizcaíno's ships returned successfully, the loss of life aboard them had been heavy, and this partially obscured the fact that Vizcaíno had achieved the objective set for him by the Spanish authorities. On the other hand, he had not seen much of significance that the Cabrillo and Cermeño expeditions had not earlier reported.

Nevertheless, the viceroy was generally pleased and planned to have Vizcaíno settle the Monterey area. In return, Vizcaíno would collect a substantial reward for his efforts by being appointed to command the Manila Galleon on an early journey. Before this could be accomplished, the King transferred Viceroy Monterey to Peru, replacing him with the Marqués de Montesclaros. Montesclaros disrupted the plans to settle Monterey, and in effect postponed the colonization of Alta California for over 160 years. The viceroy was completely unsympathetic to the settlement of California. Some contemporaries then, and historians since, have hinted that he acted out of spite, or from a desire to obtain a bribe from Vizcaíno. There is no concrete evidence to sustain these conclusions, and he may have behaved as he did from honest convictions. In any event, Montesclaros countermanded the order assigning Vizcaíno as commandant of the Manila Galleon, throwing the Basque merchant a mere sop instead—a position as alcalde mayor (combination justice and mayor) of Tehuantepec.

The Spanish court, however, unaware of Montesclaros' action, ordered that a settlement be established in California as a station for the eastward voyage of the Manila Galleon. Moreover, Montesclaros was ordered to entrust the expedition to Vizcaíno, who would captain the Manila Galleon on the run to the Philippines, and on the eastward voyage would plant the colony. This royal order was delayed by shipwreck, and did not reach Mexico until April 11, 1607. Unfortunately the Acapulco galleon had left a month before, and an embittered Vizcaíno had left for Spain. This turn of events allowed Montesclaros to make a counterproposition. He argued that the eastward voyage of the Manila Galleon was nearly over by the time a landfall was made on the California coast. The real need for a relief station was in the earlier stages of the voyages, off the Japanese coast. In this region, the viceroy continued, the islands of Rica de Oro (Rich in Gold), and Rica de Plata (Rich in Silver) were much better situated. There was only one flaw in the viceroy's plan: these two islands did not exist. They were islands described by various imaginative navigators from time to time throughout the sixteenth century. Montesclaros proposed to substitute the reality of California for two islands whose very existence was highly questionable.

A special junta considered the viceroy's proposal and endorsed it. The 20,000 pesos set aside to pay the initial costs of a settlement at Monterey were diverted to finance this island-hunting in the western Pacific. In September 1608, the junta's endorsement was incorporated into law by a royal order to the viceroy that Vizcaíno should forego planting a settlement at Monterey, and instead command the island-seeking expedition.

Three years passed before Vizcaíno was ready to lead the authorized exploration. In 1611, he sailed from Acapulco with twenty-three Japanese merchants returning to their homeland. On the outward voyage he ordered his men to keep a sharp lookout for the islands in the waters north of the Ladrones group, but they found nothing. For the next three years, until 1614, he sailed the waters that surrounded Japan, but accomplished little except to antagonize the Japanese by his unbending hauteur and undisguised contempt for their customs and government. In time the Japanese became suspicious of Spain's motives in dispatching Vizcaíno. Thus the Basque may have contributed to their decision a few years later to seal off their country from Europeans.

After approximately three years of fruitless search for the islands "rich in gold and silver," Vizcaíno returned to New Spain as a passenger aboard another vessel, for his own had become unseaworthy. He was a bitter, disillusioned man. When he died in 1628, all desire to colonize California had flickered out in Spanish official circles. Spain had turned toward South America and the mining areas of Mexico.

Sailing its lonely route in the Pacific, the Manila Galleon continued to speed down the California coast to Acapulco as fast as the westerly winds could propel it. Monterey and San Diego faded in people's memories, and in time seemed no more real than the islands of Rica de Oro and Rica de Plata. So far as is known, no ship stopped north of San Diego for over 150 years. Only in the last half of the eighteenth century did Spain rediscover its interest in Alta California.

SIX

The First Colonies

D URING the seventeenth century, the Spanish government made several contracts for the exploration and settlement of Baja California. All of these efforts proved to be blinds used by private contracting parties who were engaged in pearl fishing. Reluctantly the Spanish government concluded that it would have to provide funds, if it were ever to see enduring colonies founded there. As a result, in 1679, the Spanish king approved a new pact with Isidro Atondo y Antillón, a veteran soldier and sailor, in which the Spanish government agreed to bear most of the colonizing expenses. One delay piled on another, and it was not until 1683 that an expedition of three vessels and a hundred men could be organized.

Among the passengers with this fleet were three Jesuit priests, one of whom was the illustrious Father Eusebio Francisco Kino. A brilliant mathematician, Kino was born in the Italian Tyrol in 1645. As a young man, he had studied in German universities. Although he had originally been designated for a missionary assignment in China, his Spanish superiors sent him to Baja California under official appointment as royal cosmographer.

Beginning in January 1683, Atondo spent two futile months trying to cross the Gulf of California to Baja. Late in March, a break in the weather allowed him to cross the gulf to La Paz in four days. He found the Indians of La Paz unfriendly, because they had been badly treated by the pearl fishermen who periodically visited their shores. Although he won the hearts of some Indians with liberal gifts, many remained sullen. Like Cortés before him, Atondo soon found that lack of water could be detrimental to colonizing efforts in Baja California. This was always to be so in a land where Indian mothers bathed themselves and their children in fresh urine. Soon hunger joined thirst as a problem, and Atondo reluctantly abandoned his colony on July 14, 1683, and returned to Sinaloa.

Atondo was too persistent to give up his project so easily, however. In October 1683, he attempted to found another settlement at San Bruno, some fifty miles north of his previous attempt at La Paz. This expedition was much better equipped than the earlier had been. The potential settlers brought with them abundant food supplies, domestic animals and seeds. The San Bruno Indians, having had less contact with white men, were friendlier than those at La Paz. The Jesuits eagerly established a mission there, and soon Father Kino proudly reported that he had baptized four hundred Indians. This was only a start, since the Indian population in Baja California at the time was estimated to be between twelve thousand and fifty thousand. Kino was intellectually curious about this new land, and in addition to instructing his Indian converts, he found time to walk from the gulf to the Pacific, the first white man known to do so.

In many ways this colony was a precursor of later California settlements. Atondo and the Jesuit fathers wrangled incessantly over the perimeters of their respective authorities. Indians, once converted, sometimes relapsed, and longing for their wild ways, deserted the mission. When they did so, many found life unattractive on the outside. The memory of thick porridge dispensed by the fathers influenced many deserters to return voluntarily.

For two years the colony struggled on. Atondo energetically explored the interior of the peninsula, but to his disgust, he discovered that the midlands were arid and barren. Since the colony was an expensive financial failure kept alive only by the injection of massive amounts of outside aid, the viceroy of New Spain's attention was forcibly called to it. Upon investigation, however, he ordered that San Bruno be retained, but only until a better site could be found. Despite his decision, the colony was abandoned when provisions ran out. Missionaries and colonists alike returned to Sinaloa. A final tally revealed to the glum Spanish officials that 225,400 pesos had been poured into this futile colonial venture.

Atondo argued that he should be permitted to make another try at colonization; however, funds which had been designated for this purpose were diverted to suppress an Indian uprising in Neuva Vizcaya. The frustrated Atondo never had another chance to colonize the seven-hundred-mile-long arid peninsula of Baja California. In the closing years of the seventeenth century, Spain was locked in a deadly struggle with the fabulous "Sun King," Louis XIV of France, and was in no position to indulge in further colonization of California.

With governmental action stalled by diplomatic difficulties, the Roman

Catholic Church came to the fore. As a result of the Catholic Counter-Reformation in Europe, old and new missionary orders alike spread the Christian faith to the far reaches of the globe. Men from many countries left their homes to travel and die in remote places from Macao to Brazil in the service of their God. Rome was vitally interested in christianizing the Baja Indians, whom it regarded as ripe for conversion. The Spanish government decided that the Church would be a useful instrument in Spain's grand design for spreading Spanish colonization. It reasoned that the missionaries could be organized as an elite corps to accomplish at small cost that which large bodies of troops had been unable to do—to enlist the active cooperation of the Baja California Indians. From the days of Columbus, missionaries had been at the very elbows of the explorers, helping in the task of hispanicizing the Indians.

The Society of Jesus (Jesuits), or Black Robes, became tremendously powerful, not only in New Spain, but in South America, the Far East and Europe. The society had an international appeal and numbered among its members citizens of many European countries. As a result of this appeal, and because of its direct ties with the papacy, the Jesuit order felt it had a special religious role to play in the history of Christianity. So strong was this belief that the Jesuits and royal Spanish officials often conflicted in their attempts to handle Spain's problems. The activities of the Jesuits came into conflict with the interests of governmental officials in other European countries as well. Eventually their enemies, civil and religious, effected a campaign against them, and in the last half of the eighteenth century, the powerful order was suppressed by royal decree in many countries of Catholic Europe. The order itself was dissolved in 1773 by the Pope, only to be reconstituted on a reduced scale in 1814.

Before its dissolution, the organization had enjoyed enormous success. It was founded by a noble Basque, Ignatius Loyola, who lived from 1491 to 1556; he was succeeded by Italians who practiced a more skilful management of the order. Unlike some other religious orders, which were composed of largely uneducated men, Loyola's followers were university-trained men from the best families of Europe. Even so, they were required to take additional courses in philosophy and theology. The tradition grew and was nurtured that Jesuits (as they were first dubbed by their enemies, although in time the order came to cherish the term) were above-average men, well trained and capable of performing any assignment. They possessed a high esprit de corps. Since the order was organized along military lines, its fervent members considered themselves to be soldiers of God.

The Jesuit role in New World history began when Pedro Sanchez, their Provincial, led a band of fifteen priests to Mexico City. They were soon joined by others. They quickly obtained a generous endowment from the viceroy, the city and private citizens. For almost twenty years, they founded schools in the settled areas of Mexico, including colleges for Indians.

In 1590, the Jesuits embarked upon mission projects in an area which now comprises several modern states in northwestern Mexico: Nayarit, Durango, Chihuahua, Sonora and Baja California. They eventually set up mission sites in southern Arizona. Meanwhile the less ostentatious Franciscans—called the Gray Friars or the Brown Robes—took northeastern Mexico as their missionary domain. This area now includes the modern states of Neuvo León, Coahuila and Santander, as well as New Mexico and Texas. The Franciscans followed the precepts of their gentle founder, Saint Francis, and so drew fewer attacks from government officials.

Yet in their sphere of missionary operations, the Jesuits steadily swept the frontier of New Spain forward in two thrusts along the eastern and western slopes of the mighty Sierra Madre chain, meeting in the regions west of the continental divide near the close of the seventeenth century. In spite of the important Jesuit contribution to the colonization of California, circumstances forced them to yield their missionary task to the Franciscans, who successfully completed it.

Although not all Spanish frontiers featured a mission settlement, we can consider it a hallmark of Spanish colonization, distinguishing it from the English colonial pattern. Interestingly, during the early days of exploration the Spaniards regarded the Indians as too subhuman to have an immortal soul. A papal bull, however, established the right of the Indians to share in the benefits of Christianity. Sometimes the missionaries preceded the military in exploring an area. At other times they accompanied the soldiers into unknown lands.

In general, the Spanish king approved of the missionaries' efforts, not only because they christianized the natives, but because they also civilized and hispanicized them, making them docile laborers and taxpayers of Spain's colonial empire. When it is remembered that the Spanish were more interested in using than in exterminating the Indians (in contrast to the practice of the English settlers), the high place they accorded to the missions in their imperial design becomes understandable. Moreover, the Crown found that supporting the missions, which had their own private means of sustenance, was far less costly than advancing the frontier exclusively by means of the royal treasury.

To begin a mission, a Jesuit would travel into the wilderness, seeking potential converts. He sought first to make friends of the Indians by telling the natives about the wonders of Christianity. Then he would offer to baptize children, as well as any ill or dying adults. Since baptism, according to Christian theology, opened the gates of heaven and made Christians out of pagans, the missionaries at all stages of mission development put great stress on the number of baptisms performed. This initial phase of winning Indian confidence soon gave way to the next stage, during which the missionaries insisted that the Indians settle down in one place, preferably one with an already large native population. This type of settlement, while advantageous in many ways, was dangerous to the health of the Indians, since such closeness made them an easy prey to the diseases which white men inadvertently introduced among them. Once the Indians were collected together, the missionaries would begin to drill them in the catechism. In some places missionaries would make an effort to learn the Indian tongues, but this proved to be undesirable as a rule, because there were so many Indian dialects to learn, and because most native languages were inadequate to convey the nuances of Christian theology. As a result, the missionaries had to teach in Spanish, while they attempted also to make their converts proficient in European parlance. The Jesuits did not ordinarily permit Europeans other than themselves and a few Spanish soldiers to dwell in the vicinity of a mission, lest the whites be a distraction and a source of scandal to their neophytes. To attract the Indians, the missionaries, in the early phases of mission-founding, were as lavish as their means permitted in giving them gifts. However, once the Indians had signified their assent and settled down to the mission routine, they were no longer free to leave. If they did flee, they might be hunted down and forcibly returned for punishment. The mission was an institution for the enforced acculturation of the Indians, a process which was bound to be a painful experience for them. Many missionaries were strong, good men and the Indians loved them. Others less worthy were harsh and at times even cruel. Yet worthy or not, they were all willing to die for their religious cause, and many of them did. Fewer died as martyrs under the blows of hostile natives than through the slower martyrdom of living isolated, hard, monotonous lives which lacked many of the conveniences of civilized existence. In the earlier period of mission activity, many missionaries zealously stamped out heathen practices and destroyed what traces they could find of preconquest civilization. This policy gradually changed, and the missionaries eventually led efforts to preserve Indian artifacts and those customs not incompatible with Christianity.

While the missions in theory belonged to the Indians, in practice the missionaries ruled as absolute monarchs. Only the military forces attached to the missions enjoyed a measure of independence from the priestly rulers.

Although the missions did receive some aid from the royal treasury, the Church had its own sources of revenue including, in the California phase of Jesuit activity, the so-called Pious Fund. This endowment was raised from the faithful of New and Old Spain. The missionaries always hoped to make their missions self-supporting through farming and stock raising, but this was always a long, slow process which some missions never achieved.

By Spanish law, missions were supposed to exist for only ten years, after which the Indians were turned over to the parish clergy, and the developed lands of the missions reverted to the resident Indians. However, as the Spanish missions moved northward, the missionaries discovered that the less civilized Indians had only a limited capacity to adapt to a settled way of life. In addition, when the missionaries realized that Spanish land speculators were eyeing the developed mission lands with a view to obtaining them at the first opportunity, their natural reluctance to end their hegemony over the natives was reinforced. Therefore mere inertia, schemes of empire, and a genuine concern for the Indians all were motives for the indefinite extension of what was supposed to be a temporary arrangement.

After the failure of the Atondo expedition, Father Kino reluctantly relinquished his cherished hope of converting the Baja California Indians. Instead he was reassigned by his superiors to the Jesuit mission string in northern Sonora, called Pimería Alta, or upper Pima Land. There, for nearly a quarter of a century, Kino served as a colonizer, explorer and rancher. With only meager financial aid, he pushed the Spanish frontier ahead to the Colorado and Gila rivers. He founded numerous missions, personally baptized about five thousand converts, and distributed sheep, horses, and cattle, as well as seeds, to the Indians.

Always restless, Kino travelled on more than fifty long horseback journeys, with only a few Indian companions. In 1701 and 1702, he made two trips down the Colorado River, reaching the headwaters of the Gulf of California on his second trip. With his telescope, he provided the final proof that Baja was indeed a peninsula. His map of this region provided the basis for charts of Pimería Alta until the beginning of the nineteenth century. Father Kino may have been the first person to use the terms Alta and Baja California to designate these two coastal areas. After his great labors, Father Kino died in March 1711.

One of his comrades was Father Juan María Salvatierra. Salvatierra has been described as "square-jawed, hawk-nosed and clear-headed." He was born in Milan of noble Italian-Spanish parentage. After having joined the Jesuits, he came to Kino's area as an inspector. Kino quickly succeeded in firing him with his own enthusiasm for conversion of the natives. Salvatierra agreed to head the drive to colonize Baja. At first he faced seemingly insurmountable obstacles. Its coffers emptied by the long, unrewarding struggle with France, the Spanish government showed no enthusiasm for attempting new colonizing efforts on the arid peninsula. Even more chilling was the attitude of Salvatierra's Jesuit superiors in Mexico; they evinced no desire to spend money for the conversion of that seemingly unrewarding corner of the Spanish empire. In 1696, help came to Salvatierra from an unexpected quarter, when Father Santaella, the general of the Jesuit order, visited Mexico. Upon learning the details of Salvatierra's cherished scheme, he became an ardent advocate of missions on the Baja peninsula. With the Jesuits anxious to begin missionary activity on the peninsula, the official attitude of the Spanish government soon changed. Actually Spain had long wished to see this area carefully explored and settled, and royal officials granted the Jesuits a license on February 5, 1697, to missionize the area. Spanish officials tacked a priviso onto the agreement which stipulated that the Jesuits must find their own financial support. In return, the authorities allowed the Jesuits almost complete control of Baja California. The one check made upon their authority was the stipulation that all settlements must be made in the name of the Spanish king, and that the viceroy or other higher representatives of the Crown could issue binding directives there. All the ordinary day-to-day rules of the colonies were made by the Jesuits. Only in extraordinary circumstances would the viceroy interfere.

Father Juan de Ugarte, a member of the Jesuit college in Mexico City, suggested the establishment of the Pious Fund to obtain the money for California's colonization. The Jesuit order solicited money successfully from the "pious" laymen of both New and Old Spain. Acting as a sort of treasurer, Ugarte had the satisfaction of seeing the fund grow under his ardent direction from a single peso to many thousands.

Father Salvatierra had always hoped that Kino would be permitted to join actively with him in the christianization of Baja. This hope was never realized, however. Kino's Jesuit superiors detained him in Pimería Alta, and he never again set foot in Lower California. Although greatly disappointed, Salvatierra went ahead with his plans. Gathering a small force of Christian Indians and soldiers, he set sail across the treacherous Gulf of California. Salvatierra's rather small vessel made it across the gulf on October 10–11, 1697, but the craft containing his companions could not complete the voyage until over a month later on November 15.

Salvatierra selected a site for his first mission, calling it Nuestro Señora de Loreto; it was located about one third of the way up the peninsula. His military companions speedily constructed a fort, complete with a tiny swivel gun. Salvatierra studied the native language, and unlike most missionaries, conducted services in it. It was not long before he was joined by Father Francisco María Picolo. Then the march to the north by both priests and soldiers began.

The mother mission of Loreto, built in the first year of the settlement, remained the headquarters of the only presidio (barracks) until 1736, when a second presidio was established at La Paz. This more southerly presidio in time became the headquarters for the entire Baja peninsula.

Year after year as supply ships crossed the Gulf of California, they faced great navigational difficulties; many were lost. The gulf water could easily be whipped into a fury of thirty-foot waves by the *chubasco*, a cyclonic windstorm, most violent between July and October. As a result of its inaccessibility, starvation consistently plagued the Loreto mission, but the Jesuits refused to despair. They were able eventually to nurse the mission into a fair degree of economic health, and it persisted as a mission settlement into the nineteenth century.

As more and more Jesuits came to Mexico from all parts of Europe, the Baja mission chain grew. The usual schedule in founding a new mission was to explore the countryside until a spot with a reliable water supply and arable soil was discovered. Then gangs of Christian Indians were sent to hack out a trail, so that mule trains from Loreto could bring in supplies. Pagan Indians were drawn to the area by the offer of gifts. With the help of these new recruits, buildings were raised and farming begun. The Jesuits devised ingenious systems of irrigation to grow crops in the midst of the most parched country. Yet growing food was a never-ending struggle. Every few years a merciless drought descended over the countryside. Springs dried up, and crops withered in the fields. Many missions were forced to shift their sites again and again in the ceaseless quest for a wholly adequate supply of water. Sometimes torrential rains might wash away the mission crops. On occasion, hurricane winds leveled the crude buildings. Often, when the weather proved favorable, swarms of locusts would appear and strip the plants of their green leaves. After eight years of back-breaking labor, supplemented by 283,000 pesos (only 18,000 of which was government money), the Jesuits were able to point to fields of melons and vegetables, orchards and even some date palm trees. In time, the missionaries built up herds of sheep, cattle, horses and mules. When they had established a more or less flourishing central nucleus of missions, the Jesuits resolutely pushed out to the north and south in search of new sites.

They were compelled to revise their original purpose of converting the Indians when the Spanish government requested them to locate suitable ports of refuge for the Manila Galleon. As a result, the Jesuits expanded well out of their original area. Soon they discovered that the Cochimí Indians of the more central region of the peninsula were friendly, while the Indians to the south of them—the Guaicuro—were not. From bitter experience with sailors of all nations who occasionally stopped at the southern tip of Baja, the Guaicuro had learned to hate white men. Moreover, they had among them half-breeds and deserters, including Negroes, from the vessels of half a dozen European countries.

When Salvatierra died in 1717, the presidency or rectorship of the peninsula missions passed to Father Juan de Ugarte, one-time treasurer of the Pious Fund. Under his rule, there was no slackening of endeavor; four missions were planted in the difficult region of the south: La Paz in 1720, Santíago in 1721, San José del Cabo in 1730, and Todos Santo (which was later moved) in 1733. San José del Cabo became an important settlement, since it was accessible to the scurvy-ridden crews of the Manila Galleon, who often stopped there to get fresh water, fruit and vegetables.

This promising beginning in the south soon was shadowed by the death of Father Ugarte at age seventy in 1730. His successors were not capable men. The Indians of the Cape San Lucas area, always surly and suspicious, soon broke into revolt. The immediate occasion for the uprising was the Jesuits' attempt to interfere with the long-established Indian custom of polygamy. The rebellion was led by a mulatto, Chicori, and an Indian-mulatto, Botón. When the revolt began in the fall of 1734, there were only three Jesuits and six soldiers in the entire southern area. The Indians killed two of the Jesuits, Fathers Lorenzo Carranco and Nicholas Tameral, four of the soldiers and a large number of native converts. In 1735, when a boat from the unsuspecting Manila Galleon put ashore at Cape San Lucas, the crew was disagreeably surprised by an Indian attack which killed thirteen Spaniards. The captain of the Manila Galleon saved his vessel from capture, however, and sailed safely into port on the Mexican mainland.

Meanwhile, news of the Indian revolt had quickly traveled up the Baja peninsula. The Indians in the central and northern portions became restless when they heard that the white men had been overcome and the southern missions destroyed or abandoned. In the face of this widespread peril, the Spanish authorities temporarily abandoned all missions except Loreto. Rumors of the revolt slowly trickled back to Mexico City. When the magnitude of the Indian uprising finally dawned upon the officials of New Spain, there was still a further lag in their reaction to it. The viceroy, Juan Antonio Vizarrón, had squabbled constantly with the Jesuits, and he now appeared reluctant to take any extraordinary measures to restore their mission field. He finally sent fifty to sixty fierce Yaqui Indians, noted for their loyalty to Spain, to help in the restoration of order in Baja. Vizarrón also ordered the governor of Sonora, Manuel Bernal Huydobro, no friend of the Jesuits, to take command of the pacification expedition. After great hesitation, which subjected him to Jesuit criticism, Huydobro defeated the Indians of the south by 1737. Since the northern Indians had never joined actively with the rebels, that area did not have to be pacified. In the south, however, there remained a legacy of ill will among the Indians. The embers of the revolt continued to glow as hostile Indians drove off mission cattle and committed other isolated acts of violence. This period of unquiet lasted for another ten years and really ended only when successive waves of disease swept through the tip of the peninsula, killing off most of the hostile natives.

The Jesuit activity in the north was slower but less eventful. The northern peninsula missions, with their greater populations, drew increasing Jesuit attention during the years when the Indians of the south were dying at an unusually fast rate. By the 1760's, the Jesuits planned to link their Baja missions around the top of the peninsula with those in Sonora, but time ran out before they could do so.

During most of their control, the Jesuits severely restricted the immigration of lay Spaniards to the Baja peninsula, fearing their presence as a disturbing influence. In their last years they were persuaded to relax this ban, but even after the Manila galleons began to stop regularly on the peninsula, there was not much to attract laymen. When the Jesuits were expelled from Baja California in 1768, the lay population exclusive of soldiers included only a relative handful of settlers, miners and pearl fishermen from Spain and the Mexican mainland.

In all, the Jesuits founded seventeen missions with resident priests, fourteen of which were still in operation at the time of their expulsion. About eight thousand Indians lived at these missions.

Through the years, the Society of Jesus attracted many enemies, both lay and religious. In the years of the Enlightenment, even in Catholic countries, it was viewed as a dangerous anachronism. Many individuals in high political circles feared the power of the Jesuits and longed for an excuse to strike at them. Finally in country after country the order's enemies were able to arrange its suppression. In 1759, the Jesuits were expelled from Portugal and its colonies. France followed suit in 1764, and Spain in 1767. On June 24, 1767, the viceroy of New Spain opened sealed instructions which stated that Charles III had ordered the arrest of all Jesuits in New Spain and their expulsion from the colony by way of Vera Cruz.

The new governor of California, Don Gaspar de Portolá, carried out what was for him the unpleasant task of removing the Jesuits from Baja. The international nature of the order is strikingly illustrated by the fact that among the sixteen Jesuits assembled at Loreto to leave the mission field were five Spaniards, five Germans, three Austrians, two Mexicans and one Bohemian. The Jesuits had been accused of concealing vast wealth in Baja. This charge was proved false, for there was but one small mine at Santa Ana.

Thus, after seventy-two years of hardship and labor, the Jesuits left Baja California, many of their Indian converts weeping as they departed. Little physical evidence of the Jesuit era remains in Baja. There are a few stone churches, some orchards and piles of widely scattered ruins.

In the mission areas of Arizona, Sonora and Baja California, the Franciscans replaced the Jesuits. Although the Franciscans took over the fourteen functioning missions in Baja, they found that the system of absolute

missionary control had departed with the Jesuit priests. Governor Portolá put a soldier in charge of the administration of each mission, limiting
the Franciscans solely to religious duties. The soldiers proved to be a
troublesome element, for they insisted on searching for the mythical
hidden Jesuit treasure. In 1773–74, after the main burden of mission activity had passed to the Alta California region, the Franciscans transferred
all but one of their Baja missions to the Dominicans, who continued to
push the mission chain northward along the peninsula. In all, the Dominicans established seven additional missions between 1774 and 1797, and two
more after 1800. Ultimately their chain of missions reached to within
fifty-five miles of the first Alta California mission at San Diego. All the
Dominican missions except two lay along the coast, on the most feasible
land route to San Diego. This route, blazed by the Franciscans, became
known as the Pacific Trail.

The Dominican missions endured for well over half a century. However, their importance diminished as the Baja Indian population gradually
decreased from white man's diseases and from the shattering impact of a
new way of life.

In 1830, after Mexico had achieved its independence from Spain, it
discontinued all the Jesuit-founded missions in Baja California. Only the
San Fernando mission and six to the north of it continued to function, but
on a sharply reduced scale. By 1849 the last priest abandoned the last
mission, and all sites left in the hands of the Church were sold or granted
to private individuals.

At this point the California stage was set for the appearance of the
celebrated Father Junípero Serra. This seemingly frail little man possessed
a will which enabled him to complete amazingly difficult physical tasks.
Serra, the John Smith of California, was born on November 24, 1713, in
Petra, an inland village on Mallorca, the largest of the Spanish Balearic
islands. Mallorca possessed a soft climate, quiet fishing villages, and a lush
green countryside of flourishing vineyards and richly colored fruit orchards. Mallorca's people, dressed in quaint native costumes, were famed
for their deeply religious spirit.

Serra was born in a simple, whitewashed stone house on a narrow
cobbled street, the son of humble farmers. He was baptized Miguel Joseph on the very day of his birth. When he was a small boy, his parents
encouraged him to visit the nearby Franciscan friary of San Bernadine.
Studying at the boy's school there, the young Serra gradually decided to
become a Franciscan priest himself. At sixteen, his parents sent him to
Palma to study for the priesthood, but he looked so young and pale that
he was rejected as unready for the heavy regimen of study prescribed by
the seminary. When he finally established his true age and convinced his
superiors that he compensated for any defects of the flesh with his spirit,
he was allowed to take the habit of the Franciscans in September 1730.

All his life Serra was plagued by ill health. During his years as a novice, although he was barely able to keep up with the vigorous routine, he would not consider leaving. Gradually his health improved, and he grew to what he himself described as "medium size." However, his remains have been exhumed and measured by anthropologists, who believed he could not have stood taller than five feet and three inches. According to contemporary Spanish records, he had a swarthy complexion, black hair and black eyes.

When a Franciscan novice took his final vows, he also took a new name. Serra chose the name of Junípero, after a lay brother who was famed for his humility in the service of St. Francis.

Junípero Serra studied philosophy and theology at the Lullian University in Palma. He was ordained in 1739 and taught at the friary of San Francisco for several years. Two of his students were later associated with him in his California venture: Juan Crespi and Francisco Palóu. In 1742, according to Father Palóu, Serra earned the degree of Doctor of Sacred Theology.

Although he was a successful teacher, Serra wanted to convert pagans. When Father Palóu confessed to Serra that he wished to become a missionary, Serra confided that he had already decided to ask Palóu to accompany him into the mission field.

The future founder of the Alta California mission wrote to the administrator of Franciscan affairs in America, asking permission to come there. At first his request was denied, since the quotas were filled. Almost providentially, however, several openings developed, and Palóu and Serra departed for New Spain.

They sailed on an English packet from the Balearic Islands to Malaga. The captain, an English Protestant, soon engaged them in a violent theological dispute. According to Father Palóu, the captain lost his temper and held a knife at Serra's throat. Fortunately for the future of California, the captain did not strike Serra, but muttered a bit and then put up his knife. The two priests then journeyed to the mainland of Spain without further adventures. In August 1749, with twenty Franciscans and seven Dominicans, Serra crossed the Atlantic to Vera Cruz after a ninety-nine-day voyage.

Arriving in Mexico at the age of thirty-six, Serra labored there for the next nineteen years, until 1768. After a short tour of duty at San Fernando College in Mexico City as novice master, he went to the missions of Sierra Gordo, several hundred miles north of the capital of New Spain. He had already developed a leg affliction which plagued him at intervals for the rest of his life. Eventually he became president of the five Sierra Gordo missions in eastern Mexico. These missions were so well run that in 1770 they were turned over to the secular clergy, since the Indians were judged to be ready for life in the white man's civilization.

Previously, in 1758, the Franciscan authorities had recalled Serra to San Fernando College. They had planned to send him to missions in Texas, but when the warlike Apaches unsettled the frontier lands of New Spain, the Spanish civil authorities positively forbade sending more missionaries there. As a result, for ten years Father Serra remained on the alert for a call to the Texas frontier. While waiting, he went out from San Fernando College on assignments in southern and central Mexico. On one occasion his forceful preaching so angered someone that rattlesnake venom was placed in the sacred chalice to poison him. Serra drank the poison, stubbornly refusing any antidote when it was discovered what had happened. Somehow he recovered.

While Serra was absent from Mexico City, he was chosen as president of the Baja California missions, a post he readily accepted, since it promised the chance for converting the Indians which had been denied him on the Texas frontier. Thus at fifty-five (when life expectancy was lower than it is today) he started a new career.

With fifteen colleagues, he left from Mexico City for Loreto on April 1, 1768. Upon his arrival there, he faced a difficult situation. The glory of the Spanish had faded on the peninsula. With rare exceptions, the royal officials seemed uninspired. The spirit of adventure had flickered low. Spain, Great Britain and France, in a series of exhausting wars, had finally settled the fate of eastern North America. Great Britain had won possession of North America east of the Mississippi River and had expelled France from Canada. Spain still clung to Louisiana (transferred from the French) and Texas as buffer zones against an expanding Britain. Now a new rival appeared in the far northern Pacific—Russia.

In an important thrust, the Russians had won their way eastward across Siberia to the Pacific. A Russian expedition under a Dane, Vitus Bering (like the Spaniards, the Russians were not great navigators and leaned heavily upon foreign sailors), had sighted southern Alaska in 1741. Even though Bering died and his ship broke up on an island off the Kamchtatka Peninsula, the survivors killed some sea otters for food, and the pelts suggested a new resource to be exploited. Soon Russian fur hunters in jerry-built boats more suitable for navigation on a Russian river than upon the broad Pacific began island-hopping through the Aleutian chain. The hunters took sea-otter pelts that brought high prices in Europe and in the China market. Although the Russian effort was a small private enterprise rather than a massive governmental project, it brought Russian ships further south each year. Although Russia did not establish a base on Kodiak Island until 1784, its unprecedented movement into the Pacific so alarmed the Spanish court that an ambitious Mexican official twisted his instructions to allow an advance of New Spain's northern frontier into Alta California.

Instead of ordering the settlement of Alta California, Charles III ordered his viceroy in New Spain, Marqués de Croix, merely to guard that portion of the realm. In turn the viceroy passed the order to Inspector-General José de Gálvez who was then in Mexico to reform the colonial administration. Gálvez had been a poor boy from the petty nobility of Andalucia. As a penniless but promising youth, he was sponsored by various clerics who helped him to attain a good education. An ambitious man, Gálvez had quickly risen to prominence in the Spanish civil service. He was assisted greatly in his career by his second wife, a Frenchwoman, who taught him to be proficient in her native language.

By the late 1760's, Inspector-General de Gálvez, in his middle forties, took time off from his fiscal reformation of New Spain; he framed a grand design to subdue the troublesome Indians of northwestern Mexico and simultaneously to guard that frontier area from foreign encroachment. To achieve this purpose, Gálvez proposed a commandant-generalcy extending over the vast north and northwestern frontiers, including California. He had just developed these preliminary plans when the viceroy's order arrived and provided him with an excuse to settle Alta California.

The territory of Alta California was known mostly through Vizcaíno's report. Consulting it, Gálvez and his associates planned to occupy and settle San Diego and Monterey. Monterey was considered the key to the possession of Alta California, while San Diego would serve as an intermediate base between Monterey and Loreto.

From the port at San Blas, which was developed specifically to serve as a supply base for Alta California, Gálvez held a formal junta to plan the details of his projected voyage. Following this planning session, he journeyed to Baja California to organize its slender resources for the push northward. During his tour of the peninsula, Gálvez personally inspected even the most minute details of the expedition. Zealous, efficient, working in explosive bursts of energy, he actually aided in scraping the hulls of the expeditionary ships and boxing their supplies. He could be mean and petty also. He sternly forbade card-playing by his men, and he punished some soldiers for various minor offences by ordering them to augment the ranks of his assault on California. These men were literally "handcuff volunteers." While he was engaged in these preparations, Gálvez showed a few manifestations of the mental instability which was to prostrate him later in his career. He had a great ego which craved recognition.

As Gálvez's men probed the resources of the Baja missions to strengthen the Alta California expedition, they found the persistent rumors of Jesuit wealth to be myths. Yet the provisions of these missions were ruthlessly appropriated to furnish supplies for the new Alta California missions. Although harsh, this was the Spanish custom throughout the mission phase: to require the old missions to supply the new.

After Gálvez had launched the four divisions of the expedition from Baja California, he returned to Sonora, where he suppressed an Indian uprising. At this point the years of relentless effort took their toll. He fell victim to an illness which cost him his health and, temporarily, his sanity. Consequently Gálvez's grandiose schemes were delayed. He did not obtain his projected captain-generalcy, but he was only temporarily stopped. Regaining his health and sanity, he continued his career and in 1776 he became Minister General of the Indies, with the title Marqués de Sonora.

The governor of Baja California, Gaspar de Portolá, had volunteered to lead the expeditions to Alta California. As governor, he had become bored and now craved greater activity. An unmarried soldier of noble ancestry from Catalonia, he had seen much service with the Spanish army in Italy and Portugal. Ostensibly Portolá had been appointed governor of Lower California as a promotion, but he looked upon this position as an exile from which he might escape by rendering some signal service to the Spanish government.

The Alta California expedition left in four parties, two were to travel by land and two by sea. Commander Vicente Vila in charge of the two-hundred-ton paquebote *San Carlos*, left from La Paz on January 9, 1769, with twenty-five Catalan soldiers from Sonora and several skilled workmen. Including its crew, it carried sixty-two persons. The *San Carlos* had expected to rendezvous with the other vessel, the *San Antonio*. Storms, however, interfered with the plan, and the impatient Gálvez finally ordered the *San Carlos* to sail alone.

The voyage of the *San Carlos*, the *Mayflower* of Alta California, to San Diego took an incredible 110 days. Buffeted by adverse winds and plagued by leaking casks, the *San Carlos* often put ashore to find water. On one occasion the ship was blown two hundred leagues off course. As the *San Carlos* careened about on her erratic track, the ancient enemy of seamen, scurvy, arose to harass the beleaguered ship's company. Since the diet of Spanish sailors in the eighteenth century was deficient in vitamin C, scurvy was an unwelcome but ever-present passenger in the forecastle.

One of the difficulties endured by the sea portions of the expedition was caused by Vizcaíno's errors in charting the coast of Alta California. He had placed San Diego farther north than it actually was located, near the present port of San Pedro.

While the *San Carlos* was making its torturous way northward, the *San Antonio*, also a paquebote, but somewhat smaller than its sister ship, finally sailed on February 15 from San Bernabe Bay in Baja California. Captained by Juan Pérez, a veteran of the Manila Galleon, she carried twenty-eight men aboard. Her crew also suffered from scurvy during her passage. The *San Antonio* wandered awhile among the Channel Islands, for Pérez also expected to find San Diego some distance north of its true position. Finally, on April 11, 1769, the *San Antonio* entered San Diego Bay and anchored there—the first known vessel to do so for 167 years. Half of her crew were sick with scurvy and two had died from its effects. About April 29, a sail was sighted which proved to be the long overdue *San Carlos*. Belatedly she sailed into the harbor and dropped anchor. When no boat was lowered from the *San Carlos*, the officers of the *San Antonio* exchanged anxious glances and sent one of their own boats to board the sister ship. They found a scurvy-ridden crew too ill or exhausted to do anything more than drop anchor. In all, scurvy claimed over a third of the crews on both vessels.

A third vessel, the *San José*, had been sent by Gálvez as a supply ship to join the other two vessels at San Diego. Gálvez's workmen were unskilled or worked too hastily, for the ship proved fragile and rather unmanageable. Quickly constructed and hastily dispatched, the *San José* was loaded with supplies at several stops along the Sonora coast and at Loreto in Baja California. Heavily laden, she then set out for Alta California on June 16, 1769. Three months later she limped into Escondido, Oaxaca, with a broken foremast. Again the vessel was repaired at San Blas. She was reloaded at Cabo San Lucas, and after a delay of nearly one year, weighed anchor again in May 1770. This time she vanished at sea. Her cargo's absence caused heavy suffering to the new settlers of California.

The two land expeditions to San Diego encountered much easier journeys. They both departed from Velicatá in northern Baja California, where a new mission had been established. One party led by Captain Fernando Rivera y Moncada and accompanied by Father Juan Crespi, left on March 24. Rivera's party also included twenty-five battle-hardened *soldados de cuero*, or "leather-jacket soldiers," who wore sleeveless jackets of tough, layered deerskin and carried bullhide shields, capable of turning aside most Indian missiles. A mission father once spoke of them as "the finest horsemen in the world." In addition, this group included four hundred animals, three muleteers and forty mission Indians from Baja. Father Crespi acted as chaplain for the party and in his spare moments kept a diary which has proved to be an invaluable record of early California history. Without serious mishap, they reached San Diego on May 14, more than two weeks after the *San Carlos* had arrived.

The second land contingent, headed by Portolá and accompanied by Father Serra, consisted of about sixty persons, including Christian Indians. Since he was in his middle fifties and president of the Baja California missions, Serra could easily have remained behind fingering official papers and writing reports, but he would not hear of this. During the journey north, he developed a leg infection as a result of an insect bite. According to one story, he appealed to a muleteer for some of the salve he used upon the animals. The priest applied it to his leg and soon declared himself improved. The picture some biographers have presented of Serra tramping the entire way from Velicatá to San Diego on foot is overdrawn. In all likelihood, he rode most if not all of the way. On July 1, Serra's overland party arrived at the Spanish encampment at San Diego. It is significant that the entire expedition was purely a military and Church undertaking. There was not a single colonist included in the project.

No time could be spent in congratulations when all four sections of the expedition were united at San Diego, for the expedition was committed to push a column northward to Monterey. At this point Pérez, captain of the *San Antonio*, announced that he was ready to return to Mexico for supplies. Vila and the *San Carlos* would remain at San Diego and provide reinforcements for the expeditions. Portolá offered sixteen of his soldiers to supplement Vila's crew, if that captain would sail his ship to Monterey. Vila refused and Portolá was forced to revise his original plans. Forty men began the construction of the first rude shelters for the settlement at San Diego.

Now the original force began to scatter. On July 9, the *San Antonio* with an eight-man crew left for Mexico, bearing dispatches and reports. Although six men died on the return voyage, the *San Antonio* finally made port on the peninsula. A handful of men were left behind on the *San Carlos* which was anchored in San Diego harbor. In addition a small detachment including Father Serra remained in San Diego to hold the new settlement. On July 14 Portolá and a party of sixty-three started the long trek to Monterey.

The journey northward presented many unforeseen difficulties: in Mexico the rainy season occurred during the summer, while in Atla California, to Portolá's dismay, the summer months were a season of drought.

The explorers drove a hundred-mule pack train bearing supplies, for they believed that the *San José* would soon arrive in San Diego with additional provisions. Portolá had left orders that the ship was to be sent northward with most of its supplies, so that a mission and presidio could be started at Monterey. But the *San José* never arrived in San Diego.

Earthquakes, so much a part of the California environment, frightened and troubled them. Nevertheless the group pushed past the Los Angeles River and into the mountains of central California, finally entering the Salinas Valley. Portolá sighted Monterey Bay but did not recognize it as the fabulous harbor of Vizcaíno's report, and so trudged past it. The party moved on along the peninsula where San Francisco would one day be built. They viewed San Francisco Bay from various points, and soon realized it to be a formidable barrier against further progress northward.

As a result of increasing sickness and limited supplies, Portolá turned southward on November 11, 1769. During the last two weeks of the trip, Portolá's troops were forced to eat some of the mules in order to augment their limited food supplies. Soon, as one of the party complained, everything and everybody smelled of mules. After returning to the area near Monterey Bay, Portolá and his men decided to turn back for San Diego. At the end of ten weeks, the weary travelers arrived in San Diego on January 24, 1770.

Meanwhile, the party left behind at San Diego had not been idle. Two days after Portolá's departure, the Spaniards had raised a crude cross on the site chosen for the mission. They had completed a rough stockade, and had built a crude chapel of wooden stakes with tule reeds for roofing. Serra and his coworkers named the mission for San Diego de Alcalá. As more Spaniards sickened and died from the aftereffects of scurvy, the Indians who had been calling at the camp to gape at the Spaniards became bolder. Not understanding the European concept of private property, they stole many supplies, particularly cloth. Upon one occasion natives attempted to take the sails from the anchored *San Carlos*. One encounter occurred on August 15, when the Indians attacked the garrison. Only four able-bodied soldiers were present to meet the attack, yet they repulsed the natives. One Spanish youth died when an arrow pierced his throat; three Indians were killed at once and two others died later of their wounds.

The Indians withdrew and eventually resumed peaceful contacts with the white invaders. Serra had been hoping to make the first convert for his new mission and was bitterly disappointed at the delay caused by the Indian attack. As the Indians began to return for visits, he redoubled his christianizing efforts. Once he thought he had received the parents' consent to baptize one of their children. As he was about to pour the holy water upon the child, its parents snatched the youngster from Serra's hands and disappeared with it into a crowd of taunting, jeering natives.

When Portolá returned from his trek to the north, only about half of the men left behind in San Diego were able to greet the returning travelers. The rest were dead or seriously ill. For a short while it seemed that the whole expedition northward to Monterey had been in vain, for Portolá disgustedly reported that he had been unable to locate the legendary bay. However, when Portolá gave a more detailed account of his trip, both Serra and Captain Vila realized that he had gone by the bay without recognizing it.

The shortage of food in San Diego grew daily more acute. It may seem odd today that men should starve in bountiful California, but the Indians of the San Diego area raised no crops. Ammunition was too scarce to be used in hunting because it might be required for defense. The only feasible way for the Spaniards to obtain additional food was to trade cloth for fish and wild fowl brought to the camp by the Indians. Some of the soldiers traded in this manner until they wore only a few rags. On February 10, 1770, Rivera and forty men were sent down to Baja California to get more cattle and to bring up a pack train of supplies. Since it would have taken months for Rivera to accomplish this feat, he may have been sent away to rid the San Diego settlement of some hungry mouths, rather than in the expectation that he could return in time to rescue the survivors at San Diego.

For the next six weeks, the remaining Spaniards held grimly on in the face of continuing, nagging hunger. Perhaps the little settlement would have been abandoned if it had not been for the tenacity of its leaders. Partisan biographers of Serra insist that he and Vila talked Portolá into not abandoning San Diego. This conclusion may be an injustice to Portolá, who also showed great determination in holding on. The catastrophe of such a departure was averted on March 23, 1770, when the *San Antonio* arrived, loaded with corn, flour and rice. Her return was a stroke of luck, for the *San Antonio* had actually been bound for the mission of Monterey, which the Spanish authorities fondly supposed had already been founded by Portolá on his northern trek. Unexpectedly, Captain Pérez had decided to put in at San Diego before heading north, and so inadvertently saved the settlement.

Portolá now resolved to return and plant a settlement at Monterey Bay, according to the original plan. Taking the sixteen remaining ablebodied soldiers, he started north on April 7, after first ordering the reluctant Captain Pérez to sail the *San Antonio* to rendezvous there with him. After tramping through the countryside, Portolá reached Monterey Bay again on May 24; he was joined by the *San Antonio* on June 1. On June 3, Father Serra and Father Juan Crespi (both of whom had arrived as passengers on the *San Antonio*) founded the mission San Carlos Borroméo de Carmelo. On this same day, Portolá hoisted the royal standard over the new presidio.

After the joyous ceremony of thanksgiving which accompanied the raising of the Spanish flag, news of the occupation of Monterey was immediately sent to the authorities in Mexico. Within a few weeks, a church was built. This presidio soon settled into the military routine, as though it had been in operation for years. Heavy stands of forest which surrounded the settlement made adequate shelter easy to construct. Although the buildings at Monterey were rough hewn, they presented an almost luxurious contrast with the brush and mud lean-tos of San Diego. Father Serra found the climate and surroundings at Monterey Bay so much to his liking that he made it his headquarters for the whole "ladder" (as he styled it) of missions that he hoped to establish in Alta California.

On July 9, 1770, the easygoing yet capable Portolá, feeling that his task was accomplished, turned over the military command of Monterey to his trusted lieutenant, Pedro Fages, and sailed for Mexico and out of California history forever. Portolá arrived at San Blas on August 1. He accepted the post of governor of the city of Puebla in New Spain, after drawing some generous salary advances. Eventually he returned to Spain and died in the mid 1780's.

On August 10, after a year and a half of waiting, the viceroy learned for the first time that Alta California had definitely been successfully occupied. He ordered flags displayed, bells rung, and a special high mass of thanksgiving sung to celebrate the three-hundred-league advance of the Spanish frontier to Monterey.

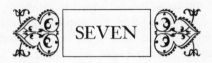

SEVEN

California Begins to Grow

ALTHOUGH Spain had extended her domain hundreds of miles north of Baja California along the Pacific coast, San Diego and Monterey remained only small enclaves in Indian territory. About forty settlers lived at Monterey and twenty-three at San Diego, and these included many Christian hispanicized Indians from Baja California.

In addition to a limited colonial population, Spain's hold on Alta California was weakened by her inability to adequately convey enough supplies to that area. Spain possessed only one tenuous supply artery, running from Vera Cruz on the Mexican east coast, through the great valley of Mexico, and then through Mexico's northern arm to the small port of San Blas on the Pacific coast. From this port the sea lanes stretched to San Diego and Monterey.

Lacking adequate supplies, the small settlement at San Diego continually faced illness and frustration. One missionary later remarked that the priests of the San Diego Mission had little sustenance except the "bread of affliction and the waters of disaster." The San Diego supply situation became less acute in June 1770, when Captain Rivera y Moncada returned from Baja California bringing cattle and other provisions.

Until 1777 there was no formal governor in Alta California. The military commander reported directly to the viceroy and paid little heed to his superior, the governor of Las Californias, who resided at Loreto in Baja California. When he departed from Alta California, Governor Por-

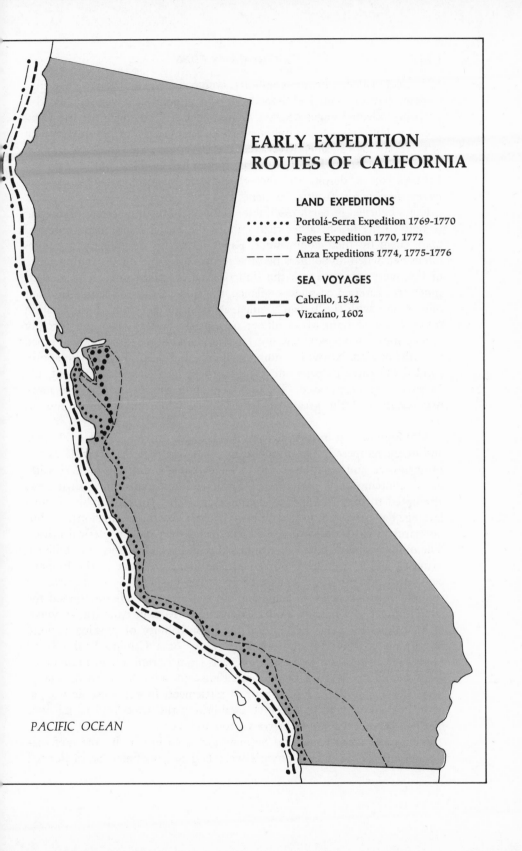

EARLY EXPEDITION
ROUTES OF CALIFORNIA

LAND EXPEDITIONS

••••••• Portolá-Serra Expedition 1769-1770
••••••• Fages Expedition 1770, 1772
— — — — Anza Expeditions 1774, 1775-1776

SEA VOYAGES

▬ ▬ ▬ Cabrillo, 1542
•—•—• Vizcaíno, 1602

PACIFIC OCEAN

tolá selected Pedro Fages as military commander. This choice chagrined Captain Rivera, who had hoped for the appointment himself. Portolá probably selected Fages because of his successful command of the Catalonian volunteers—a select military group. Fages regarded his appointment as perfectly logical, since Rivera had merely commanded the local leatherjacket troops from Baja California. Fages had nothing but disdain for Rivera's forces, despite the fact that the leather-jacket troops excelled Fages' own men as frontier soldiers.

Fages believed in harsh discipline. Many of his men deserted, preferring to take to the brush rather than endure the brutal punishments inflicted upon them by their commander. Fages found his disciplinary problems intensified when his soldiers became restless after the more exciting work of discovery gave way to the dull routine of guard duty. Unless their superiors exercised ceaseless vigilance, the soldiers caused trouble by their misconduct with the Indian women. A favorite diversion of the Spanish soldiers, out of sight of an officer or a priest, was to lasso and forcibly seduce Indian women. Once, not far from San Diego, three soldiers raped two Indian girls. Notwithstanding swift retribution by Fages, who apprehended the three culprits and clapped them into close confinement, the Indians were unappeased. They looked upon the incident as one more manifestation of the great gap between the white man's words and his deeds.

Although he was industrious and loyal, Fages proved to be troublesome and quick tempered. The Franciscans, who had regarded Portolá as too unaggressive and easygoing, found Fages equally difficult to deal with. Some contemporary partisans of Serra and historians since then have attempted to picture Fages as incompetent. This portrait of him is misleading. Fages was embroiled in many quarrels with the missionaries, but he marched to the beat of a different drum than did his clerical critics. The military commander was impressed with his lack of men and military material, and as a military bureaucrat, he looked askance at the Franciscans' demands for a quick expansion of the missions. Serra impatiently refused to brook delay in achieving his self-set goals. He envisioned the establishment of a mission ladder extending to Russian America, although in his calmer moments he realized the improbability of pushing beyond San Francisco Bay. He did speak earnestly of a Camino Real (Royal Highway) of missions located at intervals from Loreto to San Francisco— a distance of 473 leagues, or over one thousand miles. In all his dreaming, Serra never considered a new type of settlement. In this sense he was no innovator—he wanted to continue establishing the same kind of missions that had been successful in Sierra Gordo and Texas.

Friction between Fages and Serra was created in part by the fact that the military commander's powers were largely undefined. Serra insisted that Fages had no control over the friars, except indirectly through the command of the small military force stationed at each mission. This force was called the *escolta* (guard) and was composed of a *cabo* (corporal) and five privates. Fages argued that he must have control over the time and place of mission-founding, or else he could not adequately guarantee their defense. He never forgot that he had guarded San Diego and Monterey, some four hundred miles apart, with a small force of forty-three men. Three years later, after forceful pleas for more men, he could only gather sixty-one. His dispute with the missionaries continued, but for the time being Fages held the upper hand.

Despite the disputes between the military and religious authorities in Alta California, on August 24, 1771, the mission at Monterey was relocated at a new site, Carmel, five miles south of the presidio and its troublesome soldiers. During the same year, the Franciscans also started the missions of San Antonio de Padua on July 14, in the valley of Los Robles in central California; San Gabriel Arcángel on September 8, in the area east of Los Angeles; and San Luis Obispo de Tolosa on September 1, 1772, also in central California. For many years these rudely constructed missions had few converts. A report in December 1773 indicated that at all the missions combined there had been only 491 baptisms. The material development of the missions also lagged. In 1773 there were among all the missions only two hundred cattle, less than one hundred sheep, seventy goats, and two hundred pigs. Even though the Franciscans had spent 250,000 pesos upon Alta California, the development of that area was meager.

The power struggle between Serra and Fages persisted. It became acute over the issue of the projected mission of San Buenaventura, which was to have been located midway between San Diego and Monterey. The original Spanish plans had proposed founding this mission soon after the original two missions were established. The priests, the escolta and the necessary equipment arrived in San Diego, where they were detained by Fages. He averred that the thousands of Alta California Indians would not remain peaceful indefinitely and that the overriding demands of military necessity would not permit the establishment of the mission. Thus delayed, the Buenaventura mission was not founded until 1782. The conflict between the two men became even more critical when Fages declared that Serra's desire to found new missions in the San Francisco Bay area, in the face of the troop shortage, was "nothing less than the temptation of the evil one."

When the Franciscan missions in Baja California were turned over to the Dominican fathers, Serra's former student Francisco Palóu was free to join his one-time mentor. With the capable Palóu available to serve as father-president during his absence, Serra went to Mexico City to appeal to the Spanish viceroy about his difficulties with Fages in developing Alta California.

Serra arrived in Mexico City on February 6, 1773. On September 23, 1771, the vice-regal term of the Marqués de Croix had ended, and he was replaced by Don Antonio María Bucareli y Ursúa. Related to most of the old noble families of Italy and Spain, Bucareli had fought in both countries as an engineer and a cavalryman. He had served his administrative apprenticeship as governor of Cuba. From this post the king appointed him to the viceroyalty of New Spain. A man of ability and character, when he died in 1779, the king decreed that the usual *residencia*, or examination of his official conduct, be waived.

Serra and Bucareli had some unrecorded conversations about Alta California. We know something of what Father Serra urged upon the viceroy, since Serra at Bucareli's request wrote a Representación, dated March 13 and April 22, which totaled some thirty-three paragraphs embodying his suggestions for improving conditions in Alta California. Serra asked for the removal of Fages, suggesting as his replacement Sergeant José Ortega. In Serra's eyes, Ortega had proven himself a capable subordinate on the Portolá expedition. The viceroy agreed to withdraw Fages and his Catalonian volunteers, but he did not accept Ortega as the replacement, contending that Ortega did not possess sufficient rank and standing for the post. Instead, the viceroy's choice fell upon Captain Fernando Rivera y Moncada. Rivera, who had sulked when Fages was originally given the appointment, had by 1772 returned to his hometown of Compostela on the Mexican mainland. He had gone into retirement, borrowing heavily to purchase a hacienda. Therefore, this long-deferred appointment may have been no great satisfaction to Rivera; nonetheless he accepted. Borrowing more money, he journeyed to Mexico City to confer with Bucareli about his new assignment. Then he returned to Compostela to bid his family goodbye, and depart for Sinaloa to make arrangements for his new post. Rivera was sullen, quarrelsome and lazy, and Serra was to find him no easier to deal with than Fages had been.

In addition to the removal of Fages, many of Serra's other requests were granted by Viceroy Bucareli: Spanish soldiers who violated Indian women could be removed at the request of the missionaries; the army was to assign married rather than single soldiers to California, and these men must bring their families with them; the land link Serra had urged was to be opened from Mexico to California with Captain Juan Bautista Anza, commander of the Tubac presidio in Arizona, blazing the desired trail; the punishment of the Indians was to be left to the missionaries. A satisfied Serra returned to California.

Rivera traveled to Sinaloa in northwestern Mexico and began recruiting married soldiers for Serra in Alta California. He was able to assemble a party of fifty-five, who were transplanted by sea from San Blas to Loreto. Ortega (who had been promoted to lieutenant and placed in command of what would soon be the San Diego royal presidio) was ordered to escort the families from Velicatá to San Diego and Monterey, while Rivera pushed ahead more rapidly to assume his new command. This band of fifty-five were the first bona fide settlers in California. They arrived one and a half years before Anza's party, which was taken to San Francisco by the overland desert route. The Ortega party followed the so-called Pacific Trail that Portolá and Serra had blazed five years earlier. Additional colonists, many of them skilled workmen, came by sea to swell the number of Spanish settlers in Alta California.

Both the sea route from Mexico and the alternate route across the Gulf of California and up the barren California peninsula were difficult and treacherous to travel. Spanish vessels were always so small—two hundred tons or less—that cargo space was at a premium. Moreover, these ships could never be relied upon to arrive on schedule. Passage along the Pacific Trail meant traveling up the arid peninsula, if one were lucky enough to survive a stormy passage across the Gulf of California.

On May 2, 1772, a thirty-seven-year-old veteran soldier, Juan Bautista de Anza, captain of Tubac, an important frontier garrison post, proposed the establishment of a land link between Mexico and California. Anza's proposal carried weight with Spanish officials, since he was a man who had spent his life on the frontier. He came from a lineage of two generations of Indian fighters and frontiersmen, and he was no dreamer. In the recent conflict with the Pimas and Seris Indians, Anza, under the command of Inspector-General Gálvez, had recently won fresh laurels. Upon one occasion, he had killed a famous Indian chief in hand-to-hand combat.

After Bucareli received Anza's proposal for a route northwestward from Sonora to the sea, he discussed the matter with Serra. The Franciscan leader had been a staunch advocate of a land passage to California, for he and his missions had suffered many vicissitudes when supply ships failed to arrive. Bucareli was sufficiently impressed with the plan to call a junta of his major advisers to discuss the feasibility of such a land route. A resolution favoring Anza's proposal was passed which empowered Anza to recruit twenty volunteers and two priests for the expedition. The Spanish government required that Anza must personally bear all costs of the trip. The captain was not to attempt to colonize; he was only to travel to and from Monterey to test the feasibility of such a route.

Juan Bautista Valdés, a veteran of the Portolá expedition, traveled to inform Anza of the viceroy's order. Valdés later accompanied Anza on the expedition, earning the soubriquet from some historians as the "Kit Carson" of the Anza party. In addition to Valdés, Anza's band included

two priests, twenty soldier volunteers, a San Gabriel Indian from Alta
California named Sebastian Tarabal, who had run away across the
desert to Sonora and who was now pressed into service as a guide, a Pima
interpreter, and eight Indians.

On January 8, 1774, Anza's group departed from Tubac in northern
Mexico. He set out westward with thirty-five packloads, sixty-five cattle
and one hundred forty horses. The party passed through the area of the
Pima missions to Caborca, the last Spanish settlement before the Mission
San Gabriel, hundreds of miles away in Alta California. Anza had selected
the correct season to cross this territory, for the winter rains had just
filled the water holes. Anza and his party forged a trail over the Camino
del Diablo, a two-hundred-mile route across the desert to the present city
of Yuma. The area traversed by Anza was not a trackless desert. Across
its surface ran a collection of Indian trails which began in southern New
Mexico, southern Arizona, northern Chihuahua and Sonora, and ran
toward the Colorado River. This myriad of trails gradually merged
into two main routes, one of which followed the Gila River, and one
which crossed the desert from Sonoítac to Yuma. These two trails then
merged into one at the Gila and Colorado river junction. From there they
broke into many trails heading toward present-day San Diego and Los
Angeles.

Following these trails, Anza reached the Gila-Colorado junction. This
phase of the journey Anza recognized at once as being the most critical,
since he was now in the home of the powerful Yuma tribe. He realized
that if his party were to proceed, he must win their friendship. When the
Spanish officer began to encounter the curious Yuma Indians, he persuaded them to help him. The natives carried the party's baggage and one
reluctant missionary who was afraid to ford the Gila and Colorado rivers
on horseback. Once across the river, Anza followed the advice of the
Indians and descended the Colorado River until his men reached the
native village of Santa Olaya. From this point, Anza's party pushed west
into the sand-dune country of the Colorado. Soon the mules became
exhausted by the difficult terrain, and the party was forced to return to
Santa Olaya. The ten-day journey across the dunes had exacted a heavy
toll of the expedition's animals. Finally, Anza decided to leave his baggage
and cattle behind in the village along with the more worn-out pack animals. To guard this property, he detached his head muleteer and two
soldiers.

Before plunging anew into the desert, Anza's soldiers and the Indians of
the village relaxed by dancing to a violin one of the soldiers carried with
him. After this short rest, Anza and the balance of his men, the ten best
mules, and several strong horses once again attempted to cross the dunes.

To avoid the worst of the sand dunes, Anza journeyed down to the

Colorado River meadows around Volcano Lake. After six days of hard riding, he reached water and pasturage near the foot of the Sierra Nevada. One of his missionaries and the Indian Tarabal recognized the surrounding country. After six more days of travel, the party came to the San Carlos Pass which traversed the Sierra Nevada. The Anza expedition crossed the mountains by this pass into the coastal region of California. On March 22, after a seven-hundred-mile trek from Tubac, Anza's party reached the mission of San Gabriel. Then he and his men moved north to Monterey, where Anza and Father Palóu busily laid plans for a string of missions along the trail and for a mail route from Mexico to Monterey. Returning by the same route, Anza reached Tubac on May 26.

The viceroy was thoroughly delighted by Anza's report, in which he described the route with great enthusiasm, declaring that supplies could go along it without great difficulty. Anza also pointed out that the Indians along the way were weak, with the exception of the Yumas whom he considered to be relatively friendly. He did not stress the vital fact that if the Yumas ever desired to do so, they could snap the land link at the Gila-Colorado river junction.

Considering all points of the report, Bucareli authorized Anza to recruit twenty families (some accounts say thirty) as settlers to be taken to the San Francisco Bay area. In addition, Anza was to select ten trusted veteran soldiers as a guard for the party. The Spanish government promised to furnish every family with fresh supplies of equipment and clothing. Anza had warned against giving the settlers cash, for he realized that among the poor families of Sinaloa, where he would have to recruit, money would irresistibly tempt them to gamble. He had hoped to find the Sinaloa populace eager to provide colonists; instead recruits were difficult to convince.

The San Francisco Bay region had been thoroughly explored as far back as 1772, when Fages and a small exploratory party had made a cursory inspection of the area. In 1774, Rivera and Father Palóu penetrated far enough north to plant a cross above Seal Rocks. Finally, in August 1775, Don Manuel Ayala, a skillful sailor, attempted to bring the *San Carlos* into San Francisco Bay. Twice he approached the mouth of the bay, only to be driven off by strong winds. After twelve hours of maneuvering his vessel for a third try, Ayala reached a point one league inside the entrance of the bay, under what was later called Fort Point, where he anchored for the night. The date was August 5, 1775.

Shortly after Ayala's ship had passed through the Golden Gate, Anza began plans to start his trek to California early in September 1775. Preparations for the journey were delayed because of the slowness of his recruiting and an Apache raid on Anza's herd of horses. Over five hundred horses were stolen. This was a serious blow to the project, since inferior mounts had to be substituted at almost the last minute. Yet the energetic Anza labored to restore his losses.

Finally, on September 28, Anza held a review of his troops. The next day, after a mass and sermon by one of the party missionaries, his expedition departed from Horcasitas for Tubac, where more men and animals were added to the party. Anza left from Tubac on October 23, 1775, at the head of his second company, which consisted of 240 men (colonists, servants, interpreters, muleteers), women and children, and over one thousand animals. Of the soldiers in the party intended for permanent duty in California, only Lieutenant José Moraga did not take a wife with him.

Anza guided this expedition with such diligence and skill that only one life was lost during the entire 1,500-mile trip—a woman died in childbirth. Contrasted with the record of several gold-rush parties in 1849, whose ranks were decimated by the trip over the same route, Anza's record seems remarkable.

Remembering the difficulties of his first trip, Anza did not attempt to travel to Calorca and across the Camino del Diablo, but headed north instead toward the Gila River. This route allowed the company sufficient water, but proved deficient in fodder for the animals. After a march of thirty-seven days, the group reached the junction of the Gila and Colorado rivers. Anza grumbled at the slow pace set by the sick missionaries and several childbirths. He also noted with impatience that a new mother could not sit a horse sufficiently well to keep up with the party for five days after birth. Excluding nine missionaries left at the crossing of the Colorado among the friendly Yuma Indians, Anza's party was augmented by eight successful births en route and was larger at the end of the trip than at its inception.

At the junction of the two rivers, Anza was confronted by a new problem. The Colorado had risen since his previous trip, and he could not cross at the same place again. Anza successfully scouted a new ford on the river.

After several days with the Yumas, Anza pushed ahead through the desert country west of the river. Profiting from his previous experience, Anza crossed the rough country easily. He split his party into three divisions and ordered them to march on alternate days so that the waterholes would have time to refill. The third division under Lieutenant José Moraga experienced the greatest difficulty. The lieutenant suffered from the cold (it was December), and this exposure caused him severe head pains and earaches. Later in life, when he became deaf, he blamed his affliction on the hardships of this trip.

By mid-December Anza's party began ascending the mountains, where they were buffeted by icy rains and snowstorms. In the midst of the mountains, the entire company halted while one of the women gave birth to a child. Only one day of rest was permitted her before the expedition again started the jolting ride over the rude mountain trail. A four-minute earthquake surprised and confounded the group, but under Anza's wise leadership panic was averted. On January 4, 1776, the company finally arrived at the San Gabriel mission.

To their dismay, the weary party learned that they had walked into the middle of a fierce Indian uprising that threatened the very future of Spanish California. This insurrection had begun among the San Diego Indians. Originally the mission at San Diego had been located on a hill next to the presidio itself. Each day the Indians at the mission loyally trooped farther up the valley to work where more abundant rainfall and river water for irrigation were available. The missionaries argued that the mission should be located in this agriculturally more promising region, away from the distractions of the presidio soldiers. Early in 1774, the viceroy agreed to allow the Franciscans to relocate the mission.

The new mission buildings were not much of an improvement over those at the old mission site. The new site was on a slight rise located some six miles from the presidio, amidst an Indian rancheria called Nipaguay. As the molestation of Indian women continued, indignation increased among the mission natives. Added to this indignation was growing resentment among the San Diego Indians over recent atrocities committed by the Spanish. The Indians contended that one of the missionaries had threatened to burn the rancheria if the settlement were not moved further away from the mission grounds. They complained that several Christian Indians had been flogged by the missionaries for attending a pagan dance. The Indians further charged that two important Indian chiefs had been incarcerated for supposedly robbing fish from some Indian women. These imprisoned chiefs, whose Christian names were Carlos and Francisco, escaped into the interior to arouse the pagan Indians against the Spanish. Runners spread out as far as the Colorado River, urging an attack upon the hated Spaniards. Meanwhile, sympathetic mission Indians were recruited to attack the Spanish from within at the appropriate time. November 5, 1775, was a bright moonlit night. Altogether there were twenty-two Spaniards in San Diego, evenly divided between the presidio and the mission. Four of the Spanish soldiers at the presidio were ill, and two were in the stocks to expiate minor offenses. The complacent Spaniards had stationed no guards. At one o'clock in the morning, approximately six hundred Indians quietly surrounded the mission and then attacked, yelling and screaming, pillaging the church and setting it afire. A thirty-five-year-old missionary, Luís Jayme, not believing that the Indians seriously meant harm, rushed out calling to them. He was seized and dragged away. His body was found the next day, stripped, beaten and pierced by at least eighteen arrows. Other Spaniards took refuge in an adobe storehouse, from which they directed a stiff defense. Corporal Rocha distinguished himself as a musketeer by beating back several Indian attacks. Failing to take the storehouse by dawn, the Indians retreated. Two loyal Indians were sent through the lines to the presidio. Since the Indian plan to attack simultaneously at both Spanish strongpoints had miscarried, the little force inside the presidio slept through the entire affair. Once aroused, the Spanish soldiers sent out a relief force to the mission. Quickly the force found that only those Spaniards who had ventured outside the stockade were killed. Father Jayme and one other Spaniard were the only immediate fatalities, but two soldiers and the carpenter were badly wounded. Eventually the carpenter died of his injuries. After a hurried conference, it was decided to evacuate the mission personnel to the safety of the presidio.

Help came quickly. José Ortega and a handful of soldiers had gone to found the new mission of San Juan Capistrano. They received news of the attack and quickly returned to San Diego. The San Diego situation was so critical that it was nearly the end of November before Ortega could spare a runner to carry word of the disaster to Rivera at Monterey.

In a sense this attack supported Fages' fear that the Spaniards were too thinly dispersed in Alta California to defend themselves adequately. In all of Alta California, there were only seventy-five soldiers to guard five missions and two presidios. The situation might have completely deteriorated but for the timely arrival of Anza's small, picked force. Later investigations disclosed that both pagan and Christian Indians from forty different rancherias had been involved in the attack. The Spanish were lucky that the warlike Colorado Indians had been mollified by Anza's recent visit among them and had refused to join the uprising.

Rivera hastened down to the San Gabriel mission to direct operations against the Indians. Although Anza's orders called for him to proceed at once to the San Francisco Bay area, he offered twenty of his best troops to Rivera. On January 7, 1776, Rivera, Anza and thirty-five men started for San Diego. Upon their arrival on January 11, they found that the situation at the presidio had eased considerably with the arrival of two Spanish vessels and twenty-five more Spanish troops. Moreover, the Indian revolt had lost momentum. After their indecisive attack upon San Diego, the natives made no plan for future operations, and their force slowly began to disintegrate. Many Indians became disillusioned and returned to their rancherias in the interior.

To Anza's disgust, he found Rivera dilatory in his campaign against the Indians. After delaying a month at San Diego, Anza left twelve of his men with Rivera and returned to his colonists. Rivera directed his men to form patrols in order to scour the countryside for unfriendly Indians.

Hostile Indians were captured and punished with fifty lashes upon their backs. One Indian died under the lash. Another captive committed suicide. Francisco, the chieftain, was among those captured, but Carlos successfully eluded his pursuers. After months of wandering, he finally walked unrecognized into the presidio, seeking sanctuary in its church. The missionaries agreed that he could be sheltered. When Rivera learned of this, he furiously demanded that the priests hand him over for punishment. When they refused, Rivera forced his way into the building and seized the Indian. Rivera's excuse for breaking the time-honored custom of sanctuary was that the structure then used as a church was actually a converted warehouse. Father Vicente Fuster, a survivor of the Indian attack, promptly excommunicated Rivera for committing a sacrilege. When Serra supported Fuster in his action, Rivera returned Carlos to the missionaries, and his excommunication was rescinded. Carlos' ultimate fate is unknown.

The attack upon the San Diego mission gave the Franciscans their first martyr in Alta California. It also demoralized for at least a year the orderly process of Spanish settlement. The significance of this revolt of the San Diego Indians has often been missed. If the Indians had been better led, more persistent, or a little luckier, they might well have ended Spanish rule in southern California. If the royal officials had then decided that the reconquest of this area was not worth the effort, the real loser might have been the United States as Spain's eventual heir.

Upon his return to San Gabriel, Anza encountered more troubles. Five muleteers had deserted, taking with them some of the best mounts. Anza dispatched Moraga and ten men, who captured the runaways, recovered the steeds, and then rejoined Anza, who was leading his party of colonists up the coast in the face of torrential rains. They reached Monterey on March 10.

At Monterey Anza became seriously ill. When no doctor could prescribe an effective medicine, he concocted one of his own and slowly recovered. As soon as he was physically able, he started north to explore the San Francisco Bay area. Accompanied by a few men, the commander left Monterey on March 23. In the bay area, he selected sites for the presidio and one for the mission along a small stream he called Dolores. (He selected this name because March 29 was the day set apart in the religious calender to honor the sorrows of the Virgin Mary. In time the name for the stream superseded the correct Spanish name for the mission.) He then explored the region around the bay, according to his instructions. He traveled up the eastern shore as far as the junction of the San Joaquin and Sacramento rivers. From a nearby hilltop, he saw that the two rivers had widely divergent courses, but he did not see the great valley through which they flowed. Returning along an alternate route, he emerged from the hills near the present town of Gilroy and returned to Monterey by early April.

There he discovered to his indignation that Rivera wished to forbid the colonists to leave the Monterey region in order to make the Spanish hold more secure in that area. Anza had determined to lead his settlers to the bay area, but he reluctantly recognized that this move was impossible. A long exchange of letters passed between Anza and the protesting Rivera. As Anza began his return trip to Sonora, Rivera suggested a meeting between them to settle their differences. Such an interview was arranged several times at different places, only to be canceled by a petulant Rivera. The one time the two leaders did meet face to face, Rivera was so enraged that after a perfunctory greeting to Anza, he spurred his horse and rode away. After this insult Anza refused to meet with him, insisting that all their communications be written.

Unable to resolve his differences with Rivera, Anza left California for Mexico City. Before leaving he prepared a record of their conflict and left instructions with Lieutenant Moraga to proceed with the colonists if Rivera were formally pronounced mad, as Anza fully expected he soon would be.

Anza had performed a herculean feat in opening up northern California and establishing a land link with Mexico. The great early historian of California, Hubert Howe Bancroft, has said of Anza's expeditions that he had surmounted greater obstacles than those which had confronted de Soto, La Salle, Pike or Frémont.

On his way back to Mexico, Anza reëstablished his relationship with Palma, chief of the Yumas. Palma offered to return with him to Mexico City; to cultivate future good will with this tribe, Anza agreed to take the Indian with him. The Spanish officer also hoped to be sent to the Yuma country as commander of a presidio there. Instead, he was appointed governor of New Mexico, where he served for nearly a decade. After resigning as governor of that territory, Anza returned to Arizpe in Mexico. He died on December 19, 1788, and was buried in a local church. Recently his grave was uncovered under the floor of the church, and his skeleton, still clothed in his military uniform, identified.

Although Anza had no further contact with California, his ideas for a San Francisco Bay settlement were quickly implemented. An order from the viceroy to settle that area reached California soon after Anza had left. Rivera did not dare disobey it. Consequently Lieutenant Moraga with two missionaries, Palóu and Cambón, led settlers to Anza's sites. Moraga dedicated the presidio on September 17, 1776, and on October 9, Father Palóu founded the mission San Francisco de Asís. On January 12 of the following year, some of the colonists in the Anza expedition founded the mission Santa Clara de Asís. Far to the south between San Diego and San

Gabriel, mission San Juan Capistrano (originally founded on October 30, 1775, and abandoned eight days later because of the San Diego Indian attack) was reëstablished on November 1, 1776.

In addition to the founding of missions and presidial settlements, civil government was established during this period in Alta California. The first California charter of government was the Reglamento Provisional issued in 1773. This charter was primarily authored by Juan José de Echeveste, a man who had never seen California. Echeveste had obtained some knowledge of the area while serving in Mexico City as purchasing agent for Alta and Baja California. On May 19, 1773, he presented his recommendations to the viceroy. A junta modified his proposals on July 8, 1773, and on July 23 Bucareli issued the revised document. According to the terms of this charter, Baja and Alta California and the port of San Blas were put under one rule.

The Reglamento also contained estimates of the needed annual expenditures which would not be covered by the Pious Fund. The charter emphasized that the Spanish government wanted the population of Spaniards and hispanicized Indians to be greatly augmented. Anyone willing to go from Mexico to California could receive a free trip, rations for five years and a sailor's salary for two years. To be properly understood, the Reglamento must be considered in conjunction with the viceroy's instructions to Rivera on August 17, 1773. Rivera had been enjoined to christianize and hispanicize the Indians by establishing missions. Bucareli foresaw that the mission settlements would become the sites of great cities, and he ordered Rivera to plan their location with this future in mind. In addition, Rivera was to recruit soldier-settlers who would make their homes in pueblos. In California the pueblo or town was the preferred unit for frontier settlement, rather than the individual clearing or homestead of the eastern American frontier. The pueblo was a farming community. This type of settlement was transported from Spain's older frontiers to the new frontier in Alta California. Valuable inducements were offered to individuals who would inhabit these pueblos, such as individual land grants; however, these grants were governed by royal regulations. As part of his plan for civil government, Bucareli also attempted to regularize Rivera's position in Alta California. Although Rivera had to report his activities to the governor at Loreto, the governor was forbidden by Bucareli to revise any of Rivera's decisions. Thus Baja and Alta California were to have separate administrations. Rivera received strict orders not to allow any unauthorized vessels in California, except for Manila galleons and supply ships from the newly enlarged port of San Blas. Ordinary Spanish craft and foreign vessels were rigorously excluded from California ports.

In January 1776, Julian de Arriaga died and his post as Minister of the Indies passed to José de Gálvez, Marqués de Sonora. Gálvez decided to reconsider his plan for the commandant-generalcy of the frontier provinces of the Californias, Texas and New Mexico. As envisioned by Gálvez, this new command was to be independent of the viceroy. Such a command might have generated new energy into the California endeavor, if Gálvez had not appointed Teodoro de Croix to the new position. Although Croix was energetic, he was unimaginative and inefficient. Most of his effort was spent in rather inept attempts to suppress Indian uprisings in the northeastern portion of his command. Nonetheless, he ruled as commandant-general until he was promoted to the viceroyalty of Peru in 1783. Throughout his term of office as commandant-general, he flagrantly neglected California.

On September 15, 1776, the nominal governor of California, Felipe de Neve, was ordered by the viceroy to move his headquarters from Loreto to Monterey. In turn the troublesome Rivera was sent to Loreto to supervise Baja California as lieutenant governor. Monterey was now the capital of all the Californias, and Neve was ordered to direct the growth of Alta California. He did not relish the prospect of leaving quiet, sunny Loreto for an outpost on the frontier, but he dutifully arrived in Monterey on February 3, 1777.

On his way north, he observed that California needed three additional missions in the general area of the Santa Barbara Channel, as well as an additional presidio. Moreover, he proposed the establishment of pueblos on the San Gabriel, Santa Ana and Guadalupe rivers. He also suggested an increase in the military forces at San Diego, Monterey and San Francisco.

Neve's suggestions went first to Bucareli, who now lacked the authority to implement them. Bucareli carefully passed them on to Commandant-General Croix, who quietly pocketed the suggestions. Nonetheless Neve went ahead and implemented as many of his ideas as his resources would permit. Croix's one outstanding merit as a supervisor of California affairs was that he generally approved any project that Neve accomplished.

Neve had been instructed to distribute land to new colonists. Consequently he ordered Lieutenant Moraga to select five of Anza's soldiers and nine other families from the presidios of San Francisco and Monterey to found a new pueblo at San José. Neve liked the site, since it offered extraordinarily fertile land for farming.

Sixty-six settlers (*pobladores*) founded the pueblo of San José by erecting mud huts on the east bank of the Guadalupe River near the mission of Santa Clara. Serra argued that the pueblo had been placed too close to the mission. He pointed out that it was a source of distraction for the Indians at the mission and that the cattle from the two places were always becoming intermixed. Nevertheless, the settlers laid out the pueblo around a central plaza in the classic Spanish style. They dammed the nearby river for water. Each colonist's family was given probationary title. These grants were provisional for five years, after which the settlers could receive permanent title to their lands. The *suerte* (grant) was supposed to be sufficiently large to sow a fanega (about one and a half bushels) of wheat. Moraga officially dedicated the pueblo on November 29, 1777. The settlers' final title to the land was confirmed in May 1783.

Neve next revised and amplified the fundamental civil law of California which had been promulgated in 1773. His Reglamento (code of laws) was issued on June 1, 1779, and was made effective at once. Royal orders confirmed it on October 24, 1781. It became the basis for civil government in California as long as the Spanish retained control there.

While the new regulations may have seemed clear enough to contemporaries, those parts relating to land grants later gave rise to interminable litigation. According to Neve, all *pobladores* were to be *"gente de razon,"* or civilized people. Indians had to be integrated into the pueblos only after they had proven their reliability. Neve's regulations ordered that all pueblos be built around a plaza and have Spanish-style streets. Settlers recruited from the older sections of New Spain were to be granted a town lot, a farm lot and the necessary tools, seed and livestock. To gain final title, the settlers had to successfully complete a probationary period of five years. All heads of households were granted the use of common or government land for pasturage, wood and water. Any "civilized persons" already living in California, including discharged soldiers, could obtain most of these benefits.

In return for this aid, Neve laid many obligations upon the settlers. They were required to sell their surplus agricultural products to the presidios. Every *pobladore* also had militia responsibilities during emergencies. No colonist could monopolize the common land by owning more than fifty animals of one kind. Each settler was forbidden to mortgage his land. In addition he must help till the common land from which community expenses were met, and the necessary roads, canals and town buildings constructed.

Neve and Serra soon came into conflict over the administration of Alta California. Neve reported to the commandant-general, who in turn was responsible to the King and the Council of the Indies, whereas Serra, as president of the missions of Alta California, was responsible to the religious authorities of the College of San Fernando in Mexico City, and ultimately to the commissary-general of the order in Madrid. When Neve asked for annual mission reports from Serra, Serra refused until permission to do so had come from San Fernando College. The College had recently issued a rule that neither the president nor any missionary was to communicate directly with the civil authorities. Previously Serra had written to Gálvez and Croix. At other times, before the rule against this practice, he had written as a courtesy to Bucareli, giving him the latest news in California. Eventually this ban on direct communication with the California civil authorities made day-to-day living so cumbersome that his superiors allowed Serra to communicate directly with the necessary military and civil officers. They demanded a copy of all transactions.

There were other problems. Neve wanted to develop Alta California by establishing more pueblos instead of building more missions. The governor envisioned a chain of interior missions guarded by soldiers taken from the escoltas of the seacoast missions. Neve planned to finance the establishment of the additional missions by reducing expenditures at the coastal missions. Thus he wanted to reduce the number of priests from two to one at the seacoast missions, unless the second priest was also chaplain at a presidio. He intended to place these extra priests at the interior missions. Naturally the Franciscans considered Neve's plan unreasonable and refused to start any new missions during his governorship, except for the long-deferred mission at San Buenaventura, dedicated on March 31, 1782. The royal authorities finally supported the missionaries in this dispute.

Neve also wished to institute some measure of self-government among the Indians in missions established ten years or more. To achieve this form of government the Indians were to elect *alcaldes* (similar to a mayor with judicial functions) and *regidores* (councilmen). The missionaries objected to this plan by contending that the Indians were not mature enough to govern themselves. The governor ignored their objections, and whenever the alcaldes abused their power, Neve would not allow the missionaries to punish them.

In addition Neve attempted to interfere with the appointment of missionaries, claiming this right as civil governor of California. Serra objected, contending that civil patronage in appointments could be used only in the mining town of Santa Ana in Baja California, since only that town constituted a real parish. Serra further argued that the governor's power of appointment did not extend to mission affairs.

To retaliate against Neve's treatment, Serra at Monterey and Palóu at San Francisco refused to perform religious services at the presidio chapels.

Although the dispute between Serra, Neve and the other civil governors has received much publicity, there also existed some friction between Serra and the authorities at San Fernando College. In 1771, Rafael Verger, the Father Superior of the College of San Fernando, complained in various reports that the missions of Alta California were so undeveloped that they did not merit the title of mission. He predicted that they would soon fail. Father Verger blamed this failure chiefly upon Gálvez, but Serra's enthusiasm for Alta California also nettled him. Verger once dryly expressed the view that it was "necessary to moderate somewhat his [Serra's] ardent zeal."

In the meantime, Governor Neve was busy with his plans for the founding of a southern pueblo, which would be called El Pueblo de Nuestra Señora La Reina de los Ángeles de Porciúncula (Town of Our Lady Queen of the Angels of Porciúncula). On a trip south in 1777, he selected a site for the southern pueblo, near an Indian village called Yangna, which was located west of the mission San Gabriel. Near the site of the pueblo, a small river emerged from what is today called the San Fernando Valley. Neve picked this site for its water supply, good soil and favorable climate.

At Neve's suggestion, Rivera was ordered from Loreto to recruit settlers from Sinaloa and Sonora. According to his instructions, Rivera could enlist twenty-four married settlers and their families; in addition he was to recruit thirty-four married soldiers and their families, and twenty-five unmarried soldiers to replace Anza's veterans in Sonora, who would thereby be released for California duty. Rivera's soldiers moved through northern Mexico exhorting would-be settlers; they promised free land and farm animals, tools on easy credit and a subsidy of ten pesos a month.

Despite these liberal blandishments, obtaining volunteers proved to be difficult. Although Rivera started recruiting in February 1780, he did not enlist his first civilian settler until May 30. By August 1, he had only obtained seven volunteers. Soldiers proved somewhat easier to convince, and by the beginning of August he had recruited forty-five of them.

By the end of 1780 Rivera had enlisted his quota of fifty-nine soldiers, but had gathered only fourteen civilian settlers. Of these fourteen, Governor Neve sneered that only eight were of sufficient health and vitality to be "of any use." Rivera had also been hard at work collecting nearly one thousand farm animals. Early in 1781 the company started from Los Alamos. Rivera stayed behind, but he sent his settlers with an escort of seventeen soldiers to Guaymas to be ferried across the Gulf of California to Loreto. From there the party trudged along the Pacific Trail to Alta California. One of the settlers died of smallpox along the way, others deserted, and only eleven survivors remained to found the pueblo. Including women and children, the total party numbered forty-two people. Only two of the adults were Spanish; eight were Indians. The rest of the group were mestizos.

Halting their journey at the San Gabriel mission, the settlers, accompanied by Neve's soldiers moved to the locale of the new pueblo. There the Spanish officials surveyed a plaza and town lots. On September 4, 1781, the soldiers fired a salute and a missionary blessed the site. Titles to the Los Ángeles *suertes* (grants) and *solares* (building lots) were formally confirmed on September 4, 1786.

Meanwhile Rivera headed an expedition along the land route from Mexico. This party included forty-two soldiers, thirty of them accompanied by their families. These colonists were supposed to settle at Los Ángeles and at another settlement at Santa Barbara.

Crossing by way of the Colorado River country seemed to present no difficulties, for the Spaniards since Anza's day had planted settlements near the confluence of the Colorado and Gila rivers. At these settlements, Spaniards and Indians were housed in the same compound in violation of Spanish law. The military and civil authorities controlled the Indians, while the missionaries had limited authority. Despite Anza's warning that the settlements must be adequately protected, they were very weakly garrisoned. In 1780 the Spaniards had founded the mission-pueblo La Purísima Concepción. Shortly thereafter, they established another mission-pueblo, San Pedro y San Pablo Bicuñer, southwest of the original settlement. Both settlements were placed on the west bank of the Colorado River. The Spanish officials recklessly parceled out land to settlers, ignoring Indian claims.

The Spaniards had become careless in a dangerous country. The Yuma Indians who dwelt there were not as peaceful as the California Indians. They were large and strong, and could, when properly led, be hard-fighting men. The Yumas had seen enough Spaniards to regard them with less respect and awe than when the Spanish had first arrived. Their chief, Palma, had been taken by Anza to Mexico City, but the mass of the Yuma Indians felt that the Spanish had neglected them. A few trinkets had been passed out to them by the Spanish officials, but these presents were niggardly in amount and only whetted the natives' appetite for more. As the Spanish colonists continued to live among them, the Yumas regarded them with disillusionment. The colonists at both settlements were poor physical specimens, the dregs of the towns of northwestern Mexico.

The Spanish official in charge, Santiago de Islas, erred in his treatment of the Yumas. First he was too permissive with them, and then he attempted to rectify his error by becoming strict. Soon Yuma bands roamed the two settlements arrogantly jeering at the Spaniards.

An air of tension hung over the two posts when Rivera led his party to the banks of the Colorado. At that time the missionaries spoke freely concerning their fears of an Indian uprising, but Rivera, despite his reputation for caution, had become contemptuous of the California natives and did not believe they would attack. As the Yumas crowded into his camp, he distributed presents to them. Yet the Spanish budget was limited, and Rivera could not see squandering his precious supplies upon Indians, so he allotted relatively few gifts. The Yumas regarded this as a manifestation of contempt for them.

Rivera foolishly sent his main company on to San Gabriel mission, while he and a dozen men rested most of the livestock on the eastern side of the Colorado River opposite Concepción. This compounded his earlier error, since by splitting his force he was now too far away to help or to be helped by the Spaniards in the small presidio at Concepción.

The Yuma Indians unexpectedly attacked on July 17. Hitting first at San Pedro y San Pablo, the Indians surprised and easily massacred all its men, except for five colonists who were spared for various personal reasons. These five men, together with the women and the children, were made prisoners. Then the Indians repeated their performance at the other settlement, except that they varied their pattern by not immediately killing the missionaries. On the following day they returned, and at the insistent urging of a former Christian Indian, massacred the priests.

Meanwhile Captain Rivera and his men on the other side of the river were unable to help the garrison of Concepción, nor did they feel they could successfully escape from the area. They armed their camp and awaited an Indian assault. The Spaniards had dug a shallow trench in which to take refuge, but it proved to be a poor fortification.

On July 18, a howling band of Yuma Indians swept down upon the Spaniards. As the Indians charged, the Spanish fired, killing several of them. The surviving Indians continued forward. Quickly a mob of warriors surrounded the Spanish horsemen stationed outside the trench. The Indian strategy was to rain blows with clubs upon the horses' legs and bodies, until they tumbled to the ground, throwing the Spaniards helplessly upon the turf. One or two Spaniards scrambled away to fight from the ditch, but the rest were killed. Then the Yumas charged the trench where the Spanish huddled in fear. The Spaniards fired one volley and then the Indians were in among them. Rivera was struck down with his men, the highest-ranking Spaniard to fall to the Alta California Indians. Rivera's death seemed particularly tragic, since he had planned to retire to his hacienda after completing his assignment. His bloody uniform, stripped from his body, became the trophy of one of the Yuma chiefs.

Forty-six to fifty Spaniards perished under the Indians' attack. Some ninety-one others, nearly all women and children, became prisoners of the Yuma. The dead were left lying in the fields under the hot summer sun. The Yumas set fire to all Spanish dwellings along the Colorado River and withdrew with their captives.

The first news of the massacre came to Alta California after the military escort who had taken the settlers to San Gabriel stopped on its way back to Sonora at the ruins of Concepción. While they were still gaping at the ruined buildings and staring at the rotting corpses in the field, they were surprised by a band of Yumas led by a chief wearing Rivera's old uniform. The Spaniards made their escape back to San Gabriel, but not before they had lost two more men to the Yumas.

It was more than another month befort a rescue expedition left Hermosillo on September 15. This party was led by the former commander of Alta California, Pedro Fages, now a lieutenant colonel. Their first objective was to ransom the captive Spaniards. Within five days Fages' force of about 110 men picked up the trail of the warring Yumas. Skirmishing frequently with the Indians, they had rescued nineteen captives by October 18 when they halted along the banks of the Colorado.

At this point the Yumas sent a captured Spanish soldier to Fages to ask for negotiations. After haggling, the Yumas agreed to exchange forty-eight captives for corn, blankets, beads and tobacco. To keep Chief Palma in a negotiating frame of mind, Fages sent him one of his own three-cornered hats. In addition, Fages took advantage of the lull to bury some of the bodies and gather up such records as the Spaniards could find strewn about the desert.

To the delighted surprise of the Spaniards, a force of six hundred Indian enemies of the Yumas suddenly attacked. The Spanish could not resist joining in their assault on the Yumas. When the Yumas drove off their Indian rivals, the Spaniards were glad to retreat to Sonoitac. In December Fages and his force returned to bargain with the Yumas for the release of the remaining prisoners. After further haggling, the Indians released all the captives who were willing to return to the Spanish. Some of the women had found new and more likeable mates and were not willing to return to Mexico. The relief force now finished the melancholy job of burying all the Spanish dead they could find.

After the Indians finished their bargaining, they vanished, not caring to continue the fight with the Spaniards. Fages rode his men in circles vainly seeking the Yumas. Early in 1782, he was glad to lead his exhausted men back to their Mexican base.

Much of the blame for the Colorado massacre could be placed upon Rivera and the other Spaniards on the scene. Neve and his advisers could have blamed their own parsimonious government for its pound-foolish policies. Instead most Spanish officials chose to attack the soundness of Anza's original scheme to colonize the Colorado country.

Commandant-General Croix, after conferring with a junta of his leading advisers, decreed that the Colorado area was not worth resettling. Thus the Yuma massacre, which might have had only a transitory, local importance, became an important factor in the future development of California. Spanish California faced a different and less secure future after its only land link with Sonora was permanently severed.

From then on, supplies for Alta California arrived only in the holds of the small, uncertain Pacific supply squadron, or by an unreliable ferry service across the Gulf of California and then over the arid Pacific Trail.

Goods remained costly and their arrival a matter of uncertainty. In a very real sense, the future economic growth of California was stunted by the Yuma massacre. Despite some gestures in this direction, the route was never reopened during the Spanish period. As a result, California had to build itself up largely through its own resources.

EIGHT

Spanish California Flowers

WITH the severance of the Sonora link, Governor Neve's plans for the expansion of California were curtailed. Nonetheless, he was able to establish a fourth presidio in Alta California at Santa Barbara on April 21, 1782. In time a small village of military dependents grew up around the barracks.

Under Spanish rule, California was divided into four administrative districts: San Francisco, Monterey, Santa Barbara and San Diego, each with its own presidio. Los Ángeles became the fifth district after its separation from Santa Barbara. In the civil pueblos or towns, an alcalde was appointed and instructed in his duties by the governor.

The office of alcalde had developed out of the Arab-Moorish invasion of Spain. Since that time, his insignia of office had been a cane of light wood with a knob of precious metal. Below the knob were holes through which was drawn a black silk cord with tassles. Whenever conducting official business, the alcaldes always carried their canes; often when the alcalde could not be present at some official ceremony, he would send his cane.

Assisting the alcalde in his municipal duties was the *ayuntamiento* (a town council). In the early stages of pueblo life, the ayuntamiento was appointed by the governor, but afterwards was elected by the town's citizens.

Despite this degree of self-government, the pueblos of Alta California were still subject to outside control. Using a device similar to that employed by the Spanish kings to control towns in the mother country, the

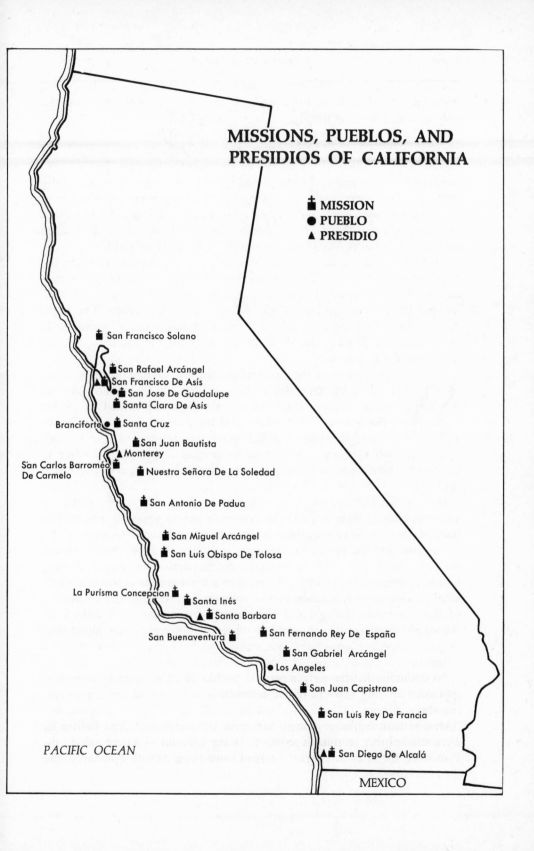

MISSIONS, PUEBLOS, AND PRESIDIOS OF CALIFORNIA

✝ MISSION
● PUEBLO
▲ PRESIDIO

San Francisco Solano

San Rafael Arcángel
San Francisco De Asís
San Jose De Guadalupe
Santa Clara De Asís

Branciforte Santa Cruz

San Juan Bautista
Monterey

San Carlos Barroméo
De Carmelo
Nuestra Señora De La Soledad

San Antonio De Padua

San Miguel Arcángel
San Luís Obispo De Tolosa

La Purísma Concepcion
Santa Inés
Santa Barbara
San Buenaventura
San Fernando Rey De España
San Gabriel Arcángel
Los Angeles
San Juan Capistrano

San Luís Rey De Francia

San Diego De Alcalá

PACIFIC OCEAN

MEXICO

California governors appointed commissioners in the pueblos. These commissioners ruled with an iron hand; an appeal to the governor was the only check on their authority.

Historian Edward Chapman has called the period from 1782 to 1810 the romantic period in California history. Prior to that time, the struggle for survival sapped much of the energy of the new Californians, but by 1782 California's settlement had been placed upon a permanent basis. Carefully nurtured crops were finally producing bountiful harvests. The number of livestock had increased. Starvation's grim spectre had at last been lifted from the colony. About 1810 the romantic period came to a close when revolutions in Latin America shattered the tranquility of California.

Even during this quiet era in California's history, disputes between the religious and secular authorities continued. Soon the bickering spread beyond the boundaries of Alta California to involve the viceroy of Mexico and the fathers superior of the college of San Fernando. The argument centered on the issue of the Franciscan missionaries' authority in Alta California. During this deadlock all plans for the founding of new missions were suspended.

To lessen the power of the missionaries, Spanish civil authorities developed a plan called the custodia, to replace the existing mission system. According to this scheme, the Franciscans were to be denied all secular control over the Indians. To the dismay of the Franciscans, some religious authorities favored this plan; the Bishop of Sonora adopted it in his diocese. Although Governor Neve was never able to put it into effect in California, dissatisfaction in Mexico with the mission system strengthened his hand.

In 1777 San Fernando College had conferred upon Serra the power to administer the sacrament of Confirmation—a power normally reserved to bishops. In 1779 Neve notified Serra that he must cease administering this sacrament until the viceroy revived his authority to do so. Serra ignored the governor's commands to surrender for inspection his patent allowing him to confirm, and placidly continued to administer the sacrament. Only after protracted correspondence between the viceroy and the authorities of San Fernando College, did Serra comply with the civil authorities. Although the viceroy examined the patent thoroughly, he could find nothing improper about the document and reluctantly returned it to Serra.

Neve diminished the power of the missionaries by forbidding them free postage, requiring them to obtain permission to leave California, prohibiting their custom of using Indians as ranch hands or messengers, and denying them military escorts for most ordinary journeys. Before he could curtail their activity further, he was promoted to a new post in the Provincias Internas. After two years of duty in his new assignment, Neve died on November 3, 1784.

Fages, who was governor of California for the next nine years, was no stranger to that area. The fiery Catalonian, who was known as "the Bear" because of his gruff manners, had married Eulalia de Callis, a Catalonian lady as stubbornly independent as himself. It is generally believed that his wife's family was instrumental in obtaining for Fages the various promotions which he received during the later years of his career. No sooner was he in California than he asked for his wife and young son, Pedro, to join him in the colony. But Eulalia, who was happy in the more civilized society of Sonora, refused to leave Mexico. Finally, after two of Fages' fellow officers, including Neve himself, wrote to her that California was much less primitive than she imagined, Eulalia agreed to join her husband in Monterey. From July 1782 to January of the following year, Doña Eulalia traveled slowly from Sonora, through Baja California, to Monterey. Along the way she was fêted and dined as the first lady of social standing ever to travel in those areas.

Governor Fages greeted a very disillusioned wife when Doña Eulalia arrived in Monterey. She considered the capital of Alta California a social desert; she was shocked by the nakedness of the California Indians, and promptly began to remedy this matter by giving them both the governor's clothes and her own. After being surprised several times to find his good clothes worn by some Indian vagrant he met in the streets of Monterey, the governor decided to end his wife's charities. He pointed out to her that both their wardrobes had been greatly reduced, and that if she did not stop her open-handed giving, both of them might be little better off than the objects of her charity, since fine clothes were unavailable in California. Doña Eulalia reluctantly agreed to the logic of his argument. Nevertheless, she was too emotional to repress her pity for the poor, and despite her shortcomings, she was always wistfully remembered by the poor of Monterey for her many kindnesses.

After the birth of a daughter in August 1784, Eulalia suffered some sort of mental disturbance. She announced that she refused to stay and rear her baby in the wilderness of California. When Fages forbade her to leave, she locked him out of her bedroom in retaliation. She also became extremely jealous, accusing Fages of lavishing too much attention upon an attractive Indian servant girl. She accused Fages of infidelity, and when the governor laughed at her accusations, she ran into the streets of Monterey, where she began telling her marital troubles to anyone who would listen. She even demanded that the Franciscan friars find a way to dissolve her marriage. The embarrassed Franciscans ordered her to return home and stay in seclusion until she had mastered her emotions.

In February 1785, Fages had to travel to southern California, so he arranged to have his wife stay at the mission San Carlos, where the missionaries could keep a watchful eye upon her conduct. Eulalia refused to leave her house and locked herself and the children in a room. At this point Fages, who had been remarkably patient with his wife, lost his temper. The governor broke down the door to his wife's quarters and loudly announced that if she would go no other way, he would bind her and carry her by force to the mission. Only then did Eulalia agree to leave. In the absence of her husband, she decided to make the friars at the mission pay for having chastised her. She made several public displays of her temper, and even complained of her situation in church. The missionaries threatened to flog her and imprison her in chains, but these threats made scant impression on the distraught señora. After an absence of more than six months, Governor Fages returned to Monterey and agreed to a reconciliation with his wife. Never again did they stage a public scene during the five remaining years of his governorship. Doña Eulalia had temporarily recovered her composure. She continued to reign as the queen of California society, since the social life of the colony revolved about the governor and his lady.

Spanish society in the New World was very stylized and rigid, positions in its hierarchy being based upon military rank and Spanish ancestry. The aristocracy consisted of all commissioned officers and high colonial officials of Spanish birth. If a man of Spanish stock were so unlucky as to have been born in the colonies instead of Spain, he was considered a Creole. A Creole was never considered equal to someone born in Spain. The Spanish-born were fond of saying that this discrimination was only fair, since long residence in the American tropics caused a man to degenerate. Below the Creoles on the social scale were the mestizos of white and Indian blood. Indians occupied the lowest position. Anyone of Negro blood suffered the same disabilities as the Indians. Creole ladies preferred to marry the meanest clerk of Spanish birth rather than the wealthiest or most handsome Creole. Likewise, ladies of mixed blood preferred the most undistinguished Creole as a husband over one of their own class. Ordinarily no one of mixed blood could break into colonial society, whatever his accomplishments. Late in the Spanish period, when Americans and Europeans of other nationalities found their way into California, they might, if sufficiently talented, win the social acceptance always denied half-breeds and Indians.

Despite the turmoil in Alta California, Serra continued to rule firmly over the nine missions between San Diego and San Francisco. Since Spanish civil settlements were few and small, the missions remained the spiritual and economic backbone of the colony. In the fifteen years of Serra's labor in Alta California, more than 4,600 Indians were induced to live at the missions. By 1784, Serra had become old and tired; his frame bent under the toil of his seventy years, the pains in his chest became worse. At two in the afternoon on the feast day of St. Augustine (August 28), he lay white and still on his bed. His companions at the mission San Carlos

Borroméo were shocked to discover that he had died, so noiselessly had he slipped from this life. Two funeral services were held on August 29 and again on September 4. The mission bells were rung and the guns of a warship at anchor in the harbor boomed in tribute to Serra. When he died, an era of California history died with him.

Serra was immediately succeeded as president of the missions by his former student, Father Palóu, who was also old and infirm. Palóu was only a temporary substitute, for within a year after Serra's death, the College of San Fernando picked Father Fermín Francisco de Lasuén of the San Diego mission as Serra's permanent successor. Palóu went down to the College of San Fernando where, two years later, he wrote the first biography of Serra.

The birth of Lasuén is a matter of dispute. Traditionally he is thought to have been born in 1720 in the Basque province of Álava. Although some historians still accept 1720 as the date of his birth, the facts of his life seem more credible if the more recent revision to June 7, 1736, is accepted as his birth date.

Admitted to the Franciscan order in 1759, he was sent to Mexico to the College of San Fernando, where he was assigned as a missionary in the Sierra Gorda region. In 1767 he left for Baja California to assist Serra in his work there. At that time he took charge of the mission of Francisco de Borja, the most northerly and important station in the Baja mission chain. For five lonely years he served as the sole missionary in that area.

When the missions of Baja California were turned over to the Dominicans, Lasuén and seven companions journeyed to Alta California. Lasuén drew an assignment at the San Gabriel mission, arriving there in September 1773. Two years later Lasuén took part in the abortive attempt to found the San Juan Capistrano mission. After this he was ordered to San Diego, which prospered under his careful administration. Lasuén's appointment as father-president of the missions came on February 6, 1785, but so slow were communications that this action did not become known in Alta California until September. Lasuén guided the destiny of the Alta California mission chain for the next eighteen years.

During his administration, the number of missions doubled from nine to eighteen. One of his first projects was to increase the number of missions in the Santa Barbara area to three. One mission, Santa Buenaventura, had been belatedly started there in 1782. On December 4, 1786, he journeyed down from Monterey to be present at the founding of the Santa Barbara mission near the already established presidio. Only a year later, on December 8, 1787, during the feast of the Immaculate Conception, Lasuén planted another mission in the same general area and named it after the feast. Next the energetic father-president turned his attention to completing the gap in the mission chain between San Carlos Borroméo and Santa Clara. A preliminary expedition had selected two sites in this region. Immediate construction was delayed because Lasuén lacked the authority to proceed. Permission from the civil authorities was not granted until July 1791. As soon as he had received the necessary permission, Lasuén traveled up from San Carlos to inspect the sites himself. He thoroughly approved of the site of the proposed mission of Santa Cruz, which he dedicated on August 28, 1791; but he disapproved of the site which had been selected for mission Soledad. He selected a new site and dedicated it on October 9, 1791.

Nuestra Señora de la Soledad, the thirteenth mission in the chain, had received its name at the time of the Portolá expedition. The party was encamped in the vicinity of the later mission when an Indian approached them. To all questions, he replied in his own language with a word that sounded like the Spanish word *soledad*. Thus Portolá put Soledad on the map as the place name for this area. Therefore, when the Franciscans decided to build their mission in this locality, the natural name for it was Nuestra Señora de la Soledad (Our Lady of Solitude).

From the days of its establishment, the mission suffered misfortunes. Royal gifts went astray, and it continued only through the charitable contributions of its sister institutions in Alta California. At its founding only a brushwood structure could be built, and this stood as the sole important building of the mission for six years.

It was 1797 before the missionaries built an adobe structure at Soledad. This building showed an alarming tendency to disintegrate under climatic conditions. The church, completely rebuilt in 1824, collapsed in 1832. After 1802 serious epidemics of disease decimated the Indian population.

In addition to these hardships, two of the most roguish Franciscans ever to serve as missionaries in California were stationed at Soledad—Mariano Rubi and Bartolomé Gili. Their tenure was brief, but they served at a critical time in the mission's growth. The two men had been pranksters while serving in San Fernando College in Mexico City. Among their feats were pilfering the storeroom of chocolate, rolling bowling balls through the halls of the dormitory after midnight, and scaling the walls of the college to spend a night in town. Their conduct at other times might have brought them a stern dismissal from the order, but Palóu, in charge at the College, was old and feeble, and the worst of the pair's exploits may have been withheld from him. They were transferred to California, and eventually to Soledad. They paid only a minimal amount of attention to their duties, being indolent and self-indulgent. After two or three years, the astute Lasuén had them transferred from California. They left 115 rather bewildered converts and some badly planted fields behind them.

Their conduct contrasts strongly with the last Franciscan priest at the mission, Father Vicente Francisco Sarría. Father Sarría, even though he had headed the entire mission chain at one time, served at Soledad when no one else could be found who would accept the assignment. When he arrived, there was little to eat and much work to be done. One morning in May 1835, Sarría fell before the altar while saying mass; that afternoon he died. His handful of faithful converts carried his body the long distance to mission San Antonio de Padua for burial. After his death the mission of Soledad closed, and its few converts dispersed to find better living somewhere else. The roofs of one building were seized to satisfy a debt, and the buildings crumbled into ruins.

In the late 1790's, Governor Borica assumed control of Alta California; he was able to achieve a more harmonious agreement with the Franciscans than had his predecessors. Lasuén received permission to found four missions in the short period from June to September of 1797: San José de Guadalupe, fifteen miles north of the pueblo of San José; San Juan Bautista, near present-day Hollister; San Miguel Arcángel, midway between San Antonio de Padua and San Luís Obispo; and San Fernando, Rey de España. This last mission had originally been intended to break the long march between San Gabriel and San Buenaventura. However, the land between the two missions was barren and had poor drainage. Lasuén therefore located the new mission south of the perfect midpoint between the two older missions.

Six months after San Fernando's dedication, Father Lasuén chose a site for a mission between San Juan Capistrano and San Diego. He rejected the former site chosen for this mission and elected instead to place it upon what had been the originally chosen site of San Juan Capistrano. He called the new mission San Luís Rey de Francia, in honor of a thirteenth-century king of France.

Father Lasuén should be credited not only for doubling the original nine missions of Serra, but also for doubling the total number of Indian converts. He directed the rebuilding of permanent adobe structures at Serra's original nine missions. More importantly, he was able to place the missions on a sound economic basis. Serra had made a small start in raising field crops and fruit trees. Many additional types of plants were added during Lasuén's administration. Lasuén also diversified mission economy by starting a number of mission industries. Some manufacturing was vital in a land where a saddle was more expensive than a horse. Skilled artisans and craftsmen of many types were brought up from Mexico to perform their special skills and to act as instructors for the Indians. Smiths, masons and carpenters entered the colony during Lasuén's term of office.

Lasuén's relationship with the civil authorities was better than Serra's had been. Fages' two immediate successors were rather mild personalities, and Lasuén was more flexible and less self-righteous than Serra had been. This is not to say that Lasuén did not campaign strongly for causes he felt were vital; for example, as a result of his experience as the only priest in charge of a mission, Lasuén was opposed to continuing this practice in Alta California. He argued that one priest, surrounded by pagan, uncivilized Indians, would have no companion with whom he could freely converse for months or even years at a time. Such a situation, he declared, impaired the performance of the missionary, as well as subjecting him to needless suffering. Similarly, he would countenance no plans which would take away the temporal power of the missionaries within the mission.

Serra's successor was a distinguished man who greatly advanced the cause of the missions. His death in 1803 ended the golden age of the missions. For many reasons, his successors averaged only two to four years in office. Never again was there a father-president such as Serra or Lasuén.

Some defenders of the mission system have pictured it as an idyllic time of harmony and peace, with the Indians working cheerfully under the direction of dedicated missionaries. Other writers have attacked the missions as institutions by which the Spaniards exploited the labor of unwilling Indians. The true picture lies somewhere between these two views.

At each mission there were usually two priests, who divided the many administrative tasks between them, frequently exchanging duties as a way of breaking the monotony. They enjoyed the use of the Indians' labor and had extensive civil authority over them. Even when the Indians were allowed to elect alcaldes and other officials, probably none were selected whom the missionaries had not approved. The only outside authority over the missionaries in their conduct of the missions was the governor, who exercised some jurisdiction over formal crimes and military affairs, and who was supposed to set overall administrative policy.

The Indians were instructed in the rudiments of the Christian religion, and as quickly as possible, a regular schedule of mission life was set up around daily religious observances. Very few of the Indians ever learned to read or write, but the Spanish missionaries did try to teach them a skill or trade appropriate to their talents and sex. With the aid of artisans from Mexico, some Indians soon learned blacksmithing, tanning, stonecutting, and bricklaying. Others were taught to work as farmers or to tend the livestock. Indian women sometimes learned the complicated arts of tailoring and dressmaking. The less skilled were taught to grind meal and weave cotton and wool. Quotas of work were assigned, or selected hours were set aside during the Indians' day when they had to perform the useful arts they had been taught.

The Indians at each mission developed different specialties. Sometimes the soil or climatic conditions dictated what the specialty would be, but sometimes it merely was the result of a particular priest's interest. San Antonio de Padua mission was famous for its Indians' skill in basketry, but even more famous for the golden palomino horses raised there. San José de Guadalupe was known for its fine all-Indian orchestra. Mission San Juan Bautista was famed for its excellent boys' choir. Mission San Miguel became legendary for its beautiful Indian painted frescos. Mission Santa Cruz specialized in the growing of wheat; San Fernando became celebrated for fine wines. All missions grew some wheat and significant amounts of barley, corn, beans, peas and lentils as well.

In all likelihood, the mission Indians were not overworked. The effective working day was from sunup to sundown. However, since Sundays and all important feast days were celebrated by total abstainence from labor, a five-day work week was not uncommon.

Since the routine of mission life was dull and monotonous, the missionaries tried to brighten life for the Indians by performing colorful religious ceremonies, that included chants, the use of incense, colorful vestments, and parades around the church. For the first time in their lives, the Indians were freed from the endless quest for food, which they had been forced to practice in the pre-mission period. By 1805 the mission fare, often a rich stew, was so heavy that a foreign observer wondered how the Indians cared to eat three such meals a day.

Yet the transition from life in the wilderness to life in a mission was difficult for many Indians. There is no doubt that the older the Indians were when they came to the missions, the more painful was the adjustment. As a rule, second-generation Indians more readily accepted mission life as a normal existence. To ease the adjustment, some missions granted two-week furloughs to those Indians who came from a long distance.

The Indian escapees were often mature men who were unable to adjust to the discipline. They had lived too long in a life of freedom from regular chores (the women and children did the routine daily tasks) to adjust to the mission routine. Runaways were not infrequent. Until 1817 records at San Gabriel mission revealed that about 8.6 per cent of the total Indians there became successful runaways. When it is remembered that the escapees were usually adult men, we can see that the true escape rate for them was much higher.

Whenever possible the missionaries with the help of the small mission guard hunted down the runaways. Interestingly, many runaways returned voluntarily when they found that the delights of life in the brush were not as great as temporary residence in a mission had led them to believe. Runaways who were recaptured were subject to confinement in the stocks or a whipping. These were cruel punishments, but since the Spaniards did not scruple to employ them upon their own soldiers, they did not view them as unusually severe.

Many students of the missions have commented upon the heavy death rate of the Indian converts. These seem to have resulted principally from the fact that the Indians were packed together densely and were exposed to diseases never known in pre-mission days. The diseases often appeared with greater severity among the Indians, for they had no natural immunity, and the missionaries had no effective remedies to cure them.

In many areas, the Christian ethic was unsuccessfully forced upon the Indians. Even the sternest mission discipline could not stop the Indians from gambling. One of their favorite games was to throw a random handful of sticks into the air and then place bets on whether the number which would fall to the ground would be even or odd. Deviation from the prescribed Christian code of sexual conduct was severely punished. An eighteen-year-old boy of predominantly Indian blood (a native of Los Ángeles) who was serving in the Buenaventura mission garrison in June 1800 was observed committing an act of sodomy with a mule. The young soldier was apprehended, tried and sentenced to be hanged in the presence of the entire garrison of the Santa Barbara presidio. Furthermore his body was burned, together with the mule who had shared in his "crime." The sentence was duly carried out.

As permanent mission buildings were erected, the Christian Indians were drawn into the communal life of the institution. Only the very stubborn Indians clung to their old life in the nearby rancherias. In time these settlements were blotted out, as outlying mission buildings were constructed. Almost all missions had an outlying ring of unconverted or runaway Indians who stubbornly dwelt along the boundaries of the mission and existed by stealthily preying upon its livestock and crops.

After a thoroughly regimented day, the Indians separated for the night. Married couples with their young children dwelt in separate small huts. The single Indians had their own special dormitories, rigorously segregated according to sex. Young girls were taken from their parents and locked for the night in large rooms with long wooden benches for beds. The missionaries hoped in this way to eliminate premarital sexual activity. Unfortunately, these dormitory arrangements crowded many Indians together in poorly ventilated rooms and contributed to the high incidence of disease.

To assist the priests in keeping order were three hundred Spanish soldiers in the missions and neighboring presidios. To supplement this security force, the missionaries eventually recruited a small special police force of trusted Christian Indians. Yet the missionaries depended also upon the docility and credulity of their charges, since a relative handful of Spaniards did keep as many as 31,000 converts in line. It should be noted that never more than one-eighth of the California Indians lived simultaneously in the missions.

Perhaps the most telling charge leveled against the missions in Alta California is that they never equipped the majority of Indians to take their place as self-sufficient individuals in a secular society. But Spanish treatment of the Indians was certainly no worse than that in other European colonies. The English decimated the Indians by war and introduced the same diseases. When the Americans came to California, they warred with the Indians and drove the small remnant of survivors onto reservations in the least desirable parts of the state. It is ironical that when the American federal government belatedly developed an interest in the Indians' welfare, it adopted a program roughly reminiscent of the mission system originally introduced by the Spaniards.

Fages' term as governor drew to a premature close. As early as October 1785, just one month after his reconciliation with his wife, she sent a petition to the Guadalajara audencia, asking that her husband be removed because of poor health. Fages knew nothing about his wife's action until after the letter had been sent. Then he had to move quickly to intercept it. Doña Eulalia could not bring herself to feel at home in California, and it seems probable that she never abandoned her campaign to have her husband accept a transfer elsewhere.

Fages liked California; he took a great interest in his estate at Monterey where he helped to oversee an orchard of six hundred fruit trees. In addition he cultivated many varieties of shrubs and grapes. Residents of Monterey remembered him affectionately as a burly governor who often belied his gruff appearance, since he seemed to have an almost inexhaustable supply of sweets in his pocket for the children he met.

Finally the constant nagging of Doña Eulalia won out, and early in 1790, Fages asked to be relieved as governor. As soon as word reached Monterey that his petition had been granted, Eulalia and the children left on a supply packet for San Blas. Although Fages had been told that he did not have to wait for the coming of his successor, he chose to stay on at Monterey until October or November of 1791, when he left for Mexico City. He rejoined his family and was making plans to return to his native Spain when he died in 1796. His term as governor saw no spectacular public events, but witnessed a slow, steady development of the province.

During Fages' governorship the commandant-general of the Internal Provinces had meddled with California matters from his headquarters at Arizpe, Mexico. With the appointment of Fages' successor, José Antonio de Roméu, Viceroy Conde de Revilla Gigedo decided to gain more control of California affairs. He was assisted in this plan by a royal order in 1793 which severed California from the commandant-generalcy and placed it directly under the viceroy.

Roméu was plagued by ill health during his entire term of office from April 16, 1791, to April 9, 1792. As an invalid, he did not desire to quarrel with the Church, so the Franciscan authorities quickly planted two new missions at Santa Cruz and Soledad. After Roméu's death in the spring of 1792, a council at Monterey agreed that the governor of Baja California should also be acting governor of Alta California. José Joaquin de Arrillaga was chosen to succeed Roméu as governor *ad interim* until November 1794, when a permanent successor was appointed. The sole noteworthy incident during his administration was an unsuccessful attempt to occupy Bodega Bay by fortifying a high point on the shore. This effort failed because of difficulties in landing supplies and ascending the mountain shore. The Spaniards finally settled for a fortification at Fort Point, at the entrance to San Francisco Bay.

Arrillaga's successor was Diego de Borica, who served until 1800. A Basque like his predecessor, Borica was urbane and witty. He worked harmoniously with Lasuén, and his governorship saw the last great burst of mission-planting activities. He boasted of Monterey's climate and lauded the good life possible in the province of Alta California. Since an increasing number of foreign ships came to California ports during his administration, he had to pay more than the usual amount of attention to coastal defense. He was well equipped to do this, for he had been a field officer in the Spanish army.

During his regime, Monterey social life reached a new peak. Borica was fond of good dining and often invited friends to share his festive table; his wife was a wealthy socialite who delighted in giving elaborate entertainments. In addition Borica's daughter was a great belle who enjoyed social festivities.

One goal Borica had set for himself was to increase the number of Spanish settlers. So far, California had grown slowly. In 1780 there were six hundred settlers and only about 970 in 1790. Borica was a propagandist for California, writing to Mexico that "all [were] getting to look like Englishmen." (The climate was so mild the Spanish were becoming light-skinned.) Still few settlers came, and by the end of Borica's governorship in 1800, the total number of Spanish settlers stood at only 1,200.

Borica supervised the establishment of the first civil pueblo since Neve's day, Branciforte, near the mission Santa Cruz. Named for the viceroy of Mexico, Branciforte was technically not a pueblo but a villa, designed for defense as well as colonization. In July 1797, Branciforte was founded with nine soldier-colonists and a total population of seventeen. These settlers were more European in origin than those of Los Ángeles and San José had been; yet the villa never prospered. Its failure is usually ascribed to the fact that the colonists who founded it were convicts sent from Mexico to serve out sentences of banishment.

Branciforte was considered an unwelcome neighbor by the Franciscans at the Santa Cruz mission. In fact, Lasuén had protested to the viceroy against the villa's founding, but had failed to convince him. The padre's worst fears regarding its proximity were realized; the settlers encroached upon the mission Indians' pasturage. When the Franciscans complained to Borica concerning this, the governor replied that since the Indians were dying out, the need for the mission would soon disappear and the matter would then take care of itself.

To obtain servants, Branciforte settlers lured the Indians away from the Santa Cruz mission. As a result the Franciscans were forced to place fresh restraints upon the Indians. This led to resentment on the part of the converts, and may have contributed to the murder of one of the missionaries, who was found dead one morning in his bed. At first the authorities decided that his death had resulted from natural causes. After two years, the actions of some of the mission Indians aroused fresh suspicion. The missionary's body was exhumed, and in California's first medical autopsy, evidence indicated that he had been murdered. Seven of the mission Indians were charged with murder. They defended themselves by saying that the priest had been guilty of excessive cruelty. Governor Borica argued that this was no justification for murder and sentenced all seven to receive a severe flogging.

Branciforte gradually passed out of existence as a settlement. Yet before it dissolved into a desolate ruin, foreign adventurers used the villa as a base for hide and tallow smuggling. By 1841 the settlement had so diminished that it was amalgamated with the mission Santa Cruz. The modern city of Santa Cruz today has grown over the sites of both the villa and the mission.

If Branciforte was an ignominious failure, it did not represent Borica's only attempt to increase the civil population of California. Between 1791 and 1798, at least twenty-eight prisoners were sent from Mexico. In 1800 the Spanish authorities sent nineteen foundlings from Mexico City to Alta California.

Civil pueblos were not the only type of civil community in Alta California. Mission pueblos grew up for the civilized Indians and other settlers attracted to the mission. The first of such pueblos was founded on September 1, 1772, at San Luís Obispo; the second came on November 1, 1776, at San Juan Capistrano. The third was a product of the Borica era, founded June 24, 1797, at San Juan Bautista. The last came at the beginning of the Mexican era of California at the Sonoma mission, July 4, 1823.

Of all types of settlements in the Spanish period, the private ranch was the least important. In 1790 there were only nineteen private ranches in existence. The number of true Spanish grants was very small; many of those so-called Spanish grants in the American period had actually been bestowed in the Mexican era. The grants in the time of Spanish control were not technically transfers of title analogous to the giving of property under Anglo-Saxon law; actually they were more similar to cattle-grazing permits.

The first provisions for granting land in California were made in 1773. At that time, Viceroy Bucareli issued an order conferring upon the governor the power to bestow land. Although the regulations permitted grants to others, most concessions were made to retired officers or non-commissioned officers of the presidio garrisons. The boundaries of the grants were only roughly measured; a rude map or even a verbal description seemed sufficient to describe the extent of the land awarded. By a law which was not always observed, the maximum amount of land which could be granted was three square leagues or about twelve square miles. The law also forbade private grants that infringed upon mission land, pueblos or Indian rancherias. As early as 1775, a soldier, Manuel Butrón, who had married a baptized Indian, Margarita Mirea, petitioned to be granted some land near the Carmel mission. Father Serra and Captain Rivera agreed to grant his request. As a result, Butrón took possession on November 27, 1775, of what was only a small 140-vara lot (about 372 feet). He later abandoned the grant for reasons that are obscure.

By contrast, the next land-grant action in 1784 dealt with giant estates. In that year Fages gave a grant to Manuel Pérez Nieto of about 300,000 acres, or sixty-eight square leagues. This was the famous Rancho los Nietos, mainly located in what is now western Orange County. In the same year two veteran soldiers, Juan José Dominguez and José María Verdugo, were the recipients of large tracts of land. Fages granted Dominguez the Rancho San Pedro near the present city of Long Beach. Verdugo was granted the Rancho San Rafael near the San Gabriel mission. Despite the vast grants, rancheros often hungrily eyed the neighboring mission lands.

The ranchero ruled like a king over many Indian *vaqueros*. Probably not more than thirty grants were ever made during the entire Spanish period. Only when Mexican rule came to California, which liberalized the granting of land and removed the restrictions on foreign trade of hides and tallow, did ranching really flourish.

Near the beginning of the nineteenth century, there was considerable turnover in both the secular and religious leaders of California. Diego de Borica retired as governor of California in January 1800 and died shortly thereafter. He was succeeded temporarily by Pedro de Alberni, a long-time officer in the Catalonian volunteers. Alberni died in 1802 after a short, undistinguished term. José Joaquin de Arrillaga took over a second time and ruled until his death in 1814.

On June 26, 1803, Father Lasuén, worn out by his long years of labor, died after a twelve-day illness. He was succeeded by Father Estévan Tápis. Tápis played mostly the role of a caretaker, although he did found one additional mission, the last of the southern institutions, at Santa Inés on September 17, 1804. This entirely completed the chain of missions from San Diego to San Francisco.

By the early 1800's, California had begun to change. The old isolation was swiftly fading. Strange tongues began to be spoken on the coast. Energetic strangers from the maritime countries of the world called at California ports. A new era had begun.

NINE

Foreign Visits and Explorations

FROM its founding until 1786, the Spanish colony of California had been a closed province. To the south lay Baja California and the territory of New Spain. Somewhere to the north were the Russians. To the east lay high mountains and seemingly impenetrable deserts. Only to the west was California open. And it was from that direction that the strangers came.

On the morning of September 15, 1786, two French ships, the *Boussole* and the *Astrolabe*, entered Monterey Bay, the first foreign ships ever to anchor there. These vessels were under the command of Jean François de Galaup, Comte de la Pérouse, who was voyaging around the world on a scientific expedition. La Pérouse had sailed from Brest on August 1, 1785, proceeding by way of Cape Horn to Chile. From Chile he sailed to the west coast of North America, after landing at the Hawaiian Islands. Since Spain and France had long been allies, Governor Fages had received orders to accord the French visitors a hospitable welcome.

In addition to surveying the flora, fauna and geology of the California coastline, La Pérouse had been instructed by the French government to report upon the adequacy of Spanish fortifications and troop strength in California, being careful not to arouse Spanish suspicions about his motives for visiting the area. Paris had also ordered him to investigate the potentialities of fur trade in the northern Pacific. It was known in Europe that the Russians were hunting otter in North American waters, and other European countries did not intend to allow the Russians a monopoly of that traffic. The French government had even considered establishing a trading post on the Pacific northwest coast. France's interest in a fur trade had been stimulated by the reports which the Englishman Captain James Cook had written during his voyage in 1776 to the northwestern American coast.

During his sixteen-day stay, La Pérouse presented the colonist with a gift which soon increased California's food supply—the white potato from Chile. This plant grew exceedingly well in many parts of the province.

In his posthumously published *Voyage autour la Monde*, La Pérouse testifies that the Spanish missionaries were dedicated men, although they held the California mission Indians in bondage analogous to that of the Negro slaves of Santo Domingo.

Having finished their observations, the Frenchmen sailed from Monterey and resumed their cruise of the Pacific. Nothing more was ever heard of the party, except for a legend about the wreckage of two French ships in the New Hebrides. The fate of La Pérouse's expedition discouraged French colonial enterprise in the Pacific.

La Pérouse had reported the extent of Russian operations in the Pacific to Fages, who communicated the information to Mexico City. Viceroy Manuel de Flores promptly dispatched two vessels under the command of Estevan José Martinez, to the north Pacific. The expedition sailed as far north as Alaska, reporting when it returned that British and Russian vessels were sailing as far south as Nootka Sound on the west coast of what is now called Vancouver Island.

Martinez was ordered to return to Nootka Sound to establish a fort and missions there as symbols of Spanish sovereignty. Landing at Nootka in May of 1784, the Spanish began to build a fort, complete with heavy artillery. Martinez discovered a brig at anchor, the *Iphigenia*, commanded by William Douglas. Martinez invited the ship's officers to visit his vessel, but once aboard the Spanish ship, the British were suddenly made prisoners and their vessel seized. Douglas soon negotiated an agreement with Martinez. Since the *Iphigenia* was flying a Portuguese flag and was registered to a Portuguese merchant, Juan Cavallo, Martinez agreed to release it if the reputed owner furnished bond to pay the Spaniards the value of the vessel. The Portuguese registry had been merely a precaution against seizure, for the *Iphigenia* was British owned. Douglas' deception went undetected by Martinez. After drawing supplies from the Spaniards, the *Iphigenia* sailed north, gathered a cargo of pelts, and then leisurely sailed for the Orient.

Soon after the *Iphigenia* sailed from Nootka, Martinez sighted another British ship, the schooner *North West America*, which was returning from a northern cruise. (This schooner's framework had been carried to Nootka by the *Iphigenia* and assembled on the shores of the Sound.) Martinez seized the vessel, which carried papers similar to those of the

Iphigenia. By this time, however, Martinez had become suspicious of ship's credentials and refused to release the vessel. Soon two vessels licensed by the East India and South Sea Company unsuspectingly sailed into Nootka—the *Princess Royal* captained by Thomas Hudson and the *Argonaut* commanded by James Colnett. Martinez discovered equipment and supplies for a settlement at Nootka and the frame of a schooner for use in the coastal fur trade. Martinez took possession of both ships, ignoring British entreaties and threats.

On July 14, Martinez placed the *Argonaut* under the command of a Spanish lieutenant and dispatched it to San Blas. Aboard the ship as prisoners were Captain Colnett, his officers and many of his crew. Martinez sent the *Princess Royal* and the *North West America* on trading voyages along the coast to gain provisions for the colony.

Martinez stubbornly believed that he had not exceeded his instructions by capturing these foreign vessels. He remained at Nootka until November 1789, when he was ordered to abandon his settlement and return with all his vessels to San Blas.

Martinez's actions had created a major diplomatic incident for the Spanish. When the captured *Argonaut* arrived at San Blas on August 16, 1789, the local Spanish officials started condemnation proceedings. The British prisoners were sent to Mexico City to be questioned by the viceroy. After a careful investigation, Viceroy Flores released Colnett and his men and returned their vessel. Flores feared the reaction of Great Britain. To save face for the Spanish, he claimed that they had only innocently violated Spanish claims on the northwest coast.

When the wildly indignant Colnett was released, he took possession of the *Argonaut* and sailed with his crew for Nootka, hoping to recover the *Princess Royal.* Discovering that Nootka had been deserted by the Spanish, Colnett sailed for China. In 1791, during a journey from Asia to the Hawaiian Islands, Colnett recovered the *Princess Royal*, which had been used by the Spaniards for two years.

Meanwhile the real owners of these two seized vessels—veteran Pacific traders Captain John Meares and Richard Cadman Etches—raised a great cry in London. Meares demanded that the Spanish pay damages to him of half a million dollars. Meares was able to pressure the British government into humiliating Spain, by obtaining considerable publicity for his charges of Spanish aggression. The British Cabinet decided to make a diplomatic issue of the case, even though plans for restitution were being made by the Spanish officials in Mexico.

British strategy in this controversy was to justify their presence in the Nootka Sound area by posing two vital questions to the Spanish. Upon these questions would pivot the issue of peace or war with Spain. They first asked if the Spanish claimed the Pacific as a closed sea. Secondly, they questioned if Spain claimed sovereignty purely upon the grounds of discovery and the ritualistic act of taking possession. Did Spain not believe that actual settlement in an area was also necessary?

Spain's first reaction to the British demands was to insist that the issue merely concerned the rightness or wrongness of the Spanish seizures at Nootka. Soon the Spanish government realized that Spain's exclusive system of interempire trade was in question. Spain quickly called upon her ally France for assistance. Britain responded by alerting its continental allies, Holland and Prussia, to the possibility of war with Spain. Parliament voted for a war budget. Learning that an imminent revolution was forming in France and that the French government questioned its legal position in the matter, Spain decided to yield to British demands. Consequently, in October of 1790, Spain signed the Nootka Convention with Britain at the Escurial. According to the terms of this agreement, Spain yielded its sovereignty on the northwest American coast. Although England agreed to curb any attempts by British vessels to trade or fish near Spanish settlements in the Pacific area, Spain reluctantly recognized the British right to fish or trade in any of the unoccupied places north of California. Tedious negotiations passed between London and Madrid concerning other facets of the agreement. In February 1793, the Nootka Claims Convention was signed by the two countries. By the terms of this document, Captain Meares and his associates were paid less than half of the damages they had claimed—about $210,000. Article V of the original treaty allowed only temporary residence for traders from Britain and Spain at Nootka. Since neither country could agree to this stipulation, the diplomats solved the problem by mutually abandoning the site. Spain was finally forced to surrender her sovereignty in the Pacific. Thus the region north of California was opened to further development by other countries.

In July of 1784, Spain decided to send out a scientific expedition, known to history as the Malaspine expedition. The expedition had two leaders, Captain Alejandro Malaspina and Captain José Bustamente y Guerra, commanding the corvettes *Descubierta* and *Atrevida*. After investigating the Atlantic and Pacific coasts of South America, these ships inspected the shore from Panama to Acapulco. From Acapulco the expedition sailed as far north as the Gulf of Alaska, and then carefully surveyed the coast as it traveled south. The vessels sighted Cape Mendocino on September 6, San Francisco Bay on the tenth, and put into Monterey on the thirteenth. At Monterey, Malaspine and Lasuén exchanged courtesies aboard the captain's ship.

Among the crew on one of Malaspina's ships was the first known American to reach Alta California. A gunner who had signed on at Cadiz, he was mentioned in the ship's records as the son of Presbyterian parents in Boston. He was listed in public records as John Groeme, although most historians assume his name was really Graham. He was buried at San Carlos mission on the day his ship arrived in Monterey.

On September 25 Malaspina's expedition set sail for Mexico and returned to Spain by way of the Philippines and the Cape of Good Hope. Malaspina compiled extensive scientific reports and wrote that he was favorably impressed by California's climate and beauty. His reports were filed away and forgotten by the Spanish.

A new foreigner soon appeared to threaten Spain in the Pacific—a Britisher, George Vancouver. Born in 1757, Vancouver joined the Royal Navy at the age of thirteen. He accompanied Captain Cook on his second and third voyages, probably learning from Cook various ways to combat scurvy. When he commanded his own ships, Vancouver fed his crew a diet of sauerkraut, soup, wheat, spruce beer, dried yeast and even seed mustard! He also encouraged cleanliness and had the crew's quarters scrubbed with vinegar. After serving in the West Indies, he led an expedition to explore the northwest coast of America.

In April 1791, he sailed from Falmouth in the sloop-of-war *Discovery*, accompanied by an armed tender, the *Chatham*. He was later joined by a supply ship, the *Daedalus*. Sailing by way of the Cape of Good Hope, he touched at Australia, New Zealand, Tahiti and the Hawaiian Islands. Approximately a year after the start of his voyage, he sighted the northwestern coast of North America and conducted what may have been the last search for the Straits of Anían.

From the vicinity of the Columbia River, Vancouver sailed south to Alta California, which he always called New Albion, acknowledging Drake's discoveries there. On November 14, 1792, he sailed the *Discovery* into San Francisco Bay on a windy night. Vancouver was shocked that his telescope could detect no Spanish town of San Francisco, which he assumed would naturally have been built at this magnificent harbor. He anchored his vessel in a cove called the Yerba Buena, for the good herb or wild mint which grew so profusely on its shores. (His was the first foreign ship to call at that bay.) In the morning when he located the mission and the presidio, he was amazed at the crudely built, unfinished appearance of the Spanish buildings.

Vancouver was given a cordial reception by the missionaries and military officials of San Francisco. The British explorer brought the Spaniards news from the world outside California. The colonists were excited by his visit, because the arrival of British seamen interrupted a boring daily routine; with the ships came tales and gossip of events in Europe and other lands. This welcome to interesting strangers in California ports continued even after stern orders from Spain decreed that colonial officials should remain aloof whenever foreigners entered their ports.

The presidio commandant, Hermanegildo Sal, and the Franciscan friars at the mission all enthusiastically greeted their visitor. They loaded his ship with fresh meat and vegetables, and gave dinners in his honor at both the mission and the presidio. On November 20, accompanied by seven of his officers, he rode on horseback to Santa Clara—the first foreigners to penetrate so far into California's interior. There he watched a small rodeo which had been staged for his entertainment.

Meanwhile the *Chatham,* commanded by William Broughham, had arrived at San Francisco and had also been loaded with provisions. The Spaniards refused to take money for the supplies, asking only for ornaments, tools, wine and rum in payment.

On November 26, Vancouver left San Francisco Bay and sailed for Monterey, where the *Daedalus* awaited him. A small Spanish squadron under Juan Francisco de Bodega y Cuadro ceremoniously saluted the British newcomers. More welcoming parties followed. When several Spanish ladies accompanied by their gentlemen visited the *Discovery* for a dinner party, they became seasick and had to leave. Five British sailors, tired of the sea and Vancouver's unique diet, deserted while their ships rested at Monterey. Vancouver became very upset when one of his few armorers jumped ship; he was mollified, however, when his hosts offered to send him the only smith at the presidio. Years later all the deserters were discovered and returned to Vancouver. After an exhausting fifty days of social events, Vancouver reluctantly left Monterey, sailing southwest on January 15, 1793.

California's Governor Arrillaga became greatly displeased when he learned of the excessive courtesies which had been extended to Vancouver. Arrillaga was embarrassed by the small, decrepit Spanish settlements and the lack of an effective defense force. The governor rebuked the commandant of the San Francisco presidio, who abjectly apologized and promised not to repeat his mistake should Vancouver return.

Leaving California, Vancouver returned to the Hawaiian Islands before resuming his exploration of the upper North American coast. Upon a return visit to San Francisco in October 1793, he was offended by the restrained Spanish reception. Although Commandant Sal visited the British ship, he sent formal letters asking for an explanation of Vancouver's purpose in calling again at San Francisco. He also informed Vancouver that only he and one additional officer would be allowed to come ashore. Incensed at what he regarded as indignities, Vancouver abruptly left San Francisco for Monterey, after having been rejoined by the *Chatham.*

Anchoring at Monterey on November 1, he successfully obtained an interview with Governor Arrillaga to obtain an explanation of this puzzling Spanish conduct. The Governor was evasive, merely remarking that only Vancouver and one or two officers would be permitted ashore during this visit also. Vancouver remonstrated by pointing out the scientific and unwarlike aspects of his expedition. Finally Arrillaga permitted the British to land a limited amount of stores and to use an observatory during the daylight hours. He granted the enlisted men the right to land and exercise, provided they did so in the area in front of the presidio. The British were also allowed to land parties for gathering wood and water, provided they did not remain ashore at night. These concessions seemed petty and ungenerous to Vancouver, particularly after his welcome the year before. The Spaniards did give Vancouver some livestock and other supplies on credit. Piqued by the Spanish attitude, Vancouver sailed on November 5, leaving ashore some of the supplies he had gathered. This aroused Arrillaga's suspicions that Vancouver was more interested in gathering information than supplies. He sent riders to the south with strict orders for the presidio commanders to refuse the British ships any further aid.

Meanwhile Vancouver leisurely sailed south, reaching Santa Barbara on November 10. The presidio commander there, Felipé de Goycoechea, was friendly, for he had not received the governor's latest orders. Although the British were not permitted on shore at night, they were allowed to buy all the provisions they needed. Hearing of Vancouver's presence, Father Vicente Santa María of Buenaventura mission drove a flock of sheep and supply-laden mules twenty miles to give gifts to the seamen. When he left, Vancouver reciprocated the padre's kindness by taking him to the mission on his way south to San Diego. Vancouver's was the first foreign ship to visit that excellent port. When he dropped anchor, he was amazed that nobody came out to greet him. Therefore, he sent one of his officers to the presidio, where he found the Spaniards politely aloof, according to the Viceroy's instructions. The presidio's commandant ordered Vancouver to leave as soon as possible, but the Britisher refused to go until he had spent twelve days in the harbor.

Vancouver had carefully noted how poorly California was defended. It seemed to him that San Diego was the most weakly held port in the province. The presidio had been built five miles from the port and possessed only three small brass cannon. Vancouver predicted that the fur trade along the California coast would prove an irresistible lure to outsiders and that Spain would be unable to keep trespassers out.

After some additional cruising in the Pacific, Vancouver arrived at Nootka Sound in September 1794. Since he was also a commissioner assigned to settle some of the details of the Nootka Sound Convention, he journeyed one final time down the coast to Monterey in early November 1794. By that time, Arrillaga had been replaced by Borica. In the climate of current political events, Borica felt that he could afford to be more cordial toward Vancouver. As a result, Vancouver spent a leisurely month recovering his previous deserters and overhauling his vessels. He even led a party into the Salinas Valley. Having shipped many provisions, he left for Great Britain by way of Cape Horn.

Upon his return to London, Vancouver found that disgrace rather than honor awaited him. A young nobleman, Thomas Pitt, claimed that he had been unfairly disciplined by Vancouver in a shipboard incident during the cruise. Now he challenged his old commander to a duel, which Vancouver refused. The young man grew bold and in a surprise attack injured Vancouver. The brilliant commander seemed never to fully recover from this incident. Growing progressively weaker, he died on May 12, 1798.

Vancouver's three visits to California alarmed the Spanish authorities. They overestimated the amount of British interest in California, and as a result, the Spanish government roused itself from its lethargy and ordered a strengthening of California defenses. When Britain and Spain went to war in the late 1790's, the Californians feared that Vancouver's reports and charts of the Pacific coast would be put to use by the royal navy. Therefore, the Spaniards took all possible precautions; they drove their livestock inland; men drilled on the presidio squares; rusty cannon were cleaned and polished—all for an invader who never came.

It was the "Boston men" who finally ended California's isolation. At that time "Boston ships" meant any New England or American merchant craft from Salem, Boston or Baltimore.

It was no accident that at this time American traders were swarming into the Pacific and along the coast of California. The years after the American Revolution were difficult times for Yankee shipping. The promises of patriotic orators, proclaiming a brighter prosperity once America had won its political freedom, soon rang hollow. Many colonial arteries of trade, particularly in the West Indies, were closed to American shipping after independence from Great Britain had been won. The New England merchants were too businesslike to allow their ships to swing idly at anchor once old markets had been closed. Very quickly they sailed to remote parts of the world to find new customers and new trade routes. Yankee traders made Boston and Salem greater names than they had ever been before, and soon brought wealth and prestige to the struggling United States.

One new path of commerce which the Yankees blazed was the fur trade between western North America and China. China was a prime market for furs, because even the wealthiest Chinese did not heat their homes. When the weather was cold, they merely piled on layer upon layer of clothing. The rich Chinese fancied furs, and more than any other they prized that most beautiful of pelts, the sea otter.

Sea otters could be captured all along the North American coast, from the chilly seas around the Aleutian Islands to Sebastian Vizcaíno Bay, halfway down the Baja California peninsula. They flourished particularly on the islands of the Santa Barbara Channel and in many sheltered coves along the California shoreline.

The animals were killed by hunters in every conceivable manner, but the chief hunting methods were shooting, clubbing or harpooning. When hit, the otters had the habit of sinking to the bottom of the water where their pelts were unrecoverable, unless the hunter had had the forethought to include in his party natives of the Hawaiian Islands who could dive for them. Hence the slaughter of the animals did not always equal the catch.

By the late 1700's, Russia had moved into the Aleutians and then onto the mainland of Alaska. Their catch of furs was excellent, but they were not allowed to monopolize the trade. The British, quick to grasp a commercial advantage, entered the fur trade along the coast of northwestern America. In the years between 1785 and 1794, about thirty-five British ships traded between the American Pacific coast and the Orient. When the Napoleonic Wars diverted British ships to the active theaters of the war, American traders crowded into the Pacific.

In 1788 two American vessels pioneered a trade route which ran from New England to the Pacific northwest and then to the Orient. Fifteen American ships followed in the next seven years. This number increased to seventy in the nine years until 1805. With this commerce passing by its shores, California could not hope to remain undisturbed; soon Yankee traders would attempt to open up commerce with the colony in spite of Spanish laws.

The first American ship to enter a California port was the 168-ton *Otter*, captained by Ebenezer Dorr, Jr., which sailed into Monterey on October 29, 1796. Although a merchantman, the vessel was well armed with six guns and a crew of twenty-six. Claiming to be a distressed ship, it remained at Monterey from October 29 to November 6. Since the craft's skipper displayed a passport signed by President Washington, the Spanish authorities decided to allow him to buy fresh supplies. When the captain then asked permission to land some English sailors, Governor Borica rejected the proposal. Before leaving, Dorr secretly landed them anyway— ten men and a woman—on the Carmel beach late at night. The newcomers had debarked quite unwillingly, for the Yankees had forced them at gunpoint to land from a rowboat. When this group was captured the next day, the Spaniards were startled to discover that they were convicts from Botany Bay in New Zealand who had stowed away aboard the *Otter*. Governor Borica was outraged at what he regarded as a Yankee trick; his temper cooled when he learned that the men were skilled workmen, always in short supply in California. He quickly put them to work at nineteen cents a day, and was genuinely distressed when royal orders obliged him to send them to Spain the next year.

The *Otter* was the first of many American penetrations into California waters. In 1798 four American sailors who had been left in Baja California by the American ship *Gallant* were taken to the San Diego presidio and put to work until they could be sent to San Blas. In May 1799, Captain James Rowan anchored his vessel, the *Eliza* or the *Hazard*, in San Francisco Bay. He was allowed to buy supplies on the condition that he would not enter any other California harbor on his cruise.

Between August 25 and September 4, 1800, the 104-ton brigantine *Betsey*, under the command of Charles Winship, obtained water and wood at San Diego. Winship was the son of a merchant who had made much money selling beef to the American army and French navy during the Revolution. He told the Spanish that he had been sailing from Hawaii to China when dwindling provisions forced him to seek refuge at San Diego. In a private letter to his brother in Boston, Winship indicated that he really had been poaching otter along the California coast.

Two months later the *Betsey* sailed into San Blas, not China. Winship had a new story for Spanish authorities. He now claimed that his mainmast had snapped, so he had come into San Blas. When a Spanish vessel suddenly appeared in the harbor, the first mate of the *Betsey* panicked and put to sea, leaving Winship and the supercargo, Joseph O'Cain, stranded on the shore. Winship died in 1800, possibly in Valparaiso, Chile. O'Cain was able to find his way back to Boston, where he obtained a vessel and returned to the Pacific. Meanwhile, the *Betsey*, under the first mate Brown, traded the cargo furs at Canton, where Brown was accused by an American representative of cheating the vessel's owners. The *Betsey* was lost off the African coast on the return voyage.

In July 1800, the 240-ton *Enterprise*, loaded with "skins and dollars" at New York, put in at San Diego, its captain claiming distress. This skipper had used the same excuse at three different ports in Baja California. Collecting an excellent cargo of furs, the ship then crossed the Pacific for Canton. There may have been some truth to her captain's tales of distress, for when the craft came along the China coast, it was taking water badly and was eventually sold.

In 1803, a 67-foot, 180-ton American vessel, the *Alexander*, possessing fourteen guns and a crew of nineteen, sailed into San Diego. In an earlier Pacific voyage, her captain, Asa Dodge, had committed suicide by jumping overboard. On still another voyage, her powder magazine had exploded, killing ten men. Now, as she lay in San Diego harbor, her captain, John Brown, convinced the Spanish that he had put into San Diego out of concern for his crew, who were ill with scurvy. Brown quickly began a clandestine trade in skins with the more enterprising of the town's inhabitants. His activities soon aroused the suspicion of Spanish officials, and they suddenly searched his vessel, where they discovered 491 skins which they promptly confiscated. The Spaniards then ordered Brown to leave the harbor at once. Brown sailed out of San Diego and journeyed to Baja California, then north to San Francisco repeating his tale of sick crews and trading whenever he could. At San Francisco the Spanish authorities, suspecting his motives for entering the bay, gave him seven days to leave. Brown set sail again and headed toward Monterey, where he prepared his vessel for a trans-Pacific crossing. He charged considerable repairs and supplies, and then quietly one night hoisted the ship's anchor and sailed out without paying for them.

The next American ship to enter a Spanish California port was the *Lelia Byrd*, a speedy brig of 175 tons. Two Americans, Richard J. Cleveland and William Shaler of Salem, Massachusetts, had bought the vessel in Hamburg, Germany, and drew lots for its command. Cleveland became captain; Shaler served as supercargo. Leaving Cuxhaven, Germany, in November of 1801, they sailed for the Pacific coast where they bought sixteen hundred otter skins from the Indians in exchange for hardware and tin. During various stops along the northern coast, Cleveland and Shaler heard rumors that there were otter skins for sale in San Diego; they sailed the *Lelia Byrd* there on March 17, 1803. Again the Americans claimed distress, but by now even the most credulous Spanish official had heard that tale too often to be misled by it again. The Spanish sent a guard force aboard the American vessel with orders to watch carefully the activities of the crew. Shaler and Cleveland attempted to persuade the lieutenant of the guard, Don Manuel Rodríguez, to sell them the furs which had been confiscated previously from the *Alexander*. Failing in this attempt, Cleveland went ashore to see if he could discover anyone who would trade skins with him. He learned that several Spanish soldiers had obtained some furs and would trade them when it became dark, if the American captain could return. Promptly that evening Cleveland sent two boats to prearranged points to collect the furs. One boat successfully returned to the *Lelia Byrd*; the other, containing a mate and two sailors, was seized by a Spanish patrol boat. When Cleveland learned of the capture, he suspected that he had been the victim of a Spanish trap. Taking four armed men, he rowed ashore just after dawn. He surprised the guards and forced them at gunpoint to surrender their prisoners, who had spent the night lying helplessly on the ground bound hand and foot. Cleveland then rowed back to the ship with the liberated men. When word of the rescue reached the Spanish fort of Guijarros on Ballast Point, the angry Spaniards opened fire on the American ship. Meanwhile, the small Spanish guard aboard the *Lelia Byrd* had been seized as hostages by the daring American seamen.

According to Cleveland's account, he ordered his crew to hoist anchor and sail into the Pacific. The fort continued to fire as rapidly as possible upon the *Lelia Byrd*. The Spanish gunners were nervous and unskilled, and their marksmanship suffered. After several volleys, the Spanish shore batteries struck the sails, rigging and hull of the *Lelia Byrd*. Cleveland feared his precious ship would be destroyed, so he ordered the Americans to fire back. The first volley scattered a crowd of spectators who had gathered on shore to watch the battle. When the second broadside was fired, the Spanish soldiers fled their stations except for one soldier who leaped upon the ramparts and madly waved his hat, as if calling for a cease-fire. The Yankee sailors safely cruised out of San Diego harbor after they had released their Spanish prisoners, who were put ashore, shouting *"Vivan, vivan los Americanos!"*

The Spanish commander Rodríguez later reported that he had never intended to prevent the departure of the *Lelia Byrd;* he had only fired in an attempt to recover his captive soldiers. When the Americans released his men, Rodríguez claimed, he had passed the order to cease firing. He dismissed the effect of the *Lelia Byrd's* attack by scoffing that the Yankee cannonballs had been totally ineffective.

Cleveland now sailed his men to the Hawaiian Islands and China. In the Orient, Shaler and Cleveland agreed that Cleveland should return to Boston by another ship to look after their business, while Shaler took the *Lelia Byrd* on a new cruise.

Shaler returned to the California coast, where he organized a clandestine fur business with the missionaries and other Californians in defiance of Spanish law. Shaler was careful this time to avoid the fortified Spanish ports. Upon his return to the United States, he published a narrative of his adventures. The account was frequently reprinted and greatly stimulated American interest in California.

Both Shaler and Cleveland had interesting later careers. Entering government service, Shaler officiated for years as American consul at Algiers. He was later transferred to Havana, where he died of cholera in 1833. Cleveland won and lost several fortunes and ended his active days in the American customs service.

Joseph O'Cain, who had been stranded at San Blas when the *Betsey* had suddenly departed, now reappeared in the Pacific as captain of the *O'Cain*, a larger ship than those which usually sailed these waters. The *O'Cain* displaced 280 tons and carried eighteen guns. O'Cain sailed his ship to Kodiak Island in Russian America, where he struck a bargain with the Russian, Aleksandr Baranov, whereby the Russians would send a company of Aleuts with their *bidarkas* (skin canoes) to California with the Americans to hunt otter jointly. "Honest Joe" O'Cain promised to share the otter skins with Baranov. From the Aleutians, O'Cain sailed for San Diego. He hoped to talk the Spaniards there into replenishing his stores. The Spanish attitude had been hardened by Yankee poaching along the California shores, however, and the San Diego officials refused O'Cain

his provisions and ordered him out of the harbor. O'Cain sailed to San
Quentín Bay in Baja California, where the authorities were more gullible.
While the *O'Cain* anchored in the bay, the Aleuts quietly scattered in
their canoes and soon captured 110 sea otters. By trading with the mission
priests on the peninsula, O'Cain obtained an additional seven hundred
skins. (The missionaries in both Alta and Baja California chafed under the
stifling Spanish trade regulations and often did business with foreigners in
defiance of civil law.) The Russian-American venture proved so successful that it marked the beginning of a long partnership to hunt otter off
the California coast.

In 1805 three vessels left Boston for the Pacific coast to hunt under
contract with the Russians. They were the *Peacock*, commanded by
O'Cain's brother-in-law, Oliver Kimball; the *O'Cain*, now captained by
Jonathan Winship; and the *Eclipse*, with O'Cain in charge. The Spanish
military officials were alert, for when the *Peacock* turned up off the
southern California coast and attempted to trade with the colony at San
Juan Capistrano, soldiers from the San Diego presidio captured three of
the crew who came ashore. In an attempt to regain his men, Kimball
sailed to San Diego and sent two letters ashore. One was intended for the
commandant; in very humble terms, Kimball petitioned him to release his
men. The other letter, which was supposed to be smuggled to the prisoners, urged them to escape to the shelter of the *Peacock*. Somehow this
second letter miscarried and was discovered by the Spanish officials. Captain Kimball then headed for the more congenial trading climate of Baja
California.

Meanwhile the *O'Cain* with one hundred Aleuts, twelve native women
and a hunting fleet of fifty bidarkas began hunting otter off the Baja
California coast. To disarm suspicion, the *O'Cain* visited Baja ports with
various tales, while the Aleuts secretly hunted off the coast. It was a
considerable period of time before the Spaniards became aware of this
deception. O'Cain cruised the California coast, anchoring just outside the
port of San Diego and sending word that he needed supplies. The Spaniards ignored his pleas. When the *Eclipse* disappeared over the horizon,
the Spanish commandant sent a corporal and four men down to Ensenada
in Baja California, guessing that the Americans would put in there.
As the Spanish scouts approached the harbor at Ensenada, they saw the
Eclipse at anchor. In a surprise attack, O'Cain's crew captured the five
Spaniards and carried them off as hostages to San Diego. As the *Eclipse*
lay offshore, out of cannon range, O'Cain released two of his prisoners
with a message for the Spanish on shore: unless the American crewmen
from the *Peacock*, held prisoner at San Juan Capistrano mission, were
released, O'Cain would hold the three remaining Spaniards and bombard the port. (O'Cain was particularly anxious to recover one of the

prisoners, a valuable pilot.) After long negotiations, all the prisoners were exchanged.

The Yankees were not always so successful; some of them were caught and imprisoned. In 1813 Captain George Washington Eayrs of the ship *Mercury* anchored near Point Concepción to obtain fresh water and oak timbers to repair his damaged vessel. Suddenly an armed Spanish longboat appeared alongside and captured his ship. The longboat had been dispatched from a Peruvian vessel, which had ventured north to California during the confusion accompanying the outbreak of revolutions against Spain in many Latin American provinces. The Peruvian officers, incensed by what they thought was another smuggler in the area, had taken the American vessel without any authorization from Spanish officials. The Peruvians turned over the ship and crew to the surprised Santa Barbara authorities, who confiscated the vessel's cargo and imprisoned Eayrs for the next two years, despite his protests that they had no right to do so. As late as 1822, the California authorities at Santa Barbara seized another American vessel, the *Eagle*, and confiscated its cargo.

Nevertheless, as Spanish authority in California weakened under the impact of the Wars of Independence in Latin America (1810–22), New England skippers invaded California waters and made Spanish pueblos their economic vassals. These were years when American commerce expanded to ports in every part of the world. The Yankees did not hesitate to defy the orders of the weak Spanish king, nor even the naval power of Great Britain.

Russian interest in the Pacific fur trade had been ignited in 1742 when the survivors of Bering's shipwrecked second expedition returned with many pelts as proof of the great number of fur-bearing animals in the waters around the Aleutian Islands. Yet the Russian government, which had financially backed the Bering expedition, was discouraged by the extent of its losses in that area and withdrew from further ventures. Development of Pacific trade east of Siberia was left to the *Promyshlenniki*—an old Russian term that denoted a free-lance exploiter of natural resources, particularly furs.

By 1745 the Promyshlenniki reached the Aleutian Islands and established themselves in temporary headquarters there. The native Aleuts were soon persuaded to hunt for the Russians in exchange for iron. In spite of recurring shipwrecks and a fierce Aleut revolt, the Russians continued to hunt in the Aleutians, and by 1763 had navigated the entire Aleutian chain.

In the 1760's Catherine the Great lifted the veil of secrecy from Russian Pacific activities, startling the ambassadors of those countries which had interests in that area. They had not realized what the Russians had been doing. The garbled reports from Russia which reached Madrid were responsible for the royal order of Gálvez, permitting the inspector-general to send the expeditions of 1769 to California.

Czarina Catherine greatly stimulated the Pacific fur trade when she struck all feudal controls from commerce and instituted more liberal policies. Soon as many as seventy-seven different fur-trading companies were sailing in the northern Pacific.

Into the commercial affairs of Russia stepped a man who yearned to exploit the resources of America, Grigorii Ivanovich Shelikhov. Born in 1747 in a small town in southern Russia, he was a merchant's clerk for many years. As a young man he came to the Siberian base of Okhotsk to learn the business aspects of the fur trade. After a preliminary trading venture to the Kurile Islands, he turned his attention to the Aleutians.

By 1781 Shelikhov had organized a partnership with two other men to plant a Russian colony in the Aleutians. In July 1784, he started a permanent settlement on Kodiak Island. Within eighteen months a small colony had been started on the island in All Saints Bay. In 1786 Shelikhov returned to Siberia, where he attempted to obtain government aid for his venture. Failing in this effort, he journeyed to St. Petersburg to lay his case before the Czarina. At first Catherine seemed interested in the colony, but the outbreak of a war with Sweden and Turkey made her refuse any financial help.

At this time the fur trade with China had slowly decreased, and it became difficult for Shelikhov to maintain what he had already established in Russian America. Nevertheless he managed to send more men, including a new manager, Aleksandr Baranov. The patient Shelikhov continued to bombard the royal court with pleas for financial assistance. Finally he was able to gain a valuable ally in Catherine's lover, the twenty-three-year-old Platón Zebov, who was distantly related to Shelikhov. Zabov persuaded Catherine to grant Shelikhov his trade monopoly in Russian America, even though it violated Catherine's cherished notions of a laissez-faire economic policy.

According to the terms of the royal grant, no competitor could operate within five hundred versts (333 miles) of his present or future posts. Shelikhov's company was supplied with a labor force of exiles, thirty serfs and their families, and missionaries from the Russian Orthodox Church to christianize the Aluets. Now Shelikhov, who had grossly exaggerated the magnitude of his colony, found the Czarina's grant to be an embarrassment of riches. He realized that he must now make good upon the plans he had so lightheartedly proposed.

In the spring of 1794, Nikolai Petrovich Rezanov, royal chamberlain of the czar, was sent to Siberia to supervise the transfer of missionaries and serfs to Shelikhov's control. Rezanov came from a family which traced its proud lineage back for nine hundred years. Unfortunately, he came from a branch which had lost its wealth, and he found himself executing a rather menial chore in Siberia. Rezanov was an accomplished linguist who spoke flawless French and tolerable Spanish. In addition, he had served his Czarina as a captain in the royal guards. However, as a poor man, he felt uncomfortable in the army, since the officer corps was dominated by men of great wealth. At the earliest opportunity, he resigned from the army and entered the civil service. There he inadvertently found himself in the midst of a squabble between Catherine's favorite, Zabov, and his own superior in the Bureau of Petitions. To escape from this embarrassing position, he requested to be sent on a mission to Siberia to arrange the transfer of persons promised to Shelikhov. In Siberia he married Shelikhov's young daughter, Anna. Part of his bride's dowry was a large share of stock in Shelikhov's trading company.

In the summer of 1795, Shelikhov died unexpectedly of a heart attack at the age of forty-eight. The future of his company became uncertain. Shelikhov's widow came under heavy attack by her husband's creditors and debtors. With Rezanov's support, however, she was able to avert financial disaster. Rezanov soon realized that Shelikhov's trading company would never succeed. He dreamed of organizing a new company, a giant colonial enterprise similar to the Hudson's Bay Company or the East India Company. The new corporation would operate from the Siberian coast eastward to the American mainland. It would penetrate as far south as possible along the American coast. Rezanov wished to see a twenty-year charter granted by the Czar. Furthermore he planned to have his stockholders elect a board of directors to supervise the colony. He hoped to avoid all but the most minimal governmental supervision; only the Imperial Department of Commerce would be able to interfere in the affairs of the colony.

On July 8, 1799, Czar Paul granted Rezanov a charter for his Russian-American Fur Company. After the accession of Czar Alexander, following Paul's murder in 1801, the company continued to operate with uncurtailed privileges under the control of Rezanov and Shelikhov's other son-in-law.

By 1791 the Shelikhov enterprise had tentatively established outposts in several areas. At that time the only post on the Alaskan mainland was Fort Alexander, a weakly garrisoned place with only twenty men. The colony had never prospered. Such was the situation when Aleksandr Baranov assumed command as manager.

His arrival in Alaska was inauspicious; he arrived delirious with fever and had to be carried ashore. Men in the colony nodded and winked to each other that this new boss would not be in Alaska for long. But Baranov clung stubbornly to life, throwing off the effects of what was probably pneumonia. His life had been one of constant struggle. Born the son of a storekeeper in 1747, at fifteen he had run away from his home town in northwestern Russia to the metropolis of Moscow. Finding work as an assistant to a German merchant, he quickly mastered German and learned many aspects of business. In his spare time he educated himself by reading widely in the area of science.

After ten years Baranov returned to his home town, married and settled down. He soon grew restless and left for Siberia, which he believed had unlimited commercial opportunities. Shortly thereafter, he drifted into the fur trade and then into Shelikhov's employment. By 1791 he had accepted a five-year contract to be governor of company affairs in Alaska.

Recovering from his illness, Baranov was soon hard at work. He inspected with discouragement the meager extent of his material resources: 110 men and an ancient sloop, the *Saint Simeon*. Even more discouraging, Baranov found that Shelikhov had maintained a policy of hiring only the most meek and inoffensive traders for his American colony, contending that they would be easy to control. Many of these recruits were indolent and unimaginative men who hindered the development of the colony. Most of the traders were so careless that they neglected the most elementary sanitary precautions and sickness was a constant problem. Baranov discovered only one man who looked as though he could be trusted with important tasks—a young clerk with a wooden leg, Ivan Kuskov.

As quickly as possible, Baranov changed the lethargic, careless ways of the colony. He instituted militia discipline, banning all alcoholic beverages except kvass, made from cranberries. Noting that the relationship between the Russian traders and the native women was a source of discord, he insisted that each man select only one woman with whom to live during his stay in the colony. The girl had to be willing to enter this arrangement, and her parents had to be given presents.

Baranov was well liked by the natives. He learned their dialects, which many Russians before him had scorned to do. Soon he had recruited nine hundred natives with 450 canoes for his main work force.

One day in 1792, a large schooner with a broken mast appeared at Nuchek Island. It was the British East India merchantman, the *Phoenix*. Baranov found the British to be friendly. The first mate of the vessel, Bostonian Joseph O'Cain, noted that the Russians seemed short of many supplies. Although O'Cain was swiftly informed that the Russians were forbidden to trade with foreigners, he eagerly began to plan future business with them.

Meanwhile Shelikhov had sent supplies and commanded the colony to start shipbuilding. Using the *Phoenix* as a model, Baranov, by September 1794, had launched his own *Phoenix*, which proved seaworthy. That winter more than 150 people from Siberia reached the Aleutians. Among them were the churchmen and serfs organized by Rezanov. Baranov soon found it difficult to feed them all.

When the serfs appeared terror-striken by the new environment, Baranov used force to send them to Yakutat Bay in the land of the fierce, unpredictable Tlingit Indians. Shelikhov's instructions had been to settle the serfs there at an agricultural colony, which he had led the Russian government to believe was already flourishing. Baranov did not dare disobey this order, and so he settled the serfs there, the first permanent mainland settlement south of Kodiak Island.

With these reinforcements, Baranov could give some attention to expanding the colony's frontiers. Using one of the two homemade sloops he had built, he went exploring down the Alaskan coast. He sought out Sitka Bay, a place often used as a refuge by ships of all flags. This region, he concluded, must soon be occupied, or it would be lost to some foreign entrepreneur. In the spring of 1799, the "Little Czar," as his men referred to him behind his back, decided that he would defer all hunting in order to have resources to settle Sitka. With the sloop *Olga* and many bidarkas, Baranov led eleven hundred men—one hundred of them Russian hunters —to Sitka. There Baranov talked the local chief into allowing him to build a settlement, which he placed under the protection of Michael the Archangel. Some thirty Russians and four hundred Aleuts were left to settle the new post.

In May of 1801, the American vessel *Enterprise* sailed to Kodiak. Aboard was Joseph O'Cain, who had traveled nine years before to the settlement aboard the *Phoenix*. He had never forgotten the great trade opportunity he had seen in the Russian colony. Therefore, when his rather inexperienced skipper Ezekiel Hubbel had trouble disposing of his cargo of hardware and other manufactured goods for pelts, O'Cain persuaded him to try trading with the Russians. The morale in the colony was so low that Baranov felt that he must try to raise it by trading his two thousand excess pelts for the cargo of supplies in the *Enterprise*, regardless of Russian law. A mutually satisfactory transaction was made. O'Cain left, vowing to return soon and trade again.

The calm of the colony was broken in the summer of 1802 when the Sitka post was destroyed by an Indian uprising. Of the 450 Russians and Aleuts living there at the time of the attack, only forty-two survived. Baranov was greatly upset by this disaster and vowed that he would recapture Sitka. Yet he was unable to do anything until 1803 when Joseph O'Cain sailed in to suggest another trade. O'Cain had a large cargo aboard his ship which he offered for pelts. Baranov, anxious to obtain sufficient supplies to attack Sitka, would have been delighted to trade, but he had recently sent off all his furs. O'Cain suggested poaching as partners off the California coast. In exchange for the services of the Aleuts and their canoes, O'Cain would share the catch with Baranov. From their share of the catch, the Russians could buy his cargo of trade goods. Baranov agreed. The voyage was a great success, for the Russian portion of the catch was sufficient to buy guns and tools from O'Cain.

Baranov, with a fleet of vessels and bidarkas, set sail for Sitka in September 1804. Before actual fighting commenced, a Russian ship, the *Neva*, arrived. It was one of the two heavily armed frigates which had carried Rezanov to Japan on a diplomatic-scientific expedition. When Rezanov heard of the massacre at Sitka, news of which eventually traveled to all ports of the Pacific, he dispatched one of the frigates to help in the attack. Baranov welcomed the *Neva*'s captain, but insisted upon keeping command of the Russian force. Despite fierce resistance by the Indians, the heavy artillery of the *Neva* soon forced them into submission. Baranov decided to build his new fort on the very island where the Indians had their principal settlement. The natives were compelled to leave, and Baranov built a fort on the island, which he called New Archangel.

Meanwhile Rezanov had journeyed to Japan, following the death of his wife Anna in childbirth. He had become despondent, and his friends arranged that he should join a naval force which would explore and make diplomatic contacts in the Pacific. Before he sailed, Rezanov had been the toast of St. Petersburg society; he was feted at receptions which hailed him as a Russian Columbus who would unlock the secrets of science and open the doors of commerce to the greater glory of the Russian empire.

No sooner had the expedition left Kronstadt when bickering began about who had the greater authority—Rezanov or the originial commander of the expedition, Captain Adam Kruzenstern. After journeying to England, Brazil, the Marquesas and Hawaii, the party reached Japan, where Rezanov found the Japanese evasive about beginning diplomatic and trade relations with Russia. After months of nervous waiting, which caused Rezanov to have an attack of ulcers, he became furiously angry at the Japanese. Finally he decided to leave. He had also had quite enough of Kruzenstern. He therefore asked the commander to land him in a seaport on the Kamchatka Peninsula. Although he had only a valet and a physician for company, Rezanov had conceived a new scheme; he would visit Russian colonies in the north Pacific before his return to St. Petersburg. He wished to see for himself the great colony which his company had founded in the New World. With his two companions, he took passage on a company brig to the Aleutians. What he found shocked him. Instead of Shelikhov's wonderful settlements, he found a few rotting shacks. Instead of the healthy, happy colonists of the glowing reports, he saw only some old and disabled Russians, or dirty and dispirited Indians. What he actually saw was the colony at its worst, since Baranov had taken away all the young and more able-bodied men to help recapture Sitka.

Yet Rezanov found the colonists overjoyed to see him. He was the only Russian noble most of them had ever seen, and he found himself playing the part of the conquering hero from St. Petersburg. He granted audiences, awarded medals and dispensed justice to the company workers. He was disturbed when he saw that the colony's only economic enterprise was the hunting of sea mammals. In August, he left Kodiak for New Archangel on Sitka Sound, where Baranov awaited him. At New Archangel, Baranov had encountered many difficulties. He found the colony short of food, because the colonists' farming techniques were careless and unproductive. He had to send as far away as Hawaii for provisions. Baranov realized that he needed a constant supply of green vegetables and other crops. Such supplies could only be gathered if he could develop a base south of Alaska, where he believed the climate and length of the growing season would be more favorable to agriculture.

In the spring of 1805, Baranov made a new contract with O'Cain's brother-in-law Oliver Kimball to continue the American-Russian cruises along the California coast. Once again these ventures proved to be profitable, and the Russians began to consider establishing a southern base for hunting sea otter.

In August 1805, Rezanov arrived at Sitka. The vain Baranov had decided to dress for the occasion to impress the great noble about whom he had heard so much. He wore his black wig, which he had tied in place with a handkerchief to keep it from blowing away. If Rezanov felt the humor of the situation, he repressed the desire to show it. Baranov, who had been crippled by rheumatism, asked to resign; Rezanov would not hear of it. Instead, Rezanov wrote asking the directors of the company to grant Baranov new authority and honors. After Rezanov had talked with Baranov, he also became convinced that expansion to the south was both necessary and desirable. Rezanov suggested two posts: one at the mouth of the Columbia River and the other just north of San Francisco.

Rezanov was eager to explore the northern Pacific coast to test the correctness of his ideas. In the fall of 1806, he purchased from an American skipper, John de Wolfe, a ship called the *Juno* and its cargo of food and trade goods. For a crew he turned to Baranov, who protested that he could spare him only thirty-three men (several of them Americans), many of whom were poor physical specimens and susceptible to scurvy. Rezanov refused to quibble, and heavily laden with trade goods, he sailed to the south on March 8, 1806.

The *Juno* was a fine ship which had been built in Bristol, Rhode Island, seven years before. It was a copper-bottomed, fast craft of 206 tons. The inadequate crew, weakened by the winter famine at Sitka, quickly fell prey to scurvy. Soon half of them were incapable of standing watch. Nevertheless, Rezanov tried three times to enter the mouth of the

Columbia River to secure a trading-post site there. He failed in these attempts and sailed south to California, hoping he could arrive there quickly enough to save the lives of his crew. Rezanov fingered copies of Vancouver's charts of the California coast, plotting the speediest course; San Francisco was his destination. He knew that the Spaniards had strict laws against any traffic with foreigners, but he had credentials as an ambassador-at-large from the Czar to the Pacific area, and he hoped the Spaniards would honor them.

Meanwhile San Francisco, which was the northern limit of the Spanish world, was inhabited by only sixty Spaniards, including the missionaries. The military commander of San Francisco was José Argüello, who took very seriously his sovereign's injunction against trade with foreigners. The same attitude was manifested by the pious governor, Don José Joaquin de Arrillaga.

Fortunately for the desperate Rezanov, both Argüello and Arrillaga were absent from San Francisco when his ship sailed through the Golden Gate on April 5, 1806. Rezanov decided to continue on into the harbor, even if he were fired at from the San Joaquin Battery at the entrance to the bay. When he was challenged from shore, he answered that his was a Russian ship and disobeyed the order to anchor until his vessel was beyond cannon range. In command at San Francisco was Alférez Luís Argüello, José's twenty-one-year-old son. Luís felt isolated in San Francisco, and was quite ready to welcome an interesting newcomer. The young lieu-tenant met the ship and invited Rezanov and his officers to take chocolate at his home. The Russian party was frankly amazed by Luís Argüello's attire. He wore a mantle of striped woolen cloth over his uniform, which reminded one observer of the "coverlet of a bed." He also wore a pair of "extravagantly" large spurs. Argüello's soldiers wore scarlet-and-black uniforms.

At the Argüello home, Rezanov met Luís' sister, María de la Concepción Argüello y Moraga, nicknamed "Concha" and often called "La Favorita." She was only sixteen years old, but she had already been proclaimed as a great beauty: she had perfect teeth, long-lashed dark eyes, a "pretty instep" and a faultless figure. Her father had given her as good an educa-tion as any boy. Concha had read widely and could carry on a conversa-tion unequalled by any young girl in all of California. However, she had few beaux, for eligible young men in her social class were scarce in the Spanish settlement. Handsome, haughty-faced and blond, Rezanov was forty-two, but he had a lean and well-preserved figure. He towered as a commanding figure above the shorter Spaniards. His polished manners and charm made him seem very much more desirable than any of the callow young men Concha had known in California. Historians have never been sure that the worldly Rezanov was interested in the girl for her sake alone. Certainly he must have realized that a marital alliance with one of the foremost California families would present trading opportunities which had been closed to him as a foreigner.

While Arrillaga and his military commander Argüello were absent in Monterey, Rezanov had two weeks to make friends and court the lonely Concha. He was a constant visitor at the Argüello house, and wooed Concha as much as Spanish custom permitted. As part of his campaign, he played for hours on his violin, and when permitted, beguiled the señorita with his courtly small talk.

The social climate turned decidedly chilly with the arrival of the senior Argüello on April 16, and Governor Arrillaga two days later. Yet Rezanov had spent his time judiciously. In addition to wooing Concha, he had been talking trade with the Franciscans. The missionaries welcomed the chance to obtain his trade goods for the use of their missions. Although the Alaskan colony desperately needed foodstuffs, Rezanov maintained a brave front. He talked of trade, not because of Russian need, but simply for demonstration purposes. Rezanov had carefully distributed gifts from his cargo to whet the Spaniards' interest. The Spanish ladies of the presidio learned that the *Juno* carried such feminine luxuries as shawls and fancy shoes. As a result, the governor found a curious alliance of missionaries and dowagers clamoring for him to allow the *Juno* to trade its cargo. For the moment Governor Arrillaga resolved that he would never permit Spain's trade laws to be violated. When Rezanov asked Argüello for his daughter's hand in marriage, the governor ordered his daughter to confession and then into seclusion. The unrepentant Concha insisted that she had committed no sin; she was only a woman in love. Moreover, she vowed that if she could not have Rezanov as her husband, she would never marry.

Argüello tried to be a stern parent, but his daughter, aided by her sisters and mother, proved too much for him to withstand. As a result, he reluctantly consented to her betrothal, on the condition that Rezanov would obtain a papal dispensation to allow his daughter to marry him, a heretic. Rezanov agreed. His plans were to return to St. Petersburg and obtain the Czar's consent to his marriage plans. He would also ask the Russian emperor for a special appointment as envoy to Spain to settle certain diplomatic issues between Madrid and St. Petersburg. On his way to Spain, he planned to stop in Italy to obtain the Pope's permission for his marriage. Then he would return to Mexico and claim his bride. Optimistically, Rezanov assured Concha he could do all this in about two years.

Now the time was favorable to trade the *Juno*'s cargo. Argüello was already treating Rezanov as a member of the family, and as a result the governor announced that for a relative of Argüello, his friend for thirty years, he would this one time permit a trade arrangement. Not even the arrival of a courier from Mexico City with news that Russia and Spain were at war in Europe as members of opposing alliances could dampen the enthusiasm of the moment. A complicated transaction occurred, and Rezanov was able to obtain supplies for the starving Russian colonies in Alaska.

The *Juno* was swiftly loaded with a cargo of grain, peas, beans, tallow, dry meat, butter and salt. On May 21, after a stay of more than six weeks, Rezanov bade farewell to his fiancée and lifted anchor for the return trip to Alaska. As he sailed through the Golden Gate, the entire Argüello family assembled outside the presidio walls to wave farewell. The Russian vessel passed the battery that had challenged him on the way in; it now fired a friendly salute. During his return voyage, Rezanov wrote a report in which he suggested that Russia found an agricultural cattle-raising empire in California, using Chinese labor.

After a stormy voyage, Rezanov reached Sitka on June 19, where he was striken by malaria for ten days. The *Juno* could not get him to Okhotsk in Siberia until September. At Okhotsk veteran travelers counseled delaying the 2,200-mile journey to Irkutsk until winter snows would allow firm sledding. Rezanov could not wait. Instead, he hired a caravan of cossacks to accompany him and pressed on, gambling that he could beat the autumn rains which turned the primitive roads into quagmires. Still weak from his bout with malaria, now chilled by the freezing winds and drenched by the cold rains, he became ill and had to rest for a time in a native hut. He arrived in Irkutsk some five months after he had started. Although it was February, he refused to wait for warmer weather. Leaving Irkutsk, he rode westward with his party of cossacks. One day he grew faint and fell from his horse; a horse's hoof accidentally crushed his skull. He was buried in the cemetery of a village of Krasnoyarsk.

Although legend says that Concha did not learn of her lover's death for thirty-five years, it does not seem to have been nearly that long. It was ten years at the most before she probably heard the details of Rezanov's fate. By that time she had already guessed that he was dead, and had put aside the wedding dresses upon which she had once sewed so industriously. She never married, rejecting many suitors, including at least one American. Eventually she joined a Dominican convent and lived as a nun until her death in 1857.

The year 1807 was one of disaster for the Russian-American company. Not only was Rezanov killed that year, but Baranov's American partner O'Cain also died. While traveling from Kamchatka to the Aleutians, Joseph O'Cain's vessel was wrecked.

Baranov now became deeply discouraged and sent a letter of resignation to Russia. When the directors termed him indispensable, he agreed to continue, although he was about sixty-one. The directors also indicated that they thought Rezanov's plans to expand to the south should be carried out.

Upon his return from California, Rezanov had urged the establishment of a colony on the coast near San Francisco. There fur hunting could be combined with farming. Therefore, Baranov sent his trusted lieutenant, Ivan A. Kuskov, to explore the coastline north of San Francisco for a favorable site for a southern outpost. By late December he had landed at Bodega Bay, which was then a well-sheltered anchorage. From there he sent out his Aleut hunters. Several temporary structures were erected and friendly contact was made with the Indians. Kuskov collected two thousand furs and returned to Sitka in October 1809. He reported that he had discovered "a fine climate, good tillable lands, plenty of fish and furbearing animals and a tolerable harbor."

His expedition had not gone unnoticed. Five or six sailors who deserted him made straight for the Spanish settlements at San Francisco where they were imprisoned. Several Aleuts had also been captured by Spanish patrols.

The Russian venture into northern California had been so successful that in 1811 Baranov sent Kuskov south to California again. Kuskov set up a temporary trading station in Bodega Bay and dispatched Aleuts to hunt for the community. Since the number of otter in Bodega Bay was relatively small, the Aleuts were sent overland to San Francisco Bay where they soon collected 1,200 skins. Lacking small boats with which to pursue the Aleuts on water, the Spaniards were at first totally unsuccessful in stopping the poaching. Later they stationed guards at all the freshwater springs in the area. Unless the Aleuts wished to be captured, they were forced by thirst to leave the region. The overall catch by this time had reached such profitable proportions that Kuskov returned to Sitka that summer.

Possibly as a result of fresh instructions from St. Petersburg, or perhaps because the Kuskov voyages had been so successful, Baranov dispatched Kuskov in the *Chirikov* with all the necessary equipment to found a permanent settlement in northern California. The Russians had explored as far as fifty miles up the Slavianka ("Charming Little One"), as they named the Russian River, but settled on a spot about eighteen miles above Bodega Bay, or Rumiantzov Bay as they called it. Although the anchorage there was not as good, the soil, water and pasture land were all better than at Bodega Bay, which Kuskov feared was too susceptible to Spanish attack. The Russians had formally purchased the land from the Indians in 1811 for three blankets, three pairs of pants, two axes, three hoes and some beads. This was the only known payment for land during the Spanish period in California.

According to one account, construction of the settlement was begun on March 15, 1812. Because of its fortifications, the place became known to the Spaniards as Fuerto de los Rusos; to the Americans it became generally known as Fort Ross. The Russians called it Rossiya, an ancient term for Russia. Work on the buildings was far enough along for a dedication of the fort on September 11, 1812, although it does not seem to have been completed until 1814. The grounds of the post covered about one thousand acres. The fort itself consisted of a quadrangle about 250 feet by 300 feet, constructed of thick redwood beams twelve or fifteen feet high driven into the ground. At the corners, diagonally opposite and facing north and south, were hexagonal blockhouses with high, sharply peaked roofs. In these towers, which commanded a view of the surrounding countryside, were mounted cannon. At first there were only twelve of them, but later they were increased to forty. Inside the stockade was a well to supply water during a siege, although ordinarily a nearby stream was the water source. A steep bluff on the ocean side and ravines on the other three sides made it very difficult for an enemy to gain easy access to the fort.

The original settlers at Fort Ross included eighty Aleuts and ninety-five Russians. California Indians were hired as laborers to supplement the force sent down from Alaska. No Russian women came to Ross until its later years, and then they were only the wives of officers.

To obtain fresh sea lion meat, a camp was established on the Farallone Islands off San Francisco. At first the catch of sea animals from these bases was phenomenal. However, the hard-hunting Aleuts soon caused a spectacular drop in the number of animals taken. Yet the Russians settled down to stay. They planted fruit orchards and grew crops for their Alaskan bases.

The newcomers were distinctly unwelcome to the Spaniards, who regularly sent orders to the Russians demanding that they leave the area. The Russians shrugged aside all these ultimatums. The Spaniards for all their bluster simply did not have a force strong enough to drive the intruders out. Spain had permanent neighbors in California. The isolation of California had ended.

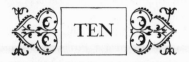

TEN

Mexico Takes a Shaky Control

WITH the wars of liberation raging in the Spanish colonies in general and Mexica in particular, after 1810 supply ships from San Blas ceased altogether for a number of years and never resumed on a regular schedule. The salaries of officials, soldiers and missionaries were all stopped. This caused a change in the economic basis of life in California, as illicit trade filled some of the vacuum.

For purposes of this trade the missions fared best, for they had the largest crops and herds. The pueblos and ranch owners occupied a middle position. Worse off were the civil officials and soldiers at the presidios. They subsisted only by forced sales of tallow and food products, paying with Spanish treasury drafts which were never honored. With few exceptions, the missionaries demonstrated genuine unselfishness by sharing their provisions with the colonists. But as is so often the case, the exceptions drew the greatest attention and publicity. This caused wide resentment among the soldiers and officials.

California remained a staunchly loyal corner of New Spain, partly because little news of the revolution reached California, one of the most isolated of Spanish provinces. The civil authorities optimistically believed every rumor that the revolts had been crushed.

Prior to 1818 there was no direct activity in California traceable to the war. During his term of office, Governor Arrillaga sent a number of exploring expeditions into the interior of California, the most noteworthy being those of Gabriel Moraga. These expeditions had little immediate impact, for California settlements continued to cluster within thirty miles of the seacoast, as if the Spaniards insisted on staying close to the sea so as to make repatriation easier.

In December 1812, an earthquake shook southern California, killing many persons at the missions of La Purísima Concepción and San Juan Capistrano. On July 24, 1814, Governor Arrillaga died. His temporary replacement was José Darío Argüello. Argüello, who was a native of Querétaro, New Spain, rose through the ranks of the officer corps of the Spanish army. He was also the father of Concepción and Luís Argüello. Luís led several exploring parties into the interior, and later was the first California governor during the Mexican period. José Argüello continued to reside in Santa Barbara, rather than in Monterey, the official capital. Retiring as governor of Alta California in 1815, he traveled to Baja California, where he served until 1822 as governor of that province without pay (because of political conditions). He died an impoverished man in Guadalajara.

His successor in Alta California was the Basque, Pablo Vicente de Solá. He was a wealthy aristocrat with a long military record. When he arrived in California, parades, ceremonies, a military review, gaudy Indian dances and speeches celebrated his assumption of office. Twenty beautiful girls dressed in white welcomed him to a reception in his honor. A great feast, exhibitions of horsemanship, a fight between a bull and a bear, and a grand ball at night were also features of his inauguration.

Solá soon faced the most serious menace to Alta California since the coming of the Spaniard—external attack. It happened largely because the American people were enthusiastic supporters of the Spanish colonial rebels. Many Americans volunteered for profitable duty as privateers (serving in private ships licensed to capture enemy vessels), preying upon Spanish commerce. These ships were often outfitted at the port of Baltimore, a practice which soon gave rise to the term "Baltimore ship," referring to any American privateer in the service of the rebelling colonists. One American vessel helped to bring the war to California in 1818.

The commander of the rebel expedition was not an American, but a Frenchman, Hippolyte de Bouchard. Along with many other Europeans, Bouchard offered his services to the new republic of Argentina, or as it was more correctly styled, "Provincias Unidas de Sud-America." He had been born about 1783 in St. Tropez and came to Buenos Aires as a young man. There he married an Argentine girl and participated in the young republic's struggle for independence as a petty officer in the navy. He received a commission as a privateer, making him an official representative of the new state and authorizing him to undertake diplomatic as well as military action in the name of his adopted country. On July 9, 1817, aboard the black frigate *La Argentina*, Bouchard began an around-the-world voyage. He sailed around the Cape of Good Hope, stopping in Madagascar, Indonesia and the Philippines. During this voyage he was constantly engaged in battles with the Spaniards. Bouchard, a brutal man of fiery temper, ran a taut ship for a privateersman. His crew feared him more than any enemy. While he was plundering ships in the Pacific, his own vessel became so heavy with booty (his enemies claimed that it consisted largely of gold chalices and silver crucifixes stolen from churches) that Bouchard sailed for Hawaii to dispose of it. He also had orders to reclaim from the king of the Islands an American ship which had been outfitted as an Argentine privateer, variously known as the *Liberty*, the *Baca*, the *Checka* and the *Santa Rosa*. The three-hundred-ton *Santa Rosa* had had a varied career before it came to Hawaii with a stolen cargo of dry goods. It now belonged to King Kamehameha, who had confiscated the ship and cargo. When Bouchard arrived, demanding that the ship and her crew be returned to him, the king quickly complied. In Hawaii Bouchard met an English soldier of fortune named Peter Corney, whom he convinced to join him as commander of the *Santa Rosa*.

Late in October of 1818, the two men sailed off to plunder the untouched Spanish province of Alta California. The *Santa Rosa* had a crew of one hundred men and carried twenty-six guns. The larger *Argentina* had thirty-eight heavy guns, two light howitzers, and a crew of 266. Most of the officers on board were Americans. Bouchard's crews, however, were as heterogenous a group as ever sailed the Pacific: eighty Kanakas (Hawaiians) who went about naked and preferred to fight with long pikes, Americans, renegade Spaniards, Spanish Americans, Portuguese, Filipinos, Malays, Negroes, Australian convicts and a sprinkling of Englishmen. These men were all held together by fear of Bouchard and the promise of plunder.

The alarm of Bouchard's coming was carried to Alta California by Captain Gyselar of the American brig *Clarion*, which sailed into Santa Barbara early in October 1818 after a fast passage from Hawaii. Gyselar's report was received by the California officials with skepticism. They had sighted suspicious ships from time to time off the California coast, and had received so many warnings from Spanish ministers that they were a bit cynical about warnings of pirate ships. Yet they dared not ignore so strong a testimony as that given by the Yankee skipper. Consequently, Governor Solá began to prepare California for the threatened attack. He ordered the sacred church vestments and chalices moved inland. He had the spare livestock driven to places of safety. The women and children either left or were warned to be ready to leave the coastal communities at a moment's notice. Extra sentinels were posted. Then nothing happened. Bouchard had sailed leisurely across the Pacific to the California coast and then beyond the northern edge of Spanish settlements to Fort Ross, where he purchased eggs and fresh vegetables. Only then did he sail south.

About the time that the Spaniards began to tell each other that the whole affair was a hoax, a lookout at Point Pinos sighted two suspicious ships; Bouchard had arrived.

The presidio of Monterey—some forty men—prepared themselves for battle. The major defensive work of eight guns was commanded by Sergeant Manuel Gómez, whose nephew, Luciano Gómez, served aboard one of Bouchard's ships. Corporal José Vallejo, brother of the famous Mariano Vallejo, commanded an improvised battery of three guns on the beach.

When the *Santa Rosa* sailed into the bay, the rebel leaders asked Solá for supplies. The governor refused them. The *Santa Rosa* then opened fire on the presidio, and Bouchard sent in six boatloads of sailors from the *Argentina* as a landing party. As the boats were being rowed in, Corporal Vallejo opened fire from his hastily improvised battery. The rebels were surprised by this return of fire, since they thought they knew the location of all the Spanish defenses. In the confusion Bouchard ordered the boats back. The *Santa Rosa*, within easy range of the shore battery, was hit several times. According to the Spaniards, Corney sent off most of his crew and then lowered the *Santa Rosa*'s flag. Since Corporal Vallejo thought this sign of surrender was a trick, he refused to cease firing, even when Gómez sent orders to do so. Vallejo suspected Gómez's loyalty and would not obey him. In great disgust, Gómez ordered his gunners in the fort to fire on Vallejo's battery. His soldiers refused. For some reason, never satisfactorily explained, Vallejo soon stopped firing. The Spaniards never boarded the *Santa Rosa*. Instead the second officer of the ship, Joseph Chapman, and two sailors came ashore, ostensibly to arrange a truce. These privateers were promptly taken prisoner by the Spanish.

The second stage of the battle opened when Bouchard sailed in with the *Argentina*. He sent a flag of truce ashore to demand the surrender of Monterey. Solá refused Bouchard's message, replying that he would fight on "while there was a man alive in the province." The privateersman then landed nine boatloads of sailors near Point Pinos. Ensign José Estrada opposed the landing with a small force, but perceiving that he was heavily outnumbered, he retreated to Monterey. Corney has reported that a party of fierce, pike-wielding Hawaiians charged the Spaniards, who fled in great haste and confusion.

Although Solá had now gathered a force of eighty men at Monterey, he felt unable to hold the colony. Carrying with him the provincial archives and some ammunition, he abandoned his capital to the enemy, retreating to Rancho del Rey near the present site of Salinas. Spanish reinforcements soon came from San Francisco.

Meanwhile Bouchard flew the Argentine flag from the flagstaffs, enjoying his possession of Monterey while the townspeople were away.

His men buried their dead and tended their wounded. The *Santa Rosa* was extensively repaired. The Hawaiians led the other sailors through the abandoned houses, looking for clothes. The Hawaiians gleefully wore any clothing that struck their fancy, men's or women's. European and American sailors looted the houses for money. The turncoat Luciano Gómez was accused by the Spaniards of leading the rebels in an orgy of senseless destruction in which buildings and orchards were burned and even gardens destroyed.

Finally, having gathered together two hundred Spaniards and many Indian allies, Solá slowly advanced toward Monterey. On December 1 he found the town in flames and Bouchard's ships gone. The Spanish soldiers captured only two men from the private ships, who loudly proclaimed themselves deserters.

The privateers next stopped at Refugio between Point Concepción and Santa Barbara. They had heard that the Rancho de Refugio, owned by the Ortega family, harbored great wealth which had been gained by smuggling. When the rebels came ashore, they were ambushed by Sergeant Carlos Antonio Carrillo, who had hastened up from Santa Barbara with thirty vaqueros. Three of Bouchard's sailors were captured with lassoes, including William Taylor of Boston. But in revenge Bouchard burned and plundered the rancho, although the Ortegas had removed all valuables. Then he reembarked his landing party, while Carrillo hastened down to Santa Barbara.

Bouchard sailed south and, after a landing at Santa Cruz Island for food and water, reached Santa Barbara on December 8. Here the Spanish Commander José de la Guerra tried to trick the rebels. He marched his small force around a hill several times to make Bouchard think that he was opposing a large force.

Undeterred, the rebels fired to gain the Spaniards' attention and sent a boat ashore under a flag of truce. Bouchard offered to give back one prisoner named Molina, whom he had taken at Monterey, if his three men captured at Refugio were returned to him. He also promised to spare Santa Barbara. After much parleying, the exchange of prisoners was concluded. Governor Solá later castigated de la Guerra for doing business with the "pirates," as he termed them. Molina, who had been recovered in the exchange, bore the brunt of Solá's anger. This alcoholic beachcomber was given a hundred lashes and a term of six years on a chain gang for his "antipatriotic behavior."

Meanwhile Bouchard had sailed south. San Buenaventura mission was abandoned at his approach, but he ignored the settlement and went on to San Juan Capistrano, arriving there on December 14.

Bouchard sent a boat ashore, saying that if he received stores he would spare the mission. The Spaniards replied that if he landed, they would give him "an immediate supply of powder and shot." Angrily Bouchard landed 140 men and two fieldpieces and brushed aside the thirty defenders, who fled after a few shots. Pillaging the town, the rebels found many stores but little money. They seized much wine which Bouchard ordered destroyed, but his command was only partially obeyed. At least twenty of the rebels became so drunk that they had to be disciplined.

Meanwhile Spanish reinforcements, summoned by a mounted messenger, marched in from Santa Barbara and Los Ángeles. Their commander, José de la Guerra, still smarted over the governor's rebuke for his handling of affairs at Santa Barbara. He sent a challenge to Bouchard to stay and fight. The insurgents chose to leave so quickly that four of Bouchard's men were captured, including two of the three previously taken at Refugio.

San Diego now girded for battle. The women and children were sent inland and a supply of ammunition was also collected. But Bouchard never landed in San Diego. Late in January 1819, his craft were seen near San Blas. The records do not support it, but there is a legend that the pirate attacked a Spanish cruiser which he mistook for a treasure ship. His ships reached Chile on July 9. Corney had quarreled with Bouchard and the two separated there.

Bouchard later became temporary commander-in-chief of the Peruvian navy, and fought in many naval and land battles. After the wars of independence had ended, the Peruvian government rewarded Bouchard for his services with a cocoa and spice plantation. In 1837 his slaves rebelled and killed him, for they had been habitually treated with great harshness. In November 1962, the Argentine navy decided to recognize Bouchard's great service. Accordingly it sent a cruiser to Peru to bring Bouchard's remains to Buenos Aires, where after a state funeral the old "pirate" was reinterred in the Pantheon of the Argentine navy.

The effect of Bouchard's raid was to make the Californians more royalist than ever in their sympathies. They had spurned all of Bouchard's attempts to subvert them.

Monterey was rebuilt with the help of the Carmel mission Indians. It was April 1819 before the town was sufficiently reconstructed to allow the women and children to return from Soledad, their place of refuge.

Santa Cruz mission had suffered great losses even though the privateers had never set foot inside it. During Bouchard's visit to Monterey, it had been evacuated, and the settlers of Branciforte and the mission Indians looted the mission buildings.

Meanwhile the mortality rate had risen among the Indians at the mission Dolores (San Francisco). Governor Solá moved a group of ailing natives to the far shore of the bay, which was sunnier. They prospered, and the mission San Rafael Arcángel was founded there on December 14, 1817, the twentieth in the mission chain. It was hoped that this settlement would serve as a buffer against the Russians in Fort Ross.

Once Bouchard had left the province, life returned somewhat to its sunny placidity. Not long afterward, this temporary calmness was disturbed by foreigners coming to live among the Spanish. During the 1800's many settlers entered California. The first permanent non-Spanish settler is believed to have been John Gilroy, a Scottish-born sailor, who as a youth of twenty landed in California. His real name was John Cameron, but he changed it when he ran away to sea. While on a voyage in an English vessel, Gilroy became ill and was set ashore in California. Recovering, he was baptized a Catholic and married a daughter of Ignacio Ortega. In 1833 he was naturalized and became a rancher. His ranch is now the modern-day California town which bears his name. Early in the American period, Gilroy fell victim to sharp land speculators. He died in 1869.

In 1814, an Irishman named John Milligan arrived in California. After many years of patiently teaching weaving to the mission Indians, he died an alcoholic in 1834.

The first American to settle in California was Thomas W. Doak, a twenty-nine-year-old Bostonian who arrived in California in 1816 aboard the *Albatross*. A skilled carpenter, Doak's talents were in great demand throughout the Monterey-Santa Cruz area. He was baptized in December 1816, taking the name Felipe Santiago. He married Maria Lugarda, the daughter of José Mariano Castro. Doak and two mission Indians painted the altar and interior of the mission San Juan Bautista. He died about 1848. Again, in 1816, the ship *Atala* landed another American at Santa Barbara, a seventeen-year-old boy named Daniel Call. Call was also a carpenter whose services were much in demand. Little is known of the later years of his life.

A more flamboyant figure in Spanish California was the American Joseph Chapman. A New Englander, he drifted to Hawaii where he joined Bouchard. After his capture at Monterey, he always averred that he had been impressed into service by the privateer. Instead of being harshly treated by the Spaniards, he soon became a general favorite. Perhaps the fact that he was extremely handy with tools in an area where skilled workmen were scarce explains his easy acceptance into Spanish colonial life. He built grist mills at several of the missions; he constructed a schooner; he planted a vineyard of four thousand vines near Los Ángeles, and he practiced as a surgeon. He was married and baptized in 1822 and naturalized in 1831. The father of five children, he lived in the Los Ángeles–Santa Barbara area, dying about 1848 or 1849.

In all, nearly twenty foreigners were living in California when the Spanish era ended.

Spanish rule ended in California when New Spain revolted and became an independent empire—Mexico.

In New Spain conservatism had been stronger throughout the wars of independence than in most South American countries; this kept revolutionary activities under such restraint that when Mexican independence was achieved, it took the form of a conservative compromise as a short-lived empire, not as a republic. The first revolution started in 1810 and was led by a gentle Creole priest named Miguel de Hidalgo y Costilla. He and other lower-class clergymen, shouting slogans in favor of the masses and the true religion, led a social, racially tinged revolt. The more powerful Creoles opposed this movement and ultimately crushed it. Ironically, after a liberal revolution in Spain in 1820, the Mexican upper classes finished the work of separation.

During 1821, political unrest spread throughout New Spain. In February, Agustín Iturbide, a colonel in the royal army in Mexico City, suddenly defected to the rebels. He formulated what became known as the Plan of Iguala, a scheme which called for an independent monarchy in Mexico. Supposedly a Spanish prince was to become king of Mexico, but when one did not promptly accept the post, Iturbide claimed the throne for himself. The Spanish viceroy signed a treaty with him accepting the Plan of Iguala in the summer of 1821.

California was so isolated that it did not hear about the independent empire of Mexico until January 1822. At first the Californios received the news with disbelief. Then, in late March, word came that they would have to swear allegiance to the new government and send a deputy to the Mexican Congress.

In April, Governor Solá convened a junta consisting of nine civil officials and a friar. This council decided to recognize the regency of Iturbide and declare Alta California a dependency of the Mexican empire.

The date usually given for the end of Spanish rule in Alta California is April 11, 1822. On that date, in Monterey, the oath of allegiance to Mexico was taken by the various former royal officials, followed by religious services, the firing of salutes, the cheering of crowds, music and fireworks. It had been 280 years since Cabrillo had first flown the Spanish flag off the coast, but only fifty-three years since Alta California had been actually settled. Later the inhabitants of other settled areas took the oath, and duly celebrated the independence they had never sought. Apparently there was no concerted protest, and with a sort of numbed acquiescence, California became a Mexican province.

Solá was allowed to remain as governor, for his loyalty to Spain had steadily declined during his term of office. In November 1822, the first gubernatorial election was held in California. José de la Guerra was considered the favorite, since he had been endorsed by the retiring governor and was the senior captain in the province. However, he was a native of Spain, and a Mexican agent in California campaigned strongly to prevent his election. As a result, Luís Argüello, a native Californian, was chosen governor. Solá immediately left Alta California for Mexico.

In a sense there was no Mexican period of California history. For two decades the sovereignty of the Mexican government was acknowledged, but Mexico was involved in its own governmental and social problems and could spare little time for this distant province. Occasionally Mexico sent governors and troops to support its waning influence, but American economic influence in California grew so strong during this period that Yankee political domination became inevitable.

The political confusion was reflected in the missions. Just as strong central control nearly vanished from California's political scene, the same changes occurred in the administration of the mission system. Ordinary priests now decided matters that they would have formerly referred to the father-president in California or to authorities at the College of San Fernando. The last mission, San Francisco de Solano, was founded in this atmosphere.

The idea of establishing San Francisco de Solano mission was formulated by Father José Altimira, a Spanish-trained Franciscan who arrived in Monterey in August 1819 for service at mission Dolores. Soon Altimira decided that the mission Dolores had been established at the wrong site; its climate was harsh, the soil poor and the number of converts small. He urged that it should be abandoned and a new mission established north of San Rafael.

Since Father Altimira suspected that the religious authorities would not approve his plan, he consulted Governor Luís Argüello, who was familiar with conditions around San Francisco Bay. Father Altimira's plan agreed with a notion the governor had long cherished: to constrict the Russians and push them out of the province by surrounding them with Mexican settlements.

In 1823 Governor Argüello presented a resolution to the Territorial Assembly in Monterey, calling for the transfer of mission Dolores to the north. The legislative body approved the plan and proposed transferring mission San Rafael as well. The secular officials had overlooked one small fact—they did not have authority to transfer missions because this prerogative lay with the father-president. This ecclesiastical office was then held by the dying Father José Senán, who from his sick bed dictated a rebuke to the governor and the rash Father Altimira. Altimira received the letter just as Indians were starting to erect structures at his new mission. He suspended work and began negotiations with the governor and Senán. The result of these was a compromise; Altimira could build his new mission, but the two older ones were to remain undisturbed. On July 4, 1823, Altimira dedicated mission San Francisco de Solano, fifty miles north of the present city of San Francisco. The mission was named for a saint who had been a Franciscan missionary to Peru.

Father Altimira was a harsh supervisor who relied more on the lash than on understanding in dealing with his converts. In 1826, an angry band of Indians stormed the mission, looting and burning the buildings. Altimira fled to San Rafael and, unable to return to his mission, eventually returned to Spain. His successors at the Sonoma mission, as it was later called, could accomplish little. Instead of resisting the Russians, in its early days the mission was able to survive only because of Russian charity in the form of bells, utensils and tools.

For many years, California felt the effects of the political vacillations which disturbed Mexico. When Iturbide fell from power in 1823, the Californios dutifully transferred their oath of allegiance to the new and weak Mexican Republic. It made little difference to California what form of government Mexico embraced, for they still remained aloof from the Mexican nation.

The greatest excitement during Argüello's term of office was an Indian uprising in 1824. In February of that year, revolts started simultaneously among the Indians at Santa Inés, Purísima Concepción, and Santa Barbara. The underlying cause of the uprisings was probably the hatred of the natives for the soldiers. The revolt began on Sunday, February 21, 1824, at Santa Inés, when one of the soldiers flogged an Indian who had been serving as a corporal in the Mexican army. The mission Indians, already sullen and mutinous, suddenly attacked without warning, having somewhere procured a sizeable supply of weapons. The soldiers took refuge in a stout building behind the church. From this vantage point they exchanged shots at long range with the Indians. Having the advantage of cover, they suffered no fatalities; two Indians were killed. Some Indians set fire to the mission buildings, partly destroying them. Once during the battle the Indians ceased fighting to save the church from the flames, for they had no quarrel with the missionaries. When troop reinforcements marched in from Santa Barbara, the rebel Indians fled to La Purísima mission. The Indians there, abetted by the fugitive rebels from Santa Inés, attacked the soldiers. By the next morning, after a night of random firing, the small garrison of mission guards surrendered. Seven Indians and four soldiers had been killed. Following a parley, the Indians agreed to allow the surviving soldiers to march out, but the rebel Indians held the mission for nearly a month. Using the building knowledge they had gained at the mission, they fortified the mission grounds by building stockades, breaking loopholes in the church walls, and mounting two old cannons, hitherto only used for the celebration of feast days.

When the news reached Santa Barbara, the Indians there also rebelled and took over the mission, seizing the soldiers' arms. Captain de la Guerra collected a force from the nearby presidio and marched to attack the mission. After a battle of several hours, the Indians fled to the hills where they eventually found sanctuary in the San Joaquin Valley. The soldiers then destroyed and looted the Indian dwellings.

When word reached Monterey of the rebel success at Purísima Concepción, Governor Argüello sent Lieutenant José Mariano Estrada with a force of one hundred men to put the rebellion down. With cannon Estrada's men attacked the walls of the Indian-held buildings. The lieutenant had also sent a troop of cavalry to surround the mission and cut off all retreat. The battle lasted less than three hours, for the Indians' inexperience in handling guns and cannon quickly compelled them to surrender. Sixteen Indians were killed and many wounded, while only one soldier was killed and three slightly injured.

Three succeeding expeditions were launched across the mountains into the Tulares to punish the fugitives from Santa Barbara. Some Indians evaded all their pursuers and were still living in the San Joaquin Valley ten years later.

The captured Indian ringleaders were quickly tried. Seven were condemned to death and the eighteen others to various terms of imprisonment.

In November 1825, Lieutenant Colonel José María Echeandía, who spoke with a pronounced Castilian lisp, came up from Mexico to serve as governor of both Alta and Baja California. He was a tall, thin man who was a notorious hypochondriac. Soon after his arrival, he announced that as governor of both Baja and Alta California, he would reside at San Diego rather than at Monterey, because the town was more centrally located for conducting the official business of both Californias. His excuse fooled no one; Californios generally agreed that he feared his health would fail in the cool Monterey region. Jealousy between north and south flared as a result of this affair.

Echeandía mishandled the missions and aroused the resentment of his unpaid soldiers. In 1828 the Monterey garrison rose in revolt against him. It was persuaded by Lieutenant Romauldo Pacheco to return to duty. In November 1829, the garrison again rose in revolt. This time the men seized their officers and followed a former convict, Joaquín Solís, who led a revolution which extended as far south as Santa Barbara. Various foreign businessmen in Monterey, suffering under the Mexican restrictions on trading, financially supported the rebels. The San Francisco garrison also joined the revolt.

Soon Solís, fearing that his uprising might lose momentum, decided to march south. Since the missionaries disliked Echeandía intensely, they received the insurgents hospitably. The Santa Barbara garrison first joined the revolt, only to revert suddenly to Echeandía's side. The governor hastened to join the troops at Santa Barbara, for he believed this settlement was the gateway to the southland, so it must be held. He arrived on December 15, shortly before Solís' small army arrived from the north. It soon became a conflict of words rather than bullets. There was a little skirmishing at long range, but a horse was the only recorded casualty. When Echeandía promised amnesty to all who would leave Solís, desertions from the rebel ranks were so heavy that Solís was forced to retreat ingloriously. Echeandía advanced upon Monterey, where he found that the foreign residents had turned against Solís. After the revolt had subsided, Solís and his fellow conspirators were arrested by Echeandía and shipped off to Mexico in irons. So ended the first California revolt against Mexican authority, and the first of many conflicts between the south and the north.

Echeandía lingered in Monterey for a year. When the newly appointed governor, Lieutenant Colonel Manuel Victoria, was sent to California, he asked Echeandía to travel to San Diego to surrender his office. The old governor refused. As a result, Victoria journeyed to Monterey in January 1831, where he was formally installed in office.

Victoria was a harsh administrator who doled out heavy sentences to wrongdoers and political opponents. His actions engendered hatred among the easygoing Californios who began a movement to drive him from office. Victoria had also annulled much of Echeandía's decree of 1831, which called for the secularization of the missions. A group of young Californios felt that this action would retard the economic growth of the province. Only the missionaries whom Victoria befriended were his firm friends. Late in 1831, a revolt broke out in the south, led by José Antonio Carrillo, Juan Bandini, Pío Pico and Abel Stearns, an American who had been in California for only two years. Leadership of the rebellion was offered to Echeandía, who had returned to San Diego after retiring as governor. Echeandía readily agreed. The presidios and garrisons at Los Ángeles and San Diego surrendered to the rebels without a fight.

With thirty veteran soldiers from the San Blas and Mazatlán companies, Governor Victoria set out southward. Many of the 150 insurgents led by Captain Pablo Portilla of San Diego had never fired a shot in anger. The two rival armies met at Cahuenga Pass, a few miles from Los Ángeles. The battle began when Victoria advanced alone, calling on the regular troops in his opponent's army to come over to his side. When they refused, he ordered his men to fire; the southern soldiers promptly ran away. Victoria then pursued his retreating enemy. Suddenly José María Avila, mounted on a fine horse, rushed forward from the southern ranks and killed a captain in Victoria's army, Romualdo Pacheco. He then attacked Victoria. Other southerners rallied to join him, and in the battle that followed, Avila was killed and Victoria was wounded in the face. The injured Victoria soon lost his desire to continue the fight. Instead of pressing on and capturing Los Ángeles, he sought refuge at San Gabriel. From there he sent word to Echeandía that he would resign and return to Mexico. Echeandía accepted his offer, and Victoria left California on a chartered vessel, the *Pocahontas*.

The Californios decided at this time to separate the administration of military and civil affairs. The provincial legislature at Los Ángeles, the Diputación, elected Pío Pico as *jefe politico* in January 1832. But in three weeks Pico resigned, since Commandante Echeandía would not co-operate with him. Echeandía seemed about to take undisputed control, when opposition developed in the north.

In the Monterey area were many Americans and British businessmen who viewed the California impulse to constant revolution with disap-proval, since so much conflict was bad for business. These businessmen had backed Victoria when he had promised order. Now they felt that Echeandía could never bring peace either, for his supporters were always bickering. The foreign community began looking for a new candidate for governor. They found one in Augustín Vicente Zamorano, former secre-tary to both Echeandía and Victoria. Zamorano realized that the populace of northern California distrusted Echeandía, since he gave every indica-tion of locating his capital in San Diego. The fiction was spread that Zamorano would only be a temporary governor until Mexico could ap-point a proper successor to the deposed Victoria. Zamorano, declaring that he was defending public order, sent Lieutenant Juan María Ibarra to defend Santa Barbara against attack by Echeandía. After securing Santa Barbara, Ibarra pushed on as far as Los Ángeles. Then word came to him that the mission Indians were flocking to Echeandía who had recruited perhaps as many as a thousand men. Ibarra then retreated. Zamorano concluded a truce with Echeandía in May 1832. The two agreed to divide California between them. Zamorano's control reached from San Fernando to Sonoma, while San Gabriel marked the northern limits of Echeandía's control.

In January 1833, Mexico sent out a new governor, Brevet Brigadier General José Figueroa. He had had a distinguished military career and had been a governor of Sonora and Sinaloa for six years. He was there-fore familiar with California's disturbed political affairs. To help establish control in the province, he brought with him an armed force of seventy-five officers and men, lately released from prison for revolutionary activity. Although he was in ill health and died after only two and a half years as governor, he accomplished a great deal during his short tenure. His conduct as governor was superior to that of previous Mexican officials. He was scrupulously honest in financial dealings; he had a talent for administration and was well educated.

His first act was to grant amnesty to all who had taken part in the recent rebellions. (This was the first document printed in California.) Another of his administrative acts was to send a party to explore the regions north of San Francisco Bay and plant settlements there to contain Russian and British encroachments. At the head of this expedition was Mariano Guadalupe Vallejo.

Vallejo held the rank of *alférez* (ensign) at the San Francisco presidio. He was the son of Ignacio Vallejo, who had come to California in 1774 with Rivera. Mariano Vallejo was a veteran of several Indian campaigns and had participated in California's political affairs, although he was only twenty-five years old. Figueroa sent Vallejo to the north bay area to select a site for a presidio. In the fall of 1833, two colonies were founded by Vallejo, one at Petaluma and a smaller one at Santa Rosa.

In May 1834, Figueroa learned that his request to retire because of poor health had been honored and that his successor would be José María Híjar, who was coming up from Mexico with many colonists. Figueroa then journeyed to the north bay area to select a suitable site for the colonists. Upon his return to Monterey, he received a dispatch from the Mexican government which altered his plans.

Ever since Mexico had become independent of Spain, the Mexican government had wished to increase the population in California, and to this end had often shipped convicts to Alta California. Seventeen had been sent in 1825, including the troublesome Joaquín Solís. During the next year, more than one hundred convicts arrived. In 1830 a shipload of eighty came into California. Then in 1833 a new colony of settlers was planned by José María Padrés, who had been banished from the territory by Victoria. While he was living in Alta California, Padrés had nurtured an idea to take over the missions under the guise of their secular administration. Padrés' scheme soon attracted adherents eager to share the spoils. Exiled to Mexico in 1831, he developed a colonization project which he planned to finance with mission funds. Padrés was backed by the prominent Mexican José María Híjar. Híjar claimed the post of civil governor and Padrés was to be his military commander. With liberal financial aid from the Mexican government, they gathered some 250 colonists of superior quality (doctors, lawyers, teachers, artisans) and left from San Blas in July 1834. One of the two ships carrying this party was the *Natalia,* believed to have been the vessel on which Napoleon escaped from Elba.

After the colonists sailed, a governmental upheaval occurred in Mexico, and the new president, General Antonio López de Santa Anna, withdrew Mexican support of the colonization project. Unable to stop the expedition, he sent a messenger over the old Anza trail, ordering Figueroa to refuse to turn the government over to Híjar, whose authority Santa Anna now revoked. The messenger, Rafael Amador, made the difficult overland journey in forty to forty-eight days, traveling alone most of the way. He was almost killed by hostile Colorado Indians, and then nearly died of thirst while crossing the desert.

On September 1, Híjar landed at San Diego. From there he traveled north by land to Monterey, telling the mission Indians along the way that he intended to free them. Aboard another vessel, Padrés landed at Monterey on September 25. Padrés' influential backers inside California deserted him when they found that he had brought with him twenty-one Mexicans to serve as mission administrators, whereas he had promised the Californios that they would fill these positions. Therefore, the Diputación voted that Figueroa should remain as governor.

Híjar unsuccessfully tried argument and bribery to persuade Figueroa to grant him the administration of the missions. Figueroa called upon the missions to supply the new colonists with food until their own crops could sustain them. The majority of these colonists were sent by Vallejo to mission San Francisco de Solano, from which they founded the town of Sonoma. When Híjar and Padrés made violent threats against the governor in March 1835, they were arrested and returned to Mexico.

During the few months of life remaining to him, Figueroa granted many tracts of land to individual settlers. In Los Ángeles, he met a twenty-two-year-old English youth, William Antonio Richardson, a mate on a British vessel who had jumped ship to stay in California. Figueroa chose Richardson to serve as captain of the San Francisco port.

Richardson moved there and, after looking over the terrain, decided not to build at either the inconveniently located mission or at the presidio. Instead, he built a rude shanty on the east side of the peninsula in Yerba Buena Cove, outside the mission and presidio compounds. This was the first building (outside these compounds) constructed in the west San Francisco Bay area. It was the beginning of the village of Yerba Buena, which in a few years became known as San Francisco.

Despite his personal predilection against it, Figueroa became remembered in California history for the secularization of the missions. The original plan for the mission system had been that after ten years the missions were to be converted to civilian towns, and the missionaries would be transferred to new posts on the frontier. This plan was never realized, for temporary missions in Alta California continued indefinitely.

In 1813, during Spanish rule, the Cortés or Parliament had passed a law authorizing the immediate secularization of all missions in existence ten years or longer. This law was not promulgated in California until 1821, and then no attempt was made to put it into effect. At the time there were no priests to replace the missionaries.

During the late Spanish and early Mexican periods, the missions reached the peak of their prosperity. Thousands of Indians still lived at mission settlements, which were the economic mainstay of the province. From 1810 through the revolutionary period, the missions supported the civil and military establishments in California. So sound was their economic health that they scarcely noticed the burden. Yet regardless of any outside pressure, the missions carried the seeds of their own destruction. For years Indian deaths exceeded births. In 1815 the proportion of deaths to births was three to two, which meant a decrease in the Indian population at the missions, even allowing for new converts. The missionaries were unable to recruit many new neophytes, because pagan Indians generally did not live in great numbers near the missions.

During the Mexican period, the missions began to feel the changed official climate in many ways. Heavier tax exactions were made on them; the friars protested but paid. In 1826 Governor Echeandía formulated a plan for the secularization of the missions. During the first phase of this plan, the Indians of the missions south of Monterey were allowed to leave if they had been Christians from infancy, or for at least fifteen years. They also had to be self-supporting. Few Indians could qualify, nor did many choose to take advantage of this proclamation. In 1827, the Mexican central government passed a law ordering all missionaries from the nation, but this rule was never enforced in California. On January 6, 1831, Echeandía issued a proclamation putting into effect his plan for the gradual secularization of the missions. The announcement of this law was in itself sufficient to cause great change. This command reflected the current attitude among Californios toward the missions. Soldiers, ill paid and ill clad, had long envied the relative opulence of the missionaries and even the neophytes. Furthermore, two generations of Spanish-Mexican colonists had grown up in California, and many men now faced an unemployment problem. Their present choice was either to join the army or do nothing. Land grants were few (only fifty ranches are known to have been operating in 1830) and so few owned or ever could own their own property. Many speculators eyed the mission settlements hungrily, for they embraced much of the best land near the coast and most of the improved land of California. The mission Indians, hearing rumors of freedom, became unruly or disinterested in their work. Gradually, the daily routine in the missions began to disintegrate.

When Figueroa became governor in 1833, it did not seem as if the final overthrow of the missions was imminent, since he had brought with him ten Franciscan friars to augment the diminished ranks of the missionaries. These Franciscan missionaries were not from the San Fernando College, which had fallen on evil days; they were Mexican clergy who came from the College of Zacatecas. The Zacatecan Franciscans, led by Francisco García Diego, were not of the same high quality as their predecessors. They had less executive ability, and in general, seemed unequal to the immense task of running the missions. They resorted to corporal punishment for light infractions and soon earned the hatred of the Indians.

Figueroa's instructions as an agent of the Mexican government had included orders for gradual secularization, but in the early days of his administration, he was supposed to restore the missions to the status they had held prior to Echeandía's term of office. Figueroa made a tour of the missions and found that discipline and morale among the Indians were low. He was convinced that immediate secularization would be a disaster. Consequently, he adopted what he thought was a compromise. He issued orders that Indians best fitted for life outside the missions were to be emancipated. Even though tools, land, seed and domestic animals were given to them, in many ways they remained subject to civil and religious authorities. Of fifty-nine family heads at San Diego eligible for this program, only two volunteered to leave. At San Luís Rey, only ten out of 108 eligible Indian families chose to become self-supporting. This convinced Figueroa that secularization must proceed gradually. At this time Figueroa also declared that mission lands were to be reserved for the Indians, and should not be given to the colonists.

Events in Mexico generally altered Figueroa's plans. In August 1833, the Mexican government decreed that the missions in Baja and Alta California were to be immediately secularized. A supplemental act in November linked colonization to secularization; wide ranges of valuable land were made available to the public. The Pious Fund was to be used to further this scheme. In April 1834, a Mexican law called for secularization within four months.

This barrage of laws left Figueroa no alternatives. He did temporize a bit. In a decree dated August 9, 1834, the governor ordered the secularization of ten missions and appointed civil administrators for them. In 1835, six more missions were converted and the remaining five in 1836.

According to Figueroa's decree, half of the mission property was to be distributed among the Indian neophytes, while the remaining land was placed under the control of the secular administrator. The income from this property was to be used to support the religious establishment and other public projects. The Indians were obligated to work on community undertakings. The former neophytes were forbidden to sell their land or slaughter their domestic animals. In the absence of parish priests, the missionaries continued in their religious ministrations.

After the death of Figueroa on September 29, 1835, the political situation in California was so chaotic that the mission administrators were only nominally supervised. Many enriched themselves and their friends from the spoils of the missions, and many were incompetents who frittered away mission properties; few seem to have been both able and honest.

The Indian labor force at the missions disintegrated. Freed from mission discipline, few Indians saw any reason for hard labor. Disregarding the provisions of Figueroa's plan, the Indians sold their land and livestock for liquor. Many Indians gambled away their possessions. When their supplies were gone, some became bond servants to anyone who would hire them. Others ran away to live with the wild Indians of the interior. Still others became beggars and lived lives of destitution, begging alms which barely kept them alive.

By the end of the 1830's, an attempt was made to run the missions more efficiently. Early in 1839, Governor Juan Bautista Alvarado appointed a capable Britisher, William E. P. Hartnell, as government inspector of the missions. After a tour of the missions, Hartnell found that while there were some exceptions, on the whole, the mission system was deteriorating. Hartnell suggested that he be made superintendent of the missions, and the administrators reduced to clerks. When the governor agreed and made the necessary appointments, Hartnell found the opposition on the part of some of the administrators so vehement that he resigned. In 1840 Francisco García Diego, a Zacatecan Franciscan, received authority from the bishop of both Alta and Baja California to use the Pious Fund to establish a cathedral and seminary for priests in California. The transfer of the mission churches to locally trained clergy seemed now at hand. Then a new president in Mexico denied the Pious Fund to Bishop Diego and turned the money over to the Mexican state treasury.

The missions deteriorated steadily. Hoping to restore them to their former productivity, Governor Manuel Micheltorena, in 1842, restored certain mission properties to the care of the friars. This action came too late to save the mission system. Therefore, to salvage as much as possible from the missions, in 1844, on the plea that the threatening attitude of the United States made war likely, Governor Micheltorena ordered all the missions sold or rented. In the next two years before the American invasion, the California government disposed of all the missions but Santa Barbara, although many titles of purchase were later invalidated by the American government.

By 1820, there were only 3,270 Spaniards in California, and relatively few foreigners (less than twenty), including such Americans as Thomas Doak and Joseph Chapman.

With the advent of the Mexican period a hide and tallow trade was established, and soon whaling ships began to visit California ports. The pace of foreign settlement was quickened. New arrivals differed from earlier foreigners; they were not homeless seamen or refugees but serious businessmen.

William Hartnell came from Lima as a representative of John Begg and Company, an English firm which opened a branch at Monterey in 1822. He was born in England and educated in Germany. He spoke half a dozen languages, including Hebrew and Russian, and became so fluent in Spanish that he wrote letters in that language to English-speaking people. He did so because he liked to emphasize his hispanization. Hartnell acquired a large library which he generously lent to friends in California. About 1825 he married a lady described as the "intelligent and beautiful María Teresa de la Guerra." Their marriage produced twenty sons and five daughters. After a trip to Lima to dissolve his business ties, Hartnell was naturalized as a Mexican citizen. The following year he began ranching, and in 1834, he patented a rancho twenty miles from Monterey. By 1849 he had eight thousand cattle and several thousand sheep and horses. He took an active role in the community and held many governmental posts.

In 1823, only eight arrivals are recorded, among them the British captain John B. E. Cooper, who came on the Boston ship *Rover*. He sold the schooner to Luís Argüello, but continued to act as its skipper. He married the "simpática señorita" Encarnación Vallejo, sister of Mariano Vallejo, and produced a socially important family.

All during the 1820's more foreigners arrived, although never more than twenty-five in one year.

In 1829 two very ambitious Americans came to Alta California, Alfred Robinson and Abel Stearns. Robinson was a native of Massachusetts, who was only twenty-nine when he arrived on a hide and tallow ship. He married Ana María, daughter of Captain José de la Guerra, at Santa Barbara. The transplanted Yankee had already been baptized and had taken the Spanish name of José María Alfredo. Robinson later wrote a book, *Life in California*, which is an excellent source of information for Mexican California. He lived on into the late nineteenth century as the oldest surviving pioneer of this period.

Abel Stearns, a Massachusetts Yankee, moved to California after three years in Mexico. Landing at Monterey, he moved to Los Ángeles where he became a leading merchant. As a result of his brushes with the Mexican law, he was banished from California briefly, but returned to lead a rebellion against Governor Victoria. The usual charge against him was smuggling, except on one occasion in 1836 when the governor accused him of taking part in a lynching. In a fight with William Day, Stearns suffered a facial wound which caused him to be called "Cara de Caballo"

(Horse Face). After marrying the lovely Doña Arcadia Bandini, he became a successful rancher. By his death in 1871, he owned more than two hundred square miles of land. Stearns, too, held a number of minor governmental posts.

In 1831, William Heath Davis, author of *Sixty Years in California*, came to the province aboard the *Eagle* from Massachusetts. He married María Jesus, daughter of Don Joaquín Estudillo. A gracious gentleman, he became famous for his delightful manners and courtesy.

In the 1830's the number of foreigners entering California annually rose from twenty-five to fifty, the Americans outnumbering the British about three to one. The several hundred foreigners in California tended to settle in the commercial centers of Monterey, Los Ángeles and San José.

As the Boston fur ships began to decline in importance, there was a transitional period during which the visits of whalers to California ports assumed some importance. Since the voyage from New England to the Pacific for whaling ordinarily lasted three years, the whalers needed a place to refit and revictual. Hawaii was the favorite haunt; literally hundreds of vessels sojourned there. California was the second most popular supply stop. Some whalers anchored at Monterey; more stopped at San Francisco Bay. After paying a nominal charge, they could barter various kinds of manufactured goods for provisions, but this was not yet the era of offshore Pacific whaling. The chief significance of these whaling visits was the American interest in California as a trading center, which they stimulated.

As early as 1813, two vessels from Lima, the *Flora* and the *Tagle*, brought up cargoes of manufactured goods in exchange for hides and tallow. Other ships from Lima followed sporadically. It was the British who first placed a commercial agent there and developed a large-scale trade with California. The Englishman John Begg had already established himself at Lima, Peru, with a flourishing trade in South American hides. Then with the softening of restrictions against foreign commerce in California, he joined with William Hartnell and a Scotsman, Hugh McCullough, to pioneer the California hide and tallow market. Their company became known as "Macala y Arnel" to the Californians. Aboard the vessel *John Begg*, Hartnell and McCullough successfully negotiated with Governor Solá for permission to make contacts with missions for hides and tallow. Soon some of the firm's dozen ships sailed directly from California to England; others began trading from Monterey to San Diego, Lima, Santiago, around Cape Horn, then up the South American coast to Montevideo and Rio de Janeiro, before the trans-Atlantic crossing to Great Britain.

The ships loaded hides for the English market and tallow to be traded in South America. In addition they carried hemp, pickled beef, suet, soap, horse hair, horns and, on occasion, wheat. In exchange the British traders offered Californios cargoes of cheap clothing, farm implements, musical instruments, cooking utensils and exotic food products, such as rice, sugar, cocoa, tea and coffee, as well as the gold and silver thread so necessary for the fancy embroidery of Latin clothing.

At first, the missions were the center of the hides trade. Later, after the break-up of the missions, private ranchos supplied the British merchants. The Yankees were not far behind the British in this traffic. The American William Alden Gale, previously engaged in the dwindling otter and seal trade along the California coast, returned to Boston with a plan to enter this new trade in hides. He persuasively argued the Boston shipping firm of Bryant & Sturgis into entering the California hide commerce. Aboard their ship *Sachem*, loaded with New England manufactured goods, Gale sailed as a supercargo on the 15,000-mile journey to San Diego. He arrived only one month after Hartnell and McCullough in 1822. Gale was called "Cuatro Ojos," or Four Eyes, because he constantly wore spectacles. Bryant & Sturgis was soon joined by other American firms eager to share in the trade's profits.

The hide trade capitalized upon one of California's few commercial assets. As far back as the Portolá expedition, two hundred head of cattle contributed by the Baja California missions had entered the province. Of all the many activities at the newly established missions, stock raising was the most successful. The lack of an adequate market limited the raising of agricultural products to that required by the small community of Europeans and Christian Indians. There was small demand for other trades and professions. The one great industry which could be fostered was the raising of beef cattle and sheep. There was almost unlimited pasture land available. Outside the missions, cattle herds could be started with a minimum of expense; often the nearest mission would give a few cattle in return for a promise to pay back the original number of cattle after a period of time, usually five years.

The original cattle multiplied by the thousands and grazed from Baja California to the north San Francisco Bay area. In 1826 it is believed that there were at least 200,000 head of cattle in California. During July, August and September, the roundup or *matanza* was held at every mission or rancho. Vaqueros (generally Indians) lassoed cattle with their *reatas*. Other Indians did the actual butchering. As a sort of side line, McCullough, Hartnell & Co. had contracted with the government of Peru to supply it with salted beef. As a result, several salters and coopers were sent from Scotland and Ireland to prepare cargoes for shipment. This portion of the trade proved to be unprofitable and was speedily abandoned. Consequently, when the cattle and sheep were slaughtered, the hides were stripped off for bartering and the best meat cut into strips to

be dried or jerked for consumption in California. The rest of the carcasses were left for the coyotes. The stench of rotting animals became so
overwhelming that in 1833 Los Ángeles passed an ordinance requiring
cremation of the animal remains, but the odor of piles of burnt meat was
a scant improvement. Although butchering was hastily done, there was
great spoilage because of the lack of refrigeration.

The animal fats were piled into the Mexican *carreta*—the clumsy two-
wheeled cart first invented about 1600—to be taken to the mission or
rancho headquarters to be made into tallow and soap.

All of the missions had elaborate brick vat systems to tan hides; most
had similar systems for rendering tallow as well. Some missions preferred
to use great iron kettles placed over large brick furnaces. The mission
laborers generally smoked and stored cattle tongues also. Some leather
was manufactured in California for use in reatas and rawhide thongs.
Sheep hides became the leather jackets of the California soldiers; the
cattle hides generally entered the international traffic. After being collected from the missions and ranchos, the cattle hides and sheep skins
were taken to about ten depots on the coast for shipment to San Diego.
Although occasionally a more direct traffic with America or Great Britain was attempted, San Diego became the chief center of the hide trade.
Tenders or smaller ships gathered the hides up and down the coast and
took them to that port. In San Diego all the Boston firms had salt vats
where sailors and Hawaiians cured the hides, and barns for storage prior
to shipment. As a warm, rain-free port with relatively little fog, San
Diego had an ideal climate and surroundings for drying, curing and stor-
ing hides.

The hide trade drew Richard Henry Dana to California aboard the
Boston brig *Pilgrim*. A young, weak-eyed scion of a prominent Cambridge, Massachusetts, family, he faithfully kept a journal from which he
wrote the classic *Two Years Before the Mast*, which has been in print
since 1840. In it Dana noted that Massachusetts men had taken over along
the California coast, from Thomas O. Larkin in the north at Monterey, to
a one-eyed Fall River whaleman tending bar in San Diego.

During the approximately twenty years of the hide trade, four Boston
firms dominated it: Bryant & Sturgis, J. B. Eaton, Appleton & Company,
and B. T. Reed.

One Boston man estimated that more than a million and a quarter hides
were shipped out of California during these years. Thirteen ships took
out more than 300,000 during the five years between 1831 and 1836. Hides
normally sold for two dollars each in California. Bryant & Sturgis bought
and exported 500,000 in twenty years. Most of the hides taken to New
England were used in the expanding boot and shoe industry of that section. The New Englander "hide-droghers" succeeded in capturing about

half of the trade away from the British, and often they had twenty or thirty ships annually engaged in this traffic. Yet not only British and American ships found profit in this commerce; some French, German, Swedish, Russian and South American ships also took part.

The secularization of the missions brought a dramatic increase in the slaughter of cattle. While the missions still functioned under a systematized administration, they were able to supply the California soldiers and officials with cash and goods worth a million dollars without seriously diminishing their resources. When the hide traffic began, the missions were able to furnish great quantities of hides without seriously impairing the numbers of their herds. Once the ranchers and former neophytes began handling herds, the desire for quick profits led to the indiscriminate slaughter of the range animals. Under the pressures of this traffic the herds diminished, for no one planned for the future. The seemingly inexhaustible supply of hides dwindled.

The hides traffic may have hit its peak in 1838, when 200,000 hides reached Boston alone. Eight years later the trade was dead. The traffic declined because of the disintegration of the mission economy, accompanied by the burdensome exactions (customs duties ranged as high as 80 to 100 per cent) and prohibitions demanded by the provincial government. Hides became increasingly scarce in the forties, and in 1842 an American naval officer estimated that only 150,000 were exported. As the trade declined, the southern ports languished, and the remaining traffic was shifted to San Francisco Bay. In 1843, hides in the Boston market still sold for eleven to thirteen cents a pound. Within two years, because of cargoes from Cuba, the price plummetted to nine to ten cents a pound—less than $2.50 a hide. As a result, there was not sufficient income to maintain a ship and crew on the California coast for two or three years. Therefore, the large Boston firms withdrew from the traffic and it virtually ceased to exist. New England turned to other parts of Latin America and the western United States for its supply of hides.

Estates in Spanish America mainly devoted to stock raising were called ranchos, while those principally interested in growing crops were known as *haciendas*. The missions normally partook of the characteristics of both. As the missions declined, the private rancho in California came to the fore as the heir of mission lands and herds.

During the Mexican period, most of the "Spanish" land grants were made. In 1824 Mexico inaugurated a liberal land policy under which Mexicans and naturalized foreigners might be granted land upon request. For various reasons this policy was not commonly implemented in California until the 1830's, when the Mexican authorities in California allowed grants composed of one league of irrigable soil, four dependent upon rain, and six fit only for grazing. Each league was 4,438 acres. After 1830, large

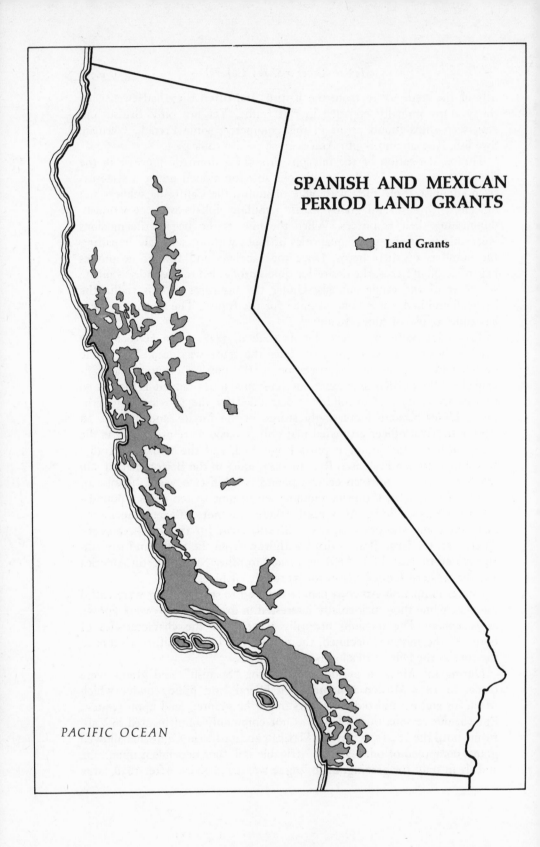

SPANISH AND MEXICAN
PERIOD LAND GRANTS

Land Grants

PACIFIC OCEAN

ranchos with ill-marked boundaries became common in California. Corner posts on a grant were sometimes marked with the owner's cattle mark. Yet often boundary indicators were much more informal, with a steer's skull or a marked cactus serving the purpose.

After the break-up of the mission system, any Californian of influence and substance had one or even several ranchos. Each rancho often had a name of religious significance (Natividad, the nativity of Christ), or acknowledging a natural feature (La Brea, the asphalt springs), or of Indian origin (Buri-Buri), or humorous, such as Las Pulgas (the Fleas).

John A. Sutter, the Swiss emigrant, obtained eleven leagues, or over seventy-six square miles. The whole East Bay across from San Francisco was once Luís Peralta's Rancho San Antonio, stocked with eight thousand cattle and two thousand horses.

According to William Heath Davis, an early American settler, 1,045 California land grants were made. Of these, eight hundred were actually stocked and worked, with an average of 1,500 cattle to a ranch, or over 1,200,000 cattle on all of California's ranchos.

The pastoral phase of California history from 1822 to 1846 is often romantically described as an idyllic time of Arcadian innocence. Yet this is an exaggeration. This was no golden age for those who lived through it. It was a time troubled by drought and political instability. It was an era when California's potential was still unrealized, as so many of its frustrated settlers discovered. Only to those who came later, or after time had dimmed the recollections of its survivors, was the golden glow added to the picture of these days.

ELEVEN

The Outsiders Arrive in Numbers

C ALIFORNIA was no longer sealed off from the East. Eventually American fur trappers came by way of the rugged mountains and across the wilderness. These men were precursors of the tide of American settlers who would soon stream west into California.

From the time of the Colorado massacre in the 1780's until 1826, there was for all practical purposes no overland contact with California. It remained for fur hunters of the Rockies to blaze a trail connecting California to the eastern frontiers of North America. These mountain men were experts in wilderness survival, for no fewer than eighty-four of them were killed by the Indians between 1822 and 1829; the weaklings or the unlucky were thus ruthlessly weeded out.

Of all the fur-trading explorers whose deeds are identified with California history, Jedediah Strong Smith was the first and perhaps the most famous. Born on January 6, 1799, in Bainbridge, New York, Smith was the descendant of old-line New Englanders. His father traced his lineage back to a settler in the Plymouth colony. Either from his parents or a neighboring physician, Dr. Titus Simons, Jedediah Smith acquired more of an education than was usual for frontier boys. He learned to read the Bible, to write and to cipher. In 1810 or 1811 his parents moved to Pennsylvania because his father had been accused of passing counterfeit money, although the charge was never proved. In 1817 they moved to Ohio.

In the early 1820's, Jedediah left his home to serve as a clerk on a

British fur-trading ship on the Great Lakes. Here he met the fur traders of the northwest who journeyed by way of the lakes to Montreal, a popular fur-trading center. These meetings provided him with valuable business experience.

When he was about twenty, he found employment at St. Louis, the new fur capital of the west, with William Henry Ashley, the greatest fur-trading explorer of the trans-Mississippi region. In this area a successful entrepreneur in the fur traffic not only had to trade for skins gathered by the Indians, but also had to find white trappers to collect pelts for him.

For Smith's purposes, Ashley was an excellent man under whom to serve an instructive, if hazardous apprenticeship. Ashley soon recognized Smith as a man of many talents. He could carry in his head an accurate picture of any map or territory he had crossed. Also, Smith gradually acquired a working knowledge of both French and Spanish. Soon Ashley entrusted important expeditions to this able young man. Smith pushed the Rocky Mountain frontier further west than anyone had before. In the spring of 1826, several trapping parties under Ashley's direction made their yearly rendezvous in the valley of the Great Salt Lake— an area Smith had been one of the first to see. That same year Ashley sold his fur interests to Smith and two other trappers, David E. Jackson and William F. Sublette. These three partners decided to search for pelts in the wilderness that stretched between the Great Salt Lake and the Mexican settlements in California. They hoped to establish a post somewhere on the Pacific coast from which pelts could be shipped directly to the Canton market.

On August 15, 1826, Smith led a trapping expedition of fifteen (some say seventeen) men from Bear River Valley in today's northern Utah, into the unknown lands to the west. Smith promised to return in time for a rendezvous in the summer of 1827 on the shores of Bear Lake in what is now southeastern Idaho. The party included fifty horses, half of them loaded with camp supplies and trading merchandise.

The party moved past Little Utah Lake, then up the banks of the Sevier River and southwestward across a mountain to a river Smith named for President John Quincy Adams. On October 4, 1826, he reached the Colorado River, which he called the "Seedskeder." Their route then took the party into the desolate land of the Mojave Indians, from whom Smith picked up a supply of corn and pumpkins as well as information that the Mexican settlements of California were nearby. Acquiring as guides two Indians who had run away from California missions, Smith recrossed the Colorado River and headed southwest into California. His route has never been traced with great exactness, but it is believed that he crossed the Sierra Madre range by way of Cajon Pass.

By mid-November, his bedraggled party reached the site of present-day Glendora, and from there they proceeded to the San Gabriel mission. The startled Father Bernardo Sánchez received his unexpected guests warmly, although he stipulated that they give up their arms to the corporal in charge of the mission guard. Father Sánchez also insisted that Smith write at once to the California governor, stating his reasons for intruding into the province. From the end of November 1826 until mid-January 1827, the trappers remained as guests at the mission. While his men relaxed, Smith rode to San Diego to meet with Governor Echeandía.

Smith tried to talk the suspicious Mexican governor into allowing the party to march northward along the California coast in the direction of the Oregon country. Echeandía refused and ordered Smith out of California, advising him to take a route that did not come near any settlements. Echeandía correctly foresaw that California's isolation from eastern North America had ended with Smith's arrival.

On January 10, 1827, Smith returned to the San Gabriel mission by way of San Pedro Bay, where he had been taken aboard an American brig commanded by Captain W. H. Cunningham. On January 18, Smith and his men began the long trek back. They recrossed the mountains by way of Cajon Pass and then slowly moved along the eastern foothills of the Sierra Nevada chain, eventually arriving at the San Joaquin Valley. Smith realized that the entire party could not successfully cross the snow-choked passes of the Sierra Nevada, and so he set up camp in the vicinity of the Stanislaus River. Accompanied by two companions, he set forth with seven horses and two mules to hike back to the site of the 1827 rendezvous. After forty-five days of travel, the small party became the first known white men to cross the Sierra Nevada. By late June, Smith reached his destination at Bear Lake.

Ten days after arriving at the meeting, Smith was ready to return to California and rejoin his men. This time he headed a party of eighteen trappers and two Indian women. As they attempted to cross the Colorado River by raft, the Mojaves, who had turned hostile, killed ten of the Americans. Smith finally led the survivors into California. Returning to San Gabriel, he obtained additional supplies and then led his party to the San José pueblo. Here Smith was arrested and sent to Monterey under guard. Imprisoned for a time, he was released only when several American ship captains posted bond for him. On December 30, 1827, he left California accompanied by nine men from his first expedition, nine from his second and two Californians who had joined him. The small company journeyed toward Oregon, trapping along the way. On June 23, 1828, he crossed out of California into the Oregon country. There on July 14, while he was encamped along the Umpqua River in southern Oregon, a war party of Indians attacked the group. Only Smith and three others survived this sudden massacre. They made their separate ways to the Hudson's Bay Company post at Fort Vancouver on the Columbia River. When Smith arrived on August 10, he received a cordial welcome. During the winter there, he recovered most of the furs he had previously lost to the Indians. He promptly exchanged his furs for $2,369.06 in a draft on London, which would be more portable now that his expedition had been largely wiped out. On March 12, 1829, Smith headed east up the Columbia River. He and one remaining companion finally rejoined his partners, Jackson and Sublette, at Pierre's Hole at the edge of the Tetons.

Smith's later career took him into other territories. After leaving the Rockies he went to St. Louis, where in 1831 he joined a large party traveling over the Santa Fé Trail to New Mexico. He was sent ahead to search for a waterhole and fell into a Comanche ambush near the Cimarron River. He was killed by an Indian arrow on May 27, 1831.

Although his colorful and important career came to a premature end, his forays to California earned him a secure place in the history of America. He demonstrated the possibilities of an overland trail to the west. Of the three main overland routes to California, Smith blazed two and traveled all three. In addition, he tied together the Rocky Mountain and Pacific frontiers, and penetrated the Pacific northwest as a precursor of the American migration that eventually spelled the doom of the Hudson's Bay Company aspirations in that area. Finally, Smith contributed significantly to the advance of American cartography.

Prominent among the American trappers who joined in the overland movement to California were the Taos-Santa Fé mountain men. The Pattie family was part of this group. The first Pattie of whom there is any record followed Daniel Boone into the Kentucky wilderness. In 1782 this Pattie saved Bryant's Station from an Indian massacre. His son, Sylvester, moved to Missouri. During the War of 1812, Sylvester dashed through the British lines during the siege of Fort Cap au Gris to seek help. After the war he returned to civilian life as a sawmill operator, caring for his wife and nine children. After his wife died during one of the many fever outbreaks that ravaged the Mississippi Valley, Sylvester reverted to his roving ways. Taking his eldest son, James Ohio, with him, he headed west.

They joined a party en route for New Mexico along the Santa Fé Trail. In the southwest they tried copper mining, but soon turned to fur trapping. In 1825 Sylvester Pattie led his son and five other trappers to the Gila River, which James Ohio stubbornly insisted on spelling "Helay." The party captured many beaver, but an Indian attack caused them to lose most of their catch. Escaping from the Indians, they disconsolately returned to Santa Fé.

In January of the next year, James Ohio Pattie, with another party of trappers whom he called the "French" party (French Canadians), returned to the Gila. Again the Indians attacked, killing many of the trappers and dividing the party. The Pattie group ascended the Colorado. The Yuma Indians along its banks were friendly and traded with the shaggy mountain men, who looked much like Indians themselves. When the party moved into Mojave country, the Indian attitude changed. At one campsite the Indians attacked, killing two men and wounding two others. After this incident the trappers moved eastward, following the rim of the Grand Canyon, which evoked little awe from Pattie, who was busy complaining about the deep snow through which the party was forced to tramp. From there the band went north to the Yellowstone and finally wandered back to Santa Fé by way of the upper Platte and Arkansas rivers. At Santa Fé the Mexican governor confiscated their furs, claiming that the pelts had been poached in Mexican territory.

Late in September 1827, Sylvester Pattie again led his son and six companions to trap in the Gila Valley. The hostility of the Yuma Indians forced them to go by canoe down the Colorado River. Using dugout canoes the Pattie group sailed on, looking for Mexican settlements which they mistakenly believed existed near the mouth of the river. They trapped many beaver along the banks of the Colorado. On January 1, 1828, about a hundred miles below the confluence of the Gila and the Colorado rivers, a sudden Indian attack showered them with arrows. The trappers replied with gunfire, dropping six of the Indians and scattering the rest. Because beavers were scarce and no Mexican settlement could be found, the trappers became discouraged, yet they continued down the river. As they approached the Gulf of California, they abandoned their canoes and set up camp. During the night their camp was flooded by a returning tide from the gulf, and they lost much of their equipment. On February 10, when the tidal forces grew worse, they buried their stock of furs and struck out for California, which they believed to be nearby.

They journeyed west across the wastes of Baja California, suffering from thirst. Finally they came upon an encampment of friendly Indians, who could not believe that the darkly sunburned trappers were white men. One of the trappers finally stripped so that the Indians might be reassured by a patch of white skin. The Indian chief offered them guides to the nearest white settlement, and the trappers pushed on. After a fatiguing journey, the men straggled into the Dominican mission of Santa Catalina, only to be arrested and imprisoned. From there the Americans were marched under guard to the San Diego presidio where Governor Echeandía interrogated them, charging them with being Spanish spies. As the weeks of imprisonment dragged by, the elder Pattie died.

The survivors continued in close confinement all during the spring and summer of 1828. Finally, in September, the other men were allowed to return to the Colorado River and retrieve their furs, while James Ohio

Pattie remained behind as a hostage. Although two men deserted, four of the party returned to San Diego. They had recovered no furs, for the river had overflowed its banks and spoiled the buried cache.

The Mexican authorities now ordered Pattie's continued imprisonment. In December a smallpox outbreak swept the northern California missions. After the governor learned that Pattie had some smallpox vaccine with him, he promised him his freedom if he would vaccinate all the California whites and civilized Indians. Pattie traveled up and down the coast of California and vaccinated some 22,000 people. According to Pattie, the Russians at Fort Ross paid him one hundred dollars for his services.

Upon completion of his task, Echeandía offered Pattie cattle, mules and land, but only upon condition that he turn Catholic. Pattie indignantly refused and left California for Mexico City to complain to the president of Mexico. He received the official's sympathy, but no money. In disgust Pattie returned to Kentucky. According to most accounts, he returned to California at the time of the gold rush in 1849 and probably died in a Sierra blizzard in 1850. He left for posterity a colorful record of his western adventure—*The Personal Narrative of James Ohio Pattie.*

In the 1830's other fur trappers followed in the footsteps of Smith and the Patties, reaching California by the routes these men had pioneered. Regular commerce was opened between southern California and Santa Fé. In the very year of Mexican independence, William Becknell took a trainload of goods into the New Mexican city. His success drew many other traders until Santa Fé became the destination for dozens of American trading caravans heading south and west from Westport, St. Louis, Franklin and other towns in the Missouri area. The city became notorious for its gambling dens, murders, all-night fandangos and dark-eyed, colorfully dressed señoritas. Santa Fé also became the equipping center for fur trappers on several rivers from the Arkansas to the Rio Grande.

Southern mountaineers with a long frontier tradition dominated the California-New Mexico trade. None was more active than Ewing Young, a native of Knox County, Tennessee.

In August 1829, Young headed a party of forty men from Taos to California. Taos was an Indian village in New Mexico, a favorite rendezvous for mountain men who wished to avoid the Mexican authorities. Young's camp boy and interpreter was the short, bandy-legged Kit Carson. Although the Young party was attacked by the Apaches in Arizona, it was able to resist them. Traveling along the Gila River as far as the present city of Phoenix, they trapped many beaver and then turned north. Their catch far exceeded Young's expectations. Since it was unnecessary to trap again on the homeward journey, he split his party into two groups. While twenty-two of them took the furs to Taos, the other eighteen men, including Young and Kit Carson, headed for California.

Young led his party across 150 miles of wasteland to the Colorado River, and then across the Mojave Desert to the San Bernadino Mountains. The men looked like skeletons by the time they wandered into mission San Gabriel in the early winter of 1830.

American mountain men had long since worn out their welcome at this particular mission. Therefore, Young quickly headed farther north. He avoided the mission San Fernando, crossing the Tehachapi Mountains to the San Joaquin Valley. From there his party trapped the streams northward to the tip of San Francisco Bay. Indians had stolen a herd of horses from mission San José, and Young won the appreciation of the missionaries when he sent Kit Carson and ten men to bring them back. The missionaries traded their horses and mules to Young in exchange for beaver pelts.

On his return trip, Young stopped at Los Ángeles. Here the Mexican authorities had decided to arrest these wild intruders who carried no passports. These plans were abandoned when the Mexicans observed one of Young's party, James Higgins, dismount from his horse and casually shoot James Lawrence, another trapper with whom he had quarreled.

Young's party then returned across the California desert. When the expedition reached the headwaters of the Gila, they had fur packs weighing more than two thousand pounds. Young feared to bring this huge catch openly into Santa Fé, lest the Mexican governor repeat the confiscation which had been the fate of the Patties. Young was also worried because he had not received a license to trap from the Mexican authorities. Therefore, he secreted his furs in an abandoned copper mine and returned to Santa Fé. After obtaining a proper license to trade with the Apaches, and after having spent several months among the Indians, Young returned with his recovered furs to Santa Fé. Other mountain men were not fooled by Young's deception. They soon became as familiar with the Gila Trail as the Missouri traders had been with the Santa Fé Trail.

Meanwhile two other expeditions came from New Mexico to California. One, consisting of thirty Mexican traders and led by Antonio Amijo, left in early November 1829 from Abiquicú. After crossing the Colorado, they traveled along what may have been Smith's route to Los Angeles.

In the fall of 1830, the first party to traverse the entire length of what became known as the Old Spanish Trail was that led by a Kentuckian, William Wolfskill, a business partner of Ewing Young. The Old Spanish Trail was not a single well-marked route, but many trails that converged and separated. It led roughly from Santa Fé to Los Angeles, wandering through Arizona, Utah or Nevada, and then into California. Although no journal was kept by any of the twenty members of this party, one of them, George Yount, later wrote an account of the trip. If he can be believed, the Wolfskill party traveled the entire route, shortening the trip by a cutoff of about 250 miles. For more than a decade Wolfskill's route was the most popular land trail to California. Wolfskill stayed in California and took a leading part in developing the citrus, wine and cattle industries in the province. When he died in 1866, he owned land worth $150,000.

In 1831 Young entered into a partnership with two other men, including David Jackson, a former business associate of Jedediah Smith, forming the enterprise of Jackson, Waldo and Young. This company sent out two expeditions. The first, led by Jackson, set out to purchase two thousand large California mules for use on Santa Fé Trail caravans. Using Pattie's old route, Jackson crossed the Imperial Valley and headed north to San Fernando mission. Jackson could find only seven hundred mules to buy. Meanwhile, a second party led by Young trapped along the Gila and Colorado rivers, rendezvousing with the Jackson party on its return trip from California. At that time the partners agreed that Jackson would drive the mules on to Santa Fé, while Young, who had been able to trap only a small supply of beaver, would continue west. Just beyond the Colorado, the Mojave Indians attacked Jackson, who escaped to Santa Fé with only two hundred mules.

Meanwhile Young entered California, and in the summer of 1832 his men hunted sea otter along the coast. When fall came, he and his party crossed by way of Tejon Pass into the San Joaquin Valley. Trapping in the northern interior, he received a cordial reception from a Hudson's Bay Company expedition on the Sacramento River. From there he moved into Oregon and then back along the Pacific coast to the upper Sacramento River. Making its way southward, the expedition passed down the San Joaquin Valley and through the mountain passes to the Colorado River and Gila Valley.

By early 1834 Young had returned to California. Near San Diego he met Hall Jackson Kelley, an eccentric American who claimed he had had a vision in 1817 that commanded him to civilize and christianize Oregon. Consequently Kelley had attempted unsuccessfully to organize various colonizing companies; in 1832 he left unaccompanied for Oregon. He traveled to Mexico and eventually arrived in California where he persuaded Young to accompany him to Oregon. Young realized that the political authorities of California were hostile toward American intruders and agreed to head north with Kelley. Governor Figueroa sent word by a Hudson's Bay Company ship that there were horse thieves in the Young-Kelley party.

Consequently when Kelley and Young arrived at Fort Vancouver on the Columbia, they were coolly received by Hudson's Bay Company officials. Kelley was shipped out of Oregon at company expense and returned to the American east coast where he became an ardent anti-British propagandist in the issue over the Oregon country. Ewing Young and his trapper companions were not so easily disposed of. The American mountain men moved into the Chehalen Valley, where they built cabins. Unable to purchase necessary supplies from the Hudson's Bay Company, they decided to make trouble. Therefore, in the winter of 1836, they constructed a whisky distillery, which angered many of the citizens in Oregon. They were finally able to convince Young to give up his still in favor of leading an expedition to California to drive additional cattle to Oregon. Young returned to Oregon to find that his status in the community had improved. He became a prosperous rancher and died on February 15, 1841.

After the Rocky Mountain trappers rendezvoused in 1833, Captain Benjamin Bonneville placed Joseph Reddeford Walker in charge of fifty to sixty men. Bonneville, a leading figure in the fur trade, gave Walker rather vague instructions about his expedition. He merely told him to reconnoitre the territory west of Salt Lake. Zenas Leonard accompanied the expedition as the official scribe, so there is a reliable narrative of the journey.

Joseph Walker was a Virginian, born on December 13, 1798. He had moved west by way of Tennessee, Missouri and New Mexico. He was a powerfully built man who stood at least six feet tall, unusually soft-spoken and deceptively gentle in manner.

On July 24, 1833, Walker's party left the Grant River to explore the desert west of Salt Lake. The headwaters of the Humboldt River in northeastern Nevada had been discovered by Peter Skene Ogden of the Hudson's Bay Company in 1828. Walker had learned of this discovery and was somewhat familiar with both the Smith and Young routes into California.

Walker followed a westward route until he came to a northern tributary of the Humboldt River, after a journey of over a hundred miles. Although the beaver were plentiful, Walker headed downstream, reaching the Humboldt River just west of the present-day city of Wells, Nevada. Pushing southwest, Walker's men found the river waters had turned brackish and that beaver were scarce. The land quickly became a desert. Naked Digger Indians trailed the party, pouncing upon exhausted or stray horses and eating them. More and more Indians trailed the party, until Walker became frightened and ordered his men to fire upon them. Over twenty Indians were killed. For years thereafter the Indians of this area were inveterate foes of any white men who strayed into their territory.

Walker's party then followed the Humboldt River until it became a shallow alkaline lake which disappeared beneath the floor of the desert.

By journeying directly south, Walker failed to find the Truckee River, which would have led him to Donner Pass. His party wandered south until it reached the northern loop of what became known as the Walker River, forty miles east of present-day Carson City. Seeing the Sierra Nevada barrier in the distance, Walker turned southwest and followed the stream into the high mountains. Without realizing it, he was following the trail pioneered by Jedediah Smith in 1827. Walker passed through the Sierra by way of the Sonora Pass and became the first white man to lead a party westward over the Sierra. He descended near the Stanislaus River and traveled into the San Joaquin Valley. The travel-stained trappers were now rewarded by a glimpse of the beautiful Yosemite Valley and its giant redwood trees.

Walker's expedition pushed on to Monterey and camped there during the winter of 1833–34. In Monterey Walker was no more cordially received by the Mexican authorities than Smith had been. In February of 1834, he led his party down the San Joaquin Valley to the site of modern Bakersfield. Not wishing to risk arrest by visiting San Gabriel, Walker turned eastward and crossed the Sierra at Walker Pass. He traveled north along the foothills of the range, until he rediscovered his previous trail and returned to Bear Lake in Utah.

In 1843, Walker led an immigrant party to California, driving several mule-drawn wagons all the way from Fort Hall in Idaho. Although he was able to get the wagons as far as the Owens Valley in eastern California, he was forced to abandon them because of the weakened condition of the animals. He also guided the pathfinder John Charles Frémont on one of his trips to California. At his camp near Pueblo, Colorado, he sold several hundred animals to the American army, which was marching to occupy New Mexico after the outbreak of the Mexican War. After having roved the western frontier for many years, he returned to California, where he died in Ignacio Valley on October 27, 1876.

Although the demand for beaver pelts decreased and the mountain men gradually dropped out of sight when silk hats became popular in the 1830's, they had performed the vital function of linking California to the interior of North America.

The ancient Hudson's Bay Company, founded in 1670, merged with its rival, the North West Company, in March 1821. George Simpson took control of the company in 1822. During the 1820's the company had many trading posts in the southern Oregon country: Fort George (the old Fort Astoria), Fort Nez Perce (Walla Walla), and palisaded headquarters at Fort Vancouver.

The chief factor of the company's Columbia River department was Dr. John McLoughlin, born in Canada in 1784. He had studied medicine in Quebec and eventually bought a partnership in the North West

Company. When the two companies agreed to merge in 1821, he joined the Hudson's Bay Company.

From Fort Vancouver parties of beaver trappers hunted in all directions. One group, designated as the Umpqua Brigade, crossed regularly into California, penetrating the Sacramento-San Joaquin Valley.

Simpson, now a knight, accompanied by Dr. John McLoughlin, visited San Francisco, Monterey and Santa Barbara in January 1842. He was distressed to learn that he was too late to purchase Fort Ross from the departing Russians. Upon investigation, he concluded that the chaotic political situation in California would make it advantageous for Great Britain and the Hudson's Bay Company to extend their influence into that area. Consequently, he arranged to purchase a store in Yerba Buena from the American trader Jacob Leese. To man this outpost, the company sent William Glen Rae, Dr. McLoughlin's son-in-law. Rae's instructions called for him to carry on both commerce and espionage. Unfortunately for the company, Rae was not able to act effectively, for he became hopelessly confused by the tortured course of California politics. He also became distracted by the charms of a lovely señorita, known in history only as Carmencita. Rae squandered company money and time courting her. Rather than face his father-in-law with an explanation of his inability to accomplish the company's objectives, he killed himself.

Although Rae had failed, the company did not immediately give up on its commercial outlet in Yerba Buena and continued to maintain an outpost there for several years. Then, assessing the San Francisco Bay area as unpromising for annexation, it withdrew. The company's trappers continued to poach in California until 1841, when an agreement with Governor Alvarado regulated the practice. Thereafter trapping in California continued until the company withdrew from Oregon in 1845. Until that time possible British influence in California continued to agitate American annexationists who wished to secure California for the United States.

From 1812 to 1840 the Russians had kept a group of Aleut hunters on the Farallone Islands, as well as at Fort Ross. These able hunters were sometimes referred to as marine cossacks. In the early period of Russian occupancy at Fort Ross, their hunters took 1,200–1,500 skins annually. After 1818, the seal herds diminished rapidly, and the yearly catch fell to about five hundred. This latter figure was too small to allow the Russian operation to show any profit. However, fur hunting was only one reason for the Russian interest in California. They urgently needed a source of agricultural products for their entire American operation. Shortly after the construction of Fort Ross, the Russians were able to exchange trade goods for grain with the Spanish settlements in the San Francisco Bay area. After Mexico took over in the early 1820's, many foreigners were allowed to enter the California market, and the Russians were unable to make any profitable deals. As a result they began growing their own grain, vegetables and fruit. All the arable land around Fort Ross was tilled. Fruit orchards and vineyards were started. While the Russians achieved some success, their harvests were generally poor. A combination of the rocky soil, blight, rust, rodents and bad weather contributed to this meagre yield. In addition, the Aleuts, Russian merchants, and California Indians at Fort Ross were not skilled agriculturalists. Even the importation of Russian peasants did not significantly increase the yield, because the peasants were unwilling to experiment amid the unfamiliar California environment.

Raising livestock also proved only mildly successful at Fort Ross. Although the Californios sold the Russians some breeding stock, lack of good pasturage kept the herds small.

Attempting to diversify their economy at Ross, the Russians tried shipbuilding. Four 160–200 ton vessels were constructed there between 1815 and 1823. Shipbuilding went slowly; one vessel took two years to complete. The primary disability under which the Russians labored was their use of redwood and laurel, two types of lumber not well adapted to seagoing construction. Pine and oak proved little better, since the Russians did not sufficiently cure the lumber. Russian workmanship was always amateurish, and the life span of these vessels was not over six years. At the end of that time, the ships were little more than rotting hulks. The Russians found it cheaper to suspend shipbuilding at Fort Ross and confine themselves to the purchase of vessels from Americans.

The Spanish diplomatic attitude toward Russian occupation of any part of California was hostile. In 1820 the Russian-American Fur Company finally offered to evacuate Fort Ross and surrender any territorial claims in return for Spanish confirmation of Russian trading and hunting rights. Governmental shuffles of Spanish personnel precluded any acceptance of the Russian offer. Therefore the Russian presence in California was never regularized by Spanish recognition. Mexico took control of California with the issue of the legitimacy of Russian occupancy still very much an unresolved question, and with the Russian flag still flying over Fort Ross.

Russian willingness to consider evacuating Fort Ross was influenced in part by the establishment of a trading post much closer to Alaska than the Russian colony in California had been. In the Columbia River area, John J. Astor's Pacific Fur Company had established productive farms which Astor hoped would allow him to sell extensively to the Russians. Negotiations for such trade began in 1812, but were broken off. In 1813 Astor sold out his holdings to the North West Company, which amalgamated with the Hudson's Bay Company in 1821. In the period between 1813 and 1820, the farm holdings of this company were very productive, and by 1820 the Russians were able to negotiate the purchase of great quantities of supplies for Alaska.

With the coming of Mexican rule in California, relations between Fort

Ross and the nearby settlements became more friendly. Trade restrictions were ignored, but duties and foreign competition kept the traffic between the Mexicans and the Russians on a modest scale.

California governors grew increasingly suspicious of the Russian operation. As a result, in June 1829, and again in September 1830, Governor Echeandía ordered the Russians either to leave Fort Ross or acknowledge Mexican sovereignty over their outposts. The Russians ignored this threat, and Echeandía was too weak to enforce it.

When Baron Ferdinand Wrangell took charge of Russian America, he decided to discuss improved trade relations with the Mexicans in California. In 1831 he sent an agent to negotiate with the new California governor, Manuel Victoria. Victoria offered trade concessions to the Russians if they would recognize Mexican independence. (The Russian government, never quick to acknowledge successful rebellions in any quarter of the globe, had not officially recognized the Mexican republic.) Such recognition touched on topics that Baron Wrangell had no authority to discuss, and so negotiations failed.

In time, Baron Wrangell decided that conditions at Fort Ross could be improved if he could expand Russian coastal holdings eastward in California. He reasoned that if he did not act soon, the incoming tide of American settlers would prevent this expansion. In order to get official Mexican approval for this increase in Russian California holdings, Wrangell proposed to the authorities in St. Petersburg that they empower him to negotiate with Mexico. The Russian czar authorized him to negotiate a commercial treaty, but not diplomatic recognition of the Mexican republic.

Wrangell dutifully resigned from his commercial post and sailed for Mexico in January 1836. He quickly determined that his mission was doomed, for the Mexicans were uninterested in discussing the expansion of Russian possessions in California. They would only discuss trade relations and insisted upon being sent a fully accredited diplomat with whom to negotiate. The matter was referred to the Mexican minister in London. Nothing more was accomplished.

The Russian establishment at Fort Ross had become a heavy financial burden. By 1820 records at the settlement showed a net loss; between 1825 and 1829, income was one-half of expenditures. By the time of Wrangell's Mexican mission, income was only one-ninth of expenses.

Therefore, on April 15, 1839, the Czar signed an imperial order at St. Petersburg, ordering the liquidation of the settlements at Fort Ross and Bodega Bay. An entire year passed before the Russian governor at Sitka received the command. When he did, he quickly carried out the order. The governor first opened negotiations to sell the colony to the Hudson's Bay Company, asking $30,000 in cash and produce. George Simpson, head of the trading company, contemplated offering $15,000 to $20,000, but after some hesitation did not press a bid, because he feared that he could never acquire title to the land and might cause needless friction with both Mexico and the United States if he attempted to purchase Fort Ross.

Then a Swiss settler in California, John Sutter, offered to purchase the livestock and other moveable property at Fort Ross and Bodega Bay. Since Sutter would not pay for anything else, the Russians notified the Swiss that his bid was unacceptable.

Much to Sutter's disgust, the Russians now turned to the Mexican authorities in California. Some months earlier the Mexicans had ignored the Russian offer to sell the colony for $30,000. Now, in July 1841, a Russian agent appeared unexpectedly at Sonoma to make a formal sales offer. General Marian G. Vallejo, on behalf of the Mexican nation, declared that Mexico must have the first option to buy. He added the warning that the Russians could sell only their livestock, not the land. In Vallejo's view, even the Russian buildings properly belonged to Mexico, for they had been built with materials gathered on Mexican territory. For what remained of the purchasable Russian assets, Vallejo indicated that $9,000 might be a fair price. Vallejo and other Mexican authorities generally felt that the Russians would never be able to find another purchaser.

At this juncture, the Mexican government gave Governor Juan Bautista Alvarado instructions to occupy the Russian settlement as soon as it was vacated, but Mexico lacked the soldiers to accomplish this occupation, or even to prevent the sale of the Russian colony to a third party.

The Russians turned to Sutter, setting their price at more than $30,000. Sutter agreed to pay this price if he were allowed credit. The Russians decided to accept this counterproposal since they believed that Sutter was a better credit risk than the Mexican authorities. On December 13, 1841, the Russians concluded a sale with Sutter. They agreed to sell all their moveable possessions, and Sutter agreed to a down payment of $2,000 cash. He would follow this with payment in produce: wheat, peas, beans, suet and tallow at San Francisco Bay to the value of $5,000 the first two years and $10,000 the third year. The fourth and last year's installment of $10,000 was to be paid in cash. In the case of the first three year's installments, Sutter agreed to remit them by September 1 of each year and to defray all duties charged against the consignment of produce by the Mexican authorities. When the Russians sent vessels to pick up the first three years' produce installments at San Francisco, Sutter agreed to pay all harbor and tonnage duties incurred by the ships. As security, Sutter pledged his extensive settlement at New Helvetia (Sacramento) as a guarantee that he would carry out his part of the bargain.

In return the Russian herds were turned over to Sutter: 1,700 oxen, cows, and calves, 340 horses and mules, including one hundred pack horses, twenty pack mules and nine hundred sheep. In addition Sutter acquired title to over forty structures and some brass ordnance at Fort Ross and Bodega Bay. After having made his cash down payment, Sutter acquired from the Russians a twenty-two-ton launch which he rechristened the *Sacramento*. He also received four smaller boats, forty-nine plows, twenty-two rakes, forty-three harnesses, fifteen halters, twenty reins, five four-wheeled carts, ten two-wheeled carts, and a machine for winnowing wheat. Although the land was expressly excluded from the deal, Sutter obtained a separate deed to it from the Russians. He hoped eventually to make good a claim to the ground as well.

Before Fort Ross was abandoned, a Russian naturalist, I. C. Vosnesensky, arrived there from a St. Petersburg zoological museum and seeing Mount Helena towering some 4,343 feet high in the distance, he decided to climb it. On June 12, 1841, he clambered to the top and named it in honor of the empress of Russia. The mountain retains that name to this day and marks the most southerly and easterly penetration of the Russians into the North American continent.

After Sutter had taken possession of the moveable property and buildings at Fort Ross, he made no additional payments to the Russians, despite his solemn contract to do so. He complained of crop failures, although he was able to pay off creditors closer to his home. By 1846–47, he had managed to pay only one-fourth of the balance he owed. By this time the Americans had taken over California, and since the Russians despaired of ever being able to bring pressure to bear directly upon Sutter, they renewed the mortgage. Meanwhile, Sutter, who had suffered financial reverses, transferred his property to his son to prevent his creditors from seizing it. The Russians remained insistent that they be paid. The Russian government had appointed a consul in San Francisco, a non-Russian, a Colonel Steward. Steward exerted so much pressure upon Sutter that the Swiss paid $10,000 in gold dust to him and the rest of the debt in notes acquired from the sale of city lots in Sacramento. Colonel Steward quickly converted these notes into cash and then absconded. Since Sutter possessed signed receipts from the agent of the Russians, they were unable to do anything to him. Thus the last vestige of Russian rule vanished ingloriously from the history of California.

When Governor Figueroa died on September 29, 1835, a victim of vertigo, California was at once plunged into a time of political trouble, which arose from the schemes of ambitious politicians, the desire for home rule for California, and the resentment against Mexican-imposed governors and other officials. The presence of a growing number of American and other foreign settlers only contributed further to the political instability.

José Castro took over as governor after Figueroa, but he soon found that several influential leaders of southern California refused to accept him as governor. One of them, José Antonio Carrillo, the provincial deputy to the Mexican Congress, quickly informed them of a congressional act which made Los Ángeles the provincial capital. The provincial council (Diputación) refused to move south and supported Castro as governor. This impasse was broken on January 2, 1836, when Lieutenant Colonel Nicolás Gutiérrez won acceptance as military commander of California. Los Ángeles, now raised in status from a pueblo to a city, was recognized as California's capital through the efforts of the powerful Bandini and Carrillo families. What many hoped would be another stabilizing move occurred in April, when Colonel Mariano Chico, a Mexican congressman, arrived and took over as governor. In three months Chico made himself the most hated man in California. He proclaimed that the new Mexican Centralist Constitution had been adopted, which purportedly gave more powers to the Mexican central government. This move reflected a recent revolutionary change in Mexico, which continued to be racked by political convulsions of its own. The Centralist document supplanted the Federalist Constitution of 1824. Chico's move was not popular, although many citizens seemingly accepted the change.

Chico soon quarreled with Abel Stearns, who had become an influential leader in southern California. Stearns was ordered out of the province by Governor Chico for what seemed to many to be an insufficient reason. Traveling south to Los Ángeles, Governor Chico outraged popular opinion when he arrested several prominent citizens who had taken part in lynching a murderer and his mistress. Then to compound his troubles, Governor Chico ordered the arrest of the father-president of the surviving missions, Father Narcisco Durán, on the grounds that the priest was an unrepentant Spaniard who had obdurately refused to take the required oath of fealty to the Mexican Republic. Finally on July 31, Chico brought his short, unhappy career to a close when he appeared at a public entertainment with his mistress, Doña Cruz, whom he tried to pass off on California society as his niece, and her friend, Doña Eldefonsa, under arrest at the time for adultery. The resulting tumult was such that Governor Chico had to flee to a vessel anchored off the coast to escape from the outraged Californios. Eventually Chico sailed to Mexico and Gutiérrez again took over as acting governor. His days of rule were few for he was also a Centralist in political preference. It is true that the niceties of Mexican politics were lost on the Californios, but they could understand that this was the party of centralized government and of the hated Chico. Also Californios felt by this time that they should have a governor of their own choosing. The young generation of California politicians resented the imposition of an outsider in this post.

The spokesman for "Young California," or at least the northern part of this group, was Juan Bautista Alvarado. Born at Monterey in February 1809, he had held several governmental posts including that of territorial treasurer. By 1836 he was president of the Diputación. Although Alvarado's father had been only a sergeant in the army, his mother came from the powerful Vallejo family. As a boy he had been a protégé of Governor Solá. With two other boys, José Castro and his own uncle Mariano Guadalupe Vallejo, who grew up to be leaders in the northern California community, he had attended a small special school established by Governor Solá, which offered educational opportunities otherwise unobtainable in the province. Here Alvarado became proficient in penmanship and arithmetic. Although books were rare in California, he was able to read *Don Quixote, Laws of the Indies, Lives of Celebrated Spaniards*, a geographical dictionary, and an early history of California. He had also obtained a copy of Fenelon's *Télémaque*, and for reading it was excommunicated by the Church.

Alvarado was more cosmopolitan and sophisticated than the average Californio of the upper classes. After the expulsion of Chico, he led a revolt against Governor Gutiérrez, a Mexican of Spanish ancestry. His old school chum, the lean, "uneasy-eyed" José Castro, helped him. His uncle Mariano Vallejo maintained a friendly neutrality. Alvarado found that his cause was popular with the foreigners in California, particularly the American settlers. Consequently, he was able to assemble a band of about seventy-five American sailors and frontiersmen under the command of Isaac Graham, an American fur trapper.

On November 3, 1836, the rebels took possession of the presidio, which surrendered on November 5 after a single cannon shot had hit the governor's house. Alvarado quickly deported Governor Gutiérrez to Baja California.

On November 6, 1836, the Diputación, chaired by José Castro, issued a proclamation declaring California a free and sovereign state under the motto "Federation or Death!" The legislative body declared that California would remain disaffected from Mexico until that country restored the Federalist Constitution of 1824. This conditional independence, nevertheless, marked a milestone in California political history and illustrated the weakness of the Mexican hold on the province.

The next day, Alvarado appointed his uncle, Mariano Vallejo, as commandante general of Alta California. On December 7, Alvarado was confirmed in power as governor, or more accurately as president, by the "Constituent Congress." To recognize the political division of California into north and south sections, on December 9 the local legislative body, the Congress, passed a law splitting California into the two cantons of Monterey and Los Ángeles. Each canton would have its own political leader. At Monterey this office was filled by Alvarado, but at Los Ángeles

Alvarado was to appoint a political leader from among a trio of candidates chosen by the citizens of the pueblo.

In a sense the creation of a political leader for southern California emphasized that this region's discontent must be appeased. Southern politicians, angered that Los Ángeles was not the capital, raised the cry that Alvarado had come to power by the strength of Yankee arms. The example of Texas was too strong for many to ignore the possibility that the Americans might try to convert California into the same type of republic. Indeed, the Los Ángeles politicans stridently argued that Alvarado had promised his Yankee followers religious toleration. Moreover, all Alvarado's talk of separation from Mexico seemed to indicate the possibility that the Yankees were using him as a pawn to attain independence on their terms.

Fearing this threat to his continued role, Alvarado with a mixed force of Californios and Americans—eighty men in all—appeared in Los Ángeles on January 23, 1837. Overawing the opposition for the moment, Alvarado offered the citizens a compact providing that none but native-born Californios could rule, and calling for a newly constituted Diputación. This body met on April 11, 1837, and passed Alvarado's revised program. Alvarado bent sufficiently into the strong political wind blowing from the south to urge that the Diputación pass a stipulation for the continued maintenance of the Catholic Church, for an undivided political leadership, and for a declaration that California was an integral part of Mexico. The Los Angelinos, despite significant concessions made to them by Alvarado, only accepted this compact with great grumbling.

Alvarado now returned to Monterey only to find that there were three uprisings being staged against him. Juan Bandini had rebelled at Los Ángeles; Captain Andrés Castillero led an uprising at San Diego and San Luís Rey; Ángel Ramirez and Cosme Peña led a revolt against Alvarado in Monterey. Alvarado easily suppressed the Monterey outbreak. Meanwhile Bandini and Castillero united their forces and threatened to engulf all southern California.

Juan Bandini had originally seized control of Los Ángeles on May 26, 1837. On June 12, Andrés Castillero appeared at San Diego with copies of the laws which had reestablished Centralism in Mexico. The southern Californios enthusiastically accepted these Mexican legal actions, not so much because they subscribed to them as a political credo, but because the laws provided a solid basis for an anti-Alvarado uprising.

Alvarado reacted quickly; he persuaded Castillero to become his representative to Mexico and on July 9 opportunistically embraced Centralism himself, hoping in this way to undercut popular support for his opponents in the south.

Meanwhile Congressman José Antonio Carrillo negotiated with the

Mexican government to appoint his brother Carlos as acting governor of Alta California, with power to establish his capital at any place circumstances dictated. On December 1, 1837, Carlos Carrillo selected Los Ángeles as his capital and took the oath of office there.

Refusing to recognize Carrillo's claims to power, Alvarado continued to maintain himself as governor in the north. Carrillo decided to fight to depose Alvarado and chose Juan Castañada as the leader of the small army he had gathered. In the interim, Alvarado had raised an army of one hundred men (about the same size as that mobilized by Carrillo) and had sent it south, commanded by Castro. The two armies met near San Buenaventura Mission, when Castro seized Rincon Pass. There on March 27–28, 1838, the rival forces clashed in a loud, noisy, smoky battle which was almost devoid of casualties; only one of Castro's army was killed. The Carrillo forces suddenly retreated under the cover of darkness. The retreat became a route and Castañada, the commander of the Carrillo forces, and seventy of his men were scooped up as prisoners as the Alvarado army pressed forward and gathered in their retreating rivals. On April 1, the exultant Alvarado forces marched into Los Ángeles.

This did not end the trouble, for the Carrillos raised a new army in San Diego and the revolt continued. Alvarado now came south to take charge of the operations against the remaining insurgents. At a place called Las Flores, south of San Juan Capistrano, the two armies met, but the result was hardly a battle. Some long-range cannon fire was the only hostile action. Alvarado persuaded Carlos Carrillo to meet him in a conference at the San Fernando mission. Whether the entire matter might have been adjusted by negotiation will never be known, since Alvarado feared treachery and, on May 20, suddenly arrested José Antonio Carrillo, Pío Pico, and several other southern leaders. He sent the prisoners up to Sonoma where they were guarded by Vallejo. Carlos Carrillo was arrested also, but was subsequently released on parole to leave for his home in Santa Barbara. Later, fearing for his safety, he fled by vessel to Baja California. Alvarado's agent, Castillero, as Alvarado had expected he would, was able to get official governmental sanction for the northerner to be governor of Alta California in August 1838. Alvarado rewarded his success by securing him a seat in the Mexican Congress.

In 1839, to gain respectability, Alvarado married his former mistress, Martina Castro, by whom he had already had two daughters. To win further popularity, he administered the Mexican policy of secularization of the missions.

Alvarado quarreled with his powerful uncle, Mariano Vallejo, the military commander of the province, over fine points of military etiquette. The most serious issue between them was who would be the administrator of the secularized mission lands. Vallejo coveted the place for himself, but Alvarado denied this request. As a result, Vallejo's support was eventually lost to Alvarado.

Alvarado also worried a great deal about the growing colony of Americans in California. It is true that these foreigners had supported him, but their very presence made him uneasy. He realized that they were probably the most determined fighting men in the province. They had helped him to become governor, and he feared that they might decide to withdraw their support. His very dependence upon them worried him. Between 1830 and 1840, Americans of a very different type appeared in the province. The earlier Americans had been sailors from the eastern United States, who were generally willing to accept California ways and settle down. They were often men of substance who had spent their energies in trade and other apolitical occupations. The later American immigrants were another breed. They were mountain men who had made their way to California, and who never seemed to settle down or have any permanent occupation. They were often noisy, quarrelsome fellows who openly disdained their Californio neighbors and were frequently in trouble. The more solid element of the foreign community looked upon these trappers and roustabouts with suspicion as a disturbing influence. Isaac Graham had indicated his capacity for mischief-making in the revolt of 1836. At this time out of a population of perhaps two thousand adult males in California, some four hundred were foreigners.

By 1840, the buckskin-clad, bearded Isaac Graham had become the proprietor of a brandy distillery at Branciforte. His nearby cabin, a kind of tavern, became the gathering place for sailors who had deserted from foreign ships, and particularly for strangers from the Rockies. Most of these men had never bothered to obtain a passport, nor had they developed any visible means of support. In time the rumor spread that they were criminals who had fled from the United States for a wide variety of violent crimes.

In April 1840, an associate of Graham's, known only as "Tom the Trapper," thought he was dying. He insisted upon seeing a priest at the San Carlos mission, Suárez del Real. The trapper babbled that an uprising of the Americans was imminent. Suárez apparently never thought of considering this information as confidential and promptly reported it to Alvarado. The governor's alarm was boundless. He had long suspected trouble from the Americans. Upon his approach they exhibited no courtesies, no bowing or scraping; instead the men seemed to go out of their way not to address him as "Your Excellency" but instead to drawl at him some greeting which they ended by calling him "Bautiste."

Alvarado had José Castro, the prefect of the northern district, investigate this rumor. Castro seized William R. Garner, one of Graham's confidents, and by threats soon extorted the information that Graham and Englishman Albert Morris were planning revolt.

Alvarado arrested all the passportless foreigners his dragnet could apprehend, 120 in all. Forty-six of these Alvarado shipped off to San Blas to be dealt with by the Mexican government. Just what might have happened to those sent to Mexico is unknown. The prisoners were transferred to Tepic where the British consul interested himself in their fate. The consul, Eustace Barron, immediately opened a long correspondence with the Mexican authorities, asking clemency for the prisoners. Eventually the British and American ministers were drawn into the exchange. Although twenty-six men had been banished from Mexican territory for life, some twenty men, including the supposed ringleaders of the plot, Graham and Morris, were adjudged innocent of wrongdoing and released with compensation for the time they had spent in jail. Therefore, in July 1841, Graham and a tattered group of released prisoners arrived in Monterey and debarked while a crowd of onlookers gaped. The Californios had never expected to see Graham and his associates again.

Alvarado, in turn, was accused of false arrest; Castro was actually tried for being cruel to the Graham men, but was acquitted of the charge. Nevertheless, the "Graham Affair" closed with Alvarado's acute discomforture. As the months and years went by, Alvarado almost ceased to lead an active life, having declined into a prematurely middle-aged, paunchy part-time governor. In September 1841, he proclaimed himself too ill to continue in office and surrendered the reins of power to the president of the departmental junta until January 1, 1842.

The rule of the native Californio ended when the Mexican government appointed Manuel Micheltorena as governor on January 22, 1842. It was September before the new appointee arrived in California to claim his post. When Micheltorena appeared in Los Ángeles, he was attended by three hundred Mexican soldiers, many former convicts.

Micheltorena had been a soldier under Santa Anna in the Mexican campaign. Gray-eyed, with military bearing, he usually impressed his visitors. In addition, he had the gracious manners of a Mexican gentleman. An educated man, he spoke French fluently and seemed to be a valuable cultural addition to California society. His only outstanding vice was indolence. Moreover, he faced an extreme shortage of money. When Alvarado turned over the California treasury to him there was the equivalent of twenty-five cents in it.

As a result Micheltorena found he could not pay his three hundred irregulars, scornfully called *cholos* by the native Californios. Soon the cholos caused him a great deal of embarrassment. Since they were unpaid, they stole from the civilians in the vicinity. They turned out to be crafty burglars who could carry off the most immoveable property. Pedestrians strolling the streets of the capital were liable to be set upon and robbed.

In reaction to Micheltorena's men, the citizens of Los Ángeles were more than willing to relinquish their city's status as capital to Monterey. In the late summer of 1843, Micheltorena moved his archives north. Soon his troops began to plunder the citizens of the new capital. In Micheltorena's behalf it should be pointed out that upon proof that his troops had robbed several citizens, he reimbursed the victims out of his own pocket.

Meanwhile, Americans continued to travel into the province. To prevent further unauthorized migration was precisely the reason that Micheltorena had brought the cholos with him. He soon found that his force was inadequate to control the activities of the foreigners in California, let alone to block the passes and halt additional migration.

Micheltorena now welcomed the Americans, even doing them many small acts of kindness. This behavior caused many Californios to raise their eyebrows. Signs of trouble began to multiply. The Indians of the interior valleys continued their depredations; the southern Californios began to complain that the capital had again been removed to the north. The capital was more than a matter of local pride; there were certain perquisites and patronage connected with being the capital.

Talk of revolution once more filled the air. In order to still the tongues of the gossips, Micheltorena married the mistress whom he had brought with him from Mexico.

By November 1844, the plotters were ready to carry out their plans. Former governor Alvarado and José Castro were the ornaments of the rebellion. From the territory north of Monterey, Alvarado was able to raise a force of 220 men. To counter them, Micheltorena advanced with 150 of his cholos. The opposing forces clashed near San José. A series of elaborate military maneuvers and issuing of proclamations ensued. Finally on December 1, the opposing parties agreed to the Treaty of Santa Terésa. By terms of this agreement, Micheltorena agreed to remove his cholos from California within three months.

It soon became clear that he had no intention of honoring his agreement. Instead, as the foreign element in the community rallied to his support, he prepared to punish his enemies.

In January 1845, John Sutter with his company of goose-stepping Indians (they trained under German and Swiss drill sergeants) took the field for Micheltorena. Isaac Graham, thirsting for revenge against Alvarado, led a party of sharpshooters for the Mexican governor. Meanwhile Micheltorena cancelled his agreement with Alvarado by a proclamation. The rebels retired to Los Ángeles, where Alvarado made a carefully worded appeal to the local assembly which placed all the blame for the hostilities upon Micheltorena. Alvarado announced in February 1845 that Micheltorena, then in Santa Barbara conferring with his supporters, had been deposed in favor of the senior spokesman of the assembly, Pío Pico.

Eventually the two opposing armies, each numbering about four hundred men, met on February 20, 1845, at the Cahuenga Pass, or more accurately at Alamos, west of the pass. A long-range artillery duel followed. The Californios had two cannon to Micheltorena's three. All the men stayed under cover, and in the cannonade the Californios lost two horses, while Micheltorena had one mule wounded. The next day, on the east side of the pass at the Verdugo Ranch, the battle was renewed.

Alvarado's contingent included a large body of Americans led by William Workman and E. D. Wilson. The Alvarado Americans opened negotiations with the Graham faction serving with Micheltorena, both groups agreeing that this was not properly their fight, so the Americans on both sides became spectators at the next encounter on February 21. Micheltorena was suffering from an illness so severe that he had not been able to ride on horseback throughout the entire campaign. Micheltorena's disability, added to the fact that the neutralized American contingent was proportionally bigger in the governor's forces, placed him at a great disadvantage. In the battle that followed there was much shooting, but no one was killed; yet Micheltorena capitulated. The two factions signed a treaty at San Fernando, and by its terms, Pío Pico was recognized late in March as governor and José Castro as military chief of California. Micheltorena and his cholos straggled up to Monterey, where they took a ship to San Blas.

The result of this last California civil war revealed the political anarchy of the province. The growing strength of the foreign element, particularly the Americans, was also demonstrated. The American migration continued. Change was in the air. The soft Spanish accents struggled for a hearing with the harsh Yankee version of English in the population centers of California.

TWELVE

The Pioneers: The Vigil of
American Rule

T HE first Americans came to California by sea, until the 1830's
when the mountain men and other overland migrants began to
arrive. The early seafaring migrants generally assimilated easily
with the Californios. Many married into Spanish families and became
Mexican citizens.

An exception among the Americans who arrived by ship was Thomas
O. Larkin. Larkin, a native of Charles, Massachusetts, came to the province in 1832. He built the first two-story timber house in Monterey with
New England green shutters. He rejected all overtures to become a Mexican citizen, nor did he take up ranching as did so many of his countrymen; instead he developed a thriving trade with Hawaii and Mexico,
exporting lumber, flour, potatoes and beaver skins. He married Rachel
Hobson Holmes, the widow of another New Englander; she had arrived in
California on the same ship that had brought Larkin. Larkin's children,
the first born to American parents in California, went to Hawaii for their
early education. For more advanced schooling, he sent them to Boston. In
1843 Larkin was appointed by President John Tyler as American consul
in Monterey. In this position, Larkin worked to annex the province of
California to the United States.

By 1840 there were perhaps four hundred Americans, ex-sailors and a
few mountain men who had arrived in California. None had brought his
family with him, nor had any come with the intention of settling. The

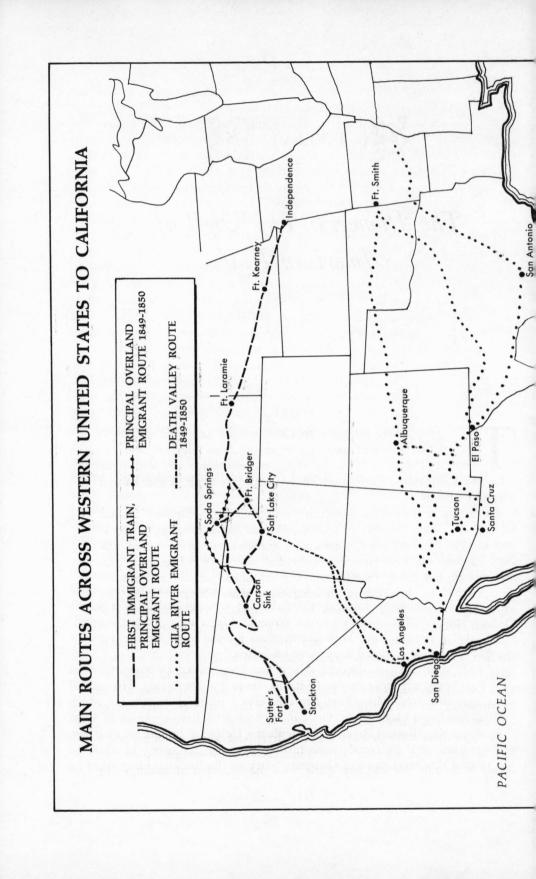

MAIN ROUTES ACROSS WESTERN UNITED STATES TO CALIFORNIA

FIRST IMMIGRANT TRAIN, PRINCIPAL OVERLAND EMIGRANT ROUTE

PRINCIPAL OVERLAND EMIGRANT ROUTE 1849-1850

GILA RIVER EMIGRANT ROUTE

DEATH VALLEY ROUTE 1849-1850

PACIFIC OCEAN

migrants were drifters, some of whom were undoubtedly wanted for various crimes in the eastern United States.

One early American who, like Larkin, deserves special mention was "Doctor" John Marsh, an eccentric New Englander. Marsh, born in South Dawes, Massachusetts, graduated from Harvard in 1823. He left New England to serve as a private tutor at St. Anthony Fort in present-day Minnesota. Marsh studied medicine for nearly two years under the fort surgeon, but his teacher died before he could complete his course of study. Moving on to Prairie du Chien, in what is now Wisconsin, he was charged with unlawfully selling arms to the Sioux. Marsh fled first to St. Louis and then to the Rocky Mountain frontier. After two short attempts at merchandising in Independence, Missouri, he wandered to Santa Fé and then to California. Arriving in Los Ángeles in 1836, he announced himself to be Dr. John Marsh, when he discovered there was no physician in the settlement. He displayed his Latin bachelor's diploma as proof of this claim. Marsh's medical services were in great demand, and within less than a year he had accumulated many cattle, horses and hides. Soon he settled on a rancho in northern California near the base of towering Mount Diablo. There he continued his medical practice and eventually became the wealthiest cattle baron in the area. After the Americans took over California, three of Marsh's own vaqueros who had a grudge against him waylaid, robbed and murdered him in September 1856.

A prominent role in California destiny was played by John Augustus Sutter. Born in 1803 in the Grand Duchy of Baden, Sutter had acquired Swiss citizenship. He was an ordinary man who upon occasion could achieve extraordinary results. From his childhood on, Sutter dreamed of seeing the American West. His daydreams of traveling seemed permanently blighted by a shotgun marriage and a son born the very day after the wedding ceremony. Then his plight grew worse as his family continued to grow while he was mercilessly nagged by his wife and mother-in-law. A fresh disaster—bankruptcy—finally forced him to flee alone from Burgdorf, Switzerland. Even then he was pursued by a fugitive's warrant which caused him to sail from Le Havre away from the continental police to New York. Sutter then journeyed to see the West of which he had read and daydreamed so often.

He went first to Missouri, which had been settled by many German and Swiss, engaging in the Santa Fé trade for two years. His second expedition from Missouri to Santa Fé was a financial disaster for which his associates blamed him. Once more fleeing his irate creditors he went across the Missouri River, living with the Delaware Indians on their reservation until he could move further west. In the spring of 1838, he joined the American Fur Company party to the Rockies. From there he went on to Fort Vancouver with a party of Hudson's Bay Company trappers. Warned against traveling south in the winter toward his goal of California he sailed to Hawaii on a Hudson's Bay Company ship. Sutter was delayed here by a lack of California-bound ships. Swallowing his disappointment, Sutter made many friends among the merchants trading in Hawaii. He influenced them to write him glowing letters of recommendation. These recommendations were placed in his pockets alongside the letters he had already extracted from Hudson's Bay Company officials. Sutter finally talked an American merchant into providing him with a brig for a trading voyage to California. Sutter first stopped at Sitka, where he received additional letters of recommendation from the Russian-American Company officials.

On July 3, 1839, Sutter arrived at Monterey waving his letters of introduction. These letters, Sutter's winning personality, and the Swiss's ability to speak Spanish, French, English and German fluently, all stamped him as a man of destiny to Governor Alvarado. As a result, the governor granted him permission to found a colony near the junction of the Sacramento and American rivers and promised that the Swiss could gain title to the land under Mexican law within a year.

Accompanied by eight male Kanakas (Hawaiians), two fair wahines, one of whom was his mistress, and three white companions, he journeyed to the American River just above its junction with the Sacramento—right where the city of Sacramento stands today. He took possession of a 50,000-acre tract he called New Helvetia (Latin for Switzerland). Once naturalized as a Mexican citizen, he began to act as a semiofficial representative of the provincial government. He purchased Fort Ross from the Russians, but it is doubtful if the buildings and equipment he bought were worth the price. Some buildings could not be dismantled without splitting the timbers from which they were constructed; much of the equipment was old and worn out. Many of the firearms had been used to fight Napoleon's invasion of Russia and had suffered through the years from hard usage and negligence.

Using the Russian materials, Sutter began construction of a fort of his own upon the lands of New Helvetia. His outpost, when finished, featured bastioned corners and adobe walls eighteen feet high enclosing a space of 150 by five hundred feet. As early as 1842, it mounted twelve cannon. Here Sutter lived in the manner of a feudal lord, on an estate which encompassed eleven square leagues. He owned 4,200 cattle, 2,000 horses and nearly as many sheep. He also developed a profitable trade in beaver skins with the mountain men. New Helvetia was a strategic trade center, because it was located on the main line of overland trade routes from Oregon and the eastern United States. He taught his Indians useful trades and organized them into military commands; they obeyed him unquestioningly.

This handful of foreigners was augmented in 1841 when the first organized overland train of American settlers entered California from the east, the Bartleson-Bidwell party of 1841.

After the Panic of 1837, hard times had settled over the American frontier in the Middle West. As the years passed with little relief, the discontent of the frontier settlers increased. These disillusioned men and women had left their homes in the East to find a land of plenty. Now disappointed, their attention strayed to the Far West. Highly colored reports and rumors of life in California traveled around the Mississippi River frontiers. There was hardly a county into which some trapper had not wandered, telling his tales of opportunities in California. These claims often found their way into the eastern newspapers and then were dutifully reprinted by frontier newspapers.

In Platte County, Missouri, a fever of excitement about California was aroused during the late summer and autumn of 1840. A fur trapper, Antoine Robidoux, who had gone to California by way of the Santa Fé Trail, started a publicity campaign about California as a place of perpetual spring. During the same year, John Marsh wrote letters to his old Missouri friends in Jackson County, in which he spoke enthusiastically about the future possibilities of California. As a result of these reports, a California-bound group, the Western Emigration Society, was formed. A pledge was signed by five hundred inhabitants of Platte County, binding the signatories to convert their property into travel gear and to join with the Jackson County enthusiasts at Sapling Grove (in present-day Kansas) on the old Santa Fé Trail in May 1841.

It seemed that all Missouri was breaking camp for the trek to California. This mass exodus upset some of the merchants of western Missouri, who set themselves the task of ridiculing the venture. They published derogatory articles regularly in the local press during the winter and early spring of 1841. Their campaign was successful, for when the appointed day of the migration came, only one of the original members appeared, a twenty-one-year-old New Yorker, John Bidwell. He had moved with his parents to Pennsylvania and Ohio, and then had come alone to Iowa and Missouri, where he taught school for a short time and then turned to farming in Platte County. After losing his farm, he decided to travel to California.

Accordingly, he organized a new migration party. Three men, Robert H. Thomas, George Henshaw and Michael C. Nye, none of them signers of the original pledge, consented to join him. Eventually, a party of forty-eight men and about fifteen women and children was formed. Their objectives differed widely: some preferred Oregon to California; others did not wish to settle anywhere, but were merely interested in the adventure of the trip.

The company organized at the Kansas River, electing John Bartleson as its captain. The majority of the party did not prefer him (many contended that he had limited capacities for leadership), but since he led the large Jackson County contingent, which declared that it would follow only Bartleson, his election was assured. Moreover, Bartleson had a letter from Marsh in which the doctor described an overland route leading directly to his rancho in California. The group then elected Bidwell to the post of secretary.

Joining the Bartleson company for the first part of the trip was an Oregon-bound party: three Jesuit missionaries, including the famous Father de Smet, three hunters, five teamsters, a lone Methodist preacher, two adventurers and three hunters bound for the Rockies. The Oregon party was headed by Thomas Fitzpatrick, a veteran mountain man, who became leader of the entire caravan since he was the only one familiar with the country to be traversed.

On May 19, 1841, the great trek west began. The missionaries with their five carts took the lead. Then came thirty-one wagons of Bartleson's company drawn by horses, mules and oxen. The route the party utilized had been blazed by mountain men and Oregon-bound settlers: up the north fork of the Platte, and then along the Sweetwater River through the South Pass, a virtual canal through the Rockies. Then the company traveled along a branch of the Green River toward the Beaver River Valley near Salt Lake. The party had thus far met no unusual hardships, except for the accidental death of one man. Two couples were married en route.

Near Soda Springs on the Bear River on August 11, the company reached the turn-off point of the Oregon Trail. Here Fitzpatrick and about half of the original party turned off northward for Fort Hall. Twelve persons who had once agreed to go to California now decided to go to Oregon. The rest of the party, some thirty-two in number, proceeded southwest toward California. Marsh had warned his Missouri correspondents that during this part of the journey the travelers must ford and follow the Mary River, because the mountains to the north and deserts to the south were impenetrable.

For ten days the party tramped down the Bear River, then turned west until they were diverted northward in a search for water. On August 27, Bartleson and a companion found the Mary River. Having run out of buffalo meat, the group began to slaughter oxen for food. Through the alkali country the travelers abandoned their wagons, packing much of their goods upon their animals. They wandered on, exhausted by the irregular contours of the terrain, choked by alkali dust and burned by the sun. It was October before they crossed the Carson and reached the Walker River, which they mistook for the San Joaquin; although they realized their mistake when they saw the Sierra crest in the distance, they determinedly moved on. It was nearly mid-October when the group began to ascend the Sierra. They reached the summit on October 18, only to find the passes buried in snow. To their relief, they came upon a river flowing south, which they followed until they came to the edge of the Sacramento-San Joaquin Valley. They looked across the valley floor in dismay, for they had expected to see orange groves and fields of grain. Instead they saw parched and barren land.

A few days later one of the group met an Indian who kept repeating "Marsh, Marsh," and offered to lead them to the doctor. They gratefully followed him, and on November 4 crossed a ford on the San Joaquin River and reached Marsh's ranch at the foot of Mount Diablo. Once more the emigrants gaped at the promised land they had entered. The countryside seemed shriveled and barren. Marsh, in the manner of a good Californian, explained that the area was experiencing unusual weather—the worst drought in California's history. No appreciable rain had fallen for eighteen months.

Dr. Marsh, who had so warmly encouraged the settlers to come, proved characteristically inhospitable upon their arrival. For a good price, he agreed to help them get settled. He sent the required notice of their arrival to the provincial authorities. The Mexican government had recently issued stern orders to the California authorities to watch and control American overland emigrants. The Mexican minister in Washington had reported rumors of the Bidwell-Bartleson party. Upon Marsh's advice, half of the party after a day's rest went on to San José, where they were placed under arrest. Commandante General Mariano Vallejo decided on his own responsibility to grant them temporary passes until such time as they could legalize their presence. In the meanwhile, older residents of the province posted bond for them. Although the members had spent most of the year together, the company was dissolved without a second thought, and the individual members scattered to all parts of California.

Another overland party, some twenty-five in number, arrived at Los Ángeles almost simultaneously with the Bidwell-Bartleson caravan. This group had been organized in New Mexico, where most of the party had sojourned for a time. Only a few men had come to Santa Fé from Missouri with the intention of going to California. These few had formed a small party which planned to rendezvous with Bartleson's group, but when they found that that expedition had already departed, they decided to take the more familiar Santa Fé Trail, rather than attempting to overtake the Bartleson company on the unfamiliar northern route.

Political motives influenced the departure of William Workman and John Rowland, the organizers of this party. There had been much excitement in New Mexico over rumors of a plot to embroil that province in the Texas revolt. The Mexican authorities suspected Workman and

Rowland of being involved in the scheme. As a result, the two Americans decided to leave the area. In September they left Abiquiú, crossed the Colorado River and in general followed the route pioneered by Wolfskill and followed by New Mexican traders. Driving a flock of sheep for food, they encountered no unusual adventures or hardships. Two of the party, including Workman himself, brought their families. Others of the expedition sent for their families soon after their arrival in California. A few drifted back to New Mexico.

Still another expedition across the mountains into California was a party of fur trappers led by Joseph Reddeford Walker in 1841. Probably none of the trappers remained permanently in California. Joel P. Walker, Reddeford's brother, led a party consisting of his wife and five children and two other settlers and their families from Oregon to Sutter's Fort in October 1841. Walker's wife became the first American woman to settle in the Sacramento Valley. She was probably the first American woman to come overland into California, arriving twenty days before Mrs. Kelsey of Bidwell-Bartleson's party.

In 1842 nearly thirty-three pioneers came to California to settle permanently. Most of them came without making any prearrangements, for there had not been time for the eastern friends of the Bidwell party to hear that his group had arrived safely. Part of the Bartleson party—some nine or ten men—left Sutter's Fort, journeying up the San Joaquin Valley, and by way of Walker's Pass, eventually reached New Mexico, using Wolfskill's old overland route. Traffic eastward and westward soon became more common.

In January 1842, a party of two hundred people, including forty non-Mexicans, came to Los Ángeles from New Mexico, most of them traders. Near the end of 1842, twenty New Mexican families came to settle permanently in California.

At the end of 1842, Almonte, the Mexican minister to Washington, published a letter in the American press warning would-be emigrants to California. Almonte wrote that many Americans were being drawn to California by false accounts concerning the Mexican governmental attitude toward settlers. The Mexican declared that his country did not want foreign colonists in California and would admit none without special permission.

Almonte's declaration may have been an accurate statement of the official Mexican attitude toward American immigration into California; in fact, most California authorities were friendly to foreigners. Governor Micheltorena treated strangers kindly and generously granted land to them.

In 1843 Mexican traders may have brought with them a few families who stayed, although detailed information is lacking. The immigration of

1843 was not as large as many authorities feared. Contradictory rumors about Mexico's official attitude had discouraged many would-be migrants, who instead went to Texas or Oregon. The hardships of the trip were exaggerated in tales which made their way east, chilling the enthusiasm of many aspiring settlers.

One party, which divided into two before reaching California, came across the plains from Missouri. A sometime lawyer and a native of Ohio, Lansford W. Hastings, left Independence, Missouri, in the spring of 1842 leading an expedition of 160 people, eighty of them heavily armed men. Their destination was Oregon, which they reached by October. There the heavy winter rains and the isolation of the country disillusioned many members of the party. By the spring of 1843, some of these dissatisfied immigrants returned to the United States, while others resolved to travel to the reputedly sunnier climate of California. Under the direction of Hastings, a party of fifty-three departed from the Williamette Valley. While most of the party had crossed the plains with him the year before, he had made some new converts in Oregon. In the Rogue River area, the party encountered troublesome but not hostile Indians. After having left the Indian country, they met some cattle drovers going north. These men were so vehement about the prevalence of Mexican oppression, citing themselves as innocent victims of official prejudice, that about one-third of the California-bound party turned back for Oregon. Despite some harassment from the Indians along the Shasta River, the company safely arrived at Sutter's Fort on July 10. They believed that they had lost two of their party who had straggled off, but these men later arrived safely in California.

In May 1843, another group, this one known as the Chiles party, was led by Joseph B. Chiles, who had been with Bidwell's 1841 expedition. The main party of fifty people came out from Independence, Missouri, by way of Fort Hall in company with several Oregon-bound groups. At Fort Hall the party divided because of the scarcity of provisions. Now Chiles led nine or ten men who had left their families and wagons behind and proceeded toward California. Chiles took his party along a new route, crossing from the Boise River to the Sacramento by way of the Malheur and Pit rivers. The exact date upon which he arrived at Sutter's Fort is not recorded.

Meanwhile the veteran scout Joseph Reddeford Walker took over the chore of leading the families and wagons left behind by Chiles to California. Walker decided to take his section of the party south along the route by which he had left California in 1834. He found the trail rougher than he had anticipated, and after entering California, the travelers were forced to abandon their wagons, the first ever brought into California by overland homeseekers. Having buried their tools and heavy equipment in the sand, the party packed their remaining supplies on horses and pushed on toward the Salinas Valley. In January of 1844, this pioneer group reached John Gilroy's ranch before scattering to different areas as individual homeseekers.

On his way south from Oregon in 1843, Lansford Hastings had encountered some settlers leaving California in disgust over Mexican oppression. Among these disgruntled Californians were Benjamin and Andrew Kelsey, who had come to the Mexican province with the Bidwell-Bartleson party in 1841. The Kelseys came back to California in 1844 with a party whose leadership is unknown. All we know is that there were thirty-six people in the party and that they arrived in the Sacramento Valley in early summer.

During 1844, another party of overland immigrants, this one led by Elisha Stevens and known as the Stevens-Murphy group since the Murphy family comprised a large part of it, left the Missouri River and followed the trail to Fort Hall. The group included over fifty men in addition to women and children. At Fort Hall about half of the group decided to go to Oregon. The remainder headed toward California, following the Bidwell-Bartleson route to the Humboldt Sink. At the foot of the Sierra, the party split again. The Murphys and a few others traversed the Sierras by way of Lake Tahoe and the headwaters of the American River, although details of the trip are obscure. The main party pushed into California by way of the Truckee River and Pass. This party is believed to be the first to reach their ultimate destination in California with wagons intact.

By 1845 the overland traffic had greatly increased. Earlier settlers sent back glowing reports coaxing emigrants from all over the United States to travel west. Lansford W. Hastings returned to the United States in 1844, and began a publicity campaign which greatly stimulated American migration. In all, about 150 men and a hundred women and children made their way to California during 1845. This number included emigrants from Oregon, as well as those who came across the Sierra. It is believed that perhaps five separate companies (excluding the exploring party of John C. Frémont) traveled overland to California that year. These companies included a group of forty-three emigrants from Oregon led by Green McMahon, who had been with the Bidwell-Bartleson party, and James Clyman, a veteran mountain man. With this group was James Marshall, the man who discovered gold in California in 1848. Another pioneer expedition in 1845 was the offshoot of an Oregon-bound party which had divided at Fort Hall, the Swasey-Todd company. This party was a small one, some twelve or thirteen young men who traveled with pack animals by way of the Truckee route. Arriving at Sutter's Fort in October of 1845 was a fifteen-member company, led by the famous fur-trading Sublette family of St. Louis. During that same year a group of fifty men and their families, the Grigsby-Ide party, was led by Captain John Grigsby along the Truckee route over the Sierra.

The last group of homeseekers to enter California in 1845 was that led by Lansford W. Hastings. Hastings had tried to persuade many settlers in the United States to come to California, but few heeded his pleas. These early settlers were more attracted by the Oregon Territory. However, by July he was able to assemble a party of twenty-two men who were willing to journey directly to California. Only ten actually left Independence with Hastings in August, far behind the last of the Oregon-bound wagon trains. Between Fort Laramie and Fort Bridger, they made a long detour to avoid hostile Indians. From Fort Hall they followed the usual pioneer trail to California. As winter approached, hunting grew more difficult and the group suffered from hunger. According to Sutter, if the party had crossed to his fort one day later, it would have been cut off by snow.

Since the Mexicans exerted pressure upon the newcomers to apply for Mexican citizenship and accept the Catholic religion, many of the pioneers who arrived before 1845 did not remain in California, but drifted into Oregon or back to the United States. Consequently, the number of foreigners in California increased from four hundred in 1840 to only 680 by the end of 1845. These newcomers refused to learn Spanish, become naturalized citizens, or turn Catholic. They married their own women and refused to assimilate into the Mexican culture of California. They avoided making homes near the Mexican settlements, and instead clustered together in the interior valleys. Later, these same settlers were instrumental in bringing California under American rule.

In 1846, five hundred California-bound emigrants left for the West. The many hardships suffered by all these travelers are overshadowed by the tragic fate of the Donner party, the worst western tragedy since the Yuma massacre.

Members of the Donner party came from the states of Illinois, Iowa, Tennessee, Missouri and Ohio. Among them was a sprinkling of foreigners from Germany, England and Belgium. The party was organized in Lincoln's home county of Sangamon, Illinois, by James Frazier Reed and two friends, George and Jacob Donner. George was sixty-two years old, Jacob was sixty-five, and James Reed was forty-six. In the party was Mrs. Sarah Keyes, over ninety years old, who died before the company left what is now Kansas. Indeed, the Donner party included a disproportionate number of elderly people, women and children—a condition which greatly slowed their progress along the overland trail.

Early in April 1846, having sold their farms and loaded their household goods into specially constructed wagons, the Donner party left Springfield, Illinois. By the first week of May, it had reached Independence. Here the party acquired additional members, so that its train eventually comprised one hundred persons. When this wagon train left Missouri, it stretched two miles in length.

By July 4, the Donner party had reached Fort Laramie. Then the caravan pushed west over the old trail up the Sweetwater River and across the South Pass. There on July 17, as the emigrants were climbing up to the Continental Divide at South Pass, a horseman named Bonney appeared and identified himself as a messenger from Lansford Hastings. Bonney delivered a letter from Hastings, describing a new route to California which he had blazed, allegedly three hundred miles shorter than the one by way of Fort Hall. This route ran north of the Great Salt Lake by way of Fort Bridger and joined the California trail on the Humboldt River. Hastings also promised to wait at Fort Bridger and personally guide the California immigrants along his new cutoff.

There was some disagreement among the members of the party concerning the wisdom of taking Hastings' shortcut. Finally, Reed persuaded the Donners and most of the others to take Hastings' advice. On July 20, the Donner caravan of thirty-six men, twenty-one women, thirty children and twenty wagons turned down the road to Fort Bridger. On the first day en route to the fort, the party elected George Donner captain of the group. The struggles of this expedition were due in part to the ineptness and lack of force of George Donner.

On July 28, 1846, the party reached Fort Bridger, only to find that Hastings had already left. The party was discouraged, but Jim Bridger and his partner Vasquez encouraged the dispirited group by telling them of the favorable conditions of the road ahead.

After resting for four days at Fort Bridger, the caravan headed west, following the wagon tracks made by an earlier party. With little difficulty the group reached Weber Canyon, through which lay the usual approach to the Great Salt Lake. There, stuck in a bank near the trail, Hastings had left a letter in which he promised to return to guide the party through a shorter route down Weber Canyon to the southern shores of Salt Lake. The travelers made camp and prepared to wait for Hastings. Messengers were sent ahead to overtake Hastings and beg him to turn back to guide them. Hastings refused to return, although he sent back details of the new route he had advised. Either the messengers misunderstood Hastings, or he did not know as much about the route as he had bragged, for when the scouts returned to the main party, they plunged the company into a wilderness of rough, almost impassable country, covered with trees and thick underbrush. The emigrants were a month, instead of twelve days as they had planned, in reaching the Salt Lake. The loss of time proved costly, for an inventory made at Salt Lake indicated that the supplies would give out before the group could reach

California. They decided to continue and hope that they would arrive in California before starvation threatened.

Leaving Salt Lake, the train rolled on over dry alkali and sand toward the Humboldt. Because of the lack of water, many of the cattle died from thirst and exhaustion before the end of September. The travelers grew gaunt and exhausted; the animal herds had been depleted. Nevertheless, the party finally reached the main emigrant trail along the Humboldt River.

The frustrating hardships of their journey caused the travelers great physical strain and mental agony. The situation grew even more tense after a quarrel between James Reed and John Snyder. Snyder lashed out and struck Reed on the head with the butt end of his whip. Mrs. Reed pushed between the two struggling men to aid her husband, and was struck upon the head and shoulders by Snyder's bullwhip. Reed, enraged, stabbed Snyder to death. The Donner party stopped to pass judgment on the murderer. By a majority vote, Reed was banished from the train. His wife and family were placed under the protection of another emigrant. With his gun and a companion, Walter Herron, Reed set out for California. It was agreed that when he had reached the settlements, he would bring help to the company. Thus his banishment would serve a practical purpose since he would act as a messenger.

The Donner party then resumed its halting progress. The Indians took advantage of the company's weakness, killing or stealing twenty-one cattle. Gradually this loss coupled with the death of cattle from exhaustion and disease left the party short of oxen to draw the heavily laden wagons. All who could were forced to walk, carrying as much as possible to lighten the burdens still dragged by the remaining oxen.

As they slowly moved toward the Sierra, one member of the party died of exhaustion; another was probably murdered. Suspicion fell upon Louis Keseberg, a tall, well-built German immigrant, but no conclusive evidence was ever uncovered.

Charles T. Stanton returned from Sutter's Fort with two Indian guides (Salvador and Luís) and five muleloads of beef and flour. This supply was to prove woefully inadequate.

Along the Truckee River, near the present city of Reno, Nevada, the emigrants camped for several days to recuperate, although clouds high on the mountains indicated that winter was approaching. A member of the party named Pike was accidentally shot and killed, leaving his wife and two small children to be cared for by other members of the party.

Finally, leaving the base of the Sierras, the company painfully journeyed up the Truckee River, crossing it forty-nine times in eighty miles. By the end of October the train had reached Donner Lake, about three miles from the present city of Truckee.

At this point a heavy snowfall descended upon the Donners. Feebly, yet determinedly, they pushed forward, trying to ascend the last few miles which still separated them from the crest of the rugged range. Heavy snowdrifts and large boulders blocked the way. At an elevation of seven thousand feet, part of the train decided to camp for the winter. They found a deserted cabin which had been used by an earlier expedition to store extra goods. It was not large enough to house everybody, but others were easily constructed. Another group, including George Donner and his family, camped at Prosser Creek six miles from the other camp. They had been prevented from going further because of a broken wagon axle. Unable to construct cabins because of the storm, this party was forced to hole up under shelters of tree limbs and canvas.

Between the two camps at Donner Lake and Prosser Creek there were eighty-one men, women and children, all desperately short of food. The party soon found that they committed another error in judgment. They had not killed their oxen prior to the heavy snowstorm, and as the animals wandered away and died, their carcasses were lost in the snow. To supplement their waning rations, the desperate people caught and ate field mice. Bits of beef hide were cut into strips, singed, scraped and boiled to the consistency of glue. Marrowless bones, already scraped and boiled, were burned and eaten. The very bark was stripped from pine trees and eaten.

In mid-December 1846, a party of fifteen from Donner Lake, including the two Indians, attempted to get out of the mountains. They had made snowshoes out of oxbow strips and rawhide thongs. This little band carried rations for six days—enough shriveled beef to cover the width of two fingers, served three times a day. This meat, plus a little coffee and some sugar, were their only rations. Each had a thin blanket. It was to be thirty-two days before the survivors of this company stumbled into a Sacramento rancho.

During their torturous hike out of the Sierra, Stanton died. By Christmas Day all the survivors had been without food for four days. The twenty-sixth was chilly and rainy; the little group tried to travel that day as usual, but its members were so weakened that after a short trudge through the snow, they crawled back to the previous night's campfire site.

The rain soon changed to sleet and then to snow, which held the hungry men and women snowbound for a week. Eventually, four members died at what was called the Camp of Death. Driven to desperation by hunger, the survivors ate the bodies of those who had died. Resuming their journey, another man, named Fosdick, died on January 4. Then the two Indians, who according to one account had refused to eat human flesh, ran away. They were soon overtaken and shot by one member of the party and eaten. Despite this cannibalism, the thin bodies of the dead were insufficient nourishment, and the party was compelled to eat moccasins, the strings on the snowshoes and even an old pair of boots. Many deer appeared along the way, only to disappear before the weakened men could shoot. On January 10, the seven exhausted survivors, two men and five women, stumbled into an Indian rancheria. Fortunately the Indians were friendly and gave the starved people acorn meal. The natives also guided the most ablebodied member of the group, Eddy, to the nearest white settlement, Johnson's ranch. A relief party went back and rescued the other six survivors.

As soon as possible Racine (Reasin) Tucker led a relief expedition to rescue the stranded emigrants at Donner Lake. Rain and snow made progress slow. Finally the horses were abandoned and each man packed on his back as many supplies as he could carry. Although some turned back, seven men reached the camp at Donner Lake.

The emigrants in this camp had been marooned for about eight weeks, surrounded by twenty-foot drifts, and eating only unpalatable, unnour-ishing hides. By the time the relief party had penetrated to the emigrants on February 19, they had little food left. It was February 23 before the trip back was begun. The relief party took with them twenty-one sur-vivors of the Donner party, many of them children. The rest, who seemed too weak to travel, were left behind. Tucker's group marched along in single file, the leader wearing snowshoes, those behind him stepping in his tracks. Food grew short and then gave out altogether. Of the twenty-one rescued people, three died on the way back. More might have succumbed if a second relief expedition had not met the party near their ultimate destination. This second party of ten men was headed by the veteran trapper Brittan Greenwood, accompanied by the banished James Reed. With the help of the additional supplies, the first relief party made it to safety in the valley below while the second rescue group pressed on toward the camp at Donner Lake. They reached Donner Lake on March 1. Leaving some of their party to care for those unable to travel, another seventeen of the survivors were led out. On the way a blizzard forced this party to seek shelter at a place called Starved Camp. Hands and feet froze; the food ran out. Three of the party died, and their bodies were eaten by the survivors. At last Greenwood and Reed took several children with them and fought their way through the snow to a relief camp. Another relief force rescued the eleven emigrants still hanging on grimly at Starved Camp. While some of the relief party took these survivors back, the rest pushed on to Donner Lake. There and in the huts at Prosser Creek, where the second segment of the original Donner party had taken refuge, only nine people were still alive. One adult and four children were taken out. Three others, including George Donner, were too ill to travel. His wife, Tamsen Donner, refused to leave him, and so she and the other three ill survivors were reluctantly left behind. This relief force safely reached the valley settlements.

When the fourth and last of the rescue expeditions reached Donner

Lake the following spring, they found only one survivor, Louis Keseberg, living in hideous squalor amid the bones of his fellow emigrants. A search revealed the skeletons of George Donner and a Mrs. Murphy, but the body of Mrs. Donner could not be found. The disappointed rescue party then turned on Keseberg and accused him of murdering Mrs. Donner and stealing her money. Keseberg denied this charge, insisting that after the death of her husband Mrs. Donner had come to his cabin, where one night she had died of starvation and cold.

The disgruntled members of the fourth relief expedition returned to the settlements and started rumors about Keseberg, who was soon shunned as a moral leper. Keseberg won a slander suit against one of his detractors, and there is no evidence that he had done any more than eat human flesh to survive.

The exact statistics of death are confused, but it does seem that of eighty-one emigrants who pitched their camp in November in the Sierras, only forty-five lived to cross the mountains. The tragic fate of the Donner party threw into sharp relief the heroism necessary for the pioneers to reach California in the 1840's by the difficult overland route.

THIRTEEN

The United States Hungrily
Eyes California

T HE laxity of Mexican control over the province made it obvious to many observers that Mexico would probably never succeed in incorporating California into its political system. Many
speculated that California might break its Mexican ties and form an
independent republic as Texas had done in the 1830's. Others contended
that the fate of the Texas Republic illustrated how difficult it was for a
large, thinly populated area to maintain its independence. They concluded
that California might well become the possession of the United States or
some European naval power.

Great Britain, the great colonial power of the nineteenth century, had
long been anxious to acquire California, thereby extending her imperial
dominion to the Pacific northwest. The British might have accomplished
their ends had they not been distracted by other imperial affairs in Europe, Africa and Asia.

Despite the earlier failure of William G. Rae to gain a toehold for the
British in the San Francisco Bay area, Britain had other, more capable
agents who looked longingly at California. Far down the Pacific Coast of
Mexico, a Scottish merchant, Alexander Forbes, cast an acquisitive eye on
California. Forbes had come to the Mexican west coast town of Tepic
during the middle 1820's. In 1831, he wrote to his American friend Abel
Stearns, then residing in Los Ángeles, asking for information about Cali-
fornia. Forbes incorporated this intelligence into a manuscript which he

entitled *California: A History of Upper and Lower California*. Finally published in 1839, the book provoked interest in California on both sides of the Atlantic. Englishmen hailed it as the first comprehensive history of California, and were particularly impressed with one chapter which discussed the possibilities of the colonization of California by Great Britain. Forbes outlined a scheme whereby British investors who held $50,000,000 in Mexican bonds would be given land in California in payment of the Mexican debt. In California, they might recover their investment by emulating the Hudson's Bay Company or the British East India Company in exploiting the commercial and agricultural resources of the province. These sentiments appealed to the London *Times*, which on September 6, 1839, pronounced the Forbes plan "well worthy of attention to the English politician." Forbes' brother John wrote a preface to the book in which he stressed the same plan.

At the time of the Graham affair, the British vice consul at Tepic, Eustace Barron, had actively intervened to help the foreigners expelled from California. Barron's diplomatic notes on behalf of Graham and his men had been channeled through the British minister to Mexico, Richard Pakenham. Pakenham wrote on August 30, 1841, to the British foreign secretary, Lord Palmerston, that "California, once ceasing to belong to Mexico should not fall into the hands of any power but England." But the aggressive Palmerston was replaced as foreign secretary by Lord Aberdeen, who refused to heed Pakenham's suggestions. In 1842 the British appointed James A. Forbes (no relation to the Forbes brothers) vice consul at Monterey. In September of that same year, a delegation of Californios called upon Forbes to ask if California might become a British protectorate, similar to that which had been established over the Ionian Islands. Forbes reported this meeting to Foreign Secretary Aberdeen, who eventually replied that the British government would ignore insurrectionary movements in California, since to aid them would be contrary to the good faith of Great Britain.

Nevertheless, in 1844 and 1845, reports of American agents in Mexico were filled with rumors that British bondholders of Mexican securities were about to "foreclose" on California. These rumors increased the anxiety of the Americans. In 1846 they again became apprehensive at the news of a British scheme to plant a colony in California. A young Irish priest, Father Eugene McNamara, after conferences with British officials in Mexico, was conveyed to Monterey aboard the British man-of-war *Juno*. After meeting with the California authorities, Father McNamara sailed to Santa Barbara to ask Governor Pío Pico for a land grant. McNamara's aim was to resettle many of his Irish countrymen, who were undergoing the sufferings of a potato famine. He proposed to plant a colony of ten thousand Irish in California on a site of three thousand square leagues. The priest selected a location which included most of the eastern half of the San Joaquin Valley. The provincial assembly, meeting at Los Ángeles on July 7, approved his request. A week later, Pío Pico backdated to July 4 his approval of the grant, so as to antedate the American naval landing at Monterey on July 7. When the Americans took over California, they claimed that the McNamara grant was invalid, since Pío Pico had predated it, and since the governor's action violated Mexican law, which stipulated that no grant could exceed eleven square leagues. Father McNamara never attempted to have his title validated by the United States, and his plan for a colony went unfulfilled once the Americans occupied the province. The notion of using Irish Catholics to advance English imperial designs has never been fully explained. Today the idea seems preposterous; nevertheless McNamara's presence seemed menacing to the Americans in California.

French interest in the province began with the previously mentioned voyage of Captain Jean François Galoup de la Pérouse in September 1786. In April 1826, Martin Lafitte of Le Havre and the Javel brothers of Paris sent *Le Heros*, a 362-ton vessel with a crew of thirty-two, on a trading voyage. Under the command of Captain Duhault-Cilly, the ship touched at several ports in South America and entered San Francisco Bay on January 27, 1827. It was too early in the season to trade hides, so the captain and crew traveled widely throughout Alta California. In October, Duhault-Cilly sailed to Callao, Peru, only to return to California in May of 1828. Trading in California until August, he then returned to France by way of Hawaii and Canton. His appearance excited great wonder in California, but his trading in the province was not successful since he carried a cargo of ill-assorted goods.

As a result of Duhault-Cilly's failure, the French did not engage in commerce with California for nearly a decade. Then in 1835 the French whaler *Gange* and a French ship, the *Leon*, touched in California. The *Leon* came to collect cattle and hay for the French army in the Pacific islands. After this transaction, French commercial contacts with California became more frequent; at least five vessels called at California ports between 1835 and 1840. In the period from 1841 to 1845 nine more ships anchored there. After the revolution of 1830 and the ascendancy of the House of Orleans, the French took more interest in Pacific lands. France sought a new colonial empire to replace that lost to Great Britain and Spain in 1763.

In October 1837, Captain Abel du Petit-Thouars, commanding the frigate *Venus* on a world tour, called at Monterey. Although du Petit-Thouars was primarily interested in the Pacific whaling industry, he carried aboard his ship a scientific corps who made hydrographic observations and surveyed the harbor of San Francisco. In August 1839, a French commander, Cyrille Pierre Laplace, sailed along the California coast from Bodega Bay to Monterey. Laplace insisted that his interests were purely scientific, but many Californios believed his voyage presaged further French colonial adventures in the Pacific.

Obvious French interest in California was indicated when Eugene Duflot de Mofras, an attaché of the French embassy in Madrid, came to report on the North American Pacific coast in 1840. During the course of his two-year journey, Mofras visited every important pueblo and mission in California. In 1844, he published his adventures in a book which noted with more than passing interest that California had two excellent harbors, at San Diego and San Francisco. Mofras also predicted a boundless future for California and suggested that the French could share in that future, since Frenchmen shared the same religion and possessed similar temperaments to the Californios. In 1843, at the request of French residents in California and French diplomatic agents in Mexico, France appointed a consul in Monterey at the then lavish salary of over four thousand dollars a year.

After 1843, most Frenchmen anticipated a confrontation between the United States and Great Britain over the issue of California. Although French warships still regularly cruised the California coast, and though French commanders were not pleased by the prospect of British or American control of San Francisco Bay, France lacked the power to challenge the United Kingdom or the United States in the contest for California.

Although several nations, even Prussia, evinced some interest in California, the territorially contiguous United States was in the best situation to exploit the near-anarchy in Mexican California.

American interest in California long antedated the period usually assigned as the beginning of their concern, namely the Jacksonian period. In the 1780's, men destined to become America's first three Presidents displayed some sentiment for the acquisition of California. On July 25, 1785, George Washington noted regretfully that the "Country of California" had already been occupied by Spain. In a diary entry of June 19, 1783, John Adams mentioned the exploration of the California coast by foreign powers and seemed concerned that America had been left out. On December 4, 1783, Thomas Jefferson wrote to George Rogers Clark, the famed conquerer of the old Northwest: "I find they have subscribed a very large sum of money in England for exploring the country from the Missisippi [sic] to California. They pretend it is only to promote knowledge. I am afraid they have thoughts of colonizing into that quarter." Nearly three years later, Jefferson began to worry about French interest in California, after the visit of Comte de Lapérouse. He then wrote, "The presumption is, therefore, that they [the French] will make an establishment of some sort on the northwest coast of America."

After the War of 1812, when America was free from the pressing international problems of the Napoleonic era, the attention of its government turned westward again. Moreover there was abroad in America in the 1830's and 1840's a kind of expansionism, different in name, appeal and theory from previous movements of this sort. This mood has been encompassed in the contemporary expression "Manifest Destiny." This phrase referred to a belief in the divinely ordained expansion of America's national boundaries to the Pacific and even to all of North America.

President Andrew Jackson made the first American effort to acquire part of Alta California. In 1835, he sent Anthony Butler as his envoy into Mexico to negotiate for the purchase of northern California, including San Francisco Bay. Butler was a poor choice; his offer of bribes offended the Mexican officials, and he returned in disgrace to the United States.

Jackson did not abandon the idea of acquiring California, however. In 1836, he sent Lieutenant William A. Slacum to Oregon and California to obtain detailed information about the Far West. After he had completed his journey to the Pacific, Slacum strongly urged that the American nation take possession of San Francisco Bay.

In 1837, when the Mexican President Santa Anna came to Washington after his defeat and capture by Sam Houston in the battle of San Jacinto, Jackson proposed that the United States mediate the war between Mexico and the Lone Star Republic. According to Jackson's offer, the United States would pay Mexico $3,500,000 if she would accept a line along the Rio Grande and then west along the thirty-eighth parallel to the Pacific as the Texas boundary. Jackson mistakenly assumed that this would give Texas possession of San Francisco Bay; and since Jackson confidently expected to annex Texas, the United States would someday control this strategic port. Therefore, Jackson urged the Texans to claim California. Yet Jackson was unable to realize his scheme, because both Mexico and Texas opposed it.

During Van Buren's presidency (1837–41), official American interest in California languished, but when John Tyler succeeded Harrison as President, this interest was revived again.

Tyler's minister to Mexico in 1842 was Waddy Thompson of South Carolina. Although he had never seen California, Thompson became a fervent enthusiast of the province, frequently pointing out the advantages of possessing San Francisco Bay. Secretary of State Daniel Webster was also in favor of annexation. He eventually evolved a scheme to annex California by means of a tripartite agreement between Mexico, Great Britain and the United States. Under this arrangement, the United States would compromise its claims to the Oregon country, accepting the Columbia River as its northern boundary and leaving the rest of the country to 54°40′ to the British. As compensation, the United States would annex Texas and California. Mexico would have its indebtedness to British and Yankee bondholders paid off by the American government. This plan failed. Many Americans objected to giving up so much of the Oregon country; the British spurned the plan, because it did not compensate them enough for their losses in the Oregon territory. Mexican officials were uninterested in this proposal, since they did not seriously intend ever to pay these debts.

An event that occurred in 1842—the Jones Affair—proved especially significant in terms of America's position in California. Commodore Thomas ap Catesby Jones was then in command of the American Pacific squadron. The American government hoped that this naval force would be able to deal with the British and French fleets in the area. Commodore Jones was understandably edgy as the American commander in the Pacific, for his task seemed formidable when compared with his resources. In September 1842, while dining with James Chamberlayne Pickett, the American chargé d'affaires at Lima, Jones received confidential dispatches from the American consul at Mazatlán, Mexico. These dispatches were three months old and announced that war between the United States and Mexico was imminent. The American consul had also sent a copy of the Mexican newspaper *El Cosmopolita*, which reprinted the diplomatic correspondence between the United States and Mexico concerning Texas. The Mexican minister of foreign affairs, Juan María de Bocanegra, had issued several bellicose declarations. Jones also received a copy of a Boston newspaper which reported that Mexico had sold California to Great Britain for seven million dollars.

Meanwhile, the British Pacific squadron put to sea from Callao, Peru. Jones interpreted this move as a possible British invasion of California. Hastily conferring with the captains of his ships, Jones decided to leave at once for California with two of his vessels, the *United States* and the *Cyane*. These two American men-of-war reached the California coast by October 18. On October 19, the brig *Joven Guipuzcoana* sailed from Monterey and was promptly captured by one of the American vessels. Under interrogation, its indignant master declared that he had not heard of a war between the United States and Mexico. Nevertheless, the Americans announced to him that they now considered his ship a prize of war. That afternoon the American warships sailed into Monterey and anchored. A small Mexican boat with two officers aboard rowed out to the American ships. When seized, the two men seemed nervous and kept insisting that they knew of no Mexican-American war. At this point, Jones contacted an American vessel in the harbor, the *Fama*. From its mate the commodore learned that there was a rumor in Hawaii that the United States and Mexico were at war, and that the British were plotting to seize California.

Jones then sent an officer and an interpreter ashore under a flag of truce to demand the surrender of Monterey. Juan Bautista Alvarado, then in charge at Monterey, tried to stall the Americans by protesting that he was no longer governor of California. The new appointee, Manuel Micheltorena, was in the southern part of the province.

Meanwhile, Alvarado's hope of standing off the Americans was dashed when one of his officers reported that the Monterey fortifications were out of repair, and that the eleven cannon in the fort had broken carriages. In addition, the officer declared, there was a grave shortage of ammunition. Alvarado sent the captain of the port, Pedro Narváez José Abrego, as a representative of the civil authorities, and Thomas O. Larkin as an interpreter, to parley with Jones. After two hours of discussion, the Mexican delegates agreed to accept Jones's original document, modified by a few minor amendments.

The next morning a Mexican panel of commissioners appeared at Jones's flagship to sign the capitulation document at seven thirty, two hours before they were due. This caused Jones to growl that the Mexicans seemed "impatient to surrender the country." About nine o'clock the articles were signed, surrendering the district of Monterey (from San Luís Obispo to San Juan Bautista) to the Americans. At 11:25 that morning, the Americans began to disembark a force of 150 sailors and marines. The Mexican garrison of twenty-nine men marched out of the fort and lowered the Mexican flag. The Americans then raised the Stars and Stripes over the old fort, which was renamed Fort Catesby.

Meanwhile, Jones kept discovering copies of foreign newspapers that showed there had been no outbreak of hostilities between the United States and Mexico. Finally Jones called a council of his senior officers, who decided that they had made a great error and recommended that Jones should send a note to Alvarado, promising to restore Mexican authority. Late in the afternoon of October 21, the disappointed sailors and marines retired to their ships and fired a thirteen-gun salute in honor of the restored Mexican flag.

Governor Micheltorena had been sojourning near Santa Barbara when he learned of Monterey's surrender to the Americans. He hurriedly traveled to the mission San Fernando Rey, where he issued a flood of proclamations, appealing to the Californios' patriotism. Then, to his relief, he received a note from Commodore Jones, notifying him that Monterey had been seized through error and had already been restored to the Mexican authorities. Micheltorena then penned two letters to Commodore Jones, in which he insisted upon a personal conference near San Fernando. He added that if Jones feared to venture so far inland, he would meet him at San Pedro Bay.

Jones was in no hurry to meet with Governor Micheltorena. After returning Monterey to the Mexicans, he cruised off the northern California coast for a time. At San Francisco Bay, he went ashore and visited at Sonoma with General Mariano Vallejo, who made no mention of his recent contretemps. Then, in early January 1843, Jones sailed for Monterey. He sent two of his vessels directly to Mazatlán, while he sailed in another for his conference with Micheltorena.

On January 17, Jones's vessel, the *Cyane*, anchored at San Pedro Bay, thirty miles from the pueblo of Los Ángeles. Twenty-five lancers in brilliant uniforms escorted the American commodore to Los Ángeles. There, on January 19, Jones and some of his officers met with the Mexican governor, who presented them with eight articles of a convention, which he requested Jones to sign. The commodore was surprised to find that one article bound him to replace completely 1,500 infantry uniforms which had been ruined when a Mexican detachment made a forced march in the rain toward beleaguered Monterey. There were not 1,500 Mexican soldiers in all of California. Micheltorena also demanded that Jones make restitution for a ruined set of band instruments, rendered useless during the same time. In addition, he asked for fifteen thousand dollars in damages for miscellaneous losses caused by the general alarm in the province. Jones refused to sign, claiming that he had no authority to bind his government in this way. Micheltorena calmly accepted Jones's decision. The two men parted amicably, and shortly thereafter Jones left the California coast.

The consequences of Jones's act were a great embarrassment to himself, the Navy and the United States government. The Mexicans were chagrined that Jones had so easily taken Monterey. Bocanegra, the Mexican foreign minister, protested to the American minister, Waddy Thompson, who replied that Jones's attack had not been authorized by the American government, and that in his opinion the Mexicans were justified in raising the question of recompense. However, Thompson pointed out that it was the bombast of the Mexican officials which had led Jones mistakenly to believe that the United States was at war with Mexico.

Although the American government offered the Mexicans a formal apology, the United States never actually paid the indemnity demanded by Mexico. However, the episode cost the Americans a great price diplomatically. From this time on, Mexican officials were on guard against American designs. To the Mexicans, Yankees were men of bad faith with whom gentlemen could not negotiate. Although Jones was recalled as commander of the Pacific squadron, his career suffered no other permanent setback. President Tyler realized his error was based on faulty intelligence and his standing orders to safeguard American interests in the Pacific. Jones's mistaken seizure of Monterey was therefore excused by the President.

On March 4, 1845, James K. Polk was inaugurated President of the United States with a platform which favored the annexation of Texas, the acquisition of the Oregon country from England and the possible purchase of California. Having been speaker of the House of Representatives and governor of Tennessee, Polk grasped the Democratic presidential nomination in 1844, when Martin Van Buren, the preconvention favorite, seemed indifferent to the demands of Manifest Destiny. As a result, there was a deadlock in the Democratic convention which was only broken when Polk, as the ailing Jackson's choice, came forward as the first dark horse in American political history. In the presidential campaign that followed, the Whig candidate, Henry Clay, seemed ambivalent about annexation. Since there were many voters who wanted the United States to encompass all the land north of the Rio Grande and west to the Pacific, they gave their support to Polk, an ardent champion of annexation. American optimism had returned after the Panic of 1837, and in this new buoyant mood there was an insistent public clamor for the acquisition of Oregon, California and Texas.

Before Polk's inauguration, the Texas Republic was annexed to the United States by the Tyler administration. This shifted American interest to the West Coast, where California and Oregon were yet to be acquired.

President Polk had never seen California, but he was certain that the United States should acquire the province before Great Britain or France attempted to seize it. Polk first hoped to purchase California, but the Mexicans refused to sell. Then Polk considered the possibility of a revolt against Mexico instigated and aided by the American residents in California. In October 1845, Polk's secretary of state penned a confidential message to Thomas O. Larkin, which stated, "If the people [of California] should desire to unite their destiny with ours, they would be received as brethren. . . ."

As part of Polk's scheme to separate California from Mexico by revolution, the presence in the province of the explorer John C. Frémont and his men was significant. Frémont was an enigmatic, but very successful young man. He was born in Savannah, Georgia, in 1813. After having become a lieutenant in the Topographical Corps of the United States Army, he married the daughter of Senator Thomas Hart Benton of Missouri. Benton, a strong advocate of expansion, sent his son-in-law into the Rocky Mountains and the Far West on government-sponsored survey trips. On Frémont's second expedition, he journeyed to Oregon, turned south into Nevada and then crossed into California's Sacramento Valley. Passing through central and southern California, he returned to the East by way of Santa Fé. His official report, ghost-written by his wife Jessie, gave the eastern United States a detailed knowledge of California's great potential, as well as how tenuous were the ties that bound it to Mexico. Frémont earned the soubriquet "the Pathfinder" from an admiring American public.

In 1845 Frémont left St. Louis with his third western expedition, ostensibly to explore the Great Basin and the Pacific coast south of Oregon. Frémont took with him sixty soldiers, scouts and topographers, and twelve Delaware Indians. The party was well supplied with two hundred horses and a few cattle to eat as food along the way. Among the company of explorers on this trip was the artist Edward M. Kern of Philadelphia, who came along to make sketches of geographical features. The Kern River in California was named for him. To guide and counsel Frémont through the wilderness was the veteran frontiersman Joseph Reddeford Walker and the experienced Christopher ("Kit") Carson.

In late August of 1845, Frémont and his party left Bent's Fort on the Arkansas River. By early September, they had pitched their camp at the Great Salt Lake. From there, Frémont decided to try a more direct route across the desert and during this journey named the Humboldt River. At Walker Lake, southwest of present-day Carson City, Frémont divided his force, hoping in this way to double the amount of information which could be gathered. The main body under Kern's guidance was to follow a trail which ran along the Humboldt and down the east side of the Sierra Nevada—the same trail over which Joseph Reddeford Walker had led the Chiles party of emigrants in 1843. Eventually, this group would rendezvous with Frémont and his band of sixteen men at a stream called "River of the Lake." Frémont decided to follow the Truckee River across the Sierra, and then enter the Sacramento Valley by way of the American River.

After a hospitable reception at Sutter's Fort, Frémont led his party up the San Joaquin toward his rendezvous with Walker. By December 22, Frémont had reached the King's River, which he thought was the river of rendezvous. Since there were several possible rivers of the same description and location, Walker chose a different "River of the Lake" than had Frémont as the correct stream of that name. After searching for the main party, only to discover snow in the higher mountain passes, Frémont's party returned to Sutter's Fort on January 15, 1846. Meanwhile, Walker's party waited for Frémont at a camp on the Kern River. Only as they roamed the valley for food did they learn of Frémont's presence at Sutter's Fort.

Frémont decided to visit José Castro, who commanded the garrison at Monterey. With a passport furnished by Sutter, Frémont journeyed to confer with the Mexican commander. During the interview, he asked Castro for permission to winter in the San Joaquin Valley and to continue his exploration in the "region of the Rio Colorado." Although his presence at the head of a band of armed frontiersmen alarmed the Mexican authorities, Castro reluctantly gave him the permission he requested, with the understanding that the American would keep his men away from Mexican settlements.

Late in February, Frémont started southward and moved into the Salinas Valley, a considerable detour from the route he had outlined to the Mexican officials. As a result of this action, Castro received orders from Mexico City to banish him from California. Castro threatened to use all the force at his disposal to drive the Americans out if they were so inconsiderate as to tarry after his order. Frémont's reponse to this threat was to built a log fortification at Gavilan (or Hawk's) Peak, overlooking the Salinas Valley. He raised the American flag and seemed ready to entrench himself there permanently. Frémont remained in his fortified camp for three days, while the Mexicans made no move to expel him. Instead, Castro gathered some of his troups and issued proclamations, branding the Americans as freebooters (*bandaleros*). Frémont realized that unless he was prepared to attempt the conquest of the entire province with his own forces, he had no alternative but to retire as gracefully as possible from the province. He slowly vacated Hawk's Peak and marched his men northward toward Oregon. They journeyed through the Sacramento Valley, crossed the Oregon border, and by May 6, 1846, were camped along the banks of Klamath Lake.

On May 9, Frémont was overtaken by Lieutenant Archibald Gillespie, a United States Marine Corps officer, with an important message. Gillespie had left Washington early in November 1845, disguised as a merchant. He traveled hastily across Mexico and sailed to Monterey on the American warship *Cyane*. There Gillespie went ashore, and after talking to Larkin, the American consul there, he set out to overtake Frémont on his way north. Gillespie produced a packet of letters from Senator Benton, a copy of an official dispatch from Secretary of State James Buchanan, and some verbal instructions from President Polk. The Buchanan dispatch talked vaguely of encouraging a revolution of Californios and American settlers, so that an independent republic might be established which could be annexed to the United States. In the absence of documentary evidence, it has never been precisely determined what orders were given to Frémont. Whatever the content of these instructions, their effect was to turn Frémont back to California, where he set up an armed camp at a place called the Buttes in the Sacramento Valley.

Frémont's return to California disturbed the American settlers who had traveled overland with their families into California. They had chosen not to mix with the Californios, and had settled instead far from any Mexican settlements. These recent immigrants into California were nervous and suspicious of the Mexican authorities, whom they felt resented their presence. In their midst were mountain men and frontier drifters, who seized this occasion to flock into Frémont's camp, where they felt certain a fight would ensue. The Americans brought alarming reports that Castro meant to attack and drive out all American settlers

who had not become Mexican citizens. Another rumor persisted that
Castro had encouraged the California Indians to attack them. Soon American residents in the nearby countryside began to beg Frémont to protect
them. Publicly he said that he would take no active measures for their
defense; however, he promised to defend them in case of an overt Mexican attack. Unofficially, he may have been even more encouraging. Many
American settlers became very bold and were anxious for hostilities to
begin.

In early June, a group of Mexican officials were driving a band of 150
horses from the Sonoma area to the Santa Clara Valley by way of Sutter's
Fort. Twelve American settlers led by frontiersman Ezekiel Merritt intercepted them south of the Sacramento River. Although Merritt's men
kept the horses, they released the Californios, who were scornfully told
to carry the details of what had occurred to Castro. Merritt and his men
then led the horses to Frémont's camp.

As word of this exploit spread, the Americans who feared Mexican
retaliation joined Merritt's marauding American band. A few days later,
possibly at Frémont's suggestion, Merritt and a force of thirty-three
leather-shirted Americans rode through the night toward Sonoma. They
galloped to the home of the former commandant general, Mariano Vallejo,
and made him a prisoner. The surprised Vallejo served his captors wine
and had a bullock killed to provide fresh meat for them. In this congenial
atmosphere, Vallejo persuaded the leaders of the band to come inside his
house and conclude an arrangement whereby Vallejo promised not to
bear arms against the insurgents, and they, in turn, promised to respect
civilians and private property in Sonoma. Vallejo in turn surrendered his
keys to the public stores in Sonoma. The mass of greasy-jacketed frontiersmen standing outside the house became impatient and selected a new
leader to replace Merritt, William B. Ide. Ide pushed his way into the
house to announce that on behalf of the men outside, he wanted more
action and less talk. He refused to accept the agreement with Vallejo and
ordered instead that he be arrested and taken to Frémont at Sutter's Fort.
Vallejo was released when regular American armed forces came into
California. Meanwhile, Ide and most of his force continued to hold the
town of Sonoma.

In the dusty plaza of Sonoma, the followers of Ide unfurled a flag
which they had improvised to serve as a symbol of their movement. It
was made of whitish-brown cotton cloth on which they had painted a
grizzly bear and a red star, made of paint or pokeberry juice. The flag's
reputed painter, Mrs. Abraham Lincoln's nephew, William L. Todd, had
inscribed the words "California Republic" upon the banner.

One of the leaders of this "Bear Flag Revolt" was Dr. Robert
Semple, a giant Kentuckian who was to become editor of California's first

English-language newspaper and president of its first constitutional convention. The other leader, William Ide, was a Massachusetts man who had wandered all over the West as a farmer, schoolteacher, carpenter and rancher, before coming to California in 1845. Ide was an idealist who communicated only with a great deal of difficulty. Consequently, he enjoyed a brief political career. In control for the moment, he issued a proclamation on June 15 which charged that American settlers had been oppressed under Mexican rule and urged all good citizens to join the insurgent republic.

Others in California had also begun to fight. The provincial government had no organized military force north of San Francisco Bay, but quickly improvised a detachment south of the Bay under Joaquín de la Torre. The approach of these troops toward Sonoma was quickly discovered by the Americans, and on June 23, the military leader of the Bear Flaggers, H. L. Ford, led a small force to repel de la Torre. A skirmish ensued at Olompali, approximately twelve miles from San Rafael. Finding that they were no match for the rifle-armed Americans, the Califorios quickly fell back. The Bear Flaggers sustained no casualties in this first skirmish.

Frémont marched into Sonoma with ninety men on June 25. At once he became known as the "Great Bear," replacing Ide as leader of the rebel movement. Ide never forgave what he regarded as Frémont's injustice to him. For years he piteously protested that Frémont had snatched the glory after others had borne the risk.

Frémont failed to prevent de la Torre's men from escaping from their exposed position in the north Bay area. De la Torre had sent a false message, ostensibly a dispatch from Castro, which announced an attack upon Sonoma once he, de la Torre, had lured the Americans away. The wily Mexican had sent this message in the care of a highly unreliable Indian, who, precisely as de la Torre had planned, defected to the Americans. Taking the captured document at face value, Frémont recalled his troops to Sonoma, and de la Torre safely crossed the Bay to Yerba Buena.

Declaring California independent of Mexico and under martial law, Frémont reorganized the insurgents by consolidating their forces with his own band of explorers—a total of 234 men. On July 4, he proclaimed this group the California Battalion.

Although the Bear Flag Revolt was one of the more romantic and colorful episodes of California history, it was of limited significance in the acquisition of California by the United States. The principal instrument by which the United States occupied California was the American Pacific squadron. At this time the squadron consisted of the following vessels: the flagship *Savannah* with fifty-four guns; the ship *Congress* with sixty guns; the sloops *Levant, Cyane, Portsmouth* and *Warren* with twenty-four guns each; the schooner *Shark* mounting twelve guns; and the transport *Erie.*

On June 24, 1845, Commodore John D. Sloat had been instructed to avoid any aggressive action against Mexico. In the event of war, he was to occupy San Francisco and the other principal ports of California. So as to better operate against California if war should come, Sloat proceeded north from the southern Pacific to the Mexican port of Mazatlán. On May 16, 1846, he learned from the American consul Parrott that fighting had begun along the Rio Grande between American and Mexican troops. News of further clashes came to him slowly. Because of the poor communications with Washington, Sloat did not learn until much later of the official American declaration of war, issued on May 13, but he decided that the news he had received of imminent hostilities justified offensive action against California. On June 7 he ordered his naval forces to proceed north toward Monterey to establish American control there. As a precautionary measure he had earlier sent several ships of the squadron to sea with orders to rendezvous at designated times and places. Sloat reached Monterey on July 2. Instead of acting immediately and possibly repeating Commodore Jones's mistake, Sloat offered to salute the Mexican flag. The Mexicans refused this request by pleading that they had no powder to return the salute. At this impasse, Consul Larkin hastened aboard Sloat's flagship to confer with the commodore. The two agreed that Sloat would treat the Californios with all possible kindness so as to win their loyalty. Larkin did not believe that war had really begun and argued that aggressive action should be postponed, since American rule would eventually be invited by the Californios. Sloat felt that his standing orders required him to occupy California ports immediately. After several days of wavering deliberation, Sloat decided to take possession of Monterey. His decision was partly motivated by the reported presence of Admiral Sir George Seymour, commander of the British squadron in the Pacific, who was keeping close watch over the activities of the American fleet.

On the morning of July 7, Monterey, with its white-balconied houses and crumbling adobe buildings, became the target of American action. At seven thirty a message was sent to the captain of the port, Silva, asking him to surrender. Silva replied that the Mexican troops had fled, and there was not even a flag left to surrender. Three hours later, Captain William Mervine, in charge of 250 marines and seamen, landed at Monterey. They marched to the small customshouse, where Captain Mervine read the commodore's proclamation. In this document, Commodore Sloat announced that he was taking possession of Alta California, since the United States and Mexico were at war. He promised to protect the inhabitants, who were free to choose their own officials, and enjoy security, religious freedom and material prosperity.

The American flag was then raised and cheered by the Americans onshore, and a salute of twenty-one guns was fired from each American vessel. Sloat immediately sent orders to Captain John D. Montgomery of the *Portsmouth* to seize Yerba Buena. The commodore also sent a courier to Frémont, informing him of the military action at Monterey.

After receiving the news that Sloat had taken Monterey, Frémont marched from Sutter's Fort with 160 picked men. Upon his arrival, he admitted to Sloat that he had no specific orders for what he had done. Sloat's reply was to dismiss Frémont and his men, refusing to accept the unit into federal service.

After the American flag was raised at Monterey, Sloat communicated with José Castro, urging him to surrender. In reply, Castro criticized Frémont and his Bear Flaggers, and declared that he would never surrender; the commodore would have to consult Governor Pío Pico and the local assembly. Sloat accepted Castro's advice and sent dispatches to the California governor. Before Governor Pico could reply, Sloat was relieved of command by Robert F. Stockton. Stockton arrived at Monterey on July 15, only a little more than a week after active operations had begun. After a series of conferences between the two commodores, Sloat turned over his command on July 23; six days later he cheerfully sailed for the eastern United States.

Although Stockton, like Sloat, was a veteran of the War of 1812, he was fifteen years younger than his predecessor. In 1844, he had been injured by an explosion of a giant cannon called the "Peacemaker" aboard the *Princeton*. An ardent expansionist, he thoroughly approved of the Mexican War. He acted vigorously, whereas Sloat urged moderation. Stockton decided to carry the war to the remaining California ports. On July 28 he issued a harsh, vindictive proclamation denouncing the Mexican government and censuring Castro for his attitude toward Frémont. The Californios now became anxious about their future under Stockton's rule.

Stockton planned an energetic campaign to drive the remnants of Mexican power from California. Castro had retired to Los Ángeles, where he industriously gathered five hundred men and seven or eight pieces of artillery. Since Castro's forces were being steadily augmented by fresh recruits, Stockton resolved to strike before they became an even greater menace. He reorganized Frémont's contingent into naval service and augmented it with eighty marines. He promoted Captain Frémont to the rank of major and made Gillespie a captain. With 220 fighting men, the battalion sailed in the sloop *Cyane* to San Diego. Their mission was to cut off Castro from support in Baja California.

After foraging for a week in the gardens and orchards of San Diego, Frémont led his men on the 140-mile march to Los Ángeles. Meanwhile, Stockton had supplanted the Mexican flag at Santa Barbara and had sailed to San Pedro Bay, eighteen miles from Los Ángeles. He landed three hundred men and several pieces of artillery and rendezvoused with Frémont, who marched in from the south. On August 13, 1846, the American naval forces moved into Los Ángeles and raised their flag without opposition. Pausing only to bury some of their artillery pieces, the Mexican forces fled in every direction. Castro hid in a desolate place overlooking the San Gabriel plain. When the Americans had stopped searching for him, he fled to Sonora. Governor Pío Pico also fled to Mexico.

Occupying the capital of Mexican California, Stockton issued a blizzard of proclamations. At first their effect was not ungratifying to the Californios, but they soon indicated that martial law would be in effect in California with Stockton as military governor. Stockton did not intend to continue long in his position as military governor of the province. He was determined to thoroughly pacify the province and turn it over to others to rule, while he carried the war into Mexico. In the meantime, Stockton partitioned California into three military districts. Stockton took command of the middle district, entrusting the rule of the north to Frémont and the south to Gillespie.

Confirmation finally arrived that the United States and Mexico were formally at war. Therefore, the Americans made provision for a long stay. The American commanders paroled their prisoners. On August 15, 1846, the *Californian,* the first newspaper to be printed in English, appeared at Monterey. This newspaper was the joint venture of Bear Flagger Robert Semple and a Navy chaplain, Walter Colton. In September municipal elections were held. Walter Colton was appointed alcalde (the Americans adopted the use of this Spanish-Mexican office) at Monterey and soon inaugurated a peaceful regime. These accomplishments were written into reports which Kit Carson was supposed to carry to Washington.

In the south, resentment at Gillespie's intolerant regime spread among the Angelenos. Since Gillespie's area was close to Mexico, the southern Californios were in constant communication with the mother country. His force, which had been reduced to about fifty volunteers, was pitifully small for the task assigned to it. In addition, Gillespie was both arbitrary and intolerant in his rule of Los Ángeles. He plagued the residents with unnecessary regulations. One of the most irksome was a curfew, originally imposed by Stockton, from ten in the evening until sunrise. The Californios, in the Spanish tradition, took a siesta during the afternoon and were fond of visiting at night. As the days passed with no visible reason for continuing the curfew, they became exasperated. Gillespie was also fond of arbitrary arrests to keep the inhabitants of Los Ángeles in awe. This practice irritated the natives, instead of making them more docile. Consequently on the morning of September 23, fifty Californios, "inflamed with patriotism and perhaps with wine," attacked the small Yankee garrison at Los Ángeles. No one was killed, but in retaliation Gillespie ordered the arrests of many citizens. One suspect, José María Flores, successfully escaped into the countryside. Flores, a former Mexican officer free on parole, began to recruit other dissident Californios to drive the Yankee invaders out. Other paroled officers and many Angelenos fled into the country to join him. When he had gathered a force of four hundred men, he moved into Los Ángeles and besieged Gillespie at Fort Hill, behind the town plaza. Gillespie rallied his troops and for a brief time stood off his attackers.

Meanwhile, another force of 110 Californios had surrounded some twenty-five American settlers at Isaac Williams' Rancho del Chino, near the present city of Pomona. The Americans took refuge in a large adobe building and faced the choice of surrendering or being burned alive, as the attackers set fire to the roof of their hiding place. The Americans held out for a short time and then surrendered. At this first triumph over the Americans, the morale of the Californios bounded skyward.

When word reached Los Ángeles, the overjoyed Californios determined to force Gillespie into surrendering. Besieged and short of water, Gillespie conceived a perilous plan. Under cover of darkness he sent a courier, John Brown, known to the Californios as Juan Flaco (Lean John), through enemy lines to Monterey to seek help. His daring ride was the most amazing single event of the war in California. Gillespie's message was written on cigarette paper and concealed in his long hair. Creeping out of the American camp, Brown was pursued for miles by fifteen Californios who had detected his escape. Brown evaded them by jumping his horse across a thirteen-foot ravine. The Californios fired on him, wounding his horse, which continued to gallop, startling Brown when it suddenly dropped dead, throwing him to the ground. His pursuers did not dare to jump their steeds across the wide ravine, so Brown was temporarily safe. Traveling on foot for twenty-seven miles, he finally reached Rancho de la Virgin, owned by Domingo Dominguez, where he obtained a fresh horse. He rode night and day for fifty-two hours, until he reached Monterey, 460 miles away. He was disappointed to learn that Commodore Stockton had returned to San Francisco Bay; so after a three-hour rest, he resumed his ride for another 140 miles until he finally reached Commodore Stockton. During his epic ride, Brown covered the distance from Los Ángeles to San Francisco in less than five days. When Stockton received Gillespie's message, he vowed to rescue the beleagured Americans and immediately began to organize a relief expedition.

But Gillespie's hilltop position had become so untenable that he surrendered to the Californios before help could reach him. According to the terms of his surrender, he was allowed to retreat with his men to San Pedro Bay, where they were to depart from the area on the merchant ship *Vandalia*.

Meanwhile, Stockton set sail aboard the *Congress* for San Pedro Bay, having directed Captain William Mervine with the *Savannah* to go to that same protected anchorage. When Gillespie reached the bay and witnessed the arrival by sea of American military forces under the command of William Mervine, he disregarded his agreement with the Californios.

On October 7, 1846, a hastily improvised force of three hundred Americans marched northward in an attempt to recapture Los Ángeles. The American route lay through large fields of wild mustard, which often grew taller than the heads of the advancing Yankees. As the American force wearily tramped along, the heat became insufferable. Consequently, the officers resolved to stop on a portion of the Rancho de Dominguez.

On the next morning, October 8, 1846, there was an engagement known as the "Battle of the Old Woman's Gun." In this conflict the Californians fought with eight-foot willow lances with blades of files and rasps. They were also armed with a four-pound cannon, their most damaging weapon. Known as the "Old Woman's Gun," this fieldpiece had been hidden by an old woman when the Americans had first occupied Los Ángeles. After the successful revolt of the Californios, the gun had been dug up and mounted on the front axle of a wagon. The Californios had only a home-made supply of powder from the mission San Gabriel.

The sixty horsemen led by José Antonio Carillo had the advantage of mobility over the Americans. Their strategy was to fire their cannon, touched off by cigaritos, and then with lassos to drag it back a safe distance from the Americans and reload it. After an hour, Mervine's frustrated force had four killed and six wounded. Finally, Captain Mervine ordered his men to retreat to their ships.

During this same interval, the Californios had driven out Lieutenant T. Talbot and a small squad which had been holding Santa Barbara. Talbot and his men escaped by fleeing into the mountains and making their way back to Monterey. At San Diego the Americans were humiliated again. A dozen men under Ezekiel Merritt had been stationed as a garrison at that port. When they were attacked by fifty Californios led by Manuel Garfías, the Americans fled to the refuge of a whaling ship in the harbor. The Californios did not dare attempt a boarding party, and for twenty days the Americans were trapped aboard this ship.

For a brief time, the territory from San Diego to Santa Barbara was controlled by the Californios, who restored their civil government. On October 20, the departmental assembly elected Lieutenant Colonel José María Flores as acting governor and commandante general. This same assembly named Manuel Castro northern commandante and Francisco Pico as his subordinate.

To recover American losses in southern California, Commodore Stockton, began planning a counterattack. Arriving on October 23 at San Pedro Bay, the energetic commodore, after surveying the situation and finding it temporarily hopeless, sailed on to San Diego. There he drove back a force of Californios and began an attack on the hills behind the town. Suddenly he received a surprising message: General Stephen W. Kearny with a small force of soldiers had arrived in California and desperately required assistance.

Stephen Watts Kearny was a veteran frontier army officer who had been born on August 30, 1794, in Newark, New Jersey; his ancestors had come from Ireland to America in the seventeenth century. Kearny was a bright child, and at fourteen he entered what is today Columbia University. After two years he transferred to Princeton, but, according to surviving records, he was never actually graduated. Young Kearny joined the New York militia, and when preparations began for a second war with Britain, he was appointed a first lieutenant in the regular army. After the War of 1812, he saw wide service on the frontier. In the spring of 1846, the War Department ordered him to march across the continent with an "Army of the West" from Fort Leavenworth in present-day Kansas. He was to seize Santa Fé and then move toward California, where he was to augment American naval forces. Kearny's small band of regular soldiers was accompanied by a large force of volunteers—in all 1,658 men and sixteen pieces of artillery. During June 1846, as his volunteers arrived and were properly organized, he sent them ahead to Fort Bent on the Santa Fé Trail in what is now eastern Colorado.

On the first leg of the journey, until the crossroad from Fort Leavenworth joined the Santa Fé Trail, the route was not well marked, and several of his units got lost. These bands of soldiers wandered in confusion until friendly Indians guided them back to the trail. Late in July, Kearny joined the force of recruits encamped near Bent's Fort. A famous trading post, the fort was the only permanently occupied settlement between the Missouri country and the province of New Mexico.

In August, Kearny's army started the long march from Bent's Fort to New Mexico. Their advance was unopposed, and by mid-August they marched into Santa Fé, to find that the Mexican governor Manuel Armijo and his small military force had already fled. For six weeks, Kearny acted as military governor of the conquered province.

From Santa Fé westward were one thousand miles of rough terrain which had never been traversed by a military force of any size. On September 26, Kearny was ready to resume the advance to California. The general rode southwest with a picked force of three hundred dragoons. Near the present town of Socorro, New Mexico, in October, he met a party of sixteen men led by Kit Carson. Carson told Kearny that he had left Los Ángeles twenty-six days earlier, carrying official dispatches from Stockton and Frémont to Washington. These dispatches indicated that the Navy, with an assist from Frémont and the American settlers, had conquered California for the United States. Since Carson told Kearny the United States was in control of California and that the war had ended there, Kearny decided to send two-thirds of his men back to Santa Fé. To continue toward California with his remaining one hundred men, Kearny needed an experienced guide. He tried to convince Carson to go west with him, suggesting that he relinquish his dispatches to others to carry to Washington. Carson did not wish to turn back, since he felt committed to carry the dispatches personally to Washington, but Kearny finally persuaded him to guide his expedition to California.

The reorganized Kearny expedition, now guided by Carson, pushed steadily westward. Forage for the mules became scarce, and to keep the animals alive, Kearny's men were forced to feed them canebrake, bark, willow and cottonwood leaves. Kearny became confused, for as he approached California, captured Mexicans told him that all of southern California was in revolt against the Yankees.

On November 25, Kearny's men forded the Colorado River and entered the California desert. Adequate supplies of water for both men and animals became a pressing problem. Finally, in December, they reached Warner's Ranch, sixty miles northeast of San Diego. The rancher in charge confirmed the earlier rumors about American reverses in California. An Englishman, Edward Stokes, who lived relatively close to the ranch, offered to carry a dispatch to Commodore Stockton. It was this message that reached Stockton on October 23 at San Pedro Bay.

Stockton quickly sent Captain Archibald Gillespie with thirty-nine men and a brass four-pounder to lead Kearny's detachment safely to San Diego. Unknown to the American marine officer, the sister of the Mexican commander in the vicinity, Andrés Pico, had seen the American force leave San Diego and understood roughly its destination and purpose. She sent this information to her brother.

Andrés Pico, the brother of the ubiquitous California politician and governor Pío Pico, was a resourceful and brave officer, but upon this occasion he did not take his sister's note at face value. He believed that Gillespie was really out on a foraging expedition; therefore, Pico decided to ambush the Americans when they returned encumbered by supplies, thus presenting a more tempting target. Therefore, Pico encamped his men at the small Indian village of San Pasqual.

Earlier the Mexican commander, José María Flores, had received word of Kearny's march toward California and had sent Andrés Pico and one hundred horsemen to reinforce Leonardo Cota, the Mexican commander who held the Americans under seige in San Diego. Yet for some reason, Pico did not credit the report of Kearny's approach and expected to fight only Gillespie's much smaller force.

Gillespie informed Kearny that it was known that Pico was in the area and that it would be necessary for the Americans to be cautious if they wished to avoid an ambush on the march to San Diego.

On the morning of December 6, Kearny's army rode through a cold rain toward San Pasqual, where Andrés Pico and his Californios rested warm and dry inside Indian huts. At dawn on December 6, Kearny ordered an attack on the Indian village, where he suspected a California force to be billeted. The resulting two-day skirmish is known as the "Battle of San Pasqual." Although the resultant fighting was only a series of hot skirmishes, it had far-reaching results upon the California campaign.

The battle was fought in the mist amid great confusion, and its details are as hotly disputed as those of the Battle of Gettysburg. As the American force approached San Pasqual, some officers advocated a surprise attack upon the Californios; others suggested a more cautious advance. Kearny adopted the safer strategy. A small scouting party rode out into the cold rainy night, leaving the main party of Americans to settle down for a few hours of fitful sleep. A Mexican deserter who had brought news of the proposed ambush guided the Americans to the outskirts of the sleeping village. Then he volunteered to go ahead and scout for them. His offer was accepted, and he disappeared into the dark. When he did not return after a few minutes, the American commander suspected that he had been a spy and gave the order to advance. The American dragoons rushed loudly into San Pasqual, awakening their sleeping foes. The Californios quickly turned out to fight, shouting, "*Viva California* [not Mexico], *abajo los Americanos.*"

Hastily mounting their well-trained horses, the Californios soon grouped into a formidable fighting force. Yet the American scouting party escaped in the confusion and reported their presence in San Pasqual. Kearny at once roused his sleeping men, and ordered his entire party to attack. As the Yankees fell in, they were disconcerted to learn that some of their blankets had frozen solid as a result of the sleety rain.

The Americans had with them two howitzers which Kearny had dragged with great exertion all the way across the continent, as well as a four-pound cannon. As the Americans drew near San Pasqual, they entered a patch of low-lying fog which obscured the battlefield. When Kearny gave the order to charge, his water-soaked forces sprang forward, but they were at a great disadvantage in the battle which followed. Many of their horses had fared badly on the cross-country march, and soon the column of advancing American soldiers had scattered. In addition, their carbines, pistols and ammunition had been soaked by the rain. The Californios met Kearny's forces with muskets and long willow lances.

Pico's men awaited the American charge in a gully which bordered the Indian village. As the first Americans approached, the Californios fired a few shots from their firearms, and then seemed to retreat from the field. Suddenly they wheeled about and charged the small lead force of American soldiers pursuing them. To their disgust, the Yankee cavalrymen learned that their water-soaked guns snapped harmlessly at the advancing Mexicans. In addition, the short cavalry sabers of the American soldiers offered little defense against the long willow lances of the Californios. The Californios also were expert with the reata or lasso, which they used to pull several Americans from their horses.

When the Americans realized that they might lose this encounter, they began to withdraw. During the confusion of battle, several Californios spied Gillespie and rushed at him with their lances. Although Gillespie fought his attackers, they were able to unhorse and wound him. Then several Californios dragged off one of the American howitzers. They were unable to fire it, and as the fight continued, they became inordinately concerned with dragging it off as a visible trophy of their victory. Meanwhile, the Americans succeeded in firing one or two shots from their remaining artillery pieces, and the Californios fled from the field. Before their attackers were repelled, seventeen Americans were killed and one more died later of his wounds. Most of the fatalities resulted from lance wounds rather than from gunfire. In all, thirty-five Americans were killed or wounded. General Kearny himself received three lance wounds. Of the seventy Californios who fought in this battle, about thirty deserted after the first encounter. Their force suffered only minor losses: one was killed and twelve were wounded.

After the Californios had retreated, Kearny gathered up his wounded men and resumed his march toward San Diego. Their progress was slow and difficult, for small bands of Californios continued to follow them. By now the Americans' guns had dried and they were able to drive off their pursuers, killing five of them. After making camp on the top of Mule Hill, they were safe for the moment, but they did not dare move any closer to San Diego. The Californios began a siege of the Americans' position.

Kearny wrote a message to Stockton requesting assistance. He sent this dispatch with Kit Carson and a companion and an Indian guide. In order to steal through the enemy lines, the two Americans removed their boots. The journey in the dark over the cacti and sharp stones of the southern California desert was extremely difficult and painful. Nonetheless, Carson succeeded in getting his message through to the commodore. In response to Kearny's appeal, Lieutenant Andrew F. V. Gray of the *Congress* marched with eighty marines and 120 sailors to rescue him. This force of sailors and marines arrived at Kearny's camp on December 11. The Californios found themselves outnumbered and lifted their siege. Kearny and his weary men resumed their march, finally reaching San Diego.

Since Kearny and Gillespie were both wounded and many of the dragoons who had made the trip from New Mexico were exhausted, it was three weeks before offensive operations were commenced. Vainly the Americans at San Diego delayed any action, hoping to hear that Frémont in the north had prepared a companion trust. At this point a dispute began between Kearny and Stockton about which of them should command in San Diego. The question was finally resolved when General Kearny accepted second place, while Stockton took supreme command. There has always been some confusion about this agreement, and conflicting claims of final authority between the two men.

On December 29, 1846, the American forces, consisting of sailors, marines and Kearny's dragoons—forty-four officers and 563 men— marched out of San Diego for Los Ángeles. As Stockton's men advanced, Flores and his Californios retreated before them. After taking the San Bernardo Indian rancheria near Mule Hill, the Americans occupied Mission San Luís Rey. Scouts reported that Frémont was approaching Los Ángeles from the north and that six hundred Californios led by Andrés Pico were riding north to counter them. Sensing that the combined American forces were too strong to defeat, Flores sent a flag of truce to Stockton, asking for negotiations. Stockton rejected these overtures.

Continuing his advance, Stockton approached the San Gabriel River. His scouts called attention to the strong force of Californios that was following them. On January 7, 1847, as the Americans approached the river, they found that the Californios were drawn up along the opposite bank. While the American force was searching for a place to ford the stream, a Yankee settler named Forster offered to show them an alternative crossing, known by its Indian name of Curunga. On January 8 the Americans forded the river, although the exact spot is still a matter of dispute. The Californios had been distracted and were guarding a lower ford of the river when the American crossing began. The Californios quickly gained the heights of the far bank before the Americans had succeeded in fording the river. While Stockton commanded the American artillery from the near side of the river, Kearny led the infantry attack. The Californios had artillery with them, but the inferior powder they were forced to use made their shooting very inaccurate. As a result, although the Americans experienced some difficulty with quicksand in crossing the one-hundred-yard river, they succeeded in gaining the far bank. Forming along the shore of the river, cheering "New Orleans" in honor of the thirty-second anniversary of that victory during the War of 1812, the soldiers, sailors and marines charged up the heights. Unable to withstand this rush, the Californios abandoned the field. The American casualties were light, while the Californio losses have never been accurately determined.

The next day the Americans began marching toward Los Ángeles. They had not gone far before three hundred Californios, rallied by Flores, once more barred the way. From a ravine, the Californios fired their cannons at the Americans. Their powder had not improved in quality, and their shots went wild. As the battle progressed, they soon depleted their supply of powder, putting their artillery completely out of action. At this point Flores decided to attack the Americans, but his men were beaten back. Then Flores rallied his forces at a point on the road to Mexico where modern Pasadena now stands. The Americans easily brushed him aside, and the Californios fled. This skirmish, known as the Battle of La Mesa, confirmed the defeat of the Californios, who scattered in all directions. Flores declared that only five of his men had been killed and twenty-two wounded in the two battles on January 8 and 9, but his records were incomplete and his casualties could have been considerably higher. The American loss for the same period was only one killed and fourteen wounded.

After these defeats, the Californios no longer existed as an organized force. Flores, seeing that there was no hope of successful resistance, and fearing that he might be punished by the Yankees for breaking his parole, left Andrés Pico in command and fled with a few men to Mexico. On January 10 the Americans marched into Los Ángeles and raised their flag once more over the government house.

As Stockton was capturing Los Ángeles, Frémont was marching from the north. Having received orders from Stockton after the uprising of the previous fall to hasten southward to join in crushing the insurgents, Frémont marched south from Sutter's Fort with 170 well-armed men. When he reached Santa Barbara, he learned of Mervine's defeat at the Battle of the Old Woman's Gun, and heard that the Californios had denuded the country of supplies. Frémont then retreated to Monterey. He scoured the countryside for adequate mounts and a herd of cattle to drive along with him for food, and ordered every available recruit sent to him from the north. Eventually he possessed a force of 430 "splendid fighters."

At the end of November, Frémont began to move south from San Juan Bautista, advancing along the San Benito River and Salinas Valley toward San Luís Obispo. The weather was chilly and the march was made in the mud. Every afternoon the battalion killed thirteen or fourteen cattle. Later they claimed to have eaten an average of ten pounds of beef per man a day.

At San Luís Obispo, Frémont captured Jesús Pico, a cousin of Andrés and Pío Pico. He was about to be executed for breaking his parole and opposing the Americans, but Frémont yielded to the weeping entreaties of Pico's wife and pardoned him.

By Christmas Day, Frémont had marched his army to a ridge behind Santa Barbara. There they were caught in a fierce storm which lasted a week. After it had abated, they marched unopposed into Santa Barbara. Resuming the push to Los Ángeles, the battalion kept so close to the shore of the Pacific Ocean that the surf at times washed their feet. Frémont had adopted this strategy so that his force would be difficult to ambush. On January 5, 1847, in sunny weather, they reached San Buenaventura. On January 11, 1847, two Californios reported that Stockton had defeated his opposition and reoccupied Los Ángeles.

Scattered fighting might still have occurred, but Frémont proved to be a peacemaker who was able to avert further bloodshed. Having camped near San Fernando mission on the afternoon of January 12, Frémont received an envoy from Andrés Pico, who suggested that the rebels were prepared to surrender. Instead of waiting for his superior, General Kearny, to arrange surrender terms, Frémont quickly arranged the Capitulation of Cahuenga on January 13. He granted generous terms to the rebels on behalf of the American government. He guaranteed the Californios' persons and property and assured them equal rights with the Americans in California. The sole requirement laid upon them was to lay down their arms and promise to keep peace. These were precisely the terms which Stockton, a short time earlier, had refused to grant. Stockton might have disavowed this document when he received a copy of the agreement. However, when he realized that if he did not accept it he might be faced with fighting another rebellion, he reluctantly accepted it.

For their part, the Californios were now ready to make peace. They felt that they had been successful in carrying off the insurgency and escaping with no punishment, and that their honor had been satisfied. It is sometimes forgotten by historians that the Californios believed that the ease with which the Americans had originally occupied California was an affront to their honor. Therefore, it was not surprising that they revolted against Gillespie's stern rule. In a sense, they needed to revolt in order to continue to live with their consciences. However, after they had rebelled and had expelled the Americans from almost all of southern California, they felt that they had won sufficient glory, and speedily realized that they could not long resist the armed might of the United States. After their revolt had begun, Mexico did not send a man or a peso to help them. As a result, they felt no compulsion to continue the struggle. They accepted the generous terms of their surrender and settled down to live in the new, American California.

Although the fighting in Alta California was over, there was continued bloodshed in Baja California. The American Navy seized several ports, and elements of a regiment of New York volunteers sent to Alta California went down to garrison them. Attempting to drive out the Yankee invaders, the Mexicans precipitated heavier fighting than had ever occurred in Alta California. In the Treaty of Guadalupe-Hidalgo, Baja was returned to Mexico. Actually, the fighting in both provinces was of slight importance, since the course of the war was determined by battles in the Mexican interior by the twin invading armies of Zachary Taylor and Winfield Scott.

If the fighting between the Americans and Californios was over in Alta California, the three-way fight between the American commanders had only begun. It is a characteristic trait of all American wars that there have always been serious controversies among the nation's military and naval commanders.

A conflict in orders from Washington led to a fierce quarrel between Frémont and General Kearny over which of California's conquerors was actually in command of the American forces. Despite his rank in the regular army, Frémont felt that he had fought under the protection of the navy, and sided with Stockton against Kearny. Stockton and Frémont also took a denigrating view of Kearny's exploits. In their eyes, the general had done nothing except be roughly handled at San Pasqual.

When the three officers settled down together in Los Ángeles, their rivalry erupted. Kearny regarded Frémont as a lieutenant colonel in the army's mounted rifle battalion, and therefore subject to his jurisdiction. Kearny also believed that according to the 1825 edition of the General Regulations of the Army, then in current use, he, as a brigadier general outranked Stockton, a commodore in the navy. Therefore, secure in his own mind that his right to command should be unchallenged, Kearny seized the initiative. In separate notes, he demanded that Stockton cease to act as military governor of California, and that Frémont make no appointments or changes in his battalion without his consent.

Frémont's reply declared that until the commodore and the general had adjusted their differences, he would continue to report and be subject to the orders of Stockton. In a personal interview, Kearny advised Frémont to change his course, and when the army officer refused, the general left in anger.

Stockton refused to pay any attention to Kearny's orders and told the general to consider himself suspended from command. He also informed him that he would write asking the President to recall him as an uncooperative officer.

Since he had so few regular troops under his command to defend his claims to supremacy, Kearny withdrew with his dragoons to San Diego. He then sailed to Monterey, arriving there on February 8, 1847. Upon

Kearny's withdrawal, Stockton relinquished his post as governor of California and sailed away, leaving California under Frémont's control as the military governor.

Upon his arrival at Monterey, Kearny met the newly arrived Commodore William B. Shubrick, who carried orders naming him to succeed Stockton as commanding officer of the Pacific squadron. After reading Kearny's instructions, and with the arrival of Colonel Richard Barnes Mason with fresh orders from Washington, Shubrick decided to recognize General Kearny as the senior military officer in California.

On March 1, Commodore Shubrick and General Kearny issued a joint circular, which divided authority in California: the governorship and the land forces were the concern of Kearny, whereas the naval forces and regulation of the ports were to be under the authority of the commodore. Kearny then issued a proclamation to the Californios asking for their help and cooperation in building a peaceful, prosperous California. Kearny was now the recognized governor of California, except in the area around Los Ángeles, where Frémont continued to rule, although he was greatly hampered by a lack of funds. How to unseat Frémont as governor was Kearny's problem. He met with Frémont on March 26 and asked him if he were now ready to surrender his office. Frémont took an hour to decide and then announced that he would give up his post.

As Kearny's deputy, Colonel Mason was sent to Los Ángeles to transfer authority out of Frémont's hands. When the two men met, they got into a heated argument. Frémont challenged Mason to a duel. Mason suggested the use of double-barreled shotguns as weapons. No definite date was set for the fighting of the duel, and the matter quietly died. After a fifty-day reign as governor, Frémont surrendered his post, but not his papers, to Colonel Mason. When Kearny reproached him for this omission, Frémont defiantly replied that he had forwarded all his correspondence to Washington and that he had nothing left to turn over.

Before leaving for the East on May 31, 1847, Kearny appointed Colonel Mason as the military governor of California. Frémont traveled overland with Kearny. Left with only a small escort, Frémont felt that Kearny was trying to humiliate him. When Kearny and Frémont reached Fort Leavenworth (outside the zone of active operations), the general put his insubordinate junior officer under arrest, as he had always intended to do when he had the chance. Kearny felt keenly that Frémont had deliberately snubbed and belittled him while toadying to Stockton. Frémont was then sent to Washington for court martial proceedings under the charges brought by Kearny.

On November 2, 1847, Frémont was formally brought to trial on three charges of insubordination and failure to obey orders. The trial caught the attention of the country and was reported daily in the press. After weeks of testimony, the court martial judges retired for three days of deliberation and then on January 31, 1848, announced their verdict: Frémont was guilty on all counts. The judges then sentenced him to be dismissed from the service. Upon review, President Polk formally announced that he approved the findings of the court, but because of mitigating circumstances would remit Frémont's punishment.

Frémont instantly tendered his resignation to the President, declaring that he would never accept Polk's clemency. After some hesitation, on March 15, 1848, Polk accepted the resignation. Frémont was out of the army, but he was still to figure in California history.

Frémont's antagonist, Kearny, never lived to return to California. He went to Mexico, contracted a fatal disease, and returned to St. Louis, were he died on October 31, 1848.

Meanwhile, California was formally passing to the control of the United States. President Polk was anxious to end the war as soon as he could achieve his territorial goals. Therefore, he sent along with General Winfield Scott's invading army the chief clerk of the State Department, Nicholas P. Trist. Negotiating a treaty under the circumstances was difficult, and Polk, disgusted by a lack of results, recalled Trist. Refusing to return home until he had concluded negotiations with the Mexicans, Trist signed the treaty of Guadalupe-Hidalgo on February 2, 1848, and forwarded it to Washington.

The terms of the treaty were far reaching. They confirmed the American title to Texas with the Rio Grande as its southern boundary. The provisions of the treaty also ordered the Mexicans to yield New Mexico, including modern Arizona and Alta California, to the United States. The American government agreed to pay $15,000,000 for the land, and to indemnify the claims of its own citizens against Mexico to the amount of $3,250,000.

In the meanwhile, Democratic expansionists, drunk with success, were starting to demand all of Mexico. Polk was dead set against what he felt would be swallowing an indigestible Mexico. Therefore, he sent Trist's treaty to the Senate, where after a warm debate it was ratified by a vote of thirty-eight to fourteen, which officially ended the war on May 30, 1848. News of California's formal status as an American territory did not reach the Pacific coast until August 6, 1848.

FOURTEEN

The Gold of Ophir

A FTER the active fighting ended in California, many discharged
veterans lingered in California, particularly those from the
Mormon Battalion. This fighting force had been recruited from
among the Mormon emigrants who had been waiting in the Middle West
for transportation to Utah. They had joined the fighting in California
with the expectation that once the government had moved them to the
Pacific coast, they could approach Utah more easily from the west.
Their families were to be taken care of by the Church of Jesus Christ of
Latter-Day Saints' ecclesiastical authorities during the men's absence. The
battalion eventually marched from the Middle West to Santa Fé, and then
to San Diego, arriving after the active fighting had ceased. As the American veterans in California were discharged, many of them stayed on, waiting for something to turn up. Something did.

Minor finds had been made prior to the discovery of gold in 1848,
mostly by mission Indians, who were cautioned by the padres not to
divulge the location of the gold, lest miners and adventurers enter and
disrupt the quiet life of the province. In 1842, one Francisco López, a
rancher, uncovered a deposit of gold in San Feliciano Canyon, in the
mountains behind the San Fernando mission. His find sparked a modest
rush. Placer mining for gold employed forty to sixty men for a few years
before the deposit gradually "played out." The first California gold sent
to a United States mint came from this lode, but by 1848 the gold ore of
San Feliciano had been depleted.

California's major gold strike was indirectly precipitated by John Sut-

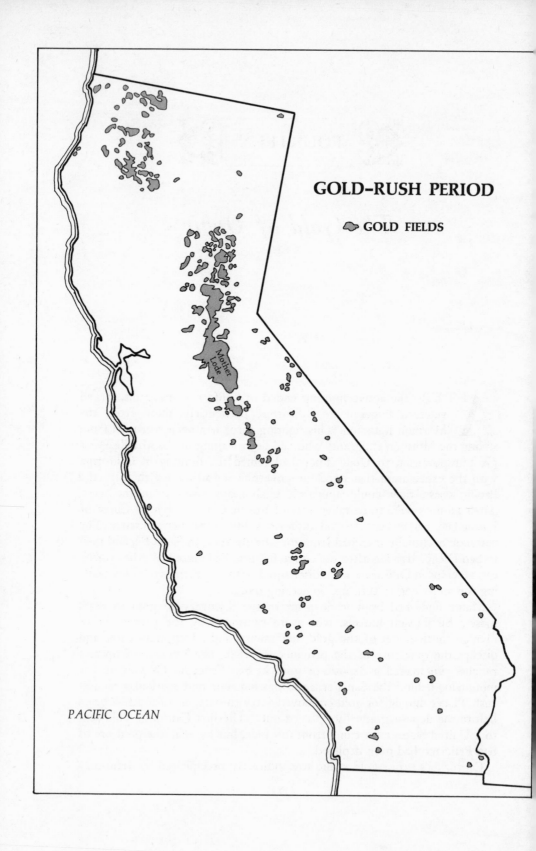

GOLD-RUSH PERIOD

 GOLD FIELDS

Mother Lode

PACIFIC OCEAN

ter. Sutter's Fort, publicized in a report by John C. Frémont, drew hundreds of American settlers who had come into California. Encouraged by increasing economic opportunities in the province and by the availability of skilled labor from the discharged Mormon Battalion veterans, Sutter decided to develop a lumber business. He hired a broody, rather eccentric carpenter, James Wilson Marshall, to select a site for his new sawmill. Marshall, a native of New Jersey, had come to California by way of Oregon in 1845. He chose a site in a small valley on the south fork of the American River, some forty-five miles east of Sutter's Fort. Local Indians called the place Coloma or "Beautiful Vale." Sutter approved Marshall's choice of a location for the mill, and on August 27, 1847, agreed to enter a partnership with him.

Marshall set out at once with a mixed crew of Indians, Mormon veterans and the Wimmer family. Some workers, disgruntled about the food or other working conditions, drifted away. but the work of building the sawmill continued.

In January 1848, although the machinery of the mill had not yet been installed, a test disclosed that the lower edge of the tailrace which turned the main waterwheel was too shallow to turn the wheel fast enough. Marshall assigned workers to dig and blast a diversion from the river into the race to deepen the bed. At night the water was allowed to flow through the diversion to scour and deepen the channel.

On the morning of January 24, when Marshall came down to inspect the depth of the tailrace, some glittering particles on the floor of the channel caught his eye. He collected them and put them into the dented crown of his hat. When he showed the pieces of gold to his men, they were curious, but incredulous. Marshall did not know if he had really found gold or not, so he rode to Sutter's Fort to show them to his partner. Marshall and Sutter applied every test for gold that their ingenuity and a handy encyclopedia could devise. Sutter finally pronounced the nuggets to be truly gold and followed Marshall back to Coloma to inspect the site of the strike.

Both men believed that the Coloma find was only a superficial deposit. The workmen at the mill were also quite casual about the discovery. Yet a change had come over the camp. On Sundays and rainy days, the laborers left the mill to pan for gold in other parts of the stream. On February 27 outsiders (friends of one of the workers who had written about the strike) came to the camp and began digging for gold. On March 11, work had progressed on the sawmill to the point where the first log was sawed. The Mormon workmen began to leave, considering their task finished. Most of them decided not to go immediately to Utah, but to try prospecting in the vicinity.

Marshall and Sutter now realized the necessity of Sutter's acquiring title to the land where the strike had been discovered, as the site was outside the boundaries of his grant.

A Sutter employee, Charles Bennett, was sent to the military governor at Monterey, Colonel Richard B. Mason, to obtain the necessary grant. He was given a gold sample and enjoined to secrecy. On his way to Monterey, Bennett stopped at Benicia. There he found the populace excited by a reported coal discovery near Mount Diablo; he could not resist the impulse to top that story. Challenged to substantiate his claim, Bennett displayed his gold sample. In San Francisco (as Yerba Buena had been renamed) Bennett repeated his earlier performance by showing his gold sample. This time an experienced Georgia gold miner, Isaac Humphrey, recognized that Bennett's sample was really gold. By early April, Humphrey had arrived at Coloma. At Monterey, Colonel Mason was unwilling to validate Sutter's title to additional land in the Sacramento Valley and the adjacent foothills.

As more and more prospectors moved into the region, Sutter at first enjoyed a modest prosperity selling to them. He even succeeded in getting out of debt, but then began to experience a series of misfortunes as his workmen ran off to mine the river and goldseekers trampled his fields. Soon every branch of his interconnected business operations gradually ceased to function.

Although the news of the Coloma gold strike had reached San Francisco by mid-February with Bennett's visit, it did not seem to engender any real excitement. On March 15, 1848, a small notice of the discovery appeared on the last page of the San Francisco *Californian*. On March 18, 1848, a similar notice appeared in the *California Star*, the other weekly San Francisco newspaper. On March 25, Sam Brannan, editor of the *Star* and a leader of a Mormon party which had arrived in California in 1846, sent his business associate E. C. Kemble to interview Sutter and Marshall. Kemble returned to San Francisco in early May, full of praise for the agricultural prospects of the country, but unimpressed by the extent of the gold strike. Brannan traveled to Sutter's Fort himself in April and went into a partnership in a store there. He then opened one at Coloma. About May 12, Sam Brannan, now a prominent merchant at New Helvetia, returned to San Francisco with a quinine bottle full of gold dust. Waving his hat, he ran through the streets of the town yelling, "Gold! Gold! Gold from the American River!"

Soon a stampede of goldseekers started, although editor Kemble continued to call it a humbug in the columns of his newspaper, which soon had to close down because of the loss of employees and subscribers. By June 1, half of San Francisco's population had left for Sutter's Fort; by the fifteenth, three-fourths of the eight hundred townspeople had left. Business halted; real estate was sold at bargain prices; seamen deserted their ships in the harbor; soldiers departed from their barracks without permission. San Jose was practically deserted; the only able-bodied men remaining were the prisoners in jail and their guards. Towns as far south as Santa Barbara and Los Angeles lost sizeable percentages of their population to the gold fields.

As this human tide surged toward the Sacramento Valley, labor became unobtainable and all construction ceased. San Francisco and Monterey soon assumed the aspects of ghost towns; buildings fell into disrepair and stores closed down. Prices for mining equipment and food supplies soared to fantastic heights. Transportation to the mines by riverboats, wagons and horses was at a premium. To some extent, these high prices sprang from the custom of reckless spending that became the rule among the goldseekers. By 1849 flour sold for forty-four dollars a barrel; sixteen dollars bought a bushel of potatoes; eggs from around Cape Horn brought ten dollars a dozen. The profit on lumber brought to California was 1000 per cent, because the miners were too busy to cut lumber from the territory's abundant forests. This situation of inflation drew goods from all over the world. Often this influx of goods resulted in a periodic glut, and prices would tumble. Then goods still in their packing cases were left untended on wharves or deliberately sunk in the mud of San Francisco's unpaved streets to provide a footing for pedestrians.

In a few months, news of the California gold strike had spread across the Pacific to Hawaii, to the northwest coast, Mexico, Chile, Peru, Australia and China. During 1848, the rush involved only Pacific countries. The Atlantic community did not take part until the next year.

From less than a hundred goldseekers in March 1848, the number rose to a few hundred in May, a few thousand in June and July, and perhaps eight or ten thousand by the end of the year. Similarly, the amount of gold extracted is something of a mystery. Estimates vary widely, but ten million dollars seems to be a reasonable guess.

The '48ers seem to have had few problems with crime. Claims were seldom jumped; bottles and bags of gold could be left unmolested in cabins and tents. Explanations for this situation are varied: some say that since gold was so easy to find, there was no reason to steal; others contend that the criminal element of the gold rush had not yet arrived; many maintain that the relatively small numbers of goldseekers caused them to possess a neighborly esprit de corps.

For a short while the extent of the gold diggings was limited to the south fork of the American River. Soon the area of mining had spread north from the American River to the Feather River and as far south as the Tuolumne River. By the summer of 1848, the entire area of the mother-lode country had been prospected, although extensive mining operations awaited the coming of the larger number of goldseekers in 1849. The so-called mother-lode country stretched for 120 miles, beginning north of Coloma and continuing as far south as Mariposa, comprising a belt of gold fields that lay along the slopes of the Sierra Nevada. This field was so named because of the erroneous belief that it contained one continuous mother vein of ore. Although the mother-lode country was the first area to be exploited, it was not the only area which drew gold miners. Some of the richest finds were discovered north of the mother-lode country and deeper into the Sierra Nevada mountains. There was also a quite separate series of diggings along the west and north end of the Great Valley of California, known as the Trinity Mines. This area never approached the output of the Sierra fields, however. Although a wide variety of gadgets and equipment were used to find and dig gold, the only mining tool employed in the early days of the strike was a knife. With a knife, prospectors would gather particles of gold which had been brought to the surface by years of erosion. Later, one of the most popular methods for washing gold ore was panning, which was probably introduced by the Georgia miner Isaac Humphrey when he arrived at Coloma. The use of the gold pan for this purpose did not originate in the American southeast, where earlier gold strikes had been made, but dated back to antiquity. The California miners soon learned to improvise if a pan was not available. Then a wooden bowl or even a basin-shaped Indian basket was used to wash water through the gold ore.

Humphrey is also thought to be the first miner in California to utilize a machine called the rocker—essentially a short trough, equipped with a handle for rocking it and a hopper at the higher end to screen out the large stones. There were cleats across the floor of the trough which trapped loose pieces of gold from the gravel as it was washed through. The same mechanical principle that caused gold to settle to the bottom of the pan could be used to trap it in the cleats. Although the rocker was an inefficient operation and allowed much gold to be lost, it was so much faster than panning that it became the most widely used contrivance of the time. Although new techniques were introduced into the mining fields all during the gold rush, however, none of them ever completely displaced the knife.

Within a few months, the gold fever spread across the continent. Missouri heard of the California strike in August of 1848. In its issue of August 19, the New York *Herald* printed a letter with a San Francisco address, which announced the gold strike. Other news items about California gold appeared frequently in the eastern press. Even wider publicity was given the event when President James K. Polk announced the discovery of gold in his official message to Congress. The dignity of a presidential message, in addition to the early arrival in Washington of a tea caddy loaded to the brim with 230 ounces, fifteen pennyweights, and nine grains of gold, banished all lingering doubts about the reality and extent of the gold strike.

Now the gold fever swept through the eastern United States, including prim New England. It invaded Great Britain and caused great excitement in western and central Europe from the Baltic to the Mediterranean. Soon everyone with the price of passage eagerly traveled to California.

There were three main routes by which the '49ers arrived in California. The first was the well-traveled route around Cape Horn to San Francisco. Even more Americans reached California by way of a sea voyage to Central America, across the Isthmus of Panama or Nicaragua, then by ship to California. Another principal route was the overland trek across the Great Plains to the Pacific Coast.

Few New Englanders elected the overland route. Instead, they became argonauts like Jason and his companions who sought the Golden Fleece, sailing around Cape Horn via the route so familiar to the Boston fur and hide ships. Many voluntary associations were formed to enable individuals to travel to California; these companies never endured once the members had arrived safely at their destinations. Then the shareholders quickly scattered to seek their individual fortunes. A few companies of goldseekers were financed by stay-at-home investors in return for a guaranteed percentage of the profits, in the same manner as English merchant adventurers had financed the Pilgrim Fathers.

In 1849, Americans formed over one hundred seafaring companies, whose records have survived. These organizations averaged over forty members, although their numbers varied from only ten to as many as 150 men. Typical of these companies was the Bunker Hill Mining & Trading Company, composed of thirty "mechanics" from Charlestown, Cambridge and Somerville, who had invested five hundred dollars each. There was the exclusive North Western Company of Boston, composed of the Adamses, Doors and Whipples, who invested a thousand dollars each, and who were able to buy a new clipper brig. Normally, these companies could not afford to buy new vessels and had to purchase instead the oldest, most decrepit and slowest ships available. The gold disease in nine months drained a port such as Nantucket of one-quarter of its voting population. During the same period, eight hundred men left New Bedford for the mother-lode country. In all, 150 ships sailed from Boston to California in 1849, and 166 more in 1850. During the entire year of 1849, 775 vessels of all types, including a few steamers, left eastern ports for California.

On the company ships, which were usually manned by shareholders, strict discipline was impossible. The stockholders elected the captain, and a majority vote decided upon the ports of call along the way. Typhus often took a heavy toll of the passengers during the five- to eight-month voyage.

The 18,000-mile voyage around Cape Horn was considered too slow by some impatient gold hunters. They usually traveled the shortcut by way of Central America. This was the more dangerous of the two sea routes, since it involved crossing Mexico or Central America where malaria was prevalent. A ship would be taken from the east coast of the United States or Europe to the east coast of Mexico, Nicaragua or Panama. A rough overland journey took the goldseekers to the west coast of these countries, where they often faced a long delay before catching a ship to California. Whereas the journey around Cape Horn was a voyage of months, the Panama-Nicaragua route could be traveled in weeks. Delay in the fever-ridden regions of Central America was dangerous and many emigrants died during the wait.

The route by way of Panama had been opened not long before the gold rush. In 1848, ostensibly to furnish mail service to California and Oregon, Congress voted a subsidy for a steamship line with Atlantic and Pacific runs to Panama.

Two steamship companies were then established, the Pacific Mail Steamship Company and the United States Mail Steamship Company. Soon the goldseekers fought for places aboard their ships, and passenger prices became exorbitant. For the regular trip from New York to Chagrés, on the Atlantic coast of the Isthmus, and from Panama City on the West Coast to San Francisco, a steerage accommodation could cost as much as a thousand dollars. The Panama route also involved travel by native boat and by mule train.

An alternative route through Nicaragua also drew some traffic. Although the land mass to be traversed was considerably wider than at Panama, there was a waterway composed of a river and a lake which could be followed to within seventeen miles of the Pacific coast. Since Nicaragua is further north, the overall journey across its surface was several hundred miles shorter than by way of Panama. This route did not really get into full operation until 1851, and then proved quicker than that through Panama. In the late 1850's, however, revolution and governmental instability in Nicaragua made this route more hazardous to follow. In 1855 the Panama route became more popular when a railroad was completed which covered the forty-seven miles across the Isthmus. The route by way of Mexico became less popular with the goldseekers, since the land mass to be traversed was greater and the accommodations more primitive than those of the Central American alternatives.

Most '49ers followed the well-established overland trails which led from the Mississippi River to California. Despite the greater delays this route imposed, arrival in California was surer and safer than along any of the sea routes.

Superficially the overland migrations of 1849 duplicated the migrations of the earlier period; actually the differences were very significant. By 1849 the danger of a serious Indian attack had been almost eliminated, and the possibilities of becoming lost greatly reduced. The routes had been so well traveled that the emigrants were often guided by wagon ruts and the discarded belongings of earlier travelers.

On the other hand, new difficulties were encountered. The Asiatic cholera traveled eastward along the overland trails with returnees from California, striking hard at incoming emigrants. The great number of pack animals diminished the grass supply along the trails. Sometimes men and animals drained the wells. Crossing the desert between the Humboldt Sink and the Carson-Truckee region resulted in several near-tragedies. As a result, a privately financed relief society was organized in Sacramento for the purpose of sending food and medical supplies to groups stranded on the desert, and bringing them safely to California.

Most overland migrants came from the Middle West, but there were many exceptions. One New England outfit, the Overland Company, composed of fifty youths from Roxbury, marched overland in gray-and-gold uniforms with seven four-horse wagons, thirty-one mules, two colored servants, four musicians and six dogs. This group walked to Sacramento after intense suffering, caused by their own inexperience and a heavy mortality rate among their mules.

Several hundred thousand people from all parts of the world poured into California from 1848 to 1854, the height of the rush. Possibly 95 per cent of the migrating population were men: Americans, Europeans and Chinese seldom took their wives with them. Only the Latin Americans often took their families with them. These men, most of them young, were goldseekers who hoped to make a quick profit and then return to their home towns. Freed from all the restraints of home, they made California a rough, bathless, masculine society. A surprisingly large percentage of the migrants were highly literate men, who graphically recorded their adventures. It was a time of extreme informality. Who you had been in the "States" did not matter. Prostitution openly flourished; excessive drinking was the accepted norm; gambling became rife; rough horseplay and crude practical jokes were an accepted form of recreation. There was no established government in the gold fields, so justice there was quick and informal.

Despite the atmosphere of fellowship and hospitality which prevailed in the mining camps, the miners were not tolerant toward all of their fellows. European miners, such as the Irish and Germans, were generally tolerated, although when the Irish emerged as the professional office-holding class in San Francisco, vigilante violence erupted against them. The clannish French were probably the most disliked of the Europeans. They were dubbed "Keskydees" from a French phrase that they seemed to be constantly repeating. The victims of physical violence and legalized dis-

crimination were the Latin American miners and the Chinese. These
groups, so different in physical appearance and customs from the Americans, were looked down upon as inferior nuisances. The Latin American
miners were specially taxed and so maltreated that they gradually left the
diggings as prospectors. The Chinese were violently discriminated against
and allowed to mine only the worked-over sites that white men had
abandoned. The Chinese were also the objects of a special tax, which was
the greatest single source of California state revenue (about half of the
state's income) between 1850 and 1870.

Of the many who came to California, some men struck it rich, or failed
and promptly went home. Others, successful or not, remained to become
permanent residents in the new territory soon to be a state, in September
1850. Still others, who did not find wealth in California, migrated to new
gold discoveries in Nevada, British Columbia and Australia.

Going to California proved to be a good way of breaking unwanted
ties with a fiancée, a wife or parents. Many men used it as a form of
Victorian divorce. Criminals, branded as undesirables in their own communities, could lose themselves in the tide of strangers surging toward
California. "Oh, what was your name in the States?" ran an irreverent
popular song.

In the early days, mining operations were characterized by vigorous
individualism. Although many mining companies had been formed in the
eastern United States or Europe by California-bound miners, once these
companies had transported emigrants to the diggings, they dissolved.
Their members each went their separate ways into the gold fields, for no
one cared to share a gold strike with others. A partner or two was
sufficient to work the diggings with a knife, pan or sometimes rocker or
cradle.

Working and living conditions in the gold fields were primitive. Food
was expensive, and most miners either would not or could not take time
to cook it properly. Upset stomachs and diarrhea were common complaints. Winters in the California mountains could be very cold, and few
miners took the time to erect any but the most primitive cabins for
protection against the weather. Most men found gold mining, immersed
to the knees or the hips in a cold mountain stream, uncomfortable work.

Very often newcomers found that the best claims had already been
worked and that the rewards of mining were uncertain. As a result, once
experienced, mining did not recommend itself to many hopeful goldseekers. Discouraged miners returned to the cities, where they found work as
merchants, gamblers or laborers. Many men, later prominent in American
politics or finance, obtained their start in shopkeeping or other forms of
small business during the California gold rush. Two men who stayed in
California to make prominent financial careers for themselves were Mark

Hopkins and William T. Coleman; two others who returned East to use their profits to launch successful endeavors in meat packing and wagon making, respectively, were Philip Armour and John Studebaker. All four men received their business start in brawling, bustling Hangtown (later called Placerville).

By the end of 1850, most of the loose ore had been panned out of California's streams, and a new phase of mining began. Incorporated enterprise with its greater capital investment gradually preempted the mining areas. The days of the small miners were over. The art of placer mining (with a pan or bowl) was never wholly abandoned, and as recently as the great depression of the 1930's, unemployed persons eeked out a living by placer-mining the worked-out areas of the mother lode.

From 1848 to 1857, California gold fields produced gold worth $370,-000,000, or an average of $41,000,000 a year. The total worth of the gold extracted through 1865 might have reached $750,000,000. The biggest authenticated golden nugget was found in the Feather River in 1849. It weighed 161 pounds and was worth $38,000. At the height of the gold rush, California produced one hundred tons of gold. In 1859 California gold mining was so extensive that three-quarters of all the metal extracted in the United States was mined in the Pacific region. Gold mining for years surpassed in value the extraction of all other mineral products in the state. Finally, in 1907, petroleum exceeded gold in value of production in California. As the twentieth century wore on, gold production sagged. With the low fixed government price of the 1930's which has continued to the present, gold mining gradually ground to a virtual halt. In all, California's total production of gold exceeded 100,000,000 fine ounces worth about $2,333,000,000.

Gold provided the basis upon which a society of hundreds of thousands of people could be founded. It had one other immediate impact—it suddenly created an urban center in the Far West—San Francisco.

Under the name of Yerba Buena, San Francisco had been rudely surveyed on January 1, 1835, when a plaza and a few streets were plotted on a piece of paper. By 1839 some mud huts had appeared facing the plaza and along the Calle de la Fundación. Bridle trails linked the mission Dolores, the presidio and Yerba Buena. These trails gradually gave way to the rough tracks of ox carts. By 1846, at the time of the American conquest, a dozen buildings of various kinds and sixty inhabitants were all the hamlet could boast.

A single American warship, the *Portsmouth*, effected the conquest of San Francisco. Its captain, John B. Montgomery, appointed Lieutenant Washington Bartlett as military commander of Yerba Buena. Bartlett thought that this name was inappropriate, and in January 1847, with a suitable escort and proper ceremonies, he renamed the city San Francisco, changed the name of the plaza to Portsmouth Square, and that of its principal thoroughfare to Montgomery Street.

By the beginning of 1848, American-occupied California was already stirring, and the increased commerce was reflected in San Francisco's growth. Wharves had been built, and along its streets were thirty-five adobe public buildings and warehouses, and 160 frame structures of various types. Nearly eight hundred people lived there.

As the goldseekers poured into San Francisco as the principal seaport on the way to the gold fields, the city grew rapidly. Its waterfront and bay were cluttered by as many as three hundred abandoned ships. These vessels stayed on as a permanent part of the city's waterfront until they rotted and sank, were dismantled for their wood and fittings, or burned in one of San Francisco's periodic fires. About six hundred structures were added to the city by the fall of 1849, many of them crudely built affairs. Some were merely tents with wooden floors and walls. The city was a veritable tinderbox. Newcomers, drunk and sober, were careless with fire; some of the many conflagrations were the work of arsonists. Between Christmas Eve, 1849, and June 22, 1851, six destructive fires burned through the city. One, called "the Biggest Fire," leveled three-quarters of the town. After each fire, San Francisco rebuilt itself, often with redwood stolen from the forests of the Contra Costa ranches owned by the Peraltas.

After the sixth fire, San Franciscans looked for more fireproof materials to construct their buildings. Granite was imported from China; Australia, Great Britain and New York sent brick; Hawaii shipped blocks of lava. Henry W. Halleck in 1853 built the old Montgomery Block, the first four-story office building in San Francisco. Its brick, plaster, window glass and iron fittings came around the Horn. Built at great cost, it was called "Halleck's Folly," yet its offices were always crowded with tenants. Members of the San Francisco bar soon adopted it, and for years it was the headquarters for the legal profession. San Francisco's beachfront was developed for additional space, and eventually the cove around which the city had originally been built was entirely filled in. By January 1850, waterfront lots sold for nearly $1,500. In 1853 ninety-nine-year leases on choice lots sold at prices from $8,000 to $27,000.

By 1850 San Francisco boasted 20,000 inhabitants, in 1852 about 36,000, in 1860 57,000, and by 1870 almost 150,000! By 1870 it had a larger population than Cleveland, Detroit or Washington, D. C.

Other important populated settlements were Sacramento, which grew up in the vicinity of Sutter's Fort on the lower Sacramento River; Marysville on the Feather River, and Stockton on the lower San Joaquin. All of these towns served as interior distribution points for the diggings. Some mining towns, such as Hangtown and Sonora, served to funnel supplies into the hills. Rude mining camps sprang up everywhere: Rough and Ready, Liars Flat, Humbug, Red Dog, Cut-Throat Bar, You Bet, Gouge Eye and Poverty Bar. In 1852, El Dorado County in the heart of the mining country was the most heavily populated county in the state. In 1860 over one-fifth of the California population lived in cities of over 2,500 people; in 1870 four out of every ten Californians lived in cities of this size.

Overnight California had gained a population of 92,000 as counted by the federal census of 1850. According to all indications, there were many persons in the hills and in other inaccessible places where the census-takers never ventured. A special, more complete state census in 1852 counted 255,000 people. Although everyone thought and talked about mining, only 100,000 men were actually engaged in this occupation in 1852. The remaining population were suppliers and servants of those who did mine. Many tradesmen, businessmen and "mechanics" were already at work in 1852. There were also gamblers, prostitutes and saloonkeepers, and many people in the service industries of the mining camps and towns. In addition, there was a large floating, loafing population, consisting of indolent wanderers who aimlessly moved from place to place.

It is probable that California's population grew at the rate of 150–175 per cent in the decade between 1850 and 1860. The California trend to urban centers was unusual in the West. This was a pattern characteristic of the eastern United States and Europe, but for this trend to develop during the first decades of California's American settlement was very unusual. Over 20 per cent of California's population was urban in 1860, while in Ohio, after the same number of years of rapid settlement, only 1 per cent of the population lived in cities. Illinois, after a decade of bur-geoning settlement, did not possess a single town as large as 2,500 people in 1830.

The California gold strike probably surpassed in worldwide signifi-cance any local event in any other American state. The major countries of the world were profoundly affected by the inward flow of California bullion and the outward flow of emigrants. There has been some differ-ence of opinion among economists whether the gold influx by itself raised general world prices. During the years 1849–57, a majority of bankers and businessmen felt that the increased gold supply meant prosperity, and their optimism encouraged widespread speculation. Today most econo-mists would say that the shift of capital and men from more developed countries to the thinly populated area of California was beneficial, since the loss in resources at the point of departure was less than the gain from their employment in the underdeveloped United States.

An unexpected by-product of the California strike was the discovery of rich placers in Australia. In the fall of 1849, a young Australian, Edward

H. Hargraves, prospecting on the Stanislaus River in California, noticed that the geological formations there were similar to those he had seen in New South Wales. He returned to Australia in 1851 and quickly discovered gold in Lewis Pounds Creek. This led to an Australian mining effort which rivaled that of California.

The American merchant marine was also profoundly affected by the gold bonanza. The argonauts sailed hundreds of ships on a one-way trip to San Francisco Bay. Much worn tonnage was thereby removed from the American merchant marine. Thus a shortage of merchant ships occurred just as the demands of the California market shot freight rates skyward. This combination of events led to the introduction of the spectacular clipper ship.

Although the clipper ship existed earlier, it was not until 1849 that it reached its highest development. The chance for profit from the California trade, the lucrative China-Great Britain commerce, and the Australian gold boom, all contributed to its growth and widespread use. Clippers were not only speedy, but also economical to operate. Since there was little except gold dust to bring back from San Francisco, the clippers generally sailed on from California to China. Cargoes subject to deterioration, such as tea, spices and dried fruits, were carried. Clippers were essentially cargo carriers; passenger traffic was incidental. The clippers' greatest year was 1853, and the short-lived clipper boom died with the panic of 1857. The clipper ship made the American merchant marine the foremost in the world.

One indirect effect of the California gold rush was the great influx of immigrants into the United States. Until 1842, the number had never exceeded 100,000 in a single year, and as late as 1847, it had been only 200,000. After the gold rush, business expanded first under the stimulus of the exodus to California and then the swelling pile of bullion. Job opportunities grew. Hired men on farms, factory hands and clerks in the eastern United States stampeded west. Consequently, new immigrants became welcome on the farms and factories of the East. Immigration into the United States rose to 408,000 in 1851 and reached a peak of 460,000 in 1854. These immigrants expanded the American home market and furnished manpower for the industrial boom of the 1850's, when Great Britain invested widely in American railroads.

The gold rush also had a stimulating effect on price structure and business activity in the United States and Great Britain. Because of its close economic and banking ties with the European continent, Great Britain spread the effects of this commercial activity throughout the western world.

The last half of the nineteenth century saw a great commercial and industrial boom and the flowering of capitalism in many western countries. As the middle class in these nations became strong both economically and politically, various types of representative government were established all over Europe. These conditions were partly caused by new inventions and widespread railroad construction during the period from 1820 to 1850, as well as by liberalized trade laws resulting from the revolutions of 1848. Still the California and Australia gold rushes, with their tremendous production of bullion, played a significant role in these developments. The gold discovery in California, and the resultant strikes in the western United States, Canada and Australia, had an impact which reverberated through the years, ending only when World War I and the Great Depression of 1929 brought the entire era to a close.

FIFTEEN

California Founds a New Economy

SOON the simple mining techniques of poking with a knife, panning gold, or using the rocker or cradle gave way to more elaborate methods which could utilize ore that was not so easily reached and could also produce gold in greater quantities. These more elaborate methods had long been known in other parts of the world. One procedure involved the use of quicksilver to separate gold from foreign matter. Quicksilver has the property of amalgamating with gold, but does not compound with the base elements. This amalgam of gold and mercury can be reduced by vaporizing the mercury in a retort. Luckily, one of the few quicksilver mines in North America had been found about 1845 at New Almaden near San Jose. Supplemented by mercury shipments from all over the world, the New Almaden mine supplied the miners' needs. Its output of mercury eventually reached 220,000 pounds a month.

Another advance in mining techniques in California was the utilization of "long toms." These long toms operated on the same principle as cradles; however, they were longer and also stationary. Long toms could work a great volume of gold ore with the help of a continuous flow of water. Later the long tom was followed by the employment of the sluice, a series of open troughs with cleats or wooden blocks on the bottom to trap the gold.

The miners were not long contented with working deposits along the banks of rivers. As early as 1849, some miners formed organizations to dam and divert rivers from their normal channels so that their beds could be worked. This process was called river mining. By 1860 the river bottoms had been picked clean of their easily obtainable ore and were abandoned to the hardworking, patient Chinese.

Deep-gravel mining attempted to tap the placer deposits washed down by prehistoric rivers and later buried under layers of rock, lava and dirt. An early attempt to exploit these deposits involved digging shafts or tunnels into the earth, a slow and expensive process. This method of mining came into vogue during the decade between 1850 and 1860. On several occasions, tunnels 1000–2000 feet long were dug. In the end, this method (also called "drift mining") was too speculative and costly to become very widespread.

Another method of attacking the deep gravel was hydraulic mining, which began in California as early as 1853. Hydraulic mining was a California innovation, whereas all the methods previously described had been known in medieval or even ancient times. In employing the technique of hydraulicking, canvas hoses were used to wash down the sides of hills overlaying placer deposits. Wooden flumes carried water to the top of a hill high enough to enable the descending liquid to build up great pressure. As the water fell through iron pipes, it was forced out through a nozzle at the foot of the hill with sufficient force to wear away hills or even mountains. After being loosened by the water, the ore was washed through a long series of sluices which extracted the gold. Because this type of mining required great capital outlays by mining operators, it was 1856 or 1857 before it became common. In addition, this method was restricted to places where conditions permitted its practice. The area north of Coloma was better suited to this technique than the area southward.

The third type of extracting gold from deep gravel was called vein, lode or quartz mining. Using this process, miners found veins from which gold had eroded, and would extract the gold from the solid rock in which it was embedded. Quartz mines were opened as early as 1849 and captured the imagination of the interested public. Californians, eastern Americans and Europeans invested heavily in quartz-mining companies. It has been estimated that by 1853 at least twenty California quartz-mining companies were being financed in London with a total capital outlay of ten million dollars. These ventures were highly speculative, and almost all the early companies collapsed in bankruptcy.

At first Californians were inept at tracing a vein, sinking the shaft, extracting the ore and crushing it. Borrowing techniques from the Spanish Americans, Cornishmen, Germans and Georgians, California miners eventually perfected this type of mining. Still this remained a time-consuming technique requiring patience and a heavy capital investment. It is doubtful if the money invested in quartz mining during the decade of the fifties ever produced a profit. However, the techniques so painstakingly developed in California were used in 1859–60 to mine the Comstock Lode in Nevada.

As the mining frontier expanded, San Francisco bankers and merchants were quick to reap its profits. At this time San Francisco was the largest city west of Missouri. It had no real rivals as a port; San Diego was located too far south of the main area of mining activity, and Portland to the north was a mere trading post at the junction of the Willamette and Columbia rivers. Consequently, San Francisco became the storehouse and trading post for the interior of California, as well as the manufacturing center for the mining machinery used in California, Oregon and Nevada. Although San Francisco financiers had recovered from their early speculative binge by the middle and late fifties, they continued to invest selectively in mining. Yet they soon developed a remarkable sales resistance to the most persuasive prospector. Since San Francisco money men extended credit to the businessmen of the mining region, they indirectly financed even more of the quest for gold than was readily apparent.

As the queen city of the Pacific region, San Francisco soon grasped control of Nevada's most spectacular mining area, the Comstock Lode, in 1859–60. The speculative urge to invest in Nevada's mineral wealth became so widespread that even sober Reverend Henry Durant, founder of the institution which eventually became the University of California, backed a mine. In a sense, the Comstock towns of Gold Hill and Virginia City became industrial suburbs of San Francisco. For a period of about twenty years, San Francisco ownership drained the Comstock wealth to construct the ornate new buildings that soon dotted the city's landscape. This city's money men also employed their profits to diversify its business and industry. By 1880, when Nevada's Comstock Lode had been gradually worked out, San Francisco's financiers abandoned the enterprise, leaving that part of Nevada to the unpromising future reserved for a worn-out mining area. It really was no exaggeration when a San Francisco newspaper boasted, "Nevada is the child of California."

Although California gold had created a few San Francisco millionaires and a fair number of wealthy men, it was Nevada gold and silver that made the multimillionaires of that city.

Nevada mining stocks were sold on the San Francisco Stock Exchange, which was founded in September 1862, largely to provide an organized mechanism for financing Nevada's boom. So great was the speculative orgy that the Exchange was kept open for both morning and afternoon sessions. In 1863 Sacramento and Stockton opened their own stock exchanges to share in the financing of the mining bonanza.

In time, what New York was to the nation, San Francisco was to the West. When the West complained of being exploited as a colonial appendage of the East Coast and Europe, San Francisco was the source through which foreign capital was lent throughout the West. That city shared in the exploitation. In 1868 Henry George wrote, "Not a settler in all the Pacific States and Territories but must pay San Francisco tribute. . . ." A smile from San Francisco's financiers and a mining region could develop; a frown from its money men and the region's development was seriously impeded. Since San Francisco capitalists preferred Nevada to Idaho or Montana as an area for speculation, these latter territories developed slowly. Even the coming of the railroads did not seriously shake San Francisco's preeminence. The habit of shopping in "the city" was difficult to break. Large importers and wholesale dealers with their headquarters there saw to it that it remained the queen city. Under pressure from the merchants of San Francisco, railroad rate schedules were so drawn that "the city" was protected from the competition of settlements in the interior.

Because of the presence of a great urban center within California's boundaries, and its quick rise to statehood, there are those who argue that the state was only geographically part of the Old West. The phrase "West of the West" has been used to describe it.

Although an indeterminate amount of gold was transported out of the state by homeward-bound miners, it is believed that even more gold entered the marts of commerce within California. Stores sprang up in the most isolated towns and camps to cater to the miners. At first these frontier stores carried only the most basic items, but they soon stocked any item for which there was a market. In 1850 the number of merchants in California was exceeded only by the quantity of miners.

Storekeepers were only slightly more respected by the miners than professional gamblers. The reasons for this thinly veiled contempt for the storekeeper were apparent. Frontier merchants sold on a strictly-cash basis, since no one dared extend credit to itinerant prospectors who might well be broke or out of the country by the next week. Prices were high both because of costs and a lack of competition. As a result, many fortunes were made from the mercantile trade, both in the mining camps and Stockton and Sacramento. This was an age in California when shirts sold for forty dollars, and a pair of boots could command twenty dollars. A loaf of bread sold for fifty to seventy-five cents; eastern whisky brought thirty dollars a quart. It was also an era when the purchasing power of money in the eastern United States was several times what it is today. At the height of the gold rush, laundry service was so costly in California that it was cheaper to send dirty clothes to Hawaii or China to be washed.

Transportation was a great problem in the early gold rush days. Yet so strong was the demand that men overcame all obstacles to furnish the speedy transportation craved by the goldseekers. From the great seaport of San Francisco, steamboat transportation ran to the central valley by way of the Sacramento, San Joaquin and lower Feather rivers. Coastal vessels and sailing craft journeyed to ports as far north as British Columbia and as far south as San Diego. After having been transported by steamboat, teams of oxen or mules dragged freight to its ultimate destination. Even the most remote mining camp had some sort of freight service along the nearest navigable river. Pack animals were used when the rough terrain made travel by wagons impossible. Soon stagecoaches carried passengers, treasure and light freight over the newly built roads. In 1849 the first stage service into the mother-lode country began when James Birch pioneered a one-man wagon line from Sacramento to Coloma. In many places ferries gave way to permanent bridges. In 1850 Hall and Crandall established a stage line between San Francisco and the state capital of San Jose. It took a stagecoach nine hours to jolt over this forty-five-mile run.

On New Year's Day in 1854, about 80 per cent of all the small stage companies traveling from Sacramento to the mines were consolidated into the California Stage Company, running stages over routes 1500 miles in length. Consolidation and extension of service grew so quickly that by 1857 a 700-mile stage line had been extended to Portland, Oregon.

The express business began in the early summer of 1849 when Alexander Todd asked payment for making the long trip from the mines to the single post office in San Francisco to collect the miners' mail. He offered to deliver any mail at the rate of an ounce of gold dust per letter. His list of clients grew until he had signed up more than 2000. Soon he added other services, which included carrying the miners' gold dust and depositing it for them in San Francisco. Thus began Todd & Company's Express, which operated until 1851. From its headquarters in Stockton, its service expanded until a daily express ran between the mining camps and San Francisco. The lucrative express business soon drew others into the field. In 1849, Weld and Company also opened an express line which ran between San Francisco and Marysville by way of Benicia and Sacramento.

Late in 1849, the powerful eastern firm, the Adams and Company Express, appeared in California. It quickly absorbed several smaller rivals. Although Adams and Company expanded their service to all corners of the state and introduced many new services to attract customers, a new rival soon appeared—Wells, Fargo & Company. This latter outfit, commonly called Wells Fargo Express, was also eastern in origin. It established branches in mining camps and towns all over the new state. The newer company multiplied its services and thereby greatly expanded its business. Adams and Company fought back, and for about three years there was a sharp contest between the two. Then on "Black Friday," February 23, 1855, Adams and Company failed and Wells Fargo emerged as the preeminent express company in California.

In the early years Wells Fargo did not usually operate its own stage lines, but utilized instead the existing facilities to transport its freight and valuables. Incidentally, the preeminence of Wells Fargo did not drive all rivals from the freight business. In 1860, 250 local express companies, many of them very small, provided freight and passenger service to the inhabitants of California.

Soon the steam railroad began to operate in California. At least as early as 1852, people, including William T. Sherman, the later Civil War general, pondered the feasibility of establishing a railroad linking Sacramento, with its excellent river steamers, to the mother-lode country. By 1854 a young engineer, Theodore Judah, was making surveys of such a route.

In early 1855, after more grandiose schemes had been scrapped, ground was broken for a railroad to link Sacramento with the railroad-sponsored town of Folsom, about twenty-five miles to the northeast. On August 9 of that year, the first rail was laid; soon a trial run by a wood-burning locomotive was made over the finished portion of the road. Finally, on Washington's Birthday in 1856, the Sacramento Valley line to Folsom was completed.

San Francisco and San Jose were linked by a railroad in 1864, the same year that a line was built linking the small dusty city of Los Angeles with the ocean at Wilmington. A gaudy black-and-gold locomotive called the San Gabriel drew cars slowly along the tracks. Scornful vaqueros used to race their mounts alongside the San Gabriel, shouting derisive and profane Spanish phrases at the puffing, cranky locomotive.

The California counties south of Monterey were not directly affected by the gold rush. This region continued to exist much as it had in pre-1849 days. As late as 1860, Los Angeles had only 1,600 inhabitants.

One way in which the southern half of California was affected by the gold rush was the great boom in California agriculture. The tremendous influx of population increased the demand for beef and raised cattle prices far beyond the peaks of the hide and tallow days. Then steers had sold for four or five dollars a head. Now the same cattle brought from seventy-five dollars to one hundred dollars in San Francisco and the mining centers of the north.

The southern ranchers scrambled to meet the northern California demand, and soon a vigorous north-south trade developed. A drover (cattle buyer) would journey down to the grazing districts of the south, carrying thousands of dollars in gold to purchase cattle for the north. Naturally he was a popular target for highwaymen and thieves. Nonetheless, until the late 1860's when the Southern Pacific Railroad was opened linking the north and south, many thousands of cattle were bought and driven from the pasture lands of southern California to the hungry miners and city dwellers of the upper part of the state. Cattle drives, much less celebrated than the ones from Texas to Kansas, stretching five hundred to six hundred miles in length, became commonplace. A trail boss and several vaqueros drove as many as two or three thousand head of cattle northward at a time.

For a few years the ranch owners enjoyed an unparalleled prosperity. Their wives covered the earthen floors of their adobes with expensive rugs. A few even put in windowpanes. Later this extravagance was sharply curtailed, when the land titles of these early ranchers were questioned under American law, and outsiders lowered the prices they could charge.

The extremely high prices for cattle attracted competition from the East. Cattle driven from the Missouri Valley, Texas and New Mexico began to appear in the markets of gold-rush California. This competition ended the cattle boom in California by 1856, when prices slumped badly.

Southern California's pastoral era came to an unhappy end for many reasons. A "great drought" scorched the pasture lands between 1862 and 1864. Swarms of locusts added to the general distress. To protect farmers, the California legislature passed a "no fence law" forbidding stockmen to allow their cattle and sheep to roam at will. These events nearly eliminated the great Mexican (Californio) landowners and ranches. A colorful era came to a close.

Sheep prices in southern California also skyrocketed with the gold discovery in 1848. During the 1840's the Californios had allowed their sheep herds to deteriorate too badly to sell them as prosperously as they had sold their cattle. Still the southern Californios drove their sheep northward in large numbers. From the east, competition was keen. From 1852 to 1857, about 500,000 sheep were brought in from New Mexico by way of Arizona. At the height of this period, one animal sold for sixteen dollars, but the price soon plummeted much lower.

After the drought of 1862–64, sheep raising expanded into the cattle lands. The demand for wool products during the Civil War caused its production to jump from five and a half million pounds in 1862 to nine million pounds in 1867, and to twenty-two million pounds in 1871. Profits ranged from 50 to 100 per cent before sheep herds suffered from a drought in 1873. Sheep raising remained an important industry until increased land values in southern California dictated a shift to other uses.

General agriculture in California first suffered from the gold rush, when settlers abandoned their holdings to rush for gold. Soon the high price of farm products from Hawaii, Oregon and South America caused many unlucky miners to return to their farms and ranches. Since most Americans felt that irrigation was too costly during the gold rush, corn production was limited to the north coast valley, the moist bottom lands on the lower Sacramento River, and the San Gabriel Valley. Wheat had been grown during the mission phase, and Sutter had grown it in quantity during the time when his empire was at its peak. In California before the influx of gold miners in March 1848, the price of wheat was only four dollars a bushel. By the end of the year the price had greatly jumped. As a result of this stimulus, by 1850 17,328 bushels had been raised, and two years later production had risen to 300,000 bushels. By the end of the fifties, California had produced about six million bushels of wheat. By 1858 California was exporting wheat around Cape Horn to New York.

During the early fifties, barley was grown in California, since it was in great demand as animal feed. By 1850 the state raised 9,700 bushels, but just two years later the total amount grown was over two million bushels.

Raising vegetables was almost forced upon California when the influx of population began. The miners at first developed scurvy from a monotonous salt-meat diet. They soon demanded vegetables to combat this disease, bidding the price of greens to phenomenal heights. American farmers reaped a quick reward. Then the market broke when Latin American miners, forcibly driven from the goldfields, began raising vegetables in great quantities. While the vegetable boom lasted, the returns were fantastic. Several farmers planted 150 acres in potatoes, tomatoes and onions near San Jose. This truck farming yielded a return of two hundred thousand dollars in a single season. Four men planted sixteen acres of potatoes in northern California and reaped forty thousand dollars.

The importance of California farming was indicated in 1851, 1852 and 1853, when Agricultural and Mineral fairs were held at San Francisco and Sacramento. Cash rewards and other premiums were offered for prize yields. In 1854 interest in farming was put on a more permanent basis when the State Agricultural Society was founded. The number of California farmers rose from less than 1,500 at the start of the fifties to over 20,000 at the close of the period. The increase in California farmers continued, until by 1870 over 57,000 claimed agriculture as their source of livelihood.

California's rich soils and favorable climate allowed its farmers to grow all necessary crops, including sugar cane, raw silk, tobacco, coffee and tea. These crops were partly or entirely abandoned in 1870 when California's isolation was ended by the building of the first transcontinental railroad. But California's agriculture received no permanent setback, since its farmers simply turned to those crops which California could grow better than the rest of the nation. The railroad link enabled California products to find markets in the eastern United States.

At first none of the infant industries of California in 1848 were able to maintain production when their employees rushed to the diggings. It was not long, however, before astute men realized that there could be as much gold in supplying the needs of miners as in panning for the precious metal.

As early as 1849, iron casting began in California when two brothers, James and Peter Donohue, opened a foundry that was one day to become the great Union Iron Works.

By the winter of 1849–50, San Francisco had become a bustling manufacturing center with foundries, flour mills, shipbuilding yards and factories. Mining tools and machinery were locally produced in San Francisco for use in the gold fields. By trial and error, foundry managers learned not to try to compete in the manufacture of products that could be made more cheaply elsewhere. Instead they learned to concentrate upon items which could not be easily transported.

Wool from California's sheep was woven into cloth and cattle hides were tanned into leather in San Francisco. Using raw sugar from the Hawaiian Islands, a refinery opened on San Francisco Bay in 1860. By 1867–68, there were fifteen iron foundries in San Francisco, employing 1,200 workers. Their combined products in 1867 were valued at over two million dollars. At that time two-thirds of all the manufacturing in California was conducted in San Francisco.

As early as 1860, there were nearly one hundred grist mills scattered throughout California. About three hundred sawmills were busy making lumber out of California's redwood, Douglas fir and ponderosa pine. While California's gold mines annually earned forty-five million dollars, by 1860 manufacturing had grown to an importance half as great at more than twenty-three million dollars.

By 1870 California had succeeded in building a multifaceted economy which supported its 560,000 people at a high level of prosperity.

SIXTEEN

California Becomes a State

C ALIFORNIA government was military in nature from the raising of the American flag at Monterey on July 7, 1846, until the inauguration of the first elected governor, Peter H. Burnett, on December 20, 1849.

This military control changed significantly after the ratification of the peace treaty of Guadalupe-Hidalgo, which formally ended the Mexican War on May 30, 1848. Prior to that time California was merely militarily occupied as one of the incidents in the Mexican War. Since California enjoyed only the status of occupied hostile territory, the military governors were not restrained in their rule by the provisions of the American Constitution, but only by their superiors, instructions, public opinion, and the laws of war. Although the signing of a peace treaty did not end military government, since California had become a United States territory, the authority of its soldier-governors became more restricted. The Constitution was now binding upon California, and local regulations conflicting with this document were illegal. American tariff laws automatically extended throughout the territory. At the same time the province's municipal laws which were not in conflict with the Constitution continued in force until Congress, distracted by debates over the extension of slavery into the conquered Mexican territory, changed them.

During the early phase of military control, Commodore Robert F. Stockton set September 15, 1846, as an election day for towns and other political districts to elect alcaldes and other local officials. Since Stockton had already appointed alcaldes for most of the important areas in the province, these elections simply confirmed his earlier choices. Stockton had appointed Thomas M. Robbins as alcalde at Santa Barbara; in Los Angeles the commodore had selected John Temple and Alexander Bell, both of them Americans. At San Bernadino, Louis Robidoux, the brother of the celebrated mountain man, Antoine, became alcalde. Stockton also appointed one native Californian to the post of alcalde at San Diego, José Francisco Ortega. At Yerba Buena, Stockton selected Lieutenant Washington A. Bartlett as alcalde for the city. At the September 15 election, the native José de Jesús de Noe was elected second alcalde. Two minor posts also fell to Americans in Yerba Buena.

One of the most important appointments made by Stockton was his choice of Walter Colton as alcalde at Monterey. Colton, the third of twelve children of Deacon Walter Colton and Thankful Cobb Colton, was born May 9, 1797, in Vermont. Young Walter attended Yale from 1818 to 1822, winning a prize for scholarship. Then the serious-minded Yankee studied at Andover Theological Seminary, where he devoted much of his time to literature. After having become a minister in the Congregationalist Church, he taught school and edited a church newspaper. In 1831 he decided to go to sea as a naval chaplain. After serving an extensive period in the West Indies and the Mediterranean, in the late summer of 1845 he sailed to California aboard the *Congress*, under the command of Stockton. Aboard ship, he impressed the commodore with his deep learning and good sense. Consequently, Stockton appointed him to serve as alcalde for the important port of Monterey. At the election of September 15 the voters enthusiastically continued Colton in office. Within the important Monterey district, an area of three hundred square miles, he was the ruling authority, checked only by the military governor.

As magistrate Colton was a great success and found time for many extra activities. In collaboration with Bear Flagger Robert Semple he published the *Californian*, the first newspaper in the territory. After a year or so of publication, the *Californian* moved to San Francisco. The columns of this newspaper were printed in both Spanish and English in a quaint topsy-turvy manner. Colton also built California's first schoolhouse and public building, named Colton Hall in his honor. In the summer of 1849, he returned to the East and wrote an account of his three years in California. On January 22, 1851, when his precarious health failed, he died in Philadelphia. He was one of the most influential Americans from 1846 to 1849, and helped by his kindly and impartial administration of justice to make American rule palatable to the Californios.

During the period of military government, Stockton decided that the Mexican tariff regulations should be modified so that American ships could enter California ports duty free. Foreign ships were required to pay a duty of fifty cents a ton, and foreign goods were taxed at the rate of 15 per cent *ad valorem*.

Shortly before Stockton left California, he appointed seven influential citizens to act as a legislative council for the governor: Juan Bandini, Santiago Argüello, Thomas O. Larkin, Juan Bautista Alvarado, David Spence, Eliab Grimes, and Mariano Vallejo. Originally scheduled to meet on March 1, 1847, the council failed to convene once Stockton had departed. Several members refused to serve, and the council never met.

Before his departure Stockton installed Frémont as governor of the province. After fifty days Frémont was supplanted by General Stephen W. Kearny. When General Kearny assumed office, he made few governmental changes. The navy men were ordered to rejoin the Pacific squadron and resume their usual duties. When Stockton's successor as commander of the naval forces in California, Commodore William B. Shubrick, recognized Kearny's right to the governorship of California, Kearny agreed that the navy might continue to regulate the use of California's ports.

Kearny was succeeded as governor by Colonel Richard Barnes Mason in May 1847. No sooner had he assumed office than he was faced with a minor governmental crisis. Although John H. Nash had been elected as alcalde of Sonoma, he had displeased General Kearny, who ordered him replaced by Lilburn W. Boggs. Then Kearny departed for the East and left Mason with Nash, who refused to surrender his office to Boggs. Mason sent Lieutenant William T. Sherman to capture the recalcitrant Nash. Boggs was duly installed as alcalde.

The alcalde remained the major administrative officer in California, following the eclipse of the Mexican period. A combination judge and mayor, the alcalde even possessed some legislative functions as well. Governor Felipe de Neve had brought the office to California in 1781, after it had long proved its worth in the administration of Spanish America. When the United States occupied California, the Mexican Constitution of 1837 was the prevailing frame of government. Two acts had been passed in that year by the Mexican Congress relegating the alcalde to a minor role and putting the principal local governmental functions in the hands of prefects and subprefects. The political anarchy in Mexico and California prevented this reform from being made effective in California. In fact, this attempted innovation in the administration of the province strengthened the alcaldes' position. Since no prefects or subprefects ever assumed office, their additional functions were assumed by the alcaldes. Alcaldes were not lawyers. Their qualifications simply required that they be civilian citizens of the pueblo in which they were elected and that they did not owe money to the government. The extent of an alcalde's jurisdiction was not always confined to a small pueblo. Often his district comprised 300–500 square miles with no definite boundary except the Pacific Ocean to the west. In the large districts, auxiliary alcaldes were often appointed. These auxiliary officials were usually the large ranchers, who were happy to enhance their already great prestige by assuming this governmental function.

Since the office combined executive and judicial functions, an alcalde might arrest a criminal, try him and then execute his sentence. Often an alcalde improvised solutions to cases. A story which made the rounds of California concerned a case tried before an imaginative alcalde. A vaquero had saved a woman from a mad bull. In the course of his rescue the man had thrown the woman from the bull's path. She was pregnant and shortly thereafter suffered from a miscarriage. Her husband sued her rescuer for damages. After hearing the case, the alcalde ruled that the husband was correct in demanding recompense, but he ordered that since the vaquero had caused the wife to miscarry, he should return the woman to the condition in which he had found her. The husband did not insist upon execution of the sentence.

After becoming governor, Mason found that his alcaldes needed more criminal jurisdiction in order to cope with an increase in crime. Mason ordered at once that the alcaldes be clothed with the necessary authority to handle these cases.

Because of the growth of the population in San Francisco, in August 1847, Colonel Mason ordered an election for a town council of six men to make local regulations and assist the alcalde. Mason appointed First Lieutenant William T. Sherman as assistant adjutant general, and Lieutenant Henry Wager Halleck to act as secretary of state. Halleck, who had a knowledge of both Spanish and international law, handled legal problems, particularly those pertaining to land. In the 1860's Halleck rose to the rank of major general in the Union army and acted for a time as Lincoln's chief of staff.

Acting with the approval of Commodore Shubrick, Colonel Mason took some liberties with his official instructions concerning foreign trade. On October 3, 1847, Mason received a tariff schedule from Washington which imposed heavy duties on imports. Mason quickly apprehended the deleterious effect this tariff would have upon California's commerce. Mason modified the port duties from one dollar to fifteen cents a ton, and lightened the *ad valorem* tax upon imports.

To finance California's military government, Colonel Mason stipulated that money collected from customs duties should be placed in a separate account to be known as the "Civil Fund." Carefully controlled by Mason and his successor, no known misuse of the fund occurred. After the discovery of gold in California, the fund grew so rapidly that it covered all the expenses of military government, including the Monterey constitutional convention, and often had excess amounts to lend to the military. After California became a state, a budgetary surplus was turned over to the United States Treasury.

The gold discovery of 1848, despite its many benefits to California, proved a complicating factor for Mason's military government. During 1848, army desertions were so frequent that it was difficult to get the most routine assignments carried out.

One wise step, which Mason took in February 1848, was to discontinue the Mexican system of filing land claims, thus preventing a few people from monopolizing the best mining areas.

On August 7, 1848, when the news of the signing of the Treaty of Guadalupe-Hidalgo reached California, Colonel Mason had to modify his conduct, since the Constitution of the United States now applied to the territory. Some critics of military government complained that the army's rule should end at once. Mason decided to continue his rule until he could learn what course Congress had decided upon for the territory's future.

Two immediate results of the proclamation of the Guadalupe-Hidalgo treaty were the exact definition of the boundary between Alta and Baja California, and a governmental communiqué by Mason which declared that all Mexican citizens residing in California must become Americans. Only by official declaration prior to March 30, 1849, could they elect to remain Mexicans.

Californians anxiously waited for Congress to give their province an official territorial organization. However, at the close of the Mexican War, the Far West and the Southwest had become apples of discord between the northern and southern United States. By this time the northern states had all passed measures of emancipation for any slaves within their various state boundaries. Most of them harbored a small but extremely vocal number of abolitionists who urged the complete extinction of the institution of Negro slavery. In addition, a considerable group of northerners, while not abolitionists, were opposed to the spread of the institution of Negro slavery into the newly acquired western lands. Southerners, for whom the institution of slavery was an accepted tradition, were indignant that the West should be closed to slavery. Many doubted that slavery could be successfully established in regions west of Texas, but southerners disliked a positive law forbidding it. Such a law strongly implied that slavery was wrong, an implication painful to many southerners. In addition, proportionately more southerners than northerners had fought in the Mexican War, and they considered it unjust that a territory won by southern sons should be closed to the spread of slavery. As a result, northern and southern congressmen deadlocked concerning the disposition of lands granted by the Treaty of Guadalupe Hidalgo. Congress adjourned without having provided for the civil government of California.

In poor health and facing a heavy barrage of criticism from the incoming flood of miners who boisterously insisted upon the right to run their own affairs, Colonel Mason asked to be relieved of his California assignment on November 24, 1848. Washington officials agreed to his request, but it was not until April 13, 1849, that General Bennett Riley replaced him. Sensing the unpopularity of military government, Riley professed to be acting only as a *civil* governor. Although the clamor among California settlers for a popular government grew more insistent, Riley continued Mason's policy of appointing and instructing such civil officers as existed in the territory.

On March 3, 1849, Congress tardily created a tariff collection district in San Francisco, and the federal government assigned a civilian collector, J. C. Collier, to assume control. Collier could not take office until November 13, 1849. Thereafter, the collection of revenue was the joint responsibility of civilian collectors and military inspectors, until the army surrendered its authority to an elected civil government in California.

Meanwhile governmental confusion became great in California, particularly in the area of the gold fields, where there were no alcaldes. During his time in office, Mason had not interfered in the government of the mining camps. These communities were often ruled by regulations adopted in open meetings. At first any serious violations of the rules resulted in a meeting of citizens who elected a judge and appointed a jury to hold a trial. As time went by, the larger mining camps elected alcaldes to act as the chief magistrates. With its limited resources, the military government confined itself to governing the coastal strip of California. There is no evidence that Mason or Riley exercised any authority over the mining camps, which enjoyed a *de facto* independence.

Thus the day-to-day government of California was carried on by the alcaldes; whether appointed by the military establishment or elected by the people, they administered Mexican law, common law and on occasion, lynch law. The oaks of the mining camps were often festooned with the cadavers of wrongdoers who had paid for their crimes with a minimum of formality.

Most Californians agreed that a more organized government was necessary, and in the last months of Colonel Mason's administration, lively popular meetings in San Jose, San Francisco, Sacramento, Monterey and Sonoma simultaneously demanded provisional civil government. Acting on their own initiative, citizens of the largest cities in northern California elected delegates to a general convention to be convened on March 5, 1849, which would frame a charter of civilian government for California. Both Mason and Riley frowned upon these informal arrangements. Consequently the movement collapsed and its leaders reluctantly announced that they would await the action of a new Congress concerning territorial government.

Although Congress debated but refused to act, the executive branch of the government faced the California situation squarely. Zachary Taylor, who was publicly inaugurated as President on March 5, 1849, was a southerner who did not insist upon the right of slavery to move west. Taylor himself was a slaveholder owning over one hundred slaves as well as land in both Louisiana and Mississippi. Yet he had been a soldier nearly all his adult life and his devotion to the Union was very strong. He believed that the way to maintain the nation was to make California a state. In that way the troublesome question of slavery during the territorial phase could be bypassed. Taylor expected that California would enter as a free state, but that did not disturb him, since he felt that preservation of the Union was the paramount question.

While avoiding speeches on slavery in the western lands, Taylor acted behind the scenes. In early spring of 1849, he chose Thomas Butler King of Georgia as his personal agent in California. Butler, a veteran Whig politician and congressman, seemed a curious choice. The President, a Louisiana slaveholder, was sending a Georgia slaveowner to conduct California into the Union as a free state.

In April, King sailed from Savannah, arriving at San Francisco on June 4. He quickly informed the Californians that President Taylor would protect them while they made their decision to remain a territory or become a state.

Such encouragement was unnecessary. When the news arrived on May 28 that Congress had adjourned without providing a territorial government for California, various political leaders exerted pressure upon Riley, who issued a proclamation calling for a constitutional convention in September of 1849. In this same message Riley argued that the legal status of California was similar to that of the Louisiana Territory after its purchase by the United States. The governor argued that the preconquest laws of California were still valid and that there was no legal way under the decisions of the federal courts for general civil laws to be made by a provisional government. Nonetheless, Riley called for a convention to set up either a territorial government or to frame a state constitution.

Riley proclaimed August 1, 1849, as election day for delegates to the Monterey Convention. At the same time, voters were to choose four judges for the superior court and various municipal officers. Although these judges and municipal officers were elected under the terms of the governor's call, such was his personal power that none of them exercised the duties of their offices until Riley had inaugurated them.

With these elected officials in power, the California government operated under a somewhat altered form of the Mexican Constitution of 1837. The principal change that occurred was that Governor Riley did not hear appeals from the alcaldes' courts; such appeals now went directly to the superior tribunal. Most American settlers grumbled about this modified Mexican government, for they felt this rule to be both "alien" and "inferior." The only deterrent to widespread expressions of popular displeasure was the early meeting of the Constitutional Convention.

The delegates were elected by all male citizens of the United States older than twenty-one then claiming California as their place of residence. The original call for the Convention had specified thirty-seven delegates to be elected from the ten districts into which California was divided for administrative purposes. However, certain districts where the gold-rush population was large took advantage of an escape clause in Riley's proclamation to elect supernumeraries who could be seated by the convention. This raised the total number of elected delegates to forty-eight. Ten delegates represented the southern districts and thirty-eight represented northern ones.

Monterey made enthusiastic preparations to host the Convention. The school in session at Colton Hall was suspended; carpenters hastily converted its second floor into a large assembly room. Merchants constructed a hotel and enlarged or started several restaurants.

Many delegates were uncertain about attending. The session promised to be expensive, and transportation to Monterey was time-consuming and inconvenient. At this point the United States Navy offered the delegates two government ships. The *Edith* carried southern delegates from San Diego; the brig *Frémont* performed a similar service for northern delegates. Both vessels encountered rough weather and were late in arriving at Monterey. Therefore, the Convention began two days late, on September 3. Some writers have emphasized this delay and commented adversely upon it. Yet the California Constitutional Convention's record for promptness compares most favorably with the Philadelphia Convention of 1787, which framed the federal Constitution. It took this convention eleven days to muster a quorum, and it had delegates arriving over a two-month period.

Of the forty-eight delegates who met at Colton Hall, seven were native Californians, and one of the "foreign-born" delegates was a Spaniard who had come to California twelve years before. Thus there were eight members in the Spanish-speaking bloc. Six of them understood English so poorly that José Antonio Carrillo appealed to the Convention to appoint an official translator who could make a running translation of the debate and motions. The Convention agreed to his suggestion, and the hispanicized Englishman William Hartnell served in this capacity. Other foreign-born delegates included a man born in Ireland but taken as a child to New York, a Scot and a Frenchman. The latter two had each lived in California for over ten years.

Of the American-born delegates, thirty-one came from the eastern seaboard, although they represented twenty-one states. Some writers have indicated that the Convention was dominated by members from the slave states. Only fifteen delegates, including one northerner who had resided for many years in Louisiana, came from the South. The southerners did have the advantage of possessing some of the best practical politicians at the Convention. William M. Gwin, a well-educated Tennessean with many years residence in Mississippi, was a lawyer by training and a natural leader. He played a significant role in the debates of the Convention.

The delegates were primarily young men. Nine were less than thirty; more than thirty were less than forty years old; only four were older than fifty years of age. The average age was thirty-six and a half. Thirty-two of the forty-eight Convention members had established themselves in California prior to the gold rush, although several delegates counted their California residency in months. The delegates included fourteen lawyers, eleven farmers and seven merchants, even though one member gave his occupation as "elegant leisure." Although most of them listed some occupation far removed from mining, most of them had mining interests.

The former Bear Flagger Robert Semple of Sonoma was chosen as presiding officer, while Captain William G. Marcy, who had come to California with the New York volunteers, was selected secretary. Other prominent delegates were José Antonio Carrillo, Mariano G. Vallejo, Thomas O. Larkin, Abel Stearns, Lansford W. Hastings, John A. Sutter and Henry W. Halleck.

The first issue considered was whether California should organize as a territory or a state. Originally many Americans had favored a territorial form of government, but when Thomas Butler King and Governor Riley suggested that California immediately become a state, the delegates quickly switched to support of this possibility.

The northern California delegates strongly supported a move for immediate statehood; a few delegates from the south, representing landowners who feared high taxes if statehood came at once, opposed this step. At that time the first of many later proposals to split California appeared. Carrillo proposed splitting the province into a northern part that would immediately become a state, and a southern portion (the part untouched by the gold rush) that would remain a territory for an indefinite period. The Convention brushed Carrillo's proposal aside and set up machinery to frame a state constitution.

Although fifteen members had migrated from southern states, they made no serious attempt to frame a constitution making California a slave state. The probable reason for this stemmed from several incidents in the mining country, the most dramatic of which had occurred only the previous July. At that time about a dozen Texans had moved to Rose's Bar on the Yuba River, accompanied by fifteen slaves. The Texans proceeded to occupy about a third of a mile of land along the river, filing claims not only in their own names, but also in those of their slaves. The miners of the district indignantly threatened the Texans. Finding themselves out-numbered, the Texans gave up the controversy. This district sent as a delegate William E. Shannon, who had been pledged to prohibit slavery in California. When the Convention was considering a bill of rights in the California Constitution, Shannon proposed language borrowed from the Northwest Ordinance of 1787 and later used by the Thirteenth Amend-ment to the Constitution to bar slavery. His proposal was adopted, but only after a provision was likewise accepted to bar the migration of freed Negroes into California. The ostensible reason for this attitude among the delegates was their fear that southerners might free their slaves, bind them into some form of indenture, and then take them to California. Once in the Far West, the former masters would be able to use their Negroes to obtain additional mining claims. Despite these protestations, the debates revealed that many who advocated barring freed Negroes simply did not wish the blacks to migrate to California under any condi-tions. After several votes and a lively debate, the provision to bar freed Negroes from California was stricken out of the Constitution. The sec-tion banning slavery was not immediately effective in practice.

The state Constitution also provided for a free public school system, directed by a superintendent of public instruction. Every school district was supposed to be in session for at least three months a year. To help finance this educational system, which for that day was a grandiose scheme, the Convention hoped that Congress, upon the admission of the state, would grant the sixteenth and thirty-sixth sections of each township to the state for educational purposes. Since the Convention thought that even this generous grant might not be sufficient for school support, it authorized the use for educational purposes of the 500,000 acres of land normally granted since 1841 to each new state for internal improvements. William Gwin predicted that these resources would give California the most well-endowed school fund in the world. Gwin's prophecy might have come true if California had followed through with careful provision for the disposal of school lands.

For most of the technical details of government, the delegates borrowed freely from the recently framed constitutions of Iowa and New York. Despite the youth of the delegates, they remembered the dreadful conse-quences of the panic of 1837, and the widespread revulsion that depres-sion had caused against indiscriminate state spending and the loose char-tering of banks. Therefore, of the 136 sections of the Constitution which finally emerged from the debates and voting of the Convention, seventy-two were plucked from the Iowa constitution and twenty from that of New York. These documents had both been framed so as to avoid the excesses that caused the panic of 1837, and the California Convention borrowed them also to avert a financial calamity in their new state.

The delegates manifested as great a suspicion of public promotion of private enterprise as they did state regulation of business. These beliefs appear most strikingly in the constitutional prohibition against banking. Bank notes were made illegal, reflecting an amorphous, but nonetheless real fear of paper money. The Constitution did provide for creating associations for holding deposits of gold and silver, much like the federal government's independent treasury system. The new state government was allowed to charter corporations, but only under general laws, and was forbidden to incorporate these groups by special act.

In many respects California's Constitution provided for a conventional government. The twelve-article frame of government provided for a bill of rights with the usual guarantees of assembly, religion and speech, but it also guaranteed foreign residents of the state the same rights of citizenship in the ownership of property. It extended the franchise to all white male citizens over the age of twenty-one who had been residents of their county for thirty days. This latter provision applied not only to American citizens, but to every Mexican who chose to become a citizen under the Guadalupe-Hidalgo Treaty.

Governmental powers were distributed among the usual executive, legislative and judicial departments. A bicameral legislature with a senate and an assembly was provided. Senators were to be elected for a two-year term. The governor was to be elected by the people for a term of two years. Other executive officials who were to be popularly elected were the lieutenant governor, a treasurer, an attorney general and a surveyor general. The governor was to appoint the secretary of state with the consent of the senate. Judicial power was vested in a state supreme court, and in district, county and justice courts.

The most vexing question before the Convention was the location of the eastern boundary of the state. Oregon, the Pacific Ocean and Mexico set the other limits. Spanish California had no settled eastern boundary; Mexican California had only the vaguest of limits with New Mexico. A "large state" party and a "small state" party were soon formed. The large-staters favored a boundary as far east as possible. Some would have welcomed a boundary at the Rockies in the middle of present-day Colorado and New Mexico. Such an extreme eastern boundary brought immediate problems. The thousands of Mormons settled around Salt Lake would have been included, although they had not been represented at the Convention. Also it was widely believed that Congress would never accept a state with such a huge area. Small-staters argued that the Sierra Nevadas should set the state's eastern limits. The small-state party was led by Semple, and the large-staters by Gwin.

The large-state forces were encouraged when Thomas Butler King urged California to include all the land possible in order to resolve the issue of slavery in the western territories. In private conversations, King emphasized that he spoke for the administrative supporters in Congress as well as for the President. The small-staters were able to capitalize upon King's heavy-handed attempts to influence the Convention by claiming that outsiders should not be permitted to sway that body's judgement. In the end, by an overwhelming vote, the Convention adopted a compromise eastern boundary much closer to the small-staters' position than to the large-state stand. The Convention adopted the present eastern boundary of the state; while it included some land east of the Sierra Nevadas, it was a relatively small strip.

Ten thousand dollars was appropriated to print one thousand copies of the Constitution in English and another 250 in Spanish. California was a bilingual state for thirty years, until the Constitution of 1879 was adopted.

The Convention finished its work on October 13, 1849, and John Sutter carried the official notification of that event to Governor Riley. Riley distributed copies of the Constitution throughout the state, and as the Convention prescribed on November 13, 1849, it was voted upon and ratified overwhelmingly by a vote of 12,061 to 811. At the same time, elections were held for the offices of governor, lieutenant governor and two federal congressmen.

In October and early November, a spirited if somewhat unorganized campaign for offices under the new Constitution occurred. On October 25, a mass meeting was held by the Democrats in San Francisco, but it adjourned without endorsing any specific candidates. Soon individual Whig and Democratic condidates took the stump without their parties' official sanction. All the candidates supported the new Constitution, and their campaigns were more an attempt to sell their personalities to the voters than a serious discussion of issues. Also the denomination of Whig or Democrat had little claim upon the voters' loyalty—a carelessness about party labels is endemic in California politics. A nonpartisan meeting was held in Monterey to rally support for responsible candidates. General Riley was nominated for governor, but he declined the honor at once. Then the meeting chose William A. Sherwood for governor, F. J. Lippitt for lieutenant governor, and Edward Gilbert and James L. Ord for congressmen. This group's nominations had little impact, for many other candidates for the various offices asserted their independence of any group's control and tirelessly canvassed the mining camps seeking votes. The usual mode of campaigning was to appear at the common tent which nearly every mining camp possessed, and while the miners rested after dinner, to harangue them using commentaries upon the Constitution and other homemade rhetoric. After his speech the hopeful candidate passed out copies of a printed ticket with the office he sought and his name printed upon it. This do-it-yourself ballot could be deposited in the ballot box.

In the gubernatorial election, Independent Democrat Peter H. Burnett, who had skillfully used his two beautiful daughters to aid his campaign, easily defeated his nearest opponent, William A. Sherwood, the candidate of the Monterey nonpartisan meeting, by a vote of 6,716 to 3,188. Three other gubernatorial aspirants divided 4,295 votes among them. They were John W. Geary, John A. Sutter and William M. Steuart. John McDougal, with 7,374 votes, defeated four other contenders for the lieutenant-governorship. Edward Gilbert (the only Monterey nonpartisan gathering's successful candidate) and George Wright were the voters' choices for Congress.

The successful gubernatorial candidate, Peter H. Burnett, was born in Nashville, Tennessee, on November 15, 1807, and had spent his youth in Missouri. Entering business in the latter state, Burnett incurred a $15,000 debt. He then became a successful attorney. The lure of free land coupled with a chance to rid himself of his debts drew Burnett across the plains to Oregon in 1843. Burnett went into politics in the Oregon Territory, obtaining an election to the legislature. There he became well known for his zeal in supporting a bill to prohibit the sale of alcoholic beverages and another proposal to forbid the emigration of Negroes, whether slave or free, to Oregon. In 1848 Burnett migrated to California, where he practiced law and acted as a business agent for John Sutter, Jr. In August 1849, he made his bow in California politics by winning an election to the superior court. While the Constitutional Convention was yet in session, Burnett began stumping the gold fields, accompanied by his winsome daughters. Besides his daughters' charms, Burnett probably owed his election to the many transplanted Oregonians who knew of his earlier political career.

Although he had no authorization from Washington for his action, Riley grasped the opportunity to lay down his burden as governor, turning over the reins of power to Burnett on December 20, 1849. Taking office, Burnett argued that the power of the federal government over the states was very limited, and so he asked the legislature to implement the new state Constitution at once. The legislature was quick to oblige.

But California's difficulties in framing a state government were by no means over. Its unauthorized action (Congress usually passed enabling legislation first) in drafting a state constitution had to be ratified by Congress. This acceptance would not prove easy, since Congress was torn asunder by the issue of slavery in the western territories and other matters at issue between the North and the South. Moreover, since 1812,

Congress had inaugurated the policy of maintaining the balance of power between the two sections in the United States Senate by balancing the admission to the Union of a free state with a slave state. In 1849, when California requested admission to the Union, there was no balancing slave area. Southerners such as South Carolina Senator John C. Calhoun argued against the admission of California as a free state, claiming that its entrance into the Union indicated a permanently inferior position for the South.

Most southern congressmen realized that California could not be kept indefinitely out of the Union, and that once it was admitted it would be as a free state. However, they were determined to link its admission to other unresolved questions between the sections in order to win northern concessions. As a result California statehood became embroiled in the passage of a bundle of other measures, known as the Compromise of 1850. At first Henry Clay of Kentucky proposed a compromise solution of which California statehood would have been a part. When his proposals bogged down in the Senate, young Stephen A. Douglas of Illinois suggested five separate laws which would accomplish most of what Clay had set out to do. One of these bills, which recognized California as a state under the Constitution it had itself framed, passed the Senate on August 13 by a majority of sixteen senators. The House later passed the same measure on September 17 by the overwhelming margin of 150 to 56, after some southern diehards had ineptly attempted to delay the bill's passage. At the same time, the House accepted that part of the Compromise setting up Utah as a territory with its legislature free to deal as it chose with slavery. Thus in one burst of energy on a Saturday, Congress had succeeded in passing two vital parts of the compromise solution. That night there was a festive air over the Capitol. A salute of a hundred guns was fired to honor California and Utah. The National Hotel was illuminated; skyrockets shot into the air. The United States Marine Band paraded on Pennsylvania Avenue playing patriotic airs. The following Monday, September 9, President Millard Fillmore (President Taylor had died in office the previous July) signed the California admission bill into law. This event is still celebrated on that day in California as Admission Day. News of California's entrance into the Union was not received in the new state until October 18. This intelligence triggered a celebration that lasted for days in all the cities and towns of the state, with drinking, parades and speechmaking.

California's congressmen had been standing by for some time in Washington, anxiously watching the progress of the admission bill. In addition to the two elected representatives, the California legislature had in December 1849 elected two senators, John C. Frémont and William M. Gwin. Without delay, Frémont and his vivacious wife, Jessie Benton

The Grizzly Giant, patriarch of the Mariposa Grove of Sequoia Gigantea, in Yosemite National Park. This great tree, estimated to be 3,800 years old, measures 209 ft. tall, 96.5 ft. in circumference at its base. It is thought to be among five largest known living giant sequoias, those sharing this distinction being the Sherman, Grant and Hart trees in Sequoia National Park and the Boole tree in Convose Basin.

Courtesy of Curry Company, San Francisco, California

An elderly Yurok Indian fishing in the native manner as late as 1900.

Ericson Collection Prints, Humboldt State College Library

Yosemite Falls in Yosemite Valley, California. In the spring and through midsummer it appears as in the photo. During late summer it becomes dry. Fall rains cause it to fill again, although spasmodically. In winter it is an ice-coated trickle. The upper fall drops 1,430 ft. There is a middle cascade of some 675 ft. and a lower fall (partially obscured) which falls 320 ft. Comparatively, Yosemite Falls is some nine times higher than Niagara, second in drop only to Angel Falls in Venezuela.

Courtesy of Yosemite Park and Curry Company,
Yosemite National Park, California

Northwest California Indian woman in the early days of the twentieth
century weaving the intricate basketry which today is almost a lost art.
Ericson Collection Prints, Humboldt State College Library

Big Willis, a prominent Hupa Indian, about 1904.
Ericson Collection Prints, Humboldt State College Library

A blind Hupa Indian woman weaving a basket. She was estimated to
be about 100 years old at the time of this photograph, in the early days
of the twentieth century.
Ericson Collection Prints, Humboldt State College Library

San Diego Mission, 1915.
Courtesy of Title Insurance and Trust Company, San Diego, California

Carreta (2-wheel cart), backbone of transportation in Spanish and Mexican California.   *Courtesy of Historical Collections, Security First National Bank, Los Angeles, California*

San Diego from the old fort (C. B. Graham litho, circa 1846-47).
Courtesy of Historical Collections, Security First National Bank,
Los Angeles, California

A New England hide and tallow ship. "The Pilgrim," litho from Dana's *Two Years Before the Mast.*
Courtesy of Historical Collections, Security First National Bank,
Los Angeles, California

1870—scene of Chinese massacre in 1871, confluence of Los Angeles Street & Alameda Street near the plaza, south of the Lugo adobe and east of the Arcadia Block. *Note:* At time of photo present streets had not been extended as in existing pattern. *Courtesy of Historical Collections, Security First National Bank, Los Angeles, California*

Wells Fargo messenger Ely Fisher, National Hotel, Jackson, Amador County, Sutter Creek & Jackson State.

Old mining equipment near Jackson, California.

Courtesy of Peter Palmquist, Arcata, California

Black Bart.
*Courtesy of Wells Fargo
Bank, History Room,
San Francisco, California*

Southern Pacific train at Wilmington Docks—about 1880.
Collection of Historical Photographs, Title Insurance and Trust Company,
Los Angeles, California

Los Angeles, 1885, north on Spring Street from First Street.
Courtesy of Security First National Bank, Los Angeles, California

San Francisco's Market Street looking west from Drumm Street near the Embarcadero in 1888.
Courtesy of Pacific Gas and Electric Company, News Bureau, San Francisco, California

HOTEL RAFAEL
SAN RAFAEL, CAL.

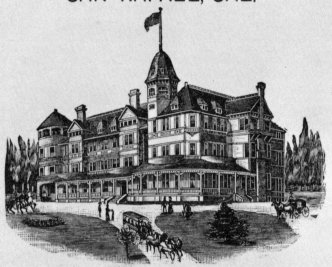

CLIMATE PERFECT — NO FOGS.

Rates—$3 to $3.50 Per Day. $17.50 to $20 Per Week
According to Accommodations.

SPECIAL RATES BY THE MONTH.

Service, Table, and Appointments not Excelled by any Hotel in the World.

THE "RAFAEL," situated just outside the town of San Rafael, is one of the best appointed hotels in this country. The grounds are spacious and beautifully laid out; the drives and scenery are unsurpassed. The hotel is located upon a knoll overlooking the valley and directly facing Mt. Tamalpais. The view from the hotel is very extensive, and its grandeur calls forth the admiration of all who have seen it. The CHEF DE CUISINE has a national reputation.

The projectors of this enterprise, recognizing the necessity of a hotel in this beautiful spot, have spared no money to make this in every particular the best hotel in America.

FIFTY MINUTES' RIDE FROM SAN FRANCISCO

by the ferry and cars of the San Francisco & North Pacific Railroad via Point Tiburon; or by the North Pacific Coast Railroad via Saucelito, both routes crossing the bay opposite the Golden Gate and running close to Alcatraz Island. The scenery along the Railroad is the most beautiful in California.

AS A SUMMER RESORT

it is an agreeable change from the fogs and smoke of San Francisco, and its warm, equable climate makes it one of the most desirable resorts in California. It has not the oppressive heat of inland towns; yet it is protected from fog and cold by the surrounding mountains.

AS A WINTER RESORT

for Eastern visitors, or for others desiring comfortable winter quarters, it has not an equal in the world. Its close proximity to San Francisco, the rapid and frequent communication with the large city, its warm winter days, and withal a magnificent hotel with every comfort and convenience that modern ideas could suggest, the Rafael has become the most popular hotel in the State.

W. E. ZANDER, Manager.

Hotel San Rafael, a resort of the late nineteenth century.
Library, University of California at Berkeley

Frémont, journeyed to Washington with many ostentatious bags of placer gold in their baggage. With Fillmore's signing of the California admission bill, the new state's congressmen at once took their seats in the national legislature.

Peter Burnett, California's first governor, found his incumbency stormy. Always unable to endure criticism, he came under heavy attack in the legislature concerning his handling of the California fiscal situation. His disenchantment with his office grew when he discovered that his $10,000 annual salary, which had seemed so large before his inauguration, was inadequate to cover his expenses. Even the gross figure was an illusion, since he was paid not in gold, but in depreciated state scrip. Consequently, on January 9, 1851, Burnett suddenly sent in his resignation, which the legislature accepted without comment. Then Burnett turned from politics to the bar, the bench and banking, dying at the age of eighty-eight on May 17, 1895.

Lieutenant Governor John McDougal, an Ohioan raised in Indiana who had come to California in February 1849, succeeded Burnett as governor. He served out his predecessor's term, which expired in January 1852. There were some constructive aspects to his year in office, but his tenure was marred by a violent controversy with the first Vigilance Committee of 1851, an extralegal body which attempted to rid San Francisco of crime. McDougal violently but unsuccessfully opposed the Committee. This action made him very unpopular. He also sought unsuccessfully to have the southern part of the state's tax burden equalized with the north's. The southern landowners found the real-estate tax unfair, since 4 per cent of the state's population paid 66 per cent of the state's taxes. McDougal fought courageously but ineptly to erase this inequity. He retired from office at the conclusion of Burnett's term. His later political career was undistinguished except for his dueling and excessive drinking. He died an alcoholic at forty-eight.

McDougal's successor was John Bigler, a Pennsylvanian, who had come to California after a sojourn in Illinois. Also a Democrat, Bigler was able to wrestle more or less successfully with the state's financial problems, so that he became the first governor to win reelection, narrowly defeating the rather lackluster William Waldo. Thus he served until January 9, 1856. His second term was undistinguished. Later he had a diplomatic career under President James Buchanan. He died on November 29, 1871, having seen the state pass under the iron grip of the Republican Party during the Civil War era. In 1854, the California legislature, dominated by his political admirers, named a large lake in the Sierra Lake Bigler. In 1870 the Republican-dominated legislature was able, in view of Bigler's faded political reputation, to strip him of this honor, and rename the body of water Lake Tahoe.

All three of California's first governors had stormy tenures of office marked by spirited quarrels with the legislature and fellow politicians. Their collective record of accomplishments is meager. Their mediocrity was not the burden to the state that it might have been because of the relative unimportance of the California state government during those years.

Despite the unequivocal wording of the California Constitution concerning slavery, those Negroes then resident in the state in the 1850's only belatedly felt the effect of this declaration. In addition, the legal rights of even freed Negroes were largely unrecognized.

At the first meeting of the anticipatory state legislature, Governor Peter Burnett recommended that laws be passed to forbid the presence of any Negroes, slave or free, in California. The legislature refused to enact this legislation, but several times bills to limit Negro migration into California were discussed, and in 1858 one was actually passed through both houses of the legislature. It happened that the two houses passed the bill in slightly different versions, and before these differences could be harmonized the legislature adjourned.

The same legislature that refused to pass Burnett's recommendation for curbs on Negro immigration was a far cry from an antislavery body. It passed resolutions deploring antislavery agitation in the North and protesting any limitation by Congress of slaveholders' rights to possess their property in the western territories.

Meanwhile many southerners immigrated into California accompanied by their slaves. In the absence of any legislation enforcing the constitutional prohibition against slavery, they were temporarily able to maintain their Negroes in bondage.

California courts were in some confusion during this period. In 1850, in the period prior to California's admission to the Union, a San Jose alcalde restored a runaway slave to his master. Yet in a case concerning a suit for a writ of habeas corpus against a master who attempted to hold a slave in California, county Judge Thomas of Sacramento decided for the Negro, declaring that slavery was illegal in California, both by Mexican law and the new state Constitution. In 1851 Judge Morrison of San Francisco ruled in a similar suit that a Negro voluntarily brought to California by his master in 1850 thereby acquired his freedom.

One part of the Compromise of 1850 was a new and more stringent fugitive-slave law. By 1852 only two states had passed acts to reinforce this federal law; California was one of them. The California law, sponsored by southern aristocrat Henry A. Crabb, provided not merely that California state officers and citizens must aid in the return of runaway slaves, but the fourth section also provided that slaves brought into California by their masters prior to the admission of the state could be reclaimed by their owners and returned to a slave state in the same manner as if they were fugitive slaves.

In August 1852, the most celebrated case on the matter of California Negro slavery, the Perkins suit, reached the state supreme court. This case concerned a Georgian named Perkins who wished to return to his native state with three Negro slaves he had brought to California in 1849. A justice of the peace and a county judge in Sacramento had both decided in Perkins' favor. As a result, the Georgian had actually placed his slaves aboard a steamer in San Francisco Bay when he was served with a writ of habeas corpus. A hearing was then held directly before the state supreme court. That tribunal ruled that the California fugitive-slave law was constitutional in all of its sections. The court argued that slaves brought to California prior to its admission on September 9, 1850, could not be freed unless their owners refused to remove them from the state after a reasonable time. Moreover, the court then declared that California's constitutional prohibition against slavery was directory only, and no slaves could be set free under it until the legislature passed laws to carry its stricture against slavery into effect. Thus the supreme court declared that slavery was still legal in California.

In April 1855, the celebrated fourth section of the state fugitive-slave law expired as the result of a time limitation, and this expiration immediately improved the Negroes' legal position. Public opinion in California because of increased northern migration was less favorable to slavery by 1855. Yet, as the Archy case decided in 1858 showed, Negro slave property was still legally secure in California. In this case there were variant opinions, but the court ruled that travelers and visitors could hold slaves in California. This decision did not end the case. When the master Stovall tried to remove his slave Archy to Mississippi, he was subject to additional legal process. Finally, after a hearing before a federal commissioner under the fugitive slave law of 1850, Archy was freed on the grounds that he had been voluntarily brought to California by his master and had not entered the state as a fugitive.

Slavery gradually ended in California as the flow of immigrants slowed. Fewer newcomers attempted to bring slaves to California as the legal climate for the institution became more chilly. Those slaves already in the state, and the number may have included several hundreds, were gradually freed in two ways: either they escaped from their masters with the help of antislavery men, or worked extra hours to earn sufficient money to purchase their freedom. Many freedom papers recorded in county archives show both the widespread presence of slaves and the large number of Negroes who bought their liberty.

In the atmosphere of California in the 1850's, freed Negroes found their rights to property and life unprotected. The California legal code forbade the acceptance of Negro testimony. Thus a Negro could be assaulted or robbed with impunity so long as there were no white witnesses willing to testify to the crime. In March 1852, freed Negroes and some whites sent a petition to the legislature to remedy this condition; the legislators indignantly spurned this petition. Year after year petitions were sent in, and yet the legislature refused to act. Only in the midst of the Civil War in 1863 was the law barring Negro testimony repealed.

In the early history of all the states, there was generally a time of struggle over the location of the state capital. A city chosen as the capital might hope through the enjoyment of the state patronage to grow quickly, enriching its real-estate owners and merchants. Several California cities eagerly contended for the privilege of being the state's permanent capital. In addition to Monterey's historic claims, San Francisco, Benicia, Stockton, Sacramento, Santa Barbara and San Luis Obispo all had aspirations.

The California Constitution had provided that the first session of the legislature should be held at San Jose with the understanding that by a two-thirds vote, the legislature could move the capital elsewhere. In fact, the capital remained at San Jose for two years, but few considered it acceptable as the permanent seat of government. Its living quarters and governmental facilities were poor; the town's distance from the center of population, as well as its inadequate transportation facilities, all doomed San Jose's chances.

General Mariano Vallejo had been trying as hard as only a real-estate speculator can to develop the north San Francisco Bay area. Vallejo proposed to the legislature that a capital city be plotted along the Straits of Carquinez on land to be selected by five commissioners—three appointed by the legislature and two by himself. He also offered the state 156 acres of land for the capital's site, and $370,000 in cash for the building of the necessary government structures.

Quickly the legislature accepted Vallejo's generous terms. A town named for its generous patron was surveyed and in January 1852, the California state government moved there. The legislature soon became disillusioned with its bargain. The capitol was a stark, unfurnished wooden building, lacking even a rostrum for the presiding officer and seats for the members. To provide seating for the legislators, boards were hastily laid upon nail kegs. Also, the town of Vallejo had no hotel, and even boardinghouses were scarce. It soon became evident that Vallejo could not raise the amount of cash for the buildings he had promised. After enduring the spartan facilities of the town of Vallejo for a week, the legislature voted to finish out its session at Sacramento, which had offered its new courthouse as a temporary capitol until a permanent building could be erected. The state capital might have remained at Sacramento after the hasty flight from Vallejo, but in the spring of 1852 a severe flood deluged the city. Therefore, the state officials selected Benicia (named for Vallejo's wife) in 1853. The legislature met there for one session. Although the legislature had an imposing two-story brick building in which to meet, the public records had to be housed in a flimsy frame structure which lacked fireproof vaults or safes. Using this insecurity of the public documents as its official reason, the legislature voted to return to Sacramento in 1854. Three years later, after an appropriation of $300,000 was made for that purpose, a permanent capitol was built at Sacramento. In the last seventy-five years both San Jose and Berkeley have staged serious attempts to get the capital moved to their cities, but the investment of the state in Sacramento was too great to allow these attempts to succeed.

SEVENTEEN

The New Society

A POLITICAL history of California during the 1850's is insufficient to recount its actual government. Extralegal bodies, vigilance committees, or men styling themselves vigilantes, meted out rough justice to transgressors in California's raw, bustling society.

During 1848 there was little violence or crime in California. With the mass migrations of 1849, this condition abruptly changed. Many criminals came to California gripped by the same gold fever that had seized honest men. When these rogues arrived, they quickly discovered that they had no taste for the hard labor of the mines and reverted to their former lives of crime. The ranks of the wrongdoers were swelled by many honest men who proved unable to resist the temptations of life in this new country. Freed from the social restraints of their home towns, many men turned to crime. Those who had unsuccessfully sought wealth in the gold fields drifted to the cities and towns. There they often found that unskilled labor was a glut on the market, and merely keeping alive was a serious problem. Since many of the same goldseekers in the British Columbian or Australian gold fields did not turn to lawlessness in large numbers, or require extralegal justice to maintain order, it seems plausible that there were elements in the political and social organization of California that encouraged crime.

Nor was this lawlessness merely an urban problem. It seems to have been concomitant with the heavy migration. A former New York schoolteacher, writing to his brother from the Feather River region in March 1852, reported that the bodies of seventeen murdered men were found in a relatively short time along one main thoroughfare in the area. Not one of the murderers was ever apprehended. Between 1850 and 1857, then lightly populated Los Angeles County had fifty murders among those elements of its population labeled white.

If crime was rampant in the gold fields and mining towns of California, the wave reached its peak in the urban center of San Francisco. Early San Francisco, as the home of the rootless, suffered from inefficient and corrupt municipal government. Migrants will tolerate corrupt politics more than settled inhabitants. At that time there was little civic pride in San Francisco. All residents thought of someplace else as home. Making money absorbed all the energies of the San Franciscans, so that any vital interest in municipal affairs was lacking.

The political confusion in San Francisco began in 1848 when the citizens of that city decided to inaugurate a more elaborate municipal government without waiting for official sanction. They elected six city councilmen to exercise power until regularly chosen successors could assume office. A few weeks later, the military governor authorized a new election for an official municipal body to replace the first officeholders. On December 28, 1848, a second council was chosen by a turnout of only 347 voters. The first councilors refused to vacate their offices.

The original council ordered a new election and on January 15, 1849, a third council was selected by a turnout of fewer voters than had voted in the previous month's election. At this point an indignation meeting of San Francisco citizens in Portsmouth Square demanded that all three councils resign, and ordained February 21 as the date for a new election. The council chosen at this new balloting tried to displace the San Francisco alcalde. The military governor reacted by resisting this move and reconstituting the original council of 1848. San Francisco municipal affairs had turned full circle.

To clarify the situation, the governor decreed August 1 as election day for a new council. Many San Franciscans could not brook this interference with their government, and by consent they designated their own election for July 9. When only 174 San Franciscans voted, a consensus of citizens agreed that they would attempt a new election on the governor's date, August 1. There were ten different slates of municipal candidates, but John W. Geary was the nominee for mayor on all of them, receiving every one of the 1,576 votes cast.

John White Geary was an unusual man. Born in 1819 in Pennsylvania, he had taught school, clerked in a store and studied engineering and law. He served with the Pennsylvania troops in the Mexican War. Then President Polk chose him to establish a postal system in California. Using this federal office as a springboard, he was soon appointed an alcalde and plunged headlong into California politics. He proved unequal to his task as mayor, yet it was not for want of ability. Leaving California because of his wife's health in 1852, he returned to the East where he served for a time as governor of the Kansas Territory, a general in the Civil War, and a term as Pennsylvania's governor.

Elected at the same time with Geary was a new council of twelve members. These men were the sixth set elected by San Francisco in a year, and the first to gain any wide acceptance. Their first action was to appropriate funds to purchase the brig *Euphemia* and convert it into a municipal jail.

The council's action seemed insignificant. Already the San Francisco newspapers were calling for a popular uprising to dispense justice to criminals who openly flaunted civic authorities. Inside San Francisco there was a city within a city—Sydney Town. Sydney Town sprawled near the base of Telegraph Hill—a collection of tents and hovels which served as the headquarters for the Australian convicts. These men were English criminals transported to Australia as punishment. They were, for various reasons, drawn to California either after escaping or after the conclusion of their prison terms. These former inmates of the Australian penal colony were called the Sydney Coves or Ducks. The Ducks roamed the unlighted San Francisco streets robbing and stealing.

Yet it was not the Ducks who precipitated the first San Francisco essay into do-it-yourself justice. This distinction was claimed by a gang popularly called the Hounds. The Hounds themselves preferred to be called the San Francisco Society of Regulators, which had a formal organization headed by a president. Operating from a canvas structure on Kearny Street called Tammany Hall, these men went out to regulate the city for their own benefit. The Hounds were the Bowery dregs of Stevenson's New York volunteers who had arrived in California during the Mexican War. Discharged from the army, they drifted about various mining camps trying to live without working. Run out of one community after another, they gravitated back to the more congenial climate of San Francisco. They augmented their ranks by recruiting desperadoes from all quarters of the globe. Eventually they numbered more than one hundred men. Prowling the streets in groups, they adopted a uniform of miscellaneous army clothes. They stole and robbed without any molestation from the authorities. Indeed, the few peace officers of the city frequently employed the Hounds to collect debts and make arrests for them.

The Hounds continued their depredations until one evening in July 1849, when they outraged even the most lenient San Franciscans. On that night they staged a raid on Chileno Village, or Little Chili. This collection of tents and shacks was inhabited by Chileans and other Latin Americans newly arrived in California. Ostensibly the Hounds had come to collect a five-hundred-dollar debt owed by a prominent Chilean, but finding most of the men away at the mines, they could not resist the temptation to steal everything of value and burn down many of the tents and shacks. They assaulted a young girl and murdered her mother, who attempted to protect her. Many other Chileans were savagely cuffed and beaten.

The citizens of San Francisco were shocked out of their apathy by this high-handed action. One such citizen was a thirty-six-year-old former Mainer, Sam Brannan, who was a prosperous merchant in the city. He had himself suffered depredations at the hands of the Hounds, and now he grasped this opportunity to break their hold upon the city. On the morning after the raid, Brannan mounted a barrel on the corner of Clay and Montgomery Streets and began to harangue the passers-by. Waving his arms and bellowing frantically, Brannan stated the alternatives: restrain the Hounds or abdicate complete control of the city to them. The crowd became too large to hear him adequately, so it passed a motion to adjourn the meeting to the plaza. Brannan made a rostrum out of the roof of the one-story office of the alcalde, from which he continued to call for action against the Hounds. That afternoon there was another mass meeting at three o'clock, also held in the plaza. Nearly a thousand people attended. Their first action was to take up a hatful of gold and silver as a contribution to help the sufferers of the Hounds' raid. Then 230 citizens enrolled themselves into a volunteer police force.

Within hours, this citizens' posse headed for Tammany Hall, which it found deserted. The Hounds had fled. At once an intensive search was begun for known members of the now proscribed organization. By evening seventeen Hounds had been arrested and put into the brig of the U.S.S. *Warren.* Samuel Roberts, the unofficial leader of the Hounds, tried unsuccessfully to hide behind bags of flour aboard a vessel bound upriver to Stockton. In all, twenty of the Hounds were apprehended and jailed. A grand jury of twenty-four citizens indicted them. With an impromptu prosecutor and two attorneys for the defense, a regular trial was held before the alcalde. Because of probably perjured alibis, only nine Hounds, including Roberts, were convicted. The convicted men drew varying imprisonments; Roberts, the leader, drew the most severe sentence—a ten-year term. Then a new difficulty presented itself. California had no penitentiary and the United States Navy refused to incarcerate the prisoners indefinitely. As a result, by popular consent the sentences were commuted to exile from San Francisco, with the threat that if any of the convicts returned, he would be summarily lynched.

As a result of this citizens' outburst, the Hounds were permanently disbanded. Although the city soon settled back into easygoing ways, the memory of the citizens' action remained as a precedent for future criminal control.

Then, in February 1851, C. J. Jansen, a prominent San Francisco merchant, was severely beaten and robbed during business hours in the heart of the city. Popular indignation soared.

When a severe conflagration caused seven million dollars worth of damage to San Francisco on May 4, 1851, many citizens suspected that the Sydney Ducks had deliberately set the fire in order to cover their depredations. Prominent citizens organized a voluntary patrol to help the local police guard the city. Yet this frenzied activity seemed insufficient to San Francisco's thoroughly disturbed inhabitants. The additional spark needed to elicit further action occurred when an arsonist was caught on June 2 after setting a fire that was contained before it had spread.

As a result of these, on June 10, 1851, an organization of two hundred prominent businessmen was formed which called itself "The Committee of Vigilance of San Francisco." The announced goal of this organization was to "bring to justice" the criminals of the city, utilizing the regular courts if possible, but more summarily if necessary.

The very night of the Committee's organization, the vigilantes were summoned to their headquarters at ten o'clock by two sharp taps of the fire bell. There they discovered that a Sydney Cove had been apprehended while burglarizing a store on Commercial Street. He was the powerfully built, wicked-looking John Jenkins. By midnight the vigilantes had tried and sentenced Jenkins. By two o'clock the next morning they had hanged him in Portsmouth Square before one thousand stern witnesses.

Although a coroner's jury subsequently blamed the vigilantes for unlawfully killing Jenkins, the San Francisco newspapers staunchly defended the lynching and nothing was done to punish the executioners. Rather, the Vigilance Committee was deluged with fresh applications for membership. Local law-enforcement officials made no effort to disband them. They selected an executive committee of twenty men headed by Sam Brannan. The mercurial Brannan remained at the head of the vigilantes only a month before he had a violent disagreement with his fellow leaders and abruptly resigned. He was replaced by the more stable Stephan Payran.

For the balance of the month of June, the vigilantes investigated the leading members of the San Francisco underworld. Four men who seemed to possess the most flagrant record of wrongdoing were sent back to Australia. Incoming vessels were extralegally checked by the vigilantes, who turned back convicts from Australia. Many criminals voluntarily fled San Francisco when they sensed the changed social climate of the city.

Nearly a month after Jenkins' execution, the vigilantes captured a second candidate for the gallows, James Stuart. Stuart had been banished from Great Britain at the age of sixteen and sent to Australia as punishment for the crime of forgery. In 1850 he left Australia for California where he became a burglar, robber and horse thief. Under intense interrogation, he ultimately confessed a string of crimes to the vigilantes. On the morning of July 11, nearly four hundred of the nearly nine hundred members of the Vigilance Committee ended several days of deliberation following Stuart's trial. Their verdict: guilty, with death by hanging decreed. After two hours' grace, Stuart was led to the Market Street Wharf, where he was hanged by means of an improvised derrick.

Stuart's execution caused Governor John McDougal to issue a proclamation deploring the activities of the Vigilance Committee. The vigilantes were unimpressed. Instead, they apprehended two Australian criminals, Sam Whittaker and Robert McKenzie, and promptly condemned them to death. With this open defiance of his authority, McDougal hurried to San Francisco to reassert his control. He joined forces with the San Francisco mayor, Charles J. Brenham, and procured a court order for the release of Whittaker and McKenzie. Acting in concert with the sheriff, the governor and the mayor went to committee headquarters and took custody of the prisoners. The vigilantes refused to be frustrated; several days later they surprised the guards at the local jail, recaptured the two prisoners and executed them.

At this, the peak of its power, the Vigilance Committee began to terminate its work. Of the eighty-nine prisoners taken into custody, they had hanged four and banished twenty-eight. One was whipped, fifteen were turned over to the regular authorities and forty-one released. So many criminals had fled from San Francisco that criminal activity dropped sharply. Despite this success, the Committee came under heavy attack from some church groups, as well as the local bench and bar. This criticism, combined with the fact that the business leaders of San Francisco were anxious to get back to their normal money-making routine, led gradually to a cessation of vigilante activity. The last entry in the journal kept by the Committee was made on June 30, 1852. Technically the vigilantes never disbanded; they simply ceased to operate by the latter part of 1852.

Several other California communities organized committees of vigilance patterned after San Francisco. Among them were Sacramento, Stockton, Marysville, Sonora, San Jose and Los Angeles. These various vigilante committees exchanged criminal records and cooperated with each other. As in San Francisco, these organizations faded way when the exigencies of the moment passed.

In this era of rough, casual justice there were many innocent victims. When able, they struck back at their oppressors. In the early 1850's several Mexicans, probably dispossessed miners, began to prey upon their

American neighbors, running off cattle, stealing horses and robbing travelers. In time the leaders of several gangs were all called Joaquin without reference to surname. The deeds of all these Joaquins were clustered around a legend concerning Joaquin Murietta, a Robin Hood-style bandit. Whether there was one Joaquin or several, the American settlers viewed these depredations so seriously that the California legislature took action. In the spring of 1853, that body authorized Harry Love, a former Texan, to raise a company of twenty mounted rangers to search for the elusive Joaquin or Joaquins. Governor Bigler approved this bill, and on his own responsibility offered a reward of one thousand dollars for any Joaquin killed or captured.

Captain Love and his men searched the region of Ponoche Pass west of Tulare Lake during late July. They discovered a party of Mexicans and shot down their leader, who was identified as a Joaquin. Also killed at the same time was a supposed lieutenant of Joaquin's, a three-fingered man. The heads of the leader and his chief lieutenant were cut off and preserved in spirits. One of the heads was triumphantly proclaimed to be that of the celebrated Joaquin Murietta by the state authorities, and they paid Love and his men the promised reward in addition to their wages. Later a grateful legislature gave Love an additional payment of five thousand dollars. The whole affair had an air of unreality about it, but Californians breathed more easily after the death of the supposed Murietta.

Crime in California continued unabated despite the efforts of California's legal and extralegal guardians. By the fall of 1855, crime in San Francisco had soared toward the heights set prior to the Vigilance Committee of 1851. Criminal acts became so common and the breakdown of law so complete, that San Francisco newspapers began to call for a revival of vigilanteism. In all, between 1849 and 1856, there were over one thousand known murders in San Francisco. The regular courts convicted only one of the murderers.

The revival of vigilanteism was sparked by a most unlikely individual—a healthseeker from Georgetown, a sleepy suburb in the District of Columbia, named James King of William. He had adopted this version of his name while growing up in Georgetown with another James King. In irritation at the confusion which resulted, he had added his father's name to his own. A dark, handsome man, he seemed the very epitome of bad luck. James King of William has best been described as "terribly in earnest." First he worked for the Washington banking firm of Riggs and Corcoran. His health became feeble and, like so many invalids of the nineteenth century, he sought recovery in travel. He went to Chile and Peru before coming to San Francisco in 1849. He soon sent for his pretty wife and small children and tried desperately to earn a living at banking. He failed. Undaunted, he turned to journalism, and on October 8, 1855, brought out the first issue of the San Francisco *Daily Evening Bulletin*. Under King's direction, the *Bulletin* was virtually a one-man newspaper. In the days of vigorous individualism in journalism, King was at home. Humorlessly and singlemindedly, he made his paper a fearless and tact-less exponent of good government. Less than six weeks after King started his newspaper, Charles Cora, an Italian gambler, shot an unarmed United States marshal, William H. Richardson. Immediately following the shoot-ing, Cora headed for the local jail, which served him more as a sanctuary than a place of incarceration. Meanwhile an angry crowd col-lected outside the lockup and began howling that Cora be taken out and lynched. Responding to the outcry, James King in the *Bulletin* called for Cora's speedy punishment.

Meanwhile Cora's beautiful mistress, a prostitute named Arabella "Belle" Ryan, the "queen" of the underworld, was busy trying to free her man. She hired a prestigious counsel, who was a close personal friend of Abraham Lincoln, the English-born Edward D. Baker. Baker proved an able advocate for Cora, and obtained a hung jury. Although Cora remained in jail awaiting a new trial, most knowing San Franciscans con-fidently expected that ultimately he would go free. In the editorial pages of his newspaper, James King continued to thunder at what he termed a miscarriage of justice in the Cora case.

On May 14, 1856, King, still stridently crusading, attacked James P. Casey, a city supervisor and the reputed inventor of an especially stuffa-ble ballot box. Casey had recently turned editor himself, and had been helping to publish the Sunday *Times*. In King's vitriolic attack, he re-vealed that Casey was a former inmate of Sing Sing. The aggrieved Casey sought an explanation for King's attack upon him, but King abruptly ordered the indignant politician from his office.

That night, as James King trudged home from his office, Casey stepped into the street from the cover of an express wagon and shot him. The badly wounded King was carried off to the shelter of the Pacific Express office. Casey fled to the local jail, where he found sanctuary from the mob that quickly collected in the San Francisco streets. At this juncture, several members of the 1851 Vigilance Committee asked one of their former associates, William Tell Coleman, to form a new vigilante organi-zation. Coleman, a college-bred Kentuckian, was a successful merchant and civic leader. Yielding to the pleas of his former associates, Coleman issued a call for a vigilante meeting the next evening. The grim-faced citizens formed a new vigilance committee with Coleman at its head. Quickly 5,500 men enrolled as members. Merchants were so prominent in this organization that the movement has been termed a businessmen's revolution. Many other San Francisco citizens expressed sympathy with the group in a very tangible way by sending large donations of money.

The prejudice of the group was starkly revealed when they closed their membership rolls to Negroes and Chinese.

The alarmed California governor, John Neely Johnson, obtained an interview with the vigilante leader, Coleman. Many variant accounts of this meeting were later given. One certainty is that Governor Johnson mistakenly thought Coleman had agreed to allow the prisoners Casey and Cora to remain in their sanctuary-jail pending trial by a regular court. Coleman had outmaneuvered the young and relatively inexperienced governor.

Yet the governor was a very remarkable man and a dangerous adversary. Born in Indiana in August 1825, he studied law, then moved to Iowa and later to California. Finding that in the California of 1849 there was no opportunity for his legal talents, Johnson became a mule skinner on a run between Sacramento and Stockton. After a brief mining career, he turned to politics and law. As a loyal Whig, he received a federal appointment from President Millard Fillmore, enabling him to devote considerable time to organizing that party in California. When the Whigs disintegrated as a national party in 1854, the so-called American Party was its heir. The American Party, the Know-Nothings as their opponents dubbed them, capitalized on antiforeign prejudice and swept Johnson into the governorship in 1855. Johnson's reward was to face the turbulent San Francisco situation. He procrastinated about what action to take.

The vigilantes did not wait for the wavering governor to take a public stand, but doggedly proceeded with their own program. Their power seemed irresistible inside San Francisco. The *Herald* had dared to condemn a return to vigilanteism in its editorial pages, and vigilante reaction was swift. Almost all the advertising was canceled in that journal, and it was very quickly forced to suspend publication. Four days after King's shooting, many of the state's militiamen, whom the governor had called out to guard the San Francisco jail, deserted to the vigilantes. (This defection occurred despite the fact that the militia commander was the tall, erect, nervous William Tecumseh Sherman. Sherman, a banker in San Francisco since he had left the army, felt keenly that taking the law into private hands was inherently wrong.) It was then an easy matter for 1,500 heavily armed vigilantes to brush aside the few militiamen remaining on duty, capture the jail, and carry off Casey and Cora. In two days they were brought before a vigilante court for trial. These proceedings were dramatically interrupted by word that James King of William had died of his wounds. In the wake of this news, Casey and Cora were summarily found guilty. On May 22, while most San Franciscans were attending King's funeral, the sentence of death by hanging was carried out. The only courtesies extended to the prisoners were to allow Cora to marry his mistress Belle and Casey to make an extended last statement in the shadow of the gallows.

This twin execution did not end the activity of the vigilantes as Governor Johnson had fondly hoped it would. Rather, the vigilantes now acted with new bursts of energy. They set up a headquarters on Clay Street, complete with armed guards, and began issuing writs of banishment, mostly to Irish criminals.

By May 27 a group opposed to the vigilantes had organized, calling itself the Law and Order Men. This committee was composed mainly of lawyers, judges and politicians who had been shouldered aside by the vigilantes. Among their number were former Governor John McDougal, a prominent local judge, Alexander Campbell, and the political boss of San Francisco in more normal times, David C. Broderick. This group drafted a letter to Governor Johnson, asking him to declare San Francisco in a state of insurrection and to suppress the vigilantes by force.

Governor Johnson felt powerless to act, since most of his militia had deserted from the state standard. He hoped that public support for action against the vigilantes might materialize now that the usual political leaders of San Francisco had denounced vigilanteism, and decided to act with the help of federal power. Accompanied by Sherman, Johnson went to the Benicia arsenal to confer with the army commander in the region, veteran soldier General John E. Wool. Johnson and Sherman were most persuasive that federal help was warranted in this impasse. Wool agreed that he would furnish federal arms to a new militia to be raised by Sherman. These plans were jeopardized when the commandant of the Mare Island Navy Yard, future Civil War hero Captain David Glasgow Farragut, declined to transport the militia from Benicia across San Francisco Bay to the city without express orders from Washington. After a minor delay, Johnson, feeling that Wool had firmly pledged his assistance, decided to proceed with his plan.

According to the governor's scheme, a friendly judge of the California Supreme Court, David S. Terry, was asked for a writ of habeas corpus in an attempt to free one of the Vigilance Committee's prisoners. When the vigilantes ignored the writ, the governor declared that the city and county of San Francisco were in a state of insurrection. According to plan, Sherman tried to turn out the militia in the city, but few men would serve. Even worse from Sherman's point of view, General Wool now announced that he would not furnish the required arms to the militia without further orders from President Franklin Pierce. Several moderate San Francisco citizens tried to open negotiations with Governor Johnson for some compromise solution to the imbroglio, but the governor, under the influence of the dueling Judge David S. Terry, refused all overtures. Terry was determined to crush the vigilantes. Terry characteristically sat with his feet up on a table, his hat pulled over his eyes, damning the "pork-merchants," as he dubbed the vigilante leaders. At this juncture Sherman had endured enough of this belligerence, and believing the governor's plans were hopeless, sent in his resignation.

Despite Sherman's defection, Governor Johnson called upon General Wool to furnish the annual distribution of arms which the federal government usually made to California. After some hesitation, Wool agreed to furnish the ridiculously small supply of 113 muskets, a horse saber and two bullet molds to the state! Johnson eagerly accepted this offer and detailed three militiamen to bring the arms from the Benicia arsenal to San Francisco. These men, James McNabb, J. P. "Rube" Maloney and John G. Philips, loaded the weapons aboard the schooner *Julia*. Unfortunately for the success of their mission, the Law and Order party had been infiltrated by informers of the vigilante committee. As a result, all details of this secret mission were known to the vigilante leaders. They dispatched John L. Durkee with a small force aboard the vessel *Bianca*, which surprised and captured the *Julia* on the morning of June 21. Durkee released the three militiamen, although he carried off the arms. After Durkee's action became known to the vigilante leaders, they decided to arrest Maloney and Philips again. For this purpose they sent out a pugnacious vigilante handyman, Sterling V. Hopkins. Hopkins had gained a measure of fame as the henchman of Cora and Casey. Accompanied by several deputies, Hopkins headed for a bank building where Maloney had taken refuge. Hopkins entered the bank and tried to arrest Maloney, but to his surprise, Maloney had many supporters with him. Hopkins was forced to leave without his intended prisoner. Then Maloney made a serious mistake. Fearing that Hopkins might return with a force large enough to arrest him, the militiaman decided to shift his hiding place. He surrounded himself with several armed men, including Judge Terry, and emerged from the bank building. Hopkins and his followers were still hovering around, and seeing their intended prisoner escape was more than they could bear. As a result, a scuffle ensued between the two groups, during which Terry wounded Hopkins in the neck with a bowie knife. In the resulting confusion, Terry and Maloney escaped to a militia armory. This refuge proved illusory, for soon a mob of shouting, wildly gesticulating vigilantes swirled around the building threatening to tear it down. Those militiamen within, frightened by the size and temper of the mob, soon surrendered. Terry was triumphantly marched off to vigilante headquarters and imprisoned there. This structure was protected by ten-foot-high piles of six-foot-thick sandbags and was known as Fort Gunnybags. Terry's trial was tempararily postponed, pending the outcome of medical attempts to save the wounded Hopkins. Meanwhile Governor Johnson raged at the capture of his chief adviser; he vainly asked the naval authorities to help him attack the vigilantes' stronghold and liberate Terry.

Late in June, while Hopkins barely continued to cling to life, the vigilantes decided to delay no longer but to try Terry, whose continued imprisonment at Fort Gunnybags was an embarrassment to them. A trial was held in which Terry boldly defended himself against the charge of assaulting Hopkins. The case went to a vigilante committee which was divided in its opinion. Some of its members wished to take this opportunity to make an example of one of the governor's advisers; others felt that since Hopkins would live, an embarrassing situation could be ended by releasing the recalcitrant judge. Finally, by a three-fifths vote, the executive committee decided that Terry should be adjudged guilty of the relatively minor charge of resisting the vigilance group's officers, and also of assault upon Hopkins. Various vigilante subgroups reviewed the verdict, wrangling interminably over the disposition of the case. Finally, since Hopkins had been pronounced recovered by his physicians, in early August the Vigilance Committee simply released Terry.

In the middle of the Terry controversy, on July 29, the vigilantes had hanged two murderers. Since public opposition to the vigilantes was gradually growing, and since they felt that they had accomplished most of their goals, they began to conclude their operations. They had hanged four men, banished thirty more from San Francisco and had caused about eight hundred underworld figures to leave voluntarily. Viewing these accomplishments as sufficient for the time being, on August 14 the vigilantes tore down their barricades, and on August 18, after holding a parade in which more than six thousand marchers passed in review, they were publicly dismissed. Yet significantly, the organization's equipment was not sold at auction until the following October; its executive committee continued to meet in modest quarters until late 1859. And it was November 3, 1856, before Governor Johnson lamely withdrew his proclamation that San Francisco was in a state of insurgency.

This was far from the end for vigilante groups in California. In Monterey in 1864, in Tulare and adjoining counties during 1872–74, and in Truckee in 1874, citizen groups arrested and tried desperadoes when official law and order seemed insufficient.

The two San Francisco Vigilance Committees of 1851 and 1856 have been excessively praised and blamed. Some historians have seen in the tribunals necessary devices for changing turbulence to quiet stability. Others, probably with more insight, have seen them as "businessmen's revolutions." In the latter view, the vigilantes are seen as upper-class citizens venting their spleen for many grievances upon lower-class foreigners. In any event, the San Francisco vigilantes set the pattern for similar actions in many mining towns in Colorado, Idaho and Montana.

In the vigilantes' actions, Californians expressed their impatience with local law. Many of them showed even more disdain for the niceties of international law by filibustering or supporting filibusters. Essentially, this class of men acted as private individuals to take advantage of the weakness of the governments of the nations south of the Rio Grande. Their forays were attempts to overthrow national governments or break off Mexican provinces, substituting foreign domination for native rule. When Americans headed these ventures, they often proclaimed them as steps whereby these areas might be annexed to the United States. These adventurers visualized themselves as latter-day Davy Crocketts and Sam Houstons.

Filibusters were restless men of various nationalities. Some, such as the French, originally came to California as goldseekers, but finding themselves discriminated against in the gold fields, they turned to vent their frustrations upon the more helpless Latin states to the south. Others, such as the Americans, were simply adventurers who widened their horizons beyond California when the easy gleanings of the early gold rush were exhausted.

The first nation threatened by filibustering was the anachronistic kingdom of Hawaii. The island kingdom seemed an obvious target for this type of activity, since its government was weak and a large American colony had settled there. Restless Sam Brannan and several of his associates were believed to have plotted the overthrow of this kingdom. Just how much truth there was to this rumor is hard to say, but the Hawaiian king reacted violently, addressing his Parliament about the peril and vociferously protesting to the American commissioner. Perhaps as a result of this publicity, nothing happened.

California's actual filibustering of the 1850's was confined to the lands of her Latin neighbors to the south. California's first filibuster was probably Joseph C. Morehead. In 1850 Morehead was invited by a Mexican faction to bring an armed force into Sonora and Baja California. Ostensibly the filibusters would come to control the Indians, although their actual purpose was revolution. Morehead, then quartermaster general of California, misused state funds and supplies to outfit his expedition, which left California in the spring of 1851. Desertions plagued the dissension-ridden force. As a result, Morehead had to flee to escape arrest and succeeded only in alarming the Mexican authorities.

Disputing Morehead's claim to be the first California filibuster is Alex Bell. Shortly after California's admission to the Union, Bell decided to reinstate a deposed Ecuadorian president. He sailed in 1851 to Panama, which he used as a base for further operations. Reinforced by Ecuadorian sympathizers, he sailed up the Guayaquil River in order to reach the country's capital, Quito. Bell soon quarreled violently with his Ecuadorian allies, whom he openly regarded as inferiors. His open disdain alienated the native sympathizers also, who eventually made a deal with Bell's enemies. Soon both Ecuadorian factions were united by their desire to oust the unwelcome Yankee intruders. Bell was lucky to extricate himself and return to Panama. The survivors of this party dissolved into small contentious groups arguing about blame for the fiasco and what should be done next. Bell himself returned to San Francisco, dying in 1859.

Morehead's attempt in Mexico alarmed the Mexican authorities, who attempted to strengthen their defenses in northwestern Mexico, and thereby inadvertently opened the door to new troubles. The decision was made to encourage French colonists from California to settle in that area to act as a barrier against the Americans. The French goldseekers, unpopular in California, were quite willing to try their luck in Mexico. They were led by a penniless but dashing marquis, Charles de Pindray. Big, physically strong and famed throughout France as a duelist, he was a natural leader for filibuster-minded Frenchmen. De Pindray reached an agreement with the Sonoran authorities to lead a force of colonists into this region. Recruiting eighty-eight French goldseekers who were disappointed with the situation in California, he arrived on December 26, 1851, at the port of Guaymas on the Gulf of California. Later arrivals boosted the French force to 150 men. This group moved inland to a tract near the old mission of Cocospera, where its members began farming. The Apaches soon fled with the stock, and the Mexican authorities did not furnish the promised supplies. In May 1852, de Pindray, while on the return leg of a trip to protest conditions in his colony to the Mexican officials, was found dead from a gunshot wound. Whether he committed suicide or was murdered is still hotly debated. His colony dissolved. Many of the survivors were bitter about their treatment by the Mexicans and readily joined future French filibustering efforts.

Another French leader who led an expedition similar to that of de Pindray was Lepine de Sigondis. De Sigondis recruited some sixty men and led them into the Mexican northwest on a treasure-hunting search. Soon de Sigondis became embroiled with the Mexicans and was forced to withdraw to save his life.

The California French had not lost their taste for adventuring south of the border. A new leader soon appeared on the scene. He was Count Gaston de Raousset-Boulbon. Although of noble family, the count's reputation was poor. He was nicknamed "the Little Wolf." He too was invited into Sonora by the Mexican authorities. The French minister to Mexico supported the count's venture. In 1852 Raousset traveled into Sonora, leading an expedition of men disguised as a mining company. Raousset probably intended to mine the Mexican coffers rather than its mountains for his silver. If he intended to carry out an innocent plan of colonization, he soon dropped it when the Mexican local officials began to harass him with a multitude of orders. Refusing to obey instructions, he was soon declared an outlaw. In retaliation, in September of 1852, Raousset proclaimed the independence of the Sonoran Republic.

While the Mexicans hesitated, uncertain about how to proceed against the French, Raousset with 240 men audaciously took the offensive, capturing the important city of Hermosillo from 1,200 Mexican defenders. The French victory, while spectacular, was barren, since the French found themselves in a trap cut off from the coast by a force of 1,200 fresh Mexican troops. Ravaged by dysentery and other illnesses, with many wounded, the French situation grew desperate. As a result they offered the Mexicans an agreement whereby the filibusters could leave Hermosillo under a safe-conduct pass to the coast where free passage to San Francisco awaited them. In return the French would release all Mexican prisoners, if the Mexicans would properly care for the French wounded who could not be removed. The relieved Mexican officials accepted these terms, and just twelve days after victoriously storming Hermosillo, the French, in October 1852, trudged down the road to the coast and sullenly reembarked for California.

After extensive preparations, Raousset in the spring of 1854 dispatched four hundred men for Mexico and joined them in Guaymas that June. Although the Mexican national authorities had invited Raousset (despite his earlier activities) and his men to establish buffer outposts against American filibusters, the local Mexican officials and the French soon became violently hostile. The result was the "battle" of Guaymas. With no more than 350 effectives, Raousset marched against the Mexican barracks on July 13, 1854. The entrenched Mexicans met the onrushing French with volleys of cannon and small-arms fire. As the French forces began to dwindle under this fire, Raousset rallied twenty fanatical followers and led a last charge. They were soon killed or wounded. Raousset himself led a charmed life, and although his clothes were riddled with bullet holes, he escaped alive from the battlefield. His flight was only temporarily successful, for his followers betrayed him to the Mexicans, who executed him on the morning of August 12, 1854. With his characteristic gallantry, Raousett waved aside the proffered bandage and bravely faced the firing squad. His men were allowed to flee. With his death French schemes for Mexican filibusters also perished.

An American filibuster who came to a quick, tragic end was Henry A. Crabb. Crabb, a native of Nashville, Tennessee, had practiced law in Vicksburg, Mississippi. While there he had killed the editor of a local newspaper in a duel. Moving to California in the gold-rush days, he served in the state legislature, where he was distinguished by his fanatical championing of anti-Negro legislation. In 1856, having become interested in Sonora because of his wife's property there, Crabb led fifty colonists to the region. A local revolutionary, Ignacio Pesquiera, had originally encouraged Crabb to come to Sonora. Once there, Pesquiera urged Crabb to return to California to obtain reinforcements. Upon his return, Crabb was dismayed to discover that Pesquiera had come to terms with his Mexican rivals and had joined them in denouncing the Yankee filibusters. On April 1, the entering American force was ambushed just outside the town of Caboroa near Point Lobos on the Gulf of California. Twenty-one men were killed or wounded, and the Americans took refuge in some well-built adobe houses in the town. There they were besieged by the Mexicans, until the wounded Crabb accepted surrender terms which promised that he and his men would receive a fair trial. Instead, the filibusters were executed the next morning.

William Walker, born in 1824, was also a native of Tennessee, but had earned his medical degree from the University of Pennsylvania. He was not a prepossessing figure—short, slight, slow in speech, with red hair, freckles and seemingly pupilless grey eyes. Walker habitually wore a white fur hat with a wavy nap. He did not stay with medicine, but studied law and was admitted to the bar in New Orleans. Moving to gold-rush California, Walker became permanently infected with the virus of filibustering.

On October 15, 1853, he sailed with forty-eight followers from San Francisco aboard the ship *Caroline*. Landing at La Paz in Baja California, he was joined by two hundred rebel Mexicans. Intoxicated with this promising beginning, on January 18, 1854, he proclaimed the Republic of Sonora, a territory which embraced both the Mexican province of Sonora and Baja California. Disillusionment was soon felt among his forces, and the Mexicans began to desert in large numbers. Walker's harsh treatment of his men did nothing to reverse this trend. As a result, Walker had only a hundred men when he attempted to invade Sonora. As he progressed, his force dwindled to only thirty-five men. Even Walker admitted the futility of continuing the operation, and he abandoned the enterprise and returned to California, where he was arrested and tried in San Francisco on a charge of violating American neutrality laws. In the temper of California public opinion, Walker easily won an acquittal. Then he worked on California newspapers while shifting his filibustering interest from Mexico to Central America.

At this time Nicaragua was torn by civil strife. One faction, the Leonese, invited the rash Walker to help them. Quickly gathering sixty men (most of them former residents of Placer County), Walker sailed on May 3, 1855, for Central America. Although his force was small, its members were heavily armed, each man carrying two or more revolvers. Thus the fire power of this small band was great compared to the single-shot pistols and muskets of the forces they faced. Walker swept aside all opposition and proclaimed a puppet to be the new president of Nicaragua. Walker's high-handed conduct, particularly the cancellation of Nicaraguan anti-slavery laws, brought down upon the filibuster a host of enemies. In addition to facing an uprising of Nicaraguan rebels, a coalition of other Central American states was formed against Walker. This alliance sent an army against him.

An even more formidable foe was Commodore Cornelius Vanderbilt, who had built a transportation system across Nicaragua. Vanderbilt turned against Walker as a divisive and troublemaking threat to his profits. Vanderbilt, a hard-driving financier of the old school, threw his financial and material resources into the struggle against Walker. Seeing the circle of his enemies drawing ever closer, Walker rather uncharacteristically surrendered to an officer of the American Navy, who was able to withdraw him safely to the United States. It has been estimated that during the time he controlled Nicaragua, he was joined in all by 10,500 filibusters (3,500 of them from California). Perhaps 5,700 of this group died from wounds or disease. This heavy toll of life might have sobered a more cautious man, but Walker speedily hatched new schemes of adventure.

After several unsuccessful attempts to return to Central America, in August 1860, Walker sailed from Mobile for Honduras. His plan was to use Honduras as a base of operations to reconquer Nicaragua. He landed with about a hundred men and seized an old Spanish fort on the north coast of Honduras. At that point, the British warship *Icarus* appeared, and its commander, Norvell Salmon, ordered Walker to leave. Salmon pointed out that Britain had a lien on the customs of the port which Walker occupied, and hence that country would not permit him to disrupt its commerce. Rather than fight the British, Walker abandoned the fort and slipped into the jungle with his men. Cornered by his enemies further along the coast, he chose to surrender to Captain Salmon aboard the *Icarus*. Although Captain Salmon extended his permanent protection over Walker's seventy survivors, he turned over Walker himself, despite the filibuster's voluble protestations, to the Honduran authorities. Six days later, on September 12, 1860, the Hondurans executed Walker. His death brought the era of filibustering to a close. As a result of the Civil War, the changed political climate made filibustering quaintly old-fashioned.

Party battles in California in the 1850's had a strange, unreal quality. California Democrats and their opponents, the Whigs and later the Know-Nothings, cherished their national labels. In the Golden State the members of these parties were often more conversant with the party stands from the days when they still lived in the East than they were responsive to national developments after their own settlement in the Far West. Thus many state political pronouncements had a curious, old-fashioned ring. The Democrats were strong in antebellum California, because they dominated national politics. Westerners who sought constant favors from the national government of course sought to remain on good terms with the ruling circle in Washington. In order to survive in California, all parties blurred their national stands and favored transcontinental railroads. The California Know-Nothing Party even equivocated upon antiforeign and religious issues in the mid-fifties, straining their dogmas so far as to nominate a Roman Catholic for governor.

Although candidates had run as Democrats as early as 1849, the party actually existed on an organized basis only after a meeting in the temporary capital at San Jose in January–February 1850. In May 1851 the first Democratic convention in California met in an Episcopal church in Benicia. In the same month, the Whigs held their first state conclave in a Methodist–Episcopal church on Powell Street in San Francisco. In the first partisan-contested gubernatorial election, the Democrat John Bigler defeated his Whig opponent, Pearson B. Redding, by slightly over a thousand votes out of 44,000 cast. By this narrow margin the Democrats moved into the state house, and as the incumbents, lost only one gubernatorial election prior to the Civil War.

Despite its slender majority, the Democratic Party felt it could afford the luxury of rampant factionalism. In 1851 the state legislature ballotted 142 times without selecting a successor to John C. Frémont, who had drawn a short term as a senator. Frémont dearly desired a reelection, even absenting himself from a session of Congress in order to spend more time politicking. While he was away on his futile campaign, courtly six-footer William M. Gwin, as California's only accredited senator in Washington, greatly increased his influence. Gwin, a strong proslavery advocate, became the leader of the dominant faction in the Democratic establishment, popularly called the Chivalry or the "Chiv." When the legislature finally acted on January 30, 1852, to select Frémont's successor, it was Gwin's lieutenant, the former Ohioan John B. Weller, who was chosen.

Gwin's position in the party was challenged by David C. Broderick, who had unsuccessfully aspired to the senatorial toga against Weller. He had learned politics in the harsh school of Tammany Hall. Broderick was an anomaly as a youth, a saloonkeeper who never drank or gambled. In San Francisco he had become a smelter of gold and silver and a wholesaler of precious metals. His faction was sneeringly called the "Shovelry" or the "Plebians." Despite this social handicap, Broderick was able to contest the control of the Democratic Party on almost even terms with Gwin.

Broderick made his power base San Francisco, serving that city in the state senate. Skillfully using local patronage, he was able to construct a political organization which rivaled Gwin's federally nourished machine. After the inauguration of Democrat Franklin Pierce as President, the Gwin faction had sole access to the California federal spoils. Pierce, a northern man with southern principles, generally approved of Gwin's political posture in California and consistently aided him.

Nonetheless, Broderick, with the advantage of remaining in California consistently while Gwin was absent for months in Washington, maneuvered his forces to best advantage. In 1853–54 Broderick forged an alliance with Governor Bigler whereby the California chief executive, defying Gwin successfully, won renomination and reelection. Savoring this victory, Broderick attempted, a year early, to have the legislature select him as Gwin's successor for United States senator. Broderick was successful in having the lower house of the legislature vote to hold the senatorial election early. In the state senate, after a maximum effort, Broderick's plan was defeated by a single vote. Broderick's attempt completely alienated the two wings of the Democratic Party.

Taking advantage of this breach in the ranks of their opponents, the Whigs showed new life. Moreover they had a new issue upon which to rebuild the opposition to the Democrats—nativism. This issue was sweeping the eastern United States where the large numbers of German and Irish immigrants had so upset the old-stock Americans that a powerful reaction had set in. The nativist movement had its counterpart in California, and there, as well as in the East, the Whig Party metamorphosed into the American or Know-Nothing Party. Using prejudice and capitalizing upon the American penchant for secret societies, the Know-Nothings perfected their organization. As a result, in 1855 the American Party elected W. Neely Johnson as governor. Johnson proved to be such an inept chief executive that he was denied a renomination by his own party.

The Gwin-Broderick feud was scarcely affected by the American Party success, since the well-entrenched Democrats continued to control the state legislature. The two factions could not agree upon a successor to Gwin, although they did unite to deny the seat to any American Party candidate. Broderick in 1856 found a challenge to his authority as boss of San Francisco when the vigilantes formed a political party and elected all their candidates to municipal office. This was a grave blow, but not a mortal one to Broderick's senatorial aspirations, since the vigilantes did not attempt to elect candidates to the legislature. As a result, in the state elections of 1856 the American Party was already disintegrating, while the nascent Republican Party was still too feeble to make itself felt. The Democrats continued their grip upon the legislature.

There were by this time two United States Senate seats at issue. Gwin's term had expired in March 1855, and no successor had been chosen. In March 1857, Weller's term would also expire. It was imperative that California's legislature break the deadlock or the state would go unrepresented in the United States Senate. Broderick aspired to Weller's seat now, since he preferred a full six-year term to the lesser four-year prize as Gwin's successor. By the legislature's meeting in January 1857, Broderick had thoroughly canvassed the Democratic legislators and had seen to it that the Democratic caucus agreed to fill the long term first. Then the caucus, by a vote of 42 to 37, nominated Broderick over outgoing Senator John B. Weller. The Democrats then closed their ranks and elected Broderick to the Senate on a joint ballot of the legislature.

The struggle then shifted to the remaining short senatorial term. Broderick was determined to drive a hard bargain with the various aspirants, since he desperately needed the federal patronage to reward his loyal followers. The municipal patronage of San Francisco was in the unfriendly hands of the vigilante group, and the state patronage was still in the hands of the American Party. Federal offices had always been denied to his faction. Indeed, so firmly had the southern wing of the Democratic Party under Gwin controlled the distribution of place that the San Francisco customhouse was known as the "Virginia Poor House." Now all that was to be changed. In the bargaining that followed for Broderick's support for the other Senate term, the winner was the most unlikely aspirant, former Senator Gwin himself! Broderick, who had little personal dislike for his rival, agreed to support him when Gwin specifically promised that the federal patronage would be exclusively in Broderick's hands. When Broderick threw his support to Gwin, the latter was elected by the legislature. John B. Weller, the other leading senatorial aspirant, consoled himself by running successfully for governor.

Broderick, who at thirty-seven was the second-youngest senator then in Congress, set off jauntily to Washington as the acknowledged political leader of California. His Washington experiences were frustrating. Gwin may have tried to live up to his bargain with Broderick, but President James Buchanan, who took office in March 1857, spurned him. Buchanan thought the brash Broderick perfidious, particularly when he attacked the administration's proslavery policy in Kansas. Also Gwin was an experienced senator who had patiently learned his way through the shoals and labyrinths of the nation's most exclusive club, the Senate, while pushy Broderick found that he could not gain acceptance from any of the Democratic Senate leaders except Stephen A. Douglas, who found that Broderick had the same loathing for the President's Kansas policy and acted with the same explosive energy as himself. The young California senator's inability to bring the state's patronage and favors to his own followers seriously undermined his political supremacy within the state. In 1859, after Congress adjourned, Broderick returned to California, a scant two years after his great triumph, literally fighting for his political life.

Broderick launched an attack upon the Gwin faction, and now that sectionalism was rampant in this period immediately preceding the Civil War, he rallied his followers with the war cry "Throw the slave-lovers out!" He traveled the length of California, urging the election of his faction's Democratic nominees for state office. This campaign became more bitter and personal than any of his previous efforts. In the course of denouncing the Chivalry's leaders, Broderick eventually found himself challenged to a duel by the California supreme court justice David S. Terry, who had deserted the Know-Nothings to return to the Gwin faction. Terry had taken umbrage at various unflattering remarks about himself made by Broderick. Meanwhile the campaign had ended and Broderick found himself a beaten man. His faction had split the pronorthern vote with the rapidly developing Republican Party in the general election and Gwin-supported gubernatorial candidate Milton S. Latham easily won.

The exchange of notes between Broderick and Terry over the proposed duel had been delayed until after the election. Then the time for the duel was fixed as September 12, 1859. An attempt by the legal authorities to interfere succeeded only in delaying the encounter until the next day.

At that time the pair met on the shores of Lake Merced. In an exchange of gunfire, Terry wounded the senator. Broderick might have recovered, but his doctor at first insisted that the wound was slight and did not attend him properly. As a result, three days after the duel Broderick died. In the Victorian age, which prized last words, Broderick was credited with having said, "They have killed me because I was opposed to a corrupt administration and the extension of slavery."

The image of Broderick as a martyr to the slavery interests was fixed in legend when Lincoln's friend Edward D. Baker delivered a moving funeral oration in which the Republican leader praised Broderick for his unequivocal stand against the spread of slavery into Kansas and charged that he had been killed because his proslavery opponents could not otherwise silence him. California public opinion was profoundly affected by Broderick's death; many citizens vented their grief by excoriating Terry and Gwin. Terry actually left the state for a time, sojourning in Nevada. Most of the Broderick Democratic faction drifted into Republican ranks and helped carry California for Lincoln in 1860.

One unrelenting issue which agitated California political life was the determined effort to split the state into northern and southern portions.

The spirit of sectionalism had been present, as we have seen, during the Mexican period. As early in the American era as the Monterey Convention of 1849 many southern California delegates favored a division of the province at San Luis Obispo. North of the line, they argued, a state could be created, but south of it they demanded that only a territory be set up. This proposal was brushed aside at the time, but the idea of division of the new state would not die. It was nurtured in the south where the area's interest in agriculture gave rise to a different basic outlook than in the more heavily settled northern part of the state, where the economic emphasis was upon mining. The southern Californians hoped a division of the state would allow them to continue the old order in their area, unhampered by the bustling, alien north. In addition, as large landowners, they felt with some justification that state taxes bore unfairly upon them. The sparsely settled south saw no reason to support a relatively expensive state government. They would have been content with a territorial government whose cost would largely be borne by the federal government.

Despite some contemporary opinion to the contrary and much historical writing since, the movement inside California to split the state owed little to a desire to establish slavery in the southern areas. However, in Congress southerners such as Mississippi Senator Henry S. Foote backed the notion of dividing California precisely for the purpose of implanting slavery in the southern part.

Yet even without this encouragement from outside, the movement to divide the state would probably not have been dampened. With this encouragement it continued as a violent issue until the 1860's. By August 1851, all candidates for the legislature in Los Angeles County announced themselves pledged to divide the state. Mass meetings were held across the southern part of California to develop support for a convention of state dividers to be held in October 1851, in Santa Barbara. At this gathering strong resolutions calling for the political division of the state were unanimously passed.

In 1852 and 1853 there was an unsuccessful drive in the legislature to call a constitutional convention which would either grant the southern Californians' demands for an end to inequities, or if necessary, divide the state. Northern Californians then in control of the state legislature were generally cool to requests to split the state, since it would diminish their own influence and prestige.

In February 1855, Jefferson Hunt of San Bernardino introduced an assembly bill which would have set up the new state of Columbia in central and northern California. The committee to which this bill was referred went even further, proposing to split California into three states, Colorado, California and Shasta. After much debate, the bill was recommitted to a select committee charged with the responsibility of preparing an address to the people of California including the proposed act and reasons justifying it. The state senate itself never acted upon the state-splitting proposal. Although most politicians believed that the session of 1856 would see legislation to divide the state, the Broderick-Gwin fight kept the legislature in such an uproar that no bill to split the state received serious consideration. In 1857, however, the tactics of the divisionists changed; then they concentrated upon trying to get a state constitutional convention approved. They failed.

In February 1859, Andrés Pico, representing a southern California constituency, introduced resolutions into the legislature separating California south of San Luis Obispo as the territory of Colorado. As a countermove, northern Californians, while this measure was under discussion, proposed to set off the area north of the fortieth parallel as a similar territory. This mocking move was only a cut above a proposal made at the same time that a state named South Cafeteria be carved out of the area south of the Tehachapi Mountains.

Despite these diversionary tactics, a majority of a special legislative committee at this session reported formally upon a bill splitting the state and setting up the proposed territory of Colorado, if two-thirds of the voters in that area voted in favor of the proposal at the next general election, and if Congress approved. The lower house passed this bill 33 to 15, and the state senate approved it 15 to 12. The governor then signed the measure. When the election was held in that part of California earmarked to embrace the territory of Colorado, 2,457 citizens voted in favor of the project and only 828 against—far more than the required two-thirds majority.

As a result, Governor Milton S. Latham, in January 1860, formally sent the election results to President James Buchanan, asking that he seek the sanction of Congress for the projected state division. Although the California legislature agreed with the governor that as a result of this election the state should be split, still no bill agreeing in details passed both houses.

It did not matter, since the attention of the federal government was riveted upon the momentous events leading to the Civil War, and it could spare no time to settle local disputes within California. Inside California as well, the swift march of events left little inclination to resolve the state's sectional rivalry. In the changed political climate of California in the years after 1861, the question of splitting the state seemed quaintly archaic. For good or ill, the two great sections of California were destined to continue their political union.

EIGHTEEN

California and the Civil War

I N California in the 1850's, sentiment grew strong for the formation
of an independent Pacific republic including the state and adjacent
areas. The reasons for this sentiment were varied. While California politically was a part of the Union, geographically the state was
isolated by hundreds of miles of mountains, desert and prairie. In addition, California was populated by rootless men who had left their
homes and families behind them. Such men, already suffering from
"anomie," found it easy to contemplate cutting their political ties with
the United States. Moreover, many Californians believed that the federal
government was ungrateful for the gold which they had mined, because
it would not build adequate transportation links for them with the East.

As early as the days of the Vigilance Committee of 1856, there had
been earnest talk about creating a Pacific republic. There were advocates
of secession on the Vigilance Committee, although opponents of the
group greatly exaggerated the separatist sentiment within the movement.
Several congressmen from the East declared that the vigilantes were
secessionists and urged that President Franklin Pierce act to suppress
them. Pierce refused, and eventually the Vigilance Committee dissolved.

In addition, prosouthern sentiment was rampant among the dominant
faction of the California Democratic Party. In 1858 the Democratically
controlled California legislature endorsed President Buchanan's proslavery Kansas policy. Senator Gwin put his faction squarely behind the

southern wing of the Democratic Party which supported John C. Breck-inridge in the presidential election of 1860. By that year the Broderick Democrats had either drifted into the Republican Party or backed the northern Democrat Stephen A. Douglas for President.

The presidential election of 1860 was an exciting contest in California. The Republicans had organized in the mid-1850's under the leadership of Leland Stanford, Cornelius Cole, Collis P. Huntington, Mark Hopkins and Charles and Edwin B. Crocker. The Republicans had made little impact on the political life of the state in the presidential election of 1856 or in the various races for governor in the fifties. In 1860, however, although two-thirds of the California voters cast ballots against Lincoln, the division in Democratic ranks allowed him to win the state's four electors.

When it became certain that Lincoln had been elected, the southern states began to secede from the Union. Soon the tide of secession ran as far west as California. In the state, however, there was less sentiment for joining a southern confederacy and more opinion in favor of an inde-pendent Pacific republic. Judge Butts, editor of the Sacramento *Standard* and also the state printer, formally proposed that a convention be called to establish such a republic. Judge Butts was merely echoing the senti-ments of former California governor John B. Weller, who had spoken out in January 1860, more than a year before. At that time Weller had prophesied that "if the wild spirit of fanaticism, which now pervades the land should destroy this magnificent Confederacy [the pre-Civil War Union] . . . [California] will not go with the South or the North, but here upon the shores of the Pacific found a mighty republic. . . ."

In late November of 1860, writing from Washington, Missouri-born California Congressman John C. Burch proposed the formation of a Pa-cific republic consisting of California, Oregon, New Mexico, Washington and Utah. On December 21, 1860, Virginia-born Congressman C. L. Scott wrote a fellow California politician and echoed a similar view. Many California newspapers editorialized favorably concerning the independ-ence of California, including the San Francisco *Herald,* the Sacramento *Standard,* the Alameda County *Gazette,* the Los Angeles *Star* and the Sonora *Democrat.*

In early 1861, several resolutions favoring a western confederacy were introduced into the California legislature. At that time state Senator H. I. Thornton and Assemblyman Zach Montgomery made fiery speeches ad-vocating a Pacific republic. Assemblyman Charles W. Piercy, a Douglas Democrat, authored an unsuccessful resolution condemning the Republi-cans as solely responsible for the secession crisis.

Opponents of the Union, whether southern sympathizers or propo-nents of a western confederacy, were swamped by a Union-minded legislative majority. In May 1861 the assembly voted 49 to 12 for a resolution strongly supporting the federal government.

Governor Milton S. Latham, who had taken his seat in the United States Senate, had previously expressed sympathy for a Pacific republic, but by December 1860, he reversed his stand and backed the national government.

Proponents of a Pacific republic soon realized that it was impossible to set up the confederacy of their dreams. At most, 602,000 people could be included within the confines of such a nation, and with a 1,500-mile coastline it would be difficult to defend. Many Californians who were opposed to this idea argued that Emperor Napoleon III of France would simply gobble up such a weak political entity.

After the Confederate firing on Fort Sumter in mid-April 1861, Union sentiment was tremendously strengthened by what most Californians regarded as an act of southern aggression. Mass meetings for the Union were held in Oakland, San Jose, San Francisco, Marysville and Placerville. Yet sympathizers with the Confederacy were numerous in California. Perhaps as many as a quarter of all San Franciscans favored secession. In addition, there were pockets of secessionists in southern California towns such as Ventura and San Bernardino.

After Milton S. Latham resigned as governor of California in January 1860 to accept election to the United States Senate, he was succeeded by his lieutenant governor, an ardent Buchanan Democrat, John G. Downey. After the Civil War began, Downey seemed to many suspicious Unionists to be unenthusiastic in his support of the federal cause. When a great mass meeting was held on May 11, 1861, in San Francisco, Downey refused to attend, sending instead a letter that lamely stated that the press of public business prevented his attendance. In this same communication, he added that he did not believe the Union could be preserved by a war. Despite a storm of criticism evoked by this statement, Downey continued in office.

Breckinridge Democrats generally applauded the governor's stand, as they argued that the South could never be successfully coerced into remaining in the Union. This faction had, however, been losing ground steadily in California, and its antiwar stand accentuated this trend. Since the overwhelming majority of Californians were of northern or foreign origin, they could not identify with the war aims of the Confederacy.

The state election of 1861 was vital to the future of California; it ended widespread talk of taking California out of the Union. In this gubernatorial campaign, Republican Leland Stanford faced two rival candidates—the Breckinridge or southern Democrat John R. McConnell, and the Union Democrat John Conness.

Leland Stanford had been born into an old New England family which had migrated as far west as Watervliet, New York. His father possessed an above-average income and had educated his son in private schools. Young Stanford eventually was admitted to the bar and practiced law in the late 1840's in Port Washington, Wisconsin. After the California gold strike, he came to the Far West with his four brothers and went into what soon became a lucrative merchandising business in Sacramento. He impressed many observers with a trait which could have been a handicap in another era. When asked anything, even the correct time, he paused and seemed to weigh his answer most carefully before replying.

Stanford fought the campaign claiming to be the candidate whose support of the Union was the most unconditional. The Republicans called the election struggle a contest between democracy and aristocracy. Between June 29 and September 2, Stanford, in company with his colleague Cornelius Cole, stumped all of northern California. He paid particular attention to the mining regions from Weaverville in Trinity County to the town of Sonora in the south. Stanford, a pedestrian speaker, also had a notable ally in the golden-tongued orator and Unitarian divine Thomas Starr King. King lived in California only four years, but he left an indelible stamp upon the state's history. San Francisco's First Unitarian Church called the young man from Boston to fill its pulpit, so well known was he as both an orator and an author. King soon played a leading role in the philanthropic and political life of California. He canvassed the state for Lincoln in 1860, and he aided greatly in carrying the governorship for Stanford in 1861. More influential to Stanford's cause than King's oratory were a group of prominent San Francisco businessmen, normally Democrats, who supported him for his strong pro-Union attitudes. These men included Henry W. Halleck, James Phelan, Henry M. Naglee and Levi Strauss. Stanford won the election with 55,935 votes. Yet the combined votes of his two opponents totaled 63,816. Stanford, like Lincoln, was a minority winner.

If Stanford's victory ended the possibility of official state action to withdraw California from the Union, it did not end the danger of subversion. Confederate sympathizers, denied a victory at the ballot box, turned to plots. Although shadowy in their existence, there seem to have been in California secret societies of Confederate sympathizers, such as the Knights of the Columbian Star and the Knights of the Golden Circle. Each had its own ritual, secret passwords and handgrips. In part they appealed to the American love for secret fraternal orders. Their numbers were never accurately ascertained, but estimates have varied from a few thousand to as high as fifty thousand. Their numbers and importance have been exaggerated both at that time and since. Yet if they never succeeded in launching any serious uprisings, they did succeed in slipping some recruits out of California into the Confederate Army. They also probably inspired some divisive unrest in two groups which had no direct connection with the Confederacy—the Californios of the southern part of the state and the Indians.

General Albert Sidney Johnston, a southerner, was in command of the Department of the Pacific at the outbreak of hostilities. Many loyal Union men leaped to the conclusion that he was plotting to deliver California to the Confederacy. Johnston, a fifty-eight-year-old Kentuckian, was a veteran soldier whose still-blond hair belied his years. He was a newcomer to California, having assumed command only a few months before on January 15, 1861. Many whispered at the time, and some historians have since hinted, that Johnston connived to get the Pacific command so as to betray California to the South. This rumor had a certain credibility, since Johnston's southern sympathies were well known; not long after leaving California he did join the Confederate Army. Yet these surface indications were misleading. Johnston himself asked to be relieved of his California command because he wished to be free to resign from the Union service and join the southern forces. In the meantime, he faithfully administered his post until he was regularly relieved. He relayed an unofficial warning to his many southern friends in California not to attempt to seize any property under his protection. Nevertheless, the Washington authorities were understandably nervous about him and quickly honored his request to be relieved. The War Department sent the barrel-chested veteran soldier Edwin Vose Sumner to succeed the Kentuckian, and he assumed command on April 25, 1861. Johnston quickly went East, where he had less than a year's service in the Confederate Army before he bled to death from a supposedly superficial wound received at the Battle of Shiloh.

If Johnston had posed no threat to California, other southern sympathizers were not so circumspect. A prominent lawyer, Edmond Randolph, a leading Breckinridge Democrat, made a fiery speech during the gubernatorial election of 1861, in which he asked for Confederate victories on the battlefield. He then said, "If this be rebellion, then I am a rebel. Do you want a traitor? Then I am a traitor." Surprisingly, since less virulent Confederate sympathizers were often summarily arrested, Randolph never ran afoul of the authorities or attracted any impromptu vigilante action.

Others not so fortunate included a leading San Francisco clergyman, the Reverend W. A. Scott of the Calvary Presbyterian Church. In 1867 Reverend Scott, at a meeting of the California presbytery, declared that Abraham Lincoln was a usurper, and favorably compared Jefferson Davis to Washington. When his speech became known about San Francisco, angry, gesticulating mobs demonstrated around his church, rattling the stained-glass windows with their shouts. In the midst of this hullabaloo, Scott resigned and left the state.

William M. Gwin was not only denied reelection to the United States Senate in 1861, but he was subsequently arrested twice as a suspected subversive and briefly imprisoned. Finally set at liberty in December of 1861, Gwin, once the political master of California, now wandered about the countryside. Finding no congenial area in which to settle, he went to Europe. After the Civil War he journeyed to Mexico and lived among the Confederate exiles. After these enterprises failed, he returned to California, where he barely managed to eke out a living as a farmer.

Another outspoken Confederate partisan who came to grief was James H. Hardy, judge of the sixteenth judicial district. After the indiscreet judge was detected cheering for Jefferson Davis, toasting the Confederacy and sneering at the American flag, he was impeached by the legislature in 1862. Declared guilty, he was suspended from office for six months. In October 1862, Assemblyman E. J. C. Kern was arrested and imprisoned for using treasonable language.

Several California newspapers openly expressed Confederate sympathies. These sheets included the Stockton *Argus*, Stockton *Democrat*, San Jose *Tribune*, Tulare *Post*, and the Visalia *Equal Rights Expositor*. As a result, in September 1862, General Sumner's successor in command of the Pacific Department, General George Wright, excluded these newspapers from the mails and expresses. The Visalia *Expositor* in particular refused to be intimidated by the general and instead became more anti-Union. As a result, in January 1863, the military authorities arrested the editors, Hall and Garrison. Hall took the oath of allegiance and was quickly released. Garrison, the more obdurate of the two, remained in prison for a time. One night in March 1863, thirty rioting soldiers from a nearby military camp destroyed the offices and press of the *Expositor*.

Several California officeholders left the state to serve in the Confederate Army. Most prominent among them were Virginia-born Congressman Charles Lewis Scott and State Controller Samuel H. Brocks. Three Californians who were flaming Confederate sympathizers deserve special mention: Dan Showalter, Judge David S. Terry and Asbury Harpending.

In some respects Showalter's career as a secessionist was the most remarkable. A Pennsylvanian, he came to California in 1852, when he was in his early twenties. He won two terms in the California legislature as a Douglas Democrat. Surprisingly, in the secession crisis of 1860–61, Showalter drifted into the position of a Confederate apologist. Then in the swirl of debate in the overheated halls of the California legislature, he became embroiled in an incident with a fellow Douglas Democrat, Charles W. Piercy. Piercy had also assumed a pro-Confederate stance during this legislative session. However, when a dispute arose concerning a procedural question at the time of the consideration of a pro-Union resolution, Showalter and Piercy exchanged hot words, leading to a duel. On May 26, 1861, the two men met in an encounter on the field of honor near San Rafael. The weapons agreed upon were rifles. There, during the last political duel in California, Showalter killed Piercy. Although Piercy himself had authored an anti-Union resolution in the legislature, the facts of the quarrel became obscured and the duel came to assume overtones of the encounter between Broderick and Terry. The rumor soon circulated that a pro-Union man had been murdered by a southern sympathizer. Piercy's earlier stand was forgotten, and he became a Union martyr.

In this inflamed state of public opinion, Showalter realized his California political career was ended. He quickly decided to leave for the Confederacy. Late in 1861, Showalter and a group of Confederate sympathizers tried to steal out of the state into Arizona with the ultimate intention of reaching Texas. Showalter's group was apprehended by a military patrol and incarcerated in Fort Yuma. Only after taking two oaths of loyalty in April 1862, was Showalter released. Because he had been forced to take these oaths under duress, Showalter did not consider them binding. Therefore, he headed for Texas where he enlisted in the Confederate Army. He fought in several battles, ultimately reaching the rank of lieutenant colonel. In February 1864, he concocted an elaborate scheme to infiltrate the Union-held territory of Arizona. With a force of one hundred picked Confederates, he hoped to seize Tucson and convert it into a base for the invasion of California. The plan failed, since the Confederacy could not raise the necessary $20,000 in specie needed to put it into effect. When the war ended, the unrepentant Showalter went to Mexico and opened a bar in Mazatlán. Not long after, he was killed in a drunken brawl with his own bartender.

After his duel with Broderick, Judge David S. Terry found the political climate of California threatening, and fled to Nevada, where he made his living as a lawyer amid the mining activity of the Comstock Lode. In 1860 he returned to California, belatedly to stand trial for shooting Broderick. At that time the secessionist-minded judge, James H. Hardy, dismissed the charges. Although he was officially cleared of responsibility for the shooting, California public opinion remained hostile to Terry. Upon the outbreak of the Civil War, he contented himself for a time by consorting with secessionist sympathizers in Nevada and California. However, when his brother was killed leading Terry's Texas Rangers in the eastern fighting, David Terry decided to play a more active role in the war. In 1863, he boarded a vessel for Mexico's west coast, making his way from there overland to Texas. After going east to Richmond, Terry saw service as a staff officer at the Battle of Chickamauga. Later he served as a colonel with the Confederate forces in Texas. Terry constantly planned to lead a conquering Confederate Army into California. However, he could never find the requisite force. After Appomattox, Terry also tried Mexico as a haven, becoming a cotton planter in Jalisco before returning, in July 1868, to a California which had grown indifferent to him.

One California secessionist who concentrated his efforts upon California was the redoubtable Asbury Harpending. Harpending was born in Hopkinsville, Kentucky. He entered college at fifteen, but ran away from home less than a year later to join William Walker in Central America. Long before he could join the filibuster, he was apprehended by the authorities and returned to Kentucky. Too restless to return to his books, he left for California at sixteen with his father's blessing. The young Asbury Harpending started for San Francisco with five dollars in one pocket and a pistol in the other. Investing his money in fruit before embarking aboard a vessel at New Orleans, he peddled these treats to his fellow passengers who quickly tired of the ship's monotonous fare. He made a four hundred dollar profit on his investment. When he arrived in San Francisco, he found the city in the grip of a depression; therefore he went off to Mexico in search of his fortune. Four years later he returned to the city as the owner of a million-dollar gold mine. At the outbreak of the Civil War, southern sympathizer Harpending was swift to answer the Unionist Thomas Starr King. He organized his own chapter of the Knights of the Golden Circle. Then he ran the federal blockade to Richmond, Virginia, to get encouragement for his secessionist schemes. He returned to San Francisco with blank letters of marque (a license to privateer) and advice from Confederate Secretary of State Judah P. Benjamin about how he might operate as a privateer without violating international law. Benjamin advised Harpending to outfit a vessel in an American port, but not to commit any depredations against American shipping until after the privateersman could reach a foreign harbor from which he could then publicly proclaim his purpose. Harpending had his eye upon seizing the gold-carrying San Francisco–Panama steamers.

Harpending recruited two principal conspirators to help him—Ridgely Greathouse, a former Kentuckian who had become wealthy banking and running a stage line in Yreka, and an English soldier of fortune, Alfred Rubery. After much searching about for a suitable vessel, the trio finally purchased a swift, ninety-one-ton schooner, the *J. W. Chapman*. Using the excuse that he planned to trade in Mexico, which was then torn by civil strife, Harpending purchased two twelve-pound cannons and many small arms. He hired a mate, four sailors and a cook, as well as fifteen "marines." The conspirators planned to slip out of the harbor on the morning of March 25 for the Mexican port of Manzanillo.

Although Harpending had laid his plans cautiously, whispers of his plot reached the Federal Revenue Service. The revenue officers alerted the San Francisco police, who maintained a day-and-night watch on the *Chapman*. As soon as the schooner's crew got the vessel away from its mooring, two boatloads of armed men from the U.S.S. *Cyane* bore down to intercept it. In order to destroy incriminating documents, the conspirators started a fire aboard the vessel. Some nervous sailor aboard one of the two Union boats called "Fire!" At once the boarding party drew back from the *Chapman*, and the resourceful Harpending used the time gained to destroy his documents, even swallowing several of them. At last the *Cyane*'s boarding party rallied and swept over the gunwales and onto the decks of the *Chapman*, only to find that all the fight had gone out of the conspirators, who meekly surrendered on demand. The *Chapman* was towed to the fortified harbor strongpoint on Alcatraz Island, where an extensive search of the schooner revealed its privateering purpose. Painfully piecing the burned and mutilated scraps of paper together, the Union authorities learned the extent of Harpending's ambitious plans. The adventurous Kentuckian had hoped to seize gold shipments and use this booty to finance the conquest of California. The crew of the *Chapman*, which included two plasterers and an attorney, but only one bona fide seaman, was released with a stern warning. The three ringleaders had to face trial before the United States Circuit Court. When two of Harpending's minor associates turned state's evidence against him, he lost all hope of an acquittal. After only a four-minute deliberation, the jury found the three ringleaders guilty. All drew the maximum sentence of ten years in jail and a ten thousand dollar fine. But they served only a brief imprisonment. Harpending and Greathouse were able to win their freedom under the terms of an amnesty act by taking a prescribed oath and posting bond for their future good behavior. Rubery, as a foreigner, was not eligible under the terms of this act, but was pardoned by Lincoln as a favor to the great English liberal leader John Bright. Harpending went on to a postwar career as a real estate operator and financier, amassing yet another fortune. He ended his days as a recluse, almost forgotten by the San Francisco which had been the scene of his adventures.

Harpending's subversive attempt greatly disturbed California's maritime interests concerning Confederate privateering, but this threat never materialized. Perhaps the closest call San Francisco ever experienced occurred in 1865 when the Confederate warship *Shenandoah* appeared in the Pacific. This commerce destroyer actually operated for months after Appomattox since its captain, James I. Waddell, had not heard that the war had ended. Captain Waddell planned but did not execute an attack upon San Francisco in August of 1865. Nonetheless, the *Shenandoah* caused some financial distress to that port when it destroyed the American Pacific whaling fleet.

One Confederate depredation which greatly excited California was the holdup of the stage from Virginia City on June 30, 1864. About thirteen miles from Placerville, robbers stopped the stage, taking from it a large amount of bullion belonging to Wells, Fargo & Company. This robbery would not have been considered unusual, except for the receipt which one of the robbers pressed upon the startled stage driver. It was signed by R. Henry Ingram, a captain recruiting inside California for the Confederacy. A group of Santa Clara County Confederate sympathizers had hatched this plot to obtain money for the recruitment of soldiers for the southern army. A great manhunt was launched to capture the culprits, and by daylight the next morning the hideout of the robbers was attacked by the lawmen. In the fight that followed, a deputy sheriff was killed, but several of the bandits were captured. The rest of the daring band fled to the vicinity of San Jose, where on July 15 they were again surprised by lawmen. This time the posse was larger, and as a result several of the holdup men were killed and most of the others taken into custody. One of the prisoners blurted out the details of the scheme, and as a result of his confession other conspirators in Santa Clara County were also arrested. On the morning of July 1, the El Dorado County Grand Jury speedily indicted ten of the holdup men for the murder of the deputy sheriff. The ten were tried separately, but only two could be convicted—Thomas B. Pool, who was sentenced to be hanged, and another man, who received a twenty-year term. Pool unsuccessfully appealed his case to the California supreme court and was executed at Placerville on September 29, 1865. As the war was drawing to a close, the remaining prisoners were not tried, and were ultimately released.

During the war, California contributed generously to the Sanitary Commission (the Red Cross of its day). In all, the state gave $1.2 million, or about one-quarter of all the money raised for that purpose. The Sanitary Commission had been established shortly after the fighting began by a Massachusetts man, Dr. Henry W. Bellows. Dr. Bellows wrote Thomas Starr King, whom he had known in Boston, asking that the San Francisco minister sponsor a fund-raising campaign in California. King became deeply interested in the fund-raising campaign and soon toured every part of the state. By September 1862, the California friends of the Commission had sent a $100,000 draft by telegraph to its eastern headquarters. The next month they transmitted a second draft for the same amount. King helped organize a committee to direct the fund-raising endeavors for the Sanitary Commission in California; later this group expanded the campaign to the entire Pacific area and Nevada. In the fall of 1863, when the demands from the various theaters of the war strained the resources of the Commission, King received a desperate appeal from the organization's leaders that California increase her contribution. The telegraphic appeal to King ended, "California has been our main support in money, and if she fails all is lost." At once King wired that he would raise at least $25,000 a month, so long as the emergency persisted. King devoted himself with such unstinting effort to the task that his health failed and he died from diphtheria in 1864 at the age of thirty-nine.

One of the Sanitary Commission's greatest fund-raising activities involved Reuel C. Gridley, the owner of a grocery store in the small mining community of Austin, Nevada. Gridley was actually a southern sympathizer, but since the Sanitary Commission helped all the wounded or ill soldiers it could reach, it was nonpartisan and therefore supported by sympathizers for both sides. In April 1863, Gridley had made an election bet that the Democratic candidate would win the first mayoralty election in Austin. When Gridley lost the bet, he had to carry a fifty-pound sack of flour (manufactured by John Bidwell of the pioneering Bidwell–Bartleson party) down a canyon to the neighboring city of Clinton, a distance of more than a mile. When Gridley had carried the sack to Clinton, he offered the flour at an auction, with the proceeds to go to the Sanitary Commission. The sack sold for $350, and was then returned to be sold again. The auction continued in this fashion for two days, raising about $4,350 in cash and even more in property.

Other Nevada mining towns decided that they too wanted the chance to bid upon Gridley's "Sanitary Sack." At Gold Hill, Silver City, Dayton and Virginia City, thousands of additional dollars were raised. Finally Gridley came to San Francisco. There on the stage of the Metropolitan Theater, he exhibited his much-auctioned sack and retold the story of his fund gathering. The audience pelted the stage with a shower of silver coins. Eventually Gridley went to the East and repeated his fund raising. In all, he gathered more than $200,000 for the Sanitary Fund. Mark Twain, who had gone to school with Gridley in Hannibal, Missouri, immortalized the grocer and his sack in *Roughing It*.

Although far from the main theaters of the war and not subject to the federal draft, California raised 15,725 volunteers for the Union Army. These troops included two regiments of cavalry, one battalion of "native" (*i.e.* Californio) cavalry, eight regiments of infantry, one battalion of veteran infantry (an organization of limited service troops), and a special battalion of mountaineers.

The battalion of native cavalry was recruited for duty in Arizona against the Apaches and the Confederate cavalry. The Union military authorities hoped that the Californios would prove effective as desert fighters. In the end military affairs dictated that this outfit be used mainly within California. Andrés Pico, the old California leader, was offered the command of this group, but ill health forbade the grizzled leader's active service. The Californios did not take kindly to the rigors of discipline in the American Army, and out of 450 men in this battalion, about 37 per cent were carried on the rolls as deserters before the group mustered out. During the entire war, the battalion of California mountaineers served not against Confederates but against the insurrectionary Indians of the California northwest.

The Confederate government planned to seize control of Arizona and New Mexico as stepping stones to California. In July 1861, Confederate General Henry H. Sibley was authorized by Richmond to organize a brigade of Texas soldiers and invade New Mexico. If Sibley had quickly succeeded in his campaign, the situation would have been very threatening for California, which had not yet replaced the regulars who had guarded it with its own soldiers. If California had fallen to the South, the Confederacy would have been able to tap the vast mineral resources of the Pacific slope.

When Sibley's force of several thousand men arrived in New Mexico about the middle of December 1861, it quickly captured Albuquerque and Santa Fé. To bolster the sagging Union position in the Southwest, a "California column" was dispatched to New Mexico. This force consisted of five companies of the First California Cavalry, ten companies of the First California Infantry, the Fifth California Infantry, and a battery of four brass fieldpieces. Dispatched in April 1862, the force was under the competent command of General James H. Carleton. Since Sibley was already desperately short of supplies and ammunition, he retreated across the Rio Grande when he learned of the approach of the California column. All the towns and forts of Arizona and New Mexico were then reoccupied by the northern soldiers. In addition to causing the Confederate retreat from New Mexico, the California column performed a valuable service in keeping the mail routes open and subduing Indian disturbances on the frontier.

Other California troops were busy fighting the restless California Indians. These Indians, particularly those in the Humboldt district, caused much fighting and some casualties. The California troops performed a real service for the federal government, since they permitted the transfer of the regulars to the main theaters of the war.

In addition, California furnished troops for theaters of the war which were far distant from the state's own borders. The California Battalion of four hundred men, and its predecessor, the California 100—five hundred troops in all—served in the east with the Second Massachusetts Cavalry. These Californians enlisted under the Massachusetts allotment because they wished to see action in the main fighting in Virginia. Since Massachusetts was anxious to obtain men to fill its quota for the Union Army, it happily promised to transport the Californians east. These transplanted Californians fought in fifty separate engagements in the eastern theater, including several against the famous Confederate raider John Mosby. Of the five hundred men who served in the East, eighty-six were killed or died, thirty-four deserted and seventeen were carried on the rolls as missing.

About the same number of Californians enlisted in eight companies which served in Washington under that sparsely settled territory's quota. The authorities in Washington Territory had been unable to raise sufficient troops and therefore turned to recruiting in California. The Californians enlisted in this organization because they expected to find greater adventure there than within their own state. They were disappointed, since they served in much the same way against the Indians as did their comrades in California. They too fought no great battles which would earn them mention in history books.

Of the approximately 15,725 men who served under California's state banners (all in some portion of the West), seven officers and 494 enlisted men were killed or died of disease. Those fighting the Indians suffered more fatalities from arrows than from bullets. Arrow wounds were not the innocuous scratches so often depicted in the movies or on television— 60 per cent proved fatal to the troops who received them.

Once the war started, there was an increase in the difference between the numbers of arrivals from the East over departures from California. This situation of population increase continued until the war ended in 1865. Then the trend was dramatically reversed as men who had sojourned in California during the war returned to their permanent homes. Yet this influx, even though much of it was temporary, allowed San Francisco to pass the 120,000 mark in population. During this wartime period it boasted over one hundred schools, twelve daily newspapers, forty-one churches, twenty-six theaters, and over two hundred bars.

The fugitives from the war-torn East often went into mining. The federal government's heavy war-related spending depreciated the paper currency which the United States so generously issued. This condition caused the price of gold relative to paper money to spiral upwards. All over the West there was a rush of prospectors to find precious metals. Besides renewed mining activity in the Golden State's mother-lode country, many mines and mills were opened in the silver fields of Nevada, California's financial satellite. In addition, considerable interest in copper prospecting developed in 1862 and 1863. Hundreds of copper-mining companies were organized to fill the war-induced demands for this metal. As a result of this activity, by 1863 California was exporting sizable amounts of copper ore.

Other migrants to California went into farming and stock raising as the voracious war's demands for wheat and wool stimulated the state's agriculture. California's increased numbers of agriculturalists not only supplied the demands of home-based troops and the growing civilian population, but also produced a surplus to ship to the East. Except for those areas of the state plagued by drought and flood, it was a time of high business activity. As a result of the increased prosperity, the state government was able to reduce its indebtedness to half its former amount.

As a specie state, California did not willingly accept the various federal laws which increased the money supply by making legal tender of the paper greenbacks. Californians, accustomed to doing business with gold, and silver, generally looked upon depreciating paper money as an unmitigated abomination. As a result of this widespread opposition to greenbacks, state officials charged with the duty of collecting taxes would not accept paper money. The minority of Californians who were debtors, or who felt that patriotism demanded an acceptance of greenbacks, took the question to the courts. On July 28, 1862, a suit was brought into the twelfth district state court by a taxpayer named Perry against a state tax collector, Washburn, who had refused to accept United States notes in payment of taxes. This court ruled in favor of the tax collector. Thereupon, Perry appealed the case to the California supreme court. That tribunal, in an opinion delivered by its chief justice, Stephen J. Field, held that the act of Congress authorizing greenbacks had not referred to state taxes. Therefore, using this evasion, the court ruled that California was under no obligation to accept paper money in payment of taxes.

Greatly encouraged by this decision, the "hard-money" merchants and financiers, in the face of paper money's continuing depreciation, decided to maintain an all-metallic currency in California regardless of federal policy. As new contracts were drawn, commission merchants and importers generally inserted in every contract a clause providing for the repayment of the credit extended in gold exclusively. Any debtor so rash as to refuse to pay in gold was blacklisted and required in any future dealings to pay for goods in gold prior to delivery. (One of the few exponents of paper money included the California attorney general, Frank M. Pixley, who argued that so long as California professed to be within the Union, it must accept federal notes.)

In this confused and embarrassing situation, the hard-money men had a bill introduced into the state assembly which recognized both specie and paper money, allowing California citizens to contract as to the media in which they would make payment. Although opponents labeled this an artful attempt to nullify a federal law, both houses passed it by overwhelming majorities, and Governor Stanford signed it into law. Although Lincoln's secretary of the treasury, Salmon P. Chase, joined some Californians in denouncing the statute, it remained on the books. Opponents of the measure appealed to the courts, but the California supreme court, in the case of Carpentier *v.* Atherton, sustained the constitutionality of the

Specific Contract Act. During the postwar period, in the cases of Lane *v.* Oregon and Bronson *v.* Rodes, the United States Supreme Court sustained the constitutionality of California's law. Despite the controversy, few doubted that the groups which profited most from the state's hard-money policy were the large merchants and bankers who bought goods in the East using depreciated greenbacks and sold them exclusively for gold in California.

California politics was revolutionized by the Civil War. The Democratic dominance was broken, never to be reestablished to the same degree. Despite the state election of 1861, which had resulted in the choice of the Republican gubernatorial candidate, Leland Stanford, it was obvious that whenever the Democrats could heal their schism, they would return the state to Democratic control. To remain in power, the Republicans decided to broaden the base of their support. As was generally true in the North, many Democrats found the name of Republican to have too strong an abolitionist tinge for them to coalesce with it. Therefore, as elsewhere in the North, the California Republicans decided to fuse with those prowar Democrats under the title of the Union Party. Yet this coalition of Republicans and Democrats was not easily arranged. At first Governor Leland Stanford himself objected to such a coalition. Yet in the end, Stanford yielded to the hard mathematics of politics. Therefore, in the campaign of 1862 to elect a superintendent of public instruction, the Republicans met as the Union Administration Party with many Democrats in attendance and nominated John Swett. The Union Democratic committee chairman, David D. Colton, refused to coalesce with the Republicans, and instead arranged a convention which excoriated the traitors who had left their ranks to join the "abolitionists." This rump faction then nominated Jonathan D. Stevenson for superintendent. The antiwar Democrats nominated O. P. Fitzgerald for the same office. In the election in September 1862, the Union Party candidate won an outright majority over both his rivals in excess of 13,000 votes. The success of the coalition now convinced the doubters. More Democrats stampeded to get into the Union Party prior to the election of 1863, and that left insufficient prowar Democrats to place their own ticket in the field that year. These bitter-enders joined the Breckinridge (southern sympathizers) faction, and together they flew the banner of the reunited Democrats. Just as the Republicans set the tone and pace for the Union Party, the old prosouthern group dominated the counsels of the reconstructed Democrats.

The Union Party organized clubs throughout California, in which lively political discussions flourished. The attention of these groups was always fixed on national issues. Patriotism was equated with support of the Lincoln administration. The growing prospects of the Union Party made its gubernatorial nomination a great prize. Leland Stanford, then the Republican governor of California, expected to be nominated for a second term by this new political amalgam, but he did not reckon sufficiently with his party rivals. Among them was Aaron A. Sargent, who had been a prime mover in the Temperance Party before he joined the Republicans. In the end, although Sargent presented his name to the convention, thereby spurning all efforts to get him out of the race, he was not Stanford's most serious opposition inside the Union Party. That honor was reserved for Frederick F. Low, an early Republican who had served one term in Congress and had then been made collector of the port of San Francisco by Lincoln. From this power base, with its important patronage, Low succeeded in grasping control of the San Francisco Union Party machinery. Stanford hoped to counter this threat by controlling the convention votes of the important Sacramento delegation. However, in the Sacramento convention to pick delegates to the state conclave, the Low supporters triumphed by sixteen votes. Sensing defeat, Stanford withdrew, and Low was nominated on the first ballot at the state Union convention. The Democrats met, nominated John G. Downey and adopted a full state ticket on a platform which severely criticized the Union war effort. In the September election the statewide Union Party candidates polled about 65,000 votes to their opponents' 44,000. All three Union congressional candidates also triumphed. An important factor in the vote was the balloting of California's soldiers. They voted 4,159 to 140 for Low for governor and supported the other Union candidates in about the same proportion. Since the state Constitution had been amended, Low won a four-year, rather than a two-year, term for governor.

In the presidential election of 1864, few expected the Democratic candidate, George B. McClellan, to defeat Lincoln in the contest for the state's electoral vote. The Democrats had suffered a blow when the chairman of their state committee was arrested and imprisoned for a month in the late summer of 1864 because of allegedly seditious remarks. Since many other prominent California Democrats had left the state to aid the Confederacy, the Union charge that the party was treasonable seemed very apt to many voters. As a result, the Union Party electors won by a majority greater than 18,000 out of nearly 106,000 votes cast. Once more all the Union congressional candidates were successful.

More fundamental for the future, a majority of Californians had become used to voting against the Democrats. It was true that the Union Party eventually foundered after the war and the Republicans had to stand alone against a revivified Democratic Party. Also the Democrats did score some local and occasional statewide successes. Nevertheless the party of Andrew Jackson never again dominated California politics as it had between 1850 and 1861.

The Civil War left its impress upon California in other respects. The effects of the war not only revolutionized the state's voting pattern, they stimulated its economy and increased its population. A transcontinental railroad was begun during the Lincoln administration, which ultimately bound California more fully to the nation. If California's military contribution to the Union war effort was modest, its help in the form of gold, copper, wheat and barley was substantial.

NINETEEN

California Land Titles and Frauds

ONE persistent problem which bedeviled many Californians was the validity of their land titles. "Whose California?" became a vital question. For thirty years after the American conquest of California, the legal status of large landholdings was uncertain. This uncertainty greatly hampered California's development.

Under the Spanish system, newly discovered land belonged to the crown. Spanish missions were permitted to use certain lands not actually granted to the missionaries. The clergy were merely trustees on borrowed land, ostensibly working for the benefit of the Indians. The mission priests fought strongly the granting of land concessions to individuals. After 1784, as we have already seen, the royal authorities made individual grants to ranchers. The secularization of the missions in the 1830's and 1840's set off a land rush in California. Population shifted. Landless Californios who had long been living with relatives in pueblos or presidios presented a veritable blizzard of petitions for various choice sites. By 1846 more than eight hundred grants had been made, embracing nearly fourteen million acres. The boundaries of these grants were loosely defined, and many of them overlapped. Some included hundreds of thousands of acres.

Soon after the American conquest, Yankee adventurers who crowded into California cast envious eyes upon the large Spanish grants, even though these holdings had been guaranteed to the Californios by the Treaty of Guadalupe-Hidalgo. American squatters, however, pushed into desirable lands near rivers or lakes, disregarding the protests of their

California owners. Americans accustomed to Anglo-Saxon legal traditions looked with disdain upon Spanish law and customs which bestowed title on the Californios. Some Americans boldly proclaimed that their conquest of California gave them the right to dispossess the Mexican and Spanish grantees. Other Yankees argued that the Californios had to be evicted in order that free, arable land be made available to them as settlers, a practice familiar to earlier western settlement.

Washington authorities were quickly forced to formulate a land policy for California. In doing so, they had the benefit of two reports concerning California land titles. The first had been filed on March 1, 1849, by Captain Henry Wager Halleck of the California military government. This report was accompanied by W. E. P. Hartnell's translation of relevant documents. In his capacity as secretary of state, Halleck had made an exhaustive study of California land claims. His report contended that the legality of most Mexican–Spanish grants was weak, because their boundaries were so vaguely defined. He also believed that there were many imperfections in the Mexican titles and that the United States could, if it wished, break these claims. Halleck's tight legal mind was horrified by the casual—even careless—manner in which the grants had often been made. For example, Governor Pió Pico had in one year bestowed eighty-seven grants upon his personal friends.

The second report on California land titles was made by a lawyer serving as a confidential agent of the American government—William Carey Jones. Jones, a son-in-law of Missouri's powerful senator, Thomas Hart Benton, was fluent in Spanish and conversant with Spanish colonial titles. In addition, he had traveled widely in California. Unlike Halleck, Jones believed that the overwhelming majority of Spanish–Mexican grants were valid, and that the few fraudulent claims would not prove difficult to detect. These opinions he reported to President Fillmore in April 1850. (Jones, however, had a conflict of interest in making this investigation, since he himself had an interest in a large Spanish grant. But at the time, no one considered anything to be wrong with Jones' dual relationship to the issue of the grants.)

Almost immediately after California's admission to the Union, its congressmen attempted to settle many land ambiguities. Senator William M. Gwin, whose views were generally those written into law, espoused the Halleck view that most Spanish–Mexican titles were defective. Therefore, Gwin sponsored a piece of legislation, which passed Congress, and became a law on March 3, 1851. This act placed the burden of proof on every Californian claiming land in the state; it ignored articles VIII and LX of the Treaty of Guadalupe-Hidalgo, which strongly guaranteed Mexican property rights.

The Act of 1851 established a commission of three members appointed by the President. The commission was originally slated to sit for three years, but when it bogged down in its hearings, its life was extended to five years. All land claimants with Spanish–Mexican titles had to present documentary proof to the commission, which was charged by law to render a speedy verdict. Decisions of the commission could be appealed to the United States District Court and then to the Supreme Court. All land for which claims were not presented or for which claims were, on presentation, held to be invalid, became part of the public domain.

President Fillmore appointed Harvey I. Thornton, James Wilson and Hiland Hall as commissioners, and hearings were begun in January 1852 in San Francisco. In March 1853, President Franklin Pierce appointed a new board composed of Alpheus Felch, Thompson Campbell (who resigned in 1854 and was replaced by S. B. Farwell) and R. A. Thompson. The commission adjourned on March 3, 1856.

California lawyers quickly formed law firms specializing in practice before the commission. Henry Halleck formed the firm of Halleck, Peachy and Billings, and by practice before the commission became a very wealthy man. Other leading law firms were Clarke, Taylor and Beckh; Jones, Tompkin and Strode; and Crosby and Rose.

Despite intense criticism that the sitting of the commission at San Francisco worked a great hardship upon the many claimants from southern California, the commission met for only one term in Los Angeles in the fall of 1852. In all, 813 claims (not the number of grants) were ostensibly filed with the board, but one was a clerical error, two were preëmption claims, and one had no Spanish or Mexican origin. Thus 809 cases involving pre-American grants were heard by the commission; 604 cases were eventually confirmed, 190 finally rejected, and the rest withdrawn. Yet in the end, all but nineteen cases heard by the commission were appealed to the District Court; of these nineteen, sixteen were governed by trial cases relative to the same grant. Therefore, only three cases were finally decided by the board.

Seventeen years was the average length of time that a landowner had to wait for a final patent after filing his original petition. Some unlucky owners had to wait as long as thirty-five years for absolutely clear title to their property. Litigation was both slow and costly. In this long interval of uncertainty, many of the original claimants were forced to sell out. The vague nature of many titles allowed the squatters an unprecedented opportunity to crowd in and cause trouble for the claimants.

Over the years, a great debate has raged between various historians and lawyers concerning the wisdom and justice of the procedures set up by the Act of 1851. In a distinct minority are those who hold the view that the federal government in requiring documentary proof under the forms of American law was merely adhering to a land policy which was already half a century old. The majority opinion has been that the Act seriously penalized the Californios, since they often could not find the certain proof insisted upon in the American courts, whose very procedures were unfamiliar to them. The inconvenience of the journey to San Francisco, the hiring of costly attorneys, and the attempt to plead his case before commissioners who were not versed in Spanish law or customs, all involved great difficulties for the Californio.

Yet if the commissioners upon occasion disallowed a valid claim, there were many attempts at fraud. Some of these attempts were temporarily successful, with devastating effects for the Californians living upon these claims. Among the largest and most insistent of bogus claimants was José Yves Limantour, a Frenchman who was a resident of Mexico. Included in two of his claims which the commissioners had allowed were 600,000 acres which included the principal islands of San Francisco Bay and four square leagues in the city and county of San Francisco. According to Limantour's story, about ten years before he had helped Governor Manuel Micheltorena, who had in return granted him extensive tracts. When the commission validated his claims, Limantour promptly asked all his "tenants" either to pay rent to him or to move from his land. Panic hit San Francisco, since Limantour's claims included the land upon which the mint, the customhouse and other government buildings stood. The federal government promptly appealed judgment of these claims in the District Court, while United States Attorney General Jeremiah Sullivan Black sent one of the greatest trial lawyers in America, Edwin M. Stanton, to San Francisco to investigate Limantour's claims, as well as those of other suspected frauds. Stanton later won fame as Lincoln's secretary of war.

Limantour had presented what appeared to be impeccable credentials. In addition to the indisputably genuine signature of Governor Micheltorena, his petitions for lands as well as the grants themselves seemed to be written on specially stamped paper provided by the Mexican government. President Arista of the Mexican Republic had himself commended Limantour's claims to the land commission. However, an employee of Limantour's, Auguste Jouan, revealed to Stanton that in 1852 the French merchant had obtained eighty blank petitions and titles, all presigned, from Micheltorena. After investigation Stanton succeeded in proving that the special stamped paper upon which the petitions and claims were written was of a later date than it would have to be if it were genuine. No substantiation of Limantour's grant could be found in the files of the Mexican archives. Finally, some of the Frenchman's witnesses were shown to be perjurers.

As evidence of fraud piled up against Limantour, his lawyers successively withdrew until there was no attorney present to present a rebuttal to Stanton's case against the claimant. As a result, Limantour's claims were disallowed by the district court, and the Frenchman himself was indicted for perjury. Limantour was never brought to trial, since he jumped his $35,000 bail and fled the United States.

Successful frauds were probably not common, yet attempts such as Limantour's alerted federal officials to the possibility of skulduggery. As a result, government attorneys appealed claims, no matter how valid, to the highest federal tribunals, never accepting defeat, and even refusing to proceed by the use of test cases. Thus 132 claimants appealed the adverse ruling of the commission to the federal courts, and 98 of them won a reversal of judgment. On the other hand, out of 417 cases appealed on behalf of the government, only five were successful.

The Land Act of 1851 had also recognized the Spanish–Mexican custom of granting to a town four leagues of land. Branciforte and several smaller towns never filed a claim. The post-Mexican towns of Sacramento and Sonora presented claims which were quickly disallowed. San Jose was in the end more successful, but its claimed tract was interspersed with private grants which caused litigation delaying final disposition of the land titles until the 1880's.

Los Angeles' and San Francisco's claims proved the most troublesome. Los Angeles filed its claim with the commission on October 26, 1852, and claimed not four square leagues, but four leagues square or sixteen square leagues. The commission speedily accepted Los Angeles' claims to be a duly recognized pueblo of the Spanish–Mexican period. The dispute between Los Angeles and the federal government centered about the extent of the pueblo's grant. After receiving depositions that the Spanish governor of California had allowed presidios to claim four leagues from the center of the presidio square, the commission handed down a decision on February 5, 1856, granting Los Angeles title to the smaller claim of four square leagues. Petitions for review and appeals to the District Court followed. In the end, the federal government and Los Angeles signed a stipulation on February 2, 1858, which accepted the board's judgment.

Los Angeles had not waited for this final decision, but as early as 1849 had employed Lieutenant E. O. C. Ord of the United States Army to survey its lands. Lots with a width of 120 feet and a depth of 165 feet sold for fifty dollars to two hundred dollars. Over the years, Los Angeles has disposed of all of its land except for Pershing Square, Elysian Park and the old Plaza.

San Francisco's claims presented an even more knotty legal problem. As the successor to Yerba Buena, San Francisco asked for the standard presidio grant of four square leagues. On December 24, 1854, the commission handed down its judgment upon the San Francisco claim, and its verdict was no Christmas present for the city. The commission confirmed the city's title only to the region north of the so-called Vallejo line, which ran from Rincon Point on San Francisco Bay to Point Lobos on the ocean. The federal government contended that as a result of a document later proved to be spurious, General Mariano Vallejo in 1834 had suggested this line to Governor José Figueroa as the boundary for the projected pueblo of Yerba Buena.

Because of the restricted award, both the United States and San Francisco appealed the commission's verdict. On September 5, 1864, after numerous delays, the case was transferred to the United States Circuit Court where a Supreme Court justice, Stephen J. Field, heard the case. On May 18, 1865, Field decided for the city's claim. While appeals were still pending to the Supreme Court, Congress passed a law which President Andrew Johnson signed in March 1866, relinquishing the four square leagues to San Francisco. The city was granted an area bounded on three sides by the high-water mark as it existed in 1846. The only exceptions to the award were the federal military reservations and a few private claims. The final granting of a patent by the federal authorities was not accomplished until June 20, 1884.

San Francisco was plagued by squatters who had taken advantage of the legal confusion to crowd into the disputed lands. As defined in 1851, the city had a large unsurveyed tract west of Larkin Street and southeast of Ninth Street. Professional real-estate operators soon moved in who did not care who won the tract, believing that their prior possession would force the successful governmental claimant to confirm their own titles. Using federal and state preëmption laws between 1850 and 1854, they filed for several hundred tracts of 40 to 160 acres each. Many speculators bolstered their claims by digging elaborate entrenchments around their land and going about heavily armed.

Although the city had no authority for the action, it decided to strike a compromise with the squatters. Three ordinances in 1855 and 1856 confirmed the title of persons who could prove possession of land in the "Western Addition" as of January 1–June 20, 1855. The city reserved only space for streets and parks. After San Francisco won its claim from the United States, city deeds were issued to the former squatters.

To the west and south of the lands of the "three ordinances" lay additional acreage within the city's four square leagues. The western boundary of this tract was the ocean, and the end of the four-square-league area was its southern terminus. Squatters had crowded into this area in the 1850's, calling it "Outside Lands." In time, as these heavily armed squatters needed funds and legal counsel, prominent bankers and lawyers obtained a hold upon many of these claims. The arms-carrying squatters were one kind of problem, but as they acquired the backing of a legal-financial battery, they became another, more serious one. As a result, the San Francisco authorities, shortly after confirmation of the city's title by the United States, declared that deeds were to be given to all squatters who could prove possession on March 8, 1866, and who had paid taxes for the five years preceding July 1, 1866. In all, several hundred persons obtained title to lands in San Francisco. The city reserved only one thousand acres for a park and other public purposes. Thus the municipality only kept what is today Golden Gate Park. There has been much criticism of this settlement, but in the climate of the times, perhaps no other solution was feasible.

Squatters were a universal abomination in the California of the 1850's. Landowners seeking redress for the squatters' trespass were soon rudely disillusioned, since squatter juries and judges elected by squatter votes proved totally unresponsive to their needs. If legal evasion was not sufficient for their purpose, the squatters seldom refrained from resorting to violence.

Sacramento was the scene of some of the worst squatter outbreaks. In 1849 many squatters crowded into the city, which was actually situated upon Sutter's grant, which he had subdivided and sold to various speculators. These squatters scoffed at Sutter's claims and also those of real estate men who had purchased land from the Swiss. These settlers loudly insisted that no one man was entitled to that much land, and squatted anywhere it was possible for them to force their way.

Holding meetings at which speakers extolled the right of "shotgun titles," the squatters in time organized to prevent their ejection. One of their leaders was Dr. Charles Robinson of Fitchburg, Massachusetts, who not long before had traveled across the plains to California. Like many of the squatters, Robinson was a restless man, constantly seeking his fortune in new places. After failing to make his fortune in California, he moved to Kansas, where he was a leader in the antislavery forces in the years before the Civil War when that territory was the scene of bloody battles. But now the testy New Englander harangued his followers in Sacramento and defied the landowners to evict them.

On June 21, 1850, an armed group of landowners and their agents tore down a squatter's shack. Meeting no active resistance, on the following day this same group spread out widely over the squatter settlement, demolishing shacks and pulling down the crude fences that marked their claims. As the summer wore on, the landowners continued to apply pressure upon the squatters, although no significant incident occurred. Then in mid-August the legal authorities, acting on behalf of the landowners, arrested two prominent squatters for resisting ejection and lodged them on a prison ship. Following this action the squatters organized a group of thirty armed men who tramped through the Sacramento streets toward the prison ship with the avowed purpose of freeing their friends. At this the mayor of Sacramento, Harden Bigelow, hastily gathered a posse and blocked access to the waterfront. When the squatters clanked up to the spot where the posse had gathered, there was an ugly moment of tension. Then, upon command, the squatters began slowly to leave the scene. Not satisfied with his triumph, the mayor, who regarded the squatters as rabble, galloped after them on his horse, calling upon them to surrender. At this action the squatters turned and mortally wounded the mayor. The mayor's posse then returned the fire. When the smoke cleared and the squatter forces drifted away, there were three squatters dead upon the field. Several others, including Dr. Robinson, were badly wounded but were carried from the scene of the fight by their comrades. In addition to the mayor, another city official had been killed. The authorities regarded the skirmish as a major victory over the squatters and decided to press their advantage. As a result, the day after the fray the sheriff, accompanied by several deputies, entered a saloon where the squatters maintained an unofficial headquarters. A wild melee followed in which shots were exchanged and uncounted casualties fell on both sides. The sheriff himself was a fatality. Just where all this violence might have ended is questionable, but the governor (himself a Sacramento real estate owner) called out the militia, and heavy reinforcements were brought in from San Francisco. This militia force, eventually consisting of five hundred men, was able to restore order by breaking the squatter resistance.

Other squatter outbreaks occurred in California at about the same time. In 1850 armed squatters moved onto the Peralta holding—Rancho San Antonio—and staked out the future city of Oakland. A long, torturous legal process was necessary before Oakland's status could be cleared. Squatters moved into the mountain areas of California as well. Some cut timber on a considerable scale in the San Bernardino Mountains without any regard for the niceties of title. Others freely used the lands of the San Gabriel Mountains. Even the islands off California's coast were not immune to them. Many squatters overran Santa Catalina Island and stayed illegally as long as they dared.

Such heavy squatter activity begat additional violence. In May 1853, a squatter, Jack Powers, barricaded himself with fifteen friends behind a crude fortification of wagons and logs on the property of Nicholas Den. From this strongpoint, Powers defied a sheriff's posse's attempts to evict him. A regular battle followed in which many men were killed on both sides.

Squatter resistance continued into the 1860's. As late as November 9, 1861, there occurred the "Battle of Waterloo" at the place of the same name, some eight miles north of Stockton. There a squatter named John Balkwill turned his home into a fort in order to defend his claim against the legal owner, who attempted to evict him with the aid of a force which boasted a nine-pound cannon. A mass bloodletting was averted only by the arrival of the local sheriff.

In addition to the use of violence, the squatters were sufficiently numerous in many places to exert political pressure in their own behalf. In the 1850's the platforms of all the major California parties promised some relief to squatters. The elected state official who showed the most solicitude for the squatter cause was Governor John Bigler. In January 1856, he called for legislation to compensate squatters if they were evicted after settling upon what they had honestly believed to be federal land. Nothing came of the governor's proposal, but that same year the legislature did pass a statute declaring that all lands in the state should be considered public until proven otherwise. Later this piece of squatter legislation was declared unconstitutional by the state supreme court.

The problem of the squatters subsided only gradually as the land commission and the courts settled disputed titles. While the 1850's were times of the greatest troubles, sporadic outbreaks continued until the 1870's. In 1877 Thomas More, the owner of Rancho Sespe in the Santa Clara Valley, was set upon by seven squatters who murdered him in the name of the Sespe Settlers League. As late as the 1920's, there was an outbreak of squatterism in southern California, but the serious problem of the squatter abated in the late nineteenth century.

All Californians suffered from the confusion regarding land titles. It was difficult if not impossible for any settler to obtain a certain title to real property. With real estate so uncertain as collateral, interest rates, always high in a new country, reached new peaks. The famous California historian Theodore H. Hittell insisted in the 1860's that the state's population was a million fewer than it might have been if California's land titles had been secure.

In 1850 California as a state owned a total of eight million acres. Between 1865 and 1895 more than half of this total was distributed to private citizens. Much of this land was unsuitable for intensive agricultural cultivation in the mid-nineteenth century. However, with the coming of non-American immigrants to California—Italians, Germans, Japanese and Armenians—these areas were brought under cultivation. Also, advances in agricultural technology such as combines, harvesters, reapers and steam plows made possible the growing of wheat in the San Joaquin and Sacramento valleys.

By 1865 it had become clear that state land policies had not achieved their stated objective of creating a community of small farms. Concentration of land ownership in the hands of a relative few remained a serious problem. In 1871 the 122 largest California farms covered an area greater than the total of the other 23,315 farms in the state combined. While factors such as climate and topography played their part, the skill of land speculators operating under the supervision of lax or bribed officials cannot be overlooked in any explanation of the state's agricultural land pattern. Inequitable distribution of the land inhibited settlement by small farmers, the group which state policy claimed to prefer as settlers in California.

One aspect of the California land problem was the question of ownership of mining claims. Along with the other uncertainties which the goldseekers faced was insecurity of title. Technically, the '49ers were merely squatters upon the public lands, under the ever-present threat of eviction. While it is true that the federal authority in remote California was so weak that this threat to thousands of miners was more theoretical than actual, nonetheless it was one more latent worry for the goldseeker.

At the time of the gold rush, the federal government had no general policy concerning mining on public lands. There existed two schools of thought: on one hand there were various federal officials who insisted upon government ownership of mineral lands, although they would permit private enterprise to develop them. Arrayed against these officials were thousands of California miners who wished to exploit the mineral wealth of the public lands with little government supervision or royalties. Speaking through mass meetings in the mining camps and their representatives in the California legislature, the miners demanded that the national government allow them to exploit the riches of California without federal royalties or regulation.

As early as December 1848, President James K. Polk had proposed that federal mining properties be sold under the preëmption system in forty-acre lots on credit. However, Missouri Senator Thomas Hart Benton, an advocate of free mining, was able to prevent congressional approval of Polk's scheme. President Millard Fillmore also unsuccessfully attempted to obtain congressional agreement for a plan similar to that of Polk's. There the matter rested. The all-absorbing pre-Civil War events and then the war itself precluded any federal legislation concerning public mineral lands. Finally in July 1866, a mining act slipped through both houses of Congress. It eluded its ardent foes by being buried among the provisions of a bill ostensibly dealing with right of way through public lands for ditch and canal owners. This bill was a complete victory for the Californians, since it ratified existing conditions in their state's mines. This act allowed anyone to obtain title to a mining tract from the General Land Office by paying five dollars an acre, if he had made more than a thousand dollars in improvements upon that claim. With improvements of less than that sum, a miner or a corporation could still obtain a possessory right to a claim. This legislation provided, in order to prevent a monopoly, that no location owned by an individual miner could exceed two hundred feet along the ore's vein and that no individual should have more than one location on the same lode. The future maximum location allowable for an "association of persons" was three thousand feet along the vein. In addition, the act provided that all local mining laws not in conflict with federal statutes were to continue in force.

The 1866 act, however, pertained only to vein mines. Its congressional sponsors believed that since placer mining sites were becoming exhausted, no legislation was needed to cover them. When this omission troubled many small miners, Congress passed the act of July 9, 1870, quieting their fears. This act ordered the sale of placer mines at $2.50 an acre with the stipulation that no individual or association could have one location greater than 160 acres. This law also stated that placer claims were to conform to local regulations. A later act of May 10, 1872, reaffirmed the policy outlined in the two earlier acts. Thus, relatively late in California's mining history, the legal question concerning the ownership of its mineral lands was settled in a manner least calculated to disturb its mining establishment.

TWENTY

California Society in
Post-Gold-Rush Days

FOLLOWING the frantic years of the gold rush, there was a period of reflection for California. Until the fever of the gold rush abated, there were few successful attempts to create a permanent foundation for California society. During the height of the rush, most goldseekers were transients who would soon return to their homes. Many of the goldseekers who left California, however, returned after they compared their sleepy New England or midwestern villages with the electric excitement of the Far West. After enduring a few eastern winters, the climate of California seemed more alluring to them. Many prospectors never left California at all, but turned to agriculture or business within the state. These men sent for wives or fiancées and settled down to a staid family existence. Soon the crude pleasures of the gold rush receded into the background. Prostitution became less blatant. The arrival of proper ladies from the East, steeped in the niceties of Victorian living, set a different tone for California. The rough, bathless society of 1849–52 became increasingly refined and perfumed.

The foundation of churches did much to stabilize California society. In a real sense, California had been Christian country since the days of the Franciscan missionaries. However, the flood of Protestant miners had quickly diminished the influence of Spanish–Mexican society in northern California, although the Latin culture continued to survive in the southern part of the state until the 1860's.

There were preachers among the earliest gold miners. In November 1848, a conclave of San Franciscans invited the Presbyterian Reverend Timothy Dwight Hunt to act as city chaplain on a nondenominational basis. By the close of 1849, twelve regular ministers were established in San Francisco. More and more ministers arrived, until by 1855 San Francisco had thirty-two churches with denominations ranging from African Methodists to Unitarians.

The first Baptist missionary to California was Osgood C. Wheeler of New York. He quickly organized the San Francisco Baptist Association and served as its first moderator. A Congregationalist minister and Dartmouth College graduate, Samuel H. Willey, arrived at Monterey in February 1849. Willey served as Protestant chaplain to the Constitutional Convention. A Bostonian, Joseph H. Benton, served with such success in the Sacramento area that he has been called the "father of Congregationalism" in California. Although an Episcopal chaplain had arrived with Stevenson's New York regiment in 1847, the first Episcopalian parish in California was not organized until April 28, 1850.

Churches were built in all parts of the state in a great variety of architectures. These edifices were unimaginatively constructed and added little to the beauty of the countryside.

The story of early Protestant Christianity in California is less a saga of formal worship in churches than it is of preaching in rural camp meetings and city streets in the manner of evangelist William Taylor. Many different Protestant sects utilized this method. In California, the camp meeting evolved from the Methodist custom of circuit riding. The meetings were natural in the rural areas of California where no buildings suitable for services existed. Families journeyed for miles, jolting in wagons over rough roads, to reach the rendezvous point. There they pitched a camp together, often in a grove of trees along a river. In this fashion, as many as ten to twenty thousand people camped and worshipped for periods as long as several weeks. The first California camp meeting may have been held in Sonoma in the spring of 1851.

The Catholic Church in California reorganized after the American conquest. It expanded and grew in northern California under the skillful direction of Archbishop Joseph Sadoc Alemany, a Spanish-born Dominican who came to California during the gold rush and served for three years as bishop of Monterey. From 1853 to 1884, he successfully ruled the archdiocese of San Francisco. Archbishop Alemany did much to expand Catholic education in his see. He helped to secure a portion of the confiscated Pious Fund from the Mexican government and devoted the money to improving the Catholic educational institutions of his archbishopric. No cloistered recluse, he became something of a fire buff and was frequently seen at San Francisco conflagrations urging on the city firemen. Over seventy when he retired, he returned to his native Spain.

Education became a hallmark of the new American society in California, since the migrants to California included many highly educated men. San Francisco in the 1850's could boast a greater percentage of college graduates than any other American city. These men appreciated the value of learning and resolved that their children, although raised on the far frontier, should not be denied the advantages of an education. Outside of the instruction of neophytes at the missions, there had been only a few feeble and intermittent elementary schools during the Spanish and Mexican periods. The only California secondary school in the Mexican period was the College of San Jose, established in the 1830's by the learned Englishman William E. P. Hartnell. This college's ambitious curriculum included several languages as well as philosophy, bookkeeping and theology!

Perhaps the first American school in California began with Mrs. Olive Mann Isbell, who migrated from Illinois in 1846 with her husband. Settling at Santa Clara, she instructed a small group of local children in the crumbling mission from December 1846 to March 1847, when she moved with her family to Monterey. She taught at Monterey for three months. William Marston, a Mormon, opened a private school with about twenty students in San Francisco in April 1847, which survived less than a year. In February 1848, a school board was elected in San Francisco, and a Yale graduate, Thomas Douglas, was selected as a teacher. This promising educational beginning was completely disrupted by news of the gold strike.

The early gold rush saw several schools started, among them that begun by the Reverend Samuel Willey at Colton Hall, Monterey, in March of 1849. Another school was started later in the same year by the Reverend Albert Williams in San Francisco. A Baptist layman from New York, John Colter Pelton, may have established the first operating public school in California. It was public in the sense that it was open to all who could afford to pay tuition fees. On December 26, 1849, Pelton opened his institution for three pupils in a small building erected by the First Baptist Church on San Francisco's Portsmouth Square. Within three months he had increased the school's enrollment to 130 pupils.

Because the delegates to the Monterey Convention had wished to encourage education, their constitution provided for a system of education headed by a superintendent of public instruction. The convention delegates also charged the legislature to promote the people's "intellectual, scientific, moral and agricultural improvement." At the first state election on October 7, 1850, John Gage Marvin, running as an independent, defeated four other aspirants for a three-year term as superintendent of public instruction. When he took office on January 1, 1851, he found a disappointing delay in the actual foundation of the public schools, since the first legislature had not implemented the constitutional provisions.

As interested citizens tried to start an educational system in those lean years, many pupils were taught in churches for lack of any other buildings, and their teachers were often the local ministers. When Marvin argued for public aid to all church schools, in an attempt to establish an educational system, many Protestants, fearful of a breach in the traditional wall separating church and state, turned against him. As a result, Marvin could not win the Democratic nomination for a second term.

In 1852 the legislature tardily voted a state school tax of five cents on every hundred dollars of taxable property to supplement the tuition which was charged pupils to maintain the common schools. This action made state money available for school aid in 1853, and by then twenty elementary school districts had been organized. The population of California contained relatively fewer children than the states of the East because of the preponderance of single men. It was therefore easier for California to educate its school-age youngsters. In 1858 there were 432 elementary schools in the state, with 517 teachers and 19,822 pupils. The percentage of the total number of children from five to fourteen years of age (very few attended private institutions) rose to nearly 64 per cent in 1860, 76 per cent in 1870, and about 95 per cent by 1880.

In 1855 the legislature authorized school district trustees to divide their schools into elementary and secondary institutions. However, no state money was provided for secondary schools. Nonetheless, San Francisco authorized the Union Grammar School with a curriculum including courses appropriate to a high school. On August 25, 1856, this institution opened its doors. On January 8, 1858, its name was changed to the San Francisco High School. It graduated its first class—twenty-two boys and thirteen girls—in December of 1859. An evening high school was begun in 1856. In time the minimum course of study in high school was the entrance requirement of the University of California College of Science. Despite this early progress, it was not until 1902 that the public high schools, which were gradually established in the larger cities, actually received state aid. As late as 1890, only 3,548 California pupils were enrolled in high schools.

These meager statistics need to be placed into perspective. California was spending more money and enrolling more students in public schools during these years than many of the older and more settled states. In the mid-1870's, California, with about the same population as Connecticut, spent nearly six times as much on its common schools. California also passed a compulsory school attendance statute in 1874, the same year as New York and before Maine and Rhode Island had enacted such legislation.

Early Californians took a great, if not always informed, interest in their schools. When the state board of education voted to replace the Mc-Guffey readers in the public schools, angry parents appealed the decision to the courts. The result was a protracted legal battle which was only resolved by the adoption of the Constitution of 1879.

California public education owes much to John Swett, who was elected in 1862 as superintendent of public instruction. Through Swett's determined efforts, he succeeded in getting all tuition charges abolished in the "common schools" of California. From that time forward, taxation supported a system of free schools at the elementary level.

Nor was California lacking in the field of higher education. The Methodist Episcopal Church obtained a charter on July 10, 1851, for what was called California Wesleyan College, but this name was soon changed to University of the Pacific. At first this institution's site was at Santa Clara, but later it was moved to San Jose and then to Stockton. There it still flourishes today. A Catholic institution, Santa Clara College (now Santa Clara University), was formally chartered on April 28, 1855.

Although in the 1850's there was a sufficient number of elementary teachers, the next decade, chiefly because of the demands of the Civil War, witnessed a shortage of teachers. To obtain the personnel needed to maintain California's elementary schools, Superintendent of Public Instruction Andrew J. Moulder caused the state to establish its first teacher-training institution by taking over Minns' Evening Normal School, a department of the San Francisco school system. It opened its doors in July 1862 with an original enrollment of one boy and five girls. In 1863 it graduated its first class of four teachers—all girls. In 1864 it graduated nineteen teachers, only one of them a male. The low pay of the teaching profession had virtually driven men from its ranks, a common national phenomenon. The fleshpots of San Francisco seemed a poor place to be instructing future schoolmarms, and so in 1871 the normal school was moved to San Jose, where it still exists today as the original California state college.

Although the Constitution of 1849 anticipated the founding of a state university, it was not actually established until March 23, 1868. At that time, with the help of the federal subsidy from the Morrill Land Grant Act, the legislature tardily chartered the University of California. This public institution absorbed the private College of California founded in 1855. The new university actually began operations in Oakland in 1869 with forty students and a faculty of ten. It became coeducational in 1870, and three years later shifted to its permanent site in Berkeley. At about the same time the fledgling university began its pursuit of excellence, the scholarly Daniel Coit Gilman was appointed its second president. The university was not ready for Gilman's ideas, and he became the target of attack by those who favored emphasizing a vocational curriculum at the new school. Consequently, after two years, Gilman left for Johns Hopkins University to develop the first genuine graduate school in the United States. Yet the University of California grew and prospered with the help of generous donors such as Mrs. Phoebe Apperson Hearst (the mother of William Randolph Hearst).

Nor did California lack other appurtenances of culture. In April 1853, seven men, including Lewis Sloat, a nephew of Commodore John D. Sloat, met at 129 Montgomery Street in San Francisco to found a society for the promotion of science—the California Academy of Natural Sciences (now called the California Academy of Science). Among the early donors of this institution, which became the most influential and firmly established scientific body of western America, were Leland Stanford and Charles Crocker. The possessions of the Academy grew from a cabinet of miscellaneous specimens in temporary quarters on Clay Street to a modern museum complex in Golden Gate Park. By the middle 1850's, there were also three public libraries: the Mechanics' Institute Library, the Odd Fellows Library, and the Mercantile Library.

Although California's two pioneer weeklies, the *Californian* and the *California Star*, ceased publication once the gold rush started, the long-term result of the influx of people was a tremendous stimulus to journalism. The publishers of the *Californian* and the *Star* merged on January 4, 1849, and brought out the celebrated successor of the two earlier papers—the *Alta California*. For more than twenty years this sheet enjoyed a preëminent place in California journalism, before going into a decline in the 1870's and finally passing out of existence in the 1880's. Nevertheless, the *Alta California*'s longevity was greater than two San Francisco papers founded during the same year. The *Pacific* lasted only two years, while a more specialized newspaper, *Prices Current*, foundered within twelve months. The year 1850 brought a notable competitor to the *Alta California;* a capable newspaperman, John Nugent, started the *Daily Herald*. The *Herald* was nearly ruined by its forthright stand against the vigilantes, but it gradually recovered its advertisers, surviving until 1862.

Despite the heavy mortality rate, additional newspapers crowded into the field. It did not require much capital then to start a paper, but in the fierce competitive jungle that San Francisco had become, it was difficult to pay the cost of operation for long. Yet in the early 1850's, the city's twelve dailies enjoyed a combined circulation of 15,000. San Franciscans proudly boasted that the number of their newspapers exceeded those of London itself. Nor was the publishing of newspapers confined to San Francisco. In most parts of the state literate goldseekers encouraged the foundation of numerous local papers. During the ten-year period after the discovery of gold, Marysville and Jackson each had seven papers;

Columbia, five; and San Andreas, Sonora and Mariposa, three each. By 1854, fifty-seven newspapers and periodicals within California served an average of 290,000 readers. As a result, for many years California could boast a per capita newspaper circulation exceeding that of the state of New York.

In the village of Los Angeles, the bilingual (Spanish and English) four-page weekly the *Star* (*La Estrella*) began operations in 1851. On July 20, 1854, it was joined by a Democratic weekly, *The Southern Californian*. This journal lasted only two years, but its staffers could tell how the paper published a graphic account of a lynching two hours before it took place, in order to meet the deadline for the steamer edition. Its backer, Andrés Pico, lost $10,000 during its brief existence. The first Republican journal in Los Angeles was the all-Spanish paper *El Clamor Público*, which published from 1855 to 1859. In 1860 the Los Angeles *News* was founded as a more ambitious semiweekly. The *News* prospered because of generous Republican political patronage, and in 1869 transformed itself into southern California's first daily.

California's polyglot population demanded the publication of newspapers in languages other than English and Spanish. As early as 1850 a French journal, *La Californian*, began publication. Two or three years later the German *Demokrat* appeared. Even a Chinese journal added to the cosmopolitan publishing within the state.

Since these papers were begun with a minimum of capital, their quality was generally poor. Many publications simply reprinted inches of trite material to fill their columns between the advertisements. News reporting was haphazard. An interesting event might be chronicled, but very frequently there were no follow-up stories in subsequent editions. A murder story might be so sparsely reported as to be meaningless. On the other hand, a barroom brawl might be described in minute detail. Most papers, as was true nationally at the time, were bitterly partisan and made no pretense of impartiality in either their editorial pages or their news columns.

In addition to newspapers, there were certain literary journals published in gold-rush California. Perhaps the most ambitious of these gazettes was the *Golden Era*. Mark Twain actually called it the best literary journal in the nation. Originally started as a newspaper, its publisher converted it to a more ornate form two years later. It divided its four pages almost equally between fiction, poetry, news and advertisements. The works of a galaxy of California writers appeared in it. Many budding authors wrote for it, but when they became established they generally switched to better-paying journals. (The *Era* paid only five dollars a column for prose and nothing for poetry.) Among those who obtained their literary start with the *Era* was New York-born Francis Brett Harte. Coming to California as a young man, Harte wandered about the state for some time before settling in Union (Arcata) in Humboldt County, where he drifted into writing for the local paper. His career in Union ended when, substituting for the regular editor, he scathingly denounced a massacre of peaceful Indians at nearby Gunther Island. Never popular, Harte felt obliged to leave town before he was murdered or lynched. Arriving in San Francisco, Harte obtained a job as a typesetter on the *Golden Era.* Soon he became a contributor of short stories. After a stint on *The Territorial Enterprise* in Virginia City, Mark Twain also contributed many items to the *Golden Era.*

The *Golden Era* had many competitors. In January 1854 the colorful, unstable Ferdinand C. Ewer launched the *Pioneer.* This remarkable literary journal survived for two years without taking advertisements. In this span Ewer went from Unitarianism to Episcopalianism, and then spent short periods as an atheist and a spiritualist before becoming an Episcopalian again. The fame of the *Pioneer* rests principally upon its publication of the *Shirley Letters* (as they are now known). These "letters," written by Mrs. Louise Amelia Knapp Smith Clappe, vividly depicted life in the Feather River mines.

Scarcely more financially successful than the *Pioneer* was *Hutchings' California Magazine.* This journal was very expensive to publish, since it relied heavily upon woodcuts for illustrations. This magazine's forte was boosterism, since it published much concerning the glories of California.

One tenacious magazine was the *Hesperian.* Originally begun in 1858, it was eventually edited by the spirited lady editor, Mrs. F. H. Day. Mrs. Day innovated greatly during her editorship—starting a juvenile department and adding many illustrations. She was able to win many women readers for her publication without completely alienating the men. Her successor as editor, Mrs. Schenk, was less successful. In 1863 the *Hesperian* passed under new ownership, acquiring both a new name, *Pacific Monthly*, and a new format. Unfortunately these alterations brought little financial success, and the magazine soon discontinued publication.

In 1864 a spin-off from the *Golden Era* was *The Californian,* started by one of Bret Harte's associates, Charles Henry Webb. Webb announced that he wanted to publish a more "high-toned" journal than the *Era.* By sparing no expense, he produced an excellent printing format. Harte and Twain both contributed to it. Nonetheless, after failing to make operating costs, it ceased publication in its fourth year.

The publication which brought California's early literary development to its apogee was the *Overland Monthly.* The *Overland* began in July 1868, and its first series continued until 1875. Its first publisher, a local bookseller, Anton Roman, made Bret Harte the *Overland*'s editor. Roman soon found the financial losses to be more than he could bear, and he passed from the scene as publisher to be succeeded by the optimistic John

H. Carmany. Bret Harte stayed on as editor, simultaneously contributing a flow of short stories, poems, book reviews and editorial comments. In 1871, when Bret Harte had sufficiently established himself in the literary world, he suddenly left for the East, and the *Overland's* fortunes turned downward. Carmany acridly remarked that he had spent $30,000 merely to make Bret Harte a national figure. Suspended in 1875, the *Overland* was revived eight years later. Doggedly published for many years until 1935 despite financial losses, the new series never gained the artistic successes achieved by its predecessor.

San Francisco was also a publishing center for books. In the city's first decade it published more books than were produced in all the rest of the western states combined.

During the Mexican era San Francisco had little entertainment for its inhabitants. Occasional fiestas, rodeos, bull, bear and cock fights, and a strolling singer or dancer were all the entertainment the place could afford. With the coming of the Americans in 1847, Colonel Stevenson's volunteers presented a series of amateur performances. In 1848, to enjoy regular dramatic performances, San Franciscans had to journey across the bay to Sonoma, where General Mariano Vallejo sponsored a theater. Then on June 22, 1849, the English entertainer, Stephen C. Massett, gave the first professional performance of the American era in a small, redwood building on the southwest corner of Portsmouth Plaza, which had also seen service as a schoolhouse and a police station. Although only charging his eager patrons three dollars apiece, Massett made a five hundred dollar profit, for he played to a full house.

Seeing the need for commercial entertainment of this type, several gambling saloons began to produce unpretentious entertainment. In only one of these establishments, the Bella Union, was this a success. That establishment continued for almost sixty years as the home of variety, minstrel and burlesque shows. One gambler-saloonkeeper, Tom Maguire, became a producer of various kinds of entertainment for twenty years while dominating the San Francisco theatrical scene. He built the first theater with elaborate fixtures and settings—the Jenny Lind. Twice his theater burned, but Maguire rebuilt. When he opened his third Jenny Lind on October 4, 1851, it was proclaimed as the ultimate in the theatrical arts. Fighting intense competition, Maguire found his establishment to be a financial white elephant. Thereupon he sold it for use as a city hall. His chief competition had been the splendid American Theater. Yet this showhouse itself was forced into darkness by the new and still more elegant Metropolitan Theater. In 1857 the Metropolitan burned down and was replaced in 1861 by another theater of the same name but even greater opulence. Maguire took advantage of the relative lack of theaters in San Francisco to open his own imposing Opera House. The theatrical history of the 1860's is largely the story of the rivalry of the Metropolitan Theater and the Opera House.

Although San Francisco was the dramatic center of California, the first building constructed for a purely dramatic purpose was built in the fall of 1849 at Sacramento—the Eagle Theater. Several other theaters succeeded this original structure. Nor were San Francisco and Sacramento the only scenes of theatrical activity. Stockton, the chief depot of the southern mines, enjoyed theatrical performances given in the assembly room of the Stockton House. The northern mining town of Marysville in 1854 opened a theater which was modeled after the San Francisco Metropolitan. Although many mining towns in the Sierra foothills could boast of crude theaters, Los Angeles had no American showhouse until 1860.

Shakespeare enjoyed a great vogue in gold-rush California. Twenty-two of Shakespeare's plays—some of them much abridged—were presented in California's theaters. Simultaneously, such well-forgotten plays as *Delicate Ground* and *The Reformed Drunkard* also played to full houses. During the 1850's the San Francisco stage presented 907 plays, forty-eight operas in five languages, eighty-four extravaganzas and sixty-six minstrel specialties.

The stars who trod the boards of California theaters varied widely in appearance, reputation and ability. There were many unknowns who assayed a stage career, found little response and retired to the obscurity from which they had briefly emerged. But there were also actors and actresses of national or even international reputation. Among this latter group was the British-born actress, Caroline Chapman. Before she came to California in 1852, she had already enjoyed a career of twenty years span with many New York successes. After a stand in San Francisco, Caroline Chapman toured the mining camps. Laura Keene, who later starred in the East, toured California, but she was widely criticized for a lack of realism in her acting. Edwin Booth, who had not yet reached the age of twenty, appeared in a great variety of Shakespearean roles, and also in blackface played the part of a banjo-thumping Negro dandy in a now-forgotten farce.

The most celebrated theatrical personality in California was Lola Montez. The popular myths about her sound like typical Hollywood publicity releases. Her publicists hinted that she was the daughter of a Spanish gypsy, a rajah of India, the sultan of Turkey—even of Lord Byron himself! Actually she had been born in Ireland in 1818, although Lola preferred to claim 1824 as the year of her birth. Early in life she married a British army officer, but this marriage soon failed. She then turned to dancing as a career, touring England and the Continent. Soon her name was romantically linked with composer Franz Liszt and the eccentric King Ludwig of Bavaria. Under the spell of her charms, Ludwig supposedly made her the Countess of Landsfeld. Then Lola got married again to a boy ten years her junior, although there is some doubt concerning this marriage's validity.

In 1851 Lola traveled to America. Despite her notorious reputation, Lola's success in the eastern United States was ephemeral. As a consequence, in May 1853, she came to San Francisco. That city's journalists showered attention upon her. Five days after her arrival, she played to standing-room-only audiences in the American Theater. Lola's specialty was the Spider Dance in which she slithered around the stage supposedly fighting off an attack by spiders.

Six weeks after her arrival in California, Lola found a third husband, Patrick Purdy Hull. Leaving San Francisco, the couple moved to Sacramento and then to Grass Valley. Lola and her husband soon parted, but she found another interest when she discovered a child prodigy, Lotta Crabtree, in the mining country. Lola taught the young girl to act and sing, launching her on a career as one of California's favorites. Lola herself returned to San Francisco in the late summer of 1856, and again appeared on stage. Although she was only thirty-eight, she had aged; nevertheless, she tried to create a new career for herself with an act in which she carried a white talking cockatoo on her shoulder. Lola was never the sensation with the cockatoo that she had been as an exotic dancer, and by October she could no longer obtain bookings in San Francisco. Soon thereafter, she quietly sailed from San Francisco, leaving her collection of strange birds to the Pacific Museum. Four years later she died, far from California. Elderly San Francisco men, as late as the 1890's, adversely compared the can-can girls to Lola Montez and her Spider Dance.

California's economic growth even after the height of the gold rush was rapid. In a real sense, California's natural resources were exploited quickly and successfully, particularly if conservation standards are ignored. These resources were also developed close to their potential, considering the times and the state of technology. The development of California was not just a local development, but was the physical extension of the growth of capitalism in the eastern United States and Great Britain. In the American period, California was not really an underdeveloped area in the present use of that term. It is true that California was dominated by what economists call primary production; in addition, much of the ownership of resources within the state was non-Californian, and Californians were often faced with unfavorable terms of trade in dealing with the powerful East. Nonetheless, California was not the downtrodden colony some then and since have pictured it. The state was settled and exploited by a series of economic booms. The mining boom, of course, overshadowed all the others. It caused a cattle boom in southern California and a farming and lumbering boom in the central and northern parts of the state. From these dramatic developments, a host of secondary industries sprang up. While some of the profits went to easterners or Britons (much wealth accrued to San Franciscans as the local agents for outsiders), since California was an integral part of the western world complex of capitalism, it shared ultimately in the general prosperity. Such a drain of profits as did occur had no long-run negative effects.

The importance of mining to California continued well after the human stampede to the placer claims had slowed in the early 1850's. After 1853, mining became a large-scale industry utilizing elaborate machinery and quartz-mining techniques. The small-scale miners increasingly became laborers for the big operators or left the industry to pursue agriculture. California gold stimulated the state's population growth, flow of capital, improved technology, and provided the basis for a greatly diversified future.

The dominance of gold mining was relatively brief. A silver rush in 1859 helped its decline. Some silver was found in the eastern part of California, south of Lake Tahoe, particularly near Owen's Lake, but the greatest amounts of that metal were mined east of the state's Nevada boundary. In addition, there was an oil rush in California that for a time caused as much excitement as had the search for the precious metals. Stimulated by the success of the oil industry in Pennsylvania, many promoters frenetically sought oil from the region of Petrolia in Humboldt County in northwestern California down through the area north of Coalinga, parts of Los Angeles County, and even as far south as San Diego. In the area of Sulphur Mountain near Ventura, instead of sinking wells, the wildcatters used tunnels to obtain oil. In the years 1865–66 more than seventy oil companies were incorporated. Professor Benjamin Silliman, a noted geologist of the time, averred that "California will be found to have more oil in its soil than all the whales [possess] in the Pacific Ocean." Hampered by lack of scientific and technological knowledge, and with insufficient capital, these early companies were uniformly unsuccessful. Indeed, it was 1876 before enough California oil was actually pumped to have the state's first commercial oil refinery constructed. Yet the petroleum boom of the 1860's stimulated many factors of economic growth, and so this premature flurry had beneficial side effects.

Supplementing California's other economic activities were the fishing and whaling industries. The Indians living along streams had always taken great amounts of fish, particularly salmon. The coming of Americans greatly reduced the fish-carrying capacities of California's streams just at the very time when the vastly increased population provided a great market. Nevertheless, many fishing companies in the northern and central parts of the state exploited California's rivers and streams so heavily as to cause concern on the part of conservationists. As a consequence, in the early 1870's Congress passed an appropriation of $15,000 for conservation, part of which went for the propagation of California shad and salmon. New varieties of fish from the East were also introduced into the state's waterways. As a result, California fisheries did not diminish under the heavy population impact. Instead, helped by these measures, California's catch gradually increased, and by 1890 California's fishing industry ranked sixth in the nation.

With the immigration of the Americans, many fishing boats swarmed out of Pacific coastal ports. By 1862, San Francisco fishermen ventured into the northern cod fisheries, and by 1866 there were eighteen vessels engaged in this enterprise. However, the long, monotonous cruise, taking from ninety-five to 193 days, discouraged a great expansion of this venture. The Italians, using their lateen-rigged vessels to fish, became a common sight in the San Francisco Bay area. Their fishing methods and experience, gained over the centuries in the Mediterranean, helped develop California's coastal fishing. In time the Italians were joined by the Greeks, the Portuguese and the Chinese.

Along the California coast, fishing gradually evolved from hand-rowed small boats to larger sailboats. Methods of catch changed from the hook and line and primitive nets to more sophisticated gear. By 1876 the Italian "paranzella," a small but very seaworthy boat, was introduced into the California fishing areas, greatly increasing the catch. Monterey emerged as a center for the sardine and anchovy fishermen, while San Pedro became a tuna-packing center. By the close of the 1880's, California fishermen had diversified their catch by taking skipjack, barracuda, albacore, rockfish and mackerel. Shellfishing for clams, abalone and crabs became important. In 1890 the industry employed 5,496 men with an investment of $2.5 million. A firm basis had been laid for the great present-day fishing industry.

Whaling vessels had often called at California ports during the Mexican period, although they did not generally hunt off the province's coast. After the American conquest of California, daring Yankee skippers used its ports as temporary bases from which to extend their whaling activities as far as the Bering Sea, the Japanese coastal waters and the shores of Peru. Until 1850 these American vessels usually claimed harbors along the eastern seaboard as their home ports. Increasingly after that date, American whaling vessels used California ports as permanent bases of operation. Many of these vessels had strikingly successful cruises. By the mid-fifties, five hundred vessels (many of them not American) used California harbors to engage in the Pacific whaling industry.

Shore stations for coastal whaling were established from San Diego in the south to Trinidad in the north. The take of whales was sufficient to serve as a supplement to the long-range whaling. Meanwhile, by the late fifties and early sixties, large whaling fleets sailed each summer from San Francisco into arctic waters. Even the losses inflicted in 1865 by the Confederate raider *Shenandoah* could not long cripple the California-based whaling industry. The whaling season's product in 1867 amounted to 13,149 barrels of oil and 186,000 pounds of bone. Yet from this peak, the whaling industry from California ports went into a slow decline, caused by the indiscriminate killing of young whales. By 1881 there were only forty vessels still engaged in the industry. The decline continued, but this picturesque industry lasted until well into the twentieth century.

The post-gold-rush period saw California finally deal with its Indian problem. When the Americans came to California, they viewed the Indian as they generally did elsewhere—simply as an obstacle to the development of the land, to be swept away as rapidly as possible. The temper of the Americans who came to California by the overland routes was not improved by the sporadic difficulties they encountered with the Pawnees and the Humboldt Sink Diggers. Once in California, the white men's frontier did not advance slowly and in a generally straight line as it had in the East. On the contrary, the whites rather quickly penetrated all parts of the state in their frenzied search for gold. As a result, conflicts with the Indians occurred in all parts of California. After the first skirmish between the goldseekers and the Indians, the original cause of the trouble was forgotten while both sides continued to retaliate for past wrongs. This revenge was often senseless, since neither the white men nor the Indians bothered to retaliate upon the individuals who had injured them, but simply attacked any convenient group of the other race. Most of California's Indian wars were carried on in this rather haphazard fashion. Almost as soon as white men had settled over the new state, they demanded that the Indians be restrained on reservations and not allowed to roam over mining claims and cultivated fields. To implement this policy of removal, as early as 1850 a United States Indian Commission of three men was appointed by the federal government. These men were Redick McKee of Virginia, Oliver Wozencraft of Louisiana and George W. Barbour of Kentucky. They arrived in California between December of 1850 and January of 1851.

Early in February 1851, the group went to the Indian country of the San Joaquin Valley to induce the red men there to conclude an agreement with the United States. After much effort, the commissioners succeeded in persuading the Indians of that region to sign a treaty. In April the commissioners moved south, making a pact with what they regarded as sixteen tribes (really bands) of Indians at Camp Barbour on the upper San

Joaquin River. In these treaties the Indians agreed to cede their lands in exchange for provisions, beef cattle, agricultural implements, hardware and a sizable reservation. As fast as the Indians signed the compacts, they were led off to the reservations selected for them.

Having acted jointly at first because of their lack of experience, the federal Indian commissioners at this point decided to act separately in order to finish their task more quickly. McKee selected northern California, Wozencraft the central part of the state, and Barbour the south. Their treaty-making activities followed the pattern already set. Eighteen pacts were concluded with 139 Indian groups and subgroups. Eighteen reservations comprising an aggregate of 7,488,000 acres or 11,700 square miles—some 7.5 per cent of the entire state—were set aside for the Indians. These treaties were duly sent to the Senate for ratification by President Millard Fillmore. Had California been a territory with no senatorial representation, these pacts would in all likelihood have been ratified. However, California's senators, following the sentiment of the state, opposed these treaties. California public opinion had turned against the Indian agents' work. Since the treaties had caused Indian depredations to decrease, there had been general approval of the pact-making. Yet when Californians gradually comprehended the full effect of giving the Indians such a generous allotment of the better lands of the state, public opinion quickly changed. When word of California's attitude reached Washington, the entire state congressional delegation steadfastly opposed the ratification of these documents. The United States Senate, strongly influenced by California's revulsion to the Indian treaties, rejected all eighteen of the pacts. An additional factor prejudicing the Senate against ratification was the Indian agents' action in obligating the United States to furnish hundreds of thousands of dollars in supplies and services to the Indians. The reaction of the Indians to this rejection of their agreements was at first bewilderment and then resentment. Most of the claims for supplies under the treaties were never paid.

The result was chaos. In March 1852, Congress passed an act creating a California Indian superintendency. Edward Fitzgerald Beale, who had been a naval officer at the time of the American conquest of California, became the first occupant of this office. Beale decided upon a fresh start. He argued for the creation of a series of small reservations with military posts on them. In this way the Indians could be controlled and also protected against white men, while they were learning to adjust to the changed circumstances in California. Upon his plea, Congress authorized five military reservations which were not to exceed 25,000 acres in extent and also appropriated a quarter of a million dollars to carry out his idea.

By August 1853, Beale put his plan into operation in the Tejon region of southern California. By late in 1854, he had persuaded the four hundred Indians gathered there to cultivate 3,265 acres of land. Beale, a blunt, outspoken man, never hesitated to reprimand either his own subordinates or white citizens whom he believed were improperly treating the Indians. Such unvarnished honesty made him a host of determined enemies. In addition he had allowed himself to become vulnerable by keeping his accounts carelessly. With inefficiency as an excuse, he was summarily removed by the federal authorities in the spring of 1854 and replaced by Thomas J. Henley. Henley proved to be a less capable man than Beale, although at first he worked diligently to implement the best of his predecessor's plans. By September 1856, four permanent reservations had been established at Tejon, Nome Lacke in Colusa County, Klamath on the Klamath River, and Mendocino on the northern California coast.

Henley also established temporary reserves, or farms, in several parts of the state. An optimist of the first magnitude, Henley reported that all was going according to schedule on the reservations and reserves. However, a special agent, Godard Bailey, after an investigation of Henley's establishments, pronounced them a failure, partly because of mismanagement. In addition Bailey declared that the Indians had proved to be poor farmers. Congress reacted to this report by severely cutting the California Indian appropriations in 1858.

Forced to operate with this small budget, Henley's successor as superintendent, James Y. McDuffie, soon reported that all the reservations except that at Klamath were badly dilapidated. He recommended that many Indian reserves and reservations be abandoned. Congress largely accepted this suggestion and passed the law of June 19, 1860, which split the state into a northern and southern district with a superintendent in each area. Attempts to maintain the remaining reservations under this plan were unsuccessful. This failure was so vexing that in the midst of the Civil War in April 1864, Congress once more reestablished a single superintendency for the state. During the 1860's almost all of the Indian agents were army officers. Their understanding of the Indians' problems was minimal. As a result, on July 15, 1870, Congress tried to improve the Indians' lot by relieving all army officers of Indian agent duty. President Ulysses S. Grant then decided to replace them with civilian agents appointed upon the recommendation of a Christian denomination. The California Indians were entrusted to the Methodists. By that time California was so well settled and the Indians so diminished in numbers by illness and war, that the final solution of the Indian problem was at hand.

The Indian wars of the American period began as early as the spring of 1848, when some former members of Stevenson's regiment of New Yorkers (many of them the later Hounds) attacked some Indians in the Coloma area. The Indians retaliated against the nearest whites and the war was on. Miners of the district organized two parties which severely punished the natives of two nearby rancherias who may or may not have been to blame.

In 1849, hostilities broke out again along the Yuba River and in the Kings River region. The Indians committed atrocities against isolated whites. In the south, around the Colorado River, the fierce Yumas attacked immigrants passing through their territory. In the region of Clear Lake north of the Bay Area, when two settlers were killed by the Indians, a revenging force led by Captain Nathaniel Lyon killed 175 indigenes.

The year 1850 saw increased fighting. Although California's first governor, Peter H. Burnett, had declared defense against the Indians to be a local problem, he was soon compelled twice to call out the state militia to punish Indian atrocities. Typical of these actions was the fighting in Yuma country. It began because the Yumas had massacred eleven to fifteen Americans who operated a Colorado River ferry. These white men were far from innocent victims, but were reputed to be cutthroats and robbers. Nevertheless, the governor appointed a future filibuster, Joseph C. Morehead, to raise a force to punish the Indians. Morehead found few recruits willing to serve from the Los Angeles area, so he resorted to drafting men from incoming immigrant wagon trains. By this means he ultimately raised a force of 125 men, which he marched to the Colorado River only to find the Indians quiet. Unable to resist the impulse to garner a little military glory, he prodded some Indians into a fight—killing about twenty of them. He then charged the state of California the very considerable sum of $76,588 for his expenses. Later Morehead allegedly sold four hundred muskets and 70,000 cartridges belonging to the state, pocketing the money for use in an ill-starred Mexican filibustering venture.

In 1850 the city of Los Angeles began the practice, sanctioned by an ordinance, of auctioning off Indian prisoners charged with drunkenness or other petty offenses to work out their fines. This practice persisted for nineteen years. Since the only pay the prisoners usually drew for their labor was alcohol, it frequently happened that the same Indians were auctioned off week after week, since they again became intoxicated and could be rearrested.

With practices such as these, many southern California Indians were sullen, only awaiting the occasion or a leader to rebel. In 1851 the Cupeño Indians of southern California arose in rebellion under an able, white-hating chief, Antonio Garrá, who had been educated at San Luís Rey Mission. Garrá wished to forge an alliance of all southern California Indians to exterminate the white men. After plundering many ranchos and murdering isolated settlers, Garrá was captured when a Cahuilla tribal chieftain betrayed him to the California rangers. A military court martial decreed his death sentence, which was carried out by a firing squad in January 1852. American attention then shifted to the rebellious Yumas. Major Samuel P. Heinzelman led a force which captured the Yuma chief. After his execution, an uneasy peace once again fell over this part of southern California.

In 1851, in the course of the "Mariposa War," Major James D. Savage led a volunteer battalion which stumbled upon the great Yosemite Valley while pursuing some marauding Chowchilla and Yosemite Indians into the Sierra. Joseph Reddeford Walker's 1833 expedition had originally discovered the valley, but its existence had been forgotten. This nasty little war went on well into the 1860's before the Indian leader, Chief Tenieya, finally surrendered.

In the early 1850's, Indian fighting known as Oregon's Rogue River War broke out. This émeute spilled across the border into California. During the winter of 1856–57, the Indians on the Pit River in northern California massacred many isolated settlers. The Indian troubles continued in northern California, and the adjutant general of the California Militia, William C. Kibbe, led a campaign in 1858–59 into the northern coastal range to break native resistance. Kibbe succeeded in killing one hundred Indians and driving three hundred others down to Humboldt Bay. These Indians were trapped against the shore, so that they could be seized and forcibly shipped south to the Mendocino reservation. Yet small-scale Indian depredations and scattered fighting continued throughout the northern part of the state.

During 1861–65 there was much fighting in northwestern California. The Hoopa Indians held out so obstinately against a specially picked mountaineer battalion of California troops that they succeeded in obtaining an excellent tract of reservation land in Hoopa Valley when peace was made. Meanwhile, the Indians of the Owens River Valley continued their raids against the ranchos of Santa Barbara and Los Angeles counties, carrying off hundreds of cattle and horses. As the line of advancing settlement further diminished the Indian hunting grounds, they turned increasingly to stealing forays against white settlements. To end this nuisance, the ranchers raised a force which harried the Indians in 1862. The desperate Indians were not long deterred by this campaign. Therefore, to end the Indian depredations, in January of 1865 the settlers attacked and killed forty Indians in a single village. The next month the settlers literally drove nearly one hundred Indians into the waters of Owens Lake and killed them. Although isolated skirmishes continued into the 1870's, this was the last important Indian engagement in southern California. In the Pit River country of northern California, the violence of the 1850's continued for over another decade and was ended only when the hard-bitten Indian fighter General George Crook led an expedition into that area in 1868.

California's last great Indian uprising was the Modoc War. General John M. Schofield, a one-time secretary of war, called it "a conflict more remarkable . . . than any before known in American history." The seeds of this war had been sown years before in 1852. In September of that year, at Bloody Point on the east shore of Tule Lake, an immigrant train of sixty-five whites was slaughtered by Modoc Indians. Ironically these Modocs were spoiling for revenge against the white men because they had been maltreated by some Americans who mistakenly thought them to be horse thieves. One white man escaped from the massacre of the immigrant train and made his way to the nearest large white settlement at Yreka. A citizen of that town, rugged, weather-beaten Ben Wright, led a party which lured forty-six of the Modocs to a parley at Black Bluff and treacherously attacked them. Only five wounded Modocs escaped to carry the word of the whites' duplicity to their tribe. Wright's expedition returned to Yreka, brandishing Modoc scalps. Its members were greeted by the citizens as returning heroes and entertained at a victory ball. Scattered hostilities then broke out. The Modocs proved to be fierce warriors, since they were proficient with the bow and arrow and carried black obsidian knives for fighting at close quarters. They also became adept at using the white man's firearms. In October 1864 the Modocs, impressed by the white man's superior force, accepted a peace treaty which bound them to move to a reservation on the upper Klamath Lake in Oregon.

Once settled upon the reservation, the Modocs quickly found trouble. They had to share the place with their natural enemies, the Klamaths. As a result, many of the young hot-blooded Modocs followed a leader, Captain Jack or Kientopoos, in plans to escape. Captain Jack gained his nickname from the whites because of a fancied resemblance he bore to a miner who lived in Yreka. On one dark, moonless night, Captain Jack led fifty braves and their families from the reservation on a journey back to their ancestral home in northeastern California. Between 1865 and 1869 various unsuccessful efforts were made to persuade him to return to the Klamath reservation. However, when a persuasive Indian agent with long experience, Alfred B. Meacham, became superintendent for Indian affairs in Oregon, he vowed to make peace with the Modocs. In December 1869 he was able to convince the runaway Modocs to return to the Klamath reservation. They found the basic situation unchanged. It was as difficult as ever to live in peace with the Klamaths. The Indian agent in charge was coldly indifferent to their plight. As a result, on April 25, 1870, Captain Jack and his band again left the reservation, vowing never to return.

By crossing into California without permission, the Modocs defied the federal government and caused military resources to be concentrated against them. To make the breach more irreconcilable, in 1871, Captain Jack became guilty of murder when, according to tribal custom, he killed a medicine man who had failed to cure his niece. When Captain Jack refused all overtures to return to the reservation, a detachment of thirty-five soldiers under Captain James Jackson on November 28, 1872, left Fort Klamath to capture the recalcitrant chief. As the army contingent advanced, it was reinforced by about twenty-five settlers. On November 30, 1872, this force came upon Captain Jack's camp in the Lost River country. At first it seemed as if hostilities might be avoided when a parley was opened between the two sides. This peaceable interchange was abruptly broken by pistol shots as the Modocs and the troops got into an argument. The Indians fell back, dragging the dead body of one of their warriors with them. Then the Modocs fired down upon the whites with their pistols and muzzle-loading rifles from behind the cover of the sagebrush, killing or wounding perhaps fifteen of their enemies. Realizing that they could not hold their position, the Indians fled toward more difficult terrain. As they went, they left a bloody trail, revenging themselves by murdering thirteen (some accounts say eighteen) white settlers.

It would not prove easy for the federal soldiers to capture the Modocs, since Captain Jack had led his band to the lava beds. This region lies between Tule Lake and Clear Lake in the extreme northern part of California, almost within sight of the Oregon boundary. The area was geologically young when the last lava flow took place about five thousand years ago. The country contains a rugged labyrinth of chasms and over one hundred caves, where the melted lava has congealed in numerous weird shapes. Most caves were formed when the lava surface hardened and the molten core ebbed away.

Despite the advantage of fighting in this rugged area, the odds were prohibitively heavy against the Indians. They numbered no more than fifty-three braves, armed only with antique muzzle-loaders, some pistols, and their native weapons. Against them the government mobilized units of the regular army, Oregon volunteers and California settlers. By mid-January 1873, two detachments of this mighty host were only a few miles apart, as they tightened a ring of iron around the Modocs. Suddenly the Modocs ambushed one detachment of four hundred soldiers. Firing entirely from behind cover, the Indians killed thirty-five whites and wounded many others, without loss to their own ranks.

As a result of the battle, the military expedition fell back in great disarray. In glee the fifty Indian braves who had routed an army danced their scalp dance. The government, in its chagrin, removed the officer who had been in charge of the military campaign.

The government at Washington appointed a Modoc peace commission eventually composed of Alfred B. Meacham, the former superintendent of Indian affairs in Oregon, General Edward Richard Sprigg Canby, commander of the Columbia Department of the Army, a Methodist minister, Eleazar Thomas, and the federal Indian agent of the Klamath Falls agency, Leroy S. Dyer.

The commissioners arranged a virtual truce with the Modocs and arranged for both sides to parley. Meanwhile over one thousand soldiers and armed settlers surrounded and cut off the Indians in their lava beds stronghold. At this point Captain Jack may have actually meant to end this hopeless war by negotiation, but his peace moves put him under fire from his young warriors. The young men would hear of no compromise. Instead they urged Captain Jack to murder the general and the other members of the peace commission when they met to negotiate.

As a result, when the long-awaited peace meetings occurred between the commissioners and the Indian leaders on Good Friday, April 11, 1873, the Modocs secretly violated the agreement to attend without arms. The Indians who met to parley all carried concealed knives and pistols. In addition, two rifle-bearing young braves were secreted in the nearby brush. When the white commissioners arrived at the rendezvous the atmosphere was tense, but General Canby produced cigars which he distributed to break the tension. For a while the Indians and whites talked listlessly; then at a given signal Captain Jack drew a pistol and shot General Canby. The wound would not have been fatal, but as the general staggered away he was pursued by other Indians who stabbed and shot him to death. Canby was the first general officer to fall to the western Indians. Simultaneously, Meacham was badly wounded, scalped and left on the field for dead. At the sounds of the shooting, the troops advanced and recovered Canby's body and rescued the wounded Meacham. Despite his grievous wounds, Meacham later recovered. Another of the white commissioners, the Methodist missionary Eleazar Thomas, was killed at the scene of the meeting. The fourth member of the peace commission, Indian agent Leroy S. Dyer, escaped by outrunning his pursuers. Although often shot at by the Modocs, he succeeded in reaching the safety of American lines.

After this act of Indian treachery, the soldiers swarmed forward to attack the Modoc position. Despite the help of artillery, the troops accomplished nothing against the well-hidden, securely entrenched Modocs, except to accumulate more of their own casualties. The soldiers then fell back to besiege the Indians. The Modocs' position had one glaring weakness—there was no adequate water supply. As a result, after three days of intermittent fighting, the Indians were forced to evacuate their position and melt away into the rough terrain.

In pressing the pursuit of the hostile Indians, one military detachment under Captain E. Thomas was roughly handled by the ambushing

Modocs. Out of sixty-six enlisted men in the party, forty-three did not answer the roll call after the battle. All five of the commissioned officers were killed or wounded. Although troop reinforcements arrived, the Modocs successfully escaped. This brief battle has been aptly named the Black Ledge Massacre.

Since the federal authorities had no hope of a negotiated settlement, they called in as commanding officer of the soldiers a tough Union Civil War general, then serving in the regular army establishment as a colonel. He bore the improbable name of Jefferson C. Davis. Davis was a hard-bitten man who, during the Civil War, had shot a fellow officer over a trifling matter and had gotten away with it! Davis went on to compile a creditable combat record.

In May 1873, Davis sent a strong detachment into the lava beds, prob-ing for the Modocs. An attempted Indian ambush was only partially successful, for the soldiers were learning to expect the unexpected. As a result, fourteen warriors of Captain Jack's band became disgruntled by the chief's leadership and deserted to the army to serve as scouts against their former comrades. Ironically, some of these Indians had been the loudest exponents of a war policy at the time of Canby's massacre.

The remaining Modocs under Captain Jack were closely pursued by the overwhelmingly superior numbers of troops. The strain of fleeing before the soldiers snapped the remaining bonds of unity among Cap-tain Jack's band. Soon the Modocs had broken into very small groups, all of which were frantically scrambling to escape. Thus by late May the Modocs were being hunted down and killed or captured as individuals. On June 1, Captain David Perry's detachment captured Captain Jack. A dirty, weak, disheveled fugitive, the Indian chief bore little resemblance to the cunning leader he had so often shown himself to be. At the time of his capture, Captain Jack was accompanied by only two warriors, five squaws and seven children. Within the next four days, all the important Modoc leaders were apprehended. In early July, under orders from Washington, Colonel Davis transported his prisoners to stand trial before a military tribunal at Fort Klamath, Oregon. Captain Jack and five other Modoc chiefs were given death sentences. Ironically, several of the Modocs who had committed some of the worst atrocities, but who had then abandoned Captain Jack before the end, were never brought to trial. At the last minute before their execution, two of the Modocs had their sentences commuted to life imprisonment, and were sent to Alcatraz to begin their sentences. The other four condemned Indians, including Cap-tain Jack, were hanged on October 3, 1873. The remaining Modocs were moved hundreds of miles to a reservation in the Indian Territory.

The Modoc War was the nation's costliest Indian conflict since the Seminole War of the 1830's. The monetary cost of subduing this handful of Indians (only fifty-three warriors) was over half a million dollars; the human cost was the lives of at least eighty-three whites. The Modocs themselves lost only seventeen warriors killed in battle or executed. It was all a tragic waste, since if the Modocs had been allowed to live on their own land, a strip of relatively worthless territory in the lava beds, the whole conflict would have been avoided.

The California Indians by the 1880's had become more an object of pity than of terror. This change in public opinion was partly brought about by two of authoress Helen Hunt Jackson's works—*A Century of Dishonor* (1881) and *Ramona* (1884). Other humanitarians made the same point, namely, that the Indian had been shamefully mistreated and must now be helped by the whites. The end result of this agitation was the passage by Congress of the Dawes Act of 1887, by which the federal government assumed responsibility for the Indians and authorized the granting of land to individual Indians. Nevertheless, the path of Indian adjustment to white society has been strewn with failure.

TWENTY-ONE

Links to the West

AMERICAN California and the eastern states were too closely linked by business ties for Californians to remain content with their inadequate overland links with the outside world. Although the lonely distances that stretched eastward from California were endless and awesome they were far from a trackless wilderness. From the earliest times, there were a number of primitive thoroughfares trodden by the buffalo and the Indians. These routes were later used by the trappers, traders and goldseekers as they pressed west.

Of the most important land routes linking California with the East, special mention should be reserved for the Oregon–California Trail, or as it became increasingly known after 1850, the Central Overland Road. This trail was heavily used by immigrants, since it was the best direct road to the California gold fields and a branch of it led to Oregon. It began at Fort Kearny, two hundred miles west of Omaha, then ran west along the Platte River through South Pass to the upper Snake River. From the vicinity of this river, it branched west to Oregon and southwest to California.

Overland caravans with their creaking, rattling, weatherbeaten covered wagons carried settlers and goods slowly west. The wagon-freighting business utilized hundreds of prairie schooners which had been modeled after the famed Conestoga wagon and modified for western conditions. The wide variety of cargo carried by these vehicles included groceries, clothing, tobacco, rope and hardware, hauled overland from the Missouri River to California. The striking feature of the overland traffic was its

LAND LINKS FROM EASTERN UNITED STATES TO CALIFORNIA

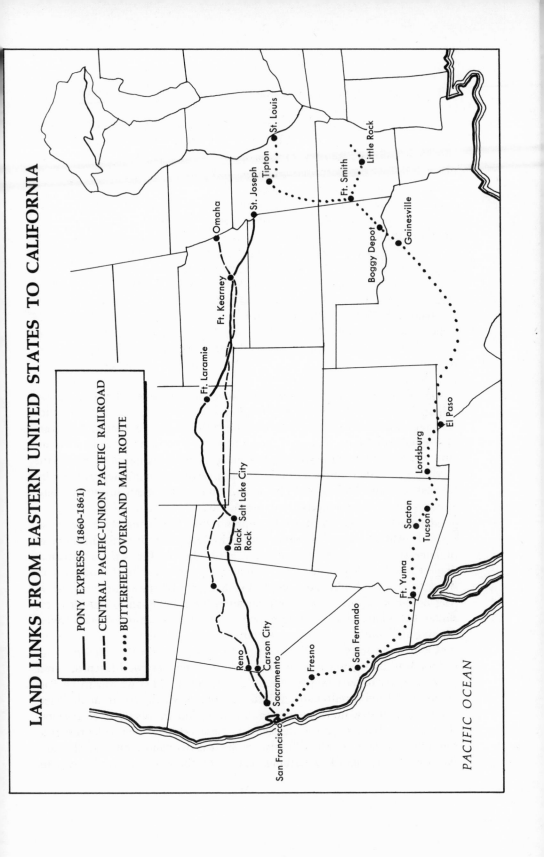

PONY EXPRESS (1860-1861)

CENTRAL PACIFIC-UNION PACIFIC RAILROAD

BUTTERFIELD OVERLAND MAIL ROUTE

St. Louis
Tipton
St. Joseph
Little Rock
Ft. Smith
Omaha
Gainesville
Boggy Depot
Ft. Kearney
Ft. Laramie
El Paso
Lordsburg
Salt Lake City
Black Rock
Sacton
Tucson
Reno
Ft. Yuma
Carson City
Fresno
San Fernando
Sacramento
San Francisco

PACIFIC OCEAN

primarily western direction. Seldom was anything except buffalo hides or military supplies carried eastward.

Travel along this route was both slow and expensive. Under favorable conditions, it took a prairie schooner one hundred days to complete the two-thousand-mile journey to California. While rates were neither fixed nor regulated, the customary charge was one dollar per one hundred pounds for each one hundred miles.

Distressed by their isolation from the outside world, Californians in the 1850's clamored for better overland transportation and communication. By 1851, although there were only thirty-four post offices in California, a mail contract had been let between Sacramento and Salt Lake City to speed mail to the Golden State. A thirst for cheaper, faster mail service was unslaked by this action, and in 1856 a petition bearing 75,000 signatures was presented to Congress along with a request for daily mail service from the East. Finally on March 3, 1857, Congress passed the Post Office Appropriations Bill with an amendment authorizing a subsidy of $300,000 a year for semimonthly mail service from the Mississippi River to San Francisco, $450,000 for weekly service and $600,000 for semiweekly service.

At this juncture, since stagecoach and mail service supplemented each other, James E. Birch, a transportation magnate, entered the overland mail business. As a very young man, Birch had been a stagecoach driver in Providence, Rhode Island. Moving to California to seek his fortune in July of 1849, Birch opened a stage service from Sacramento to the foothills of the Sierra, which featured an old, springless ranchwagon drawn by four half-wild Mexican broncos. He soon replaced his primitive conveyance with elegant eastern coaches, such as the famous Concord. With good equipment and prompt, efficient service, Birch quickly built up a business valued at over a million dollars. By late 1853, he had persuaded a number of his competitors to merge with him to form the California Stage Company—a giant enterprise which encompassed well over half of the stage lines in California and monopolized the business in the northern part of the state. At the age of twenty-five, Birch served as president of this corporation, which boasted that it was the largest staging company in the world.

When word reached California that Congress had finally acted in 1857 to establish faster mail service to the West, Birch resigned his post with the California Stage Company and traveled to Washington to bid on the contract. The postmaster general of the United States, Aaron V. Brown, favored a southern route for the new service. Apparently as a preliminary to the larger contract, Postmaster General Brown awarded Birch a $15,000 contract for monthly mail stages over a route that was dubbed the San Antonio and San Diego Mail. Critics tartly called the 1,476-mile road a trail from nowhere to nowhere. Until March 1858, the line did not even offer stage accommodations, but instead utilized pack trains. Although it employed both horses and mules, it was also derisively called the "Jackass Line." Because it lay so far from the heavily populated areas of California, most Californians benefited little from the service. Its only justification consisted in being a subsidiary of the larger overland service which was still to be established. Nonetheless, service began on August 7, 1857, and continued despite various vicissitudes until August 1861. The line survived the untimely death in September 1857 of its founder James Birch, who perished in a shipwreck. His associates reorganized the corporation after his death, and it became known as Giddings and Company.

Yet even before Birch's death the line had already failed in the pursuit of the coveted contract for the main overland mail service. As a result of the intervention of President James Buchanan, the contract had been granted to a combine headed by John Butterfield. Associated with Butterfield were men representing all the leading express companies, particularly Wells, Fargo & Company. The terms of the contract called for service to be performed by a "good four-horse" coach able to accommodate passengers and mail on a trip that was to take no longer than twenty-five days.

At first Butterfield dominated the combine, and the company was widely known as the Butterfield Line. Butterfield was born near Albany, New York, on November 18, 1801, and began his staging career as a driver. He quickly moved into the executive end of the business and became preëminent controlling the traffic west from Albany. When the government suggested the western stage and mail service, the experienced Butterfield decided to organize a group to bid for the contract. Actually Butterfield and his associates were not happy with the southern route advocated by the postmaster general, but since Brown would hear of no alternative, they acquiesced in his choice. The route covered a 2,700-mile-long trail, which looked on a map like an oxbow or a horseshoe, from the railroad's end at Tipton, Missouri, through Arkansas, the Indian Territory, Texas, New Mexico and on into California by way of Fort Yuma. Then the route ran on to Los Angeles and up the San Joaquin Valley to San Francisco. The route had one great advantage: year-round passability. To obtain this advantage, it ran at least six hundred miles south of the track favored by most bidders for the contract, and one which necessitated a heavier than necessary expenditure for equipment and personnel.

Within a year after the granting of the contract, under Butterfield's supervision, the route was surveyed, the necessary roads, ferries, bridges and stations built, over one thousand horses and mules collected, and nearly one thousand employees hired. The line was divided at El Paso (Franklin) into eastern and western halves; the western half was manned by Californians. In all, perhaps a million dollars was invested by the company before the first stage rolled west from Tipton, Missouri, in mid-September of 1858. At the same time, a coach rolled eastward from San Francisco. The westward trip was finished in twenty-four days, eighteen hours and thirty-five minutes—just inside the agreed upon time. To accomplish this feat, the coaches had to run night and day, stopping only to change teams, or at greater intervals, coaches. The average speed of the stage had to be approximately five miles an hour. At the line's two terminals—Missouri and California—brightly colored Concord coaches still redolent of paint and fresh leather were used. On the rougher parts of the road, more durable vehicles, such as the Troy carriages or "Celerity" wagons, were employed. The Concord coaches could accommodate, with some squeezing, six to twelve passengers on the inside and even more on the roof seats, although coaches were seldom that crowded.

In the beginning, Butterfield's 139 to 165 stations were about eighteen miles apart, although in some parts of Texas stations were over sixty miles from one another. Four to twelve men generally staffed these lonely outposts.

Within California the Butterfield stage provided what had never existed before—regular, fast service between San Francisco and Los Angeles. This link between the two cities caused some dislocation in the established paths of commerce, since San Francisco now obtained certain specialized items from southern California instead of from her former northern California sources.

On the Butterfield line, the mail went through handily. Passengers, however, did not fare nearly so well. Since there were no stopovers except those necessary to keep the coaches rolling, passengers had to catch such catnaps as they could within the jolting coaches and wagons. The only food service consisted of poorly prepared meals, hastily eaten at way stations. Experienced travelers often carried some cold food with them to eat during the long intervals between stations. The price of a meal—not included in the fare—ranged from forty cents to one dollar, which was quite high for the time. The standard menu consisted of jerked beef, fried pork, corncakes, raw onions and coffee. Since drivers and way-station agents were more concerned with handling the mail and horses, they paid scant attention to the comforts of the passengers, who had to be hardy to survive. Although some enthusiastic travelers praised the stage ride as an exhilarating experience, others found it a grueling ordeal. One sensitive journeyer went mad during a trip. Two other passengers so grated upon each other's nerves that they arranged a duel.

Nor was this jolting, uncomfortable ride inexpensive. At first the fare from St. Louis to San Francisco was $200, while the eastbound charge was only $100. Heavy criticism by westbound passengers caused the line to equalize its fare at $200 regardless of direction. Before long, to woo more passengers, the fare was slashed to $150. For short distances (and many travelers did not go all the way across the route) the fare was ten cents a mile. Each passenger was allowed forty pounds of free baggage.

Contrary to popular fiction, the Butterfield stage in its less than three-year history on the southern run was seldom bothered by Indians and hardly at all by highwaymen. The company's generous policy toward the natives accounted for this relative freedom from harassment. The line distributed over $10,000 worth of beef to hungry Indians along its route. Once a large band of Comanches stopped a stage and forced the driver and his passengers to wait for five harrowing hours while the Indians carefully inspected the strange vehicle and its cargo. At last they released the coach with the instructions, "You go! Go swift!" The greatest depredation that the Indians committed was the occasional theft of spare horses from the lonely way stations. Only one stage was openly attacked. This incident occurred at Apache Pass in the early part of 1861, when the withdrawal of United States troops from the southwestern posts emboldened the Indians of that area. Highwaymen did not molest Butterfield stages since company policy forbade the carrying of specie.

In March 1860, Wells, Fargo & Company became dissatisfied with John Butterfield's lavish business policies, which kept the combine from making the expected heavy profits. As a result, the express company was able to oust Butterfield from his position as president in favor of the vice-president, William B. Dinsmore. Butterfield suffered a physical breakdown, and he was only able to operate for the remainder of his life on a schedule of reduced activity. In October 1867, he suffered a stroke, and died an invalid in November 1869.

The approach of the Civil War shadowed the future of the reorganized Butterfield Line. In March 1861, with Fort Sumter already under siege, the federal government ordered that service on the southern track be discontinued. In recompense, the government offered the company a mail contract for service over the central route. This new contract included several other interesting changes. Letters were to be carried from the Missouri River to California on a twenty-three-day schedule with daily service. Newspapers and other second-class matter were allowed to fill the minimum of one thousand pounds of mail daily. If space were really at a premium, second-class matter could be allowed as long as thirty-five days for the transcontinental trip.

In order to help defray the expenses of the relocation of the line, the government allowed the company a bonus of a month's extra subsidy ($50,000). Also, the Post Office awarded the company an annual subsidy of one million dollars. The stage company needed this help, since it had suffered substantial losses in both real estate and chattels when it was forced to relocate.

The Overland Mail Company, still headed by William B. Dinsmore, retained for that company the stretch of the central route from Salt Lake City to Virginia City, Nevada. It sublet the rest to other companies. As a result of these arrangements, by mid-July of 1861, stage-coach mail service had been restored from Missouri to California.

By the close of 1861, a wealthy businessman, Ben Holladay, took over the Central Overland and Pike's Peak Express Company, and with it the mail contract from Missouri to Salt Lake.

Holladay found his stage line much harassed by Indians, grown bold since the withdrawal of the regulars to fight in the Civil War. To counter these attacks, Holladay hired the toughest gunslingers he could find. These men often knew little about staging, and the mail was sometimes lost by their careless or corrupt handling. Passengers were relatively few, and the line was shut down for weeks at a time by Indian uprisings or threats of Indian rebellion.

During the Civil War years, the route between Salt Lake City and California fell under the control of the giant express corporation Wells, Fargo & Company. This company seldom operated coaches under its own name inside California, preferring to work instead through subsidiary companies. Not realizing this practice, many historians have been misled to undervalue the company's role in western staging. Yet through its great control of capital, it took over the Pioneer Stage Company (a California corporation) and then the original Overland Mail. This put Wells Fargo in control not only of the western section of the overland mail route, but also, through its connections with many ostensibly independent connecting stage companies, in control for a while of the entire transportation complex of the Pacific area.

Holladay and Wells Fargo then battled each other for dominance in western staging. The rivalry abruptly ceased on November 1, 1866, when Holladay accepted a Wells Fargo offer to buy him out for $1.5 million in cash, $300,000 in the company's stock and a seat on the company's board of directors. By this stroke, Wells Fargo took over control of all the major western express and stagecoach companies. With the completion of the transcontinental railroad and the transfer of the mail contract to it, the stage lines were reduced to a supporting role. Nonetheless, as Wells Fargo had shrewdly anticipated, there was still a profit to be made running connecting stages to the various railheads. In this manner, staging continued to be important in the overall transportation picture of the West.

To keep the transcontinental stage lines in perspective, it must be re-called that while they gripped public attention, California mainly depended upon the steamers plying to the Isthmus of Panama for passenger travel and cargo-carrying. A railroad linked the Pacific and Atlantic Panamanian ports, allowing a transit to be made in a matter of hours. From the Atlantic ports there was excellent steamer service to the East

Coast of the United States. The fare for this voyage decreased by the late 1850's and 1860's, so that it was competitive with stage travel. In addition, the steamship magnates were able to cut passage time from thirty-four days to a very competitive twenty-one. The Pacific Mail Steamship Company took over the Pacific run exclusively in 1860, and five years later it bought out the ownership of the Atlantic fleet as well. It has been estimated that one-half of California's population increase in the 1860's came over the Isthmian passage. Steamer patronage did not begin to decline until after the completion of the transcontinental railroad in 1869. During the last full year of nonrailroad competition—1868—the passenger total carried by the Isthmian steamers reached its peak. Even after the completion of the railroad, traffic declined very slowly over the Isthmian route.

One overland mail service to California, the Pony Express, even though its life was measured in months rather than years, has received more attention than any other American communications link. This rapid communication service was called the Pony Express both by the firms engaged in it and the general public, yet there were as many horses as ponies used in this endeavor. The Pony Express originated because of the demand for more rapid communication between California and the East than the fastest stagecoach or Isthmian steamer could provide.

Actually the Pony Express had many forerunners. As early as 1858, Postmaster General Brown contracted with John M. Hockaday for a weekly service from Missouri to Utah, and with Major George Chorpenning for service from Utah to California. This central-route service brought the mail through in less than the thirty-eight days the schedule allowed. Upon one occasion in December 1858, these firms carried one of President Buchanan's state addresses through in just seventeen days. Perhaps a swifter schedule would have resulted, but the death of Postmaster General Brown in 1859 brought in an economy-minded successor, who eventually deprived Chorpenning of his mail contract.

At this point fresh men and capital joined the race with time across the plains and mountains to California. In February 1859, the veteran wagon-freighter William H. Russell formed a partnership with another experienced freighter, John S. Jones, to form the Leavenworth and Pike's Peak Express, which ran a line of stages from Leavenworth in Kansas Territory to Denver. Russell had previously formed a wagon-freighting partnership with Alexander Majors and William B. Waddell, but these two men feared that the stage from Leavenworth to Denver was too risky, and so Russell began this line as an independent venture with the more speculative-minded Jones. By October, Russell's independent venture was in deep financial trouble, even though it was busily engaged in carrying freight as well as passengers and had taken over the J. M. Hockaday Company's mail contract. Majors and Waddell realized that they could not allow Russell to fail because of the disastrous financial consequences to themselves. Therefore, they, in partnership with Russell, obtained full control of his ailing firm, forming a new Kansas concern called the Central Overland California and Pike's Peak Express Company to carry on its operations. This company soon developed a flourishing business between the Colorado mines and Salt Lake City. After Chorpenning lost his mail contract in 1860, the COC & PPE Company took over his franchise, thus giving the firm the right to carry mail from Missouri to California.

Raising the necessary capital during the spring of 1860, Russell and his associates ordered a survey of the trail between St. Joseph, Missouri, and the vicinity of Sacramento, California. In all, the route measured 1,966 miles and passed through Fort Kearny, Fort Laramie, Fort Bridger, Salt Lake City, Carson City and Placerville. Along the route, Russell and his associates established stations approximately ten miles apart. To handle the five hundred ponies and horses, several hundred horsetenders, horsemen and stationkeepers were hired.

The Pony Express actually began on April 3, 1860, with riders starting from both ends of the line, carrying the mail in relays. To lighten the load, wiry but hardy men and boys were hired as riders and furnished with the thinnest possible clothes and the lightest equipment. The mail itself was wrapped in oiled silk to protect it from the elements. A normal cargo consisted of between forty and ninety letters, but within a year as many as 350 were carried at one time. The fee was high—from ten dollars to two dollars an ounce.

The schedule called for the run to be made in ten days. To maintain this pace, a rider was expected to average about nine miles an hour, night or day, and to take no more than two minutes for changing horses. Each rider drove his horse at a gallop for the ten miles between stations. At the way station a fresh horse was already saddled and held ready for mounting. Quickly the mail pouch was flung across the saddle, while the rider vaulted upon his new pony and then raced away to the next station. Each rider covered between seventy and one hundred miles, depending upon the roughness of the terrain. Then he rested until it was his turn to ride the return run. Usually eighty riders were working on the line in relays. This romantic run typified the western spirit, and it is probably no accident that the one man who came to personify the West to easterners was a former Pony Express rider named "Buffalo Bill" Cody.

During the period from April 1860 to the early months of 1861, Russell, Majors and Waddell operated the Pony Express without official recognition or financial support from the federal government. They hoped, of course, that they would so demonstrate the feasibility of their service that it would qualify for a federal subsidy. Despite the high fees charged for postage on the Pony Express, expenses generally exceeded income.

Yet early in 1861, when Russell, Majors and Waddell became insolvent, it was caused not so much by the financial strain of the Pony Express as by their other unsuccessful business operations. In March 1861, Russell and his partners made an agreement with the Overland Mail Company, then controlled by Wells Fargo. The Overland Mail Company, which had an officially subsidized mail contract, was able to drive a hard bargain with Russell and his associates: Russell's group could run the Pony Express to Salt Lake City, while the Overland Mail operated it from Salt Lake westward. Russell and his partners were to retain 70 per cent of the income from the eastern part of the route, giving 30 per cent to the Overland Mail Company. The Overland Mail shared none of its revenue with Russell and his associates. This unequal arrangement remained in effect for the last one-third of the Pony Express's life.

In the end it was the advantages of another form of communication—the telegraph—and not heavy costs, that finished the Pony Express. Ten weeks after the Pony Express riders began their run, on June 16, 1860, Congress authorized a transcontinental telegraph. This bill instructed the secretary of the treasury to give a subsidy of $40,000 annually for ten years to a transcontinental telegraph line.

This congressional action, taken only sixteen years after Samuel F. B. Morse invented the telegraph, caused the incorporation of two companies to build the transcontinental wire. The Pacific Telegraph Company, a Nebraska firm under Edward Creighton, built westward from Kansas City toward Salt Lake City. Simultaneously, the Overland Telegraph Company of California began building eastward from Fort Churchill in Nevada Territory. The Overland Telegraph was the result of a consolidation of several local California telegraph companies. As the building of the two connecting lines continued, it turned into a race to see which line could reach Salt Lake City first. Creighton's company won the contest when a crew planted the last pole at the Mormon capital on October 20, 1861. Four days later, the Overland Company's crews reached the same city, completing the system. San Francisco was linked to New York City by wire; instant communication coast to coast was at last a reality. The Pony Express ceased almost at once, as soon as the last of its 34,753 pieces of mail could be delivered.

Within California, telegraphic service began as early as September 1853, when a line was stretched between Point Lobos and San Francisco to provide shipping information and weather data. San Francisco was linked to San Jose by October of the same year. The first telegraphic message from San Francisco to San Jose was not profound, but was typical of thousands of routine business communications tapped out over the line. One G. H. Bodfish ordered ten half-barrels of "clean pork." By October 1860, San Francisco was linked with Los Angeles. Consequently, the cross-country line to San Francisco also linked many other California cities with Chicago and New York.

With instant communication now available to them, Californians were ready to concentrate upon faster overland transportation by rail. Actually the idea of a transcontinental railroad had been talked about ever since the steam locomotive had proved its practicality. As early as 1836, the *American Railway Journal* published an article concerning "an Atlantic and Pacific Railroad." In 1845, Asa Whitney presented to Congress his idea for a railroad from Lake Michigan to the mouth of the Columbia River. No idle dreamer, Whitney actively lobbied for his proposal, which was completed within a quarter of a century. Before the gold rush, planners dreamed of linking Oregon with the Midwest; after 1849 the transcontinental railroad was projected west to California.

During the 1850's, various governmental surveys were undertaken to decide the best route for the railroad. In the end these surveys indicated only that there were several alternative routes, each with its own advantages and disadvantages. Meanwhile sectional jealousies were aroused; northerners generally favored a central road across the continent, while southerners favored a southern track to the Pacific.

By 1854 the first eastern railroad reached the Mississippi River, but then progress westward slowed down. The problems, engineering and financial, of pushing a railroad through the lightly settled or unoccupied mountains and desert were enormous. Investors faced the prospect of scant revenues for many years while the land remained unsettled, and most feared that the project represented too great a risk.

In the midst of 1850's, however, a young New York construction engineer became an ardent advocate of the transcontinental railroad. Born in 1826, Theodore D. Judah enjoyed a considerable career in the East before coming to California; he had worked at rebuilding portions of the Erie Canal and constructing railroads and bridges in New York and New England. In 1854, when the builders of the pioneer Sacramento Valley Railroad ran into engineering problems, they interested Judah in coming to California to help them. Judah supervised the construction of this railroad from Sacramento to Folsom—a distance of less than twenty-five miles. When the company proved unable to build the line farther on to Marysville because of lack of money and interest, Judah left its employ to devote his efforts to planning a transcontinental railroad. At his own expense, he surveyed possible passes through the mountains. Moreover, he went to Washington to lobby for his project. Since Judah burned with enthusiasm for the transcontinental railroad, he talked of nothing else. Ostensibly more practical men called him "Crazy Judah." The financiers of San Francisco scorned his dreams and refused to back him.

Judah remained resolute. He drew up articles of incorporation for

what he called the Central Pacific Railroad of California and attempted to
interest the leading men of Sacramento in his scheme. In a memorable
meeting in an upstairs room at 34 K Street in Sacramento, Judah elo-
quently harangued a dozen men, including future United States Senator
Cornelius Cole and four powerful merchants. The latter four included a
politician and wholesale grocer named Leland Stanford. Another was a
dry-goods merchant, Charles Crocker. Two others, Mark Hopkins and
Collis P. Huntington, were partners in a hardware store. In his speech,
Judah argued for the financial feasibility of his road. He claimed that his
railroad would certainly tap the profits of trade with the enormously
profitable Comstock Lode in adjoining Nevada; he also predicted that
the federal government would shortly grant a sizable subsidy to aid in the
railroad's construction.

After hearing Judah's plea, six Sacramento merchants, including the
four mentioned above—soon to be known as the "Big Four"—agreed to
subscribe to eight hundred of the 85,000 shares in the Central Pacific
Railroad. Nevertheless, to safeguard their investment, they insisted that
they be given places of power in the new corporation. As a result, when
the Central Pacific was formally organized on June 28, 1861, Stanford
was president, Huntington vice-president, James Bailey, another Sacramento merchant, secretary, while Hopkins took the post of treasurer.
Judah was content with the title of chief engineer. After further surveys,
Judah went again to Washington.

In the fall of 1861, Washington was a changed city from the sleepy
southern village it had been in prewar days. Its streets rang with the tread
of thousands of troops, and its hotels were crowded with contractors
seeking war contracts. The whole atmosphere was one of crisis and
urgency. Military necessity made federal officials more ready to listen to
Judah's pleas for a transcontinental railroad. Suavely, Judah argued that
California must be bound to the Union by a railroad. Such a link would
provide ammunition to answer those disloyal Californians who talked of
secession and the southern Confederacy, or who argued for a Pacific
republic.

Judah also had become an accomplished lobbyist. He knew which congressman to see and how to cut his arguments to move his auditor. As a
result, he wrangled appointments as a clerk on key congressional committees and subcommittees in order to help a bill granting federal aid and
subsides for a Pacific railroad. This bill passed Congress and was signed
into law by President Abraham Lincoln on July 1, 1862. This measure
named two companies, Judah's Central Pacific and the Union Pacific, to
build and operate a railroad from the Missouri River to Sacramento. It
provided for lavish grants of federal aid; the government donated a strip
of public land for a right of way and made additional grants of five

alternative sections per mile of public domain, with only trivial exceptions, on each side of the line for the entire length of the railroad. Moreover, the United States agreed to lend the two companies money through the device of thirty-year bonds at 6 per cent interest. These would be granted at the rate of $16,000 to $48,000 per mile, depending upon the nature of the terrain over which the railroad was built. Two years later a second Pacific Railway Act doubled the land grants and provided that the federal government would accept a second instead of a first mortgage upon the railroad's assets. In all, the government gave the two companies over 45,000,000 acres of land (11.5 million acres in California) and loaned them about $60,000,000.

The Big Four and their associates actually invested about $159,000 in the Central Pacific, which eventually reached a capitalization of $139,000,-000 under their control. In addition to the federal government's aid, the Central Pacific was the recipient of much help from western states, including California and many of its cities and counties. For instance, Los Angeles alone granted the Central Pacific $602,000, nearly four times the stake invested by the Big Four's combine.

Building westward, the Union Pacific broke ground at Omaha in Nebraska Territory on December 2, 1863. Company finances were inadequate, and its track-building soon ceased. The additional federal aid in 1864 attracted more capital, and by 1865, 247 miles of track had been placed in operation. A company, the Crédit Mobilier, served as the construction agency for the Union Pacific. The Crédit Mobilier made great profits for its owners, a combination of Union Pacific officials and congressmen. In 1866, General Grenville M. Dodge as chief engineer successfully organized hundreds of Civil War veterans into crews and pushed the work of railroad building across the plains of Nebraska into the more difficult mountain area of southern Wyoming. The Union Pacific's construction proceeded so well that most bystanders assumed that this firm would easily win the race with the Central Pacific to reach Salt Lake City.

The Central Pacific had begun construction on January 8, 1863, with whatever help seven speeches from an assembly of dignitaries could give it. The most important address was made by Leland Stanford, who wore two hats—one as president of the Central Pacific and the other as governor of California. Stanford, operating in a day when the idea of a conflict of interest was absent, never bothered to hide his official solicitude for the welfare of his own railroad. The Central Pacific had its equivalent of the Crédit Mobilier, a construction company headed by hard-driving, iron-nerved Charles Crocker. It too made vast sums for insiders such as the Big Four. Judah objected to Crocker's company as the construction agent for the railroad, and he began to bicker with the Big Four concerning construction details. A rupture between Judah and the Big Four could not be averted, after the chief engineer defied his associates by refusing to certify to the government officials that the Central Pacific entered the Sierra over twenty miles sooner than was actually the case in order to gain a greater amount of federal bonds allowed for mountainous terrain. Even without Judah's testimony, the Big Four succeeded in "moving" the Sierra into the middle of the great valley, thereby winning the larger government subsidy.

As for the disgruntled Judah, in October 1863 he accepted $100,000 for his interest in the Central Pacific and took an option to buy out the Big Four for $100,000 each. In order to secure eastern capital with which to take over the Central Pacific, Judah sailed for New York by way of the Isthmus of Panama. He contracted yellow fever on the Isthmus, but pressed on to New York, where he died on November 2, several months before his thirty-eighth birthday. The Big Four never so much as named a siding for him, and, of course, never shared a penny of their future profits with his widow.

With Judah now gone, the 250-pound Charles Crocker took over supervision of the Central Pacific's construction. He was capable of great bursts of furious energy, followed by periods of lassitude. As the railroad extended into the Sierra, he found many problems to tax his ingenuity. He was ignorant of the techniques of engineering, but he could bluster and bully those who did know the art of construction. He faced a chronic shortage of labor. All his unskilled laborers tended to drift off to the Comstock Lode in Nevada until he hit upon the idea of employing the Chinese. These docile, hard-working men, who usually made no demands for higher wages or better working conditions, proved ideal railroad builders. When Crocker had hired all the able-bodied Chinese he could find in California and still needed more, he sent away to China to bring in all the help he required. In time, he mobilized a force of perhaps ten thousand Chinese workmen, who were known to the disgruntled white laborers of California as "Crocker's Pets."

Crocker found that the heavy winter snows of the Sierra would frequently close the railroad with heavy drifts. As a result, wooden snowsheds were built enclosing the tracks to keep them clear. The rock of the Sierra proved to be a great problem for tunnel boring. Foolishly, Crocker eschewed the use of steam drills and depended instead upon gangs of rock-chipping Chinese.

Finally, by June 1868, the railroad between Sacramento and the California state line was completed. Then construction was able to proceed more quickly across the Nevada desert.

As the Union Pacific built toward the west and the Central Pacific toward the east, both companies made plans to build on past each other.

As a result, on April 10, 1869, Congress designated Promontory Point, six miles west of Ogden, as the rendezvous point of the two companies. By early May the tracks of the two railroads had approached each other. However, the official ceremonies for the meeting were delayed several days because the officials of the Union Pacific were late in arriving. San Francisco and a score of lesser California cities could not wait, and on Saturday, May 8, 1869, there were bands, fireworks and parades. "California annexes the United States" boastfully read one of the transparencies in the San Francisco parade. In truth, California was firmly joined to the Union, and talk of a Pacific republic was permanently silenced.

On May 10, the formal ceremonies included the driving of a golden spike by Leland Stanford, marking the junction of 1,085 miles of Union Pacific track with that of 690 miles of Central Pacific line. Stanford's hammer and spike were both equipped with telegraph wires, so as to record the event all over the United States. More at home behind a desk than swinging a hammer, Stanford missed! A quick-thinking telegrapher simulated the blow, causing a magnetic ball specially installed for the occasion atop the Capitol dome in Washington to fall from its pole, bringing cheers from thousands of bystanders. In time the golden spike was duly tapped into place.

Now that the heady excitement of railroad building was over, the important but humdrum business of operating the transcontinental railroad was at hand. The actual operation of the railroad was delayed somewhat, since the remainder of 1869 was spent in rebuilding makeshift fills and bridges, placing the roadbed in a condition to pass federal inspection and obtaining the necessary equipment and rolling stock.

The Union Pacific officials lost no time in selling out their interest in the company, taking their profits in building it and turning over the plucked cadaver of the railroad to others. The Union Pacific insiders accomplished the looting of their railroad when they formed a construction company—the Crédit Mobilier—to build it at exorbitant rates. They presented their claims to the railroad, which uncomplainingly paid these high charges out of the government funds that they had been advanced. Of course, only a relatively few top officials and other key individuals controlled the Crédit Mobilier. They used their positions within the Union Pacific and in Congress to insure that their exorbitant charges were never effectively questioned. In a similar manner Crocker's construction company was very well rewarded for actually building the railroad. The Big Four had expected to make their money constructing the railroad, not in the painstakingly long period of its operation. The Big Four would have liked to act in the same manner as the Union Pacific officials and unload their completed and heavily mortgaged railroad upon some guileless takers. There were no investors, however, who seemed willing to pay the Big Four's price. Hence, they had to continue operating the railroad themselves. The thought of so much desk activity was too much for rotund Charles Crocker, who liked to be out in his shirt-sleeves directing outdoor work. As a result, in 1871 Crocker sold out his original interest in the Central Pacific to his three partners, although he retained the large blocks of stock that he had gained by heading the construction company which built the railroad. The Big Four were reduced to the Big Three. Not for long, however, since Crocker, after a long travel vacation, returned to become a director of the Central Pacific and its second vice-president.

In its early years, the transcontinental railroad had few passengers, and much freight was still transported by alternative systems. In addition, the paralyzing panic of 1873 slowed business and tightened credit. Finally, the opening of the Suez Canal in 1869, the same year as the transcontinental railroad's completion, ended the hopes of American entrepreneurs since Judah's day that travelers from the Orient would elect to go to Europe by way of the transcontinental railroad.

As a result, the Big Four reluctantly concluded that they could never build up a great volume of passenger travel until the population along the route was increased. Consequently, the railroad made an effort to bring in easterners and immigrants from Europe in special, low-cost trains to settle upon company lands. Unfortunately these accommodations were not merely economical, they were substandard. The coaches were old and dilapidated. The passage was slow, and the coaches were often attached as parts of slow freight trains. In addition, on these immigrant trains the travelers were often victimized by confidence men and gamblers who were tolerated or in partnership with the train's crew. Only belatedly, after many complaints, did the Central Pacific move to clean up these abuses.

In the early years of the Central Pacific's operation, its schedule allowed four and a half days between Omaha and Sacramento. At first the terminus of the two lines remained at Promontory Point, where a rude shantytown grew up. Later the junction point was shifted to Ogden. The Central Pacific had no Pullmans, but instead offered what were called Silver Palace cars. Their name was the grandest thing about them, for they lacked most facilities, including good springs to cushion the rough ride. The trip through the alkali dust of Nevada seemed a horror to the more sensitive travelers. The discomforts and dangers of the Sierra crossing also made a great impression upon many passengers. Spectacular train wrecks in the Sierras, which were described in copious detail in the nation's press, also helped to discourage passenger travel on the transcontinental railroad.

Meanwhile, the Big Four were consolidating their hold on transportation within California. Since they were forced to operate the railroad or sell out below actual value, they decided to run it at the greatest possible margin of profit, regardless of the long-run consequences. They quickly realized that their railroad needed to control access to the San Francisco Bay area. Before the end of the 1860's, therefore, they purchased the California Central and the pioneer Sacramento Valley Railroad, which were adjacent to the line's terminal at Sacramento. In 1871, they acquired the California Pacific, which operated between Sacramento and Vallejo on San Francisco Bay. Ferries linked Vallejo with San Francisco.

This access did not long satisfy the Big Four, and they decided to acquire facilities along the Oakland and San Francisco waterfronts, so that vessels from the Orient could dock at wharves adjacent to the Central Pacific's tracks. The Big Four not only wanted these facilities for themselves, but they also planned to deny their use to others. Using a subsidiary, the Western Pacific Railroad Company, which had a charter to build from Sacramento to San Jose, the Big Four not only constructed this track, but also laid a branch line from Niles to Oakland. Through this company the Big Four were able to establish a stronghold on the land along the Oakland waterfront. Nearly thirty years passed before a competitor could squeeze through what became known as the "fence" around Oakland.

Obtaining the same kind of monopoly in the flourishing city of San Francisco was another matter. The establishment of San Francisco looked upon the Sacramento Big Four as upstarts. As a result, San Francisco's leaders blocked efforts to take over San Francisco's state-owned waterfront by way of legislative grants. When the Big Four attempted to persuade Congress to grant them the federally owned Goat Island in the Bay, the San Francisco newspapers successfully fought this effort. In the end, the Big Four succeeded in controlling the peninsular traffic into the city by purchasing the San Francisco and San Jose and two smaller lines which circled around the southern tip of San Francisco Bay.

Besides dominating the San Francisco complex, the Big Four reached into southern California. As early as 1865, they obtained a charter for the Southern Pacific Railroad Company, which was used as a vehicle to amalgamate a number of southern California railroads purchased or built by the Big Four. Originally the Southern Pacific was scheduled to build a line down the coast to San Diego. However, in the early 1870's the Southern Pacific announced a reconsideration of its earlier plans, and declared that it would build south by way of the valley route instead. The California population would have been better served by the coastal route, but along the right-of-way were approximately 350 privately owned ranches. By contrast, the valley route lay through government land where grants could be obtained. Actually, under the terms of the

Railroad Act of 1866, the federal government had bestowed land grants upon the Southern Pacific, because it was scheduled to build from the Bay area south to Los Angeles and then veer eastward to the Colorado River in order to link up with the land-grant Atlantic and Pacific Railroad, building westward across New Mexico and Arizona. The Big Four had other plans, as we shall see. As they built southward, they let it be known that if cities and towns along the way did not subsidize them, they would bypass them. Such sharp practices were not original with the Big Four, but nonetheless this kind of blackmail caused great exacerbation. Los Angeles, the biggest city in southern California, was threatened, along with smaller towns. For Los Angeles the price of linking the city to the Southern Pacific was stiff. Los Angeles had to give up its short line, the Los Angeles–San Pedro Railroad of some twenty-two miles, grant the Southern Pacific sixty acres of land in the center of town for a depot, and pay a subsidy of $600,000. Only after the city officials complied did the Southern Pacific's first train pull into Los Angeles in September 1876. When San Bernardino's city fathers did not seem properly appreciative of the coming of the Southern Pacific, the railroad built its own junction point three miles away at Colton.

Having for the time being guaranteed themselves against unwanted railroad competition, the Big Four did not neglect other competing systems. As early as 1869, they bought the profitable California Steam Navigation Company, which enjoyed almost complete control of California's inland waterway traffic between San Francisco and interior towns. Then they shifted their attention to the Pacific Mail Steamship Company, which had continued to operate financially profitable ships between California ports and the Isthmus of Panama. It remained a formidable competitor for its share of the Atlantic-to-Pacific passenger and freight business, since its rates were generally below those charged by the transcontinental railroad. The Pacific Mail Steamship Company operated steamers between San Francisco and the Orient, and it was against this facet of its operations that the Big Four first struck. They joined with the Union Pacific to establish a competing line of trans-Pacific vessels— the Occidental and Oriental Steamship Company. Cutting rates below operating costs, the new company drove the Pacific Mail from this commerce. Then the Big Four notified the Pacific Mail that they intended to operate a competing line to Panama. At this threat, the Pacific Mail capitulated. In return for raising its rates approximately to those charged by the transcontinental railroad, the Big Four promised the steamship company an agreed-upon monthly profit from its Panama ships.

There was yet another obstacle to Big Four dominance of the California area. The Union Pacific began building what it called the Oregon Short Line from Granger, Wyoming, to Portland, Oregon. There was danger that if this were done the Union Pacific Railroad would feel strong enough to challenge the Big Four by transporting California-bound goods to Portland and then south by steamer to the Golden State. To forestall this threat, at least partially, and to claim some of the land grants for themselves, the Big Four bought the California and Oregon Railroad and built tracks northward from Sacramento to link up with it. In 1887 the tracks were joined at Ashland, Oregon, allowing the Union Pacific access to the Portland market.

Meanwhile the Big Four had not neglected the southern route to the East. Rather than tie in with the Atlantic and Pacific Line and thereby open their empire to competition, the Big Four decided that since they had obtained lucrative land grants, they could make their own crossing of the Colorado River at Yuma and build eastward. Huntington, with the support of the territorial governments of New Mexico and Arizona, convinced Congress that the Southern Pacific Railroad should be allowed to build eastward all the way to El Paso, Texas. Then the Southern Pacific acquired the Galveston, Harrisburg and San Antonio Railroad, which gave it access east from El Paso as far as New Orleans, over what the company called the "Sunset Route."

In 1884 this mighty but sprawling and complicated railroad empire (including the original Central Pacific Company) was amalgamated into a new Southern Pacific Company. The new company was incorporated in Kentucky on August 14, 1884. Leland Stanford, president of the new company, thought of using it not only to effect more cohesion between the various parts of the far-flung railroad empire, but also to continue unchallenged control of the Central Pacific in the hands of the Big Four, despite sale of great quantities of its stock to British investors and other outsiders. His scheme was a great success.

Stanford continued in office as president of the new Southern Pacific Company until 1890, when having won the unrelenting enmity of Collis P. Huntington, largely because of his own political ambitions, he was unceremoniously turned out of office. Huntington took over as president and ruled with an iron hand until his death in 1900. At one time it was said that Huntington controlled enough railroad track to connect the North and South poles. By the time of his death, his personal wealth was conservatively estimated at seventy million dollars.

The Southern Pacific's iron hold on the economic life of California was not seriously shaken even when another transcontinental railroad, the Atchison, Topeka & Santa Fe, belatedly reached the state. After a slow start, the railroad (chartered in 1859) built east from Topeka to the bustling Missouri River port of Atchison and simultaneously westward. By the end of 1872, trains could run from Atchison, Missouri, to the Kansas state line. Pushing on by the late 1870's, this road crossed the vital

Raton Pass and built on into Albuquerque. Despite its name, the main line of the railroad never ran through Santa Fe. Sending out a westward line from Albuquerque, the Atchison, Topeka & Santa Fe successfully battled the influence of the Southern Pacific, reaching Los Angeles by way of San Bernardino in 1887. Eventually the Santa Fe built northward to San Francisco, but the strain of heavy constuction costs, the dogged opposition of the Southern Pacific, and the great depression of 1893, caused it to fall into bankruptcy. It was reorganized and continued to operate. However, even such feeble competition as it offered to the Southern Pacific virtually disappeared when the two railroads made a peace pact, with two men from the Southern Pacific interests taking their seats on their rival company's board of directors. The dominance of the Southern Pacific thus continued in California. No other company ran trains eastward from San Francisco until 1910, or north from the city until 1931!

With its monopolistic control, the Southern Pacific did not have an enlightened rate policy—generally charging all the traffic would bear. It has been estimated that from the middle 1870's until about 1910, the greater share of the profit of every California business found its way into the pockets of the Southern Pacific's controlling group. Its charges were so high that, according to a Sacramento newspaper, at the peak of its power it demanded higher freight rates between Sacramento and adjacent Nevada points than had been asked by wagon trains in the years before the railroad was built.

Nor was this all. In the 1860's the Big Four had gone into the political arena in order to get federal, state and local subsidies. Once they had gotten their friends into high places, they continued to use them for political favors to strengthen their transportation monopoly. Thus the Southern Pacific controlled city and county officials, members of the state legislature and state courts, and governors. California congressmen were also often "railroad men." Two California United States senators during this period, Cornelius Cole and Aaron A. Sargent, were cronies of the Big Four; Leland Stanford himself was twice chosen to the Senate to represent California.

The railroad that so many hoped for turned out to be a hated "octopus" when it became a reality. The transcontinental railroad bound the state to the Union, but the chains were those of economic and political bondage.

TWENTY-TWO

California: Growing Pains
and Social Unrest

THE Union Party, which controlled California in the middle
sixties, was a strange conglomerate of opinions. It included former
Democrats and Whigs whose views on Negro slavery were less
enlightened than those of Jefferson Davis, and radicals from across
the political spectrum who favored freedom for the Negro and
his immediate enfranchisement. Nonetheless, the Union Party served as
a convenient device for rallying all Union-minded men during the Civil
War. However, as soon as that conflict ended, internal stresses began
to tear the party apart.

Two factions had gradually developed within the party: the "short
hairs" and the "long hairs." These names were given to the two factions
during the 1864 session of the legislature. At that time those legislators
who favored legislation redistricting San Francisco into wards were
labeled by their opponents within the Union Party as professional politicians, or "short hairs." Their opponents became known as "long hairs."

The short hairs were mainly composed of former Democrats who had
followed Stephen A. Douglas, "the Little Giant," in the immediate prewar period. The leaders of the short hairs were United States Senator
John B. Conness and Governor Frederick Low. Conness wished to capture control of the Union Party at the July 1865 convention so that he
could dictate the election of Governor Low as his colleague in the Senate
from California. To Conness, a Senate seat was like a lieutenancy in an

eighteenth-century army. The long hairs opposed this power play. This group consisted primarily of former Republicans and was led by John Bidwell and Cornelius Cole.

During the spring and early summer of 1865, control of the Union Party was bitterly contested in county primaries and conventions. An additional ideological difference was injected into the struggle; the short hairs had no sympathy with Union congressional leaders' demands that in the remaking of the South after the Civil War, Negroes should be granted civil rights. In general, the short hairs approved of President Andrew Johnson's mild reconstruction policies.

In July 1865, at the Sacramento County convention, the two rival factions came to physical blows; a wild riot resulted in which inkstands and spittoons were thrown and canes were wielded freely. The long hairs were literally driven from the hall. Refusing to accept defeat, they made plans to contest at the polls those short-hair candidates nominated by the rump convention. The Sacramento situation with rival Union Party candidates was duplicated in many parts of the state. With party unity in tatters, Governor Low announced that he was stepping out of the senatorial race to heal the breach. His gesture was futile, since the short hairs transferred their senatorial preference to a wealthy attorney, John B. Felton.

Meanwhile the regular Democrats, who had suffered one electoral defeat after another at the hands of the Union Party, looked with smug complacency at the disunity manifested in the opposition party. The regular Democrats decided that, except in isolated areas where they had survived as the dominant party, they would make no nominations, but would support candidates from the Union Party faction who were ideologically close to their own position—the short hairs.

In the September general election for the state legislature (which would choose the next United States senator), the fusionists (Democrats and short hairs) carried the cities of Sacramento and San Francisco, but lost the east bay, the mining country and Los Angeles. As a result, the long hairs controlled the legislature and elected their man, the Big Four's business associate, Cornelius Cole, to the United States Senate.

The legislature heeded Governor Low's pleas and ratified the Thirteenth Amendment to the Constitution, which abolished slavery everywhere in the United States, but later refused to ratify the Fourteenth Amendment. This amendment proposed by the reconstruction Congress provided federal guarantees for the rights of citizens. It was aimed primarily at securing rights for southern Negroes, but many Californians did not favor this amendment because of the implications regarding Indians and Chinese. Eventually the amendment became part of the Constitution by the action of other states.

Because of the continuing schism in the Union Party ranks, Governor Low refused to become a candidate for reelection. Since the election of 1865, Senator Conness and the short hairs had been gaining ground within the Union Party. Conness backed George C. Gorham for governor, a man who had served a long political apprenticeship, relishing the meanest chores in his scramble for place. The long hairs contested this office by putting forward John Bidwell, leader of the pioneer Bidwell-Bartleson party. Since coming to California, Bidwell had become a wealthy landowner. At the Union state convention in June 1867, Gorham defeated Bidwell by the narrow margin of 148 to 132 votes. Many of Bidwell's disgruntled supporters withdrew from the convention. The bolters abandoned the Union Party and the next month held a nominating convention for a resurrected Republican Party. That convention offered its nomination to a perennial officeseeker, Caleb T. Fry. The Republicans could not possibly win, but they hoped that by splitting the Union vote they could punish the Gorham faction.

Meanwhile, the confident Democrats nominated Henry H. Haight for governor. A New Yorker, Haight had been born in 1825 and had studied at Rochester College and Yale. He practiced as a lawyer in Missouri before coming to California in 1850. After settling in San Francisco, Haight speedily entered politics. In the 1850's he frequently shifted his party affiliations; he was in turn a Democrat, a Whig and a prewar Republican. He entered the Union Party only to leave it in 1863, after the Emancipation Proclamation. In Haight's view it had become an abolitionist party, and so he returned to his former Democratic allegiance.

While Gorham equivocated concerning his position on minority rights, the Republicans, consistent with national policy, declared for "suffrage without distinction of color." The Democrats, however, erected a platform, upon which Haight proudly stood, which called for equal opposition to Negro, Chinese and Indian voters.

Haight's racist stand drew many Irish and German voters in California cities to his standards. These foreign-born workers feared Chinese competition for jobs and had become violently anti-Oriental. With California citizens voting their prejudices, Haight polled nearly 50,000 votes to 40,000 for Gorham and a scant 2,000 for Fay. The entire state Democratic ticket was swept to victory, and the lower house of the legislature passed into Democratic control. The Union Party quickly dissolved after this defeat, and its members found a future political home within either the Republican or Democratic parties.

Despite Haight's victory in 1867, the Republican Party soon obtained a solid hold upon California in the national elections. Only once in the presidential elections between 1868 and 1888 did the Democrats carry the state for their national candidate; in 1880, by a paper-thin margin, the Democrats succeeded in capturing five of the state's six electoral votes.

Nevertheless, during the Haight regime the state was firmly under Democratic control, during which the Democrats named Eugene Casserly as Conness' successor in the United States Senate. As governor, Haight continued his racist pronouncements and focused his attention on national rather than state issues. The governor strongly backed the embattled President Andrew Johnson in his struggle with Congress over reconstruction. Consistent with his view on race, Haight urged the legislature to spurn the Fifteenth Amendment, which had been passed by Congress and sent to the states for ratification. This amendment attempted to guarantee the right to vote for all citizens, regardless of race or color. Since the amendment might be used to allow Chinese or Indian voting in California, the legislature indignantly refused to ratify it. Like the Fourteenth, this amendment became part of the nation's organic law despite California's disapproval.

While Haight was rousing the rabble against minority races, he also posed as a violently antirailroad politician. On the campaign platform and in his official papers as governor, he often scathingly denounced governmental subsidies to railroads, as well as the high rates the railroads charged. Although he bluntly vetoed several individual railroad subsidy bills, on April 4, 1870, he signed a measure empowering counties, if their voters approved, to subsidize railroads to a maximum of 5 per cent of their taxable property. This opened the door to many county subsidies of railroads.

In 1871 when Haight tried for a second term, he found himself facing a revitalized Republican Party. To embarrass the governor, the Republicans called for an end to all governmental subsidies of railroads. The Republican choice for governor was Newton Booth, the uncle of novelist (Newton) Booth Tarkington. Romauldo Pacheco, a native Californio, and the son of a Mexican captain killed in the California civil wars of the 1830's, was nominated for lieutenant governor.

Booth was born in Indiana in 1825. He graduated from what is now De Pauw University. He came to California as a lawyer in 1850. However, for a time he operated a thriving wholesale grocery business in Sacramento. He was a Democrat until 1860, when he campaigned for Lincoln. Although he had once been a vociferous advocate of the Central Pacific Railroad, he was repelled by that company's excesses. As a result, he quickly adopted an antirailroad stance.

The campaign of 1871 was unusual because both Haight and Booth preached the same political sermon as opponents of further Chinese immigration into California, and both were avowed antirailroad men. Since the California public in those years never granted a governor a second term, Booth and his running mate Pacheco won with approximately 62,000 votes to 57,000 for their Democratic challengers.

Once in office, Booth proved to be rash in council, but irresolute in

action. Notwithstanding this, Booth nurtured senatorial ambitions. Since
he believed that he was unpopular with the Republican inner circle, he
forged an alliance with a crusading farm organization, the Grange, or to
give it its more proper title, the Patrons of Husbandry. This coalition of
antirailroad reformers and farmers was called "the Dolly Vardens," a
name given it in derision by the Republican regulars. The title was
derived from the soft-hearted but scheming character in Charles Dickens'
novel *Barnaby Rudge*.

The Dolly Vardens' objective was to control the legislature so that in
1875 Booth could be elected to the United States Senate. Although the
Democrats had controlled the state senate, following the elections of
1873, the Dolly Vardens displayed such strength in electing members to
the lower house that they chose the speaker. Actually a United States
Senate seat fell vacant sooner than anyone had anticipated. Democratic
Senator Eugene Casserly, whose term would expire in March 1875, resigned in November 1873 because of ill health. It appears that behind the
scenes the Democrats and the Dolly Vardens struck a bargain. For the
remaining months of Casserly's term, Democrat John S. Hager was
chosen as senator. However, in the contest for the new six-year term,
Booth easily defeated an organization Republican and a Democrat. In late
February 1875, Booth resigned to accept the post as United States senator. Lieutenant Governor Romauldo Pacheco, the first native son to hold
the office of governor in the American period, served out the remaining
months of Booth's term. Pacheco had a caretaking tenure as governor, for
the legislature never met during his time in office.

In this period, California politics seem dreary, since the politicians
could not bring themselves to grapple with the real problems troubling
the state's gangling, adolescent society. California only reflected the prevailing national political arena where campaigns resembled "masks in a
pageant." It was a time of partisanship without a significant difference.

Part of California's problem, of course, was the railroad monopoly.
Wholesale merchants who purchased goods from the East found freight
bills so high that in order to sell their stock they had to nearly eliminate
any profit. San Francisco businessmen found that the railroad agents kept
a close watch upon market fluctuations. At times the railroad ratemakers
even insisted upon examining their shippers' books. They then set rates
calculated to exact the utmost in profit, while still keeping the shipper in
business. Charges for the transportation of agricultural products were set
on the basis of existing market prices. Prices and rates moved together as
if by magic.

Nor was this all of California's problem in the 1870's. The winter of
1876–77 was unusually dry and had ruined California's grain harvest.
Thousands of farmers and farm laborers left the land and tramped to the
cities, particularly San Francisco, vainly seeking work.

Simultaneously, California felt the adverse effects of a turndown in the national business cycle. Despite local ups and downs, California had previously suffered from only one severe economic jolt. About 1855, when placer mining largely gave way to quartz operations, this dislocation caused much financial distress. Many of California's economic troubles resulted from the national panic (as depressions were then quaintly known) of 1873. Since the panic struck first along the Atlantic seaboard, Californians winked to each other complacently about the troubles "back East." After two years, in August 1875, depression conditions reached California. The powerful Bank of California collapsed in late August of 1875, taking with it many lesser financial institutions and business houses. Simultaneously, mining stocks tumbled on the San Francisco and allied exchanges. Stocks valued at $300,000,000 in the mid-seventies declined to a market value of $30,000,000 by 1887.

As a new state, the stringency of credit imposed more severe conditions upon California than it did on the eastern states. Retail prices, which had been declining since the end of the Civil War, slumped rapidly to a low point, from which they did not fully recover until the boom times of World War I.

The resulting financial distress gripped all parts of the state. Industries closed down. Ten thousand hungry workingmen were on public relief in San Francisco alone. Men fought for jobs paying two dollars a day. Crime flourished. The seventies became popularly known as the "Era of Good Stealing."

During this critical period, the stage robber continued to operate in California. In fact, one of the most successful practitioners of that art earned his reputation at this time. His professional name was Black Bart. Bart, a most improbable bandit, was skinny, short and bald. He wrote bad poetry and did not even own a horse. He walked to his crimes, carrying a shotgun that was so rusty that he could not have fired it. Covering his head with a flour sack with two holes cut in it for eye slits, Bart waited along the roadside for a stage to approach. When it did, he stepped from behind cover, pointed his shotgun and cried, "Throw down the box!" In the eight years between 1875 (when hard times began) and 1883, twenty-seven stagecoach drivers threw down the Wells Fargo box of valuables. On Bart's twenty-eighth robbery in November 1883, somebody had thoughtfully bolted down the valuable box to the floor of the stage. Surprised by this precaution, Black Bart lost valuable time fumbling with the locked box. In the midst of the robbery a rabbit hunter came upon him and drove him off with some well-aimed shots. Bart fled, leaving behind various articles of clothing, including a handkerchief. Now Black Bart had previously left some doggerel behind near the scene of the robberies, signed with his name and the title "Po8," but these planted notes had never provided a firm clue to his identity. His abandoned handkerchief had a laundry mark upon it, and a check of San Francisco laundries led to the capture of Black Bart, or Charles E. Bolton, a some-time mining engineer. Bolton pleaded guilty only to his last attempted robbery and drew a six-year prison sentence. He quietly served his time and then vanished upon his release.

Black Bart was not unique. Between November 1870 and November 1884, the total amount taken from Wells, Fargo & Company in the single department of San Francisco (which included more than California) by stage robbers, train bandits and burglars was in excess of $415,000. During that time the number of successful stage robberies carrying Wells Fargo express funds reached 313. There were also thirty-four attempted stage robberies and four attempted train robberies, four successful train rob-beries and twenty-three successful burglaries. In all, 240 robbers and burglars were caught and convicted. These totals pertained merely to crimes against Wells, Fargo & Company valuables; there were many more committed in the state of California.

One of the last great robber groups of California was that led by Tiburcio Vásquez. Vásquez was probably born in Monterey on August 10, 1835, although this is not entirely certain. For a Californio, Vásquez was fairly tall—about five feet, five inches. He often wore a suit, tie and polished boots and carefully trimmed his full beard and moustache. When only seventeen, he and two friends attended a *fandango* in Monterey and killed a constable who tried to arrest them during a disturbance. Vásquez became an outlaw. Moving to southern California on July 15, 1857, he and a companion attacked a ranch in Los Angeles County, driving off a herd of horses. While trying to sell the stolen animals, they were arrested. Tried in Los Angeles in August 1857, Vásquez pleaded guilty and was sentenced to five years in prison. Before he had served two years, he escaped in a general prison break on June 25, 1859. He went to Amador County in the mother-lode country and was there recaptured after seven weeks of freedom, when he unsuccessfully attempted a horse theft. Returned to San Quentin, he completed his original sentence plus an additional year before being re-leased in August 1863. Vásquez again turned to horse stealing and cattle rustling in Contra Costa, Sonoma, and Mendocino Counties. Captured by a posse early in 1867, he was tried and sentenced to three and a half years in prison. Until this time his career had been spectacular only in its lack of success. Once more at liberty in June 1870, he began a four-year reign of terror. He rentlessly robbed stages, stores and inns. Whereas previ-ously his luck had been bad, now he seemed to lead a charmed life. Apparently he and his gang were harbored by the Mexican Californians to whom they were heroes. Finding central California too dangerous for him, Vásquez decided to stage one more robbery at Snyder's Store in

Tres Piños and then transfer his operations to the vicinity of Los Angeles. On August 26, 1873, Vásquez and his men swooped down on that hamlet. They had anticipated that this would be only a routine robbery, but they were interrupted. In the confusion they killed three people before they succeeded in escaping. The gang took with them eight horses, $1,200 in cash and other valuables.

When news of the Tres Piños "tragedy" (as the newspapers of the time called it) traveled the length of the stage, a demand for vengeance rose from many citizens. The governor of California put a price of $8,000 on Vásquez's head. Despite the hue and cry against him, Vásquez did not remain long in hiding. In December 1873, he and his men attacked the town of Kingston in Fresno County. They captured and tied up thirty-five men, while leisurely plundering a hotel and two stores of $2,500 in cash, and followed that exploit with two stage robberies.

In mid-May 1874, Vásquez's career came to an end in Los Angeles County when a cockold husband betrayed his hideout. He was wounded and captured by a small posse. Removed to San Jose for trial, Vásquez was hanged on March 19, 1875.

To alleviate the frustration and despair of their economic situation, many Californians turned to crime. Others acted out their frustrations in acts of violence against the Chinese.

The Chinese had long been a target for discrimination and abuse. For a short time during the early gold rush, they were welcomed as additional labor. However, as they began to enter California by the thousands, their Caucasian neighbors swiftly changed their attitude. Orientals were allowed to mine only the worked-out claims, and they were subject to a discriminatory tax. However, when Crocker began to bring them from China in order to give him a sure and docile labor supply to build the Central Pacific Railroad, feeling against "coolieism" reached new heights. A treaty negotiated between China and the United States in 1868 expedited the immigration of the Chinese. To the Anglo-Saxon Californians, the Chinese were hopelessly different and unassimilative.

The Chinese laborers were exploited in a manner that their employers were unable to achieve in the case of white workers. Thirty dollars a month was their pay for a workday of twelve hours. The industrious Chinese gradually won more than their share of work in the fields, service trades and light manufacturing industries of California. In 1872 they comprised one-half of all the factory workers of San Francisco. Their numbers, almost all men, rose from 35,000 in 1860 to nearly 74,000 in 1880. Contemporary unofficial estimates of their numbers ran much higher, and it is possible that the official census-takers drastically undercounted them.

The plight of the Chinese won no pity from the white workingman, nor did he feel any solidarity with them. As a result, by 1867 anticoolie clubs were being formed all over California. These organizations bore such names as the Workingmen's Alliance, the Anti-Chinese Association, the People's Protective Alliance, and the Supreme Order of Caucasians. They generally had as their purpose intimidating the local officials to discriminate against the Chinese. Whenever legal pressure was deemed insufficient, outbreaks of direct violence flared against the Orientals. In December 1867 the Chinese were forcibly driven out of French Corral in Nevada County. On October 23, 1871, about twenty Chinese were killed during a fierce race riot in Los Angeles.

Anti-Chinese feeling was not, however, the controlling factor in the election of Democrat William Irwin as governor in 1875. The Democratic state convention in that year, while declaiming against the evils of Chinese labor, stressed equal taxation of real estate and less tangible forms of wealth and opposition to the Central Pacific monopoly. The Republicans nominated Timothy G. Phelps on a platform that stressed national issues, but also promised to fight public fiscal support to sectarian schools. The sonorous platitudes denouncing the Central Pacific were also inserted into the Republican platform. The Dolly Varden faction, or People's Independent Party, nominated pioneer John Bidwell for first place on the state ticket and former governor Romualdo Pacheco for lieutenant governor. Their platform called for governmental reform and rigid control of the railroad monopoly's excesses. After a bitter campaign, Irwin won with about a hundred votes more than the combined total of his opponents, out of 123,000 ballots cast.

With the advent of hard economic times, anti-Chinese agitation grew more violent. Workingmen's discontent centered in San Francisco, where there were an estimated 16,000 unemployed in 1877. These idle men spent most of their time voicing their grievances. Although some of their wrath was directed against the large employers who hired Chinese laborers in preference to white workers, most of their spleen was vented directly upon their Oriental competitors for the relatively few jobs remaining on the farms and in industry.

Across the street from the San Francisco City Hall, on what became known as the "sandlot," six or seven thousand unemployed or underemployed workmen gathered on the evening of July 23, 1877. The meeting was ostensibly called to express the sympathy of California workers with a great railroad strike then going on in the East. Various speakers harangued the workingmen concerning their grievances. Then suddenly a bystander fired into the crowd, wounding two of the laborers. Quickly the deranged assailant was arrested and hustled away by the police before the mob could lynch him. Order was restored and the meeting passed several scorching resolutions decrying monopolists and demanding better conditions for average Americans. Satisfied with this action, the group began to disperse. Some excited members of the crowd destroyed some Chinese laundries, but the police acted quickly to avoid further trouble.

These happenings were in retrospect not very fearsome, but they greatly alarmed some of the most influential San Franciscans. As a result, these men held a gathering of their own on the afternoon following the workingmen's meeting. This assemblage, actually called by a brigadier general of the local militia, met in the austere chambers of the Chamber of Commerce. This conclave of "the better class of citizens" included several old vigilante leaders such as William T. Coleman, who became the presiding officer. A group of twenty-four men were speedily selected as a committee of public safety. Within twenty-four hours this committee had recruited a force of five thousand men. A war chest of $100,000 was also raised from the frightened "better" citizens of San Francisco. For five days this host—many armed with hickory pick handles—patrolled the streets of San Francisco. Although they suppressed any overt manifestation of the workingmen's anger, they only dampened the flames of discontent.

Watching Coleman's vigilantes at work, many workingmen decided that rather than risk a civil war by colliding with them, they should instead turn to the slower process of political action. Among the workers's leaders who talked most violently, although he actually relied upon political action, was nervous, active Denis Kearney. Kearney, a native of county Cork, Ireland, had come to San Francisco as a young sailor of twenty-one in 1868. He soon established a profitable business as a drayman. Although a latecomer to the cause of the workingmen and therefore suspect in the eyes of some, Kearney was an excellent platform orator. By the late summer and early fall of 1877, he had attracted a wide following. Addressing the workers at Sunday afternoon meetings on the sandlot so that those workers who still had jobs could also be present, Kearney saw everything in terms of black or white, while using language that never lacked pungency and heat. Kearney became the favorite of the Sunday afternoon crowd. He cleverly injected massive amounts of anti-Chinese propaganda into his tirades. Repeatedly, to the cheers and applause of the crowd, he shouted his slogan, "The Chinese must go!" His favorite platform pose was to stand with a noosed rope clutched in one hand and bellow that it was his program for action. Upon one occasion, he advised every workingman "to own a musket and a hundred rounds of ammunition." Despite his inflammatory talk, Kearney only intended political action and so organized and became president of the Workingmen's Party of California, which had no direct descent from any earlier party. His party demanded an eight-hour day, direct election of United States senators, a compulsory education law, state regulation of banks and railroads and a more equitable system of taxation. These demands read tamely today, but in the 1870's Kearney seemed a flaming radical.

Meanwhile Governor Irwin was bending into the political wind. He successfully exhorted the 1875–76 legislature to authorize a board of transportation—the O'Connor Act. The act was not really new, for almost all of its provisions had been utilized earlier to regulate roads, ferries, and canals.

Perhaps the most important bow Governor Irwin made in the direction of change was to sign a bill calling for a state constitutional convention. For many years Californians had argued that the simple document of 1849 could not be used indefinitely to govern the state. The early Constitution's unrealistic public finance limitations and its lack of any regulatory powers over banks and railroads were its most glaring deficiencies. The population of California had grown from about 100,000 in 1849 to over 800,000 in 1878, with a complexity of economic and social problems the Monterey delegates could not have envisioned.

While many Californians, even among the upper classes, had long foreseen the need for a new constitution, the prospect that this Workingmen's Party of urban laborers, acting in concert with the Grange, might control the Constitutional Convention appeared intolerable to many.

As a result, the "better" people of both the Republican and Democratic parties decided to present a united front against the farmer-worker threat. Although the Republicans and Democrats were never able to agree entirely upon one ticket of delegates for the Constitutional Convention, this lack of unity was partly offset by the fact that the Workingmen's Party was torn into rival pro-Kearney and anti-Kearney groups. As a result, in the June 19, 1878, election for delegates, the Workingmen's candidates won only 51 out of 152 delegates. Yet their cause was not hopeless, for among the seventy-eight nonpartisan delegates elected were many members of the Grange. In addition, eleven delegates were elected as Republicans, ten as Democrats and two as avowed independents.

The Convention convened on September 28, 1878. Work was parcelled out among twenty-three committees. Interestingly, only two of the delegates were native-born Californians; all were Caucasians, neither California Indians nor Mexicans being represented. Thirty-five of the delegates were foreign-born, mainly of Irish and German origins; fifty-nine were lawyers, and thirty-six were farmers.

There were roughly three groups at the Convention. The first faction contained the representatives of the establishment, mostly lawyers. The second group represented the workingmen's organizations. This group included many foreign-born and men with little formal education. They possessed a handful of experienced leaders who were usually lawyers. The third group were either farmers or spokesmen for that group. Whenever the second and third groups of delegates agreed upon an issue, they could gain their objective. However, they were an unwieldy coalition, and the representatives of the establishment were often able, by cunning parliamentary leadership, to blunt and blur the demands of the farmers and workers.

The Constitution as written was in reality a bundle of compromises. In an effort to bind future governors and legislatures, the California Constitution became too detailed. Under the stress of producing immediate results, too many incidental provisions were written into a basic document of government. As a result, the Constitution's wordiness guaranteed that as conditions changed it would be heavily amended and, on occasion, ignored.

The Constitution of 1879 made relatively few changes in the general structure of California government. The executive, legislative and judicial branches remained much as they had been except that popular distrust, particularly of the legislature, led to some definite restrictions of power. Many Californians felt that their legislature was corrupt, and that their lawmakers had needlessly meddled in local government through the device of special laws. To remedy these abuses, the legislature was forbidden to make gifts of public funds or to appropriate money for any institutions not under state control except for orphanages and homes for the indigent. All state laws regarding local government had to be general. In addition, the legislature was suspect since it had so often sold out to special interests; therefore, some provisions of the Constitution were made self-executing.

If the powers of government were contracted in some respects, they were stretched in others. Railroads, gas companies and telegraph companies were subject to regulation. A state railroad commission was created. All tangible and intangible property was made equally subject to taxation. Since many farmers and workingmen believed that corporations such as banks and utilities had evaded their fair share of taxes, this provision was insisted upon by their representatives. Corrupt lobbying and bribery were labelled felonies.

The rural delegates were able to frame provisions putting water for irrigation under governmental regulation, and requiring the legislature to protect a portion of the homesteads of heads of families from forced sale.

The workingmen sacrificed much to obtain a number of anti-Chinese clauses. One provision prohibited the employment of Chinese by corporations, and another forbade their employment as labor on public works.

The California frame of government guaranteed its citizens all the rights in the federal Constitution and some not included there, such as the right to fish. Although Wyoming had accepted woman suffrage as early as 1869, the Constitutional Convention turned this idea down; women could not vote in California until 1911.

In March 1879, after six months of deliberation, 120 of the 152 members of the Constitutional Convention signed the new charter of government. The document had opponents on both the left and the right. There were workers and farmers who felt that there had been too many compromises and that the finished Constitution did not go far enough in taxing the rich and regulating monopoly. On the other hand, members of the "better class" of citizens felt that such novel experiments as the Railroad Commission and the state Board of [Tax] Equalization made the Constitution a recipe for chaos. Governor Irwin, who had signed the act authorizing the Convention and who had acted as temporary chairman, turned against the completed document. Nevertheless, on May 7, 1879, in an election with a potential electorate of 161,000, some 145,000 Californians voted, ratifying the new charter of government by the slim majority of 11,000. San Francisco—the scene of the most intense workingmen's agitation—showed its disapproval of the document by voting against it by a majority of 1,600 votes. To his disgust, Governor Irwin had to issue the proclamation putting the new Constitution into effect on July 4, 1879. Under it the new state officers were to assume their posts in January 1880. Thereby Irwin gained the longest single gubernatorial term in California's history.

The Constitution proved a disappointment to its most ardent friends. The problem of railroad regulation continued to be acute well into the twentieth century. The state Railroad Commission proved singularly inept in controlling oppressive railroad practices. Although Charles J. Beerstecher, a prominent lawyer-leader of the Workingmen's Party, was elected in 1879 to the commission, the wily railroad lawyers found ways to evade the orders of the regulatory group. The impotence of the Railroad Commission was due primarily to the inexperience of the commissioners and the skillful intransigence of the railroads. A certain cycle developed as commissioners came and went. A new commission started its activities with a burst of energy, then quickly ran into legal obstructions which brought its activities to a virtual halt for the remainder of its term. Until 1911, when the commission was made appointive, the railroads generally had the upper hand.

The constitutional provisions for taxing railroads did not prove effective. As soon as a levy was made upon a railroad, its attorneys went to court, fighting through the state courts and into the federal judicial establishment. The state habitually lost. During the long legal struggle, California was forced to accept such pittances as the railroads deigned to pay as taxes. When a final settlement was reached years later, the assessment figures for the value of railroad property were much lower than those originally made.

Hope for the heavier taxation of corporations was likewise dashed. A large California corporation won a suit denying the power of the state Board of Equalization to change assessments set by local assessors. Since local assessors habitually discriminated in favor of powerful corporations, their actions were not subject to effective review at the state level. These efforts to tax intangible wealth, while not altogether ineffective, were far less fruitful than their ardent proponents had hoped.

Other aspirations of the Convention delegates were in the main unrealized. Although deprived of the power of special legislation, the legislature soon found a loophole by contriving classifications to meet particular instances, and then passing what appeared to be a general law to achieve its purposes. The legislature was quick to evade many duties placed upon it by the Constitution. It never found a way to exclude Chinese immigration into the state, or to pass legislation authorizing cities and counties to accomplish this end. The constitutional prohibition of corrupt lobbying became a dead letter.

As time went by, the Constitution's length and excessive detail led to demands for a better charter of government. Five times the question of a new constitutional convention was placed before the voters: in 1898, 1914, 1920, 1930 and 1934. The first four times the people heartily voted down the proposal. In 1934 it passed by a narrow margin. However, the proposition was only in the form of an authorization for the calling of a convention by the legislature. That body refused to act.

In September 1879, the first governor was elected under the new Constitution, Republican George C. Perkins. A Mainer by birth, he had run away to sea, arriving in San Francisco in 1855 at the age of sixteen. He became first a prosperous merchant and then a shipping magnate. He had long served the Republican Party and the state in various minor offices. Perkins was an ardent foe of the new Constitution, which he viewed as a dangerously radical innovation. His campaign ignored the issues and concentrated upon pageantry. Perkins' supporters used a nautical theme, borrowed from Gilbert and Sullivan's operetta, *H. M. S. Pinafore*, to dramatize his campaign. Facing candidates from the Democrats, a proconstitutional party and the Prohibitionists, Perkins polled almost 68,000 votes—a plurality out of a total of approximately 160,000 votes cast.

His administration saw the disappearance of the Workingmen's Party, which had already amalgamated for the 1879 gubernatorial campaign with the proconstitution party. For a short while after the adoption of the Constitution, Kearney had continued his agitation against the Chinese, and sought to have the anti-Chinese features in the Constitution implemented by the legislature. But he acted so boisterously that he was barred from the assembly floor. His heyday soon passed. Kearney had always been suspect in the eyes of other Workingmen's Party leaders; rumors said that he was in the pay of the railroads. Then a great schism developed within the Workingmen's Party concerning the group's political future. Kearney advocated a tie with the national Greenback-Labor Party; other leaders favored affiliation with the Democrats. When the Democratically oriented leadership assumed control, they deposed Kearney. The movement then became so fragmented that it completely disappeared by 1882.

Thereupon, Kearney retired from politics. Successively he became a real estate agent, stockbroker, and operator of an employment service. Then he inherited a fortune and lived a quiet, untroubled existence. Shortly before his death in 1907, he was asked how he had reconciled his later career with his earlier views. He shrugged and said, "Oh, you know, somebody had to do the work. What's the use?"

In the end it was not by California state action that Chinese immigration was stemmed. California congressmen, along with other interested politicians, pressed President Rutherford B. Hayes, so that in November 1880 he concluded a new treaty with China which permitted the United States to "regulate, limit or suspend" the immigration of Chinese laborers. To implement this treaty, the Congress in the spring of 1882 considered a bill calling for Chinese exclusion. To help this cause along, Governor Perkins on March 4, 1882, declared a legal holiday for demonstrations against the Chinese. On May 6, 1882, the federal bill became law, forbidding Chinese immigration for ten years. In 1892 the ban was extended for another ten years. In 1902 and 1904 additional legislation put Chinese exclusion on a permanent basis.

That the California Constitution had not won the fight against monopoly was clearly demonstrated by a spectacular incident, the "battle" of Mussel Slough. This action occurred in May 1880, in an area now called Lucerne Valley near Hanford, California.

During the early 1870's, the Southern Pacific ran a railroad line south through the San Joaquin Valley. The railroad, anxious to populate the region, advertised widely throughout the East about the fertility of the area south of Fresno. Since the railroad offered the land at cheap prices, many settlers were attracted to this part of California. Although the railroad had earmarked certain lands for its grants from the federal government, the Southern Pacific did not wish to take immediate title to the real estate for tax reasons, so it made a gentlemen's agreement with the settlers. The railroad agreed that when it perfected its title to the government land, the settlers would be allowed to purchase their holdings at an average price of $2.50 to $5.00 an acre. Ten dollars was the greatest amount specified by the Southern Pacific. Thus the settlers would not be charged because they had improved their holdings with houses, barns and irrigation ditches. Although making a living at first was difficult in the southern San Joaquin Valley, often sarcastically called "Starvation Valley," by 1877 the settlers had won their fight to establish prosperous farms there. Then the railroad announced that it had taken title to the land from the federal government and formally issued its terms for the sale of the property to the settlers. To the consternation and anger of the farmers, prices had been raised to a range of $25 to $35 an acre, with all the land to be sold on the open market to the highest bidder.

Refusing to be thus taken advantage of, the farmers of the Tulare Basin formed a Settler's League. Hiring counsel, they fought their case through the courts to the United States Supreme Court. The railroad decided not to wait for the completion of the judicial process, but while the case was awaiting a hearing before the Supreme Court, began to move in new settlers upon the disputed land. When this happened, the original settlers banded together and descended upon two of the newcomers' houses, burning them as a warning to the others.

In retaliation, the railroad secured eviction notices for several of the original settlers in favor of two supposed purchasers, Walter J. Crow and Mills P. H. Hartt. Crow and Hartt were experienced gunfighters. Leaving the nearby town of Hanford on May 11, 1880, a United States marshal named Alonzo W. Poole, the railroad's land agent, William H. Clark, and Hartt and Crow traveled in two buggies to evict the defiant farmers. A mounted group of armed settlers intercepted them at the Henry Brewer Ranch.

The farmers crowded around the buggy containing the United States marshal, warning him not to evict anyone until the Supreme Court had the opportunity to decide upon the case. If the marshal would surrender peaceably, they declared that they would escort him without harm to the nearest railroad depot. While this was happening, the other farmers turned their attention to the buggy occupied by Crow and Hartt. They angrily called to the two men to surrender their weapons. Suddenly some unidentified person pulled a trigger. At this, everyone began firing. In a minute, five farmers lay dead or mortally wounded; one settler had been injured, but later recovered. Hartt, who had been slow to leap down from his buggy, was fatally wounded by a pistol shot in the abdomen. Almost miraculously, Crow escaped from the hail of gunfire and hid in a wheat field. He was tracked down an hour later by one of the settlers (no one would ever say whom) and shot dead a mile and a half from the main encounter. This ended the battle of Mussel Slough. Since the railroad controlled the telegraph lines, the complete story of the encounter was slow to reach the rest of the state. When four of the five dead farmers were buried on May 13, their funeral cortege contained so many mourners that it stretched for two miles over the countryside.

Under indictment for resisting a federal officer, seven of the settlers were arrested and taken away to San Francisco for trial. Eventually five of them were convicted and sentenced to eight months in a San Jose jail. In the eyes of many antirailroad Californians, the farmers were martyrs. When they had served their terms, three thousand people assembled to welcome them back to their homes.

This battle later inspired two novelists. Josiah Royce wrote *The Feud of Oakfield Creek,* and Frank Norris penned his more famous, searing novel *The Octopus.* At least three other novelists have also written at length about the incident. But the real-life aftermath of the struggle was less satisfying. Lack of funds and plummetting morale caused the farmers to end their resistance. They abjectly withdrew their pending case before the Supreme Court. Ironically, other settlers from another county won a similar case several years later. As a result of the bad publicity and unrest, the Southern Pacific made a token reduction of 12.5 per cent in its land prices in the Tulare Basin. Those settlers who could accepted these terms. The others left and peace descended over the valley.

To place this incident in proper perspective it should be noted, however, that this was the only violent occurrence of this type during the period.

The troubles of the "Terrible Seventies," or the "Discontented Seventies," only slowly gave way to relative stability during the eighties. Better times were more the result of external forces than anything specifically done within California. State government continued to be out of touch with the rapidly industrializing economic and social conditions in California. State and local government remained in the hands of mediocre men with false nostrums, supported by constituents who suffered from wrongs they did not really comprehend.

TWENTY-THREE

A New Agricultural California Arises

D URING the 1860's, the cattle-raising economy of southern
California was permanently changed. Ranching had long been
California's main business, but during this period a combination
of adversities combined to virtually eliminate the old-fashioned cattle
industry. Weakened by competition from cattle ranchers outside the
state, years of land litigation with squatters and the federal government, heavy state property taxes, ruinous interest rates and the devastating drought of 1863–64, the rancheros gradually sold out or lost title
to their holdings, and their easy-going, graceful way of life vanished.

American purchasers quickly stepped in to buy their land at forced
sales where prices were often as low as twenty-five to fifty cents an acre.
A syndicate of San Francisco financiers, including the redoubtable Sam
Brannan, incorporated themselves as the Los Angeles & San Bernardino
Land Company, which purchased Abel Stearns' rancho of 200,000 acres
in the area north of the Tehachapi Mountains. Stearns received the unusually high price of $1.50 an acre for his land. In 1868 the corporation
divided the rancho into tracts of forty acres, which it retailed to purchasers. Utilizing a mammoth advertising campaign, the company was
able to obtain from two to ten dollars an acre for this land. As the area
became more settled, the company was able to increase its prices. As a
result of these carefully controlled sales, the financiers and their heirs
were eventually able to realize a profit of two million dollars on the
transaction.

The disappearance of the old Californio rancho brought about a new kind of cattle business run along more efficient and businesslike lines. The practice of allowing cattle herds to roam over vast, unfenced ranges soon ended. If allowed to roam at will, the best breed of cattle deteriorated, so the new landowners accepted farmer-inspired state laws requiring fenced-in ranges. After 1870 the system of free pasturage on vast holdings of federal land in California gave way to private ownership and government leases. Government land in California soon dwindled as railroad grants, veterans' warrants, agricultural college scrip, and homesteading all took their share. Disregarding railroad grants, in 1866 only 147,000 acres were sold for cash or homesteaded. Just three years later, the amount of land homesteaded or purchased with either scrip, military warrants or cash reached the record amount of 2.4 million acres. Although the acreage of public land claimed by these methods declined after that record year, in 1873, 658,000 acres were claimed—four times greater than the purchases of 1866. In Kern, San Diego and San Bernardino counties, almost all the free land was controlled by a few large companies who, by owning the strategic water sources, exercised a virtual monopoly over the nearby government land. At the Tejón Rancho in Kern County, Edward F. Beale ran cattle on some 200,000 acres of land. In addition he controlled the springs and water holes for an adjacent 300,000 acres of public land.

Powerful companies or individual land barons continued to dominate agriculture throughout the rest of the 1800's. The *Pacific Rural Press* in 1875 demonstrated that only forty-five men controlled four million acres of California land.

The most elaborate ranch-farm enterprise was that owned by Henry Miller and Charles Lux. Miller, born Heinrich Alfred Keiser in Brackenheim, Würtemberg, in July 1827, came to San Francisco in 1850. Once in the state, he adopted the name of a chance acquaintance whose nontransferrable ticket he had used to come to California. He soon became the leading wholesale butcher on the Pacific coast. In 1857 he entered into a partnership with his only real rival in San Francisco, Charles Lux, to raise livestock and farm on a grand scale. This combine lasted until Lux's death in 1887. Energetic Charles Lux was also an interesting figure. Born in Alsace, he worked at his father's trade as a wheelwright until he emigrated to New York at the age of sixteen. In America he found employment as a butcher's apprentice at six dollars a month. In 1849, he moved to San Francisco, and by 1850, he had also established a wholesale meat business and had amassed a small fortune.

When Lux and Miller became partners, they quickly proceeded to become proprietors of a land empire that staggers the imagination. For thirty years the two partners avidly collected real estate and cattle. Using their own names or those of their employees, they acquired preemption rights and homestead title to land which stretched from Oregon to Mexico. They also bought up land warrants originally issued as a form of bounty to veterans of wars from 1790 through the Mexican War. These veterans' warrants had originally sold for $110–$115 in the market, but they could be used to buy as much as $200 worth of land at the going price of $1.25 an acre. In addition, Miller and Lux cleverly purchased swampy areas and lands bordering on rivers, which the federal government had granted to the state, which now sold them for a maximum of $1.25 an acre. Moreover, under California law, which sought to encourage reclamation, the partners could count the purchase price as money spent to reclaim the lands and then obtain a repayment of this sum from the state.

They had another clever device to gather additional holdings. They often purchased the interest of one member of a Californio family who was in financial distress. Thus they might buy a one-eighth or one-tenth interest in a large ranch. Since Californio custom allowed them unlimited grazing rights, they could run large herds of livestock on the ranch, crowding out the cattle of other members of the family. Rather than fight Miller and Lux, the other owners usually sold out for purely nominal amounts.

At its height, the "Kingdom of Miller and Lux" included one hundred miles of land along the San Joaquin River and a fifty-mile strip along the Kern River. Since they used so many dummy purchasers, it may never be known just how much land they actually controlled. It has been conservatively estimated that they controlled 750,000 acres in nineteen different counties of California. They also owned 250,000 acres of land in Nevada, Arizona and Oregon.

The Miller and Lux herds, marked with a double-H brand, included at one time perhaps one million head of livestock. Their sale of meat in 1888 amounted to a million and a half dollars. The partners also grew many crops, including wheat, upon their holdings. Upon Lux's death, after protracted legal maneuvers, Henry Miller bought out his dead partner's heirs and continued to rule over his great empire (estimated to be equal to the size of Belgium) until his demise in October 1916.

With the subsidence of the cattle boom (although, as we have seen, a new kind of cattle raising partially replaced it), there was a great wheat boom. Wheat had been grown earlier in California, but after 1865 it became one of the great grain-producing states of the Union. Because of climatic and economic conditions existing within the state, wheat was the logical successor to cattle as the preeminent concern of California agriculture. Grain did not require intensive methods of cultivation; it could be grown without irrigation by dry-farming methods, and it was not dependent upon local markets, being a staple of international trade. The long, hot California summers in the San Joaquin and Sacramento valleys were ideal for producing a hard, dry wheat which could stand the long sea voyage to Europe without deterioration. Since there was little danger from rain during the harvesting season, grain could be left in the fields until it was ready to be shipped to market.

Starting about 1860, the ratio of grain crops in California was about two to one in favor of wheat over barley. In 1860 California produced six million bushels of wheat, nearly five times as much as all the rest of the United States west of the Rockies. By 1870, California's wheat production had been raised to about sixteen million bushels. Annual production grew from this amount to twenty-nine million bushels in 1880. By 1890, California produced forty million bushels and ranked second among all the states in wheat production. Some 2,750,000 acres of California land were devoted to growing that grain. Then a reaction set in. Although the actual wheat production decreased to thirty-six million bushels, relatively speaking the decline was even more pronounced. Wheat had decreased in acreage partly because barley had become more profitable in the drier regions and because irrigated crops had become more important.

Although the wheat boom was short-lived, it spawned its own king just as the cattle industry had. He was German-born Isaac Friedlander, who came to San Francisco in 1849 at the age of 25. A giant of a man, he stood six feet, seven inches. Very active in the social life of San Francisco, he was the friend of many prominent politicians. Friedlander was often associated with another real-estate operator, William S. Chapman, in his business dealings. Friedlander purchased 196,000 acres with agricultural college scrip (the result of the Morrill Land Grant Act). On this land, he became a wheat operator who had a near monopoly of the grain trade between California and Europe. Friedlander was not able to found an enduring empire such as Henry Miller had, because his holdings were too heavily mortgaged. The drought of 1877 seriously impaired his wealth, and he died the next year, leaving only a modest estate.

In the wheat period and continuing on into the later stages of California's agricultural history, a heavy reliance upon machines developed. Indeed, much of California's early manufacturing industry was centered about the production of agricultural machinery.

In preparing the soil, these American successors to the early rancheros utilized steam plows. In 1868, Philander Standish built the Standish steam rotary plow, the Mayflower, at Pacheco, California. It was offered for sale in a variety of sizes, from ten to sixty horsepower. Its operating speed was from 1.7 to 3.4 miles an hour; its plowing rate was as high as five acres an hour.

A successful wheat combine had been built in Michigan as early as 1836, although local conditions in the Midwest mitigated against its successful use. When the Michigan combine was shipped around Cape Horn to San Francisco, it harvested several hundred acres as early as the season of 1854. In California, a more favorable climate, larger acreages, and the Californians' love for the gigantic put this large piece of machinery into general use. California-made versions of the combine began to appear in a few years. As many as forty horses were utilized to pull the large fifteen-ton machines, which could cut a swath thirty-five feet wide. By 1880 there was an improved version of the combine ready for the California fields. This machine cut a swath from twenty-six feet to twice that distance. It was propelled across the grainfields by a steam tractor, threshing and bagging the grain as it went, sometimes at the rate of three 150-pound bags a minute.

In the early twentieth century, wheat growing in California stabilized itself at less than 750,000 acres. The transition from a heavy reliance on wheat to more diversified agriculture came about gradually between 1870 and 1900. Although much wheat was sent around Cape Horn in sailing ships destined for the eastern United States and Europe, even more of it in time proceeded eastward over the transcontinental railroad. This situation put the wheat growers at the mercy of the Southern Pacific. While it is true that agricultural barons such as Miller and Lux could demand rebates from the railroad on carload and trainload lots of wheat, individual farmers were not so fortunate. Also the world market for California wheat became less steady. New grainfields in the Mississippi Valley and Russia became tough competitors for California. The rapid growth of population in the state increased the price of land to the extent that in many parts of California it was not profitable to cultivate wheat. Moreover, some of the yields of wheat per acre began to decrease when the constant planting of that grain began to exhaust the soil.

In addition to the factors working against the continued dominance of wheat, there were factors working for the cultivation of the new, more diversified crops. Mass production in California's vineyards and orchards pointed the way to new profits. One favorable factor working for diversified agriculture was the attitude of the railroads, which decided to foster (at least in the beginning) these new crops. Although the coming of the transcontinental railroad ended the growing of some crops for the local market (since out-of-state growers were able to produce them at lower cost), it opened world markets for crops previously undreamed of as California produce. Also, as American farmers learned more about California's peculiar soil and climatic conditions, they discovered the possibilities of a number of diversified crops. Finally, as large irrigation systems were constructed, the emphasis turned away from crops specializing in dry farming.

These new crops were raised on rather large farms, often owned by a company rather than a single individual. This sort of corporate commercial agriculture, or agribusiness, as it came to be known in the twentieth century, abandoned the narrow bases on which California agriculture had rested in the previous stages of cattle raising and wheat growing. The success of this kind of commercial farming, with emphasis upon raising domestic staples and exotic delicacies, had three results: it consigned the family farm, which dominated so much of American agriculture outside of California, to a diminishing, relatively insignificant place; it tied California agriculture firmly to the mass markets; it made harvesting dependent upon great seasonal peaks of manual labor.

This last factor heavily influenced the social structure of the California rural scene, since the need for seasonal labor meant that not only would the farmers' women and children find employment at harvest time, but many more hands would be needed. At first the California Indians filled this need, then successively the Chinese, Japanese, Filipinos and Mexicans.

Before finding successful crops, there was a time of experimentation. Among the crops tried and discarded in the latter nineteenth century were tobacco, silk and cotton. The first tobacco crop had some success during the Civil War, when normal southern production was cut off, but California could not compete in the tobacco market once the original sources were again available. Silk growing had an involved history in California. The legislature offered aid in great amounts to encourage the production of silk. Some silkworm eggs were raised and sold as a short-time commercial success. However, there never was a successful market for California silk and the artificially stimulated industry eventually collapsed. California climatic conditions were such that the types of cotton produced at the time did not grow well. A limited amount of cotton was grown in the post-Civil War period, when southern farming was still disorganized, but once conditions in Dixie again became normal, California could not compete in the world cotton market. (In the twentieth century, California has become a great cotton-producing state, but that is because of greatly changed technological conditions.)

Although mission agriculture had prefigured the cultivation of many "new" crops, large-scale California farming actually owes much to the conscious efforts of the "fruit pioneers" of the American period. In particular the work of Luther Burbank was important to the development of California agriculture. Burbank, a famous American plant breeder, was born at Lancaster, Massachusetts, on March 7, 1849. Here he attended public school and Lancaster Academy. In addition he learned much about plant life from residence on a farm. The reading of one of Darwin's works was a turning point in his life. From then on he became an avid reader of plant and agricultural treatises. Burbank was no textbook farmer, for when he was twenty-one, he bought seventeen acres of land near Lunenberg, Massachusetts, and began his life's work of plant breeding. There he developed the Burbank potato, which he later brought to California.

In 1875 he followed his three brothers west to California and settled in the Sonoma County city of Santa Rosa, which he called "the chosen spot of all this earth. . . ." There he established a small nursery garden with a greenhouse. Here, and at an experimental plot a few miles away, he worked uninterruptedly for fifty years, developing a long series of flowers, fruits, vegetables, grasses and grains. Burbank was very pragmatic. He did not conduct his experiments to test or prove any general scientific theory or hypothesis; his work had as its only aim the production of better varieties of cultivated plants. Forty years of his attention was given to growing at least forty new varieties of prunes and plums. For thirty-five years he experimented with various kinds of berries, producing ten new types. Among the fruits which he introduced were many varieties of nectarines, quinces, peaches, apples and cherries. Among vegetables, he produced new types of potatoes, tomatoes, squash, corn, asparagus and pears. In the production of flowers, he specialized in lilies, although he also developed the large, beautiful Shasta daisy. Burbank remained at work continuously until his death on April 11, 1906.

California's climate had early been recognized as favorable for growing vegetables. By 1859, market garden produce had already passed the one million dollar mark in value. During these early years, vegetable production, except for potatoes, was almost entirely for local consumption. Numerous market gardens ringed California's larger cities. With the coming of the railroad and refrigerated freight cars, by 1879 California vegetables reached Cheyenne and Denver nearly twelve months of the year. By 1881 steamers were carrying California vegetables to British Columbia, Washington and Central America. As a result of these wide markets, vegetable production moved out of the market-garden stage. By 1899, the value of California vegetables had reached nearly six million dollars. Carloads of vegetables daily reached eastern markets. When a large tract of peat soil in Orange County was cleared, it brought such an increase in celery production that about two thousand carloads were shipped east annually. Vegetable production spread along the coast and into the interior valleys. Fall and winter tomatoes were grown near Los Angeles for shipment all over the country, and shortly after the opening of the twentieth century, vegetable production developed in the Coachella and Imperial valleys.

But it was orange growing in California on a commercial basis that captured the attention of farmers all over the United States. They anticipated financial rewards from irrigated, intensive citrus growing. The mental picture conceived by the eastern farmers of orange groves set in hot valleys with a background of snow-peaked mountains accorded perfectly with the California image. This vision gripped men's imaginations in a way reminiscent of the gold rush; California was accepted generally as a veritable Garden of Eden.

Oranges supposedly were introduced into California in 1770. A flourishing grove existed at Mission San Buenaventura as early as 1792. One of the earliest orange groves in California was that planted at the San Gabriel mission in 1804. Here four hundred sweet orange seedlings were set out over a six-acre plot. Thirty trees, all in poor condition, were still bearing fruit as late as 1885.

About 1834 several garden plantings of oranges were carried out in Los Angeles by Louis Vignes and Manuel Requena. In 1841 the first commercial grove, a two-acre tract, was planted by a former trapper, William Wolfskill, using trees acquired from the San Gabriel mission. Eventually he expanded his orchard to seventy acres. The lack of important markets, however, prevented Wolfskill from greatly expanding his orange-growing operations. As a result of this factor and a lack of sufficient capital, the California orange industry slumbered until after the completion of the transcontinental railroad, which enabled Californians to tap the eastern markets.

Early in the 1870's, a number of ambitious experiments were undertaken to raise citrus fruit commercially in California. In March 1870, Judge John Wesley North, then living in Knoxville, Tennessee, suggested an agricultural colony in California. He attracted a good deal of attention and even some capital. In September 1870, North and several associates journeyed to southern California, where they purchased the rights and real estate of a defunct silk-growing plantation. The price for the times was not cheap—$43.50 an acre. The tract itself was four thousand acres of barren, dry tableland or mesa, which had never been cultivated. Oldtimers liked to say that coyotes carried their own canteens when they ventured across it. The nearest railroad was at Los Angeles, sixty-five miles away. Supplies and produce would have to be taken that distance on a dusty wagon ride. However, in 1870–71, colonists who had migrated to the area constructed an irrigation canal from the Santa Ana River at a cost of $50,000. The colonists had originally intended to grow oranges, but the dreary prospect of waiting eight or nine years from seed planting to fruit harvesting caused some of them to despair and turn to more immediate harvests, such as the raisin grape. Others persevered.

Next, a colony of settlers from Indiana purchased four thousand acres of the Rancho San Pasqual along the Arroyo Seco, east of Los Angeles, establishing both a town and an agricultural settlement. Since some of this acreage was devoted to orange cultivation, the colony was renamed the

San Gabriel Orange Grove Association. Eventually this settlement became known as Pasadena. In addition to the two colonies already mentioned, in the next few years a number of other orange groves were founded at such places as Ontario, Redlands, Placentia, Anaheim, Duarte, and in the San Gabriel Valley. By 1874 it was estimated that mature seedling trees were producing at a net profit of $20.50 a tree, or $1,435 an acre. The chief market in those days was San Francisco, but oranges were already being shipped from that port to places as far away as England. There were about 90,000 orange trees in the state, but many of them were not bearing. Nearly 65,000 of that number were in Los Angeles or San Bernardino counties. A great impetus was given to the infant orange industry at the close of the 1870's, when a series of annual fairs were held at Riverside. Simultaneously a new variety of orange was exhibited, the Washington navel, which bore a seedless fruit. Credit for introducing this new orange goes to Luther Tibbets and his wife Eliza who, in December 1873, received a package of three small orange trees from Washington, D.C. These trees had been brought into the United States from Brazil by the federal Department of Agriculture. Tibbits and his wife tenderly cared for the new trees, but not until 1878 did the two surviving trees bear fruit, and then there were only two oranges to a tree. To introduce the four seedless oranges to California, a party was held by the Tibbets' with Mrs. Tibbets as "orange hostess." The reception by California farmers of the seedless oranges was enthusiastic. Then Tibbets and his wife visited Santa Barbara, Pasadena and Los Angeles in a buggy, promoting the new orange. California's climate and soil seemed ideally suited to the Washington navel. Demand for the seedless orange rose in the East, and the high prices paid for them greatly stimulated California production. By 1889, over one million seedless orange trees had been planted, and by 1900 five and a half million trees were bearing fruit.

In 1880 at Placentia, R. H. Gilman planted California's first commercial grove of Valencia oranges, introduced from Europe. This first grove of these excellent juice oranges was a modest four rows of trees, eighty-five trees to a row. In addition to its excellent juice, the value of the Valencia orange was that it matured in the summer and early fall, supplementing the Washington navel, which was marketed between December and April.

It was 1877 before a full railroad car of oranges was first shipped to eastern markets. The first special orange train left Los Angeles on February 14, 1886. In the 1880's refrigerator cars made it possible to deliver fresh fruit to the East in the summer months. By 1892, California oranges reached London by way of New York. Then the orange growers found that their profits from the golden fruit were being dissipated by the excessive charges of commission merchants and the high railroad freights rates. Therefore, a few farm leaders such as William H. Mills advocated cooperative marketing. As early as 1892, a local cooperative organization known as the Pachappa Orange Growers' Association was formed. The next year, growers' associations were started at Claremont, Duarte, San Bernardino, Orange and San Antonio. It was quickly seen that an even wider pooling of fruit was desirable. As a result the Southern California Fruit Exchange was started in 1895 and in 1905 was broadened into the California Fruit Growers' Exchange.

Orange growing in California faced significant natural hazards. First there was the cottony scale, which had come to California from Australia and spread throughout the orchards of southern California. At first poisons were used against these insects. However, the exasperated farmers could find nothing that would kill them without also killing the trees or damaging their fruit. Then in 1888 the United States Department of Agriculture imported the small ladybird beetle from Australia. This beetle was the natural enemy of the scale insects and soon effectively solved the problem. Second, there was the black scale, which also seriously damaged citrus trees. At the beginning of the twentieth century, citrus growers turned to spraying tree trunks with distillate oil and using fumigation. These techniques provided relatively effective remedies.

After the troublesome frosts of 1895, many orange growers experimented with oil burners to heat their groves during freezing weather. However, even with cheap oil it was still too expensive to try to heat "all outdoors," and therefore, the effective use of smudgepots had to wait until the twentieth century.

As late as 1909 the California production of oranges was only five million boxes, valued at less than thirteen million dollars. Greater advances were yet to come. Between 1890 and 1900, lemon growing took a prominent place in California citrus areas. G. W. Garcelon at Riverside spent fifteen years experimenting to bring the California lemon to the point where it could compete with foreign fruit. One variety, the Lisbon, was grown successfully, but bore lemons only in the winter. The Eureka, which bore fruit all year round, had the disadvantage of setting its lemons on the very tips of its branches, which overexposed its fruit to the sun's rays. It was discovered that by constant pruning, this difficulty could be overcome. A process was also discovered whereby winter lemons like the Lisbon could be cured and held over for the summer market. The quality of California lemons was also improved considerably.

Although the lemon had been planted in the 1870's and 1880's, it did not fully share in the citrus boom of that period. Not until orange prices declined somewhat did lemon raising in California come into its own. An additional incentive was provided by a great freeze in 1894–95, which virtually wiped out the Florida lemon crop and discouraged its revival for nearly forty years. In 1882 the lemon industry in California could count 62,130 bearing trees, 48,350 of which were located in Los Angeles County. Nineteen years later, lemon production had spread from San Diego to Tulare County, with over 805,000 trees. By 1909 the California lemon crop was valued at nearly three million dollars.

Grapefruit culture was introduced into the state in the 1880's. The demand for California grapefruit also improved with the Florida freeze of 1894–95. In the late 1890's, California production rose when the Marsh seedless grapefruit was introduced into the state. When experimentation finally proved that the fruit from several areas of the state was not satisfactory until late spring or summer, the areas where successful early bearing was possible prospered. In the 1920's grapefruit culture extended into the Imperial and Coachella valleys over an area of 15,000 to 20,000 acres. This region, which ripened its fruit in winter, was an excellent supplement to the other citrus areas of California.

A particularly important and colorful part of California agricultural history was the cultivation of the grape. In 1770 the Franciscans set out the first California vineyard—a small patch of grape cuttings—at San Diego. Each mission in time developed its own vineyard and winery. This stock was known as the Los Angeles grape. It was of Spanish origin, but had been much changed during its cultivation in Mexico. It was a reddish-black berry which had a sweet juice. About 1820 a grape called the Sonoma was introduced north of the Bay area. This grape produced a lighter wine than did the Los Angeles grape. Both of these types were indiscriminately called the Mission or California grape. Los Angeles soon became the center of the early grape industry. In 1831, Louis Vignes, a Frenchman, established the largest vineyard in California. His nephew, Louis Jean Sainsevain, is generally credited with producing the first California champagne. About 1840, a large vineyard was planted in the Cucamonga district a few miles west of San Bernardino from San Gabriel cuttings. This tract contained 125,000 vines by 1859. The census of 1850 credits Los Angeles with producing nearly 58,000 gallons of wine that year. Sonoma was also already famous for the wines which it shipped to gold-rush San Francisco to help slake that city's thirst.

The real father of viniculture in California is Agoston Haraszthy, a Hungarian immigrant who settled in San Diego, where he planted a vineyard in 1851. He had brought with him a cutting of the Muscat Alexandria grape, which began California's raisin-growing industry. He also introduced the Zinfandel red wine grape. Eventually he imported some 200,000 vine cuttings, including all of the best-known European varieties. He moved to Sonoma in 1856, where he operated a vineyard in partnership with a man named Delmas. Becoming the leader of California grape growers, Haraszthy campaigned vigorously for state aid to viniculture.

Since he was active in politics and had a position of importance within the dominant Democratic Party, Haraszthy was in a strong position to secure state help for his industry.

In 1859, Haraszthy gained his first political success when a law was passed instructing county assessors to exempt growing vines from taxation. In 1861 the governor appointed Haraszthy to a special commission for the promotion of the wine industry. Although the legislature refused to pay his expenses, Haraszthy went to Europe at a cost of $12,000 to gather various strains of grapes, which he then introduced into California. Upon his return from Europe, the commission recommended to the legislature that a broad program of state aid be voted for vineyardists. However, the legislature was unsympathetic, for the timing of this request was wrong. Haraszthy was a well-known prosouthern Democrat, and the Civil War had just started. With the legislature firmly in the grip of northern Democrats and the Republicans, it declined to pay serious attention to Haraszthy's ideas. This refusal of further state help seriously hindered the growth of the grape industry.

However, it was only a temporary setback. Even during the Civil War, the grape growers persisted in forming informal associations to seek state help in promoting the grape industry. In 1862 the California Wine-growers' Association was established to obtain a state board of viticulture to foster the industry and enforce disease-control measures. (Although viniculture may have been a better word to use in connection with this board, the Victorian Californians preferred to call it viticulture, thus emphasizing the use of the grapes as fruit.) Nothing was accomplished then. Haraszthy himself vanished in July 1869 while on a trip to Nicaragua. Nonetheless, by 1870 grape lands were paying a return of better than a hundred dollars an acre, and wine was selling at twenty-five cents to a dollar a gallon. At this time there were twenty-five million grapevines in the state.

This promising beginning was darkened by the appearance of a dread pest, the phylloxera, in 1870. These plant lice were first discovered in Sonoma, but they quickly spread despite all the winemakers' efforts. Finally, in April 1880, the legislature created the state board of viticulture to combat the grape pest. The board had some success in controlling the phylloxera, until it was abolished in 1895 after a dispute concerning whether its primary concern should be to foster research or to promote the sale of California wines.

Until 1885 southern California enjoyed a time of preeminence in the wine industry. After that year, Napa, Sonoma and El Dorado counties, as well as areas in the Sacramento Valley, seriously challenged its leadership. In 1871 there were 139 major wineries in California with a capital investment of half a million dollars. Continuing at a steady growth, the value of

California wine jumped from $600,000 in 1880 to nearly three times that amount in 1890. By the opening of the twentieth century, the state had a yearly output of nearly nineteen million gallons—over 80 per cent of all the wine manufactured in the United States. It was worth nearly four million dollars.

The raising of raisin grapes (viticulture) had lagged behind the wine establishment (viniculture). It began in Los Angeles in 1859. As late as 1872, the raisin crop totaled a mere sixty tons. In 1880 the yield increased to 750 tons and by 1890 had risen to a respectable 19,000 tons. During this time, the raisin-growing region had pushed north from southern California into the Sacramento Valley. By 1900, 43 per cent of all grapes raised in the state were made into raisins—some 47,000 tons. Only 12,000 tons of table grapes were produced. The rest of the grapes were manufactured into wine.

Grapes were dried on sun-drying trays, but in years of early rains, natural draft-type blowers without fans were also utilized. In time more elaborate mechanical blowers came into use.

For a time, there was a considerable apple boom in California. Actually, as late as 1880 there were more apple trees in the state than those of all the other deciduous fruits combined. The Franciscans had grown some apples in their orchards at the missions, as did the Russians at Fort Ross. General Vallejo in 1830 made extensive apple plantings on his rancho in the Sonoma Valley. Yet the apple industry of California was virtually created at the beginning of the American period by Martin De Long, who came to the Far West with Stevenson's regiment of New Yorkers during the Mexican War. Tradition has it that De Long brought with him a small lot of French varieties of apple and planted them in Los Angeles.

In the fall of 1849, W. H. Nash, in partnership with R. L. Kilburn, ordered a box of thirty-six assorted fruit trees, many of them apple, from a nursery in western New York, and planted them in the Napa Valley. Other apple trees were brought from nurseries in Oregon. By 1880, California had 2.4 million apple trees, the majority of them in north-central California. However, the fact that the California apple was judged to be inferior in flavor to apples elsewhere in the country caused the importance of this fruit to decline after 1880. By 1890 there were only 1.3 million bearing apple trees in the state.

The peach had grown in the mission gardens. More peach trees were brought from Oregon by Seth Lewelling in 1851. In the early days of the gold rush, peaches commanded the fantastic price of $1.50 a dozen. However, after the gold excitement died, the young peach industry disintegrated. As late as 1880, peach trees numbered only 800,000, or about a third as many as the apple orchards could boast. The coming of the transcontinental railroad with refrigerated cars and the rise of canning combined to stimulate the demand for California peaches. By 1892 there were nearly 34,000 acres of bearing trees. By 1900, 1,361 railroad cars of peaches were shipped outside the state. By 1890, twelve and a quarter million pounds of peaches were dried annually. Nearly all of these drying peaches were grown in the San Joaquin Valley.

The pear had been featured at the San Diego mission; San Juan Bautista had pear trees which lived to be over 150 years old. In the early days of American California, pear trees were planted in the mother-lode country and as far north as Shasta County. These early pear orchards never attained commercial significance. Yet the high prices the fresh fruit commanded after 1850 caused an increase every ten years in the number of bearing pear trees. Therefore, by 1880 there were 350,000 pear trees in California. The orchards spread from the valleys into higher ground. The Sacramento Valley and Contra Costa County raised what became the dominant type of pear—the Bartlett. The public so identified this pear with the state that it was commonly called the "pear of California." By 1900, California had 2.5 million pear trees producing nearly one-fifth of the nation's output.

Prunes or dried plums became another successful fruit crop of California. Louis Pellier, a Frenchman, came to California seeking gold. He noticed that the miners paid high prices for fruit and that at that time a grower might more surely make a fortune than a miner. As a result, he left the mines and went into the orchard business around San Jose, where there was already a small French colony. In 1853, Louis Pellier financed the passage back to France of his brother Pierre so that he might return with seeds and cuttings from his mother country.

In 1856, Pierre Pellier returned to California, and Louis was able to plant an orchard area called "Pellier's Gardens," which revolutionized agriculture in the Santa Clara Valley. Pellier soon produced a strain of plum tree that produced fruit that dried into a prune without the development of any fermentation. Soon he was selling many trees to his neighbors. In 1863, California dried prunes were exhibited at the state fair in Sacramento. They attracted considerable attention, and the area of their planting increased. By 1866 the state had 650 acres of prune trees, but the number grew to 90,000 by 1890. Ten years later, there were nearly ten million plum trees, producing 65 per cent of the plums and prunes in America.

The apricot—a native fruit of Asia—was probably bought to California by way of North Africa and Europe by the missionaries. In 1880 there were a quarter of a million apricot trees in California. By 1891, 6,750 tons annually were dried and sent to market, principally in the eastern United States. By 1900 over 14,000 tons were produced, and the number of apricot trees had risen to 4.2 million, producing 95 per cent of American apricots.

The growth of the California fruit industry caused an increase in the number of canning establishments in the state from twelve to 136 between 1880 and 1900. In the latter year, California was processing one-quarter of all fruit and vegetables canned in the United States.

A number of exotic crops sparked California's agricutlural development in the latter nineteenth century. Walnuts had been grown at the missions, and as early as 1843, a grove had been planted at Warner's Hot Spring in San Diego County. By general consent, the early walnuts were considered inferior. In 1868, Joseph Sexton planted the soft-shelled Chilean variety near Goleta. A French variety was grown at about the same time near Nevada City. The English walnut was introduced in the 1860's, but became commercially important only in the next decade. Since the English walnut seemed best suited to California, by 1881 there were more than 100,000 trees of this variety in California. The average yield was ten pounds a tree. In 1899, 5,400 tons of walnuts were produced in the state.

Nursery plantings were made of almonds at the Santa Barbara mission soon after its founding. The results were unsatisfactory and the trees were abandoned. But Jean François de Galaup, Comte de la Pérouse, is supposed to have given the padres a better kind of almond. Starting in 1843, a number of experimental plantings were made of almond trees in Placer County, which did so well that nuts from these trees won a prize at the first state fair. Plantings of the almond tree became more common in the 1860's, and they were commercially grown by the 1870's. For a time the almond tree outstripped the walnut in numbers, and by 1890 there were 650,000 almond trees in California. Ten years later their number had grown to some 1.6 million. However, the almond proved to be more difficult to grow, and by 1900 it had fallen to second place behind the walnut tree yield. In 1910, to upgrade the almond crop, the California Growers' Exchange was formed. It set high standards and marketed its almond crop under the trade name Blue Diamond.

The olive became another ornament of California agriculture. The olive cuttings and seeds brought from Mexico as early as 1764 were important during the mission period because the olive was frequently used in religious ceremonies. In the last decade of Mexican rule, small groves of olive trees were planted on the ranchos, and the oil became a common commodity. In 1849, T. K. Stewart planted olive trees along the American River, thus proving that the tree could grow in northern California. Still, few people fancied the olive for food, and only the demand for salad oil accounted for the presence of the few trees in the state. In the 1870's tracts of olive trees were planted in the San Joaquin and Sacramento valleys, and even as far north as Shasta County. The boom continued on a modest scale until there were about 13,000 trees in 1885, 275,000 in 1890 and 1,530,000 in 1900. The olive oil market (all of the eighty varieties of California olives were primarily of the oil-bearing

type) could not stand this heavy production, for the successful competition of cheaper salad oils caused the state's industry to diminish in the
early years of the twentieth century. A revival set in after 1910, when the
pickling and canning processes made the olive itself palatable as food.

The mission fathers introduced the fig to California, and this "mission"
fig was the only variety known in California for about eighty-five years.
By 1850, fig trees were common from San Diego to the north Bay area.
Figs were grown experimentally in combination with citrus fruits in
southern California in the 1850's and 1860's; continued experimentation
increased the number of trees to 110,000 by 1890. Then a mild boom
caused by rising interest in the fruit increased the number of fig trees to
190,000. Production remained limited, however, because fresh figs could
not be shipped long distances without deterioration. Thus the eastern
market remained tantalizingly out of reach. Since dried figs could not
compete in the world markets with those imported from the Near East,
the modern California fig industry had to wait for the technological
advances of the twentieth century.

As the population of the state increased, so did the demand for dairy
products. Little use was made of milk or butter during the Mexican
period, but in the American era the demand for all kinds of dairy products increased steadily, although slowly. The goldseekers brought the first
good milk cows overland to California. Soon the eastern rim of the state
had dairy herds located close to the mining centers. Scrawny Mexican
cattle along the coast helped satisfy the San Francisco demand for dairy
products. In 1857 there were 130 dairies, with herds as large as two hundred cows, shipping butter, cheese and milk to San Francisco. As long as
butter sold at a dollar a pound and other dairy products at a comparable
price, dairying with the poor-quality Mexican stock was feasible. By
1860, when outside competition caused prices to drop, this pioneer dairying could no longer pay its way.

In the 1860's in the coast region, better milk cows were imported and
sufficient buildings and other equipment were erected to start a more
efficient operation. From 1866, local production of butter increased and
the importation of the commodity into the state dropped. Yet it was not
until 1878 that local production of butter equaled consumption. As early
as 1866, the dairy industry produced more cheese than Californians cared
to eat.

Between 1880 and 1890 there was a transition period in dairying. Cream
separators were introduced in 1881. Refrigeration allowed less spoilage.
The alfalfa area of cattle feed was increased by the use of irrigation. After
1890 the California state government provided rules to insure the purity
of dairy products. The new government standards and refrigeration allowed longer shipments. In the 1880's and 1890's the immigration of

Italian-Swiss dairymen into California helped promote that industry. New country north of San Francisco, even regions as far from the city as Humboldt County, became dairying centers, as did coastal areas as far south as San Luis Obispo. By 1895, California had 203 creameries producing over thirty-one million pounds of butter.

Poultry raising was also influenced by California's growing population. The missionaries and the rancheros raised poultry, but records of specific amounts are virtually nonexistent. By the middle fifties, the state fairs featured poultry exhibitions. The growth of the Californians' taste in poultry is illustrated by the fact that in 1867 there were barely one million chickens in California. That number more than quintupled by 1910. In the same period, the number of turkeys remained almost constant and the number of ducks and geese actually declined. By 1880 the Petaluma area in southern Sonoma County, connected as it was by both water and rail routes to San Francisco, became a leading poultry- and egg-producing region.

As the mining and cattle era of California drew to a close, and agriculture increasingly dominated the state's economic scene, the issue of water became more acute. No technique except irrigation could produce commercial crops in much of central and southern California. Actually, irrigation began in California during the mission phase. San Diego mission, for instance, built an elaborate irrigation project between 1776 and 1781. There was actually some irrigation at all missions that had their own orchard and vegetable patch.

In the American era, one of the first regions to undergo reclamation was an area in the San Joaquin Valley in 1853. A ditch was dug from Mill Creek near Visalia to carry water for grainfields and gardens. The first irrigated settlement or colony in California was carried out as a result of the founding of Anaheim. In 1857, fifty German settlers constituted the Los Angeles Vineyard Society, which purchased a tract of 1,265 acres some thirty miles southeast of Los Angeles near the Santa Ana River. The property was surveyed into fifty twenty-acre farms around a town site. A twelve-mile main ditch and laterals were built to carry water to the orchards of the settlement.

In the Sierra Nevada, some of the earliest irrigation companies began by carrying water to the gold mines. The mines bore the heavy initial cost of financing the projects, and only gradually were agricultural clients added. In 1856 and 1859, a number of canals were constructed to irrigate wheat in Yolo County. At that time there were additional irrigation diversions from the Kings, Tule, Kaweah and Kern rivers of the San Joaquin Valley. The larger cooperative companies were not founded until the 1860's and 1870's. Yet in this early period, some irrigation was also developed along the basins of the Santa Ana and San Gabriel rivers.

By 1870 irrigation was practiced on about 60,000 acres out of some five million under cultivation in California. At that time the size of the average farm in the state was 482 acres. By 1900 the area of the average unit had fallen to 397 acres, as water made intensive cultivation of farm land more profitable. Water also allowed a greater variety of crops to be grown in California.

The utilization of irrigation on a large scale created legal problems. California common law had recognized riparian rights, or the doctrine that the landowners along the banks of a stream had the right to an undisturbed flow of water. Then in 1872 the California legislature adopted the New York civil code, which allowed the appropriation and diversion of water by upstream users. This confused the legal situation in California. Great landowners, such as the cattlemen who enjoyed vested water rights, favored continuing riparianism. Newcomers to agriculture favored the appropriation doctrine, which allowed the impounding or diversion of water flowing through the public domain from its natural course and its application to beneficial private use. In this way, these later settlers could gain access to water. Between 1872 and 1878, the two rival groups, the riparians and the appropriationists, fought it out in the legislature. In the end, all they could agree upon was a proposal to make a comprehensive study of the water problem by a new official, the state engineer. This officer, William Hammond Hall, made an exhaustive investigation of the irrigation problem. His conclusion was obvious; the riparian and appropriation doctrines could not be reconciled. Hall recommended that the California state government impose controls upon water diverted from streams. A regulatory state agency would insure riparian users of the water that they needed, while giving a share to owners dependent upon a public source under the doctrine of appropriation rights.

The leading landowners in California were out of sympathy with Hall's suggestion. Two of them went into court over the question. James B. Haggin, with the support of his partner Lloyd Texis, challenged Miller–Lux over the waters of the Kern River upon which they held adjacent properties. This legal "Battle of the Giants" was begun in 1879 and reached the California Supreme Court in 1885. It took more than a year for the court to write what was then the longest decision rendered by the tribunal. After involved reasoning, the court upheld Miller–Lux's claims and the doctrine of riparian rights.

Haggin's associate, J. B. Carr, started a political crusade to reverse the court decision. With help from irrigation conventions that backed the appropriation doctrine, Carr was able to mount an impressive attack. As a result, a special session of the legislature repealed Section 1422 of the civil code which protected riparian rights. State Engineer Hall had irritated both the riparians and appropriationists, and so they both agreed that his office should be abolished. Having accomplished this, the Legislature could not agree upon a policy of water distribution. The problem was left to the courts; either the doctrine of riparian rights or that of appropriation came to be applied in thousands of court decisions, reflecting the different geographic conditions in the state.

Meanwhile the development of irrigation projects went on. In 1871 the largest irrigation project in California was begun. It involved the San Joaquin and Kings River Canal Company which included among its investors Henry Miller, Charles Lux, William S. Chapman and San Francisco banker William Ralston. It was extended from the San Joaquin River for nearly seventy miles. The total cost of the enterprise was $1,300,000. Several similar projects were begun from the Kern River northward. As a result, by the 1880's, 190,000 acres were irrigated in the San Joaquin Valley. In the far south of the state, the San Diego Land and Town Company also furnished irrigation water for farming.

Prior to 1887 all irrigation projects were private. The legislature, by the Wright Act of 1887, provided for public operation of irrigation by voluntary districts. Fifty or more landowners could ask the county board of supervisors to form an irrigation district. If their petition was approved, all the landowners of the district elected a board of directors. If the voters concurred, the directors could issue bonds and construct irrigation works. They could tax landowners to pay interest on district bonds. This act served as a model for later legislation in the United States, despite the fact that its operation revealed some weaknesses.

The Wright Act was not an immediate success. Although fifty irrigation districts were formed by 1890, many of them existed only on paper. Inexperience hampered their successful flotation of loans. Meanwhile the depression of 1893 destroyed the money market for new bonds. In order to dispose of their paper, some districts in desperation turned it over to contractors at prodigious discounts. One of the most unsuccessful districts was the Central Irrigation, located in Tehama and Glenn counties. This district was organized in 1887, but did not actually provide any water for irrigation until eighteen years later. For years mutual companies operating under state charters dominated irrigation rather than the districts formed under the Wright Act. Gradually the amount of land irrigated by both public and private agencies grew, until by 1919 the land so watered in California came to over four million acres.

As farming came to play an increasingly important role in the California economy, gold mining fell to a subordinate position. Yet, utilizing new techniques, gold miners tried valiantly to continue their work as a major industry of California. These new techniques brought the miners and farmers to loggerheads—a battle of gold versus grain.

Hydraulic mining, which utilized streams of water to wear away hillsides, thus exposing the gold-bearing ore, was begun in March 1853 at American Hill, north of Nevada City, by Edward E. Matteson. This type of mining quickly became very popular. Water was needed on a large scale, and the first engineering projects to carry it long distances were begun in California. By 1857, seven hundred miles of ditches wound around and across the rolling countryside of Nevada County. Despite becoming a fad, hydraulic mining was not successful once the lightly packed topsoil and gravel were washed away. The lower levels of gravel were more densely compacted and not easily broken down. The drought of the early sixties also slowed this type of mining. In 1865, with increased capital and great technological advances, hydraulic mining became more successful. One problem which became acute as the hillsides were washed away was the problem of tailings or debris. In the middle and late 1860's, mountain streams were choked with gravel, mud and sand.

The mines continued to enjoy unusual prosperity, while blithely ignoring the tailings which drifted into the rivers and streams of the Sacramento Valley. As this debris choked the streams in flood times, it caused them to overflow their banks, depositing a slimy sediment called "slickens" over the flat land. As the slickens covered fruit orchards and wheat fields, they caused crops to die. Yuba and Sutter County farmers suffered the most. Since it was usually difficult to tell whose tailings caused what damage, and the economic climate was one of laissez faire, nothing was done for years, despite the damage this type of mining caused.

Then in 1873, when the large Spring Valley Mine began dumping tons of debris along Dry Creek in Butte County, A. J. Crum, in behalf of the farmers' cause, brought suit in the local court. He claimed the mine was destroying his peach orchards. A jury turned down the farmers' complaint. Crum and his associates were not satisfied, so they organized to sue once more after suffering additional damage because of new flooding in January 1874. The Spring Valley Mining Company acted to head them off by buying all the land injured by mining debris. To eliminate the problem in the future, the company constructed the Cherokee Canal, which carried the tailings into the tule swamps along the Sacramento River in Sutter County. This action solved the mining debris problem in southwestern Butte County. The Spring Valley Mining Company operated successfully until 1887, when it ceased mining because production costs had become too high to allow a profit.

The farmers of Yuba and Sutter counties watched the solution in neighboring Butte with interest. Yet their problems were more complex. There were many large and small mines which poured waste into the Feather, the Yuba and the Bear rivers.

Then in January 1875, Marysville was virtually destroyed, and at least one life lost when a flood deposited tons of mining debris upon the city. Still nothing was done. In November, the uncontrolled Sacramento River overflowed its banks throughout the lower valley. In December, a farmers' meeting was held in Yuba City, at which gathering speakers pointed out that 15,000 acres of farmland had been destroyed along the Yuba River, 11,000 acres along the Bear River, and that a half million dollars worth of destruction had been wrought along the Feather River. As a result of these statistics, the meeting decided to demand that the legislature and the federal government prevent further loss. Since the two governmental bodies were slow to act, in July 1876, James Keyes, representing the Bear Valley farmers, sued nineteen mining companies and individuals of the Bear River basin, asking for both an injunction to prevent future injury and damages for past wrongs.

In reply, the miners formed the Hydraulic Miners Association in September 1876 to fight the farmers' suit and to counter their political pressure. The rules of organization provided that every corporation had one vote for every $5,000 in capital. Thus the large companies controlled the association.

In November 1876, when the miners' attorneys argued against the Keyes suit, they declared that the case belonged in a federal court. Two years went by before this matter of jurisidiction was settled. In January 1878, the Supreme Court itself decided that the Keyes suit was not a matter for the federal courts. In July 1878, the Keyes suit was heard upon its merits in the court at Yuba City. To carry on their fight, the farmers organized themselves into the Anti-Debris Association. Assessments were levied upon the members in order to raise a respectable war chest. Keyes himself became the president of the Association. In mid-March of 1879, the state court decided the Keyes case in favor of the farmers, issuing a restraining injunction. However, on appeal in November 1879, the decision was reversed by a higher court on the technical ground that the miners were not liable to be enjoined from carrying on their activities.

At this point there is some evidence that the Big Four aided the farmers to continue their struggle against the miners. The latter had incurred the wrath of the Big Four because, in an attempt to protect their pioneer railroad—the Sacramento Valley—they had fought the building of the Central Pacific.

Finally, with renewed financial help, the Anti-Debris Association was able to get its case into the United States Circuit Court in San Francisco. After one year of study, in January 1884, Justice Lorenzo Sawyer granted a perpetual injunction against all hydraulic mining. At that the Hydraulic Mining Association surrendered, and by the end of 1884 all the major mines had closed in obedience to the Sawyer decision. The miners did not give up completely, however, but instead asked for governmental regulations under which they could resume operations. The federal government appointed the Briggs Commission, which issued a report after four years of study. The commission proposed that the government allow hydraulic mining to be resumed, but that it build dams and other retaining devices to hold back the debris.

Encouraged as a result of this report, in January 1892 a group of hydraulickers organized the California Miners Association. They were successful in persuading the federal and state governments to enact legislation allowing hydraulic mining under rigid safeguards. Nevertheless hydraulic mining never regained its former importance. Several hundred mines reopened after 1893, but most of them were small. The larger companies had spent so much money in fighting the farmers that they lacked the means to reopen. A combination of the lack of capital and the heavy taxes levied to provide for debris control crippled the industry. Finally great technological advances in quartz-mining techniques allowed greater profits to be made in that manner. Hydraulic mining became obsolescent.

The importance of agriculture rather than mining in California's economy between 1870 and 1900 was reflected in the result—in the end the farmers defeated the once all-powerful miners in both the legal and political arenas. The farmers' wheat was prized more highly than the miners' gold.

TWENTY-FOUR

The Healthseekers, the Real Estate Promoters and the Land Boom

C ALIFORNIA continued to gain population after the gold rush had ended. Between 1860 and 1880, the population of the United States as a whole grew at an average rate of 26 per cent. In general, during the same period California's population expanded at about twice the national average. The hard times of the 1870's produced a delayed reaction after 1880, which then adversely affected California's growth rate. In the early years of the 1880's, California immigration slumped badly. There was an upward change in the middle years of the 1880's when there was a rush to southern California. Between 1880 and 1890, California's population rose from 864,000 to 1,213,000 persons.

Between 1860 and 1880, the proportion of people living in rural areas declined successively from 79 to 63 and then to 57 per cent of the total population. The growth of San Francisco and other California cities was more stimulated by the completion of the transcontinental railroad than it was retarded by the decline of mining. Furthermore, California's rise to importance as a wheat producer stimulated the growth of the state's seaports and market towns. Despite the widening settlement of the interior valleys, California cities continued to grow so fast that the percentage of rural population declined to a bare 51 per cent of all the citizens of California in 1890.

In the days of the gold rush, 1850–60, San Francisco, Sacramento, the

Sacramento Valley and the Sierra may have contained four-fifths of the state's inhabitants. Except for San Francisco, these regions depopulated appreciably after 1860. The population of the Sierra actually declined by 24 per cent between 1860 and 1870. As late as 1900 the Sierra had a population less than 10 per cent greater than it had had forty years earlier. The decline of mining meant the end of growth for the mountainous area of California. By contrast, the San Francisco region continued to grow so quickly that in 1880 the locality contained 40 per cent of the state's total population. Almost five-sixths of California's population increase between 1860 and 1880 took place in the northern areas of the state. Yet the north's preeminence was soon seriously challenged by the south's rising population. Here the superior climate for most types of agriculture began to lure farmers. Yet as late as 1870, 491,000 Californians lived in the northern counties as opposed to 69,000 in the south. After that date, immigrants began to settle in the south in ever-increasing numbers.

Between 1880 and 1890, all the southern metropolitan areas grew in size, but the growth of the Los Angeles region was particularly striking. Still, as late as 1900 the population of the Los Angeles area was only a little over a third as large as that of the San Francisco region.

In its own way the population growth of the south was startling. Kern County at the southern end of the San Joaquin Valley grew from a population of 2,925 people in 1870 to over 37,000 forty years later. Between 1860 and 1900, Los Angeles County grew from 11,000 people to an aggregate of 101,000. During this time span San Diego County grew from 4,000 people to 35,000.

What drew this large number of migrants to southern California? It was not merely chance, for Californians worked hard to persuade newcomers to settle in the state. In October 1869, the California Immigrant Union was founded by a group of distinguished citizens, including Leland Stanford, Mark Hopkins and William T. Coleman. This association hired permanent agents at Copenhagen, Hamburg and Bremen, as well as a traveling representative in Germany. A general agent spread the glories of California throughout the eastern states. There were also a number of other propagandists for California, both paid and volunteer. In *The Resources of California*, which was originally written in 1863 and went through several editions, John S. Hittell decribed the state's climate as "the most conducive to health and the most favorable to mental and physical exertion. . . ." He also claimed for California "the largest specimens of fruit and vegetables on record. . . ."

The Southern Pacific, with over ten million California acres to dispose of, supported extensive propaganda to induce settlers to come to the state. The railroad wanted settlers who would both buy its land and then utilize its services, thus contributing to its operating revenue. The Southern Pacific opened a land office at Sacramento, under the supervision of the tireless Jerome Madden, who issued a veritable stream of propaganda. Madden acted in the same manner as a modern public-relations man. He advertised in many California newspapers and in eastern journals and magazines. He composed special pictorial editions for newspapers such as the San Francisco *Spirit of the Times*. During the 1880's he had many illustrated pamphlets printed and distributed by railroad ticket agents all over the country. Finally, in 1890 he wrote the book *California: Its Attractions for the Invalid, Tourist, Capitalist, and Homeseeker*. However, he did not have to carry the load of boosterism alone. He soon had a galaxy of stellar journalists who described the glory of California. German-born Charles Nordhoff (a grandson of the same name co-authored *Mutiny on the Bounty*) wrote *California for Health, Pleasure, and Residence: A Book for Travellers and Settlers* in 1874. This work was so well received that Nordhoff composed a sequel in 1883, entitled *A Guide to California, the Golden State*. Nordhoff had a great literary reputation prior to his California writing, since he had served during the Civil War as managing editor of the New York *Evening Post* under William Cullen Bryant. An important newspaperman and also a minor politician who wrote this kind of propaganda for the railroad was Rhode Island-born Major Benjamin Cummins Truman. He had taught school and set type before the Civil War. In that conflict he was attached to the staff of four Union generals. Truman served President Andrew Johnson as a confidential agent and later came to California where he became the head of the Southern Pacific literary bureau for eleven years. In 1874 he authored *Semi-Tropical California*. Nine years later he wrote *Homes and Happiness in the Golden State of California*. I. N. Hoag, a professional emigrant recruiter, penned *California the Cornucopia of the World* in 1884. The Southern Pacific also founded *Sunset* magazine to further detail the splendors of California's climate.

Volunteer authors composed tributes to the Golden State which were hardly less fulsome. Ohioan Benjamin F. Taylor in 1878 wrote *Between the Gates*, a lyrical tribute to southern California. W. H. Bishop in 1883 narrated the story of *Old Mexico and Her Lost Provinces*. An Austrian archduke, Ludwig L. Salvator, authored a California tribute entitled *Eine Blume aus dem goldenen Lande: oder, Los Angeles*, published in Prague in 1878. The Los Angeles Chamber of Commerce founded a publication which dealt in superlatives, *Land of Sunshine*.

Voluntary promotional groups, usually called "state societies," of former residents of states such as Illinois and Indiana wrote letters and columns in their hometown newspapers extolling the climate of California. Paid lecturers traveled through the eastern United States, retelling before appreciative audiences their wonderful experiences as sojourners in the Golden State.

In the later nineteenth century, there was a health rush to the West in general and to California in particular. At first, southern California was too rough and remote to attract the healthseekers. Physicians frequently prescribed travel to alleviate illnesses whose causes and cures they did not know. As a result, many patients, upon their doctor's advice or their own initiative, journeyed west to seek a cure for everything from tuberculosis to rheumatism. Starting in the 1870's, healthseekers poured into southern California for the next thirty years. Once there, although many quietly died from their diseases, many invalids, whose ills may have been psychosomatic, announced that they felt greatly improved. They wrote the folks back home concerning the magical, curative effects of California's sunshine and mild climate.

Since Los Angeles society was still too crude in the 1870's to possess first-class hotels, invalids crowded into boardinghouses, attracted by the supposedly therapeutic value of the dry, warm air. The San Francisco *Alta California* sneered that they came to California not to buy land but lungs. The boosters of southern California were ambivalent about the healthseekers, since their presence might drive away tourists and investors. Still, many of the healthseekers had sufficient means and energy to contribute substantially to the development of the region. They formed a labor pool, glad to work for lower wages than prevailed in more unionized San Francisco. They often became ardent advocates of both southern California's climate and agricultural prospects.

Many invalids sought water cures, or balneotherapy, as this medical fad was then known. They frequented spas such as Byron Springs, Palm Springs and Calistoga. This health boom faded with the end of the nineteenth century, when new medical theories and methods changed doctors' attitudes toward the effectiveness of a warm climate and the baths.

Touting the delights of southern California living, the railroads began to organize tours to Los Angeles with the completion of transcontinental rail connections. As early as 1880, the first glamorous resort hotel, Hotel del Monte, was built near Monterey by the Southern Pacific Railroad. The Raymond was built at Pasadena in 1886 by the son of the senior partner of the Boston travel agency Raymond and Whitcomb. The luxurious Coronado Hotel was started on a sandbar off San Diego. Santa Barbara, which was called the "Italy of America," drew many tourists to its resort accommodations.

After travelers and tourists returned to the sooty, dingy cities east of the Mississippi, they looked back upon their California sojourn through golden memories of flowers and sunshine. As a result, many returned to settle in California. Whether aboard deluxe accommodations in palace cars or in dirty, noisy, slow immigrant trains, in 1885, more than 50,000 tourists and settlers entered California.

Nevertheless it took a rate war between the Santa Fe Railroad and its archrival, the Southern Pacific, to develop the population boom of the middle eighties. The Southern Pacific Railroad refused to concede its rival half of the southern California business and over a quarter of its northern California traffic. Angry at this rebuff, the Santa Fe in late 1885 began a rate war. Both passenger and freight charges were involved in this struggle for traffic. As fast as the Santa Fe cut its rates, the well-entrenched Southern Pacific followed suit. The passenger charge from the Midwest to Los Angeles started at about $125. It was successively slashed until it reached $17. Nor did it stop there. The rate kept being shaved until it ultimately reached the ridiculously low figure of one dollar in the spring of 1886. So many passengers and so much freight were carried by the two railroads during the rate war that all scheduled trains had several sections. Salt from New York was carried to California for sixty cents a ton. Illinois coal was transported to Los Angeles for a dollar a ton. In 1887, over 100,000 visitors and immigrants came into California. Since the two railroads patched up their differences when they judged the rate war to have gone far enough, some citizens then and historians since have argued that it was not a real struggle between the two rail-roads, but a disguised collaboration to populate southern California and dispose of the surplus railroad land.

In any event, a tremendous real estate boom was generated. It seemed legitimate enough in the beginning, since it started with a mighty influx of purchasers. However, the shrewd real estate operators, called "Escrow Indians," proclaimed that this excitement was merely the prelude to a real boom. Using methods that sound surprisingly modern, these promoters reaped a quick harvest of sales. Many of the real estate men were themselves from the Midwest. They brought with them to California techniques borrowed from the more settled parts of the country. These practices flourished in the wildly optimistic atmosphere of southern California.

An enterprising real estate operator's first step was to gain title to a plot of land upon which his development could be projected. Many of these tracts were on swampy, rocky or hilly land, which made them poor homesites.

Prices of Los Angeles city lots skyrocketed from $500 to $5,000 within a year. Garden land, vineyards, and orange groves worth about $350 an acre were plotted into lots whose total asking price was $10,000 an acre. Gridirons of sidewalks were laid out in the desert scrub brush.

The newcomers to California included gullible farmers and rustic shop-keepers from the Midwest. These unsophisticated people proved to be easy targets for the promoters. The wealthier immigrants paid $20,000 to $50,000 for ocean lots on remote beaches. For instance, Redondo-by-the-Sea drew investors because the promoters declared that engineers had found a submarine oil well off the Redondo coast which kept its water placid, making it an ideal harbor. Widney-by-the-Desert was another hopeful tract. At first it attracted only minimal interest, because it was located amid a wasteland filled with spiny, misshapen Joshua trees. These gaunt trees gave the plot a stark effect. Then some enterprising promoter thought of putting oranges on the prickly trees and sold the site as a citrus grove to some unwary purchaser.

One newspaperman discovered a piece of unoccupied land on the Santa Fe railroad. He founded a town which he called Gladstone, after William Ewart Gladstone, the famous British statesman. The promoter widely advertised that he had deeded a lot to the British politician and that Gladstone would soon build a magnificent residence there. A rival newspaperman exposed the promoter's sharp practice. As a result, the real estate operator lost his land, which he was buying on time, and the site was then planted in barley.

The town of Azusa, in the rich valley of Azusa de Duarte, was plotted and the lots advertised for sale as of a certain date. All during the night before the sale, a queue of hopeful purchasers formed. A buyer far back in line offered the second man a thousand dollars for his place, but he was refused. The fifth man in line did sell out for $500.

Paper cities such as Border City and Manchester made money for their promoter Simon Homberg. He bought quarter-sections of railroad land forty and forty-three miles northeast of Los Angeles. He paid only the first payment of twenty-five cents an acre, so his four thousand tiny lots cost him only two cents each. He sold them in northern California, Oregon and the east for a profit of nearly $100,000. During the height of the speculative orgy, the record for real estate transfers in a single day rose to $664,000, then to $730,000, and then to $930,000.

July of 1887 may have been the peak of the frenzy, when land sales in Los Angeles passed the two hundred million dollar mark. From January 1887 to July 1889, sixty new towns were laid out containing a total acreage of 79,350. By early 1888 the boom finally collapsed. However, it did not end in one wild day of falling prices. Rather it slowly collapsed like a punctured balloon. Some speculators escaped, enriched by their profits. Some purchasers paid their debts and faced a barren future. Others defaulted on their payments, preferring to lose their land rather than continue to make payments based on the inflated value of the real estate. There were a few suicides. Then life returned to what passed for normal in southern California.

Despite the business failures and the departure of many disgruntled real estate plungers, southern California permanently benefitted from the land boom. Cities and towns complete with governmental and municipal services quickly sprang up across the southland. New businesses and banks were begun. Additional transportation and agricultural facilities were permanently established. Relatively little industrial production resulted from the boom. Nevertheless southern California became more than a tourist resort or a sanitarium for invalids.

The character of the newcomers changed after the 1880's. Before this decade, migrants came principally from New England, New York, Illinois or Ohio. Now they increasingly came from the central Midwest—Kansas, Missouri, Iowa or Nebraska. The newcomers no longer settled in northern California, but went to the San Joaquin Valley or California south of the Tehachapi. By 1890, 43 per cent of Californians of American birth came from the Midwest, but this percentage rose to 47 per cent by 1900 and to 51.9 per cent by 1910. From 1860 to 1900, more native-born Americans living in California claimed New York as their home than any other single state. However, by 1910, Illinois took over this distinction and retained it until 1950. The percentage of newcomers from New England and the South Atlantic states was cut in half between 1860 and 1910.

In southern California these midwesterners made the region Protestant in morality and outlook and gave the area a distinct populist tinge. Southern Californians were more likely to favor prohibition or even women's suffrage. In 1896, southern California approved giving women the ballot, only to see foreign-born, Catholic San Francisco voters defeat it. In the matter of divorce though, the more easygoing San Franciscans, despite their Catholic background, were more liberal than the more straitlaced south. There was one divorce for every five marriages in San Francisco in 1911, as compared to one to eight in more conservative Los Angeles. After the collapse of the real estate boom in the eighties, the state began again to make economic progress, only to fall victim to the deleterious effects of the national panic of 1893. This panic was touched off in California by the failure of the Riverside Banking Company, which precipitated a chain of banking disasters across the state. Agricultural prices dropped to less than half their former levels. Excellent crops rotted in the fields because farmers could not pay the cost of transportation and harvesting. Laborers' wages fell from a quarter to a half of the rates prevailing in 1892. By the fall of 1893, thousands of unemployed men, following the sun as they traditionally had since the completion of the transcontinental railroad, caught rides on freight trains and rode to California. These refugees from the East's cold climate and severe unemployment conditions complicated California's uncoordinated relief activities. Bread lines were opened in all major California cities.

The local and state governments instituted programs of work relief. Private charities also did their best to help the migrants, but thousands of ragged, hungry men aimlessly tramped the countryside.

In 1894, when Ohio's "General" Jacob Coxey announced his plan to march on Washington to demand relief measures from Congress to combat the ravages of the depression, units were formed among the homeless of California. As this army of broken veterans of the industrial army passed through California communities, there was much apprehension that violence would erupt. Instead, outside of some raids on henhouses and ripping up of fences for firewood, little damage resulted. As the army straggled into the forbidding Colorado River desert region, most of its followers dropped out to remain in the more hospitable parts of California. A few hardy souls made their way to Washington with Coxey, only to share his fate—arrest for trampling upon the Capitol grass.

The Pullman strike of 1894 also had an adverse effect upon California. This industrial battle began with a strike by its workers against the Pullman Palace Car Company in the company town of Pullman, Illinois. The cause of the Pullman workers was championed by the American Railway Union led by Eugene V. Debs. Consequently, when the railroads backed Pullman, the result was a paralysis of transportation over most of the United States, including the areas around Sacramento, Oakland and Los Angeles. Although the strike was eventually broken by the use of federal troops in the East and the militia inside California, much economic dislocation resulted. In California the interruption of transportation facilities caused heavy losses to shippers of perishable goods. Untended refrigerator cars were left on sidings and their fragile produce spoiled. California farmers had to absorb the losses. In addition, 10,000 laborers lost about a million dollars in wages.

Then in the mid-1890's there were three years of devastating drought bankrupting many stockmen and farmers and causing severe water shortages in many towns and cities. California, as did the nation generally, recovered in the late 1890's. By 1896 there was a crop failure in India which caused world farm prices to rise. Nonetheless, the price of agricultural products continued to be disproportionately below the highs of the 1860's. Yet even this partial prosperity was welcome to the American farmer. The decade between 1900 and 1910, except for the relatively mild panic of 1907, was a time of economic advancement.

California boosterism gamely struggled during the depressed nineties to sell the state's attractions to tourists and settlers. Chambers of commerce, with railroad help, staged campaigns to draw tourists to California festivals, conventions and expositions. Generally the Californians chose dates in the winter or early spring when they might be most successful in luring easterners. For instance, Michael H. de Young, publisher of the San Francisco *Chronicle,* who served as custodian of the California exhibits at the Columbian Exposition at Chicago in 1893, learned that several foreign governments wished to exhibit after the fair closed. Quickly de Young proposed that San Francisco invite these governments to stage exhibits in 1894. He did this not to bring culture to California, but to draw tourists to the Bay area. Christened the Midwinter Fair, it opened on January 1 and closed six months later, after drawing over two million visitors.

Despite this ingenuity, the nineties was not a good decade for California. Its population grew at the rate of 22.6 per cent, which was less than 2 per cent above the nation during that period. From 1,213,000 Californians in 1890, the number rose to only 1,485,000 in 1900. California's economic progress was similarly hobbled, although the total value of California farm products reached a new high of $130 million. The decade between 1900 and 1910 saw much greater population growth; California gained over 700,000 people, a growth rate of over 60 per cent. The 1910 census counted 2,634,000 Californians. Economic good times had restored the westward flow of population.

In the latter part of the nineteenth century, one new industry developed that helped greatly to stimulate the economic growth of southern California—petroleum. We have already discussed the pioneer beginnings of this activity, but as late as 1875, the cumulative amount of oil in barrels pumped in California totaled only 175,000, with a value of less than half a million dollars. In 1876 the first truly commercial oil well was drilled in Pico Canyon; it eventually reached production of 150 barrels a day. By the end of the seventies, a pipeline had been laid from the Pico Canyon oil field to a commercial refinery at Newhall.

In the early eighties, the growth of the petroleum industry was steady but rather unspectacular. Wells were dug, but they were shallow until 1885, when at Puente in Los Angeles County, one was bored as deep as 1,600 feet. The speculators delightedly found that this deep oil was lighter and easier to refine into kerosene and the other lubricants which still formed the bulk of the demand for petroleum products. From then on, the genuine petroleum industry grew, eventually taking a significant place in the state's economic life. Improvements in technique and technology, together with unflagging persistence in wildcat drilling, opened extensive new fields. In 1890 the number of barrels produced rose to 307,000 annually with a value in excess of $384,000.

The nineties saw the petroleum industry grow as its products came to be used for energy and heat. Also, another use was expanded, the technique of mixing the nonvolatile oil residue with sand to make asphalt for street and road paving. In 1892, California's first gigantic oil well gushed forth. It was Adams No. 28 in Adams Canyon near Santa Paula in Ventura County. This well originally had a flow of 1,500 barrels a day.

Simultaneously, markets for the flow of black gold were opening up.

Railroad locomotives were developed that could use oil for fuel; oil burners were installed in the electric power plants of Los Angeles. In 1893 the extensive Los Angeles–Salt Lake oil field was brought into production. Soon other large-scale developments were made at Coalinga in the San Joaquin Valley, in Fresno County's Kern River oil field, and in the Midway Sunset field in Kern County. The latter contained the greatest gusher in California petroleum history. On March 15, 1910, the Union Oil Company's Lakeview No. 1 errupted. In its first twenty-four hours, it produced 125,000 barrels. According to official records, until June 12, when production began to drop off, it produced 48,000 barrels per day. The well continued to flow for a year and a half, and its total production was nine million barrels.

California's petroleum industry became dominated by two great companies. One stemmed from the firm which had drilled the Pico Canyon well, the California Star Oil Company. This corporation eventually reorganized into the Pacific Coast Oil Company. Then about 1900 this company passed through a quick series of reorganizations and bewildering name changes which culminated in the Standard Oil Company of California. The second preeminent corporation was the Union Oil Company, which was founded at Santa Paula in 1890 through the consolidation of several smaller organizations, principally the Harbison and Stewart Company. As a result of these developments, California petroleum production zoomed to 4,319,000 barrels worth $4,152,000 by 1900, and to 77,697,000 barrels worth $37,689,000 in 1910. This early-twentieth-century increase was less the result of new fields being discovered than of the more efficient utilization of the old fields by drilling more and deeper wells.

Los Angeles, which grew to become a city in the 100,000 class with 123,000 in its metropolitan area, began to expand geographically, as well as in number of inhabitants. Los Angeles did not start its eventually great program of annexation until 1895. In that year it annexed the Highland Park region, which adjoined the original Spanish pueblo upon the northeast, thus adding 904 acres to the city. To the west, the city, in need of harbor and water frontage, took in Wilmington and San Pedro in the early years of the century. In 1910, Los Angeles annexed Hollywood, the first action that brought in many people to the city. In that year, Los Angeles could count 319,000 people within the city and 438,000 in the metropolitan area. In May 1915 the greater area of San Fernando was joined to the city. As Los Angeles had the water and other municipal services these areas needed, it was able to absorb neighboring towns. By 1920, Los Angeles had 578,000 in its central city and 879,000 in its metropolitan area. Still Los Angeles continued to grow geographically, until after ninety-five separate annexations, it had succeeded in expanding its original twenty-eight miles to an extent of 442 miles—an area three times the size of Chicago.

Around the beginning of the twentieth century, the big red cars of the electric interurban railroad tied together the scattered communities of southern California. In the years before the private motorcar gave southern California an automobile-oriented culture, the Pacific Electric, styled "The World's Greatest Interurban Railway," carried passengers to and from the beaches, mountains and cities of the region.

The Pacific Electric was the creation of Collis P. Huntington's wealthy heir and nephew, Henry E. Huntington. Actually, the family relationship was closer than uncle-nephew. Henry Huntington's first wife was the sister of Collis' adopted daughter; his second wife was Collis' widow. A New Yorker by birth, Henry Huntington held a wide variety of railroad posts in the eastern branches of his family's empire. Between 1892 and 1900, he occupied various positions with the Southern Pacific, rising to become a vice president of that line. He was quick and decisive in action. When Collis P. Huntington died in 1900, his heir, Henry Huntington, might have continued in control of the Southern Pacific, but instead he shrewdly chose to sell out to E. H. Harriman at a handsome profit.

Seeking new interests, Huntington purchased the pioneering interurban line, the Los Angeles–Pasadena. Within ten years, despite some interruption in expansion caused by the panic of 1907, he built his interurban system into a mighty network which linked Los Angeles with a host of lesser communities. Huntington closely coordinated his electric railroad activities with his widespread real estate interests. The advance of the big red cars into an area meant that Huntington's Pacific Electric Land Company was busy subdividing and selling his holdings to hopeful suburbanites. Since southern California was then undergoing considerable growth, Huntington was able to turn his dual interests into lucrative avocations.

In 1910, Huntington tired of his electric railroad interests. While retaining a majority interest in the Los Angeles city streetcar lines, he sold out to the Southern Pacific Railroad. The next year the Southern Pacific merged the Pacific Electric with other neighboring and competing systems into the largest electric railway system in history. After this consolidation, there was some additional construction. In 1914 a main line was opened to San Bernardino. The next year a direct line was laid to Riverside via Rialto.

At its height, Indianapolis surpassed Los Angeles in the geographical extent of its interurban service, but the California city's electric railroad hauled larger numbers of passengers. Nearly 10 per cent of American interurban investment was in the Los Angeles system. In 1914, some 1,626 trains, consisting of 5,262 cars, daily entered or left Los Angeles. The Pacific Electric Railroad, at its greatest extent, owned more miles of track, operated more cars, and carried more freight and passengers than any other interurban service. The distance of track from San Fernando on the northwest to Corona on the southeast was 105 miles. From Redlands to Owensmouth, the line ran for 97 miles. From the shore at Balboa to the Highlands at the base of San Antonio Peak was over 103 miles.

The Pacific Electric had a four-steel-track layout which permitted speeds up to sixty miles an hour. Nor were the passenger cars all ordinary utility coaches. Gleaming parlor-observation cars had lecturer-guides who harangued goggle-eyed tourists concerning the wonders of the southern California landscape through which the trains sped. Wonderfully appointed private cars clicked over rails, carrying railroad officials to their appointed places of business. Many special excursion trains were run for singing trolley parties, Sunday School picnics, and moonlight streetcar excursions.

In downtown Los Angeles, the Pacific Electric eventually built not one, but two major passenger terminals. Los Angeles' first skyscraper and, at the time of construction, its largest building was a Pacific Electric passenger station. The interurban had both elevated and subway lines into Los Angeles.

In addition to its considerable passenger service, the electric line carried freight, express and mail to all the cities of the system. Railway post-office cars were part of trains on all important routes. Linking the industrial centers of southern California, the Pacific Electric carried so much freight that it became California's third-ranked railroad in this category. Much freight traffic was interchanged with the major transcontinental systems. Despite increasing competition from private motor vehicles, as late as the 1920's the interurban system embraced 1,200 miles which served forty-five incorporated cities with more than 3,700 trains entering and leaving Los Angeles daily. At that time its physical assets were valued at over $88 million.

Between 1880 and the outbreak of World War I, southern California changed from an isolated rural community into an area tied into the mainstream of the nation's commerce. Tourists discovered the area; promoters successfully sold its real estate to investors and healthseekers. In those years southern California experienced its own version of the gold rush of 1849, which had so transformed the north of California.

TWENTY-FIVE

The Second-Generation Californians: 1875-1920

AS the pioneer days passed, Californians had an increasing opportunity to turn their interests from mundane affairs to more
refined cultural matters. Nevertheless, cultural development in
California moved slowly. Contemporary observers of the cultural
scene remarked that the rawness of life in the state impeded its
cultural growth. As late as the beginning of the twentieth century,
Benjamin Ide Wheeler, president of the University of California, but
an easterner in origin, felt the state to be a cultural backwater, where
few sophisticated people came except to sojourn for the winter. Wheeler
lamented the fact that New York newspapers only mentioned California
when they recorded an earthquake, a murder, or some other freak
occurrence. While President Wheeler's statement contained a kernel
of truth, for a new state California did possess more than the beginnings
of culture and learning. Culturally speaking, until late in this period,
there were two Californias—San Francisco and the rest of the state.

Painting was one art in which Californians regularly dabbled. Among
the early artists was Charles C. Nahl, who had been born into an artistic
family in Germany. Possessing some knowledge of European technique
and traditions, he painted the California scene extensively. His best works
were *Sunday in the Mines* and *The Fandango*.

Three painters of the school of heroic landscape were Albert Bierstadt,

Thomas Hill, and Thomas Moran. Bierstadt was born in Germany in 1830 and came to America as a child. Until his death in 1902, he enthusiastically depicted the wonders of Yosemite and the Sierra. His contemporary Thomas Hill (1829–1913) started his artistic career as a coach painter. Switching to more serious work, he began painting canvasses of mountain views. Although mildly popular in his own day, his work is now largely ignored. Thomas Moran (1837–1926) studied painting in Europe. In California he painted western scenes. Although in his most creative period he was not as well received as Bierstadt or Hill, later critics have ranked him above his two contemporaries.

William Keith (1838–1911) may have been the most distinctive of all California landscape artists. It has been reported that the famous landscape artist George Inness once remarked, "I am the greatest artist in America, and the second greatest is William Keith of San Francisco." Keith was jointly influenced by his friend Inness and the French Barbizon school. He sought poetic mood and subjective harmony in his work. Avoiding the massive scenes of Bierstadt and Moran, he painted instead quiet groves, hillsides and brooks. His pictures were remarkable for their effects of light and shade.

With the decline in popularity of California landscape artists, new influences from the eastern United States and Europe affected California painting. In the late nineteenth century, impressionism, eclecticism, Munich genre painting and French romanticism, all influenced California artists. The Bohemian Club of San Francisco—with a membership of both artists and patrons—was founded in the early seventies. This organization fostered a host of minor artistic figures working in what was called the "new art." In 1874 the influential California School of Fine Arts was established. Other events which nurtured popular interest in the arts were the organization of the San Francisco Institute of Arts in 1874, the establishment of the E. B. Crocker Art Gallery in Sacramento in 1884, and the founding of the M. H. de Young Memorial Museum in San Francisco in 1895.

With the population growth of Los Angeles in the last years of the nineteenth and early part of the twentieth centuries, artistic activities were gradually fostered in southern California. The Southwest Museum was established in 1903 and was followed by the Los Angeles Museum of History, Science, and Art, established in 1913. The Los Angeles Art Association was organized in 1923.

California's first widely recognized sculptor was Douglas Tilden. Born in 1860, Tilden received his education at Berkeley and Paris. He received his greatest acclaim for *The Football Players* in Berkeley and San Francisco's *Mechanics' Fountain*. Among other California sculptors, the work of Arthur Putnam has won wide recognition. Putnam, born in Mississippi in 1873, came to San Francisco at the age of seven. His childhood was darkened by accidents and poverty. Nonetheless, as a young man, he became an art student whose figures of wild animals were acclaimed even by Parisian art critics. Putnam was stricken with a brain tumor in 1911, which left him a partially paralyzed invalid, unable to sculpt any longer. He lived out the last nineteen years of his life a bitter, wasted man.

California strongly influenced one of the most original of American thinkers—the unorthodox Henry George. Born in Philadelphia in 1839, George came to California at the age of nineteen. Working as a sailor and then as a printer, he moved freely around California. All his life Henry George would be impetuous and nervously active. He then became a reporter and an editor, eventually settling in San Francisco. George, who was a strident social critic, favored the San Francisco workingmen's cause, staunchly arguing for immediate reforms such as the eight-hour day. Soon noting the contrast between the wealthy landowner with his high-priced land and the penniless workers, George diagnosed the extent of the social illness and advanced a cure—the single tax. This was one of the few original economic theories formulated by an American. Actually George's diagnosis of the causes of poverty was more profound and sophisticated than his cure. George decried what he called the unearned increment which accrued to landlords, who did little to improve the value of their land, yet reaped a rich reward when the growth of California made their holdings more valuable. George proposed a single tax on this unearned increment, which would be sufficient to support all necessary government. George claimed his panacea would lift the burden of taxation from most people, destroy monopoly, eliminate speculation and restore economic equality. Although it sounds wistfully inadequate today, his proposal, which found its best expression in *Progress and Poverty*, published in 1879, struck a responsive chord all over the world. Over two million copies of the book were quickly sold to poor Kansas farmers, as well as to slum dwellers of London, Paris, Moscow and Shanghai. Poor men painfully sounded out the words of George's vision of a better human society. Admiringly called the "Bayard of the Poor," George influenced men as diverse as Americans Hamlin Garland and Clarence Darrow, Bernard Shaw and Sidney Webb in England, Count Leo Tolstoy of Russia, and Sun Yat-sen of China. George quickly became an international figure and moved to New York, where he became a professional lecturer. In 1886 he unsuccessfully ran for mayor of New York. He died in 1897, leaving behind him many ardent disciples who tirelessly spread his doctrines.

Another California thinker of a novel turn was Josiah Royce. Royce was born in Grass Valley, California, in 1855. Twenty years later, after graduating from the University of California, Royce studied abroad at

Leipzig and Göttingen and then returned to study at Baltimore's Johns Hopkins University, where he earned a doctor of philosophy degree in 1878. After four years of teaching English at the University of California, Royce took a lectureship in philosophy at Harvard. He based his theories of philosophy upon the concept of individuality and human will—a sort of monistic idealism. Royce, like Henry George, was distressed by the abuses of land monopoly and railroad control that he saw in his native state. Royce published his first essay in the *Overland Monthly* as early as 1875, following this with a long, versatile publishing career in several different literary forms. When the Houghton Mifflin Company sponsored a series concerning all of the American states—the *American Common-wealths*—they asked Royce to contribute the volume on California. In 1886, Royce wrote *California*, in which he presented the state as graphically demonstrating the American character. As an idealist and nonconformist, Royce found much to criticize in the building of California. Royce's reforming tendencies found better expression in his novel *The Feud of Oakfield Creek*, which described the struggles of farmers with the railroad. Since Royce did not write in a popular style, his writings did not circulate as widely as George's had. Royce lived out his life at Harvard, writing upon philosophical subjects until his death in 1916.

At Stanford University, two unorthodox thinkers briefly taught during this period. They both left, after having offended sensitive trustees. They were Edward A. Ross (1866–1951), who taught at Stanford between 1893 and 1900 while writing his iconoclastic volume *Social Control* (1901), and Thorstein Veblen, who taught there from 1906 to 1909. Veblen had already written *The Theory of the Leisure Class* (1899) and *The Theory of Business Enterprise* (1904).

During the late nineteenth and early twentieth centuries, one of the most creative groups in California were the writers. They enjoyed the heritage of the gold-rush writers, as well as the stimulation of the presence of the short-term Californians, Bret Harte and Mark Twain. In addition the literary journals of San Francisco were less stodgy and more ready than eastern magazines to publish the work of unestablished writers.

Great literary figures also visited California and wrote there. Motherly Helen Hunt Jackson, who wrote of the mistreatment of the California Indians, was a New England writer of children's stories. In 1884 she wrote *Ramona*, which became immensely popular. Ironically, the authoress wrote the novel to arouse the public's indignation about the plight of California Indians. Instead, the reading public accepted it as an idealization of California's Spanish past, and the book fostered the growth of a romanticized Spanish tradition in southern California.

Robert Louis Stevenson visited California in 1879–80, living for a time in San Francisco and Monterey. Several of his later works had California themes. A young British journalist, Rudyard Kipling, found San Francisco inhospitable because, during a brief visit, he failed to interest the city's editors in his writings. Another writer, Gelett Burgess, who made a name for himself as a humorist, lived in California for a few years around the turn of the century. While editing *The Lark* for a San Francisco publisher, he gained a measure of fame with his nonsense rhyme—"Purple Cow."

The Polish novelist Henryk Sienkiewicz also briefly visited California. His visit was related to the utopian Modjeska colony. Sienkiewicz, who later became world famous by writing *Quo Vadis?* and many other novels, was then only thirty years old. As one of a group of eleven Poles who emigrated from Russian tyranny in their native country, he sought a haven in California in 1876. The party was headed by Helena Modjeska, Poland's leading actress, her second husband, Count Chlapewski, and her son, Ralph Modjeska. They found refuge in the little Orange County German-settled community of Anaheim, because they had heard stories of its favorable climate and thought they would face fewer problems there than in an English-speaking settlement. They attempted a sort of Brook Farm experiment, but personality conflicts and lack of agricultural experience eventually forced them to abandon their enterprise. Modjeska returned to the stage. After living for awhile in a hut at Anaheim and working as a salesclerk in Los Angeles, Sienkiewicz returned to Europe. He drew upon his California sojourn as background for some twenty essays and short stories, including "A Comedy of Errors" and "Orso." Although he could not resist some caustic comments on California life, because of his disillusioning experiences in southern California, he always maintained a romantic view of the state as a sunny haven.

Prominent among the writers who claimed California as their home, even though they were born elsewhere, was author Frank Norris. Born in Chicago in 1870, Norris grew up in California. Leaving the University of California, he went to study art in Paris, where he fell under the spell of the French realistic novelist Émile Zola. Returning to California, he became a leader in the movement toward realism in American writing by producing novels, *McTeague* in 1899, *The Octopus* in 1901, and *The Pit* in 1903. The last two books were part of a trilogy which Norris never lived to complete. His death at thirty-two cut short a brilliantly begun career as a romantic realist.

Writing in the same vein of social criticism, but even more bitterly and vindictively than Norris, was Ambrose Bierce. With his tart wit and acid pen, Bierce for decades dominated the California literary world. He spent a boyhood of poverty on farms in Ohio and Indiana before enlisting in the Union Army, emerging as a brevet major in 1864, while still only twenty-two. Coming to San Francisco, he took a job as a watchman at the Mint, but soon began working for various California journals. He joined the tide of California writers who went to Great Britain to become curiosities and pets of British drawing-room society. After four years his popularity faded, and he reluctantly returned to California. He then attempted writing poetry, epigrams and realistic Civil War tales. He also posed as the "Devil's Lexicographer," writing such ironic definitions as "A saint is a dead sinner revised and edited." In time he wrote a column, "Prattle," for William Randolph Hearst's San Francisco *Examiner*. Too misanthropic to be a really likeable character, Bierce was respected and read by most literate Californians. In 1913, when he was past seventy, he decided to cover the Mexican revolution. He disappeared south of the border into the "good, kind darkness," amid the maelstrom of the Mexican civil war. He was never again heard from.

Of a much different sort was another California literary figure, Joaquin Miller. Born Cincinnatus Hiner in Indiana around 1839, he was probably taken to Oregon in 1852. A heavy curtain of Miller's tall tales obscures the details of his early life. From Oregon, he wandered into Lassen County, where he lived with the Indians and reputedly fathered a half-breed daughter. After a time, he probably drifted back to Oregon for further schooling. In 1870, clad in leather clothes and uttering boisterous war whoops, he descended upon San Francisco, where he was soon included among the literary men of that city. In the same year, he published at his own expense *Pacific Poems*, which won him wide attention in literary circles. Capitalizing upon his fame, he went to Great Britain and toured the island, reading his poetry at literary gatherings of lords and ladies. At these soirées he dressed picturesquely in what the Britons believed was typical miner's garb. In time Europeans tired of his flamboyant theatricals, and he returned to California in 1885. He bought cheap land in the Oakland hills and built "The Hights" (as he spelled it), where he hoped to found a literary colony. He took the name of Joaquin, after the California bandit, Joaquin Murietta, who was the hero of his longest poem. He also became the literary editor of *The Golden Era*, and when that journal moved south, he went with it. However, since the San Diego land boom had about ended by the time he arrived, he returned to Oakland. He lived out his life in his Oakland retreat, dying in 1913.

Another poet associated with California was Edwin Markham. Although born in Oregon in 1852, Markham moved as a child to California. He worked on ranches and studied at San Jose Normal School (now San Jose State), and became a teacher in Oakland. In 1899 he wrote *The Man with the Hoe and Other Poems*. Markham's inspiration for the title poem came from a picture by the French painter Jean François Millet. Written in blank verse, this poem of protest against the "lords and rulers in all lands" won Markham instant fame. It was translated into more than forty languages and ultimately earned for him over a quarter of a million dollars. The success of Markham's poem alarmed conservative Collis P. Huntington who offered a $750 prize to the poet who would write the best answer to "The Man with a Hoe." John Vance Cheyney, a minor poet from San Diego, won the award, but his counterattack upon Markham's poem did nothing to dim its popularity. As a result of his international reputation, Markham moved to New York, where he resided until his death in 1940. Interestingly, Markham sang the praises of California from his self-imposed exile in a highly laudatory book, *California the Wonderful,* published in 1914.

Another California poet was Edward Rowland Sill. The Connecticut-born Sill was educated at both Yale and Harvard. In 1862, in his twenty-third year, he came to California and worked as a cowboy and postal clerk in the Sacramento Valley. Later he taught school in Oakland and became a professor of English at the University of California from 1874 to 1882. He left teaching to become a full-time writer. Two of his poems, "The Fool's Prayer" and "Opportunity," became standard pieces in contemporary anthologies.

Nor were poetesses absent from the California literary scene. Ina Donna Coolbrith enjoyed a great vogue as a writer of sentimental poems. Born Josephine D. Smith, she was the niece of Mormon leader Joseph Smith. Her mother, Agnes Coolbrith, had married the Mormon prophet's younger brother, Don Carlos Smith. Four months after Ina's birth in 1841, her father died. Her mother broke with the Mormon Church and with her child left its settlement at Nauvoo in Illinois. In St. Louis, Agnes Coolbrith met and married a lawyer, William Pickett. With her mother and stepfather, Ina was brought to Los Angeles.

Ina later liked to boast that she was the first student in a Los Angeles school and the first woman to be both married and divorced in Los Angeles County. After an unhappy marriage in 1861, Ina Coolbrith, as she now called herself, went up to San Francisco. She had already published verses in the papers of southern California and had enjoyed some local fame in Los Angeles as a poetess. In San Francisco, she continued her writing career, eventually acting as a sort of den mother to a number of younger literary figures. Mary Austin, Jack London and George Sterling all accepted help and encouragement from her in launching their writing careers. In 1915 she was made the first poet laureate of California—an honor she cherished until her death in 1928.

Mary Austin's bitter experiences with poverty warped and twisted her writing into something grotesquely beautiful. She was born in 1868 to a Yorkshire emigrant father and a pioneer mother. Growing up in Carlinville, Illinois, Mary Austin, then Mary Hunter, was a bookish, homely girl who was never accepted by her family, including her widowed mother. With her family, Mary came West in 1888, during the land boom in southern California. After a sojourn in the boom town of Monrovia, the Hunters moved into the hill country that lay between Los Angeles and the San Joaquin Valley. They soon discovered that inexperienced home-steaders were a poor match for the drought and loneliness of the country. In 1892, Mary Hunter married Stafford Wallace Austin and settled at Lone Pine in the southern end of Owens Valley. In the next fifteen years, the Austins suffered from both poverty and an unhappy marriage. Mary taught school in several California towns and turned for solace to her writing. In 1903 she wrote *The Land of Little Rain,* a series of sketches of life in the Owens Valley desert. For several years she sought refuge in an artist colony in Carmel, and after 1911 lived abroad much of the time. In all, she wrote eight books with a California background.

The dashing, colorful Jack London was a native Californian who was born in San Francisco in 1876, the illegitimate son of an astrologer and a spiritualistic medium. Jack London was largely self-raised, and while still very young worked as a roustabout and small-boat thief in the Bay area. He shipped out on a long, Pacific sealing trip, and later took part in the Klondike gold rush. Back in California, he fell under the influence of Ina Coolbrith and the poet George Sterling. From them he learned what books to read and acquired a veneer of learning. His writing he learned in a painful, self-taught manner, which he described in his autobiographical novel *Martin Eden* (1909). His popular novels *The Call of the Wild* (1903) and *The Sea Wolf* (1904) established him as a well-known writer. His literary style was uneven, but at his best he captured the smell of the sea and the sound of twigs snapping in the cold, as few other authors ever have. For a time, London was an aggressive socialist, but he died at forty, disillusioned by all "isms." His literary output of fifty books in seventeen years was amazing, considering his precarious health and constant battles with alcoholism.

Poet George Sterling is more important as a sort of literary catalyst than as a poet of light odes and sonnets. Born in 1869, Sterling came from a wealthy family, but he spurned a business career to live in a world of books. He numbered among his friends in literary circles such diverse types as Edwin Markham, Mary Austin and Joaquin Miller. He was per-haps as close to Ambrose Bierce as anyone ever got. He also served as guide and father confessor to Jack London. Sterling founded a literary colony at Carmel, where he gave sanctuary to both London and Austin. His colony drew budding novelist Sinclair Lewis and the crusading writer Upton Sinclair. The latter was Sterling's more successful rival in a torrid love triangle which adversely affected Sterling's literary output and general health. Nevertheless, he survived his friends, growing ever more lonely and sad. In 1926, Sterling killed himself with poison in his room in San Francisco's Bohemian Club.

As for Upton Sinclair, he had already gained a measure of fame before he came to California with his muckraking novel *The Jungle*. Sinclair settled in Pasadena and wrote many books. In the 1930's, he stepped out of his literary role to make a memorable, though unsuccessful, try for the California governorship.

Gertrude Atherton was born in San Francisco in 1857 and lived out her life in the Bay area. She began her literary career in the late 1880's, and among her early successes were several novels of Spanish California. In 1914, Gertrude Atherton wrote an unconventional but interesting account called *California—An Intimate History*.

A host of minor popular writers either visited California or made the state their home. California's literary output was amazing in quantity, even if it was of widely varying literary merit.

California journalism, which had enjoyed such a lusty beginning in the gold-rush decade, did not slacken in pace during the succeeding years. In 1865 in San Francisco, two young brothers, Charles and Michael H. de Young, founded a paper which they called *The Dramatic Chronicle* and whose initial issue appeared on January 16, 1865. It began as a four-page newspaper with sheets ten by thirteen and one-half inches. As its name implied, it was principally interested in theatrical activities, although from its inception it carried some general news. As a result, in April 1865, when several Democratic journals in San Francisco had been sacked by rioting mobs seeking vengeance for Lincoln's assassination, the *Chronicle* decided to exploit the circulation gap caused by their disappearance from the newsstands by printing extra editions which described the melancholy events in Washington following that presidential tragedy.

However, it was over three years later before the *Chronicle* dropped the word "dramatic" from its title and styled itself *The Daily Morning Chronicle* to signify its conversion to a general newspaper. Bret Harte was among the early contributors. The *Chronicle* made history when it became the only important San Francisco daily to support the ratification of the California Constitution of 1879. Its reputation grew steadily and the distinguished British observer of the American scene, James Bryce, said of it ". . . it was ably written and went everywhere. . . ." The decline and ultimate disappearance of the formerly preeminent newspaper, the *Alta California*, left a vacuum which was partially filled by the rising *Chronicle*.

Another paper which filled the void left by the *Alta*'s demise was the *Examiner*. This latter sheet was founded in 1865 upon the wreckage of an earlier Democratic paper. In 1887, wealthy mining investor and United States Senator George Hearst gave it to his son, William Randolph

Hearst. Young Hearst then launched himself upon a publishing career which was to make his name internationally famous. Hearst, who started as a militant crusader, ran the *Examiner* with a staff recruited from his college classmates. The *Examiner* literally made news when a reporter dived from a ferryboat to test the vessel's lifesaving procedures. The reporter's colleagues stood by with stop watches to time the efficiency of the operation. Lurid and sensational feature stories became the order of the day. With these techniques, the *Examiner* drew thousands of readers and became the mighty senior paper of a far-flung chain owned by Hearst.

Outside of San Francisco, journalism in California also recorded many advances. The McClatchy family founded the influential Sacramento *Bee* in 1857. In time the cities of Modesto and Fresno had their own counterpart *Bees*. The McClatchy family soon became noted for its independent journalism, as it spoke for and to the great valley. The McClatchy family championed the cause of the small farmers against the large ranchers. Editorially, they thundered for a heavy real-estate tax that would break up the land monopoly.

In Los Angeles a new figure appeared upon the journalistic horizon—the bombastic, personal journalist Colonel Harrison Gray Otis. Otis had been born in 1837 on a farm near Marietta, Ohio, and was named for an uncle who had been a Massachusetts senator. Otis attended a country school until he was fourteen, when he left home to work in a print shop. Later he attended an academy. At twenty he married. Four years later, when the Civil War broke out, he enlisted as a private. Taking part in fifteen battles, he was wounded several times and ultimately reached the rank of lieutenant colonel. Back in civilian life, he obtained a few minor political posts, serving for a time as editor of the Union veterans' organ, *The Grand Army Journal*. In 1870 Otis crossed the continent and became editor of a weekly, the Santa Barbara *Press*. In 1882, after failing to obtain any patronage post of his choice, he bought a one-quarter interest in the Los Angeles *Times*, which had been started the previous year. By 1886 he had obtained control of the paper.

Otis was a large, aggressive man who wore a walrus mustache and a goatee. In his booming voice and in the editorial columns of his newspaper, he declaimed about the future greatness of southern California. With his paper, he helped to build it into a region worthy of his dream. He made the *Times* into the mightiest daily in Los Angeles. In addition, he molded the paper into a rabid antilabor, antisocialist organ. The colonel equated any anti-Republican or anti-laissez faire politician or public figure with the devil himself. Until Otis's death in 1917, he was the preeminent journalistic figure in southern California.

Only a few years after Otis acquired the *Times*, he hired a circulation

Overland travelers at Palm Springs about 1898.
*Collection of Historical Photographs, Title Insurance and Trust Company,
Los Angeles, California*

Old Town, west from Presido Hill, 1898.
Courtesy of Title Insurance and Trust Company, San Diego, California

A group of loggers sitting and standing in the undercut of a giant redwood just before it was felled in the northwestern California of the late nineteenth or early twentieth century. *Ericson Collection Prints, Humboldt State College Library*

The port of Arcata, since closed by silting of the channel in Humboldt Bay, in its heyday a lumber-shipping center.

Cleaning up the rubble following the San Francisco earthquake
of April 18, 1906.

Fires on Market Street following the San Francisco earthquake of April 18, 1906.
Courtesy of Wells Fargo Bank, San Francisco, California

San Diego railroad station (no date).

Plank road and telephone poles across the sand dunes between the
Colorado River and Imperial Valley.

Old Fisherman's Wharf, Monterey, California.

Courtesy of Monterey Peninsula Chamber of Commerce,
Visitors and Convention Bureau, Monterey, California

manager, Henry Chandler, who three years before, at eighteen, had left Dartmouth College and had come West to seek a cure for his tuberculosis. Young Chandler regained his health and worked so efficiently as circulation manager that he soon was noticed by Otis himself. Otis beamed kindly upon this energetic young man and interposed no objection when Chandler married his daughter. In time, Chandler became Otis' chief assistant and, in due course, his heir.

An expression of the growing cultural sophistication of California was the increased development of colleges and universities. The spectacular growth of population in this period, in addition to the growing American tendency to seek an education, contributed to the expansion of higher education.

At the University of California at Berkeley, after Dr. David C. Gilman had resigned as president in 1876, he was succeeded by an eminent scientist, John Le Conte, famous for his work in electricity. During Le Conte's five-year term as president, he succeeded in attracting some of the nation's leading scientists to Berkeley. A number of mediocre presidents followed him at the University until 1899, when Benjamin Ide Wheeler was chosen to preside there. Wheeler was an aggressive president and often rode a white horse around the campus to better supervise all details of campus life. He was born in Massachusetts of a pioneer New England family and had graduated from Brown University in 1875. In 1885 he gained his Ph.D. in linguistics from Heidelberg and then taught at Cornell for thirteen years, until he was called to the presidency of the University of California. Wheeler quickly grasped day-to-day control of the school away from the regents. As the regents surrendered many prerogatives to him, the understanding was, of course, that Wheeler had to assume full responsibility for all operations of the institution. This arrangement worked well. From the two thousand students largely concentrated at Berkeley (there were only a few students of agriculture at Davis and of medicine at a medical center at San Francisco), the university expanded to 12,000 at all of its branches by the close of his presidency in 1919. In addition many physical landmarks were added to the Berkeley campus during his tenure of office, such as the Campanile and Sather Gate. Wheeler also instituted a summer session, which became increasingly popular over the years, and permitted the first real student self-government through the organization of the Associated Students. The last years of Wheeler's presidency were shadowed by his stridently pro-German opinions. Wheeler had developed a great affection for imperial Germany when he had studied there in his youth, and had often subsequently visited there. As a result, when World War I broke out, his voice was raised to defend the Kaiser's conduct of the war. This jarring note was shrugged off by regents, students and faculty until after the United States entered the war on the Allied side in April 1917. Then Wheeler's utterances became a seemingly intolerable burden to the regents and faculty. In a violation of academic freedom which hopefully would not be tolerated today, Wheeler was shunted aside from the active management of the University. An advisory council of three prominent faculty members, well known for their pro-Allied views, exercised the real executive power of the University until Wheeler's retirement at age sixty-five. In 1927, Wheeler died while living abroad.

A branch state normal school was opened in Los Angeles in August 1882, as a sister institution to the normal school then functioning at San Jose. In 1919 this institution was elevated to the position of the southern branch of the University of California. In 1927 it was made coordinate with the campus at Berkeley under the title University of California at Los Angeles, or as it is more popularly known, UCLA. Other normal schools were established during the late nineteenth or early twentieth centuries at Chico, San Diego, San Francisco, Santa Barbara, Fresno and Humboldt in Arcata. In 1921 these normal schools became teachers colleges, and in 1935 state colleges.

As for private institutions, by 1870 the Catholics had added St. Mary's, Saint Ignatius (now the University of San Francisco), and Loyola of Los Angeles to their original men's college at Santa Clara. A Catholic girls' school, College of the Holy Names, also was founded during the same period. Mills College began as a young ladies' seminary in Benicia. In 1865 a former Hawaiian missionary and his wife, a Dr. and Mrs. Cyrus T. Mills, taught students those subjects fit for genteel young ladies. In 1871 the school was moved to its present site in Oakland and in 1885 was elevated to collegiate status as a Christian but nonsectarian institution. In 1887 a charter was obtained by a group of Presbyterian ministers and laymen as Occidental Presbyterian University of Los Angeles, later called Occidental College. A few months after Occidental's founding, a group of New England Congregationalists started Pomona College. At the Quaker colony at Whittier, a college gradually evolved during the nineties. In 1909 the Baptists started Redlands University, which held its first classes in a church.

Generally, all of those colleges had the goal of teaching the liberal arts. A different kind of institution was started by Amos G. Throop at Pasadena about 1890. It evolved from Throop Polytechnic Institute to Throop College of Technology to the California Institute of Technology, with emphasis upon scientific and engineering subjects. In 1921 the great physicist Robert A. Millikan came to Pasadena and accepted the chairmanship of the executive council of the California Institute of Technology. With his connections in the world of science and with the help of various philanthropists in southern California, by the time of his retirement Millikan had succeeded in building Cal Tech into a world renowned leader in scientific education and research.

The University of Southern California, a Methodist Episcopal church-related institution, was started in 1879 by the donation of some land in southwestern Los Angeles by a Jew, a Catholic and a Protestant. The first college of USC, that of the Liberal Arts and Sciences, was opened on October 4, 1880. Its early years were ones of struggle. In 1891 it had only 192 students studying in its college preparatory school and only twenty-five full-fledged collegiate students. Only after World War I did its student enrollment boom when the university became known to all sports fans in the nation for the excellence of its athletic teams.

However, the greatest private institution of higher learning started in California during this period, and the one which attracted the greatest attention, was Leland Stanford Junior University, started by the Leland Stanfords in memory of their son. In 1885 they announced that they intended to found what would be the mightiest university in America. They conveyed property to the school worth six million dollars, and added another million and a quarter dollars for buildings. In all, it was expected that the new school would boast an endowment of $30 million, or six times as much as either Columbia or Harvard could count. The cornerstone of the first building was laid with appropriate ceremonies in 1887.

The Stanfords selected as president of their new institution the remarkable David Starr Jordan. A New Yorker by birth, Jordan had attended Cornell, Indiana Medical College and Butler University. By speciality he was an icthyologist, but he was also a man of wide interests. In 1885 he had become president of Indiana University. Six years later, he was recruited by the Stanfords to head their university. He served as president of Stanford until 1913 and as chancellor until 1916. There had been some skepticism that Stanford University would ever find sufficient students to justify the superior faculty which had been gathered. These fears proved groundless. The University started with 559 students and by 1894 had 1,100 enrolled. Ironically its early problems centered around the problems of finance. The panic of 1893 and the death of Leland Stanford threatened to dissipate what had seemed to be an inexhaustible pool of wealth. Mrs. Stanford came to the rescue by supplementing the university's funds with income from her husband's estate. She practiced all manner of small personal economies in order to devote extra funds to the university. In the end, despite some anxious days, it survived with its excellent faculty intact. Herbert Hoover was among the first graduates of Stanford.

Although California did not actually establish the first junior college in

America, it did pioneer in their development. Today these colleges call themselves "community colleges" and have their own state-level board of governors. The California junior college came to offer the first two years of standard collegiate academic fare, as well as a terminal vocational curriculum. In 1907 the California legislature authorized public junior colleges. Fresno was the first area to take advantage of the law, founding a junior college in the spring of 1910. In 1913 the first junior college to be supported by a school district opened in Fullerton. Soon public junior colleges were common in most parts of California. By 1940 there were forty-two junior colleges in the state.

The oldest scientific body in the West, the California Academy of Sciences of San Francisco, continued its growth during this period. Medical doctors were prominent in its early history, since theirs was the most common type of scientific training then available. As we have already seen, the society was founded in 1853 and opened a one-room museum at 622 Clay Street. After the founding of the University of California, there was some discussion by the regents of that institution and leading Academy members concerning the possibility that the two institutions might merge. Nothing was decided, however. In 1872, with financial help from Charles Crocker and Leland Stanford, the Academy opened its first formal museum in a rented building at the corner of California Street and Grant Avenue. In 1891, through the philanthropy of eccentric millionaire James Lick, the Academy found a new home in a large museum building on Market Street. The San Francisco earthquake and fire of 1906 destroyed the Academy's library and museum, which had been half a century in the building. It was not until 1916 that the Academy was able to open its doors in a new and more modern museum. In a few years, through the generosity of Ignatz Steinhart, the Academy added to its holdings the first large public aquarium west of the Atlantic seaboard. By the late 1920's, the Academy could boast a membership of 1,200.

California libraries have been handicapped by the fact that great libraries are only built over a long period of time, and California has lacked this time. The State Library at Sacramento is the oldest research library in the state. However, in its early days, political appointees were its librarians and grossly mismanaged the instituton, so that the effects of its early start in the 1850's were largely vitiated. With the purchase of the Bancroft Collection of western Americana, the University of California at Berkeley Library became preeminent as a center for the scholarly study of this subject. Stanford University in time acquired the materials for the Hoover Library of War, Peace, and Revolution, which furnished vital information upon aspects of the First World War, the Russian Revolution and various relief efforts after these events.

Perhaps the most unique library in California is the Henry E. Huntington Library and Art Gallery in San Marino. Henry Huntington, the transportation and real estate millionaire, collected books, rare manuscripts and art treasures. Between 1917 and 1922, by various deeds of gift, he put his collection and a two-hundred-acre estate to house it in the hands of five trustees who were charged to maintain the art and book treasures for public use. At Huntington's death, the library and art collection were valued at 30 million dollars with an endowment of 8 million dollars. There are three principal divisions of the physical properties—the Library, the Art Gallery and the Botanical Gardens. The library contains a 1455 Gutenberg Bible and the Ellesmere Chaucer on vellum, as well as hundreds of thousands of books and thousands of letters and documents concerning English and American history. It has a collection of California material second only to the Bancroft collection.

Although not in the halls of higher learning or in literary societies, the history of California was already being written on a heroic scale. While it is true that the first general history of California was Franklin Tuthill's *History of California* (San Francisco, 1866), this work was not comprehensive and is rarely referred to today even by the most erudite historians. It remained for Hubert Howe Bancroft to attempt the task of writing the first definitive history of California, from its exploration to settlement.

Bancroft was born at Granville, Ohio on May 5, 1832, of New England ancestry. He received only a common-school education before he left home to enter business as a bookseller for his brother-in-law in Buffalo. He was attracted to California by the gold rush. In 1865, after some time spent in and around the mines, Bancroft, with a loan of $5,500 from his sister, established H. H. Bancroft & Company in San Francisco. This firm both published and sold books and soon became enormously successful. As a personal hobby, he began acquiring books about the history of the Pacific coast. When he sold his library to the University of California in 1905, it contained 60,000 volumes.

At first, in the late 1860's, Bancroft planned to use his collection to publish an encyclopedia of the Pacific coast. Soon he realized that a multivolume history of the region would be a better vehicle to propagate the information in his library. From 1874 to 1890, Bancroft issued thirty-nine volumes under his own name. Seven are labeled as the history of California. Actually, he only wrote a small portion of the total work, using many literary assistants who authored the bulk of his volumes.

Bancroft seems consistently to have toadied to the important people of the regions about which he wrote (or had written for him). Despite this defect, his works had great value as a pioneering attempt to write the history of the Pacific coast area of North America. Bancroft, as editor and promoter of this mighty enterprise, made available a monumental amount of information. In addition to his other services, he preserved a mass of priceless historical source material which might otherwise have been lost to future generations. While his product was uneven in historical quality and literary workmanship, it contained a vast mine of minutiae. If it was not well digested and conformed to no overall view of history, it was still a compilation of historical knowledge which can never be safely ignored by later historians.

A second historian who worked generally at the same time as Bancroft was Theodore H. Hittell, a San Francisco lawyer. Hittell was born in Pennsylvania in 1830, but was raised in Ohio. His father was a doctor who enjoyed such prosperity that he could send all of his four sons and two daughters to college—a rarity for that time and region. After attending Oxford College (now Miami University) and Centre College, he transferred to Yale, where he was graduated in 1849. Then he studied law in Ohio and was admitted to the bar. After practicing law in Ohio for three years, he became dissatisfied and migrated to California to join his brother John, who had entered the newspaper business in San Francisco. Hittell had planned to go to the mines, but instead he entered the newspaper field in San Francisco, replacing James King of William as city editor of the San Francisco *Bulletin* after King's assassination. In 1861 he returned to his law practice, specializing in civil cases. In addition to building a lucrative practice, he was interested in writing upon legal subjects, and between 1863 and 1880 he compiled twelve volumes dealing with California and Nevada law. He continued to practice law sporadically as late as 1906, but increasingly from 1880 on gave more and more time to his historical writing. Hittell had always had some interest in history, but his desire to probe more deeply into California history was a result of the exhaustive research he had to undertake as background for the San Pablo land case. This case, first taken to court in 1868, was not settled until twenty-seven years later. During this time, Hittell had to consult extensively the 250,000 handwritten pages of records in the United States Surveyor General's office in San Francisco.

Hittell wrote steadily in the evening hours and by 1885 had published the first two volumes of a projected four-volume history of California. The first volume covered the Spanish period and the second dealt with the later Spanish and Mexican periods. In his last two volumes, published in 1897, Hittell carried the story of California to 1890. It was a more popular and manageable history than Bancroft's. For years it has remained the standard reference source and the most comprehensive history of the state.

The professional study of the history of California also began in this period. In 1907, the Native Sons of the Golden West proposed to endow a chair of California history at the University of California, but president

Benjamin Ide Wheeler demurred, probably because he doubted that a suitable occupant for the place could be found. In 1911, however, the history department brought Herbert E. Bolton to Berkeley for the very purpose of directing graduate research in the treasures of the Bancroft Library. Bolton was born in Wisconsin in 1870 and earned a bachelor's degree at the University of Wisconsin and a Ph.D. at Pennsylvania. Before coming to the University of California, he taught at Texas and Stanford. In Bolton's long career, he produced works on Kino, Anza, Crespi and Palóu. Before his death in 1953, he directed scores of doctoral dissertations in California history and also in Hispanic-American history. The era of the professional historian of California had flowered.

With the impetus of its gold-rush theater, San Francisco had become the foremost theatrical center in the West. Regularly, touring theatrical companies made the Chicago to Salt Lake City to San Francisco circuit. Theatrical fare in the city was increased in 1869, when the California Theater opened, under the joint direction of two actors, Lawrence Barrett and John McCullough. It became the scene of many stage successes. This theater was completely rebuilt in 1888 and remained popular with drama lovers until it was destroyed in the fire and earthquake of 1906.

San Francisco in 1877 was the scene of Helena Modjeska's debut in an English-speaking play. She journeyed to the city from Orange County, after her ill-starred attempt to found a utopian colony there. She had a successful stand, whereby she earned enough money to return to Europe.

For a time David Belasco, on the threshold of a notable career as an actor-producer, managed a San Francisco theater and directed a play in 1878 on the beginnings of Christianity that created a storm of controversy in the San Francisco press and pulpits.

Other theatrical notables who played San Francisco in the late nineteenth and early twentieth centuries—the "champagne days"—were Edwin Booth, Lillian Russell, Julia Marlow, Otis Skinner, De Wolfe Hopper, Sarah Bernhardt and John Barrymore.

While San Francisco was the center of the theater on the Pacific coast from the gold-rush days, the cities of southern California did not enjoy the same rich theatrical fare. Although minstrel shows and circuses went south after touring San Francisco, the first professional dramatic troupe to reach Los Angeles, according to the records, was the Stark and Royer Company in November 1860. At that time the troupe played to enthusiastic audiences in makeshift quarters called the Temple Theater. San Diego was visited in 1868 by a professional company who performed plays in both Spanish and English. For years thereafter, Los Angeles depended for its actors on thespians from San Francisco. Regularly, when the coastal steamer from San Francisco was late, the curtains in Los Angeles theaters had to be held. Actually Los Angeles did not have any elaborate theaters until the land boom of the 1880's greatly increased its population. Show folk did not consider Los Angeles a good theatrical city until after 1900.

One type of drama which enjoyed a great vogue in California was the outdoor theater based on Greek or Roman forms. The Greek Theater of the University of California in Berkeley became a favorite site, and Sara Bernhardt and Maude Adams both appeared there.

After 1900 the motion picture theater increasingly competed for the entertainment dollar with the legitimate stage in California, as it did throughout the nation. As a result, live drama vanished from the stages of the small California cities by the 1920's. Even San Francisco supported fewer productions than it formerly had. The golden age of the legitimate theater had passed.

In the "champagne days," California, and particularly San Francisco, did not fail to appreciate the musical arts. The Grand Opera House in San Francisco seated three thousand patrons and boasted that it possessed the largest cut-glass chandelier in America. Originally the Opera House was dedicated to dramatic performances, but then it switched to housing the opera. On the night before the San Francisco earthquake of 1906, Enrico Caruso and an all-star cast appeared there in *Carmen*. Perhaps the greatest musical theater of them all was the Tivoli. It started as a public beer garden in 1877. There the good burghers of San Francisco drank beer and listened to aggregations such as the Vienna Ladies' Orchestra. In 1879 the management decided to try a more elaborate production, Gilbert and Sullivan's *H. M. S. Pinafore*. This musical proved to be such a triumph that it ran for eighty-four consecutive nights. As a result, the Tivoli switched to presenting light and even grand opera during twelve-month seasons. The Tivoli, for twenty-six years after 1879, gave year-round performances which, it has been stoutly averred, constitutes an American theatrical record. The impresario of the Tivoli was the irrepressible "Doc" Leahy. The Tivoli charged low prices—only a quarter to a half dollar for admission—and catered to lower-middle-class and even day-laborer audiences. Its atmosphere was very democratic, and nobody "dressed" for the opera. It greatly popularized attendance at serious musical performances. Alice Nielsen rose to stardom from the ranks of the Tivoli chorus; Luisa Tetrazzini first came to musical prominence in a performance as Gilda in *Rigoletto* on the Tivoli stage in 1905. She became such a sensation in San Francisco that a gourmet dish—Chicken Tetrazzini—was named for her. Supposedly the first regular performance of Pietro Mascagni's one-act opera *Cavalleria Rusticana* was played there in 1890. The Tivoli's curtain went down on its last musical performance in November 1913, after the Italian composer Ruggiero Leoncavallo conducted his own opera *I Pagliacci*.

In San Francisco, opera faded in popularity after inroads caused by the depression of 1929 and the rise of talking movies. In the 1930's, the San Francisco Opera Association could only manage a season of a few weeks.

San Franciscans heard their first symphony orchestra in 1865 and from that date on have been interested in serious music. In 1911, the San Francisco Symphony became the first such musical organization to be aided by public funds.

Inhabitants of Los Angeles were handicapped in the enjoyment of operatic performances, since the city lacked an adequate opera house in this period. The Los Angeles Philharmonic was founded in 1919 and became a permanent fixture on the musical scene. The Hollywood Bowl was established in 1921 by an unpaid musical buff, Artie Mason Carter. When she failed to get support for her idea from the wealthy patrons of the arts, she built the bowl from contributions and tickets of the average symphony-goer. In time six-week summer concerts were given under the stars to as many as 25,000 people.

One form of theatrical pageant that is uniquely Californian and popularly plebian in taste is the Tournament of Roses, held in Pasadena on New Year's Day. In time this pageant also spawned the practice of sponsoring bowl games to match leading collegiate football teams. This affair had originally been suggested by the flower fetes in Nice. It began in 1890 as a kind of village festival to celebrate the midwinter flower season. In the beginning, residents decked their buggies with roses and went picnicking. In time pretty girls were placed on elaborate flower floats and paraded through the streets. Eventually the floats became more and more numerous, as entries came from all prominent California cities and even from foreign countries. Themes were chosen for the floats and decorations. High school marching bands came from all over the United States to parade. In 1902, to climax the festivities, the University of Michigan football team was invited to play Stanford University in what was called the Rose Bowl. A 49-to-0 victory for the midwesterners dampened the occasion. As a result, the Tournament of Roses officials turned to chariot races instead of football for the next dozen years to round out the day's festivities. Finally, as the result of the growing popularity of college football, in 1916 the Rose Bowl game was reinstituted as a permanent feature of the celebration. The Tournament of Roses thus became firmly fixed on the California scene as one of the hallmarks of the state's popular culture.

California's cultural growth between 1875 and 1920, while uneven, was on the whole impressive. In particular the institutions for the popular diffusion of culture became firmly established during this period. Brilliant individual practitioners of the performing and creative arts who lived in California would have been a credit to any region emerging from the frontier phase. California had successfully built a cosmopolitan society in which artistic skills from many areas joined and formed a new subculture in America.

TWENTY-SIX

Political Uprisings: The Progressives

DURING the period 1880–1900, the California political arena
continued to echo with the clash of partisan arms. For a time
this political era seemed to be as barren as the previous decade,
but soon public opinion clamored for a new morality in government.
Such a political situation was not achieved until the next decade, however.

Although George C. Perkins retired from the California governorship
at the close of his term in 1883, he did not retire from an active political
life. In 1893 he was appointed to the Senate upon the death of Stanford
and was reelected several times until 1915. He was commonly considered
the Senate spokesman for the Southern Pacific.

In the 1882 gubernatorial election to select a successor to Perkins, the
outspoken former Union general and perennial railroad commissioner
George Stoneman successfully opposed the rather colorless Republican,
Morris M. Estee, and two minor party candidates. Stoneman, a New
Yorker by birth, had graduated from West Point and had served a long
career as a regular army officer. During the Mexican War he served as an
officer in the Mormon battalion. In 1870–71, after a Civil War record that
was uneven in performance, Stoneman fought against the Apaches in
Arizona. He was suddenly relieved of his command amid growing complaints that he spent too much time at his ranch in California's San Gabriel Valley, hundreds of miles from the scene of active operations. After
having retired from the army and settled in California, Stoneman was
appointed in 1876 by Governor Irwin to serve two years as a railroad

commissioner. In 1879, under the new Constitution, Stoneman was elected railroad commissioner. In this post Stoneman was stridently anti-railroad, although the commission was able to accomplish little effective regulation. Consequently Stoneman enjoyed a popularity which did not coincide with his accomplishments. In 1882 he was easily nominated for governor by the Democrats over the wealthy George Hearst. Stoneman defeated his three opponents in the gubernatorial election, polling 90,000 votes out of 165,000 cast, setting the pace for a statewide Democratic sweep. Part of the Republicans' failure in this election was attributed to their part in the miner-farmer hydraulic-mining debris issue.

Although Stoneman had a detailed program for combatting the state's economic problems, he was singularly unsuccessful in persuading the legislature to pass much of it. Still Stoneman pursued an independent course as governor, and this action cost him a renomination when the Democratic Party bosses turned against him. Between 1882 and 1891 San Francisco's Democratic boss was a near-blind Irish saloonkeeper, Christopher A. Buckley. Buckley was always able to accommodate the railroad interests, and since that group feared Stoneman, Buckley gladly helped to turn him out of office. Despite his handicap, Buckley ruled the city's politics with an iron hand until 1891. At that time he hurriedly left the state while a grand jury investigation of his affairs was in progress.

The next successful Democratic gubernatorial candidate was a party hack with a distinguished appearance, Washington Bartlett. In the election Bartlett won with a minority of the vote because of minor party candidates. In his brief eight-month tenure, Bartlett ignored the railroad and corporation tax questions with which Stoneman had so unsuccessfully grappled. In September 1887, Bartlett was afflicted with Bright's disease and became the first California governor to die in office. He was succeeded by his lieutenant governor, Robert W. Waterman, who was a Republican. Bartlett had defeated the Republican gubernatorial candidate John F. Swift by only 654 votes and had been unable to carry his candidate for lieutenant governor to victory with him.

Before running for office, Waterman had been in the mining business and had obtained little experience in politics. Waterman spent most of his term as governor replacing Democratic appointees with deserving Republicans and preaching the virtues of rigid state economy. Waterman hoped to be nominated for a term in his own right, but the Republicans had been unimpressed with his record and so passed him over in favor of Henry H. Markham.

Markham, also a New Yorker, was a Civil War veteran who had moved to Pasadena in 1879. An attorney, he soon became involved in real estate and banking in the Pasadena area. In 1884 he won a congressional election in southern California, but after only one term, he retired to supervise his far-flung business interests. In 1890, as evidence of the growing political power of southern California, Markham was nominated to the Republican gubernatorial candidacy, despite the determined opposition of northern California Republican leaders. In the election, Markham defeated the Democratic candidate, Edwin B. Pond, mayor of San Francisco. The issues debated in this campaign included Markham's late arrival in California, his Civil War record, and his opponent's position concerning Chinese immigration into California. As evidence of Markham's political outlook, Senator Leland Stanford widely campaigned for him, as did Markham's old crony, Harrison Gray Otis of the Los Angeles *Times*. When he garnered 125,000 votes to Pond's 117,000, Markham became the first successful Republican gubernatorial candidate from southern California. While the voting trend across the nation eastward from the Rockies was primarily in favor of Democratic candidates, the Republicans triumphed in California. There was now a Republican governor, an overwhelming margin of Republicans in the California legislature and four Republicans in the state's six congressional seats.

Although Markham's accomplishments were minimal, his term of office was a troubled one. The panic of 1893 had struck California, and from 1893 to 1895 there was chronic labor unrest in the state. Markham's response was to call out the state militia to break a strike. During his tenure as governor, Markham's one notable accomplishment was to veto more appropriations than had any other governor in a single term. These bills which he vetoed were primarily public works projects which sought to relieve the ravages of unemployment plaguing California.

This unrest and dissatisfaction in California allowed the Democrats to win in the gubernatorial election of 1894. The successful Democratic candidate was James H. Budd, the last Democratic governor for forty-four years. As governor, Budd enjoyed another distinction—he was the first University of California graduate to become the state's chief executive. Born in Wisconsin, Budd was brought to California at the age of seven. Graduating with the first class from the university, he became an attorney, deserting his law practice for a single term in Congress. Although it was no secret that he was the Southern Pacific's choice for governor, in one of the many anomalies of the times he won the Democratic nomination. In order to still the cries that he was a tool of the Southern Pacific, he campaigned throughout the state, uttering antirailroad slogans.

Fearful that Budd seemed to be making headway among the voters, the Republicans spread rumors that Budd was a philanderer who had seduced a girl in his youth. Budd attempted to counter these charges by posing as a good family man as he toured the state in a buckboard with his wife. Evidently Budd was successful in combatting the smear campaign against him, for he defeated his Republican gubernatorial opponent by the close margin of two thousand ballots. Republicanism in California had become so pronounced by this time that two years later California, in the presidential election, voted contrary to the trend in the West and preferred goldbug William McKinley over William Jennings Bryan and his free silver platform. As a gold- rather than a silver-producing state, California had less incentive to support Bryan than did the Rocky Mountain area.

As governor, Budd accomplished little since his Republican legislature opposed most of his policies, among them a graduated tax on corporate profits. Budd retaliated by vetoing many appropriation bills favored by his legislative opponents. Since both his health and his political prospects were poor, Budd abandoned all attempts at reelection.

Like so many successful gubernatorial candidates, Republican Henry T. Gage was a transplanted New Yorker who had come to southern California at age twenty-two. As a lawyer he soon became identified with the Southern Pacific's interests and was their choice for governor. To clinch his nomination, Gage apparently made an agreement with Michael H. de Young, the publisher of the San Francisco *Chronicle*, whereby if the newspaperman would support him for the governorship, Gage would in turn back him for the United States Senate. During his campaign, Gage advocated a platform which ignored state issues in favor of attention-getting but irrelevant national problems. He faced formidable opposition —a jerry-built political coalition of Democrats, Populists, and Silver Republicans who were united behind a single gubernatorial candidate, San Francisco Congressman James G. Maguire. Maguire ran on a platform which vaguely condemned railroad, land and water monopolies. A third gubernatorial candidate, who illustrated the growing radicalism of some California laborers, was Socialist Labor Party member Job Harriman, who attracted more attention than votes.

Maguire tried to pin the railroad label upon Gage, but seemed unable to get his message to the electorate. This coalition was handicapped by the fact that, except for William Randolph Hearst's San Francisco *Examiner*, no major California newspaper endorsed Maguire. Predictably Gage won 148,000 votes to Maguire's 129,000. The Republicans also controlled the legislature.

The senatorial election (still accomplished by the legislature, since the direct election of United States senators was not achieved until the Progressive era) evolved into a great political deadlock. Gage broke his promise to support de Young for the Senate and as a result, no choice for senator had been made after 104 ballots. Eventually the legislature agreed upon an obscure Ventura rancher, Thomas R. Bard. The governor and the Southern Pacific interests generally regarded this choice as a defeat—a harbinger of more difficult political times for the railroad.

As governor, Gage suffered many embarrassments. When a bubonic plague broke out in San Francisco in 1900, the governor denied its existence because he correctly feared it would depress business conditions in the West Coast's busiest port. When caught in this lie, he suffered an additional loss of prestige. To the governor's intense disgust, an anti-Gage Republican club was organized by the reform mayor of Sacramento and a young maverick attorney, Hiram W. Johnson. Other anti-Gage clubs were organized throughout the state. Gage had counted upon a renomination in 1902, but he found that he simply could not command a majority of the delegates to the Republican state convention. The Southern Pacific had no intention of sticking with a losing candidate; it switched to a more attractive vote-getter, George C. Pardee, who easily won the party's gubernatorial nomination. Pardee became the first California governor to have been born within California since the American conquest. He was also a University of California graduate and had earned a medical degree from Heidelberg. Later Pardee enjoyed a prominent career in Oakland municipal politics.

Pardee was embarrassed in his campaign by the open Southern Pacific intervention upon his behalf. Nonetheless, he was able to convince enough of the electorate that he would be his own man as governor. When the results of the election came in, Gage had defeated the Democrats and their candidate, Franklin K. Lane (later a member of President Wilson's cabinet), by 146,000 to 143,000 votes. The Democrats were quite bitter over their narrow defeat and unsuccessfully challenged in court the validity of some five thousand ballots from Oakland and Los Angeles.

As governor, Pardee seemed to have trouble discerning the important issues and spent a disproportionate amount of his time selecting suitable textbooks for use in the state schools and getting the golden poppy made the California state flower. Yet he did succeed in establishing a progressive tax program for corporations, direct inheritances and insurance premiums.

On the whole, Pardee was a better than average governor, and normally could have anticipated a renomination. However, he had demonstrated too much independence for the Southern Pacific, and at an infamous Republican state convention at Santa Cruz in 1906, he was unceremoniously dumped in favor of a more pliant northern California congressman, James N. Gillett. Gillett was overwhelmingly nominated on the first ballot.

Gillett was born in Wisconsin, where he studied law, and then worked in the Pacific northwest lumber industry and eventually drifted southward to Eureka, California. He entered politics, won a number of minor offices, and then in 1902 he was elected to Congress and reelected two years later. In 1906, to the surprise of some political observers, he gave up his congressional seat to run for governor. The usual explanation was that he wanted the state office as a springboard to the United States Senate.

Gillett's selection as a candidate of the Union Pacific caused more than the usual indignation. Gubernatorial candidates of both parties ever since the 1860's had been tapped for the honor by the railroad without generating much in the way of resentment among the electorate. Yet the winds of change were blowing over California, and Gillett's nomination caused black headlines and scolding editorials in the press. California was becoming too populated to remain the fief of any one interest, no matter how powerful. Gillett might very well have been defeated except that William Randolph Hearst's ambition stood in the way. Hearst was unhappy with the Democratic gubernatorial nominee, Theodore A. Bell, who was opposed to his own aspirations. Bell had been busy uttering the right antirailroad slogans and might have been victorious had Hearst not split the anti-Republican vote. The publisher managed this split by forming the Independence League, which supported a spoiler candidate, William H. Langdon. In the election, Gillett polled 125,000 votes to Bell's 117,000, while Langdon picked up a decisive 45,000 ballots. Thus Gillett became the winner with a bare 41 per cent of the total votes cast.

As governor, Gillett tried to preserve a semblance of independence from the railroad. Although he did vainly call for a state pure food and drug law, his conservative frame of reference would not allow him to get in step with the progressive drumbeat of the times. In October 1907, Gillett faced a problem not of his own making when the financial panic of that year traveled west and caused several San Francisco banks to fail. Gillett was forced to ask the legislature, which he had called into a special session, to enact several palliative measures. These measures included extending the due period of state taxes and granting the governor the power to declare several additional commercial legal holidays to help the banks through the period of panic. Fortunately the economic turndown proved short-lived and California did not require additional measures to weather it successfully.

Some progressive measures were passed during Gillett's administration. In 1908 a direct primary law replaced the nominating convention with its smoke-filled rooms and closed-door bargaining. In addition the legislature enacted laws which established the beginnings of California's great network of highways.

By the end of Gillett's term, the Progressive movement had fully developed. The relics of the old political order were soon to be swept into the dustbin of history. This change was inevitable, for the railroad domination of California had become too obvious and heavy-handed. By 1910, Californians had come to blame the Southern Pacific for every ill that afflicted their state. It did no good to talk to them of more sophisticated causes—of fluctuations in international trade or the defalcations of local politicians. Many Californians saw railroad meddling in every falling price or shady deal. The image of the Southern Pacific had become one of a stone-hearted colossus.

Earlier there had been more substance to this image. In the early twentieth century the Southern Pacific had organized its political apparatus more tightly than ever. At the top its arch-political mechanic was its chief counsel, William F. Herrin, a nominal Democrat. An Oregonian by birth, Herrin had come to San Francisco after graduation from law school. Once established in San Francisco, he married a judge's daughter and joined a prestigious law firm. By 1900 he headed the Southern Pacific's "Political Bureau," as it was popularly known.

From the railroad's San Francisco headquarters, Herrin's influence extended into both major parties. Herrin's principal lieutenant was Walter Parker, who directed railroad political activities in southern California. The two men worked closely with Senator George C. Perkins, who functioned as the Southern Pacific's ambassador to the federal government.

The Southern Pacific's domination had finally developed strong counterforces within California. For decades the Southern Pacific had played Gulliver to the other Lilliputian corporations. The disorganized farmers, however, spoke with no single voice. In the early twentieth century the railroad found it had to deal with tightly knit cooperatives such as the Southern California Fruit Growers' Association and the Deciduous Fruit Protective League. The Los Angeles Chamber of Commerce also welded many divergent interests into a unified force. Since the inhabitants of Los Angeles had a strong tradition of antipathy to the Southern Pacific, it was possible to rally many shipping entrepreneurs who opposed the iron control the Southern Pacific had so long riveted upon the state.

The character of the California electorate was slowly changing also. They were becoming both more educated and more politically independent. Since Californians were very urban in their population distribution, many of them read a daily metropolitan newspaper; their children went to newly established high schools and colleges. California's literacy rate was high even in areas such as San Francisco, where the percentage of foreign-born citizens had been high. An informed electorate was certain to refuse to accept machine control indefinitely.

The Progressive movement in California and along the Pacific slope in general (Washington and particularly Oregon had powerful progressive coalitions) was created by such forces as the religious and moral influences brought from New England, interest in mass education, and the legacy of previous reform groups such as the Populists. A study of Progressive leaders has revealed them to be under forty, natives of the Midwest or California with northern European names. They were most often Congregationalists, Unitarians or Christian Scientists.

The Progressive movement in California had its genesis when two youthful crusading newspapermen, Edward A. Dickson of the Los Angeles *Express* and Chester H. Rowell of the Fresno *Republican,* became disgusted by the machinations of the 1907 meeting of the legislature. Dickson had already led a nonpartisan fight against the Southern Pacific in Los Angeles; Rowell then suggested to him that the two collaborate in a statewide effort against the railroad influence. After a preliminary organizational meeting in Los Angeles, the League of Lincoln–Roosevelt Republican Clubs (named for the Civil War president and the Progressives' idol, Teddy Roosevelt) was formally organized in Oakland on August 1, 1907. It became popularly known throughout the state as the Lincoln–Roosevelt League. Within a month, over thirty California newspapers pledged their support to the new movement, including at least one major journal in every important city, such as Los Angeles, San Francisco, and Sacramento.

As early as 1908, the League had organized to the point where it could nominate a complete slate of candidates for both the Republican primaries and conventions. The results were uneven. In a close vote the League lost thirteen out of eighteen assembly districts in San Francisco. Los Angeles also spurned the League's candidates that year. Yet many local successes were recorded in Fresno and Long Beach, and in county conventions including Humboldt, which was Governor Gillett's bailiwick.

Although they constituted only a minority in the 1909 legislature, the Progressive reformers were very noisy and attracted much attention.

When President Taft, originally elected as a Roosevelt protégé in 1908, seemed to swing toward the right during his first year in office, California Progressives talked of supporting a Roosevelt boom for a third term in 1912. Linking this national objective with their state goal of eliminating the Southern Pacific's influence in California, the Progressives prepared to challenge the regular Republicans at every level.

The Progressives had long been searching for a man to head their state ticket in 1910. After rejecting other candidates, most leaders came to believe that the man who could lead the League to victory was the short, stocky San Francisco lawyer Hiram W. Johnson. Johnson had a round, florid face that seemed to glow with his love of political combat. His public image was that of a deadly earnest man who would never compromise. He seemed just the man to lead a reformers' crusade. He was no intellectual, and in the last half of his life he consistently preferred movies to books.

Johnson was born in Sacramento on September 2, 1866. A precocious youth, he graduated from high school at sixteen and then worked in his father's law office for a year. In 1884 Johnson entered the University of California, only to drop out in his junior year to marry Minnie L. Mc-Neal of Sacramento. To support his new bride, young Hiram worked as a shorthand reporter and as a clerk in his father's office. Admitted to the bar in 1888, he went into partnership with his father, Grove L. Johnson, and his brilliant but unstable brother, Albert M. Johnson. For a time the three men worked in harmony, Hiram and Albert managing their father's successful try for a congressional seat in 1894. Two years later the idealistic sons advised their father not to seek a reelection, since he had become a tool for the railroad interests and was now vulnerable to defeat. The father indignantly rejected his sons' advice and was beaten in his bid for another term. Embittered, the elder Johnson savagely turned on his sons. This family feud erupted into the open in 1900 when Hiram Johnson backed a reformer, George H. Clark, for mayor of Sacramento. Grove Johnson, a member in good standing of the Republican machine, vociferously campaigned for the regular nominee. When Clark won, he appointed Hiram Johnson as corporation counsel for the city at the sum of $75 a month. In this office, Johnson opened a legal attack upon the gambling interests which then controlled Sacramento. In the bitter campaign which Clark waged for reelection in 1902, Grove Johnson bitterly denounced his sons, who were actively supporting the incumbent. One night the rival tent meetings of Grove and his sons were less than a block apart. At that time Grove referred to his "two chief enemies down the street, one Hiram, full of egotism, and the other Albert, full of booze."

Once more the sons triumphed over the father when Clark was reelected. Nevertheless, the sons decided to leave Sacramento for San Francisco, where they opened a law partnership. Here Hiram was quickly recognized as one of the best trial lawyers in the city. While his brother was drinking himself into an early grave, Hiram Johnson devoted himself to his passion—reform politics. At this time San Francisco was busy trying its one-time boss Abe Ruef and associates on various charges of graft. In the courtroom the chief prosecutor, Francis J. Heney, was shot in the face and nearly killed. Quickly the reformers looked about for a replacement. They offered the place to Hiram Johnson. He also became active in the Lincoln–Roosevelt League of San Francisco. The fearless young crusader quickly caught the eyes of the managers of the League. At first Johnson was reluctant to run because success would bring him back to Sacramento with its painful memories, and because the financial cost would tax his modest resources. Assured of adequate financial backing, Johnson reluctantly agreed to make the race.

He eschewed the niceties of the Progressive platform. He hammered at one issue which he believed the people completely understood. His stock campaign cry was "Kick Herrin and the Southern Pacific out of the government of the state!" Johnson was encouraged in his battle in the primary because several candidates were running, which made it difficult for his opposition to effectively support any one of them against him. Since this was the first statewide nominating primary, Herrin found it difficult to coordinate the railroad's forces to nominate a pliant Republican candidate.

Meanwhile Johnson was in his element. He campaigned over all parts of California in a bright red Locomobile which he had chosen to emphasize his complete independence of the railroad. He equipped his flashy automobile with a brass bell to summon crowds to his meetings, which were held at every crossroad. During his campaign, he traveled 20,000 miles, mostly over unpaved roads, to bring his message to the electorate.

Despite his crowds, Johnson was worried, for he had an important problem in southern California. Harrison Gray Otis, although no friend of the Southern Pacific, had been ignored in the formation of the Lincoln–Roosevelt League, and he regarded this as a personal insult. Moreover, the crusty publisher of the Los Angeles *Times* regarded the reformers as wooly-headed thinkers who were indirectly promoting the cause of the Socialists. As a result, the columns of the powerful *Times* contained many stories hostile to Johnson.

Nonetheless, Johnson's slashing attack on the Southern Pacific produced results in the August primary. He polled 101,000 votes—a plurality out of the 215,000 votes cast. The crusading attorney carried with him almost all members of the Lincoln–Roosevelt state ticket. An analysis of Johnson's vote shows that he ran very strongly in the San Joaquin Valley and, despite the *Times*, very well in southern California. Johnson was relatively weak throughout all of northern California except for Alameda County. And he had run badly in his home town of San Francisco.

Although the general election in November was an anticlimax after the emotional August primary, Johnson maintained his momentum and continued his one-theme campaign with gratifying public response. He dramatized the fact that he was the candidate the Southern Pacific least desired to see in the governor's mansion. He continued his colorful campaign tactics, employing bands, fire and his red automobile. The Democratic candidate, Theodore A. Bell, was no railroad lackey. However, he had lost the governor's chair in 1906 because of Hearst's petulance, and he was now attempting to claim his rightful prize. After 1900, the Democratic Party had seemed to possess a more responsible attitude about the issues of monopoly and railroad control than had the statewide Republican apparatus. Therefore, an impartial observer only months before the election might have wagered that if the people of California craved reform, they would choose the Democratic Party as the vehicle by which it could be accomplished. Bell conducted an educational campaign, discussing a wide range of issues in contrast with Hiram Johnson's narrow approach. Bell was hurt rather than helped when Hearst and the Southern Pacific belatedly threw their support behind him.

With the luck that was to grace the remainder of his political career, Johnson won the gubernatorial contest because of the split in his opponents' ranks. Johnson defeated Bell with 177,000 votes to Bell's 154,000, but the Socialist and the Prohibition tickets together pulled some 53,000 ballots. The entire Republican slate of state executive officers, seven out of the eight congressmen, and substantial majorities in the legislature were also returned. Interestingly Johnson carried San Francisco by a paper-thin margin, but he lost twenty-one out of forty-nine northern California counties. By contrast, he won a greater majority in the nine southern counties than he had polled in the more populous north.

Moving into the governorship in January 1911, Hiram Johnson launched one of the most successful political careers in the history of the state—serving as California governor and United States senator for thirty-four years until his death in 1945. Along with Earl Warren, he became the only California governor to achieve national political stature. Johnson also became the first governor since John Bigler in 1853 to be reelected and the first four-year-term governor to gain this distinction. Within a year and a half after his election, Johnson was nominated as Theodore Roosevelt's running mate on the third party Bull Moose or Progressive ticket. This ticket carried California by the narrowest of margins. Nonetheless, it was a Democratic year nationally and Woodrow Wilson claimed the White House.

When Johnson became governor, the average citizen assumed that he would have to do battle with the Southern Pacific for mastery of the state. Actually, for the past decade the railroad's power had been steadily declining, although at times, as in 1906, it could still dictate the choice of a governor. Yet overall it was no longer the octopus with tentacles in all directions against which Frank Norris had railed in frustration. As a result, the forces opposed to Johnson were weak and disorganized. The chairman of the Republican central committee, Meyer Lissner, had feared that the new state administration would not have a detailed series of proposals to submit, and so had appointed committees of specialists to plan the work of the legislature shortly after the election. These sessions of the new California legislature marked a watershed in the legislative history of the state. The legislature proved to be very cooperative with Johnson and enacted a long overdue series of laws. Among the acts passed during the first Johnson administration were those strengthening the primary law and establishing the initiative referendum and recall. Other accomplishments included a water power and conservation act, a state board of control to draw up a systematized budget, a blue-sky law to protect the public from wildcat stock, the extension of the civil service over most state employees, a pure food law, an honest weights and measures law, laws setting up minimum wages and maximum hours for women, employers' liability laws covering the injury of employees, tax reforms, free school textbooks, child-labor legislation, antiusury laws, reform of the criminal code, nonpartisan election of judges, pensions for teachers, improvement of state highways, and an effective Railroad Commission (whose power was later extended to all utilities) to fix rates and other conditions of railroad service. Johnson finally laid the bones of Frank Norris' octopus to rest.

Many of these laws were passed at the first session of the 1911 legislature, whose record Theodore Roosevelt characterized as "the most comprehensive program of constructive legislation ever passed at a single session of any American legislature." No other state with any considerable population had ever accepted so sweeping a progressive program of political and economic reform.

In 1914, Johnson considered running for the United States Senate, but instead sought a second term as governor. Although a law which went into effect in 1913 permitted cross-filing (whereby a member of one party could file in the primaries of other parties), Johnson chose to file only in the Progressive primary. He campaigned upon his record and did not specify any new advances of Progressivism. In the election in the fall of 1914, Johnson polled 460,000 votes and carried all but four counties; he just missed a majority of all the votes cast.

While Johnson had shown great personal strength in California, nationally the Progressive Party had made a poor showing. Johnson was the only governor elected as a Progressive. In congressional races, the Progressives had fared badly. And in California, although Johnson had pulled most minor Progressive candidates to victory with him, a Democrat, James D. Phelan, had defeated the Progressives' senatorial choice, the noted reformer-prosecuting attorney Francis J. Heney.

As a result, some of the steam went out of the Progressive movement. The 1915 legislature passed much less legislation than had its immediate predecessors. An attempt to make all state elective offices nonpartisan failed. Among the accomplishments of this legislature was a law encouraging cooperative marketing and one establishing a commission on colonization and rural credits. Despite this slowdown, in his term and a half Johnson had recorded an almost incredible record of accomplishment.

With the disbanding of the Progressive Party, Johnson successfully ran for the Republican senatorial nomination in 1916. Johnson did not enthusiastically follow Theodore Roosevelt back into the Progressive

Party in 1916, and many of his colleagues in the Progressive movement refused to accept the Republican presidential candidate, Charles Evans Hughes, preferring the liberal Democrat Woodrow Wilson. Although Wilson's narrow margin of victory in California assured his gaining a second term in the White House, this phenomenon has sometimes been attributed to Hughes' snub of Hiram Johnson. According to this story, the barnstorming presidential candidate, Charles Evans Hughes, was staying by chance at the same hotel as Hiram Johnson. Hughes never did invite Johnson to see him, and as a result, Johnson and thousands of his supporters in anger turned against Hughes, costing him California's electoral votes and with them the election. The real story of Hughes' defeat in California is much more complicated. The Republican Party in California was all but obliterated in 1912. In that year Taft received only a token vote in the state. This meant that when the national Progressive Party disbanded in 1916, the Republican Party in California had to be largely reconstituted. If the regular Republican leaders and Charles Evans Hughes could win over the overwhelming majority of the former Progressives, they could win the state. Yet too much bitterness had been engendered in the recent campaigns to make this more than a possibility. Hughes himself was not popular within the state. Moreover, whatever Johnson's personal feelings toward Hughes, the governor played down his support for Hughes in the campaign to avoid antagonizing his supporters who were backing Wilson nationally. Johnson was always something of a "loner" in his campaigning methods, and it would have been surprising if he had been too vociferous in his support of the Republican national ticket. As a result, Johnson was elected senator by about 300,-000 votes, while Hughes lost California by about four thousand ballots. It is too much to say that California decided the election any more than several other states, most notably Ohio, which had usually gone Republican, but this time voted for Wilson. Simply because California's election returns were the last to come in did not in the final analysis make it any more important than any other large state.

After Johnson's senatorial election, he resigned on March 15, 1917, to take his seat in Congress, and turned over the governorship to his lieutenant governor, William D. Stephens. With his departure for the national scene, an era of California history ended.

While this frenzied politicking was going on at the state level, California's two principal cities, Los Angeles and San Francisco, were undergoing trials of their own.

Los Angeles at this time was pursuing its quest for an adequate harbor. It had grown up as a landlocked city, but it became clear that its future would be limited if it had no access to a good port. It was true that since the days of the Spaniards there had been a port at San Pedro Bay, but this harbor was only a little better than a deathtrap for mariners. Richard Henry Dana had complained about it in 1835. Nonetheless, a settlement, San Pedro, eventually faced the western rim of the bay at the edge of the San Pedro Hills. As early as 1852 the harbor became a port of call for a shipping line to and from San Francisco. On the flat ground facing Terminal Island there was established a settlement of sorts, largely through the single-minded efforts of Phineas Banning. In the 1850's, Banning with several associates bought a 2,400-acre parcel of the old Rancho San Pedro and laid out a town called first New San Pedro and then later Wilmington. A stage line in the late 1850's and in the 1860's linked the port with Los Angeles. During the Civil War, two army installations were built there, Camp Drum and Drum Barracks. In 1869 Wilmington was linked to Los Angeles by rail. The channel of San Pedro was deepened by federal appropriations as early as 1877. Despite this, San Pedro was considered so poor a port that most freight shippers bound for Los Angeles shunned it completely, choosing instead to unload their cargo at San Francisco and complete the journey by rail. Similarly, most exports from Los Angeles went by rail up to San Francisco for loading aboard ship.

Los Angeles citizens had long agreed on the necessity of a deep-water port, but in the same vague manner that they discussed the need for a trans-Nicaraguan canal or the irrigation of the Mojave Desert. In time most southern California chambers of commerce, the railroads and the newspapers supported the idea of a good port for Los Angeles. This harbor, all agreed, should become a reality with federal appropriations.

The method these southern California boosters employed was to commandeer any influential politician or congressman who came to the Pacific coast and take him by special train to San Pedro Bay. There the visitor was overwhelmed with statistics that seemed to prove that Los Angeles already had a thriving port which unfortunately was slightly inadequate, a deficiency that could easily be remedied by modest improvements.

One sunny morning in 1889, the Senate Commerce Committee journeyed all the way to Los Angeles to view San Pedro for itself. The chairman, a crusty, dour Mainer named William P. Frye, was completely unimpressed by what he saw. He complained that the citizens of Los Angeles had the gall to demand a harbor from the federal government since God had denied them one naturally!

In 1890 Congress appropriated $5,000 for harbor surveys along the Los Angeles area coastline without specific reference to San Pedro Bay. For the first time there was some serious thinking done about possibilities other than San Pedro. One group of investors decided that the ideal port was at the beach town of Redondo, which was closer to both Los Angeles and San Francisco than was San Pedro. These investors quickly formed the Redondo Railway Company and constructed a small wharf over a submarine canyon where there was deep water. This provided a fairly safe anchorage except when really large storms prevailed. A narrow-gauge railroad connected the port with Los Angeles. The Santa Fe railroad, after a study of Redondo's possibilities, decided that it was the place for the Los Angeles port. Thereupon, it built a second wharf along the coast there. Soon considerable traffic was using the new port.

Another group of investors refused to believe that any place other than San Pedro would be picked so long as the Southern Pacific wanted it there. They organized the Terminal Railroad, made a jerry-built road to San Pedro and constructed wharves. Soon the company succeeded in winning a share of the business away from its giant rival, which of course already controlled a line into the port.

The Southern Pacific was annoyed by this competition, and in 1892 suddenly proposed Santa Monica as the site of the new deep-water port. The railroad management argued that Santa Monica was even closer to San Francisco than Redondo Beach, and therefore much time could be saved in shipments between the two ports. This action confused the issue even further, so that Congress voted to have a board of army engineers judge between Santa Monica and San Pedro. Meanwhile the Southern Pacific bought all the land upon which wharves could be built. If it was successful in making Santa Monica the deep-water port, all rivals would be excluded.

After deliberation the army board reported favorably in 1892 upon the claims of San Pedro! This did nothing to dampen the claims of the rival ports. Soon the battle to locate the artificial harbor at one site or the other reverberated across the continent to Washington. Proponents of the various ports began to collect petitions to send to the national legislature.

In May 1896, the matter was finally settled when Congress appropriated nearly three million dollars for an artificial harbor at San Pedro. When the news was flashed to Los Angeles, the city celebrated its victory in obtaining a "free harbor." Three years later on April 26–27, 1899, Los Angeles celebrated its Free Harbor Jubilee with a barbecue and speeches at San Pedro. The Southern Pacific officials, angry at the turn of events, boycotted the function. Nevertheless, the crowd gathered on schedule near Point Fermin, where the first barge loaded with stone from Catalina Island was ready to be dumped as the first step in the building of the port. Across the continent President William McKinley pushed a button that was supposed to dump the stone into the water. Something went wrong, and there was an embarrassing delay. Finally the stones were pushed over by hand. The fight for a free port had been won.

The president of the Southern Pacific, Collis P. Huntington, had lost the battle. This unusual experience has been credited by some with hastening the old curmudgeon's death in 1900. Santa Monica was destined to remain a pleasure beach, served for a time by Southern Pacific trains and then by the interurban cars of Henry Huntington's line. As the era of the interurban faded, the rails were left to rust.

Since Point Fermin only inadequately protected San Pedro, the work of building a breakwater went on, until by 1911 it jutted into the Pacific over 11,000 feet. Eventually the breakwater, forming an outer harbor, extended as far as Long Beach. The federal government's investment at San Pedro grew from the original $2,900,000 in 1896 to $36,500,000 by 1950. The Los Angeles Harbor Commission and the city of Long Beach spent additional sums.

San Pedro and Wilmington were annexed to Los Angeles in 1909 and connected to it by a 500-foot shoestring of land that extended about sixteen miles.

Only a few years later, the West Coast's preeminent port and long-time queen city, San Francisco, was plagued by a natural catastrophe—a disastrous earthquake and fire in 1906. This disaster was the result of the earth's shifting along the San Andreas Fault, a rift in the earth's crust. The quake was felt from San Juan Bautista on the south to Fort Bragg on the north—in all, some 210 miles. Some damage was reported for thirty miles on both sides of the fault.

On April 18, 1906, at 5:13 A.M., San Franciscans were startled by a heaving and rolling of the earth's surface of a much greater magnitude than the city had ever before experienced. (The city's last important earthquake had occurred a generation before in 1868.) A scientific investigation later revealed that the initial movements of the earth had lasted forty seconds, then diminished in intensity for ten seconds and then recovered their original force for another twenty-five seconds before gradually subsiding.

Although San Francisco itself was badly shaken from the quake, the damage was not very great. Some casualties were caused by brick chimneys crashing down upon sleeping occupants of top-floor bedrooms. Yet if it had not been for the disastrous fire which followed the quake, the total damage and deaths might have been modest.

By midmorning following the quake, the survivors observed clouds of smoke rising from several sections of San Francisco. The fires were caused by overturned wood-burning stoves, broken gas lines and damaged electric wires. Despite the fact that the fire-alarm system had been knocked out of commission, and that the San Francisco fire chief, David Scannell, was killed during the earthquake, squads of firemen answered the calls for assistance. The fires were nearly under control when the water supply failed. The water mains had been broken in so many places that the pressure had drastically fallen in the entire system.

Fires in the industrial portion of San Francisco blazed through the untended shops and factories south of Market Street. From there the flames licked their way to the city's center. For three days and two nights the disastrous fire fed on the wrecked buildings of San Francisco before burning itself out. In all, 514 city blocks containing 28,000 buildings were destroyed. About 450 citizens died in the quake and fire, and property damage, while variously estimated, reached at least $350,000,000.

Refugees camped in Golden Gate Park. The regular army and the Red Cross stepped in, and while nobody starved, many of the refugees were hungry until relief activities were established. The Southern Pacific, by this time more damned than loved, displayed a kindlier side when, under the personal direction of E. H. Harriman, men and materials were rushed to relieve the prostrate city.

After the immediate emergency-relief needs were provided for, the city began to dig out. Clearing the burned-over district took many months and cost at least twenty million dollars. Although some skeptics had predicted that San Francisco could never be rebuilt, it soon was. At first there was great apprehension that the fire-insurance companies could never pay their claims. Yet it is believed that in the end, out of $175,000,-000 in claims filed, about $167,000,000 was paid. With the help of these funds and additional new investments, within three years after the fire 20,500 of the 28,000 buildings destroyed had been replaced. In general the new buildings were superior in materials, design and workmanship to those they replaced.

Unfortunately, since the merchants were in such haste to return to business, they were powerful enough to prevent any important improvement in the city's design. It had been proposed that the downtown streets be widened and that new thoroughfares be cut to speed traffic flow in the areas north and south of Market Street, but these changes all became casualties of the speedy drive to rebuild.

San Francisco was faced with a more prodigious task than rebuilding. Since the gold-rush days, the city had experienced alternating periods of graft and reform. But the periods of corruption had become longer. After the blind boss Buckley had fled San Francisco in 1891, just one jump ahead of the revelations of a prying grand jury, there was a reaction against the Democrats that swept the Republicans into office. A Republican boss, Daniel Burns, soon filled the vacuum left by Buckley's sudden departure. Burns's sway was short, for he was tried for graft in 1894. Although he managed to win an acquittal, he decided to take no further chances and speedily left California's legal jurisdiction. After a period of political confusion in 1897, a young scion of a socially prominent family, James D. Phelan, announced his candidacy for mayor. As an idealistic reformer, Phelan emphasized his interest in ending the rule of the "California Tammany." He sincerely believed that the corruption in municipal politics could be lessened if city utilities were publicly owned, since it often appeared that utility magnates bribed mayors and supervisors to obtain special favors. Therefore, Phelan ran for mayor on a platform calling for a new city charter that would permit the public ownership of utilities. A San Francisco Merchants' Association was formed from the city's leading businessmen, which helped Phelan to win handily. A new city charter was eventually adopted, making Phelan's goals attainable.

With Phelan as mayor, San Francisco for a time enjoyed honest government, but in the summer of 1901, civic harmony was rudely shattered when a general strike of the labor unions broke out against the tightly organized Employers' Association. For two months there was one outbreak of violence after another. Phelan, of course, was closely identified with the organized employers. Therefore it was not surprising that the Phelan administration hired special police ostensibly to keep order, but in the eyes of the labor unions, to break the strike. Angrily the unions charged that Phelan was controlled by the employers. The temper of the labor unions was not improved when Governor Gage intervened to effect a settlement of the strike in October 1901. Few workers believed that they had won anything significant.

In their mood of frustration, the union leaders decided to enter municipal politics and so obtain a friendly city administration. Thus the politically inexperienced labor leaders played into the hands of a Republican politician, Abraham ("Abe") Ruef. Ruef had little real sympathy for labor, but he saw a rare chance to gain power. Ruef was a little-known attorney from a wealthy family and a graduate of the University of California. Quietly he had built up a flourishing law practice. Ruef offered his services to the union leaders to reform the Union Labor Party. To run for the office of mayor Ruef chose Eugene E. Schmitz. Schmitz, a fiddler and president of the Musicians' Union, was a political novice. Yet he looked like a mayor should, for he was a large, hearty, handsome man—a perfect front for Ruef's scheme. In the ensuing election, Schmitz and several other Union Labor candidates won. Ruef used his leadership of the local San Francisco party to enhance his position within the state Republican organization. Soon Ruef, who wanted no office for himself, gathered the real power of the city into his hands. He was too shrewd to accept money that could be easily labeled a bribe. Instead, in exchange for favors, he asked that corporations and individuals pay him generous legal retainers for his services as an attorney. In 1903, Schmitz won a second term, despite the mutterings of reformers.

By 1905 a counterforce to the Ruef machine began to form. A coalition was created, consisting of Fremont Older, editor of the *Bulletin*, a "good government" organization under the direction of former Mayor Phelan, the public-service corporations (who with fine impartiality were also paying out bribes to Ruef and his associates), and William F. Herrin, the political boss of the Southern Pacific. This motley array was united only by a desire to end Ruef's reign as the uncrowned king of San Francisco. These powerful men were able to persuade the Democrats not to split the opposition vote to Ruef by running a candidate of their own. As a result, the Republican mayoralty candidate, John S. Partridge, carried a fusion banner against Ruef's perennial candidate, Schmitz. The result was a frustrating defeat for the reformers and a smashing Union Labor Party victory. The utilities and even the proud Southern Pacific hastened to make their peace with Ruef, now grown more cocky than ever. The grafters became more flagrant in their wrongdoing, and Ruef basked in a false sense of security.

The earthquake of 1906 seemed like a stroke of good luck to Ruef and his cohorts, since Schmitz as mayor had displayed unexpected qualities of leadership during and immediately after the disaster. Then, in September of 1906, fissures began to appear in the seemingly monolithic structure of Ruef's power. After the Republicans' state nominating convention at Santa Cruz, several of Ruef's lieutenants became disgruntled when the boss would not share the money paid him by the Southern Pacific to throw his support to the railroad gubernatorial candidate, James Gillett. These unhappy lieutenants babbled freely to the hostile press, thus arousing public opinion against Ruef.

Perhaps this internal dissension could have been resolved, but the outside pressure on Ruef's organization continued. Fremont Older had never paused in his crusade against Ruef. He had already talked to reform-minded attorney Francis J. Heney, who was a determined foe of the grafters. Heney convinced Older that if anything effective were to be done to expose the graft of the Ruef machine, a war chest of $100,000 was needed to investigate and prosecute the grafters. In addition, Older arranged with President Theodore Roosevelt for federal attorney Heney to take part as needed in the San Francisco graft investigation. Phelan persistently continued his opposition to Ruef. Yet more help was needed now that the utilities and the Southern Pacific had defected from the reformers' cause.

Help appeared in the person of Rudolph Spreckels. Spreckels was the son of a Hawaiian sugar king who at the age of nineteen had quarreled with his father and stalked from his family home vowing to make his own way in the world. His father expected him to return soon as a chastened prodigal son. To the older Spreckels' surprise, his son quickly made a fortune in his own right. Busy with his business interests, thoroughbred horse breeding and an extensive social life, Spreckels had paid scant attention to municipal politics. He was rudely jolted out of his complacency when Ruef brazenly proposed to include him in a scheme to defraud the city. Angered, Spreckels then offered to help Older and Phelan in their drive to rid the city of Ruef.

The three reformers still needed an additional break to launch a legal attack upon Ruef. The labor ticket elected in 1905 had included (by mistake) an honest district attorney, William H. Langdon. Langdon allied himself with the reformers, calling a grand jury to probe graft charges and appointing Heney as a special prosecutor.

By late 1906 the graft trials began; they continued intermittently for the next five years. These were years of high drama; witnesses were suborned; jurors were bribed; documents were lost or stolen; Fremont Older was kidnapped and then released after a chase over half the length of the state; the house of a Ruef henchman who had turned state's evidence was bombed; chief prosecutor Heney was gunned down in open court and severely wounded. The grafters' power was starkly revealed when Heney's assailant, who had been captured, was allowed to commit suicide or was murdered while in a local jail. Heney's place was taken by Hiram Johnson—no net gain for the grafters.

As a result of the relentless probing, the Ruef associates began to weaken and confess. The entire board of supervisors turned state's evidence. As a result of their damaging testimony, Ruef, in return for at least partial immunity, also offered to talk. Bit by bit the whole sordid story came out. It was revealed that many important officials of the public utility companies had proffered bribes to members of the machine. The reformers, not content with snaring relatively small fish like the grafters, pressed on to attempt to convict some of the most prominent of the San Francisco community for offering bribes. Quickly the solid support which the first citizens of San Francisco had given to the reformers was shattered. To members of San Francisco society, it was one matter to convict petty politicians of accepting bribes, but quite another to prosecute their friends and neighbors.

As a consequence, some hoped-for results were not realized. In the political arena the Good Government League (as the nonpartisan coalition of reformers styled themselves) did win the municipal election of 1907, but because so many important people had defected from the reformers' ranks by 1909, the Union Laborites elected their candidate for mayor. The new civic head, P. H. McCarthy, announced his program for making San Francisco the "Paris of America." If anybody lost the real meaning of this statement, the Union Labor–Republican district attorney spelled it out in detail by announcing that he was abandoning new graft trials.

The legal results were also disappointing to the reformers. Of some three to four hundred indictments, only four convictions were ever gained. Three of these, including that of Schmitz, were later set aside by higher courts. Schmitz himself never suffered any penalty except that of removal from office. Ruef alone went to the penitentiary, and he might have escaped had not the decision of a majority of the California supreme court been thwarted by a legal technicality. Not one of the accused bribers was ever convicted.

Yet all was not lost. Many of the reformers, frustrated in their attempt to cleanse San Francisco, transferred their efforts to the successful state-wide Progressive revolt in the immediately succeeding years.

Nor was the cause of good government in San Francisco completely lost. San Francisco's Mayor P. H. McCarthy, who put an end to the crusaders' municipal control, was himself defeated for reelection in 1911. His successful opponent in that election was James Rolph. Rolph, whose nickname of "Sunny Jim" accurately described his character, came in for a tenure of nearly twenty years as mayor, which ended only when he was elevated to the governor's office. Rolph, while not a great mayor, steered a steady course between making San Francisco a "closed town" and allowing the blatant vice of earlier eras to continue.

TWENTY-SEVEN

The Ugly Shadows of Racism and Labor Unrest

CALIFORNIA'S traditional anti-Oriental prejudice found a new victim in the late nineteenth and early twentieth centuries. Those discriminatory practices which once had been manifested toward the Chinese were now directed against the Japanese. During the gold rush, Japan was still isolated from the rest of the world, and so the Japanese did not participate in the immigration to California. Even after Commodore Matthew C. Perry opened Japan to foreign contacts in the middle 1850's, Japanese immigration into the United States was slight. As late as 1880, there were fewer than 150 Japanese in the entire United States.

Until the 1890's the small number of Japanese who had migrated to California received no attention. After 1891, Japanese immigration into the United States increased markedly, when several landowners brought Japanese laborers into California. At first Japanese laborers came directly from Japan, but after the acquisition of Hawaii in 1898, a heavy influx of Japanese migrated to California from these islands, where they had been employed as agricultural laborers. The early Japanese immigrants were skilled agriculturalists and industrious workmen. California newspapers hailed them as a valuable addition to the labor force of the state; steamship companies encouraged Japanese migration by charging them relatively low fares. Thus encouraged, Japanese migration during the 1890's rose to about one thousand new arrivals a year. Prior to 1900 the overwhelming majority of the Japanese who came to the United States were peasants who were content to work as farm laborers. As a result, they were not the threat to American workmen that they later came to be.

By 1900 there were over 12,000 Japanese in California; by 1910 the number rose to 41,000, and to nearly 72,000 by 1920. Although this amounted to a very small percentage of the total population of California, strong opposition to the Japanese began to be heard throughout the state. While their number was small, the Japanese received public approval. However, as they continued to enter the state, they became the victims of outright discrimination. To many Californians, the arguments against the Chinese seemed equally plausible when directed against the Japanese. They were so different in skin color, language and customs that the Caucasian Californians claimed that they could not possibly be assimilated into American society. Because of their tendency to congregate in a few areas of the state, the Japanese became more conspicuous than their total population warranted.

In 1886, when the number of Japanese in California could not have exceeded four hundred, the cry of ousting the "Japs" was already beginning to be heard. Yet the general public attitude toward them did not become significantly hostile until the turn of the century. In May 1900, during a mass meeting in San Francisco, there was great public discussion that they be subject to an immigration ban under the same terms as the Chinese exclusion law. Although the Japanese labored under the same handicap of laws that had excluded other Orientals from citizenship, to many Americans this amount of discrimination was not enough. Patriotic groups, labor unions, and merchant associations clamored for the total exclusion of the Orientals, shouting "California shall not become the Caucasian graveyard!"

As middle-class Japanese began to migrate to California, they were not content to be hired as laborers for others. Many bought or leased tracts of fertile land, and entire Japanese families toiled in the fields. The industry and aggressiveness of the Japanese soon gave them a near-monopoly in the raising of berries, potatoes and flowers. In many California cities, the Japanese middle class opened stores, restaurants, hotels and banks. Nor did the mass of Japanese laborers leave the fields of gardening and domestic labor, which in time they came to dominate. Using San Pedro as a base, the Japanese also became very active in the commercial fishing industry.

This unabated arrival and success of Japanese laborers led to increased agitation against them. In 1905 various trade unions formed the Asiatic Exclusion League. The San Francisco *Chronicle* added to the hostility by running a series of articles which warned of the dangers of the "yellow peril." The *Chronicle* and other California newspapers took up the cry that the Japanese be excluded.

A state law already on the statute books empowered local school boards to establish separate schools for Indians and Orientals. In October 1906, while San Francisco was rebuilding after the disastrous fire, the San Francisco Board of Education, then particularly responsive to union hostility to the Japanese community, established a school to be exclusively attended by Chinese, Korean and Japanese children. Some ninety-three Japanese pupils were involved. Other Oriental groups in California, such as the Koreans and the Chinese, were too downtrodden to protest, and in addition their governments were too weak to attempt effective diplomatic support of their nationals abroad. The Japanese proved to be another case.

First among their complaints was the bitter resentment they felt at being classified with the Chinese and Koreans. They denied that the law should apply to them, for they insisted that they were not Orientals as defined by the law. Moreover, they had the support of their national government. After defeating Russia in the Russo-Japanese War, Japan was not afraid to protest what it regarded as a slight to its national honor by the United States. Viscount Aoke, Japanese envoy to the United States, vehemently protested that Japan's treaty rights were violated by the San Francisco school board action. The international situation grew tense as Japan, flushed with its recent military victory, refused to rescind its diplomatic protests. In Tokyo a photograph of Mayor Eugene E. Schmitz was circulated with the caption that this was a portrait of a true devil. Japanese public indignation mounted. Finally, the Japanese authorities banned such activities, for they feared that rioting might be provoked. President Theodore Roosevelt became sufficiently alarmed to confer with Admiral George Dewey concerning Pacific fleet dispositions.

President Roosevelt was unwilling to sacrifice good American–Japanese relations to increase the prestige of local California officials. He therefore attempted to pressure the San Francisco Board of Education to modify its order. This presidential effort failed to impress San Francisco's local politicians, however. At this point, San Francisco Congressman Julius Kahn invited the San Francisco school board to Washington to negotiate with the President and the secretary of state. Whether he acted upon his own authority or whether Roosevelt himself had charged him to try this method has never been fully ascertained. Mayor Schmitz, then in the midst of the graft investigation that ultimately toppled him, made haste, as the contemporary press put it, "to butt in." He also journeyed to Washington to reap what prestige his presence there might lend.

In two White House conferences, Teddy Roosevelt bluntly laid down the law to the San Francisco Board of Education. It had been easy to defy

Roosevelt at a distance, but under his stern gaze in the White House, the school board agreed to a rather one-sided compromise. According to the terms of this agreement, San Francisco schools were opened to all Japanese students, except a few over sixteen who were seeking to enroll in the primary grades because of deficiencies in their previous education.

Part of the bargain included the understanding that Roosevelt would find a way for the national government to stem the flow of Japanese immigration, although the President acidly remarked at the time that he did not think California politicians were as interested in actually excluding the Japanese as they were in merely agitating the question. Congress hastily passed an amendment to the Immigration Act of February 20, 1907, which allowed the President to refuse entrance to the continental United States to immigrants with passports for any country other than America. Roosevelt speedily applied this provision to Japanese coming from Hawaii, Mexico or Canada, but not to those arriving directly from Japan. To eliminate this last category of immigration, Roosevelt negotiated a "Gentlemen's Agreement" with the Japanese government in 1907. This unwritten agreement provided that Japan would not object to the presidential restriction of Japanese coming to the American mainland from Hawaii, Mexico or Canada. In addition, Japan agreed not to issue passports to laborers wishing to come to the continental United States, except for returning immigrants, and the parents, wives and children of Japanese nationals already living in America. The United States agreed not to exclude the Japanese by domestic legislation.

To anti-Japanese agitators in California, this agreement of 1907 failed to accomplish the Japanese exclusion they desired. Many Japanese found loopholes in the agreement, by which they illicitly entered the country. One such loophole was provided by the Japanese custom of contracting "picture-bride" marriages. According to this custom, a Japanese laborer in America, unable to return to Japan to be married, could make the acquaintance of his future wife through a marriage broker who arranged an exchange of photographs. A marriage ceremony was performed in Japan and the girl entered the United States as the bride of a Japanese male already resident in America. This procedure allowed hundreds of young Japanese women to come to America and to increase the population of the Japanese community. (The birth rate of these Japanese women was three times that of Occidental mothers.) After 1920 the Japanese government no longer issued passports to "picture brides." But many Japanese were still smuggled across the Mexican border into California.

Meanwhile, except for the relatively short period of time during World War I when the United States and Japan were allies against Imperial Germany, anti-Japanese agitation continued. Although the threadbare issues of coolieism and cheap labor were exploited, it was really the success of the Japanese as entrepreneurs that excited real animosity. Organizations as disparate as the Native Sons and Daughters of the Golden West, the California Grange, and the American Federation of Labor united to achieve anti-Japanese legislation.

In 1913 the California legislature considered the Alien Land Act, better known as the Webb Bill (so named for California's attorney general, U. S. Webb). This bill sought to prevent Oriental aliens who were ineligible for American citizenship from owning farm land or leasing such land for more than three years. Although couched in general terms, everyone was aware that the Japanese were the intended targets of the bill.

In addition to religious organizations, several California newspapers opposed the Webb Bill because of its adverse impact upon American-Japanese relations. The Japanese government predictably protested. President Woodrow Wilson responded by sending Secretary of State William Jennings Bryan to confer with Governor Hiram Johnson and to lobby with legislators against the Webb Bill. The state legislature ignored Bryan and passed the Webb Bill by a vote of 35 to 2 in the senate, and 73 to 9 in the assembly. Despite Bryan's appeals and several last-minute messages from President Wilson, Johnson calmly declared that eight states and the District of Columbia all had statutes similar to California's proposal, and signed the measure into law in August 1913.

There was protest from the rest of the country that California was sacrificing the national interest in order to pander to its own prejudice. Even so conservative an organ as the Chicago *Tribune* bitterly editorialized that California "when it is not scared to death itself is scaring the rest of the nation to death. . . ."

Although the Webb Act remained on the books, there were ways in which the Japanese could evade its provisions. Six years after its passage, Japanese individuals and corporations owned or leased 535,000 acres of agricultural land in defiance of the Act. Soon Japanese farmers tended crops in the rice regions of Colusa, Butte and Glenn counties, in the orchards and vineyards of Tulare and Fresno, in the berry gardens and vegetable plots of Los Angeles and Orange counties and down to the Imperial Valley. In 1922 it was reported that 80–90 per cent of the tomatoes, celery, asparagus and strawberries of California were grown by the Japanese. These crops brought over sixty-seven million dollars into the wallets of their growers. At this time the Japanese, with only 2 per cent of the state's population, owned 11 per cent of the state's land.

In the last years of the decade, the United States and Japan were at war against Imperial Germany. In 1919, during the delicate peace negotiations between the various Allied powers, including the United States and Japan, the California legislature suddenly injected a jarring note upon the international scene. It proposed a harsher alien land law in order to close the loopholes of the 1913 act. Secretary of State Robert Lansing successfully appealed to the California lawmaking body to delay consideration of this measure.

However, no such sensibility to foreign relations prevented the California electorate from approving an initiative measure in 1920, which ostensibly strengthened the Webb Act. Although the constitutionality of this legislation was repeatedly challenged in the California and federal courts, it was not until 1952 that the California supreme court finally invalidated the Webb Act.

The prohibition of Japanese immigration still loomed as an inviting prospect to most Californians. Starting in 1911, various proposals to exclude the Japanese were introduced into Congress by Californians. All these measures failed until the act of May 26, 1924, when Congress passed a general immigration law setting limited quotas for most of the world's nations. California's congressmen joined other West Coast senators and representatives in writing into the bill a stipulation forbidding the entrance into the United States of Oriental aliens ineligible for citizenship.

During the approximately fifteen years that the Gentlemen's Agreement had been in operation, the total Japanese migration into the continental United States was only 8,681 individuals, while the number of Japanese moving to Hawaii was 7,415. After the passage of the Immigration Act of 1924, the number of immigrants admitted to the United States was actually exceeded by the number of Japanese returning to their homeland. The California Japanese increased as a result of births, so that by 1930 there were over 97,000 of them, and by 1940 their number had increased to 120,000. These Japanese, feeling isolated and hated, looked for advice to Japanese consuls and business corporations in Japan. Following the advice of Japanese consuls, the majority of Japanese immigrants did not settle in widely scattered parts of the country, but moved into the heavily concentrated Oriental communities in California and other states in the Far West.

When the attack upon Pearl Harbor occurred in December 1941 (this catastrophe was in no way deterred by California prejudice against the Japanese), the torrent of ill will against the Japanese residents of California allowed federal and state action to be directed against them in the form of forcible relocation.

One effect of the Gentlemen's Agreement and the Immigration Act of 1924 was to make transient Japanese laborers scarce in California. Consequently, many prominent agriculturalists had to seek other sources of labor to work their lands. In the 1920's the number of Filipinos in California greatly increased. In 1923 some 2,426 Filipinos were brought into California, and by 1930 their number stood at about 35,000. The Filipinos went through the same cycle of acceptance and rejection by the white

Californians as did the Japanese. Barroom fights between Americans and Filipinos over the affections of white dancehall girls at Watsonville in 1930 and at Salinas in 1934 prompted cries for the exclusion of Filipinos. Their numbers decreased in 1935 when what became known as a "free transportation" act went into effect. This act stipulated that no Filipino who accepted free transportation to the Philippines could return to the mainland of the United States. Under this measure, thousands of Filipinos were deported upon one pretext or another and then forbidden to return.

Although many Californians romanticized the days of Mexican California, this did not make them any more tolerant of the Mexicans in their midst. Most of the old Californio families had dissolved, and relatively few of them survived into the twentieth century. In 1900 the total number of Mexican-born Californians was 8,086. Mexicans were employed as a source of transient labor only in the Imperial Valley. Some were brought from Mexico to work on railroad tracks, but they attracted relatively little attention from white Californians, since they often lived in boxcar settlements that moved from place to place. By 1910 their number had risen to 33,694. During World War I there was an acute shortage of workers, and thousands of Mexican laborers were brought into California under temporary waivers of the immigration laws. Many Mexicans went home after the close of the conflict, but many others stayed on and settled in the Los Angeles area. By 1920, California agricultural harvests were worked more and more by use of Mexican labor. By 1925 the Mexican community in Los Angeles was the largest aggregation of Mexicans outside of Mexico City. By 1930 it was believed that at least a quarter of a million Mexicans were residing in California and providing the agricultural interests of the state with a vast source of unskilled labor. Like all other casual laborers in California, the Mexicans suffered from chronic underemployment and low wages.

By the late 1920's, the latent hostility toward the increasing Mexican population became overt. During the depression of 1929, Californians objected to keeping aliens on relief during the winter months so they could serve as a source of cheap labor on farms in other seasons. As a result, thousands of Mexicans were quietly deported for a variety of fabricated reasons, and the border was more carefully patrolled to discourage illegal entrants. The number of Mexicans in California diminished, and their jobs were claimed by Dust Bowl refugees from Oklahoma and other plains states.

San Francisco had known labor unions as early as 1850 when a printers' union had been established there. Other trade unions soon followed. Labor unions in San Francisco benefitted from the presence of many European-born workmen who believed in the importance of worker organizations. San Francisco thus acquired a reputation as a union town, unmatched by any other California city. During the first two decades of its existence, the union movement lobbied through important labor legislation, such as laws providing for the prompt and full payment of wages, a mechanic's lien, and an eight-hour day for government workers. Nowhere else outside California did so many workers enjoy an eight-hour day as they did in San Francisco.

In the 1870's the developing labor movement was diverted from its course by the anti-Chinese activity which engaged many white California laborers during the career of Denis Kearney. When Kearney's popularity faded, his place as a labor leader was taken by the man who had been his severest critic—Frank Roney. A native of Ireland, Roney had been an agitator for Irish independence in his youth. Finding this cause to be both frustrating and dangerous, Roney migrated to the United States, where he became a national leader in the iron moulders' union. Arriving in San Francisco, he took an active part in the Workingmen's movement of the 1870's. His most distinguishing trait was his unrelenting hostility to Kearney, whom he considered to be a fraud.

Following the collapse of the Workingmen's Party, Roney was elected president of the Federated Trade and Labor Unions of the Pacific Coast. This organization evolved into the San Francisco Central Labor Council. Twice previously, a union had attempted to organize the seamen of San Francisco, only to win ephemeral success. Now Roney was given the difficult task of reorganizing them. By this time San Francisco had earned a reputation as the world's worst shanghaiing port, where an alliance of shipowners and underworld elements preyed upon sailors. Once he became president of the Seamen's Protective Association, Roney began a campaign against poor shipboard conditions and low wages which allowed the filling of crews only by resort to kidnapping. Roney's union brought suit against cruel ships' officers in the names of individual seamen. In addition, the union lobbied vigorously for laws to protect seamen from oppressive officers and poor working conditions.

In 1885, when the shipowners cut seamen's wages, the Coast Seamen's Union was formed with the help of the Knights of Labor—a national union then at the peak of its strength in California. Also active within the ranks of the seamen's union were Socialists from the International Workingmen's Association; five of them served in the union's original advisory committee. This union was effective in halting the employers' drive for wage cuts by organizing branches at all leading Pacific ports. In 1887 the union launched the *Coast Seamen's Journal*, the region's most influential labor paper for many years. In 1891 a rival Steamship Sailors' Union amalgamated with the Coast Seamen's Union to form the Sailors' Union of the Pacific.

With the establishment of an effective seamen's union, waterfront unions became strong in San Francisco's total labor movement because the pile drivers, ship caulkers and longshoremen had already been unionized.

The growth of organized labor in San Francisco did not proceed without generating intense opposition. To counter the growing strength of organized labor, which had staged a waterfront strike and brewery work stoppage in 1886, and a bitter labor battle fought by the metalworkers in 1890, a Board of Manufacturers and Employers was created. In 1893 the two groups met in conflict, a battle which the workers might have won if some of their partisans had not bombed a nonunion boardinghouse on Christmas Day, killing eight people and injuring many others. Public opinion immediately shifted from sympathy for the workers to violent hostility toward them, thus preventing a union victory.

The Spanish–American War and the Klondike Gold Strike caused great economic activity in San Francisco and encouraged labor to make new demands. To coordinate their efforts, the waterfront and seagoing laborers joined together in the City Front Federation, which was declared to be the strongest union organization in the West, and perhaps in the whole United States. A counterforce, the Employers Council, was quickly formed.

When the San Francisco teamsters were locked out on July 30, 1901, the City Front Federation called a rash of sympathetic strikes. Many employers, who had raised a war chest of a quarter of a million dollars, fought back stubbornly. The strike's real issue concerned whether management could succeed in establishing an open shop (no union recognition) throughout the city of San Francisco. Strikebreakers were brought in and protected by the police at the order of Mayor James D. Phelan. Ugly violence broke out. About three hundred assaults were recorded on the police blotter, and five men were killed. In October the strike ended in a stalemate when the governor intervened. The labor leaders were very bitter, feeling that they could have won if it had not been for the police intervention sanctioned by Mayor Phelan's administration. The result of this conflict was the formation of the Union Labor Party, which collapsed in a welter of ugly scandals after almost a decade of power. In the long run, the effects of the strike of 1901 favored labor. The unions remained strong, and eventually, in a series of smaller labor disputes, they succeeded in making San Francisco the first closed-shop city in America.

While labor was winning in San Francisco, it fared poorly in Los Angeles, where the union movement had a weak tradition and the open shop was almost an article of faith with large employers. As early as 1890, when employers threatened a 20 per cent wage cut, the typographers on four Los Angeles newspapers walked off their jobs. Three of the papers quickly capitulated to the union demands, but the *Times*, controlled by Harrison Gray Otis, who would never employ union printers, continued stubbornly to hold out. Otis hired strikebreakers from as far away as Kansas City. In retaliation, the unions attempted a boycott of the *Times* and its advertisers. Because Otis could find new advertisers in the speedily growing Los Angeles metropolitan area, and since he retained the loyalty of many farm readers, he successfully rode out the storm and defeated the strikers.

He then took advantage of the antilabor feeling engendered in southern California by the Debs Pullman strike. He violently attacked the unions for what he called their "robber rule." Soon he organized an aggressive employers' group called the Merchants and Manufacturers Association, which had six thousand dues-paying members. This association organized a counterboycott of any business that weakened in the face of union demands. Otis' success was galling to the state's labor leaders, because San Francisco's employers had argued that they could not be expected to pay a wage differential forever, and if labor leaders did not organize Los Angeles, they would themselves try to reestablish the open shop in San Francisco.

Faced with this threat, the Bay area union sent organizers to Los Angeles in June, 1910. This attempt to organize Los Angeles merged with a national labor problem when 1,200 workers of the International Association of Bridge and Structural Steel and Ironworkers went out on strike in the Los Angeles area. This international union had been organized in 1896. Because structural ironworking was dangerous, casual and migratory, the union at first displayed little stability. For six years it remained weak, until 1902, when it defeated the American Bridge Company in a strike. At that time American Bridge was the industry's leading company, and its defeat caused a union shop to be established in the entire industry within a year. The employers refused to accept this situation and instead formed the National Erectors Association. This association was successful in infiltrating the union with its own agents, and using an extensive black list, succeeded in gravely weakening the workers' organization. In desperation the union turned to terrorist tactics. Between 1908 and 1911, there were forty-three dynamitings on projects of the Erectors Association and an additional twenty-seven on jobs of nonunion independent contractors. In all these explosions no lives were lost, and relatively little property damage resulted. Los Angeles furnished a strikingly different incident, however.

At the Los Angeles strike of the Structural Ironworkers, there was violence on both sides, and many pickets were arrested by the police. Since the juries regularly refused to convict the pickets, many labor leaders felt confident that they would win. Their most articulate foe was

Harrison Gray Otis, who fought with his newspaper against the structural workers' strike as he had against the printers' union.

If public opinion had been sympathetic toward the strikers, it quickly changed when, at seven minutes past one on the morning of October 1, a series of explosions rocked the *Times* building and gutted it with fire. Twenty-one men were killed and seventeen injured. Otis branded this incident as another example of the violence of the ironworkers and blamed the union for dynamiting his plant. Labor leaders indignantly retorted that escaping gas had caused the explosion and that Otis was guilty of criminal negligence in the upkeep of his plant. Police and grand jury investigations supported Otis' contention that the building had been dynamited. Public opinion remained confused and uncertain about what to believe.

Meanwhile the Erectors Association and the Los Angeles Merchants and Manufacturers' Association hired a former Treasury agent, William J. Burns, then running his own private-detective agency. A countywide manhunt for the dynamiters was conducted. Seven months after the explosion, the *Times* announced that William J. Burns's detectives had taken into custody three union men. In Detroit, Ortie McManigal and James B. McNamara had been secretly arrested for the crime. A few days later, a brother of one of the arrested men, John Joseph McNamara, a secretary-treasurer of the Ironworkers Union, was suddenly apprehended at union headquarters in Indianapolis. All three men were promptly removed to California. Union men across the nation complained that the rights of the three suspects had been violated by the lack of extradition proceedings. Meanwhile, in a flurry of publicity, Burns announced that McManigal had turned state's evidence and that his confession had named J. J. McNamara as director of the terror campaign and J. B. McNamara as the man who had dynamited the *Times* building.

The arrest of these union men was a grave shock to the entire American labor movement. The removal of the three men from the Midwest to California convinced most union leaders that they were innocent. The American Federation of Labor employed the renowned defense attorney Clarence Darrow to defend the McNamaras, who were indicted for murder and a series of other dynamiting crimes in the Los Angeles area. Their trial began in October 1911 and became a contest for prestige between management and labor groups. The National Manufacturers' Association and various local antilabor groups helped the prosecution. The trial was the scene of political maneuvers. Job Harriman, an attorney for the defense along with Darrow, was also a Socialist candidate for mayor of Los Angeles. In the first decade of the twentieth century, the Socialists demonstrated considerable political muscle in local California elections. Consequently, Harriman and his backers expected a victory to use as a springboard for statewide power. This possibility greatly frightened men like Harrison Gray Otis.

No sooner had the trial begun in earnest than Darrow realized that his clients, particularly J. B. McNamara, had a very poor case. Therefore the noted attorney attempted to arrange a settlement to save his clients' lives. His opponents were most anxious that labor be discredited and that the threat of a Socialist political victory be dissipated. Hence they were more eager than usual to strike a bargain. Therefore a behind-the-scenes agreement was eventually reached.

On December 1, to the consternation of many individuals not on the inside, the McNamara brothers appeared before the court and changed their plea to guilty. Two days later, the judge sentenced J. B. to life imprisonment and J. J. to a term of fifteen years. This last development was shocking to the defense, since they believed that the deal had provided that J. J. would draw only a ten-year term.

Organized labor and the Socialist Party had badly underestimated the impact upon their fortunes of the McNamaras' confession of guilt. Harriman was badly defeated in the mayoralty election, and the Socialist Party's hopes for statewide success were permanently blighted. Organized labor's progress in the Los Angeles area was severely retarded for twenty years. Los Angeles employers gleefully pushed the advantage of the McNamaras' conviction in their struggle to maintain the open shop in southern California.

A militant workers' organization, the Industrial Workers of the World (often called the "Wobblies"), was formed late in June 1905. This group hoped to organize an industrial union to include all skilled and unskilled workers. Its professed goal was a federation of industries owned by workers. To gain its ends, the I.W.W. advocated strikes, boycotts and sabotage. Never actually stronger than seventy-five thousand or one hundred thousand members, the I.W.W. depended upon the militancy of its adherents to place it in the forefront of labor struggles. It attempted union organizing in areas previously neglected by organized labor. It sent organizers into the Pacific northwest labor camps and into California, preaching fiery doctrines to lumberjacks, agricultural workers and miners.

In 1910, Fresno decided to suppress its Wobblies by passing an ordinance to abridge their right to hold public meetings. The Wobblies decided to make a fight on the issue of free speech and adopted the idea of passive resistance. They permitted themselves to be arrested in such large numbers that they filled the Fresno jail. There they sang and chanted, despite the police strictures to be silent. Finally their enraged prison guards turned a fire hose on them. Anti-Wobbly vigilantes took impromptu counteraction by burning the laborites' headquarters. After several months of turmoil, Fresno authorities surrendered, offering concessions to the Wobblies.

Encouraged by their success in Fresno, the I.W.W. decided in 1912 to launch a similar campaign in San Diego, which had adopted a comparable ordinance against Wobbly meetings. Since San Diego was not a mining or agricultural center, a word-of-mouth campaign was launched to bring Wobblies to the southern California seaport from all parts of the West. The San Diego police were undaunted, and soon began to arrest the incoming Wobblies. Again this did not intimidate the members of the I.W.W., who hoped to fill the jails to overflowing in San Diego as they had in Fresno. The San Diego police were not gentle in their methods; one Wobbly was beaten and kicked to death by policemen. With the tacit approval of the authorities, vigilantes began to take bold anti-Wobbly action. Tar and feathers were meted out to some intransigent Wobblies as punishment. Another large mob of vigilantes seized several hundred Wobblies and made them run a gauntlet in groups of six or eight. On two sides of the fleeing man, vigilantes struck them with clubs and blacksnake whips, eventually running them out of town. Despite eight months of disorders in San Diego, the Wobblies were unable to repeat their earlier success in Fresno.

The Wheatland riot in August 1913 pointed up the gap that existed between an itinerant farm worker's way of life and a reasonable standard of living. Prior to the 1913 hop-harvesting season, a rancher named Richard Durst, who owned a very large farm near Wheatland in the eastern Sacramento Valley, advertised widely for workers. He misrepresented information in a number of ways, a common practice among agricultural employers. His circulated notices stated that he could use twice as many pickers as he really needed, that he could give steady employment to nearly all workers who applied, and promised higher wages than he had any intention of paying.

As a result of Durst's far-flung advertising 3,800 hop pickers of all races descended upon his ranch. Hindus, European immigrants and native Americans jostled each other for places in his work force. While many itinerant workers were single men, others had families with them. As the pickers arrived, they were herded onto a treeless hill on the Durst ranch. There in pitiful tents or in makeshift cloth-walled accommodations that were open to the sky, the workers and their families dwelled. Eight small toilets had to serve this horde of people. No provision was made for the disposal of garbage. Soon waste of all description littered the countryside. The water supply was located away from the fields where the workers toiled, and no water was regularly sent to them; only lemonade allegedly made of citric acid was sold to them. The wages were not those advertised—between seventy-eight cents and a dollar a day. A company store which gouged on prices was the only available grocery facility. Finally, in exasperation at their plight, thirty workers formed an I.W.W. local. On August 3 the local called a meeting to demand better living conditions. An I.W.W. leader, Richard "Blackie" Ford, harangued the crowd. Then as the meeting was closing with one of many rousing Wobbly songs, the sheriff of Yuba County, the district attorney and a posse arrived in automobiles. Their object was to disperse the mob and apprehend Ford. As the I.W.W. organizer's arrest was being made, one of the deputies fired a shot into the air. At once a wild riot resulted. Before it subsided, the sheriff, the district attorney and two workers (one a young boy) were killed. Many were injured. The posse fled in wild disarray from the camp; the workers also swiftly left, hoping to escape before any efficient dragnet could be thrown out. The state militia were quickly ordered out and patrolled the area for a week. Meanwhile the Burns private-detective agency roamed the state, arresting Wobblies and detaining them without benefit of warrants. Not only was Blackie Ford arrested, but a colleague of his, Herman Suhr, was apprehended in Arizona. Without any legal formalities, Suhr was thrust into a boxcar and returned to California. After a quick trial, both Ford and Suhr drew life sentences, while other apprehended rioters were given long terms in the state penitentiary.

A more constructive result of the riot was the first law concerning the welfare of itinerant workers. A Commission of Immigration and Housing, with Simon J. Lubin as chairman, was appointed. The commission was charged with the duty of inspecting labor camps to see that minimum standards of health and sanitation were observed. While this law was only a beginning in efforts to help the migrants, it marked a significant step forward.

By 1916 there were many in the United States who favored a strong national military policy, since America might enter World War I. These individuals and groups sponsored what became known as "Preparedness Days." The feature of these events was a large parade through the streets of the nearest large city. One such parade was scheduled for July 22, 1916, in San Francisco. In that city, employers who equated unionism with un-Americanism had grasped the occasion to use it to further the open-shop campaign. As a result, union men, who were often pacifists, openly damned the parade as a disguised antiunion demonstration. Warnings were issued that if the parade were held as scheduled, violence would result. The warnings were disregarded and the parade was held on schedule. As columns of marchers stretching for miles moved down Market Street, a bomb was exploded near the Ferry building, killing six persons and fatally injuring four others. Over fifty people suffered injuries.

There was so much confusion and excitement after the blast that most on-the-scene evidence was lost. It was believed that an iron pipe filled with dynamite and loaded cartridges had been detonated. Even the exact way in which the bomb was delivered was unknown. It may have been planted in a suitcase or dropped from a window or roof.

Citizens of San Francisco from all levels of society were outraged by the tragedy. As a result, four days after the blast, six thousand San Franciscans gathered in the Civic Auditorium to pledge themselves to a "relentless pursuit" of the bombers. Coming only six years after the destruction of the Los Angeles *Times* building, citizens of San Francisco naturally assumed that radicals in the labor movement had perpetrated the crime.

Suspicion quickly settled upon two men closely linked with the militant wing of the labor unions—Thomas J. Mooney and Warren K. Billings. Mooney had been a friend of J. B. McNamara; he had defended the I.W.W. leaders charged with the Wheatland riot only three years before; he had many known anarchists among his acquaintances and had contributed articles to an anarchist journal called *Blast*. Most damning of all, Mooney and Billings had both previously been tried for sabotage. Mooney had been charged with dynamiting transmission towers during a strike of electrical workers, and Billings had been accused of the unlawful possession of explosives. Mooney had been acquitted of his charge, but Billings had been convicted with a two-year prison term. At the time of the bombing, Billings had only recently been released from the penitentiary.

The San Francisco district attorney, Charles Fickert, soon decided that Mooney and several of his friends were responsible for the crime. He has since been severely criticized by historians, because once he had made up his mind about Mooney and Billings, he did not seriously consider other possibilities. In the end, Fickert arrested Tom Mooney, his wife Rena and Billings. As a man with a previous conviction, Billings was tried separately. He was quickly convicted of second-degree murder and sentenced to life imprisonment in September 1916. The case against him was based upon the testimony of extremely dubious witnesses.

In January 1917, Mooney was brought to trial. At that time the prosecution charged that Mooney, his wife and Billings had originally intended to hurl a bomb down upon the parade from a roof, but at the last minute had changed their plans and had driven in a car to the scene of the explosion. There they allegedly planted the bomb along the parade route. A surprise witness, Frank C. Oxman, testified that he saw Mooney leave a suitcase containing the bomb at the scene of the explosion. In February, Mooney was found guilty of first-degree murder and sentenced to be hanged.

Quickly Mooney's case passed out of the category of a local event; in the eastern United States and in many other parts of the world, demonstrations broke out against his conviction. In time the Mooney affair, which has been called an American Dreyfus case, became enshrouded in a fog of controversy. After Mooney's trial and sentencing, the presiding judge asked the California attorney general to have the case retried. The California supreme court refused to allow a retrial on the ground that the appeal court could not consider evidence that went beyond the court record. This was the ruling when the defense tried to show that new evidence indicated that the witness who had so positively linked Mooney with the crime had lied. The accused witness was then tried for perjury and promptly acquitted!

Adding to the confusion was the fact that Rena Mooney was tried on the same evidence that had convicted her husband only a month earlier and was acquitted by a different jury. Two other of Mooney's friends who had been charged as accomplices in the crime were subsequently either acquitted or freed for lack of evidence.

Both Billings and Mooney had their convictions upheld by the California supreme court, while the United States Supreme Court refused to intervene.

Because of his personal concern and because of international ramifications, President Woodrow Wilson, in November 1918, successfully appealed to Governor William D. Stephens to commute Mooney's sentence to life imprisonment. Labor and liberal groups never ceased to chant "Free Tom Mooney!" Each incoming California governor received piles of petitions for this purpose. The two men, Mooney at San Quentin and Billings at Folsom Prison, became symbols of the antilabor groups' hatred and oppression. As time went by, Billings became less and less prominent in the continuing agitation, which became known as the "Tom Mooney Case."

Mooney, as a radical leader, had been the principal target of the prosecution. Moreover, Mooney was an extraordinarily energetic and domineering person with greater drive, more family and more friends than Billings. Also Billings, as a man with a prior conviction, did not fit the role of a martyr as well as did Mooney. Both Mooney and Billings were adamant in refusing paroles, which to them were admissions of guilt.

Finally, nearly a quarter of a century after the Preparedness Day bombing, Governor Culbert L. Olson, on January 7, 1939, granted Mooney a full and unconditional pardon. The event was broadcast by radio throughout the nation. Nine months later Billings had his sentence commuted to time already served and was released. Because of his previous record, Billings was considered ineligible for a pardon. Once freed, both men were quickly forgotten. A few years after his pardon, Tom Mooney died, on March 6, 1942, from complications of a stomach ulcer.

Billings worked in a watch repair shop for years while steadily battling for a full pardon which in December 1961 Governor Brown finally granted him. The questionable conviction of Billings and Mooney created sympathy for the hard-pressed California labor unions during the twenties and thirties.

The climate of American opinion during the years immediately following the First World War was decidedly hostile to organized labor. Ordinary unionism frightened many conservatives, but labor groups had a noisily militant wing which sent shivers up the spines of most members of the general public. The Russian Revolution seemed to demonstrate that all shades of liberal dissent were suspect, since any sustained criticism of the existing society might lead to a bloody upheaval. In this period, California was no exception to the national trend. In 1919, California passed a criminal syndicalism law similar to those passed by twenty-one other states. Noteworthy was the change in political climate evidenced by the passage of this act. The sponsor of the measure had been chairman of the committee that had killed a similar previous bill in 1917. Moreover, the legislator in question had a reputation as a friend of labor and a supporter of progressive legislation. Now he sponsored a measure on criminal syndicalism which defined this term so broadly as to include any doctrine advocating crime or sabotage to effect political change. Under this statute, guilt was equally attributed to advocating a deed, doing it or belonging to an organization which so advocated it.

In many states, when this type of law was placed upon the statute books it remained a dead letter. This was not so in California. There, in the first five years after its passage, 531 persons were arrested under its provisions, 264 of these were tried, and 164 convicted.

Meanwhile the I.W.W. continued to upset many Californians. During the First World War the conditon of many laborers improved, for there was general prosperity. When the I.W.W. seized the opportunity caused by the shortage of labor to strike, it was generally condemned as unpatriotic. Its reputation in these years outstripped its power. Many things for which it was not really responsible were blamed upon or credited to the influence of the I.W.W. As a result, in 1918 the federal government prosecuted 105 top leaders of the movement and convicted all but thirteen of them. Thousands more Wobblies were arrested. Their best leaders were in prison when the war ended. As an organization, the I.W.W. still seemed formidable to its conservative opponents in the postwar years, but it was only a semblance of its former self. Even this remnant was sharply divided between centralists who wanted strong central direction and the autonomists who wanted more local control. As a result, the I.W.W. lost both membership and financial resources. In California it was not strong enough to effect the tasks it undertook, nor to withstand the fierce counterattack launched upon it. It was responsible for the strike in 1922 of 1,700 construction workers who were building an aqueduct to carry water to the San Francisco Bay area from the Sierra. This strike failed when the California criminal syndicalism law was harshly applied. A strike of three thousand longshoremen in San Pedro met the same fate. Hundreds of strikers were arrested and taken away to stockades hastily constructed in Griffith Park. Within a month, that strike had been broken. California also fought the Wobblies with professional witnesses; when juries became more skeptical and harder to convince that they should convict individuals, the authorities turned to a new weapon. They obtained an injunction which barred I.W.W. union organizers from seeking new members. Any Wobbly brash enough to disobey this order was jailed for contempt of court without the necessity of a jury trial. By 1924, the I.W.W. was reduced to the leaders who were in jail and a handful of hard-core supporters. These supporters, now left leaderless, soon split among themselves over whether jailed leaders should accept pardons, if they could get them. The I.W.W. became a corpse—the victim of a relentless drive to persecute it and of its own doctrinaire inability to heal dissensions in its own ranks.

With the obvious decline of the Wobblies as an effective force, the criminal syndicate law of California was not repealed; it merely ceased to be actively employed against dissenters.

The entire California labor movement remained impotent for nearly twenty years after World War I. Even San Francisco's vaunted status as a closed-shop town was thoroughly undermined, while Los Angeles continued as an undoubted bastion of the open shop.

TWENTY-EIGHT

California Rides the Wave of Prosperity

DURING the era of World War I, California enjoyed a period of feverish expansion. From 1910 to 1920, industrial output, wages, employment and construction of industrial plants soared spectacularly, and the assessed value of California real estate and personal property doubled.

In 1914 the opening of the Panama Canal promised California a solid economic future and made Los Angeles one of the world's most important harbor cities. Ten to twelve years after the canal was in operation, Los Angeles passed San Francisco in total annual tonnage and became the most important port on the West Coast. Los Angeles' location on the great circle route to the Orient made it the port many had always proclaimed it would be. The city was expanding both in area and population in an exploding labyrinth of steel, cement and stucco. Because of its sprawling growth in all directions, and because it seemed to have no central section, Los Angeles was referred to as "a series of suburbs in search of a central city." By contrast, San Francisco refused to annex anything except the offshore Farallon Islands, and remained with a land area of less than forty-five square miles.

Although California was geographically remote from the theaters of combat during World War I, the state's industrial pace was markedly stimulated by wartime demands. Prior to World War I, California's industrial employment had been concentrated in food-processing industries and finishing the products of extractive industries. Lumbering, mineral extraction and oil production were also major industries. These activities continued to flourish during the war and encouraged greater industrial diversification. Eastern corporations established branches and offices in California, particularly in the San Francisco Bay area. The result of this industrial migration westward was to integrate California more closely into the nation's economic life.

Agricultural activity in California was also stimulated by the war. Great quantities of grain, meat, fruit and vegetables were sent to the eastern United States, as well as to the war-ravaged countries of Europe. The production of cotton became important. Special representatives were sent to California by the Department of Agriculture to experiment with the growth of a long, staple, tough, elastic variety of cotton used for cord-tire fabric and the covering of airplane wings and fuselages. Cotton was also required to meet the urgent demands for millions of army uniforms. Between 1916 and 1920, the average cotton planting in California covered 90,000 acres a year with an average yield of 48,000 bales. While it is true that after the war the competition from Egyptian cotton pushed the price of California cotton below cost and threatened the state's cotton industry, nonetheless California had become a major cotton producer.

In manpower, California contributed over 150,000 men to the American armed forces. The Ninety-first Division (California's own) served on the western front during the Battle of the Argonne. Since the war against Germany was relatively popular in California, the state was able to exceed its quota in both the Liberty and Victory Loan drives. Two Californians, Herbert Hoover and Hugh Gibson, served important roles in postwar relief activities.

The automobile has played a vital role in California's history. During World War I, the age of the railroad gave way to the age of the motorcar. Although the Detroit area became the first automobile-manufacturing center, the Bay area and the Los Angeles region both experienced some minor activity in motorcar production. For their specialty, Californians concentrated primarily upon the design and construction of racing cars.

By 1898, California had developed its first successful car, the harbinger of millions to come. W. L. Elliott was responsible for it. To the utter disbelief of onlookers, it steadily chugged along the cluttered streets of Oakland. In September of 1898, Elliott successfully navigated his car on a 56-mile run to Mount Hamilton. Elliott's successful trip changed the minds of many skeptics, and soon wealthy Californians began to order automobiles.

During the San Francisco earthquake, the more serious uses of the motorcar were demonstrated. Federal troops from the Presidio were rushed by automobile to the scene of San Francisco fires and looting.

Many refugees packed their cars with families and friends and drove from the scene of the catastrophe to outlying areas.

Notwithstanding its beneficial uses in San Francisco, for many Californians the automobile had to prove itself as more than a rich man's toy. As late as 1910, there were only 36,000 motor vehicles registered in California. By 1912 the first paved California highway especially for autos was opened. Early speed regulations were severe: eight miles an hour in residential areas, six miles an hour in business districts, and four miles an hour at street intersections.

However, the benign California weather allowed open automobiles to be operated the year round, and the great distances to be traversed within the state stimulated a growth in the sales of automobiles. By 1920 the number of automobiles in California exceeded 604,000. California had become a state on wheels.

The automobile diffused population even more widely than had the interurban railroad. New suburbs sprang up. Isolation broke down as long-distance travel for both business and pleasure became common. For a short time, the automobile actually reduced urban congestion before making it worse than anyone had dreamed possible. It also enabled thousands of tourists and migrants to come to California by car. The long-distance auto traveler was encouraged by events such as the cross-country drive in the summer of 1911 from Atlantic City, New Jersey, to Los Angeles.

In 1920 the census showed that California had a population of less than three and a half million people and claimed eighth place in the roll of states. During the twenties many people drove to California, and the state gained more than two million people, pushing the total population to 5,600,000 and making California the sixth most populous state in the nation. The newcomers settled generally in southern California, drawn there by advertising such as that put out by the All Year Club, which worked unceasingly to draw tourists and residents to the region. Once they had seen southern California, many tourists returned to settle there. Los Angeles had a growth of 114 per cent in the twenties.

Between 1920 and 1924, at least one hundred thousand people a year poured into Los Angeles itself. Naturally a real estate and building boom ensued. The changing value of building permits tells the story of this real estate boom. In 1919 permits were worth $28,000,000; the value rose to $60,000,000 in 1920 and doubled to $121,000,000 by 1922 and $200,000,000 in 1923. Only the great metropolises of Chicago and New York exceeded this last total. Although 1,400 housing tracts were opened in Los Angeles during the early twenties, this building boom did not have an immediately disastrous aftermath. Although building and real estate activity declined somewhat, until the stock market crash of 1929, bank clearings and retail trade continued at a high level in southern California.

Along with this increase in population, the flood of autos showed no letup. In 1929, when the number of automobiles owned nationally came to something over twenty-three million, nearly one auto in eleven was owned by a Californian; nearly two million cars were registered in the state. On a per capita basis, California automobile registration became the highest in the country. There were many effects of this massive concentration of cars. First, many accidents occurred, and the phrase "California driver" to describe a reckless driver became part of the national vocabulary. In an effort to cut down highway slaughter, California pioneered in the use of highway center lines and automatic traffic signals. Even so, by 1936 California exceeded New York in the number of traffic fatalities.

The sale of automobiles and accessories became a big business in California. In Los Angeles, whole boulevards, such as Figueroa and Alvarado, and Van Ness in San Francisco, were given over to car dealers' showrooms. The radio industry came to California almost as a by-product of automobile sales activities. For years KFI, Los Angeles' largest station, was owned by a leading southern California Packard dealer. A Cadillac dealer operated still another of the most powerful stations in southern California.

Many auto assembly plants were built in Oakland, Long Beach and Los Angeles, providing more work for the increasing California population. However, they did not make it cheaper to own a car, since dealers generally charged buyers the freight rate from Detroit in addition to the retail price of the car.

At first, Californians had to struggle to keep their cars running on muddy roads during the rainy season when winter rains turned the dusty horse-and-wagon trails into quagmires. Improvements were made when irate auto drivers and bicyclists vociferously complained to their state officials. The California Highway Commission was set up by a statute approved by Governor James N. Gillett in 1909 and later ratified by the people. This commission was authorized to issue $18 million in bonds for surfaced road construction. At the time, this sum seemed enormous, but for the task involved it was a mere pittance. In 1916 the voters approved the issuance of an additional $15 million of highway-construction bonds, and three years later, they voted another $40 million. Soon the habit of voting ever-increasing sums for highways became common to the California electorate.

As a result of the insatiable demand for highways, California cement production soared until it became second only to that of Pennsylvania, at times approaching thirteen million barrels a year.

California agriculture became increasingly important in the initial quarter of the twentieth century. As late as 1909, California stood seventeenth in the roll of states in the production of vegetable crops. Because of its excellent climate and the increasing demand for vegetables as the American public learned about the value of vitamins, California soon ranked much higher in the growth of perishable vegetable crops. Moreover, after 1909 the improving facilities for refrigeration allowed the transportation of spoilable crops from California to the eastern states.

The census of 1919 showed that California led the nation in the production of miscellaneous vegetables; during that year the state had 217,179 acres of truck crops. Los Angeles County boasted the greatest truck-garden acreage—closely followed by San Joaquin, Sacramento, Imperial and Stanislaus counties.

Lettuce, which was raised in insignificant amounts prior to 1910, assumed a new importance. While asparagus had been grown in California as early as 1852, its serious cultivation within the state occurred only after 1890. In 1892 the first large asparagus cannery was opened on Boulder Island. Soon great crops of white asparagus were grown in the Sacramento Delta. In the early years of the twentieth century, rust became a severe problem for asparagus growers. After 1906, when the rust problem was lessened, there was a more or less steady increase in the growth of asparagus, until 1931, when there was a peak production of 2,633,000 cases. The subsequent decrease in demand for this crop during the great depression of the thirties caused a slump in asparagus production to about two million cases. Production remained at that level until after World War II. Green asparagus was canned only experimentally in California before 1930, but after that date California was canning half of the green asparagus of the United States.

Although tomato canning was begun in the Santa Clara Valley in 1880, it was only after 1900 that it became important. At first canned tomatoes were only processed in California, but eventually half of the processed crop was used for paste, catsup and juice. Although the state of Indiana actually pioneered in the production of canned tomato juice, it quickly became a California staple. In 1929 only 185,000 cases of tomato juice were packed in the United States. By 1931, California alone packed 419,000 cases; this figure climbed in 1940 to 2,723,000 cases. Tomato shipments to the East became important in 1902 or 1903. By 1917, southern California was supplying 90 per cent of tomato shipments in the United States. California preeminence in this field of agriculture has continued.

In 1901 cantaloupes were first grown commercially in the Coachella Valley. Then in 1905 additional acreage was planted in the Imperial Valley. As a result, the average annual acreage climbed until 1927–36, when California's annual acreage was 37,430, while the annual average market value was over six million dollars.

Rice was another crop that became important in California only with the advent of the twentieth century. Although there had been experimental attempts to grow rice within the state; it was not until 1906 or 1907 that its production became significant. At that time the Japanese introduced rice into the Sacramento Valley. Although the acreage involved was relatively small, the yield per acre was high. By 1937 the rice harvest exceeded ten million bushels.

Cotton in California after World War I had to adjust to increased foreign competition. In order to meet this challenge, the farmers of the southern San Joaquin Valley switched from growing the Pima to the Acala variety of cotton. Between 1926 and 1930, 217,000 acres of cotton were planted and 183,000 bales were produced annually. Although cotton could be grown in many parts of California, the cotton fields of the San Joaquin and Imperial valleys predominated. In this period, California cotton production leaped ahead of that of Virginia and Tennessee and began to challenge the cotton crops of Georgia and the Carolinas.

Fruit and nut crops contributed greatly to California's commercial agriculture. Between 1895 and 1930 the average rate of growth in these crops was 5 per cent a year. In the fifty years between 1895 and 1945, the production of fruits and nuts increased ten times—eventually reaching the enormous total of more than five million tons during World War II. Nut production increased almost twenty times in the same fifty-year period; citrus production increased twenty-five times. In the same time span, the growing of grapes increased eight times. Deciduous tree fruit production rose from 300,000 tons to more than two million—a sevenfold increase.

The growing of grapes for the flourishing wine industry of California received a severe check when the Eighteenth Amendment went into effect. After this enactment, the California wine industry continued on a small scale by selling grape concentrates, which when mixed with water produced a sort of wine, and by selling pressed grape bricks which could be changed into a kind of wine. With the repeal of Prohibition, California's wine industry recovered its former preeminence and eventually was producing 90 per cent of the wine manufactured in the United States.

Perhaps a third of California agriculture was concentrated in livestock and poultry. By 1940 only eight midwestern states surpassed California as dairy producers. Meat production took second place to dairying on California livestock ranches. Nevertheless, California had more cattle than any state in the Confederacy, or any state west of Kansas. Hens and eggs were raised on small poultry ranches clustered around centers such as Petaluma, north of the Bay area. A 1929 census revealed a California egg count of 159,000,000 dozen.

By 1937, California crops reached a value of $648,200,000, putting the state first in agricultural production in the nation. This phenomenal growth was caused by intensive agricultural research at the University of California and other educational centers; a willingness on the part of California farmers to try new farming methods and crop varieties; and a readiness on the part of landowners to adopt industrial farming methods. California agriculture soon became efficient, specialized farming, far removed from the stereotype of the one-family, all-purpose farm.

In California a problem closely related to agriculture was that of adequate water supply. The vast immigration into the state's relatively arid areas, such as Los Angeles, soon created an acute demand for water to provide for increased individual, domestic and industrial purposes. It might be supposed that this problem should not exist in California, since the annual seasonal runoff from the state's rivers and streams approaches seventy million acre feet. However, since this heavy winter runoff occurs in the north, away from the centers of population, it does not help during the long, dry summers of southern California. As a result of this condition, during the last years of the nineteenth century, Los Angeles not only needed to create an artificial harbor to continue its growth, but also needed to supplement its water supply. From 1892 to 1904, southern California suffered a long drought. It seemed that the city of Los Angeles might have to stifle further growth by stabilizing its population at 200,-000, because the Los Angeles River and artesian wells could not provide more water.

To the civic boosters of Los Angeles, such a state of affairs was intolerable. One man, hard-headed, belligerent William Mulholland, came forward to suggest a way out of the water dilemma. An Irish immigrant, Mulholland had arrived in Los Angeles in 1877 with only ten dollars. Eventually, as an on-the-job trainee, he became an employee and then superintendent of the water company of Los Angeles. In 1902 the company was purchased by the city, and Mulholland became the supervisor of the entire municipal waterworks.

While looking for a new source of water for Los Angeles, Mulholland's attention was drawn to Owens Valley. This area on the eastern side of the Sierra Nevada was a green oasis in a desert where freshly melted snow flowed into the Owens River, traversed the valley, and poured eventually into the Owens Lake. The valley had been settled since early 1860. Near the Owens River, they had begun growing crops by irrigation, fighting continuously against dust, heat, floods and disease. Finally the settlers won and the desert began to produce crops. Mulholland soon realized that here was a water supply for perhaps two million people. Moreover, it could be brought to Los Angeles by aqueduct. Since this would provide more water than the city would need for years, the surplus could be sold to the farmers of the San Fernando Valley on the outskirts of the city. The charge has been made that much land in the San Fernando Valley was quietly purchased by insiders before the news of Los Angeles' water plans became known. The property was supposedly purchased at the rate of $50 an acre; with a bountiful water supply assured, it would have become ten times that price in value.

When the Los Angeles *Times* in July 1905 broke the news that the city planned to tap the water of Owens River, Los Angeles boosters could not restrain their jubilation; but the aroused citizens of Owens Valley vowed that the city would never get a drop of their precious water. The initial skirmish for the project was fought in Congress, since Los Angeles had to acquire a right-of-way for the aqueducts across federal land. In June of 1906, Congress passed the necessary legislation. Then, two years later, Los Angeles got the Federal Reclamation Service to extend national-forest boundaries into the flat land of Owens Valley, so that private claimants to the public domain could not harass the city's plans.

Meanwhile, Mulholland had had twenty-five million dollars authorized by the voters in two bond elections to build a ditch across the approximately 240 miles from Owens Valley to Los Angeles. Mulholland supervised an army of workers building a vast network of tunnels and trenches across the Mojave Desert. This feat was completed on November 5, 1913. Los Angeles changed from an area of water famine to one of water glut.

For a time the controversy between Los Angeles municipal authorities and Owens Valley settlers slumbered, but in the early 1920's the issue erupted in several violent incidents, precipitated by a variety of factors. First, a number of abnormally dry years left an inadequate water supply for the agricultural needs of Owens Valley, particularly now that the insatiable demands of the expanding city of Los Angeles had to be met. Secondly, Los Angeles had failed to build a promised large storage reservoir which would have helped to maintain an adequate supply of water. Third, Mulholland's aggressive tactics had embroiled him in personal feuds with other Los Angeleans, as well as with Owens Valley inhabitants.

Although Los Angeles had over the previous decade acquired nearly one hundred thousand acres of Owens Valley land, in 1923 the city inaugurated the policy of purchasing irrigated ranches there in order to obtain surface and underground water rights. As the number of ranchers and farmers in Owens Valley decreased, the businessmen of the area began to suffer. Bitterness against Los Angeles now pervaded the entire valley. Finally, in the spring of 1924, a small dynamite charge was detonated against the wall of an aqueduct near the town of Lone Pine. This violence eventually led Los Angeles officials to offer compromise terms to the settlers. Indignantly the Owens Valley inhabitants spurned their offer and demanded millions as reparations for damages and compensation for their property. On November 16, 1924, a band of organized Owens Valley protesters opened the waste gates of a large spillway in the Alabama Hills and diverted the entire flow of the aqueduct into the Owens River. For four days the settlers occupied the spot and left only when the Los Angeles Clearing House Association promised to use its good offices to obtain adequate compensation for them. The Alabama Hills incident turned the spotlight of national publicity upon the controversy. The *Literary Digest* discussed the struggle in an article, and at once Los Angeles reaped a harvest of unfavorable national publicity.

In 1926 and 1927, a series of dynamite explosions blew out sections of the aqueduct, damaging powerhouses and destroying all of Los Angeles' newly drilled wells. Although it was common knowledge in the valley who was behind the sabotage, no one was ever arrested or convicted.

At this point an event occurred which left the valley settlers stunned and leaderless. Two brothers named Watterson, who controlled the local bank as well as many other valley businesses, were charged in August 1927 with violating the state's banking laws. After an investigation, they were indicted and convicted. The fall of the Wattersons bankrupted some of the settlers and left the remainder ill prepared to carry on their struggle. Consequently, Owens Valley became a colony of Los Angeles. By 1931 the city owned over 200,000 acres of rural land in the valley. Los Angeles also acquired additional water rights in the Mono Basin. Not long thereafter, an eleven-mile tunnel was constructed to bring additional water from this area into the Owens Valley system.

While the repercussions of the Owens Valley controversy were still reverberating, southern California was trying to acquire still more water. In December 1928, Congress passed and President Herbert Hoover signed the Boulder Canyon Project Act, sponsored by Congressman Philip D. Swing of San Bernardino and Senator Hiram Johnson. This act authorized the construction of a dam which was actually located in Black Canyon rather than the Boulder Canyon. In September 1930, the Secretary of the Interior named the dam after President Hoover, but it was years before this name was recognized by Congress. Actual construction of the dam began in February 1931 and was completed in March 1936. The completed dam measured 1,282 feet long, 727 feet high, and 660 feet thick at the base. It was capable of holding over thirty million acre feet of water. This dam was built to provide a water reserve for several states other than California, to protect the Imperial Valley against flooding, and to generate water power. Hoover Dam provided a precious flow of water without which southern California cities from Ventura to San Diego would not have been able to expand.

Because of its growing population and manufacturing activities, San Francisco also had to seek an additional water supply. As early as 1901,

San Francisco's mayor, James D. Phelan, had appointed a committee of engineers to survey the Sierra Nevada as a future source of water. These engineers recommended taking water from the Tuolumne River above scenic Yosemite Valley and routing it along 150 miles of aqueduct to San Francisco. Although Phelan's original application to take water from the river was denied, in 1908 the Department of the Interior authorized San Francisco to acquire several storage reservoir sites along the Tuolumne in Hetch Hetchy Valley. This federal action aroused protests from the famous naturalist John Muir, who condemned what he called the "spoliation" of the Hetch Hetchy area. In 1913, Congress passed an act which granted San Francisco permanent water rights to approximately 420,000 acres of public land.

To start the work, in January of 1910, a seventy-mile railroad was constructed into the mountains from the San Joaquin Valley to carry both workers and supplies to the dam and reservoir sites. The route of the 156-mile aqueduct was next surveyed. Then the World War I moratorium on most kinds of civilian building delayed the rest of the project. In 1919 the work was resumed and was finally finished in 1934. Since the aqueduct route dropped from an altitude of 3,800 feet at its source to a point below sea level where it passed beneath San Francisco Bay, the falling water generated electric power for city lights and energy to operate the municipal streetcar system.

The California petroleum industry enjoyed its third boom immediately after the close of World War I. By 1920 annual production passed 100,-000,000 barrels a year. During these years California's greatest oil discoveries took place, particularly in the Los Angeles Basin. Among the most important discoveries were those at Huntington Beach, Santa Fe Springs, Signal Hill, Torrance and Dominguez. Ventura and Kern counties were also the scenes of significant discoveries.

Pipelines and refineries were built at a feverish pace. In 1927 seventy-eight refineries produced over 209,000,000 barrels of crude oil. The new wells in the Los Angeles region produced an oil of lighter consistency than that of the San Joaquin Valley. As a result, a higher proportion of gasoline and light distillates could be obtained from this oil. The opening of the Panama Canal made it possible to ship California's surplus oil to refineries and markets on the Atlantic seaboard. Shipments to the East leaped from less than a million barrels in 1920 to over forty-four million barrels in 1929. At that time more gasoline was shipped to the East than was consumed along the entire Pacific coast. As early as 1924, California ranked first in the nation in the production of petroleum products.

By 1930 California's petroleum production had soared to 227,000,000 barrels—a figure that it did not achieve again until 1937, because of the adverse effects of the depression and the competition from Mexican and South American oil. In 1937 the production of natural gas in California was 335,420,000,000 cubic feet. Lacking adequate sources of coal for power, California led the nation in the daily consumption of natural gas.

Banking flourished too in booming California. From 1900 to 1917, California's banking resources grew steadily from $384,785,000 to $1,682,000,-000, while the number of banks increased from 269 to 718. By 1927 banking resources had risen to $3,833,957,000. This increase had been stimulated by various bank mergers, by the importation of capital from the East, and by the inauguration of branch banking. By 1928 the Bank of Italy (later renamed the Bank of America), under the guidance of Amadeo Peter Giannini, became the fifth-largest bank in the nation, with some 280 branches in the state. Paralleling the growth of the banking system was the rise of building and loan companies whose resources grew 100 per cent from 1895 to 1920. Their assets increased fourfold from 1920 to 1927.

The early twentieth century also saw the rise of the movie industry in California. As early as 1901 two large companies—Biograph and the Thomas Edison Company of New Jersey—were filming crude moving pictures to be exhibited in penny arcades and cheap vaudeville houses. The low-income segments of society were the principal viewers of these early films. Their tastes were unsophisticated, and they demanded make-believe to brighten their drab lives.

Edison's company, which held most of the basic motion-picture patents, and several other big film companies soon formed a close monopoly called the Motion Picture Patents Company, which tried to collect royalties from independent producers. A five-year war developed between the trust and the independents. This conflict combined every known form of legal action as well as chases, camera snatching, and even camera smashing. It seemed logical to many independent film makers to move west, because of southern California's year-round sunny weather, and because a hard-pressed independent producer could rush across the Mexican border whenever the legal process servers swarmed too menacingly.

One independent producer, William N. Selig, fled from Chicago process servers and established himself in Santa Monica. There in 1908 he completed *The Count of Monte Cristo*, which is usually accepted as the first commercial movie made in California. The first film made in Hollywood itself (which incidentally did not contain a single motion-picture theater at that time) was produced by the Horsely brothers from New Jersey, who leased an old tavern and barn at Sunset and Gower Streets. This epic was called *The Law of the Range*. Although there was some early picture-making activity at Niles Canyon near Oakland, as well as at some other places in the Bay area, other locales eventually lost out to the Los Angeles region because of its superior climate and the proximity of the Mexican border.

As late as 1913, movie making was still widely scattered throughout the state. Places outside of California, such as Chicago and Philadelphia, still had some studios, as did such California towns as San Diego and Santa Barbara. By the end of the decade, Hollywood had become the nation's film capital.

In an attempt to dodge movie-patent suits, the independent producers turned increasingly to films longer than two reels, which were billed as features. These films became financially successful and the full-length motion picture became firmly established.

While many movie entrepreneurs either misjudged what the public wanted or operated with such scanty capital that they were failures, the more shrewd and grasping became rich and famous. Some early film profits were fantastic. An obscure company, Kalem, began in 1905 with a total cash investment of $600. Three years later the company was earning $5,000 a week. In 1913, Samuel Goldfish (later changed to Goldwyn), Cecil B. de Mille and Jesse Lasky raised $6,000 and produced *The Squaw Man*. Three years later the capital of these three men was estimated at $4 million. In 1915, David Wark Griffith, son of a Confederate colonel, produced *The Birth of a Nation* at a cost of about $100,000. Despite its racist tones, in fifteen years it had grossed $18 million.

Because of profits as great as this, outside capital soon flowed into the movie industry. As evidence of their economic respectability, Hollywood film companies were listed on the New York Stock Exchange. By 1926 investment in moving-picture studios, theaters and subsidiary enterprises totaled $1.5 billion to $2 billion. By 1923 motion pictures accounted for one-fifth of the annual manufacturing production in California. Two years later there were seventy-two movie companies with 3,722 people employed, turning out a product valued at $63 million.

A phenomenon which the movie industry fostered was the "star." Mary Pickford, Tom Mix and Douglas Fairbanks were familiar to millions. Fan clubs were organized. Movie columns appeared in newspapers to chronicle the doings of this new elite group, and movie magazines were published for the seemingly insatiable fans of the silver screen. These new film celebrities were able to make this adulation pay at a rate stage stars could only envy or hope to emulate by making movies themselves.

Around 1927–28, Hollywood experienced a great crisis with the introduction of talking pictures. Some acting careers, such as that of John Gilbert, were aborted, but new careers in movies were launched by personalities who could sing. Al Jolson became a bigger celebrity with his first talking picture than during his long career in the theater. The movie companies reorganized by hiring sound technicians to supplement their staffs. After a period of adjustment, the movie companies were commanding high profits once again.

Even the long depression of 1929–39 did not stunt the growth of the movie industry. Few people were so poor that they could not find enough money to see at least one picture a week. Theaters cooperated by making attendance seem a great bargain. There were many give-away programs and double features. Usually the double feature included a relatively strong first film and an inexpensive, amateurish second attraction. The lure of two for the price of one brought crowds of people into theaters.

By 1939, according to an estimate of the California State Chamber of Commerce, Los Angeles County studios incurred production costs of $216 million—some 87 per cent of all such productions in the country. More than 31,000 persons found jobs in the industry, with annual wages of $133 million.

In the rootless society of southern California, the old established religions did not satisfy many. Often migrants turned to strange sects with bombastic names such as Firebrands for Jesus, the Psychosomatic Institute, and a sect labeled Nothing Impossible. While not strictly typical of the new type of religious leaders who sprang up in southern California, surely the most publicized in the twenties was Aimee Semple McPherson. Born in Canada in October 1890, Aimee was converted to religion at an early age while attending a Salvation Army meeting. When she grew older, Aimee met a young Holy Roller pastor, the Reverend Robert Semple. Eventually Aimee married him, and they both went to China as Pentecostal missionaries. After the Reverend Semple died of malaria, Aimee returned to America, marrying a clerk named McPherson. Since Aimee continued as an itinerant preacher, she had little time for her new husband, who ultimately obtained a divorce upon the grounds of desertion. Meanwhile, Aimee had embarked upon a great career in Los Angeles. Although she started her crusade on a street corner, she soon had a $1.5 million temple from which she preached her Foursquare Gospel.

Although not a pretty woman, she was an arresting personality who knew how to support her excellent rhetorical efforts with a brass band, an organ and a choir. Aimee preached an uncomplicated gospel of love, and her adherents gained a spiritual peace that they had never known in more orthodox sects. While more sophisticated people laughed at her, bewildered Kansas farmers and elderly Missourians transplanted to southern California found her message uplifting and edifying. She turned to radio preaching twice and three times a day—never failing to win large audiences. Donations rained upon her, as her 35,000 hard-core converts gave so that Aimee might press ahead with the Lord's work. Her real estate holdings at the peak of her prosperity were conservatively estimated at $300,000 and could easily have been a million.

Aimee's popularity even withstood a curious happening. In the spring of 1926, she went swimming in the Pacific Ocean and disappeared. After a thorough search, no trace of her was found. Then she turned up in the desert of Sonora, Mexico, telling a wildly improbable tale of having been kidnapped. Her critics pounced upon this opportunity to discredit her; she was charged with a conspiracy to defeat justice. This move failed for want of evidence. Then a charge of subornation of perjury was filed against her. Again this attempt met with no success. Despite the cries of hoax, Aimee's followers remained faithful. While she never surpassed her following of the twenties, until her death in September 1944 she remained popular. At that time there were two hundred branches of her temple around the state.

Politics from the time of World War I until after the great depression can be easily summarized as a time of growing Republican influence. The Democratic Party had been so thoroughly defeated that it almost ceased to be an effective opposition. For a time orthodox Republicans and Progressive Republicans provided the only effective opposition to each other.

When Hiram Johnson resigned as governor in 1917 to claim his seat in the Senate, his state post devolved upon William D. Stephens, his lieutenant governor. Stephens, born in Ohio in 1859, ended his formal education with high school. Later he studied law. During the land boom of the late 1880's, he moved to southern California. There he entered the grocery business and became a force in the unofficial governing body of southern California—the Los Angeles Chamber of Commerce. When the mayor of Los Angeles resigned under fire in 1909, Stephens was appointed interim mayor. Joining the Progressive revolt, he was elected three times to Congress. In response to demands from southern California, Johnson selected Stephens as his lieutenant governor. As acting governor, Stephens attempted with some success to coordinate California into the national war effort. In 1917, Stephens vetoed twenty bills and pocket-vetoed many more as frivolous expenses.

Stephens had been carefully laying the groundwork for his own re-election in 1918. He announced a program supporting American participation in World War I, suppression of the I.W.W., and support for Prohibition. He also declared that he would continue in the reforming tradition of Hiram Johnson.

The primary held in August 1918 was an exciting affair, and the Progressive's scheme of cross-filing hopelessly tangled the results. On various tickets, since the principal candidates had cross-filed, the Progressive Stephens opposed the Republican mayor of San Francisco, James Rolph, and Francis J. Heney, a Democrat. The result was confusion. Stephens won the Progressive and Republican primaries; Rolph, whose votes were split into three totals, actually won the Democratic nomination. However, under the rules, Rolph, as a registered Republican, could not have the Democratic nomination, since he had lost his own party's primary. An appeal to the state supreme court brought the decision that the Democrats could not have any candidate printed on the general election ballot.

In desperation the Democrats backed their veteran leader Theodore Bell as an independent candidate for governor. Stephens defeated him by a margin of nearly two to one and entered the governor's mansion. He was the first governor since 1898 to have won an outright majority of the votes cast in the general election.

Among Stephens' contributions in his second term was a state enforcement act to supplement the federal Prohibition Amendment. Stephens also signed the criminal syndicalism bill which ultimately destroyed the California Wobblies. The governor also persuaded Washington to make the Japanese government curtail the practice of sending picture brides to California. One of Stephens' habits as governor was to proclaim special days. Other governors had done so previously from time to time, but Stephens added many extra days, such as "Go to Sunday School Sunday" and "Ripe Olive Day."

In 1922, Stephens sought another term, only to be defeated in the Republican primary by Friend W. Richardson. Stephens had abandoned the Progressive Party for the Republicans, and as a result, he may have harvested the antagonism of many party stalwarts who had been waiting for years to collect some Progressive scalps. Another factor in his defeat was his overenthusiastic approval of Prohibition, which was already starting to fade in appeal within California. California's tradition of defeating its incumbent governors was once again maintained. Stephens went into law practice in Los Angeles, until his death at the age of eighty-five in 1944.

Stephens' successful opponent, Friend William Richardson, was born in a Quaker colony near Ypsilanti, Michigan, in December 1865. He moved to San Bernardino where he graduated from an academy; later he studied law. He entered the field of journalism and ultimately became publisher of the Berkeley *Gazette*. Entering politics in 1910, Richardson was defeated by a small margin for the post of superintendent of state printing. When the incumbent unexpectedly resigned, Richardson was appointed by the governor to fill out the unexpired portion of the term. From here,

Richardson moved up to the office of treasurer, and then won a reelection. Although he had been a Progressive from 1911 to 1918, in the latter year he returned to the Republican Party, where he became closely identified with the ultraconservative wing. Bushy-browed, heavy-set Richardson proved to be an effective campaigner. His only important stand was to call for stricter economy.

After defeating Stephens for the Republican nomination in 1922, Richardson easily beat an obscure Democratic candidate by nearly 230,000 votes. As governor, Richardson proposed slashing educational appropriations, and unsuccessfully tried to close California Polytechnic School and Humboldt State Teachers College. He succeeded in cutting some state services, calling his election a mandate for rigid economy. His program was generally negative. He quickly established himself as a vetoing governor by pocket-vetoing about 40 per cent of the nonfiscal legislation sent to him, and by returning nearly one bill out of every ten sent to him with an outright veto. In addition, Richardson used the item veto on budget legislation forty-nine times.

In 1926, Richardson ran in the Republican primary for renomination. To his shock he lost to his own lieutenant governor, Clement C. Young, by a narrow margin. The powerful Bank of Italy, which at that time was expanding branch banking to all corners of the state, felt that Richardson's attitude had been unfriendly. Former Progressives in the Republican Party united to defeat the man they felt had repudiated the Johnson tradition. Richardson went into a well-earned obscurity, broken only by a term in a minor post during the Merriam administration of the 1930's. In 1943, he died of a heart attack.

Clement C. Young, the successful Republican gubernatorial nominee in 1926, was born in New Hampshire fifty-seven years earlier. As an infant, he had been taken to California by his family. He graduated from the University of California in 1892. Becoming a secondary-school teacher, he wrote a textbook on English poetry. After the 1906 earthquake, there was great activity in the real estate and insurance businesses, and Young left teaching to take part in these more lucrative vocations. He eventually entered politics and won several assembly terms, ultimately reaching the position of speaker. A Progressive during the Johnson era, Young reentered the Republican Party in 1920. After two terms as lieutenant governor, he was ready to challenge Richardson for the Republican nomination. In the general election, Young captured 71 per cent of the vote, easily defeating a weak Democrat and author Upton Sinclair, the Socialist candidate.

In the November 1926 general election, the voters approved an initiative measure which placed the state legislature on the federal plan. Prior to that time, the members of California's legislature had been elected on a population basis from forty senatorial districts and eighty assembly districts. Each senatorial district included two assembly districts. The less populous counties were dissatisfied with this system, since a few of the more populous counties could often effectively control the legislature. As a result, the rural areas proposed that while assembly seats should be apportioned strictly on a population basis, senatorial districts should be divided along county lines. Of the forty senatorial districts, twenty-seven would contain one county, eight would include two counties, and five would embrace three counties. The formula upon which the legislators were elected between 1928 and 1965 rested upon a theory of balance between sectional interests; the senate represented the rural areas and the assembly spoke for the urban centers. A geographical division was also implicit in this arrangement: more than three-quarters of the senators represented counties north of the Tehachapi Mountains, whereas a clear majority of the assemblymen were elected by the southern counties.

Entering upon his duties in 1927, Young's administration was more positive than Richardson's had been. Young added four new administrative departments to the state government—industrial relations, natural resources, public health and social welfare. As a former English teacher, Young seemed ever vigilant to veto what he regarded as carelessly expressed legislation. Yet he was sparing in his use of the general veto, employing it against merely 3 per cent of the bills passed by the legislature during his term. He was more vigorous in his use of the pocket veto, and employed it 362 times on about 16 per cent of the bills sent to him. He had an able but colorless administration. Californians had become bored, and when the governor entered the Republican primary to win the nomination for another term, he was soundly trounced by "Sunny Jim" Rolph. Young returned to private life and supervised his business interests until his death in 1947.

Rolph, a native San Franciscan born in 1869, went into the shipping business as a young man. Following the earthquake of 1906, he first caught the public eye while heading a relief committee. After his election as mayor of San Francisco, he continued a successful business career. He established a shipyard on Humboldt Bay and built many wooden ships there. The market for this type of craft collapsed with the armistice which ended World War I. It took Rolph nine years to recuperate from his financial losses.

Meanwhile he became mayor of San Francisco for five terms between 1911 and 1927. After his defeat in the gubernatorial primary in 1918, he stayed out of state politics until 1930. Then, judging the time propitious to defeat the colorless Young, he once more tried for a state office. He was a colorful campaigner who dressed flashily and spoke humorously. He always placed a carnation or gardenia in his buttonhole and wore cowboy boots. Campaigning against Prohibition (a federal question), he traversed the state in a private airplane. In the general election, Rolph polled 72 per cent of the vote—the largest gubernatorial margin to that time.

Rolph had the misfortune to be governor during the depression. Taking office in January 1931, he had to face declining state revenues and increasing relief problems. He might have been an adequate governor in normal times, but he was beyond his depth in trying to administer California during the years of the great depression. Moreover, he was inept in his dealings with the legislature. Although neither Richardson nor Young had ever had a veto successfully challenged, the unhappy Rolph had seventeen of his vetoes overridden by the legislature.

Rolph's attempts to travel through the state undisturbed by the suffering of the depression brought him much criticism. His jovial appearance, which seemed so fitting when times were good, now seemed out of place. In addition, charges of graft and corruption were aimed at some officers of his administration. The state treasury became depleted, and the governor seemed uncertain what course to pursue in an attempt to replenish it. He announced plans to seek a renomination in 1934. However, in the spring of that year his health failed after a bout with pneumonia, and he died in office.

TWENTY-NINE

The Dark Era of the Great Depression

AS in the nation generally, the economic prosperity of the twenties was uneven in California. Although speculative gains were enormous between 1923 and 1928, wages increased only 12 per cent. The great majority of the industrial and agricultural workers were unorganized and hence vulnerable to employer pressure should the job market seriously falter. Even in boom times, many California workers were either unemployed or underemployed. Just before the collapse of the stock market in October 1929, California consumer purchasing power rested upon a precarious basis.

Prior to the depression, hundreds of thousands of Americans traveled to California and opened many small businesses such as roadside stands, restaurants, gasoline stations and small shops. Other newcomers started "poultry ranches," purchased on the installment plan with relatively heavy mortgage payments. These individuals faced economic ruin from a prolonged depression. After the stock market crash in the autumn of 1929, tourism in California ceased to exist. Since many small businesses in California depended heavily upon the tourist trade, its decline forced these businesses to close down. With their collapse, the full impact of the depression fell upon the people of California. Banks and building and loan associations failed; their depositors' life savings disappeared. Despair replaced the boundless confidence which had been the trademark of California.

During previous depressions, California had been somewhat insulated from their effects by time and distance. This was not the case with the depression of the thirties, for California's economy had been too closely integrated with that of the rest of the nation. The numbing effects of the business depression quickly spread across the state. Factories closed; the lines of unemployed workers grew longer. Both the federal government under President Herbert Hoover and the state government under Governor Rolph were slow to take any effective palliative measures. Between 1929 and 1933, per capita personal income in California fell 29 per cent. Migrations into California during the 1930's dropped to only 40 per cent of what they had been during the twenties. The Japanese invasion of China after 1931 disrupted Asian trade and added to the economic gloom.

In Los Angeles the economic situation became so depressed that the city, which had once solicited tourists and residents, in February 1936 stationed 136 of its policemen along the main rail lines and highways entering California from Oregon, Nevada and Arizona. These policemen had orders to turn back all vagrants. Such action signaled the extent to which official Los Angeles policy had changed. The city no longer advertised for newcomers other than tourists. Instead, civic leaders concentrated on attracting industry, for they believed that new companies would bring their employees with them. No jobless migrants to raise the total of the unemployed were welcome. The great human flood to Los Angeles was reduced. The population of Los Angeles County grew by only 577,000 between 1930 and 1940. In the same period the city of Los Angeles grew by a mere 266,000. Surprisingly, however, the Los Angeles area still grew at a pace three times that of San Francisco, although its growth fell by a quarter from that of the previous decade.

Despite the barriers to migration in the thirties, thousands of newcomers from the Dust Bowl area of the Midwest crowded into California. Their migration was precipitated by one of the oldest historical causes of population shifts—the necessity of fleeing a land made unproductive by drought. By the early thirties, a long cycle of arid years turned many of the western prairie states into a wasteland swept by wind-blown dust. Agriculture—even the grazing of livestock—became an impossibility. Many of the farmers, tenants and sharecroppers of this area traveled west to California, drawn there by rumors of high wages and comfortable conditions. Piling all their worldly possessions on the tops and running boards of their rickety old cars, they made the long trek to California. Crowded into these cars were entire families—no one seemed too young or old to join the migration. Scornfully called "Arkies" or "Okies," because of their origins in Arkansas and Oklahoma, they crowded into California's great valley, seeking menial jobs on the ranches of the region.

Novelist John Steinbeck has vividly described their plight in his novel *The Grapes of Wrath*. Although their numbers were never accurately determined, there may have been 285,000 Dust Bowl migrants entering California between 1935 and 1939.

This influx of unskilled laborers into the farm regions of California had a tremendously adverse impact upon the agricultural labor market. Many migrant workers could find no jobs and so became objects of governmental or private relief. As a result, outraged and impatient Californians demanded that their state government pass a law closing the borders to indigents. The legislature enacted number 2615 of the Welfare and Institutions Code of California. Popularly known as the "anti-Okie" law, this statute provided that any person or corporation bringing an indigent migrant into California was guilty of a misdemeanor and could be sentenced to six months in jail. This law supplemented the many unofficial roadblocks set up by the Los Angeles police and various county sheriffs. By these measures, many would-be migrants were turned away from the borders of the state. California was not alone in passing such an ordinance, for more than twenty other states passed similar legislation.

In December 1939 a man named Edwards left his home in Marysville, California, and went to Spur, Texas, where he picked up his wife's brother, an unemployed laborer named Frank Duncan. Edwards transported Duncan back to California in his private car in January of 1940. Once in California, Duncan could not find a job, and since his meager savings were exhausted, he sought help from the Federal Farm Security Agency. At once a complaint was filed in the justice court of the area against Edwards for having violated the "anti-Okie" law. Although Edwards was convicted in a local court, he appealed all the way to the United States Supreme Court. In 1941 that court ruled the law unconstitutional, for it obstructed interstate commerce. A minority of the court contended that the statute violated the privileges and immunities of a citizen as guaranteed by the Fourteenth Amendment. This decision precipitated several pages of constitutional law, although this legal action did not come in time to help the migrants.

Even those migrants who successfully crossed the border and were able to obtain employment in California suffered from the critical economic conditions. In 1935 the typical family of itinerant farm workers averaged $289 a year—less than half the amount estimated by California state authorities as necessary for a subsistence living standard. On the ranches where they were employed, the workers lived in crowded, filthy camps. Attempts to unionize them were pitifully ineffective. Higher wages and better working conditions could not be attained as long as so many available people would work for starvation wages and under any conditions.

When neither farm owners nor local government officials seemed able to remedy the conditions of the farm workers, the Federal Farm Security Administration intervened. This agency built model workers' camps in the Sacramento, Imperial and San Joaquin valleys. The migrant farm workers were able to better their economic condition only when the quickening demand for labor after 1940 on both the farms and in the factories of California provided more and better jobs for them.

Even nature seemed to be conspiring against California during this era. The Long Beach earthquake of 1933 killed 120 people and caused forty million dollars in property damage. One beneficial result of this tragedy was a serious revision of California building codes and specifications.

Labor became very restive during the great depression. With wages falling nationally, many California employers took advantage of the situation to slash wages, lengthen hours and crush unionism. In San Francisco, despite its long history of unionism, between 1921 and 1933, employers converted the city into an open-shop community. However, with the coming of Franklin Roosevelt's New Deal, the political climate abruptly changed. With the passage of the National Recovery Act, including its vital Section 7A, labor was permitted to select a collective bargaining agency. Some San Francisco waterfront laborers decided to use the International Longshoremen's Association as their vehicle for organization. In September 1933 these men obtained a charter from the international union and proceeded to organize the majority of the workers along the docks. One of the organizers of the new local was an Australian ex-sailor, Harry Bridges, who had been working along the San Francisco waterfront as a hydraulic-winch operator ever since his arrival in the United States a dozen years before. Dark and "razor-faced," with the quick movements of a fencer, he soon acquired a wide following among union members.

The waterfront workers demanded that the prevailing weekly wage of $10.45 be substantially raised, that the work week be shortened to thirty hours, that a coastwide labor agreement be negotiated, and that the union be vested with control of the hiring halls. When the employers refused to grant the longshoremen these substantial concessions, the International Longshoremen in San Francisco struck on March 7, 1934. By May 15, the revived seamen's unions had also entered the maritime strike. Later the ships clerks' and licensed officers' labor union followed suit.

On July 15, 1934, "Bloody Thursday," a violent encounter between the strikers and the San Francisco police erupted. Two union pickets were killed, and another hundred union men were gassed or clubbed. The San Francisco unions answered this violence by calling the second important general strike in American history. Nearly 127,000 workers left their jobs, paralyzing the entire city of San Francisco from July 17 to July 19.

Stores were shuttered and factories padlocked; public transportation was halted.

The strike made newspaper headlines from coast to coast. The administrator of the National Recovery Administration, frightened by the extent of the labor disturbance, hastened to California to denounce the general strike. Finally a growing wave of national disapproval caused the sympathetic strikers to return to their jobs. Only the waterfront workers continued to strike. They returned to work only when it became clear that there would be mediation of the main points in dispute. Eventually the mediators made an award which gave unions control of the hiring halls, as well as other concessions.

Harry Bridges came to the fore of the leadership of the longshoremen's union. He took the union into the C.I.O. rather than the more conservative A.F. of L. Bridges soon became a Pacific coast director of the C.I.O., and as a result of his strong pro-C.I.O. stance, a number of jurisdictional squabbles occurred between Bridges and the seamen's union, which had elected to continue with the A.F. of L. Because of Bridges' aggressive union leadership and provocative statements, many employers and government officials charged that he was a Communist. As a result, Bridges became involved in a long legal battle to prevent his being forcibly deported. This attempt to remove Bridges from the United States failed.

During the 1930's, California labor unions were revived. Increased unionization in San Francisco led to worker demands for more union control in southern California. In Los Angeles, bastion of the open shop, unionization spread by way of its port at San Pedro. Union-organizing drives also extended into the inland valleys, where unions had never before shown much strength.

California had long sheltered utopian social and economic schemes. During the late nineteenth and early twenieth centuries, Henry George had advocated an appealing single-tax theory, and many communal colonies had been established. Even during the relatively prosperous twenties, many Californians had shown a tendency for religious and social reforms. With the advent of depression conditions, the intellectual ferment in California increased. Now the receptivity of many Californians to schemes for curing economic and political ills of the nation proved remarkable.

Among such schemes was the movement known as Technocracy, the first major utopian plan to sweep across California during the depression. It had actually begun at New York's Columbia University at the time of the First World War in a scholarly study of the theory that all civilization was founded on physical energy. By the early 1930's, this cause had become the principal concern of Howard Scott, an engineer who had pioneered discussion of the subject at Columbia. The Technocrats proposed that the government be placed in the hands of engineers and skilled technicians. The price-and-profit economic system was to be abolished, and machines were to be devoted to the satisfaction of human wants. No longer was physical wealth to be measured in terms of gold or money, but in units of energy.

Under Scott's enthusiastic aegis, Technocracy won a wide following in California. In addition, E. Manchester Boody, the owner-editor of the Los Angeles *Daily News*, enthusiastically championed this idea in the columns of his newspaper. Although Pismo Beach was the headquarters for this movement, its strength lay principally in the communities to the south—particularly in Los Angeles.

Technocracy soon had to jostle with the Utopian Society for public attention in California. This movement had skyrocketed to prominence by July of 1933. Its creed was a strange mixture of many ideas—some of the tenets of Technocracy and state socialism, wrapped in mystic rites and initiation ceremonies reminiscent of the Ku Klux Klan. At its peak the Utopian Society claimed half a million adherents; no single auditorium in Los Angeles was adequate to hold all the zealots who desired to attend its meetings.

Great social ferment of this nature was bound to have extensive political repercussions. Along with a majority of Americans, most Californians voted for Franklin D. Roosevelt and his New Deal in 1932, the first time since 1916 that California had voted Democratic in a presidential election. The solid grip in which the Republicans had held California all during the twentieth century now seemed in peril. In 1932, California had also elected the old Wilsonian, William Gibbs McAdoo, to a senatorial seat. Nevertheless the Democratic Party had become so moribund that, despite this tremendous opportunity, it had difficulty gaining substantial victories at the state and local levels.

When Governor Rolph died in June 1934, he was succeeded by his Republican lieutenant governor, Frank Finley Merriam. Born in Iowa, he attended local schools and graduated with a bachelor of science degree from Lennox College. After holding jobs as a teacher and an administrator in the public schools of Iowa, he became the editor of his hometown newspaper. Entering Republican politics, he won a seat in the legislature and two terms as state auditor. He married and moved first to the Oklahoma Territory in 1904 and then to California six years later. Here he joined the business staff of the Long Beach *Press*.

Merriam's Iowa Republican background was no bar to his entry into California politics, for he won five terms in the assembly, eventually becoming speaker of that body. In 1926 he lost the Republican lieutenant governor's nomination, but four years later, he was successful in gaining that office. After Rolph's death, Merriam served as acting governor, rather than actually ascending to the gubernatorial office itself. Always a conservative, during his brief term as "acting" governor, he showed little sympathy with labor or economic innovation. In 1934 he won the Republican gubernatorial primary, although in the Democratic primary, author, vegetarian, ascetic Upton Sinclair, a former Socialist, garnered more votes than did Merriam in his race.

Sinclair's strength stemmed from a far-reaching campaign program which attacked the problems of unemployment and the depression. He published a pamphlet entitled *I, Governor of California, and How I Ended Poverty, A True Story of the Future,* in which he discussed twelve measures to "end poverty in California." He suggested state land colonies for the unemployed; he proposed using idle factories for the same purpose. He wanted to repeal the state sales tax, sharply increase the inheritance and public utility taxes, and institute an income tax. He also advocated the exemption of owner-occupied homes and small ranches from taxation. Borrowing a leaf from Henry George, he suggested taxing unimproved lots and idle farmland. Lastly, Sinclair proposed modest pensions for the aged and physically disabled. To his EPIC ("End Poverty in California") plan, Sinclair added the slogan "I Produce, I Defend," illustrated in publicity releases by an emblem of a golden bee. Sinclair also founded an End Poverty League whose members heavily contributed to his campaign.

During the campaign, thousands of conservative Democrats deserted their party's gubernatorial nominee, joining the Republicans to "save the state." One Democratic leader quipped that he preferred catalepsy with Merriam to epilepsy with Sinclair. At the same time, the movie industry turned its cinematic weapons upon Sinclair, issuing propaganda as vicious as it was effective.

Merriam won the election because the protest vote against Republican state rule was split between Sinclair, who garnered 879,000 votes, and the Progressive gubernatorial candidate Raymond L. Haight, who received 302,000 votes. The victorious Merriam captured 1,138,000 ballots. California had bucked the national trend in favor of the Democrats.

As governor, Merriam was nearly the direct opposite of Sinclair. He believed that if he could put California on "a sound financial basis," he could find the key to economic recovery. He adopted Sinclair's proposal of a state income tax, which the legislature eventually enacted.

While the exciting gubernatorial election of 1934 was still being waged, Dr. Francis E. Townsend, a retired physician who sold real estate in Long Beach, came forward with a scheme designed both to end the depression and provide monthly pensions for all citizens over the age of sixty. Officially the movement was labeled Old-Age Revolving Pensions, Limited, but it soon became known as the Townsend Plan. Townsend suggested a federal sales tax of 2 per cent on all of the nation's business transactions. With these funds, the federal government would pay eligible individuals a monthly pension of $200 in scrip, provided it was spent within a thirty-day period. According to Dr. Townsend, this money would insure both gracious leisure for the aged and a firm basis of demand for the nation's goods and services. With the help of a weekly newspaper that described how to start a local club, the Townsendites were quickly organized across the nation. In the end, although the movement was denounced as California's phony nostrum gift to the nation, the Townsend Plan helped to focus attention on the plight of indigent, elderly citizens.

Townsend's idea paved the way for various other visionary schemes. In 1938 a promoter named Robert Nobel suggested paying $50 every Monday to all citizens over the age of fifty. An "engineer-economist," Roy C. Owens, and two brothers, Willis and Lawrence Allen, revamped this proposal and sponsored it under the title "The Thirty Dollars Every Thursday Plan." The Allen brothers' scheme called for a state constitutional amendment to authorize that thirty one-dollar state warrants be issued to all retired persons over the age of fifty. A special two-cent stamp tax was to finance this venture. When someone said that this pension movement would become as well known to Californians as ham and eggs, it was nicknamed the "Ham and Eggs" plan. Using this short slogan as their battle cry, supporters of the plan quickly obtained 700,000 signatures to place the idea on the ballot as an initiative constitutional amendment. In the campaign that followed, money was freely spent by both sides both to promote and discourage the plan. The scheme drew 1,143,-000 votes, meeting defeat by a relatively small margin.

Immediately the backers of "Ham and Eggs" announced a new drive for a 1939 election. A somewhat revamped initiative, now called Retirement Life Payments, secured 1,103,000 signatures by May 1939. The advocates of this pension scheme hoped that the governor would call a quick special election to vote on it. To their dismay, Governor Culbert L. Olson put the measure on the November election ballot. This delay in voting caused many of the electorate to have second thoughts about the benefits of this scheme. As a result, the measure obtained only 993,000 out of the 2,975,000 votes. This ended "Ham and Eggs" as a serious political issue, but it did not end the economic and social unrest in California. As late as 1940, a survey in *Fortune* indicated that the Pacific coast harbored more fears about the future and more disillusionment concerning the success of the American capitalistic system than any other section of the country.

Meanwhile California had cast its electoral votes for Roosevelt in his 1936 landslide. In California, the Democrats continued to control the congressional delegation as they had since 1932; however, they were not nearly so successful at the state level. Although the Democrats, for the first time in years, succeeded in winning control of the lower house, they were unable to shake the solid Republican control of the upper house of the legislature. Merriam continued to sit in the governor's mansion, appointing Republicans to those offices within his purview.

Nevertheless, in 1938 the Democrats were ready to vote Merriam out of office. Postmaster General James Farley, the leading architect of Democratic national victory, had listed Merriam as one of the Republican governors the national Democratic Party wanted to see retired. Since Merriam's administration had disgusted many Republicans, they rallied to the support of Lieutenant Governor George J. Hatfield of San Francisco for the gubernatorial nomination. Although Merriam won the bitterly contested primary over his lieutenant governor, the party was now too disunited to meet the Democratic challenge in November.

The Democratic Party had by then enjoyed enough success so that it could reasonably hope to elect its gubernatorial choice. In 1938 that choice was the veteran politican Culbert L. Olson. Born on November 7, 1876, near Fillmore, Utah, Olson had enjoyed a varied career. He had worked as a young man on a farm, on construction jobs, and on a railroad. He had also found time to attend Brigham Young University for two years. In 1897 he moved to Washington to serve as secretary to his congressman-cousin. He eventually graduated from Columbia University (later George Washington University) Law School. Practicing law in Salt Lake City, he soon became one of the leading members of the bar. Here he earned the means to invest extensively in both mining and real estate. Olson participated in Utah politics, although as a Democrat, he met with only modest success. In 1920 he moved to Los Angeles, where he came to the political fore with the resurgent Democratic Party of the 1930's. Although Olson managed Upton Sinclair's EPIC campaign for governor, he was more successful in his own campaign for the California senate.

In the legislature, Olson became the leader of the anti-Merriam forces. Becoming well known for his liberalism, Olson began regular radio broadcasts to all parts of the state, in which he criticized the Republicans for a lack of initiative and proclaimed his own plans for solving the state's depression problems. As a candidate for governor on a generally liberal platform, Olson faced stern competition for the Democratic gubernatorial nomination. Popular congressman, John F. Dockweiler, an ardent "Ham and Egger," challenged Olson in the battle for the nomination. Although he gave the impression that he also favored the "Ham and Eggs" pension scheme, Olson managed to straddle the issue well enough so that he could collect the votes of any Democrats who were dubious about the efficacy of the plan. By this stratagem he defeated Dockweiler, a feat which was all the more remarkable when it is recalled that in the Democratic senatorial primary, Sheridan Downey, a "Ham and Egger," defeated Democratic incumbent William Gibbs McAdoo.

Merriam tried to fight off Olson's challenge by advocating congressional acceptance of the Townsend Plan. While California business leaders still preferred Merriam, they did not attempt to make the election the holy crusade that they had waged four years earlier. In the November election, Olson defeated Merriam by 1,391,000 votes to 1,171,000. Olson's lieutenant governor was the only other member of the Democratic statewide ticket to win in the election. The Republicans also managed to maintain a slender control of the state senate.

As the first Democratic governor since James L. Budd in the 1890's, Olson believed that he would have a successful reform administration, and many observers agreed with him. But he failed to get the principal parts of his program through the legislature for a number of reasons. His election in 1938 was one of the few victories in the country for the Democrats; generally that year saw a turning away from the New Deal and the scoring of fresh Republican gains. The steam had gone out of the New Deal, and it was against this background that Olson had to operate in California. The Democratic resurgence in California had come too late. As a result, Olson's vaunted "Little New Deal" for California was defeated in the legislature by his opponents, who successfully constructed temporary coalitions to defeat his program. In addition, Olson's health failed. He was not an able administrator and so had difficulty in conducting the day-to-day surveillance necessary for supervising the executive branch of the state government. He also lacked tact in dealing with the leaders of his own party, thereby alienating many of them before he had ended his term as governor. Moreover, he lacked newspaper support. He even alienated some of his supporters when he seemed to equivocate in support of the "Ham and Eggs" pension scheme. Despite his elaborate plans, Olson was able to translate few of them into concrete legislation.

Although Olson vetoed 208 bills, he was overridden by the legislature eleven times. In addition, he employed the pocket veto 229 times. When legislation that he desired was passed in a form that he disliked, Olson was placed in a cruel dilemma. If he vetoed the bills, he might get no legislation; if he signed them, it would look as if he approved of their details. Throughout his term, he let sixty-one bills become law without his signature.

As governor, Olson pardoned Mooney and commuted Billings' sentence, as he had announced that he would during his campaign. He also succeeded in liberalizing the state's treatment of convicts and the mentally ill. He appointed some liberals to state office, and he attempted to protect the rights of labor and minority groups (except for the Japanese, after the outbreak of World War II). Yet his total record of accomplishment in the one term granted to him by the California electorate was frustratingly small. His overall importance in California political history lay in his suggestions for many social programs, which his Republican successor, Earl Warren, succeeded in putting into practice.

Amid the troubles and frustrations of the depression decade, there were some notable advances in California's transportation system. Increasing sums were spent by the federal and state governments upon highway construction. The legislature doubled the extent of official state highways to about 14,000 miles of road. In 1940 the first California freeway was completed and named the Pasadena Freeway. The decade of the thirties also saw the erection of two great bridges across San Francisco Bay, which greatly facilitated automobile travel in that area. The San Francisco–Oakland Bay Bridge, completed in 1936, is eight miles long. It is the world's longest, biggest, and most expensively built bridge. Its cost in depression dollars ran to $79.5 million. The Golden Gate Bridge, completed in 1937, is the largest, highest single-span suspension bridge ever constructed. Its towers are 746 feet high and the bridge is suspended 266 feet above the water. It has been called "the bridge that couldn't be built," because the engineers who designed it had to solve unique construction problems. Among them was the construction of a bridge pier into the open sea. The span claimed a dozen lives among the men who built it. Over the years, this bridge has attracted hundreds of suicides, and is perhaps the most photographed bridge in the world. Both the Bay Bridge and the Golden Gate Bridge handle a much greater volume of automobile traffic than was ever imagined when they were built. The Bay Bridge is double-decked and has been able to keep pace with traffic demands, but there is serious concern that if improvements are not made, automobile traffic between San Francisco and Marin County may soon be more than the Golden Gate Bridge can comfortably handle.

THIRTY

California in World War II

WHEN Japanese dive bombers attacked Pearl Harbor in
Hawaii on December 7, 1941, they scattered the embers
of war all over the Pacific. Among the first casualties of
the combat were the Japanese–Americans. At that time there were
127,000 of them living in the United States; more than 112,000 were living
on the Pacific coast. Of that number, 73.8 per cent were concentrated
in California. Among these Japanese–Americans were *Issei* (persons born
in Japan), *Nisei* (American-born Japanese) and *Kibei* (American-
born Japanese partly educated in Japan after the age of thirteen).

The number of Issei in America was about 40,000, most of whom had
lived in the United States for twenty-five years. Despite their exclusion
from citizenship and laws designed to cripple their economic activities,
they raised their families and had become economically strong. In southern California, about 85 per cent of the Japanese–Americans were engaged in farming. They were also prominent in the state's wholesale and
retail vegetable and fruit trade. Most of the 70,000 Nisei were teen-agers
or young adults. Except for certain racial characteristics, they were indis-
tinguishable from other Americans of the same age. Less than nine thousand were Kibei. Americans suspected this class of Japanese–Americans
the most, since it was believed that they had been indoctrinated with
warlike attitudes during their education in Japan.

Immediately after the Pearl Harbor attack, a series of security measures
were taken against the Japanese–Americans. About 1,500 "enemy aliens"
who were thought to have close connections with Japan were speedily

interned by the federal Department of Justice. Their businesses were
shuttered and their bank accounts blocked. The remaining Japanese–
Americans, aliens and citizens alike, were required to register and carry
identification cards, while surrendering to the local police their cameras,
binoculars, radios and firearms. In addition, they were restricted to an
area within a five-mile radius of their homes and ordered to stay indoors
between eight o'clock at night and six o'clock the next morning.

As the war continued, and Japan successfully overran the Philippines,
Thailand and Singapore, American public opinion became increasingly
suspicious of the Japanese–Americans as "fifth columnists." The American public had been fed a stream of unsubstantiated reports that sabotage
and undercover Japanese–American activities assisted the Japanese planes
in their Pearl Harbor attack. Reports of enemy submarine sightings off
the Pacific coast led many to believe a Japanese-led invasion was imminent. Even the liberal pundit Walter Lippmann proclaimed the Pacific
coast a combat zone, in a column written with a San Francisco dateline of
February 1942, and captioned "Washington Fails to Cope with Western
Fifth Column." He also declared that Japanese-Americans should be interned since "Nobody's constitutional rights include the right to reside
and do business on a battlefield."

On the day following the appearance of Lippmann's column, seven
members of Congress from Pacific coast states sent a letter to President
Roosevelt, urging the "immediate evacuation" of all Japanese and other
subversives from California, Washington, Oregon and Alaska. Simultaneously from San Francisco, Lieutenant General John L. De Witt, the
commanding general of the Western Defense Command, wrote an urgent
message to the War Department with a similar recommendation. General
De Witt justified this action in a later statement that "A Jap is a Jap. . . ."
He declared that naturalization did nothing to destroy a Japanese's primary allegiance to his emperor and that sabotage and espionage would
continue until the Japanese were removed from the Pacific coast area.
Earl Warren, California's state attorney general, agreed with De Witt
that California was "the most likely objective" in the nation for sabotage.
He added that Japanese–Americans were distributed in places where they
could inflict the most damage.

Not all Californians clamored for indiscriminate removal of the Japanese. Because Japanese truck farming was so widespread and so successful, many state officials urged moving the Japanese away from the coast
to the agricultural regions of California's interior. These officials were
concerned that a removal of the Japanese would leave an agricultural
labor void that could be only inadequately filled by other sources of
labor.

Nonetheless, in the early weeks of World War II, President Roosevelt agreed to issue Executive Order 9066, by which the army was given power to "solve" the enemy alien situation. On March 2, 1942, General De Witt issued Public Proclamation No. 1, by which the western half of Washington, Oregon and California, and the southern third of Arizona were declared a "military area." All Japanese-Americans were banned from that region. To supervise the evacuation, the WCCA (Western Civilian Control Administration) was created under the directorship of Milton Eisenhower, brother of General Dwight D. Eisenhower. Tom Clark, later a United States Supreme Court Justice, was a civilian coordinator with the army who helped carry out the relocation program. These distinguished Americans, and others, would later regret their part in this operation.

Scholars have since determined that the overwhelming mass of Japanese–Americans had shown a remarkable ability to adapt themselves to life in the United States. No reliable evidence has ever been unearthed to show that they deliberately lived near strategic areas in order to commit sabotage. Nor were they in any other communication with the Japanese war machine. The few potentially disloyal Japanese could have been screened by the FBI in the same manner as Italian and German aliens were investigated. The cost of carrying out these screening operations has been alleged as the reason they were not attempted. Yet the construction of sixteen assembly centers and ten relocation camps cost about $70 million. Maintaining the evacuees during their three years of internment cost an additional $150 million. The entire cost of the operation may have reached $350 million. Moreover, although the Japanese numbered 37 per cent of the population of Hawaii, only 1,118 were ever evacuated or interned there.

At first the Japanese–American evacuation was voluntary, and almost five thousand Nisei and Kibei moved out of the prescribed area—mostly to Colorado and Utah. Their reception in these states was often openly hostile. Consequently many Japanese in the Pacific area stayed where they were already living.

On March 27, 1942, the program of voluntary evacuation was suspended, and the army ordered compulsory internment for the Japanese in the interior of the United States. This entire operation was to be accomplished by June 5, 1942. The Japanese generally accepted this arbitrary decision with an attitude of *shikaganai*, or "realistic resignation." One Japanese family who had leased some land near the Los Alamitos Naval Air Station were never allowed into their fields to harvest their crop of celery which stood ready for cutting. The Japanese were generally given a week's notice before they had to move, but many received less warning than that.

Among the effects of this expulsion were tremendous property losses suffered by the evacuees. It is estimated that the Japanese owned hundreds of millions of dollars worth of property. Included were 250,000 acres of fertile land, about 20,000 automobiles, several thousand miscellaneous businesses, as well as the usual personal property acquired over the years.

Taking advantage of the forced evacuation, unscrupulous second-hand dealers followed the federal notifying officers around, declaring that the government intended to confiscate Japanese household goods. They would then offer four or five dollars for goods worth a hundred times that amount. Real estate men purchased Japanese–Americans' homes and farms for a small fraction of their real value. Only belatedly was the Federal Reserve Bank of San Francisco authorized to provide warehouse storage facilities for the personal effects of interned Japanese. A mere three thousand families were able to take advantage of this service. One Japanese family had a retail store in Sacramento, which they had to liquidate in a few days. When they sold their stock, they received only twenty-five cents on the dollar for their inventory. Their furnishings and furniture they sold for "nothing."

By August 7, 1942, over 110,000 Japanese—half of them in their teens or early twenties—had been processed through sixteen assembly centers and sent to relocation camps located in Arizona, Idaho, Wyoming, Colorado, Utah, Arkansas and the interior of California. These assembly centers, located at livestock exhibition halls, race tracks and fairgrounds, were surrounded by white military police and barbed-wire fences. From these assembly points, the Japanese were herded into ten internment centers—two at Manzanar and Tule Lake, in the interior of California. Manzanar, the first of the ten centers, was opened in Inyo County on March 21, 1942, and operated until November 21, 1945. At the peak of the relocation activity, it harbored 10,046 Japanese internees. The relocation camp at Tule Lake in Modoc County began operations on May 27, 1942, and continued until March 20, 1946. It was the largest relocation center, housing 18,789 internees at the peak of its activity.

It was not until three years after Pearl Harbor, on December 17, 1944, as General Douglas MacArthur's troops were fighting their way toward Manila, that the Western Defense Command lifted its alien exclusion order. It took many months to discharge the Japanese from their incarceration; the Tule Lake center did not close down until March 20, 1946.

In the summer of 1942, the War Department began a program to recruit carefully screened Nisei citizens for the army. Japanese–Americans were needed to teach the Japanese language to American military personnel. The Kibei furnished most of these translator–teachers. Later some of the Japanese–Americans served as translators on the battlefield, where they were often shot at by Japanese and Americans alike. Some five thousand Nisei were already in American uniform at the time of the Pearl Harbor attack. After the bombing, induction of Japanese–Americans into the armed forces was not allowed. In 1943 the army decided to allow carefully selected Nisei to serve in an all-Nisei army unit. Thus, the 442nd Regimental Combat team of five thousand men was organized in April 1943. It served with distinction during the Italian and French campaigns, its members collecting 3,690 citations and decorations during the war. The 442nd won more presidential citations than any unit of its size. One of its heroes was Daniel K. Inouye, who came back from overseas to become United States senator from Hawaii. On January 20, 1944, Japanese–American males were again made subject to involuntary induction through Selective Service. Starting in July 1942, carefully selected evacuees were granted leave to work outside the relocation centers. Many were sent to Chicago, Denver and Salt Lake City; others worked as agricultural laborers in rural areas. By the end of 1943, over 17,000 Japanese–Americans were on leave from incarceration areas.

Of the final total of 120,313 Japanese in WRA custody, only 4,724 chose repatriation to Japan when the chance came for the exchange of civilians. Despite the frustrations of relocation, the overwhelming majority of Japanese chose to remain in the United States.

The *Kokufuku*, or return of the Japanese from their internment, was complicated, despite the fact that racism had died down in California during the war. The Chinese had become accepted as allies during the conflict, and now labor leaders spoke out for the repeal of Chinese exclusion laws. In 1944 the California attorney general ruled that Chinese aliens might own land.

When Japanese evacuees returned to California after the war, they found their homes sold or confiscated. Many had been deprived of their homes under an escheat law passed in 1943, which had been aimed at immigrant parents who had purchased land in the name of their citizen children, a practice already forbidden by California law. About 40,000 southern California Japanese were among the evacuees of 1942. Harry Honda of the Japanese–American Citizens League has estimated that about ten thousand of them did not return after the war. A few of these had gone back to Japan, but many relocated in other areas that had accepted them during the war. Many Japanese who had lived in Washington and Oregon before the war settled in northern California once their incarceration had ended.

Consequently, at the present time there are more than 100,000 Japanese in southern California; 80,000 of them live in the Los Angeles metropolitan area, according to the Japanese Chamber of Commerce. What used to be "Little Tokyo" in Los Angeles is now a few blocks of restaurants and small shops. At night the Japanese disperse to their homes, which are scattered all over the Los Angeles area. By 1950 there were more Japanese–Americans living in San Francisco than there had been before the war. Here a Japanese settlement called "Jay-Town" is located in the heart of the heavily Negro Fillmore Street district. It consists of just a few commercial buildings, since the Japanese live in homes dispersed throughout the city. Thus, one good result of wartime relocation was a wider dispersion of Japanese throughout the population of California and the rest of the United States. Now, twenty-five years after relocation, 60 per cent of the Japanese in the continental United States are estimated to be living in California, in contrast to 75 per cent in 1942. For example, Illinois, which had only a handful of prewar Japanese inhabitants, currently has over fifteen thousand.

During the war the Japanese–Americans suffered a property loss estimated at between $350,000,000 and $500,000,000. In 1948 a repentant Congress passed the Evacuation Repayment Act to partially compensate the evacuees for their lost property. This act applied only to the approximately 75,000 evacuees who were American citizens. When the last of 26,500 claims had been settled in 1965, about $38,000,000 in property claims had been paid out by the federal government. This amounted to about one-third of the 1941 valuation. Some Japanese–Americans complained that they were paid only ten cents on the dollar. The federal government also made slim restitution for the amount of money lost by Japanese–Americans in confiscated bank deposits. In 1958, 7,500 Japanese–Americans were offered yen or dollars for confiscated deposits at an exchange rate of 361.55 yen to the dollar. Thus a $12 deposit in 1941 was worth fourteen cents in 1958. Only 1,817 depositors accepted the offer in the United States; 1,600 in Japan took yen. One Japanese–American group sued, and the government settled their deposits on a dollar-for-dollar basis at the 1941 rate of exchange, 4.3 yen per dollar. Nearly four thousand small depositors at the California branches of the Yokohama Specie Bank sued for the same settlement, but they were turned down because they had filed their claims too late. In April 1967, the United States Supreme Court ruled that these individuals should be paid in full (but without interest). This ruling was based on the Federal Bankruptcy Act, whereby tardy claimants can share "remaining assets."

Meanwhile, in 1952, Japanese–Americans were again allowed the privilege of naturalization. The older Issei—almost all of whom immigrated to America before the 1924 exclusion act and who had been denied citizenship until then—have steadily diminished in number. The businesses they built, which were lost during the evacuation and then rebuilt, have been taken over by the Niseis, who display the same shrewdness and energy as their elders.

Whereas 85 per cent of the Japanese–Americans were farmers before World War II, today only 10 per cent are agriculturally employed, although agriculture remains their most productive single industry. The postwar increase in professional people among Japanese–Americans is reflected in census figures which show that by 1961, one out of six Japanese–American men were in professional fields, as compared to one out of twenty-two in 1950. The 1960 census also disclosed that 56 per cent of the Japanese–Americans held white-collar jobs, compared to the Caucasian figure of 42.1. At present, Japanese–Americans dominate the floral industry and nursery business, operating both as growers and wholesalers. In addition many own valuable income property. There are approximately five thousand members of the Japanese Gardeners Federation of Southern California, many of them prewar farmers who found postwar mechanization costs too great to allow a return to farming.

Stressing as they do the virtues of thrift, industry and cleanliness, the Japanese have won widespread acceptance in recent years from their white California neighbors. Their willingness to assimilate has been very high. They are one minority group which has a low rate of crime and delinquency. As a result, the status of Japanese–Americans is many times better now than it was in 1940.

The mass relocation of the Japanese–Americans can only be compared in American history with the forced removal of the civilized tribes of Georgia from their land in the mid-1830's. Few Americans remember that event; fewer still care to recall the World War II relocation story. Hopefully these experiences will stand as a warning to the thoughtful not to repeat this folly in any future national crisis.

The Mexicans also experienced some difficulty in World War II California, although it was a time of full employment. Between 1900 and 1942, many Mexican migrants drifted into California. When the demands of war called for a great pool of casual labor, this haphazard migration of workers had to be better regulated. Between 1942 and 1951, an emergency plan was established that provided for a series of agreements between the United States and Mexico to admit casual labor into the state. According to this plan, the federal government arranged to supervise and regulate the flow of Mexican migrant labor. This contracting of Mexican labor under government supervision was a great success. On forty-eight hours notice, farmers in northern California were supplied with needed workers from centers eight hundred miles away. No crops were lost, and Mexican laborers proved to be tractable and cheerful. In addition to the Mexican workers brought into the state legally, thousands of "wetbacks" smuggled themselves across the border by fording the Rio Grande.

Employers brought the Mexicans into California cities in great numbers, making this minority group noticeable to many Californians for the first time. As a result, particularly in Los Angeles, great tension erupted between war-workers and members of the armed forces from the South or Southwest who resented the presence and affluence of the Mexicans. These servicemen were in the forefront of rioting against the Mexicans in June 1943.

The roots of this incident lay in the social structure of these new Mexican communities, where many young Mexican men were organized into gangs. The members of these gangs wore a distinctive costume—a long coat, tightly buttoned pants and a flat broad-brimmed hat. Often a long key chain was part of this so-called "zoot suit" collection. In the late spring of 1943, several servicemen were beaten and robbed by Mexican youths wearing zoot suits. Immediately, at service camps near Los Angeles, plans were made to strike against the Mexican youths. The military authorities, who must have been aware of the agitation gripping their men, did not confine their troops to the bases. Instead leaves and passes were granted as usual. Meanwhile, many Los Angeles newspapers printed inflammatory stories and editorials concerning the criminality of the Mexican youths. For two hot nights in June there was vigilante terror in the streets of that city. The servicemen traveled about the city in cars followed at a distance by squad cars of the Los Angeles police. Whenever any Mexican boys were spotted, the vigilantes swarmed around them, striking and clubbing their victims. After they had finished, the police would step in and arrest the Mexicans for rioting or disturbing the peace. From the center of Los Angeles, the vigilantes fanned out to every part of the city where Mexicans had been observed. After two nights they had driven the Mexican youths, ranging in age from twelve to seventeen, completely from the streets. This outbreak against the Mexicans was reminiscent of the same type of riots that almost simultaneously occurred in several industrial cities of the eastern United States. Here the victims were generally Negroes.

As a result of the heavy migration of war-workers into southern California, the character of the southern California population changed from a preponderantly older society to one which was younger in many cities than the national average. San Diego was transformed from a sleepy town with sailors to a bustling port with a great industrial complex. In 1940, San Diego had about 25,000 war-plant workers, whereas three years later it had 90,000. Its prewar population of 200,000 nearly doubled. Apartments and rentals were at a premium. Newspaper advertisements often carried notices offering rewards of from ten to one hundred and fifty dollars for anyone who could provide rentals for newcomers.

Actually the Second World War wrought the most drastic changes in California since 1849. In 1943 (the year of peak mobilization) the San Francisco *Chronicle* called the migration a second gold rush, during which many California industries grew at a fantastic rate. From a mere four thousand Californians working in shipbuilding in 1939, there was an increase to a peak of 282,000 in August 1943.

Wartime shipbuilding contracts in California totaled over five billion dollars. The region of San Francisco Bay had the greatest concentration of shipbuilding in the nation. As early as 1941, the Todd and Bethlehem shipyards built vessels in the Richmond, Oakland and San Pedro shipways. With the help of financial assistance from the United States Maritime Commission, shipbuilding facilities at Sausalito and Vallejo were reactivated for the first time since World War I. The Bay area soon accounted for about 60 per cent of the nation's shipbuilding contracts; Los Angeles had $1.7 billion in such contracts.

The mud flats of the east Bay at Richmond were soon covered by jerry-built housing developments and trailers. Here children went to school in shifts; streets cracked under the heavy traffic of cars and heavy trucks; overloaded sewers backed up; electrical utilities frequently failed. Even though twelve movie houses sprang up, there never seemed to be enough recreation for the tin-hatted workmen of the area. These deficiencies were created by the unprecedented population growth which made Richmond's population quadruple in less than three years.

By 1944, American shipbuilders had delivered 2,158 Liberty cargo carriers; some 53 per cent of these were built on the West Coast, and 23 per cent were built at Richmond. More than 100,000 people worked at Henry J. Kaiser's Richmond yard. Kaiser enterprises also controlled Calship, which built many vessels in the Los Angeles area. Two hundred and fifty miles north of San Francisco, the Chicago Bridge and Iron Company exploited a labor surplus area in Eureka and built some of the largest ships launched during the war.

In other areas of industry, California both reconverted and expanded. The gold industry was shut down and shifted to war work. The Yuba Consolidated Gold Fields Limited converted from making placer-mining dredges to manufacturing howitzers.

In 1939 there were only two nationwide steel corporations with plants in California—Bethlehem and United States Steel. In addition, California had 675 small plants producing and fabricating iron and steel. The total capacity of all California plants was below a million tons of ingots annually. This amount of steel was insufficient for the vast amount of war work which California needed to do. As a result, shipbuilder Henry J. Kaiser, liberally subsidized by the Reconstruction Finance Corporation, built the West Coast's first completely integrated steel mill, with a capacity of 700,000 tons. Although it was dependent upon coal from Utah and iron ore from Eagle Mountain 150 miles away, it nonetheless successfully produced steel. It was built at Fontana on the site of a vineyard and soon employed about seven thousand workers. By 1945 this plant was making 42 per cent of California's steel. California iron production tripled during the war to the amount of 1.4 million ingots. The war brought new heavy industry to California, some of which continued during peacetime. Yet to keep these figures in perspective, by 1945 the state still produced only 1.8 per cent of the nation's pig iron. Among those industries that profited from the wartime stimulus were machinery, textiles, chemicals and metal products.

In all, factory output rose from a value of less than three billion dollars in 1939 to more than ten billion by 1944. In 1940 only 461,000 Californians were engaged in manufacturing; that number had increased by 1943 to 1,186,000. California's total employed labor force rose from 2,703,000 in 1940 to 3,854,000 in 1944. From 380,000 unemployed in 1940, California's total fell to just 25,000 in 1943.

The petroleum industry was greatly stimulated by World War II, since California's geographical position made it the logical center for military fuel in the Pacific war theater. The growth of defense industries throughout the West Coast and the heavy burden on railroads and shipping also gave a tremendous impetus to the demand for fuel oil. All these factors worked together to cause increased crude-oil production in California. At first, war demands reflected the needs of the naval establishment and the transportation industry for fuel oil. With the tremendous expansion of air fighting in the Pacific theater, the need for gasoline greatly increased. To meet these requirements, total petroleum production in California increased from 224,000,000 barrels worth $226,000,000 in 1939, to 284,000,000 barrels worth $289,000,000 in 1943, and to 326,000,000 barrels worth $378,000,000 by the end of the war.

It was California's aircraft industry that was most stimulated by the war. Actually, the aviation industry had its pioneer beginnings in California. According to some accounts, the first public aviation meet in America was held at the Dominguez ranch near Los Angeles in 1910. This event drew 200,000 spectators who saw Glenn Curtis make the first successful heavier-than-air flight on the West Coast, that lasted for two minutes. Louis Paulham, the chief aerial attraction of the meet, was paid $50,000 for the occasion.

When more serious aviation activities came to southern California, the airplane builders soon noted that the region possessed excellent flying conditions. There were as many as 350 clear days a year in those presmog times. Even more important, airplanes could be constructed largely outdoors.

One of the pioneers of the California aviation industry was Donald Douglas who had learned his craft with Glenn L. Martin, an established aviation engineer. Martin founded his own company in 1912 at Los Angeles, but in 1929 he moved his operations to Baltimore. Meanwhile the energetic Douglas had set up an aircraft factory of his own in 1922 at Santa Monica. He reportedly built his first plane in sections in a second-floor loft and then lowered the parts to the ground in order to assemble them.

In the next decade Douglas was joined by the Lockheed Aircraft Company and San Diego's Ryan Aeronautical Corporation. The Lockheed Company, founded by Malcolm and Allan Loughead, was sold for only $40,000. One of the new owners, Robert E. Gross, helped it to become a successful aircraft company. Ryan Aeronautical is chiefly remembered for having built Charles A. Lindbergh's "Spirit of Saint Louis," which the "Lone Eagle" flew on his famous solo, nonstop flight from New York to Paris in May 1927.

Soon aircraft engines and instruments were brought from the East to be assembled in the milder climate of southern California. Southern California soon demonstrated that it had another asset—the California Institute of Technology, which could provide the necessary consultants for the fast-growing aviation industry.

Another aviation corporation which developed in southern California was Consolidated Vultee, started by California Institute of Technology graduate Gerard Vultee. During the depression, when this remarkable entrepreneur was unemployed, he started his own aircraft company. It expanded during the thirties because of heavy foreign military orders. Even Vultee's death in a crash in 1938 did not stop the company's progress, for a syndicate continued its operation. This corporation eventually merged with Consolidated Aircraft of San Diego to become one of the giants of California aviation.

By 1935 the aviation-production output of the state had reached a value of twenty million dollars. Two years later, California became first in the nation in aircraft manufacturing activity. As the world began to rearm in the late thirties, the output of California's aircraft factories soared. By the time of Pearl Harbor, orders placed by the Allies, as well as by the American government, had already greatly expanded the industry.

After America's entry into the war, the federal government made $150 million available to the aviation industry for plant expansion. To this was added $80 million in private investment capital. Great camouflaged plants were erected at San Diego, El Segundo, Long Beach, Inglewood, Santa Monica and Burbank. Companies such as Douglas, Lockheed, North American, Vultee and Hughes all took a leading part in the expansion. From fewer than 20,000 workers in 1939, the aircraft industry reached a peak of 243,000 workers in 1943. Lockheed alone employed 90,000 persons and turned out 6 per cent of the total national production. These thousands of workers were recruited from all parts of the country.

By the middle of 1945, some $2 billion in federal aircraft contracts had been let in San Diego County, and another $7 billion in Los Angeles County. Using assembly-line techniques, airplanes were produced by the hundreds. The Lockheed Corporation alone built 20,000 planes during the war. California's aircraft industry might have expanded even more if the federal government had not insisted upon artificially dispersing aircraft plants around the country for security reasons.

California's agricultural industry also greatly expanded during the war. The state's widely diversified agriculture could be utilized to feed the needs of the Allied nations, as well as those of the United States armed forces. Yet the increase was uneven. Some crops, such as sugar beets and strawberries, were reduced in acreage planted, probably because of lack of labor. At the same time, the growing of flowers upon a commercial basis was deliberately curtailed.

Among those crops whose acreage greatly expanded were a harvest acreage of potatoes from 71,000 acres in 1941 to 119,000 in 1945. Alfalfa acreage jumped in the same period from 797,000 to 1,026,000; tomatoes from 90,000 to 121,000; lettuce from 95,000 to 107,000; carrots from 22,000 to 31,000; and peaches from 78,000 to 86,000.

On the whole, California's agriculture prospered greatly. Income from beef cattle, hogs and lambs more than doubled between 1940 and 1944, eventually reaching $175,000,000. Poultry income during the same period rose two and a half times to $119,000,000. Cotton income increased two-fold to $51,000,000. Other field crops more than doubled to $161,000,000, and vegetable income increased from $123,000,000 to $284,000,000. Citrus income nearly tripled; grape income went up five times, nut income nearly tripled. The total amount earned by the California farmer tripled from $626,000,000 in 1939 to $1,744,000,000 in 1944. While California could only climb to ninth among the states in industry, it continued to hold an undisputed first place in agriculture.

For a short while in the early weeks of the war, California was a zone of active operations. Japanese submarines cruised off the coast. A tanker was sunk near Crescent City; several shells were fired from the deck guns of a Japanese submarine at the Goleta oil fields. Airplane alerts often occurred. On February 25, 1942, the "battle" of Los Angeles was fought. On that date antiaircraft fire suddenly sounded. After the shooting stopped, no one knew if the Japanese had attacked or not. After the war, the Japanese denied having caused the disturbance. Gradually, after the battles of the Coral Sea and Midway, the Japanese were pushed to the west, and the inhabitants of California coastal towns began to relax.

California enthusiastically espoused the cause of civil defense. California householders bought and stocked the recommended fire-fighting equipment. Airplane spotters contributed many volunteer hours gazing skyward for attackers that never came. In the end the bomb shelters stood unused, but the whole effort probably contributed to civilian morale.

While some 700,000 Californians served in the nation's armed forces, the citizens of the other forty-seven states manned the various installations in California. As a result, many of them stayed in California after their discharge. Long before Pearl Harbor, the army had opened several large camps in the state. The tempo of activity at these new installations was quickened after the formal declaration of war. Camp Roberts in central California at times housed as many as 50,000 men. Fort Ord near Monterey was another large army installation. The marine base at Camp Pendleton trained leathernecks for their major role in the Pacific campaign. Naval installations at Mare Island, Long Beach and San Diego were greatly expanded. Treasure Island, the site of the Golden Gate International Exposition in 1939–40, was permanently converted to a naval station. Airbases at Sunnyvale, Hamilton Field, El Toro and Alameda were exceedingly busy. It has been estimated that during the war perhaps one out of every ten training centers was located in California.

Both the San Francisco Bay and the Los Angeles areas served as troop embarcation centers for the Pacific theater. Supplies and ammunition were also shipped overseas in enormous quantities from California ports. In July 1944, at Port Chicago in the Bay area, a disastrous explosion aboard two munition ships killed 322 men and battered the town.

California's population grew at a prodigious rate during World War II. Californians had grown accustomed to a rapid growth of their numbers. Between 1900 and 1940, the population of the United States increased about 73 per cent, while that of California alone increased 365 per cent, and that of southern California more than 1000 per cent. Since 1860, Californians had seen their numbers double every twenty years. Even against this background California's total population increase during wartime was spectacular. California's total population, including members of the armed forces, grew from 7,237,000 persons in 1941 to 9,344,000 in 1945. In the single year of 1943, California's population grew at a 10 per cent rate.

California soon became a state of war-enriched citizens. The average weekly earnings of manufacturing workers in 1939 was $27.80; that figure was raised in 1944 to $55.21. Total personal income in California rose from $5,257,000,000 in 1939 to $15,294,000,000 in 1945—virtually a threefold increase in six years. Total California bank deposits went from $4,132,000,000 in June 1939 to $13,267,694,000 on December 31, 1945. Despite some inflation, these figures reveal the good life that most Californians enjoyed. The most noticeable exception was the agricultural worker, whose wages did not equal the national average, since the large influx of Mexican labor depressed wages in this field.

Many doomsayers predicted that this wartime boom would be unhealthy for California's economy and that a severe postwar depression would result. Their gloom was ill founded. California's modern growth and development date from 1940. The war opened a time of expansion which has not yet come to a close.

THIRTY-ONE

An Uneasy Peace and Its Problems

DURING World War II, there had been much speculation concerning the process of reconversion from a war-stimulated economy to a peacetime one. Many observers feared that when the war ended California and the nation would be plunged into a depression similar to that of 1929. Consequently, financiers were understandably slow to invest in war-born industrial plants that would probably cease production once the war had ended. Some observers argued that even if the nation as a whole avoided a depression, California, which had so thoroughly specialized in war production, would probably cease production once the war ended. However, the impact of peacetime conversion had been cushioned in some areas, since the federal government had subsidized many shipbuilding yards which would not be needed after peace came.

In 1943 the California legislature created the State Reconstruction and Reemployment Commission to cooperate with various legislative committees and to supervise a program of postwar economic conversion. In addition to making plans for postwar spending, the state government also designated funds for various kinds of heavy construction work that could not be accomplished during the war because of the shortage of men and materials. A schedule of projects for elementary and secondary school construction, for buildings at the University of California and the state colleges, and for new highways was prepared. Wartime governor Earl Warren resisted suggestions that he cut state taxes. Instead, during the war he built up the sizable reserve of $400,000,000 to meet peacetime requirements for economic readjustments.

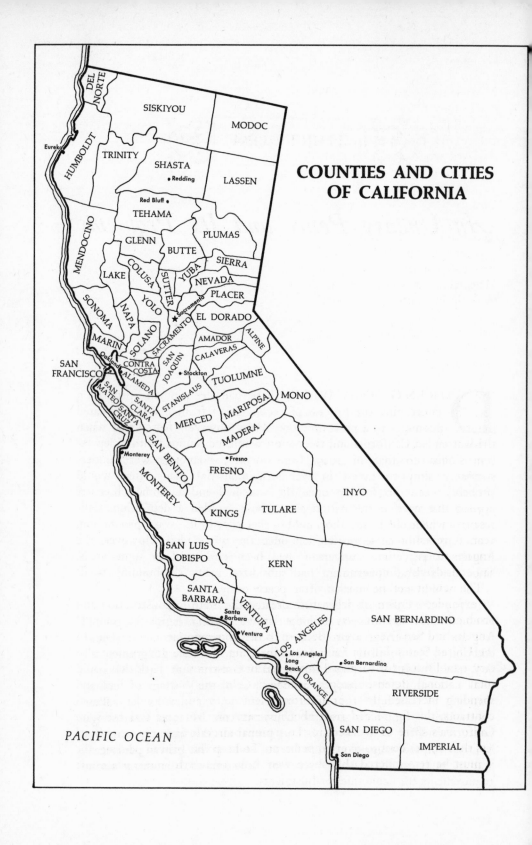

COUNTIES AND CITIES OF CALIFORNIA

Actually, demobilization and a slackening of industrial war efforts had begun long before the technical end of the fighting. In California, both shipbuilding and aircraft production reached a peak two years before V–J Day. By the time Japan had surrendered, there were only 128,500 shipyard workers still on the job, as compared with 282,000 workers in the years of peak wartime employment. Similarly, in 1943 there were 243,000 aircraft workers, whereas at the end of the war only 111,200 persons were employed by this industry. In California's training camps and staging areas there was also a decrease in personnel prior to the technical end of hostilities.

Although some war-workers left California when their jobs had been terminated, many of these same individuals later returned to the state. Many veterans, and their families, from other parts of the country chose to settle in California once they had received their discharges. This migration into the state continued at a slower pace after the war. During the last year of the fighting, 365,000 persons migrated into California. In the next year 99,000 persons entered the state. By 1947 the number of immigrants had risen to 123,000.

With this growth in population unemployment increased also. In March 1946 the ratio of claims for unemployment benefits by non-veterans to the number of covered employees in the twelfth Federal Reserve district was 11.6. Despite this situation, many individuals found satisfactory work in new jobs created by peacetime conditions—in residential construction projects, and in service and retail trade agencies. The number of employees in California's manufacturing industries fell from 881,000 in 1945 to 731,000 in 1946. By 1947 this figure had risen to 754,000 and to 771,000 by 1948. Total civilian employment in California rose from 3,849,000 in 1946 to 4,026,000 in 1947, and to 4,137,000 the next year. A recession in 1949, that saw 178,000 workers unemployed in Los Angeles County alone, was short-lived. By 1950 the employment situation had considerably improved.

The new peacetime economy that emerged in California was more than an expanded version of what had already existed in 1940. In 1947 the production of aircraft was still the largest single industry in the Los Angeles and San Diego areas. Because of the uncertain international peace the United States did not fully demobilize, but maintained a greater military establishment than it had supported before the war. Even when the total national defense budget declined, California's share of military spending increased. In 1951 California had 13 per cent of all military contracts; this figure had risen about 25 per cent by 1959. Interestingly, California's share of workers in the national aircraft industry rose from less than 19 per cent to over 30 per cent. To keep this gain in perspective, it must be remembered that there were only one-sixth as many aircraft workers on an average in this postwar period as there were in the last full year of World War II.

California's agricultural industry did not face the reconversion problem that other industries did. California farm cash income increased from $561,300,000 for livestock and livestock products in 1941 to $653,300,000 in 1946, and to $858,700,000 by 1948. The cash value for crops rose from $1,271,400,000 in 1945 to $1,505,700,000 in 1946, although it declined to $1,295,900,000 in 1948.

Personal income in California during the postwar period increased from $16,084,000,000 in 1946 to $27,432,000,000 in 1954. Total bank deposits in California increased from $13 billion in 1946 to $18 billion in 1954. Included among the new banking institutions of the state was the Bank of America, which by the middle forties had become the largest bank in the world with branches all over California and subsidiaries in Oregon and Nevada.

Organized labor also increased from about 200,000 members shortly before the war to 1,566,100 members in 3,384 locals in 1954. Since the total working force at that time numbered about five million, union membership during the war and postwar periods rose to include three members out of every ten workers.

As a result of this booming economic situation, the state's population quickly increased. Between 1940 and 1950, over three and a half million people entered the state and became residents—an increase of nearly 54 per cent—while the national population increased only 14.5 per cent.

Politically, California in the 1940's was dominated by Earl Warren. Warren was born in Los Angeles on March 19, 1891. After attending public schools in Bakersfield, he enrolled at the University of California, where he majored in political science. He graduated in 1912 from Boalt Hall (the law school) at the university, and was admitted to the bar. Interrupting his legal practice, he served in the army during World War I.

In 1919 Warren began his political career by serving as clerk of one of the legislative committees. He was then employed as deputy city attorney in Oakland and later as deputy district attorney of Alameda County. At thirty-three he was appointed as the district attorney of Alameda County. His marriage to Nina Palmquist Meyers produced six children who became a political asset because they were so photogenic. Numerous photographs of the Warren family pictured them as a "typical" American family.

In 1926, Warren was elected as district attorney, winning reelections in 1930 and 1934. For his crusading zeal as district attorney, Warren gained a national reputation and subsequently became president of the State Association of District Attorneys.

When the incumbent state attorney general announced that he would not seek another term, Earl Warren entered the three major party primaries and won them all—Republican, Democrat, and Progressive. In the general election he triumphed without real opposition, although Democrat Culbert L. Olson won the gubernatorial chair that year.

As California's attorney general, Warren reorganized the office and its staff. He fought bookmakers and gamblers and closed down the luxurious gambling ship *Rex* that had been anchored in international waters near Long Beach. Unfortunately for his record as a consistent liberal, Warren approved of the relocation of the Japanese. During the war, he became embroiled in serious wrangling with Olson, which led him to attempt to unseat the governor in 1942.

Tired and unsuccessful, Olson was no match for the vigorous, crime-chasing attorney general in the gubernatorial election of 1942. In this election, Warren revealed what was to be his political technique as governor. Although a regular Republican, he muted his partisanship and ran an independent campaign, largely ignoring the other Republican candidates for statewide office.

Inaugurated as governor on January 4, 1943, Warren soon revealed himself to be an excellent politician within the framework of the essentially nonpartisan western political tradition. With the departure of Hiram Johnson for Washington, the state government had fallen into the hands of narrowly partisan Republican governors. This kind of partisanship could be afforded in the days of majority Republican registration, but when the party became a minority in California in 1934, a new type of politician, exemplified by Warren, was essential for Republican success. Moreover, Warren was able to seize the center of the political road from the Democrats because his opponent Olson seemed to be far too liberal for most Californians.

The great middle area of the political spectrum had remained unclaimed for about two decades before Warren planted himself there. In state affairs, Warren restored the chief executive's office to a moderate progressivism. Ignoring the far left of the political spectrum as well as the far right, Warren concentrated upon a moderate nonpartisan approach to California's governmental problems. In time, conservatives in his own party came to abhor him, since in the postwar period Warren espoused a number of liberal programs. He repeatedly advocated a program of compulsory health insurance. This scheme was successfully fought by those politically to the left and right of him. Those to the left charged that his program was an insufficient sop for California's medical problems, while conservatives equated it with socialism. In other state matters Warren made an impressive record as a builder of highways and state buildings. Helped by a record prosperity, he was able to accomplish this construction and still maintain a balanced state budget. He also substantially raised old age pensions, broadened unemployment insurance, urged industrial safety measures, and effected far-reaching reforms in the state's penal system.

Under Warren, the State Conciliation Service, whose good offices were purely voluntary, was particularly effective. Out of 1,420 cases handled between 1947 and 1952, strikes or lockouts occurred in only forty-one cases.

Warren's relations with many Democratic legislators were better than they were with the more conservative members of his own party. In general, he worked well with the legislature, vetoing less than 2 per cent of the bills sent to him; he never had a veto overridden by the legislature. His appointments to office were generally hailed as excellent and were made in keeping with his policy of nonpartisanship.

As a result of his appeal in the primary elections of June 1946, Warren won an unprecedented victory, taking both the Republican and Democratic gubernatorial nominations. This feat was remarkable, since he was opposed in the Democratic primary by Robert W. Kenny, a leading member of that party then serving as the state's attorney general. In the general election of 1946, he amassed 92 per cent of the vote, defeating a weak candidate put forward by the Prohibition Party. In 1950, Warren won an unprecedented third gubernatorial term, defeating Democrat James Roosevelt, the popular son of Franklin D. Roosevelt, by a majority of 1,127,000 votes.

Interestingly, while Warren displayed a policy of nonpartisanship on the state level, he was able to operate on the national scene very effectively as a partisan Republican. In 1944, when Thomas E. Dewey was nominated as the Republican standard-bearer by the national convention, Earl Warren was the keynote speaker. He then delivered what may well have been his most partisan speech. In a slap at FDR and his drive for a fourth term, he called for "indispensable principles" over "indispensable men." (He also attacked Washington New Deal bureaucrats.) As a result of this speech, the Republican Party booked Warren for five addresses, in which he denounced the Democratic Party as an amalgam of left-wingers, conservative southerners and impractical dreamers.

Because of his national efforts and his tremendous personal popularity, the Republican presidential candidate Thomas E. Dewey secured Warren's consent to take second place on the national ticket in 1948. Before Warren would agree to run for Vice-President, he obtained assurances from Dewey that, in the event of success, the office would be given additional responsibilities. The vigorous Warren did not want to disappear into the obscurity of the traditional duties of the vice-presidency. Despite Warren's presence on the Republican national ticket, President

Harry S. Truman captured the electoral votes of California in the political upset of the century when he defeated Thomas E. Dewey.

In 1952, Earl Warren succeeded in obtaining California convention delegates pledged to his presidential candidacy, despite the opposition of the conservatives in his own party. However, the Republican presidential nomination went to war hero Dwight D. Eisenhower. Nonetheless, Warren's reputation as leader of California's Republicans probably influenced his nomination by President Eisenhower as Chief Justice of the United States Supreme Court.

While Governor Warren generally won high encomiums for his administration as governor, the same cannot be said for his legislatures. Because party discipline was weak during his years as governor, the members of the legislature were especially susceptible to the blandishments of lobbyists.

Lobbyists were not new in California. They had become so common and were considered so much of a problem that the California constitution of 1879 actually declared lobbying to be a crime. This provision had always been a dead letter, however. In the latter part of the nineteenth century, the Southern Pacific maintained a powerful lobby, until the Progressive revolt of 1910. These lobbyists made a strong comeback in 1926 when the legislature became less representative of the people. In the 1930's, when horse racing and the legalized sale of liquor touched the political scene, lobbyist activities became more financially rewarding.

The archlobbyist of this era was Arthur H. ("Artie") Samish. Born shortly before the beginning of the twentieth century, Samish started his political career as a $170-a-month clerk in the San Francisco tax collector's office. In 1918 he obtained a position as a clerk in the legislature. In 1926, Samish was one of the men who helped defeat Governor Friend Richardson in his bid for a renomination in the Republican primary. After this taste of political manipulation, Samish designated himself as a "public relations counselor," and by 1930 his career of political lobbying was in full bloom. Samish's method of operation was well within the law. In time he became a public relations counselor for beer and liquor interests, motor carriers, banks, cigarette companies, railroads, race tracks, building and loan companies, and chemical industries. Working through various front organizations, Samish made contributions to individual political campaigns, retained a large staff of lawyers who were also legislators, and entertained important people. Samish and his clients asked legislative favors that concerned details of legislation which were remote from the concerns of the various legislators' constituents.

Samish's activities were first detailed by detective H. R. Philbrick's report to the Sacramento grand jury. Philbrick reported that nearly half a million dollars from clients who wished him to influence legislation had passed through Samish's accounts. Samish's technique was to funnel contributions to newspapers and radio stations to be used to pay for various candidates' advertising expenses. A Samish-supported candidate could advertise at no expense on the four thousand billboards provided by Samish's clients. Samish was no partisan, however. He backed candidates who might be useful to him, regardless of their party affiliation. He often backed both candidates in a political race. In one primary race he was known to have backed all five candidates.

During his political career, Samish sought publicity and freely granted interviews to reporters. Upon one occasion he posed for a picture with a dummy on his lap, labeled "Mr. Legislature." Actually Samish believed that the publicity would further enhance his power. Yet articles by Carey McWilliams in *The Nation* and Lester Velie in *Collier's*, appearing in the summer of 1949, exposed his lobbying practices. As a result of his publicized bragging, Samish was barred from the floor of the legislature in 1949.

In December 1949, stung by the magazine articles, the legislature passed and the governor signed three antilobbying bills. Although they were impressive, these bills did not really touch the source of the lobbying evil. As a result of this widespread publicity about political lobbying, the Kefauver Senate crime investigating committee examined the California lobbying situation. Eventually the federal Internal Revenue Service interested itself in Samish's affairs, and in 1953 he was convicted of evading payment of $71,000 in income taxes for the years 1946–51. He was fined $40,000 and given a three-year prison sentence. By appealing to higher courts, Samish remained at liberty until January 1956, but then he was forced to serve twenty-six months in McNeil Island Federal Penitentiary. This conviction and incarceration broke his former power.

Lobbying, of course, continued into the post-Samish era. Despite the fact that most lobbyists avoided the excesses that had characterized Samish's operations, almost four hundred organizations maintained lobbies of one sort or another at Sacramento in order to influence California legislation.

This postwar period was the era of the tidelands oil dispute. In the 1940's, California had leased tideland drilling rights to private oil companies and had collected large royalties from these leases. Suddenly California authorities received a federal summons to vacate the three-mile strip of territorial waters, because federal rights were preeminent there. California's original constitution of 1849, approved by Congress in 1850, had defined the western boundary of the state as extending three miles out into the Pacific. Since 1850 the federal government had negotiated with California for the lease or purchase of areas in this new, disputed strip; therefore, California authorities had assumed that the state's authority over the tidelands was completely accepted. Since California felt it had an excellent case against the federal government, it consented to a suit against the state by the federal government on the tidelands issue. To the consternation of state officials, the United States Supreme Court ruled in 1947 that the federal government had "paramount rights" in this belt of territorial waters.

Californians had no intention of accepting this decision as final. Joining with other states who had tideland claims, such as Texas and Louisiana, California congressmen pressed for a bill that would award tideland rights to the adjacent seaboard states. Although Congress passed such a bill in 1952, President Harry S. Truman vetoed the measure. As a result, this veto became one of the more important campaign issues in the presidential election of that year. Republican candidate Dwight D. Eisenhower proposed that these tideland oil reserves be given back to the states, in line with his party's philosophy of states' rights. This campaign stand undoubtedly helped the Republicans to win California's electoral votes from native son (born in Los Angeles) Adlai E. Stevenson, the governor of Illinois.

The Eisenhower sweep and the changed political complexion of Congress made it virtually certain that the tidelands question would be settled in a manner satisfactory to California. In May 1953, the Holland Bill became law. According to the terms of this statute, the federal government was instructed to surrender its claim to the three-mile tidelands strip. The law also provided that states which could prove title to an even greater tidelands territorial claim could obtain their "historical" boundaries. As a result of this provision, California authorities discovered a basis for claims as far out into the sea as thirty miles. The legal status of these additional California claims is still uncertain.

Despite the heavy Democratic registration which had risen to nearly a 900,000 majority by 1940 and then to over a million majority by 1950, Republican officeholers flourished at all political levels in California. William Knowland, son of the publisher of the Oakland *Tribune*, was appointed to the Senate in 1945 as the successor of Hiram Johnson. Republican Knowland easily won additional terms in 1946 and 1952. When "Ham-and-Egger" Sheridan Downey retired in 1950, after a particularly rough campaign, a young, southern California Republican congressman named Richard M. Nixon defeated Representative Helen Gahagan Douglas for his senatorial seat. Two years later Nixon was elected Vice-President as Eisenhower's running mate. Republican congressmen in California were as numerous as Democrats, and the Republicans regularly controlled the legislature.

A number of factors accounted for this political phenomenon. Since many registered Democrats came as immigrants from the South or Southwest, they felt more comfortable registering in the party that had traditionally controlled their home states. But in general elections, they were generally conservative and could easily be persuaded to break party ranks and vote for Republican candidates. Furthermore, the Democrats attracted many nominal members who sympathized with the New Deal in general and so registered as Democrats. These people often saw little connection between national presidential politics and electing Democratic congressmen and state officials. In addition, the Republicans, as a minority party, were better organized and had more ample political funds. Since Republicans were more often incumbents at the time the big shift in registration took place, they took advantage of the cross-filing law to remain in power. Since party affiliation was not printed upon the primary ballot, an incumbent Republican could file in the Democratic primary and win on the basis of his name, despite partisan considerations. Thanks to this device, as many as 50 per cent of the congressmen and 80 to 90 per cent of the state legislators were actually elected in the primaries when they captured the nominations of both major parties.

From 1932 to 1948, California's electoral votes were cast for Democratic presidential candidates. However, only in 1936 was the vote markedly one-sided. In both 1952 and 1956, Californians registered a heavy preference for popular "Ike" Eisenhower over the Democratic presidential candidate, Adlai E. Stevenson.

California politics saw the rise of private publicity organizations which took over the campaigns of many candidates in the absence of strong party organizations. The firm best known for this kind of work was Whitaker and Baxter, which chalked up an excellent record of winning elections for its clients. Other public relations firms entering the political field were Baus and Ross and Keene Associates. Democrats as well as Republicans came to use the services of these organizations. In addition, these firms became adept at winning the initiative elections that Californians so delighted in waging.

The postwar period in California was marked by many fears and tensions. The cold war with Russia, the war with the Chinese in Korea, and the fear of Communist infiltration of the national government were sufficient to cause some Californians to clamor for their state government to protect them against the subversion of the American system in California. Modeled after the Dies congressional investigating committee, a California legislative committee was created for this purpose. Known as the Legislative Fact-Finding Committee on Un-American Activities, or the Tenney Committee for its chairman, Senator Jack B. Tenney, it was very active from 1941 to 1949. At first Tenney's committee seemed to be gathering data for possible legislation, but soon the hearings became legislative trials of organizations and individuals. Senator Tenney himself stepped down from his post as chairman in 1949, when several subversive control bills which he had strenuously backed were rejected. His committee then came under the control of Senator Hugh M. Burns, who continued the work of investigating subversives.

One common device for rooting out subversives in California was to require public employees to sign a "loyalty oath" denying Communist affiliation. These oaths were also required in certain private industries; for example, the powerful Los Angeles radio station KFI required loyalty oaths from its two hundred employees. In 1947, Los Angeles County required its employees to sign a non-Communist oath; the city of Los Angeles required oaths from its personnel the next year. It was at the state level that such oaths became the topic of controversy. Responding to the public demand for such oaths, in 1949 the regents of the University of California imposed a special loyalty oath on its professors. Many professors refused to sign, and the resulting legal battle raged in California for the next three years. The question of academic freedom at the University was debated throughout the state. In 1950, the state legislature required a more elaborate oath of non-Communist affiliation of all state employees.

Those University of California professors who had been dismissed for failing to take the required regents' oath sued the regents. On April 6, 1951, Justice Paul Peek of the Third California District Court of Appeals sustained the University of California professors who had refused to take the oath. Justice Peek argued that the loyalty oath required by members of the faculty was invalid, since it was in conflict with the California constitution. The case was then carried to the California supreme court. In October 1952, that body vacated Justice Peek's decision, but they came to the conclusion that the loyalty oath exacted by the university was invalid. The California supreme court declared that when the legislature passed the Levering Act in 1950, it had preempted the field of loyalty oaths. Furthermore, they declared that the regents of the University of California could not require an additional oath of their own. As a result, the faculty members who had been discharged were eligible for reinstatement with back pay from the date of their separation. Despite this vindication of the professors' stand, much damage had been done to the university. Twenty-six professors had been discharged; another twenty-seven had resigned, protesting the regents' action; forty-seven scholars who had been invited to join the staff of the university declined because they disapproved of the loyalty oath. Some fifty-five courses were dropped from the university's schedule when many professors proved to be unobtainable.

Despite these decisions, the state of California extended its program of oath requirements. The state legislature required a non-Communist oath from religious groups and from all veterans seeking tax exemptions. This oath was struck down by the United States Supreme Court in 1958. By the 1960's, California's interest in loyalty oaths had abated.

The Korean War, which raged from June 1950 to July 1953, had a stimulating effect upon California's economy. Industrial production rose as defense activities were renewed. California also provided military staging areas and embarcation points. By 1953, California pushed New York from its position as the nation's leading state per net value of military prime contract awards for supplies, services and construction. During this period the general economic level of the country also remained high, which meant increased tourism and accelerated demands for California's products and services.

The number of California workers employed in aircraft and other allied industries rose from 115,900 in 1950 to 293,700 in 1953. Total civilian employment rose from 4,154,000 in 1950 to 4,858,000 in 1953. The percentage of unemployed workers fell from 7.7 per cent to only 4 per cent in 1953. California's personal income rose from $17,835,000,000 in 1949 to $26,642,000,000 in 1953. California's percentage of the total United States personal income rose from 8.6 per cent to 9.2 per cent. During the same period, weekly California manufacturing wages rose from less than $62 in 1949 to nearly $79 in 1953. This constituted a gain of 12 per cent over the national average.

Crude oil production in California rose from 327,000,000 barrels in 1950 to 365,000,000 barrels in 1953. California electric power production rose from 22,112,000,000 kilowatt-hours in 1947 to 35,064,000,000 in 1953.

California's agriculture also enjoyed great prosperity. In 1950, livestock and livestock products raised on California farms rose from $847,600,000 in 1950 to $973,700,000 in 1953. Total crop value rose in somewhat the same fashion from $2,297,400,000 in 1950 to $2,639,500,000 by 1953.

As a result of the general prosperity in the state, California's population grew from 10,337,000 persons in 1949 to an estimated 12,101,000 in 1953. About one million of these persons immigrated into California.

Californians continued to own cars in great numbers. The number of passenger cars in the state rose from 2,500,000 in 1945 to 4,000,000 in 1950, and to 4,700,000 in 1953. In 1947 a ten-year highway construction program costing $3 billion was voted by the legislature. By 1955, including federal highways and city streets, as well as state thoroughfares, California could boast 136,570 miles of roads throughout the state.

Commercial aviation also flourished within the state. In 1947, 117,000 passengers used the Oakland International Airport. By 1950 the number of passengers had risen to 297,000 and to 515,000 by 1953. Similarly, the San Francisco International Airport saw its passenger traffic climb in the same period from 905,000 to 1,198,000 and then to 1,927,000. During the same period the Los Angeles International Airport saw its passenger traffic increase from 1,234,000 to 1,349,000 and then to 2,508,000.

Between 1945 and 1953, in peace and in war, sparked by progress in both industry and agriculture, California continued to prosper and grow.

THIRTY-TWO

Culture in Contemporary California

C ALIFORNIA is in the laborious process of building a sub-culture of its own, as part of the overall American cultural scene, while it is simultaneously attempting to take care of the material demands of its rapidly growing population at a standard of living unparalleled in modern history. If the *nouveaux riches*, a traditionally persistent class in California, form an impediment to the growth of culture, then California has a problem in its struggle to build cultural foundations of lasting value. The accomplishment of this task has been assisted by the Californians' reverence for all levels of education and the traditional willingness of westerners to spend money for the trappings of culture.

During their history, Californians have generally been willing to support public education, although very recently there has been a growing taxpayers' revolt that threatens to tarnish California's record in this area. While the grade schools of California have been the primary responsibility of local school districts, in modern California large amounts of state aid to education have become necessary. To encourage districts to enforce compulsory attendance, state aid has been dispensed to school districts on the basis of average daily attendance (A.D.A.). The amount appropriated for this purpose rose during the first half of the twentieth century. In 1920 it was $30 for each unit of A.D.A. By 1933 it had risen to $80, and to $120 in 1946. The demands for school support in the postwar period increased this figure to $180 by 1952.

As early as 1940 the per capita expenditure on education was second only to the state of New York. These advances in California's educational system were made during 1914–40, when the California school population doubled in number. In 1940–41, there was a total average daily attendance of 1,121,000 in California public schools. This number continued to rise dramatically to 1,244,000 in 1945–46, to 2,750,000 in 1956–57, to 3,562,000 in 1960–61, and then to 4,393,000 in 1964–65. By the midsixties, California had 1,179 elementary school districts, 201 high school districts, 51 junior college districts, and 155 unified school districts. In 1965–66, about 185,000 personnel were employed in California's public schools.

The custom of local districts furnishing the buildings and physical facilities continued until the mighty influx of population during World War II created a crisis in school housing. In the years 1947–48, the state granted $55 million to help financially distressed districts. In 1949 a quarter-billion-dollar bond issue was voted for this purpose. This sum was soon exhausted. When the California legislature would not agree on an extension of this program of state aid, a constitutional amendment was voted in 1952, that made such aid a permanent part of state assistance to education. Under this 1952 provision, a series of bond authorizations totalling $1,640,000,000 had been voted by 1967. Such state assistance has been an essential factor in financing a 300 per cent increase in California school plants in less than a generation. By the 1965–66 school year, California had 163,200 classrooms, a total greater than that of any other state. By way of comparison, New York had only 124,660 classrooms. In that same school year, California built 7,100 classrooms, a total greater than that possessed by the state of North Dakota. Because of state assistance, the serious overcrowding of California schools, which had been great during the war and the immediate postwar years, was no longer a major problem. In 1955, state-aided districts reported that only 23 per cent of their pupils were attending half-day sessions. By 1966 the comparable figure had dropped to less than 2 per cent.

Total expenditures of the California public schools rose from $315,000,-000 in 1946–47 to $950,000,000 in 1956–57 and to $2,198,000,000 by 1964–65. This tremendous increase caused the local share of payment for schools to balloon despite state aid. The state's share of the cost of educating the children of California on a percentage basis declined. As a result, local taxes, particularly the property tax, became a heavy burden, especially for elderly people living on fixed incomes. A widespread revolt against increased school appropriations caused many local tax and bond measures to fail in the elections of 1966. If the state should prove unable to grant substantial property tax relief by providing additional state funds, it appears possible that the excellence of California public education will eventually suffer. Yet, although Californians groan under what they regard as intolerable taxation, they are less burdened than many other Americans in this respect. In 1966, California's state debt placed it twenty-fifth among the fifty states; its tax burden per $100 of personal income ranks it thirtieth.

Because of California's effort in education, by 1960 it ranked well above the national average. According to the census reports, Californians over twenty-five years of age had completed a median of 12.1 school years as compared to a national average of 10.6 years. Only 5.7 per cent of Californians over twenty-five had less than five years of schooling, compared to a national percentage of 8.4. Some 89.7 per cent of Californians between the ages of fourteen and seventeen were enrolled in school, compared to the national average of 87.4 per cent. Despite these impressive figures, many Californians were concerned about the quality of their schools. In 1962, Dr. Max Rafferty won election as Superintendent of Public Instruction by campaigning on a platform of eliminating the "frills" of progressive education and bringing back renewed emphasis upon the "3 R's" in California schools. In 1966, still stressing his efforts in this direction, he was easily reelected to a new four-year term. In the spring of 1968 he was a conservative rival of Senator Thomas H. Kuchel for the Republican senatorial nomination.

There were some worrisome indications that California's educational system possessed certain weaknesses. A study in 1966 of first and second graders' reading abilities showed that 62 per cent of the pupils could not read as well as other students across the nation. In 1964 the high school drop-out rate in California was 25 per cent. Moreover, California education, despite its many achievements, was not reaching its minority groups —the Negroes and the Mexican-Americans. Seventy-five per cent of the nonwhite population over the age of twenty-five were without a high school diploma and more than one-third of these had not obtained an eighth-grade education.

In its program of higher education for all qualified students, California has led the nation. Public education in California has been divided into a system of junior colleges or community colleges (two-year institutions), state colleges (essentially centers of undergraduate education, but granting the master's degree), and the University of California, which has all the functions of the first two but also awards the doctorate degree and has prestigious professional schools. All segments of public higher education have grown rapidly throughout the twentieth century. By the 1950's, there was a scrambling for funds and prestige among these various collegiate systems. To end this confusion and competition, in 1960 the California legislature passed the Donahoe Act, that tried to define and limit the scope and function of the various segments of higher education. It set up a master plan to chart the future of higher education in California. According to this plan, high school graduates in the upper eighth of their graduating class could go directly to the University of California for their education. Those in the upper third of their graduating class could enter the state colleges. The remainder had to begin their college education at the junior college level. Those junior college students who had acquired good records could transfer to a state college or the university.

An assignment of functions was also part of this plan. The university was recognized as the primary state-supported institution for research. It was awarded the function of granting the doctorate, although the provisions of an extremely cumbersome arrangement allowed the state colleges and the university to jointly grant a limited number of doctorates. The university was to continue to have jurisdiction over professional schools. The state colleges were assigned the bulk of undergraduate instruction, as well as the awarding of master's degrees in many fields. The junior colleges were assigned the task of terminal vocational education, as well as the task of lower-division college instruction.

In California junior colleges, attendance rose from less than 40,000 before World War II to 72,000 students in 1946. Students continued to seek this type of education and the enrollment of these institutions swelled to 117,000 in 1954–55 and then to 289,000 in 1965–66. Styled "community colleges," they won their own statewide board of governors in 1967. State college enrollment has also increased by tremendous numbers. As late as 1954–55, the state college system enrolled only 45,000 students on ten campuses. By 1966–67, eighteen campuses of California state colleges enrolled 193,000 students, making this the largest system of higher education in the United States. The state colleges won their own board of trustees under the master plan of education and are now headed by a chancellor, Glenn S. Dumke, a former professor of history at Occidental College.

The University of California, capstone of the state's public education system, has enjoyed the most spectacular growth. After Benjamin Ide Wheeler's retirement as president of the university in 1919, its next chief executive was a man markedly different in type—David Prescott Barrows. Barrows was a retired army general, a political science professor, and a columnist for the Hearst newspapers. It was during his presidency that the Los Angeles branch of the university was opened. William Wallace Campbell (1924–30), an astronomer, was selected as Barrow's successor. He greatly developed the University of California's Lick Observatory during his tenure. From 1930–58, Robert Gordon Sproul served as president, the longest term in the university's history. An eminent faculty was gathered during his term of office, particularly in the natural sciences. Enrollment at the university rose from 18,600 in 1941 to 34,500 in 1954–55, and to 42,000 in 1957–58. Upon his retirement Sproul was succeeded by an industrial relations expert, Clark Kerr, who also presided over an expanding university. By 1966–67, the University of California had expanded to nine different campuses with an enrollment of 130,000, making it the fourth largest educational system in the United States. In quality it ranked very high. A survey of graduate education in the middle sixties ranked the Berkeley campus as perhaps the strongest overall university in its various departments.

Yet trouble has plagued the University of California. In a sense it has always been a different type of state university, since it derives only one-third of its budget from state funds and relies heavily on private grants and federal funds for most of its support. As a result, the university became essentially an "Ivy League" institution, oriented toward academic research and liberal in its treatment of controversial issues. It contrasts sharply with sister land-grant institutions, such as Michigan State and Ohio State, which are more service-oriented to fulfill the immediate needs of the states that support them.

It has always been questioned whether any state with California's turbulent party politics and vociferous pressure groups could allow such a liberal and independent academic atmosphere to continue. The University of California has survived thus far because of the institution's long tradition of free inquiry, its constitutionally preferred status in the state's organic law, and the long terms of its Board of Regents. The Board of Regents, because of its prestigious members, has been likened as the closest thing in California to the British peerage. However, as a result of a series of controversial events on the Berkeley campus of the university in December 1964, there is now some question whether the university will continue to function in the future as it has in the past.

The material for this trouble had been long gathering. The Berkeley campus, down through the years, has attracted a host of nonstudents who live on the fringe of the campus, enjoying its free lectures and concerts, and frequenting its off-campus hangouts. Most of these people at one time were students of the university—most of them at the graduate level—and have dropped out of the academic scene but not entirely out of the academic life. No longer serious candidates for degrees, they live on allowances from home (most are of middle-class or financially affluent backgrounds), or by performing such odd jobs as they can find. Many of these nonstudents, so long a part of the university scene, felt that they had a special stake in the governance of the university. They also had the time and the maturity to provide leadership for the younger students on campus.

In December 1964, there was a student uprising at Berkeley, ostensibly over the matter of free speech on the campus. The students and other demonstrators seized Sproul Hall and "sat in" for over eight hours, allegedly disrupting the administration of the university. The chancellor called in 367 lawmen to arrest the demonstrators and clear the building. Hundreds of demonstrators were arrested, tried and sentenced. Despite lengthy appeals, a number of them began serving sentences by the summer of 1967. Yet because the students received concessions following this incident, the Berkeley campus has become a springboard for increased political activity for such causes as civil rights and ending the war in Vietnam.

This widely publicized event attracted the attention of the California public, long grown accustomed to noticing activities on the Berkeley campus only on the sports pages of California newspapers. Rudely confronted with this campus activism, many Californians reacted violently against allowing these protests to continue. Then, in the winter of 1965, a handful of students and nonstudents attracted widespread attention with what was dubbed a "Filthy Speech Movement." These individuals insisted on chanting and displaying four-letter words. These few were quickly arrested, but the attention of the public was again dramatically drawn to student activities at the university. As a result of widespread criticism of his handling of the situation, President Clark Kerr announced that he would resign. Some of the regents had become disenchanted with him and were ready to accept his resignation. However, Governor Brown and his faction on the Board of Regents rallied to Kerr's support, and he continued in office. Meanwhile, many California legislators had become convinced that Berkeley was a haven for Communists and homosexuals, and so called for a study of the matter. The report of the state senate subversive committee convinced many citizens that these accusations were true.

As a result of this report, the university became a lively issue in the gubernatorial campaign of 1966, during which the Republican candidate Ronald Reagan promised to cleanse the university of subversive and immoral elements. When Reagan triumphed at the polls, it was clear that he would take some action against the university's administration. The Berkeley activists played into his hands when, during the fall term of 1966–67, there were new student demonstrations and a short-lived student strike over navy recruiters being given special privileges in the student union building.

Much student discontent had been traced to the student feeling that the "multiversity" was so busy with faculty research that students were considered by many teachers to be simply a nuisance. Various attempts to dispel this notion were belatedly put into effect. In addition, there was some decentralization of authority around the campuses as well as various curriculum and educational reforms. Nonetheless, President Clark Kerr was dismissed in January 1967, shortly after the new Reagan administration took office. The anti-Kerr faction on the Board of Regents had been so bolstered by the new administration that Kerr was dismissed by a vote of 14 to 8. An interim regime was installed. In September 1967 the Regents unanimously selected the university's vice president for finance, Charles J. Hitch, to become president on January 1, 1968. Hitch typified the demand for a new university leader who would be a pragmatic manager.

Almost simultaneously with the firing of President Kerr, Governor Reagan demanded heavy budget cuts in the amount of money to be expended in 1967–68 for the university and the state colleges. The governor also demanded the imposition of tuition at these schools. This last issue was obscured by the fact that while the university and state colleges were both technically tuition free, various fees were already charged which made the student cost equivalent to tuition charges paid in some other states. The two issues became linked in the bargaining between the leaders of higher education and the governor. In the end Reagan gave way on the matter of tuition for the time being, although he vowed later to reopen the issue. The state colleges and the university were ultimately forced to accept severely shorn budgets of $187 million and $250 million, respectively. Reagan's budget proposals for the university and the state colleges for 1968–69 were again far below the amounts needed to operate the schools at previous standards. The atmosphere of conflict in 1967–68 and the governor's insistence upon budget cuts hardly promised a serene future for California higher education as blueprinted in the Donahoe Act. While the university and state colleges could continue ahead on their previous momentum for some time, the result of this hostile political climate would inevitably be mediocrity, if the state administration's policies were adhered to over several successive years.

In addition to the institutions of higher learning, the California Academy of Sciences continues to share in the cultural growth of California. Since 1940 it has added a new wing to its museum in San Francisco's Golden Gate Park. This addition contains a planetarium, an auditorium, a hall of botany, and a library. Its membership had increased from a depression low of seven hundred to slightly over four thousand members by 1966. In addition to its membership dues, the academy has been supported by endowments, as well as by an annual subvention in the San Francisco city budget to sustain the institution's free public services.

California journalism has continued on its rather freewheeling course. Although a national figure, publisher William Randolph Hearst made his headquarters at San Simeon, California, where he maintained a baronial estate of opulent luxury. He continued to build new structures and collect more furnishings for this estate until the end of his life. In the course of his publishing career, he maintained his nationwide newspaper chain in impressive style, although it would seem that his press holdings were never profitable and drained away much of his wealth. By the 1930's, Hearst had become very conservative and increasingly hostile to Roosevelt's New Deal. In the period before World War II, he was vigorously isolationist. Hearst's peculiar beliefs—some would have termed them prejudices—led him to espouse causes such as opposition to vivisection of animal for experimental purposes. His great influences was often frittered away on trivial or inconsequential causes, and as a result he failed to make a significant impression upon the country. After his death in 1951, his complex of mansions at San Simeon became a state monument and his heirs greatly retrenched his far-flung newspaper chain.

While the Hearst empire was contracting, in Los Angeles County an old newspaper family (the heirs of Harrison Gray Otis) was enjoying increased success. After Otis' death, his succeeding publishers, son-in-law Harry Chandler and grandson Norman, made no startling innovations in the very successful Republican Los Angeles *Times*. The *Times* might easily have maintained its pronounced tilt to the right and editorially stodgy ways, except that the ill health of Norman Chandler brought his young son increasingly to the forefront after 1961. Young Otis Chandler speedily made a number of changes in the paper's format and policy. The editorial pages remained conservatively Republican, but the news pages displayed a new impartiality toward Democratic candidates and pronounced liberals. To enrich his paper's coverage, Chandler added a string of twelve overseas news-gathering bureaus. Other new features were adopted. As a result, a recent Sunday *Times* contained twenty-three sections with a total of 472 pages, giving a breadth of coverage unmatched in the western United States. The *Times* has led the nation's dailies in advertising lineage and had reached a daily circulation of 847,000 in 1967. Until 1960 the *Times* was the backbone of the Chandler enterprises—the Times-Mirror Company. Since that time the company has become diversified. By the mid-1960's, thirteen new subsidiaries of the newspaper published everything from novels to telephone books.

In the field of magazine publishing California houses the nation's most persistently gadfly journal—*Ramparts*. This publication exists partially in the muckraking tradition of journalism. Started in 1962 in the San Francisco area, the magazine later received national attention with its exposés of CIA activities. The magazine has not been a commercial success, and its founder, Edward M. Keating, was removed in the spring of 1967 as managing editor. Nonetheless, the journal continues to give evidence of a sprightly nonconformity.

California has continued as a haven for authors. About the time of World War I, there were estimated to be about 1,400 writers living and working in the state. Today there are probably three to five times that number. California's literary interest is high; over one-fifth of all the books sold in the nation are purchased within the state. According to *Who's Who in America*, more writers presently live in California than in any other state except New York. California has long maintained a tradition of being hospitable to new authors and of inspiring established literary figures. Thus authors have flocked to the state, causing California's literary production to increase.

One popular California wrtier was Zane Grey (1875–1939). Settling in California before World War I, this one-time Ohio dentist and professional baseball player began writing popular novels about the West at the rate of one or two a year. His most popular work, *Riders of the Purple Sage*, appeared in 1912. Writing in the same vein was Harold Bell Wright (1872–1944), whose *The Winning of Barbara Worth* was published in 1911 and has sold more than a million and a half copies. Two writers of more literary substance who settled in California late in their careers were Hamlin Garland (1860–1940) and Theodore Dreiser (1871–1945), though both produced only minor works while residing in California.

California has produced several native writers in the more recent period. Robinson Jeffers (1887–1962), whom many have hailed as California's most important poet, was born in Pittsburg, California, in 1887. After leaving college in 1912, Jeffers went to live at Tor House near Carmel. He turned out many volumes of verse, among them *Roan Stallion* (1925), *The Women at Point Sur* (1927) and *Thurso's Landing* (1932). Among the native-born California writers of recent years, John Steinbeck (born at Salinas in 1902) is among the most famous. He has often drawn upon the people and the setting of Salinas Valley for his novels. *The Grapes of Wrath* (1939) stirred the conscience of the nation with its tale of the Dust Bowl migrants who searched for a new start in California. His later works have been of uneven quality, although he won the Nobel Prize for literature in 1962. Also drawing upon his California boyhood, William Saroyan has turned out significant pieces concerning the San Joaquin Valley, where he was born of Armenian parents in 1908. Although primarily a poet and essayist, he won the Pulitzer prize for drama in 1940 for *The Time of Your Life*.

Among writers drawn to California from other states is Upton Sinclair (1878–   ). He turned from politics in his later years again toward letters. He wrote a series of best-selling novels dealing with a character, Lanny Budd, who was supposedly a figure in international politics before and during World War II, one of which (*Dragon's Teeth*, 1924) won a Pulitzer prize.

F. Scott Fitzgerald (1896–1940), the novelist famous for his characterization of the Jazz Age, came to California in the 1930's. By that time his need for money to care for his invalid wife and young daughter caused him to write movie scenarios. He steadily deteriorated under the pressure of his fast-paced life and his alcoholism. When he died in 1940 he was attempting to write a novel about Hollywood. This incomplete work, along with his notes, was published in 1941 as *The Last Tycoon*. Fitzgerald was joined by many other writers drawn to California to work for the movie industry and then later for television. Non-native California writers who have also won renown both as novelists and as screenwriters for the movies are Jessamyn West (1907–) with *The Friendly Persuasion* (1945) and James M. Cain (1892–) with *The Postman Always Rings Twice* (1934) and *Mildred Pierce* (1941).

Earle Stanley Gardner, born in New England in 1889 but a California literary figure for many years, has turned out many successful books and stories for the movies and television. Based upon crime themes, these stories deal most notably with his lawyer-sleuth Perry Mason.

New York-born Budd Schulberg (1914–) has lived intermittently in California since 1936. He is a screenwriter of note, having written the award-gathering *On the Waterfront* (1954). As an author he is best known for his *What Makes Sammy Run?* (1941). Since the riots in the Negro section of Los Angeles (Watts) in August 1965, Schulberg has devoted many Friday afternoons to teaching a class in creative writing for ghetto-scarred blacks. In this manner he has discovered several promising poets and playwrights.

A migrant author to California is Henry Miller (1891–) who spent his youth in New York and then moved to France where he wrote his famous novels *Tropic of Cancer* (1931) and *Tropic of Capricorn* (1939). For years these books were banned in America because of their themes and language. Miller found himself one of the better-known writers of unpublished works in his native land. In the more relaxed atmosphere of the recent past, his novels have been published and sold widely in the United States. He has moved to Big Sur, California, where he has lived in semiretirement as a literary figure and draws thousands who come to stare at his central California retreat.

California's institutions of higher learning have likewise attracted some writers of superior quality. Walter Van Tilburg Clark (1909–), born in Maine and raised in Nevada, taught for a time on the staff of San Francisco State College. He is perhaps best known for the stirring *The Ox-Bow Incident* (made into a successful movie). Iowa-born political scientist Eugene (Bud) Burdick (1918–1965) wrote much significant fiction, as well as many pieces for magazines. Although an excellent classroom lecturer and capable political scientist, Burdick found time to turn out novels (some of them with co-authors) such as *The Ninth Wave* (1956), *The Ugly American* (1958) and *Fail-Safe* (1962). His untimely death of a heart attack in 1965 was a loss to both the California academic and literary communities. Wallace Stegner (1909–) also a native of Iowa, has taught at Stanford since 1945. Stegner has written several colorful works on the American West—most notably *Beyond the Hundredth Meridian* (1954) and *The Gathering of Zion* (1964). He is also a stimulating teacher of young authors.

Foreign-born writers, such as Christopher Isherwood (1904–) and Thomas Mann (1875–1955), have also spent considerable time in the state. An American citizen since 1946, Isherwood penned, among other works, *Goodbye to Berlin* (1939). A fragment of this novel became the celebrated play and film *I Am a Camera*, and now serves as the basis for the musical *Cabaret*. Aldous Huxley (1894–1963) lived in California for a time and became noted for the acerbity of his remarks about southern California culture. The area similarly affects British-born author Gavin Lambert (1926–) who has taken up residence in Santa Monica Canyon and has become an American citizen. He considers Los Angeles as a Theater of the Absurd brought to life. Several of his writings have southern California backgrounds. His most notable work is *Inside Daisy Clover* (1963) which was also a successful movie. Playwright and poet Bertholt Brecht (1898–1956) fled Germany after Hitler's rise to power and after some wandering settled in Santa Monica, California. Although the critics would later label him the "Einstein of the new stage form" he found that there was little he could do in films. In California he wrote or rewrote half a dozen plays. While one, *Galileo*, reached Broadway, the rest, like *The Caucasian Chalk Circle*, were performed in small out-of-the-way theaters. During his California stay he also began work on a book concerning the aesthetics of the theater. After World War II, the political climate for Brecht, an avowed philosophical Communist, was sufficiently chilly so that he left America in November 1947. He returned to East Germany, where the *Berliner Ensemble* was created for him. Until his death he was the cultural showpiece of the East German regime.

Two recent serious California writers, Jack Kerouac and Allen Ginsberg, reflect the influence of Henry Miller. Kerouac was born in Massachusetts in 1922, and after a residence in California moved to New York. After attracting attention with *On the Road* (1957), he published two California books—*The Dharma Bums* (1958) and *The Subterraneans* (1958)—that brought Kerouac's unconventional literary style to a unique peak. Ginsberg was born in New Jersey in 1926 but found himself as a writer during a stay in San Francisco. An outstanding example of his work is *Howl and Other Poems* (1957). As spokesmen for what became known as the Beat Generation, Ginsberg and Kerouac confused and shocked many staid Californians.

California's most unusual writer of serious nonfiction is Eric Hoffer (1902–). Hoffer worked regularly as a longshoreman on the San Francisco waterfront and in his spare hours penned his books. His most important work is *The True Believer* (1951). His appearance in an hour-long TV interview in the fall of 1967 sparked new interest in his writings.

California has continued to add greatly to its musical heritage. The opportunity to work for the movies and television has drawn many musicians and composers to California. In addition the state has proved a haven for great foreign-born artists such as Igor Stravinsky (1882–). Moreover, the avant-garde musical center of western universities is now located at the once exclusively agricultural campus of the University of California at Davis (near Sacramento). Mills College in Oakland continues to attract many high-caliber graduate students in composition. Under Joseph Krips as conductor the San Francisco Symphony Orchestra is continuing in its role as a capable and tradition-oriented organization. On the other hand, the Los Angeles Philharmonic under Zubin Mehta is less hidebound and more dashing. At a less celebrated level, there are at least sixty-three community orchestras in California.

A number of cultural and recreational centers have been constructed in California. Spurred by Mrs. Norman Chandler of the *Times* Chandlers and by department store executive Edward W. Carter, Los Angeles finally opened a worthy music-and-drama complex in 1966 and 1967. A corps of fifty-eight guides handle the many free tourist tours of the music center. Musical comedies, operettas, operas and ballets play in the 3,200-seat Dorothy Chandler Pavilion. This building is a distinguished structure of marble floors, crystal chandeliers and a black marble bar. The center also includes the Mark Taper Forum, whose foyer walls are covered with abalone chips. It is billed as a "theater of involvement," and its resident company performs in an unusual amphitheater set with blue and purple seats. A short distance away is the Ahmanson Theater with its unusual espresso-colored walls, painted so as to give the illusion of melting away once the house lights are dimmed.

Six miles away is the new County Museum, designed by architect William Pereira. Here are exhibits which range from Renaissance statuary to contemporary sculpture by American artists of the 1960's. Los Angeles has also become the scene of a large number of private art galleries along La Ciénega Boulevard, once known as "Restaurant Way." These galleries hold open house on Mondays and serve drinks to their patrons. Sears, Roebuck & Company has its own gallery that sells paintings on credit. Fresno has recently completed an $8.5 million community and convention center, complete with theater and exhibition hall. The new Oakland museum is intended to house collections of art, natural science and western history.

The city of Long Beach purchased the Cunard liner *Queen Mary* for

$3,450,000. In December 1967 when the city took possession of the ship, it began to spend a sum over twice that great to convert the liner into a marine-oceanographic exposition center and a hotel-convention complex.

Less highbrow are the new baseball stadiums at Candlestick Point for the San Francisco Giants, Dodger Stadium at Chavez Ravine, home of the Los Angeles Dodgers, and the California Angels' ballpark at Anaheim. Oakland, which now has a major league baseball team, the Athletics, and professional football and basketball teams, has built a $30 million Oakland-Alameda County Coliseum. This structure contains a 53,000-seat, night-lighted stadium and a separate, 15,000-seat indoor arena.

In 1955, Walt Disney opened his super-recreational plant—Disneyland—in Orange County. On his visit to the United States, Nikita Khrushchev complained bitterly when he was unable to visit this mecca for children of all ages. To build and rebuild this recreational center, Disney spent the staggering sum of $95 million. Six million visitors a year pass through its portals, and its success has led to a host of imitators throughout the nation.

Californians are noted for taking their recreation in other than sedentary ways. Always outdoor livers, Californians in the mid-1960's enjoy twenty-five million acres of land set aside for recreation. On pleasant summer weekends, California's 120 state parks and eighteen national forests are heavily utilized. Californians have taken out enough fishing licenses to lead the nation in the collection of fees for that purpose. Golf has also been a leading pastime ever since the first golf courses were installed in southern California in the 1890's. Some Californians have taken the game so seriously that by 1962 they had won the USA open championship six times and have been United States amateur champions eight times and professional golf champions four times. California has produced more champion tennis players than any other single area of the world. Up to 1963, twelve men and eleven women had won national singles championships. In track and field, California has produced more champions than any other state. In college meets, the track teams of the University of Southern California and Occidental College have been outstanding for years.

Many professional baseball players have claimed California as their home, among them the DiMaggio brothers and Ted Williams. In football, Jackie Robinson, who went on to fame as a professional baseball player, was an outstanding college player at UCLA. Jackie Jensen played in the Rose Bowl for the University of California and then played professional baseball well enough to play in the World Series. Many collegiate and professional football players have learned their skills on California football fields. Other sports in which Californians have excelled are racing car driving, archery, badminton, sports car racing, and swimming. Surfing was carried to California from Hawaii in 1907 and quickly became a favorite in the warm waters of southern California. In 1950, a Californian revolutionized the design of surfboards and, thanks to publicity in movies and television, the manufacture of surfboards has become an important business. Another, more unusual, sport in California is glider flying. There is even an Associated Glider Clubs of Southern California which holds annual championship meets.

Formal religion in California is declining in influence, despite exhortations of the successors of Aimee Semple McPherson, as well as those of clergymen of older sects. One California clergyman who caught the headlines frequently with his original proposals was the Episcopal bishop of San Francisco, James Pike. After a number of years of service he retired in the mid-sixties to become a foundation scholar at Santa Barbara. Most Californians do not belong to a church and, according to attendance reports, they seem to be growing increasingly indifferent in the matter of religion. This general trend has not kept exotic religious sects from flowering in California's balmy climate, however.

Californians who once welcomed the gospel as preached by Aimee Semple McPherson have now turned in some numbers to more complex and sophisticated spiritual guides. Alan Watts has found a base of operation at Sausalito in the Bay area. Although English-born, Watts since 1951 has made his home in California. A one-time Episcopal clergyman, he has delved deeply into Far Eastern thought and religion. From 1951 to 1957 he was connected with the Academy of Asian Studies in San Francisco. Since the latter date he has devoted himself to lecturing and writing.

Although Watts interpreted Zen Buddhism to the Occidental world, by the time of his coming to California he refused to label himself as a member of that or any religious sect. By the late fifties, Zen Buddhism drew many followers in California, as indeed it did throughout the United States. As an authority on the study of Zen, Watts became the acknowledged leader of its cultists. The Beat Generation, the forerunners of the hippies, admired his writings greatly.

After 1952 Watts broadcast weekly half-hour talks over a Berkeley radio station that were taped and rerun in southern California. A series of programs on philosophy by Watts was originally presented over San Francisco's educational television station and taped for widespread distribution. Although identified in the popular mind with Zen Buddhism, Watts has also evinced interest in Taoism and Vedanta. His "in" status with nonconformist Californians has faded somewhat over the years as new figures and movements have crowded onto the scene.

Less cerebral and more gaudy has been the devotion of many Californians to the cult of Scientology. A kind of religion which has been defined as "the common people's science of life and betterment," it claims to be able to cure 70 per cent of man's ills and raise a person's I.Q. This cult is the creation of Lafayette Ronald Hubbard, an orange-haired Nebraskan born in 1911. After writing movie scripts and serving as a naval officer in World War II, he moved about Los Angeles and Pasadena where he took to writing science fiction. About 1950 Hubbard wrote *Dianetics: The Modern Science of Mental Health*, which became a best seller. Dianetics swept the United States as a short-lived fad. When the public interest in it faded, Hubbard converted the science of Dianetics into the religion of Scientology. Although Hubbard eventually moved to the United Kingdom to make his headquarters near London, his California faithful continued spreading his ideas. The unaccredited Sequoia University in Los Angeles awarded Hubbard a Ph.D. Orgs (as Scientology groups are styled) flourish in Los Angeles and San Diego. One of two American Scientology Academies (which institutions are usually a mark of a large org) exists in Los Angeles.

California has continued as the center of the entertainment industry. Great studios with stables of stars under exclusive contract became a thing of the past after World War II because of the competition of foreign movie-makers and television. The typical Hollywood movie of the thirties and the forties could no longer command success at the box office. American companies soon shot many of their films abroad in Spain, Greece and Finland. Many film stars became producers in order to take advantage of income tax laws which made the take-home residue of capital gains preferable to even astronomical salaries. While some of the old Hollywood studios were closed and their land sold for valuable real estate property, others simply reconverted to making pictures for television. The demands of television for films has become insatiable. After the backlog of old Hollywood films had been shown repeatedly on the late show, television stations demanded full-length movies made primarily for showing on television. In 1964, 305 California corporations engaged in motion-picture production reported a net income of nearly $16 million.

The first California commercial television station was granted a license to operate in the Los Angeles area on January 22, 1947. Very quickly, other stations came on the air; in February 1964, thirty-nine television stations were broadcasting, four of them being of the educational, noncommercial type. More importantly, Los Angeles now shares preeminence with New York as a studio for network shows. Affluent California families, with two and even three television sets, have become ardent viewers. Portable television sets are carried to the beach or on picnics so that favorite programs will not be missed.

Much more important than the movie-television industry in California is the defense-space industry. California, as we have already seen, obtained more than its share of defense contracts during and immediately after World War II. This trend has continued. In 1952 the dollar value of prime defense contracts which were awarded (those over $10,000) swelled to almost $5 billion—nearly 13 per cent of the nation's total. Although the total national defense budget was slashed after the Korean War, this downward trend did not continue in California. In 1955, California still possessed nearly $3 billion of defense contracts—over 20 per cent of the total number of contracts awarded. The value of these contracts rose to over $5 billion in 1961, and California's share consistently remained at the 20 per cent figure. Then a politically inspired drive to spread defense spending more equitably around the country caused this amount to drop slightly.

If one looks at the more restricted area of prime defense contract awards for research, development, test and evaluation work, California has claimed a high percentage of this category. In 1960, California had 42 per cent of these awards, and even as late as 1965, she claimed 31 per cent. In 1965, nearly half of California's prime defense contracts involved missile and space systems. Other categories of defense work included ammunition, petroleum, photographic equipment, electronics and communications. California's share of prime defense contracts in 1966 was 18.3 per cent, with a value of $5.8 billion. New York in the same year had attracted only $2.8 billion; Texas claimed $2.29 billion in such contracts.

An estimated 40 per cent of California's space industry orders are nondefense oriented. In the early sixties, California had won over half of the prime contract awards made by the National Aeronautics and Space Administration. As late as 1965, California had garnered nearly 46 per cent of these contracts. Total employment in California aerospace manufacturing industries was 131,000 in 1950, 461,000 in 1960, 482,000 in 1965, and 544,600 in 1966. The aerospace industry has employed the talents of the many scientists attracted to California's universities and colleges by the many opportunities to do consulting work for industrial firms. In 1964, 26,645 scientists lived in California—about 12 per cent of the total in the United States. About 17 per cent of all the mathematicians and scientists trained in space research work in California. On the roster of the National Science Foundation, California leads all other states with 13,668 members. Almost half of the American Nobel Prize winners and 22 per cent of the members of the National Academy of Sciences live in the state.

Space and defense needs have created special types of corporate organizations. The aerospace industry grew logically out of the aviation or manned aircraft plants which had been part of the California scene for most of the twentieth century. In 1942, the Aerojet General Corporation spun off from the California Institute of Technology. As time went by, it became known as the Jet Propulsion Laboratory and is today a leading center of applied research. It worked first on defense projects, but lately it has switched to NASA projects.

Two California Tech graduates, Simon Ramo and Dean Waldridge, began working in the scientific research and development aspects of Hughes Aircraft in the post-World War II era. In the 1950's they left Hughes to set up a technological firm of their own called Ramo-Waldridge. An auto and aviation parts firm, Thompson Products, had a financial connection with Ramo-Waldridge and they merged in 1958, setting up an independent subsidiary—Space Technology Laboratories. Two years later, as a result of complaints that a profit-making firm was engaged in this type of operation, a nonprofit firm, Aerospace Corporation, was created to take over STL's work. Recently the Aerospace Corporation reported an employment list of 1,900 scientists and engineers, nearly half of whom had advanced degrees. These nonprofit organizations are a key feature of the science-defense industry in California.

A discussion of this organizational structure demands some mention of the Rand Corporation. This company had its genesis after World War II, when General H. H. Arnold became concerned that the defense industry should not lose the civilian experts who began to work for it during the war. Therefore, he took most of the Air Force's civilian experts and contracted with Douglas Aircraft to set up a special plant in Santa Monica. Various difficulties developed, and this operation soon became the nonprofit Rand Corporation, with assistance from the Ford Foundation. In the mid-1960's, a new Rand president, Henry S. Rowen, helped to turn Rand away from exclusively defense projects to other national interest work. At that time, Rand employed a staff of 1,100—one-half of whom were professional experts.

Presently, the central Los Angeles telephone directory lists two columns of entries beginning with *aero*. Ten to twelve thousand firms in southern California are in some way engaged in aerospace work.

Union membership grew in post-World War II California. However, only about one-fifth of union members were women. This factor helped to limit the unions' growth, since more and more women had entered the California labor force. In 1950 there were 3,164 locals with a membership of 1,354,500. By 1965 the number had grown to 3,865 locals with 1,871,-000 members. Despite this gain, the unions had lost ground. In 1950 about 29 per cent of the California work force were union members, but by 1965 only 25 per cent were. One of the reasons for the relative lack of success of unions was the fact that a high proportion of California workers are white-collar employees, rather than the traditionally union-oriented blue-collar laborers. The unions still tried to exert political influence, but union causes or candidates seldom have attracted heavy voter support among union members or their families in California (except in campaigns such as that in 1958, when a so-called right-to-work law was an issue).

The direction that California unionism has taken is well illustrated by the recent actions of the International Longshoremen's and Warehousemen's Union. Since 1960 this union has wrung from its employers contributions averaging nearly $7 million a year for a fund that guarantees that some 15,000 longshoremen—including any displaced by automation—will receive a $13,000 lump sum payment when they retire, in addition to excellent pension payments. In return, the union has given the employers the right to automate the waterfront as rapidly as they deem necessary.

Despite the state's heavy spending for freeway construction, its roads and highways are becoming choked with automobiles, particularly in the vicinity of the big cities. As a result, the San Francisco Bay area has decided to drastically remedy this situation. The voters of the area have set up the Bay Area Rapid Transit District or, as it has become better known, BART. This became the first new mass transit system since 1907. It will have computer-operated trains to carry commuters when completed. Costing a billion dollars to construct, it will connect San Francisco with Oakland, and will run additional lines into the suburban regions. Technically BART will be a marvel. Engineers are currently engaged in laying seventy-five miles of special wide-gauge tracks, and burrowing and digging sixteen miles of tunnels so that cars can be dispatched at seventy miles an hour every ninety seconds. Hopefully, passengers will be transported so comfortably they will give up commuting by car. Although construction began in 1964, bitter disputes and costly delays have plagued the project. Its cost has increased at least 20 per cent since its planning began. Originally it was scheduled to be completed by 1971, but delays have made this goal impossible.

The greater Los Angeles area, which is much behind San Francisco in its attempt at mass transport, has plans for a sixty-two-mile combined subway, surface and elevated system with three hundred miles of feeder bus lines. This rapid transit system, costing $1.57 billion, will be submitted to the voters of the Southern California Rapid Transit District in November 1968. If the legislature refuses to authorize a sales tax on gasoline or the use of tidelands oil revenue, the system will be financed by a property tax.

The automobile has continued to dominate the transportation scene in California, despite recent plans for mass transportation systems. In 1951 there were 5,303,000 registered motor vehicles in California. This number had increased to 8,681,000 by 1950 and to 11,333,000 by 1965. Recently,

California has acquired more new automobiles than residents. In 1965, Californians and visitors to the state traveled some 47 billion motor-vehicle miles on the state's highways.

One California subculture that has caught the national attention is that of the hippies. Hippies, of course, are a national or even international phenomenon, but the San Francisco colony in the Haight-Ashbury district has been celebrated throughout America as a kind of capital of the movement. Individuals in revolt against society's standards are nothing new. The beatniks of the late 1950's had centered at North Beach in San Francisco. Across the Bay, the Berkeley rebels or activists have continued in the same general tradition. Hippies dress in old clothes and sandals and wear their hair long. Male hippies affect mustaches and beards—often these are the only signs which distinguish hippie boys from the girls. Hippies stress love as a force in human affairs. They are young people for the most part—a guess has been made that inhabitants of the Haight-Ashbury district average about twenty years of age. They carry flowers and bells and speak of "flower power." Unfortunately, their eccentric characteristics include a propensity to smoke marijuana and to take various psychedelic drugs as part of their withdrawal from the conforming American society, which they view as irredeemably distasteful. The hippies have congregated in the forty blocks of older homes and shops where Haight and Ashbury streets cross each other. By the summer of 1967, some 16,000 to 20,000 hippies had managed to crowd into the district. San Francisco municipal authorities have complained that their overcrowding and unhygienic habits are a menace and are costing the taxpayers extra money. Nevertheless, the Haight-Ashbury hippies became a great tourist attraction. Bus tours of the district were organized by enterprising guide lines, but the hippies have objected so violently that the bus tours have been dropped.

The great impact of the hippies seems to be their gradual effect upon the Berkeley activists. Whereas the activists wish to change society, the hippies want to withdraw from it, because they see it as essentially unreformable. As some of the activists have trooped across the Bay to the San Francisco quarter, some of the steam has begun to disappear from the Berkeley activist movement. As this trend continues, the orientation of New Left politics is drastically changing.

In addition, California has gangs of both young men and women who center their activities around motorcycle riding. Traveling in packs through many California communities, these groups seem to be an intolerable menace to many older and more sedentary Californians. Most motorcycle clubs seem typical of a technologically oriented juvenile delinquency which embraces youths from white-collar families. The most publicized of these gangs is a group known as the Hell's Angels. According to California's Attorney General Lynch, this group is far from a harmless, noisy aggregation. He has charged that the group has 466 members with records, which include 874 felony arrests, 300 felony convictions, 1,682 misdemeanor arrests and 1,023 misdemeanor convictions.

California's culture and society are big, malleable and ebullient. The old taboos do not often apply to life there. A great deal about the state defies easy generalization. All that can be said with certainty is that much of what was true yesterday will not be true tomorrow. While much that caustic critics deplore is unquestionably deplorable, much that is worthwhile and challenging is also occurring within the borders of the state. Since as a settled region, California is very young, it still has much to learn. However, the overwhelming mass of Californians still have hope—there is yet time to build a utopia according to their individual blueprints.

THIRTY-THREE

Contemporary California
and Its Problems

ONTEMPORARY California politics began in October 1953 with the appointment of Earl Warren as Chief Justice of the United States Supreme Court. His lieutenant governor, Goodwin J. ("Goodie") Knight, succeeded him in the governorship, earning a reputation as a conservative, but soon moving into the middle of the political road to claim the space vacated by Warren.

Born in Provo, Utah, on December 9, 1896, Knight moved with his family to California when he was eight years old. He attended Stanford University until navy service in World War I interrupted his college career. After receiving his undergraduate degree, Knight earned a scholarship to Cornell University, although he ran out of money before he could earn a law degree. Returning to California, he worked in a law office until he was admitted to the bar in 1921. Soon he built a prosperous law practice and purchased some gold mines in Kern County. In September 1935, Governor Merriam appointed him to the Los Angeles County superior court. During the next ten years, Knight rendered some seven thousand decisions, few of which were ever appealed to a higher court.

During his years as an attorney, Knight had been very active in Republican politics; however, as a judge he felt constrained to seek less partisan publicity. Therefore, Knight carved out a career for himself as a public affairs radio moderator. In 1946, utilizing the services of the public relations firm of Whitaker and Baxter, he won the Republican nomination for lieutenant governor and then easily defeated Democrat John F. Shelley of San Francisco in the general election. In 1950, Knight won both the Republican and Democratic nominations for lieutenant governor, and in the November election, Knight polled over three million votes—a record for any state official. As governor, Knight not only retained his predecessor's principles, but his appointees as well. Besides establishing himself as a moderate administrator, Knight presented himself as an energetic one by making eighty-four speeches in his first twenty-nine days in office.

Knight and Republican Senator Thomas H. Kuchel (appointed to Nixon's Senate seat when the latter was elected Vice-President) faced more formidable Democratic opposition than any other Republicans since the halcyon days of the New Deal; that slumbering giant, the California Democratic Party, had finally come awake. Imitating the California Republican Assembly, which long had focused the minority party's support in the critical primaries, the Democrats belatedly formed the California Democratic Council (C.D.C.) in 1953. In addition, the Democrats also profited from an initiative measure adopted in 1952 which required that a candidate's party affiliation be printed after his name on the primary ballot. As their gubernatorial candidate, the Democrats chose a former Republican, Richard P. Graves, who had only recently changed his party affiliation. While Graves had never held an elected office, he had been active in public affairs and was known as an associate of Earl Warren.

While Knight won the Republican primary over Graves by a ten-to-one margin, he lost the Democratic primary by a small number of votes. To make this strong showing, Knight won strong labor support from the AFL. After a vigorous campaign in which he generally ignored his lesser-known opponent, Knight defeated Graves by a 551,000 majority. Kuchel was successful in defeating his Democratic challenger, the veteran politico Sam Yorty.

In his full term as governor, Knight continued to follow the moderate trail blazed by Warren. He advocated increased spending for education and augmented unemployment benefits. He dipped heavily into the "Rainy Day Fund" in order to avoid new taxes. In his public pronouncements, he also promised labor that he would fight attempts to cripple the unions' effectiveness by enacting right-to-work laws. He worked so well with the moderates of both parties in the legislature that he employed his full veto only thirty-five times. His vetoes were never overridden.

In August 1957, Knight announced that he would attempt to win another term. However, his future as governor appeared tenuous because veteran Senator William F. Knowland also coveted the governor's seat. It was rumored that Knowland would run for the state post on a platform which endorsed a right-to-work law. Most observers believed that Knowland was vacating his Senate seat and his post as Senate minority leader only because he believed that the governorship was a more certain step-ping-stone to the Republican presidential nomination in 1960.

The Republican leadership in California was horrified at the prospect of a party-splintering primary clash between Knowland and Knight. In the fall of 1957, in a behind-the-scenes deal, Knight agreed to forego his ambitions for a gubernatorial reelection and to seek instead the Senate seat which would be vacated by Knowland. Knight became bitter at this engineered change in his plans; therefore, while Knowland announced his support of Knight for the Senate the governor did not reciprocate, but fought his own campaign for the Senate with scarcely a mention of Knowland.

Opposing Knowland for the governorship was Democrat Edmund G. ("Pat") Brown, a second-generation Californian, born in San Francisco on April 21, 1905. After attending public schools in San Francisco, Brown obtained his LL.B. degree in 1927 from the San Francisco College of Law. In 1930 he married a San Francisco police captain's daughter, Bernice Layne, and became the father of three daughters and one son. Originally a Republican, Brown became a Democrat in 1934. In 1939 he attempted to unseat a veteran San Francisco district attorney. When he failed, he tenaciously tried again four years later, winning this time. He continued in office after an unsuccessful try for the state attorney generalship in 1946. In 1950 he was successful in his try for the state attorney general's post and then won a reelection in 1954. In October 1957, Brown an-nounced his decision to run for governor of California. Campaigning upon a generally liberal platform, he vociferously condemned a right-to-work constitutional amendment which had been endorsed by Knowland and which was listed as Proposition 18 on the ballot.

In the election of 1958, Brown was greatly aided by a revivified Demo-cratic Party and by greatly increased labor union political activity. The unions were unusually successful in arousing their membership to vote against Knowland and his antiunion constitutional amendment. Another important factor was also working for Brown. California voters, who careen independently in a general election, had become incensed at the brazen deal whereby Knowland had run for the governorship. Refusing to be manipulated by Knowland's supporters, they joined union men in voting for the entire Democratic slate, except for the candidate for secre-tary of state. The right-to-work amendment was also defeated. Knowland himself lost to Brown by a million votes. While Knight ran better than Knowland, he too was toppled in defeat. His opponent was a northern California congressman, Clair Engle. Engle was so little known in south-ern California that at the beginning of his campaign a sizable part of the electorate actually believed he was a woman! Not only did the Demo-crats sweep to victory in the statewide races, but for the first time since 1889, the Democrats had majorities in both branches of the legislature.

Knight bowed out of office with grace and retired to southern California, where he appeared as a television commentator and now functions as president of an insurance firm. In both 1961 and 1965, he announced his possible candidacy for a new gubernatorial term. During the first election, an attack of ill health forced him to postpone his campaign; on the second occasion the rise of Ronald Reagan as a candidate caused him to withdraw from the gubernatorial race.

As governor, Brown moved to implement his program of what he called "responsible liberalism." In the 1959 session of the legislature, Brown laid the foundation for his tenure as governor. Out of forty measures endorsed by Brown, the legislature enacted thirty-five. Brown successfully requested a record budget of $2 billion and was able to get some $200 million in new taxes approved by the legislature. He also succeeded in getting a fair employment practices act on the statute books and influenced the enactment of the Burns-Porter Act for the state construction and operation of a giant power and water project. The Democratic legislators also succeeded in abolishing the practice of cross-filing. This practice had long plagued them and many Democrats believed its end would usher in a long era of absolute control by their party. Their roseate dream was not to become a reality, however.

Brown met a major setback when he worked to abolish capital punishment. He had long questioned the value of capital punishment as a deterrent to crime, and so he granted a sixty-day reprieve to the convicted kidnapper-bandit Caryl Chessman, who had become a successful author while living in Death Row. The governor then asked the legislature in a special session to abolish the death penalty. Brown's action was applauded by foes of capital punishment, but many citizens and legislators viewed the governor's action as evidence of his "softness" for criminals. An uproar soon occurred in the legislature. Brown saw his hopes dashed for the end of the death penalty when the senate judiciary committee killed an anti-capital punishment bill. In due course, Chessman was executed and Brown had lost not only the fight against the death penalty but prestige as well.

The governor's image was further tarnished in 1960 when a slate of national convention delegates that he headed was given an unexpectedly stiff contest by old-age pension promoter George McLain in what was billed as a "gray-haired revolt." At the Democratic convention in Los Angeles, Brown attempted to deliver his entire delegation to the presidential candidacy of Massachusetts Senator John F. Kennedy, but he was only partially successful. In November 1960, Kennedy won the presidency over Californian Richard M. Nixon, but after the absentee ballots had been counted, California had voted by a razor-thin margin for the Republican presidential candidate.

Limping away from these defeats, Brown, in 1961, asked his

Democratically controlled legislature to implement additional features of his program. He asked for a far-reaching reorganization of the executive branch of the California state government. Although he did not get all that he wished, Brown was able to accomplish a considerable reorganization. A new teaching license bill was passed which reduced the number of California educational credentials from forty to five and called for greater academic content in teacher training.

Meanwhile, Brown found spirited Republican opposition to his plans to seek reelection in 1962. Richard Nixon, in need of a new power base, announced in October 1961 that he would attempt to wrest the governorship from Brown. Many California Republicans dismissed Nixon as an "Eisenhower liberal" and backed the attempt of conservative Assemblyman Joseph C. Shell to win the nomination. Although Nixon was able to defeat Shell by a two-to-one margin in the June primary, it became apparent that many conservative Republicans would never give him more than token support in the November election.

Brown was lucky in this election. He could point to his accomplishments as governor, while denouncing Nixon as a carpetbagger from Washington, D.C., who only sought the governorship of California to advance his ambition for the presidency in 1964.

Apathy on the Republican right, the independent voters' feeling that Nixon's candidacy was an attempt to manipulate them, and the relatively strong support of the Democratic organizations for Brown's candidacy, all combined to defeat Nixon. Brown's margin of superiority over Nixon was only 300,000 votes, but the Democrats managed to retain control of the legislature.

In 1963, California's budget soared past the $3,250,000,000 level—the largest state budget to that time ever submitted in the United States. In that same year, the legislature passed the fiercely controversial Rumford Housing Act that sought to outlaw racial discrimination in most private and public housing. This act directed the Fair Employment Practices Commission to hold hearings on complaints of discrimination and then to enforce its decisions.

Relations between Governor Brown and the chief legislative Democrat, Jesse M. Unruh, speaker of the assembly, had cooled, another factor which disrupted the Democratic Party in California. In addition, Senator Clair Engel had suffered an illness which incapacitated him and ultimately caused his death in mid-1964. Although ailing, Engle refused to withdraw his name from the June 1964 primary ballot, but his obvious physical weakness led others to seek the senatorial nomination. Controller Alan Cranston drew support from Governor Brown, while President Kennedy's former press secretary, Pierre Salinger, with support from Jesse Unruh, also entered the Democratic senatorial primary. When Salinger defeated Cranston, it was regarded as a defeat for the governor as well.

Meanwhile storm clouds were gathering for the Democrats in California. The passage of the Rumford Act had provoked a major reaction. Californians moved often; in Los Angeles, one voter in four moves every year. Since many citizens bought and sold their equities in homes several times while raising their families, they were particularly moved by charges that open housing would lower property values. As a result, there was soon open strife in California "between principle and interest," as James Fenimore Cooper once phrased it. With the help of the organized realtors of the state, a drive was successfully launched to put Proposition 14 on the election ballot, a measure which would void the Rumford Act. Although Brown was not running for reelection in 1964, he criticized this proposition, as did senatorial candidate Pierre Salinger. Spearheaded by their senatorial candidate, the ex-Hollywood movie actor George Murphy, the Republicans supported Proposition 14 on the grounds that a man's right to property should not be limited.

The result of this excitement over Proposition 14 was to diminish Salinger's chances of winning. However, there were many other factors that also worked against him. He seemed to be a one-note candidate who reiterated the slogan "I knew Kennedy." This refrain had been enough to carry him past the lackluster Cranston, but it palled on the voters during the long campaign. Salinger also made the tactical mistake of debating Murphy on television, exposing himself unfavorably in contrast to the genial Republican. The crowning blow to Salinger's hopes came, ironically, at the hands of Robert F. Kennedy. When Kennedy resigned as Attorney General in the late summer of 1964 to seek a senatorship from New York, critics declared Salinger to be a carpetbagger who hoped to serve as a proconsul for the Kennedys in California. A vote for Salinger, so they said, was a vote to create a Kennedy power base on the West Coast. Moreover, Salinger's opponent George Murphy skillfully exploited many Californians' concern over the end of the Mexican *bracero* program on the state's farms. From a solidly right-wing stance, Murphy had shifted toward the center of the political spectrum and so gained votes at Salinger's expense.

The 1964 election was a mixed bag for the Democrats. While President Johnson was sweeping the nation in his bid for reelection against Barry Goldwater, he rather unspectacularly won California's electoral votes. In the two worlds of California politics—the liberal north and the conservative south—Johnson ran very differently. His showing in southern California indicated future trouble for the Democrats. In northern California, Johnson commanded a lead of about 850,000 votes—nearly double his southern California figure, despite the larger voter registration in this area of the state. Johnson won 66 per cent of the vote in the Bay area and 63 per cent in other northern California counties. In southern California, Johnson garnered 58 per cent of the votes of populous Los Angeles

County, but received a narrow margin of 51 per cent in the other southern California counties. In suburban Orange County, just south of Los Angeles, Goldwater swept the countryside, winning 56 per cent of the total vote. Although Proposition 14 won by an impressive two-to-one margin throughout the state in this election, it garnered 10 per cent more votes in the south than in the north of California.

It was in the Murphy-Salinger race that the undertow of Republican resurgence in southern California was clearly demonstrated. Salinger actually won by 150,000 votes in the north, only to lose by over 350,000 votes in the south. Murphy triumphed in the classic tradition of California Republicans; he was able to obtain the support of one-quarter of the Democratic voters while losing only 14 per cent of his own party registration to Salinger. The lack of Democratic power in California is illustrated by the fact that over half of the Republican incumbents for Congress and the state assembly actually won their districts by a greater margin than they had in 1962.

Future trouble for the Democrats could be forecast from the 1964 returns, which showed that the large group of low-income Democratic voters in southern California showed wide deviations from their party position in the presidential, senatorial, and Proposition 14 contests. Democratic gerrymandering of the legislature kept that body firmly in the party's hands in 1964, however.

In 1965, the California legislature showed an increasingly large economy bloc. This group became concerned because the governor's budget not only totaled over $4 billion, but it gave an increasing share to the needs of social welfare. The 1965 legislature had to grapple with the problems of reapportioning the state legislature in accordance with the Supreme Court's one-man, one-vote decision. Since reapportionment along population lines would throw control of the state legislature to southern California, some northerners advocated secession before submission to this measure. The talk of breaking California into two states was never translated into action, for between the north and the south there were too many strong ties to be so easily broken.

Although the budget had grown, the Democratic state leadership resisted imposing new taxes before a state election. Even with California's expanding economy, the old levies did not bring in sufficient revenue to balance the budget. As a result, in 1966 Governor Brown had to resort to several fiscal devices to keep the state solvent, a move which caused his many critics to cry "financial gimmickry."

Although Brown's relationship with his legislature somewhat deteriorated in his second term, he vetoed only .005 per cent of the total number of bills which were sent to him. His infrequent vetoes were never overridden.

After 1964 the state Democratic Party became divided over the issue of President Johnson's foreign policy. Perhaps nowhere in the nation was Johnson's decision to intervene with American troops in Vietnam more attacked by Democrats than in California. The California Democratic Council, once a bastion of administration power, was now rent by dissent. Some of the most active volunteer workers from Berkeley and other liberal centers around the state became disaffected because of the national foreign policy. When Brown announced his support of the President their anger was then directed upon him. The dissidents had nowhere to go politically, but they could and did refuse to work for Brown in the 1966 campaign.

Meanwhile, a new political personality, Ronald Reagan, had captured the attention of California conservatives and had become this group's choice for a gubernatorial nominee. Once known as a movie star and then as a supporter of conservative causes and candidates, Reagan captured national attention when he appeared on national television on behalf of Barry Goldwater in October 1964.

Reagan was born in Tampico, Illinois, on February 6, 1911. He graduated in 1932 from Eureka College in his home state. Then he became a radio sports announcer on the NBC network. Traveling to California for the spring training of the Chicago Cubs in 1937, Reagan made a successful screen test and signed a contract with Warner Brothers as an actor. Reagan appeared in over fifty movies between 1937 and 1964 as a "good guy" who did not often get the girl. During World War II, he served in the Army as a noncombatant. In the immediate postwar period, Reagan was very active in the leadership of the Screen Actors Guild and became involved in many liberal causes.

From 1954 to 1962, Reagan was employed as the host and occasional performer on a weekly television show, *General Electric Theater*. Between television appearances, Reagan toured the United States in behalf of the General Electric Company's personnel relations program, visiting its many far-flung plants. In his talks to General Electric's employees, Reagan stressed the blessings of free enterprise and the evils of big government. After his earlier marriage to actress Jane Wyman ended in divorce, in 1952 he married the daughter of a politically conservative neurosurgeon. His switch from liberalism to conservatism occurred when he campaigned for Eisenhower in 1952 and 1956 and for Nixon in 1960. In the early sixties he formally switched to the Republican Party. From 1962 to 1965, Reagan appeared as host and performer on the television program *Death Valley Days*. In 1965, a group of businessmen in California organized a committee, The Friends of Ronald Reagan, and hired the public relations firm of Spencer-Roberts and Associates to prepare Reagan's image for the 1966 gubernatorial election.

For a time it seemed that Senator Thomas H. Kuchel might challenge Reagan in the Republican gubernatorial primary, but when the senator declined to run, it was clear that the moderate wing of the Republican party had no one who could defeat Reagan. In the June 1966 primary, Reagan easily defeated the former mayor of San Francisco, George Christopher, by a total of 1,417,000 votes to 675,000.

Meanwhile, Governor Brown, who had been unable to groom a suitable Democratic successor, tried for an almost unprecedented third term. In the June Democratic gubernatorial primary, when Brown defeated his opponent, conservative mayor of Los Angeles, Sam Yorty, by the narrow margin of 1,334,000 to 994,000, he was quite obviously in deep political trouble.

During the course of his campaign, Reagan gave variations upon what some of the newsmen who accompanied him called "The Speech." This address touched upon wasteful spending, high taxes, rising crime rates, increasing welfare costs, and the student revolts at the University of California. Brown struck back by hitting at Reagan's lack of political experience. The Republican candidate countered these attacks by admitting that he was no politician, but simply a citizen interested in righting the wrongs which existed in California. In his television appearances, Reagan appeared fresh and vigorous. Brown, in reality not much older than Reagan, seemed like a tired politician. To further sully his political image, Brown had allegedly been guilty of several off-the-cuff, mirth-provoking remarks which were eagerly repeated by his growing legion of detractors. Although Reagan eschewed racism in his campaign, his talks on law and order seemed to indicate that he would vigorously suppress race riots. Reagan did not favor enforced open housing, a stand which appealed to many Californians who could not forget Brown's enthusiastic opposition to Proposition 14 in the 1964 election. Since it had been conclusively demonstrated between 1958 and 1962 that the Democratic ratio of registration of 60–40 translated at the polls to a figure of only 53–47, the serious Democratic defections, which became obvious as the campaign developed, indicated a staggering defeat for the majority party. Outside the state most observers began to predict a Reagan victory, but argued that the election might be close.

As a result of these omens, Brown turned increasingly to television programs on which he gibed that Reagan was a politically untrained actor who would be a puppet for the radical right. This tactic proved to be ineffectual. Several prominent Hollywood actors made films and tapes for Brown, declaring that Reagan could play at being governor, but he could never be a real executive. Perhaps nowhere else in the country could these gibes at an actor have so little impact. Many California voters saw Reagan as a leading personality in an important California industry—movies and television.

Consequently, on November 8, 1966, Reagan was easily elected governor by a count of 3,127,000 votes—about 58 per cent of the total—against a mere 2,282,000 votes for Brown. Reagan carried every county except three in northern California. All statewide executive offices, except for the attorney generalship, passed into Republican hands. The Democrats, because of an artfully contrived reapportionment technique, were able to cling to a razor-thin margin of 21–19 in the senate and a minuscule 42–38 control in the lower house. This campaign was undoubtedly the most expensive in California history. The Republicans reported spending $2.7 million in the congressional and assembly races, while the Democrats admitted spending $2 million in the same contests.

Brown retired from office to accept a partnership in a Los Angeles law firm. Even as governor-elect, Reagan began to issue a barrage of statements indicating that he was a "true believer" in his economy pledges. As his staff began conversations with the Brown appointees in order to plan the transition between administrations, Reagan began to utter forebodings about the gloomy financial picture of the state.

In his inaugural speech, Reagan stressed again his campaign theme of a "Creative Society." The inauguration ceremonies set off a week of elaborate events that Sacramento observers declared were reminiscent of no inauguration since that of Governor Rolph. A week of early prayers, late balls, formal dress concerts and cocktail parties followed. Jack Benny played a violin solo at one concert; Walt Disney Productions turned out a twenty-four-page brochure of the inauguration festivities. Before his inauguration, Reagan had already indicated that he would not include in his first state budget any sums for an increased work load unless specifically required to do so by law, and included in his ban the requests of the university and state colleges for new teachers to handle the increased enrollment. Reagan's tactics in pushing for economy were patterned after those of Republican Governor James A. Rhodes of Ohio. One leaf which Reagan attempted to borrow from Rhodes' book was his request that the California employees voluntarily work on Lincoln's and Washington's birthdays. In Ohio the state employees had bowed to their governor's demand; in California, they indignantly refused this request. Quickly, Reagan announced a spate of economy measures. He placed a freeze upon the purchase of certain types of office equipment and banned the hiring of replacements for state employees unless their positions were vital. As a result, between January and June of 1967, California hired only 1,836 new employees as compared with 6,350 during the same period in 1966.

In addition to cutbacks in higher education, Reagan trained his economic guns upon the state mental health establishment. Since there had been a drop in the number of mental patients which this department now handled, the governor decreed a budget cut of 17.7 per cent for the 1967–68 fiscal year, thus eliminating some 3,700 jobs in the state mental health program. After much deliberation, the legislature passed a record budget of $5,126,834,709. All Republican members of the legislature voted for the budget, except for Orange County's Senator John G. Schmitz, an avowed member of the John Birch Society who felt that despite Reagan's cuts the budget was too large. Interestingly, Schmitz was joined in his opposition by twenty-two liberal Democrats—seven senators and fifteen assemblymen—who voted against the budget on the grounds that it was inadequate for the needs of the state. When the budget went to Reagan for his signature, only hours before the deadline of midnight on June 30, he signed it into law, after using the item veto to eliminate $43.5 million— mostly at the expense of the budgets for higher education and the Department of Mental Hygiene. Although Reagan reaped a harvest of praise from economy-minded citizens, his cuts in a budget which was higher than he had requested in a number of areas totaled less than 1 per cent. In addition, although the governor declared that he considered California's system of higher education to be one of the state's greatest assets, he stubbornly insisted upon fiscal cuts in this area. It remains to be seen if California's program of higher education can maintain its excellence indefinitely on such short fiscal rations. Since there is a close link between California's "think" industry and the state's system of higher education, it is possible that California's economic well-being might eventually become a casualty of the governor's actions.

According to polls throughout 1967, Reagan still maintained his popularity with the voters who had chosen him as governor in 1966. Injured cries erupted from some political quarters, however, and there was talk of demanding Reagan's impeachment. A recall petition was actually circulated in the Bay area, but there was little doubt that he remained a popular, if controversial, figure upon California's political scene.

In other matters, the legislature passed and Governor Reagan signed a bill liberalizing California's abortion law. The governor and the legislature also agreed to allow night horse racing and an extended race track season for California—items which had long been fought by certain church groups within the state.

Reagan as California governor became a national political figure. Throughout 1967 he was invited to speak in all parts of the Union. Although in accepting many of these engagements Reagan acted like a candidate, he denied that he sought the office of President. In the summer of 1967 his political stock rose even higher when the Republicans won a state senate seat in Democratic San Francisco—a victory which gave them a tie for control of the upper house of the legislature. However, Reagan's hope to gain a place on the 1968 Republican national ticket seemed dependent upon the collapse of the Nixon-for-President boom, since both men appealed to essentially the same kind of Republicans.

In November 1967, Californians reassured those Americans who had become concerned that the state's politics might be dominated by former movie stars. At that time, Shirley Temple Black, the one-time child movie star, now a society matron living on the San Francisco peninsula, was soundly defeated for the Republican congressional nomination in a special election to fill a vacancy. Her successful opponent, Paul McCloskey, who favored the arguments of the doves on the conduct of the Vietnam war then, easily defeated his Democratic opponent in the December 1967 election.

Despite the attention seized by its political affairs, California also faced important race-relation problems. Since the gold rush, California's racial minorities have experienced discrimination, but for the first time at least one minority group—the Negro—was refusing to accept its designated place in California's power structure. Negroes did not come to California in significant numbers until the twentieth century. As late as 1930, only 1.4 per cent of California's population was Negro. The pull of the increased industrialization of California and the push away from the overt discrimination of the South all combined to build the Negro population in California to 2.8 per cent by 1940, to 4.3 per cent ten years later, and to 5.6 per cent by 1960. Moreover, the Negro population of the state was concentrated in ghettos in California's major cities. Only 5.6 per cent of Negro Californians lived in rural areas in 1960.

Out of the estimated one and a half million Negroes who left the South during the decade from 1955 to 1965, one out of four came to California. Los Angeles County was the favored southern California area of settlement. In 1965 the county's Negro population stood at 650,000, an almost tenfold increase since 1940. Of the total Los Angeles Negro population, almost 89 per cent live in 46.5 square miles of south-central Los Angeles. A portion of this neighborhood had been the site of the original Negro settlement in this area, Watts.

In 1964, white Californians administered a slap to Negro citizens when they voted in overwhelming numbers for Proposition 14, which sought to nullify the Rumford Fair Housing Act. Despite the action of the California supreme court in declaring Proposition 14 unconstitutional in May 1966 and concurrence by the United States Supreme Court in 1967, the damage in California race relations had largely been accomplished. The political setback of the Negroes in regard to Proposition 14 only underscored the economic difficulties under which the Negro labored in ghettos such as Watts; the median family income only reached the figure of $2,370. Nearly half of the adult members of the Watts community did not own cars and were severely handicapped in their ability to locate and hold jobs. Moreover, nearly two-thirds of the people in Watts received no unemployment benefits and less than 14 per cent of the unemployed received public welfare assistance. Watts was not greatly dissimilar from

Negro districts in Oakland and Long Beach. One problem which the Los Angeles area Negroes faced in the 1950's and the 1960's was the fact that their migration did not come in response to specific demands for their labor. As a result, no segment of the white community felt any particular interest in their fate.

Negro violence in great cities was still a relatively new phenomenon when disorders broke out in the Watts area in August 1965. The Negro community in Watts seemed an unlikely place for it to happen, because with all its imperfections, the community lawns, trees, and rows of single family homes seemed at a glance far superior to the Negro tenements of Harlem. Yet with Negroes pouring into Watts at the rate of almost a thousand a month, the area soon reached the point of human saturation. It all began one hot Wednesday evening, August 11, when an officer of the California Highway Patrol arrested a young Negro for driving while intoxicated. This arrest was made near the Watts district. The arrested man's mother appeared and began berating her son. The mood of the scene soon changed and became angry. A crowd of about a thousand Negroes gathered. The crowd eventually became a mob throwing rocks at the police. Despite the best efforts of the Los Angeles police, this mob violence evolved into a full-scale riot. By Friday, August 13, Lieutenant Governor Glenn Anderson, then acting governor in the absence of the vacationing Brown, was asked to call out the National Guard. Anderson hesitated some hours before the Guard was actually sent in. Despite the action of the nearly 14,000 members of the National Guard, it was Tuesday, August 17, before the uprising was actually suppressed. In all, 3,438 adults and 514 juveniles were arrested. Also, 2,278 felony cases and 1,133 misdemeanor cases were filed against arrested adults. The human cost ultimately reached thirty-four persons killed and 1,032 injured. The property damage was estimated to have amounted to $40 million—with more than six hundred buildings destroyed by looting and burning.

Soon various state and federal programs aimed at curing the chronic unemployment affecting the area were begun. Some progress was made, although improvement was disappointingly slow. It remained a sort of uneasy truce. How easily it might all be kindled again was shown in June 1966 when the killing of a Negro by the Los Angeles police again touched off sporadic rioting.

Similar but less widespread and costly rioting broke out in Negro ghettos in San Francisco in late September of 1966 and May of 1967. Fresno was rocked by minor outbreaks of violence in mid-July 1967. In April 1968, after the assassination of the Reverend Dr. Martin Luther King, Jr., in Memphis, several northern California cities were shaken by minor disorders although Watts did not erupt. The main point made by these post-Watts outbreaks was that while some symptoms had been treated in California Negro communities, the basic problem of pockets of poverty in an affluent society remained. It was the poverty of joblessness, undereducation, discrimination, hopelessness and frustration.

These racial tensions bred extremists among both whites and Negroes. For example, the Negroes of the East Bay area formed an organization called the Black Panthers, which, in the spring of 1967, staged an armed march through the halls of the state capitol at Sacramento. Their action only succeeded in prodding the legislature to consider a bill banning the carrying of weapons in public places. Negro violence encouraged some California whites to join organizations such as the Ku Klux Klan. In September 1966, the Klan made one of its rare California public appearances when a brief but disorganized rally of perhaps 250 Klansmen was held at Saugus in Los Angeles County. At that time a Klan cross glowed feebly through the darkness, not with fire but with artificial red lights because of the restrictions of California fire laws.

California's minority groups are badly fragmented and do not present a united front. The Japanese and the Chinese are uninterested in making common cause with the Negroes. Many Mexican-Americans feel that the Negroes, by their violence, have succeeded in attracting too much publicity and too many government jobs. A study of precinct returns in 1964 seems to indicate that the Mexican-Americans supported the passage of Proposition 14 against open housing.

With all its human problems, California has been troubled by growing problems with its environment. One of the most difficult problems has centered about California's everlasting quest for an adequate water supply. California's Central Valley has been the scene of much planning and work to bring the excess water of the rainy north into the arid southern part of the valley. As early as 1933 the legislature passed an original Central Valley Project. Although the state stood ready to use California funds if necessary, federal money completed this initial project. Private utilities such as the Pacific Gas and Electric Company opposed the federal government's action, but by 1951 all the developments of this initial Central Valley proposal had been finished. As is usually the case, by the time the project was completed it was becoming obsolescent.

The pressures for more and more water for California have continued unabated. In 1960, 90 per cent of California's water requirements were used for agricultural purposes and only 10 per cent were needed for homes and industry. This proportion may change by 1990 to 79 per cent for agriculture and to 21 per cent for home and industrial use. Most of California's cities need about 150 gallons of water per inhabitant, but industry is even thirstier. To process one barrel of crude oil, forty barrels of water must circulate; to make one ton of steel, 100,000 gallons of water are needed; to can one case of lima beans requires 250 gallons. As a result, by 1957 a new California water plan to provide for California's domestic, industrial and agricultural purposes was created by the state's experts which greatly dwarfed the original Central Valley Project. This plan also ran into political trouble as California's representatives in the legislature bickered over its details. Governor Brown, then in his first term, stepped in and used his prestige to have the Burns-Porter Act passed by the legislature. It authorized a bond issue of $1.75 billion which was thereupon approved by the voters by the narrow margin of 174,000 votes out of 5,750,000 ballots cast in November 1960. This amount, plus the proceeds of a proposed electric power revenue bond program and some nonbond funds, were to be used to finance construction. This State Water Project is sometimes called the Feather River Project, because the key unit is a dam on that river near the city of Oroville. By 1962 a contract had been signed for the construction of the Oroville Dam. Some private interests did not appreciate the construction and operation of this water system by the State Department of Water Resources and sued to prevent its establishment. The issue was carried to the California supreme court, which decided in February 1963 that the Burns-Porter Act was valid. Meanwhile construction of the project went ahead. It was planned that the Oroville Dam, when completed, would be the highest earthfill embankment dam in the world, impounding water in a reservoir with a storage capacity of 3,500,000 acre-feet. Work on the dam has proceeded satisfactorily and it is believed it will be completed in 1968. Water released from the dam will generate hydroelectric energy and then flow into the Sacramento–San Joaquin Delta region. From there the water will be carried by way of the 444-mile California Aqueduct down the Central Valley, over the Tehachapi Mountains at an altitude of more than 3,000 feet and then down to the thirsty cities of southern California. It is planned to deliver water by means of this system to Kern County in 1968, to Los Angeles County in 1971, and to Riverside County in 1972. By 1990, sixteen dams, twenty-five power plants, and 650 miles of aqueducts will deliver 4,230,000 acre-feet of water each year to water-deficient areas.

California and Arizona have continued to squabble over the use of the Colorado River. In 1963 the United States Supreme Court ruled that Arizona was entitled to 2.8 million acre-feet of water from the Colorado River. California was authorized to take 4.4 million acre-feet and Nevada could tap 300,000 acre-feet of the Colorado's so-called normal 7,500,000 acre-feet of flow. Hearings continue to be held on federal legislation to implement the Supreme Court decision. In these hearings, California officials have insisted before Congressional committees that California must have its annual guarantee of water before Arizona can claim its share.

California has also looked forward to obtaining fresh water from the ocean. As early as 1958, Congress authorized the construction of one of five experimental facilities to make fresh water from the sea at Point Loma in San Diego. This plant was constructed only to be dismantled and reassembled in 1964 at Guantanamo Bay in Cuba. A San Diego saline water test facility was built to yield information from test plants and modules so that someday large-scale desalinating plants with capacities of 50 million gallons per day could be constructed. By the early 1970's it was hoped that the Metropolitan Water District would build a desalinating plant on a man-made island off the Orange County coast. The city of Coalinga has been experimenting in the use of a reverse osmosis desaliniza-tion process to utilize waste and brackish waters to supplement its munic-ipal water supply. Although the price of water obtained by desalinization remains so high it is impractical for irrigation purposes, at some future date the Pacific Ocean may provide much of California's industrial and human water needs. Someday, nuclear explosions deep under the Mojave Desert may provide an additional source of water. Another possibility for the future source of water is rain-cloud milking. If California's population continues to grow at a great rate, some of these devices would be needed to provide sufficient water for its future population.

Water is a problem to California in yet another way, for the state has had to battle to preserve its rivers and lakes from pollution. The classic example of water pollution is Lake Tahoe, whose waters are shared by both California and Nevada. This lake in the early 1940's was a diamond-clear body of water, high in the mountains—almost untouched by man. In the period after the end of World War II, many summer homes, ski lodges and hotels were built there. Weekend summer populations in and around the vicinity of the lake climbed to 150,000. Soon the pollution seeping into the lake seriously threatened its purity. As a result, a Lake Tahoe joint study committee was established by the concurrent action of the California and Nevada legislatures in 1965. This body capped a year of hearings with the conclusion that the sixty-one existing local govern-ments and special districts in the two states cannot serve the needs of the five-hundred-square-mile Tahoe Basin. Instead, it recommended the crea-tion of a Tahoe Regional Agency with Basin-wide jurisdiction in both states. The efforts of the two states to accomplish the protection of the lake remained in doubt by the spring of 1968, for some local agencies and large landholders in the area have strenuously fought any attempt to establish adequate controls.

Not only does water pollution plague California, but its very air is being poisoned. Los Angeles has attracted widespread publicity for its noxious smog. About the time of World War II the clear skies of Los

Angeles became polluted. Industrial smoke, backyard incinerators and the exhaust from millions of automobiles were the major sources of this air pollution. The atmospheric conditions that caused temperature inversions and allowed stagnant air masses to hang over the city for long periods of time resulted in a condition called smog. In 1947, Los Angeles established an air pollution control district which was empowered by law to declare alerts when the ozone content in the county reached 0.5 parts per million parts of air. Should the ozone content reach 1.0, the area's industrial establishment would be closed down and all automobile traffic halted. Despite what has been done, burning eyes and a hazy, brownish cloud of smog have become all too common there.

The four million cars of Los Angeles County burn more than eight million gallons of gasoline each day and send an estimated 13,000 tons of pollutants into the air. As early as 1960, the state legislature passed a bill which required most automobiles in the state to be equipped with exhaust devices. Automobile control measures have so far not been very effective. However, more strict standards are slated to go into effect with the 1970 car models. In the end, the only certain palliative may be to ban the internal-combustion engine car from urban areas. The smugness of San Francisco and other northern California cities toward smog has disappeared, for these air problems have appeared to some degree in all major California cities.

California is also faced with sagging land surfaces in many parts of the state where petroleum production has been great. In the San Joaquin Valley, farmers are losing one million dollars worth of water wells a year because of the phenomenon known as subsidence. In the Long Beach area, where oil has been pumped from underground domes for over thirty years, the land has sunk until a bowl twenty-six-feet deep now covers an area of twenty-two square miles. In downtown Long Beach, subsidence has exceeded six feet; damage has exceeded $100 million. Protective measures, however, have finally checked the subsidence process there. In Long Beach, nine pumping stations are counteracting subsidence by pouring half a million barrels of filtered seawater into the earth each day through high-pressure injection wells. The water serves a dual purpose: It keeps the upper rock formations from buckling further and it increases oil yields from the underground formations. Despite these ingenious efforts to prop up the sagging surface of the earth in California, the state is still afflicted by dangerous and damaging land slumps.

The lack of planned or rational use of land surface has also plagued California. The state is faced with spreading "slurbs"—sprawling tracts of houses, virtually unplanned and almost uncontrolled. Many of these houses were poorly built or unwisely constructed along the hills and ridges where landslides have become a problem. It has been labeled the "ticky-tacky" style by its critics. California has been built in a series of unplanned booms, but it is now a question of whether this luxury can still be afforded. For every 1,500 new residents who settle in California, about 375 acres of its greensward are converted to urban use. Time is running out to do anything effective in the way of rational planning for the future.

Other California resources whose eventual disappearance concerns not only Californians, but people all over the world are the remaining virgin redwood groves of northwestern California. Federal bills to set up a national redwoods park in the area were not enacted into laws. The state of California and the federal government have wrangled over the location and extent of a national redwoods park. Various conservation groups who might otherwise have effectively pushed the program have been snarled in their efforts by the rival plans they have proposed and great confusion has reigned concerning this issue. The citizens of northwestern California are rightly concerned about the economic future of their region if lumbering is greatly curtailed. Meanwhile, a partial moratorium on cutting in the area of a proposed park is only temporary, and there is the possibility that if some action is not taken soon, eventually the only area of virgin redwoods that could be included in a future national park are those lands already protected by state parks.

Concern over the misuse of California's natural heritage has been highlighted in several recent books, the most notable of which is Raymond Dasmann's *The Destruction of California*. Hopefully, books such as this will arouse Californians to insist upon conservation measures to protect the state's natural beauty while there is still time to do so effectively.

California has had to face a labor problem connected with its agribusiness. Mexican migrant laborers—the *braceros*—have become an important part of the California agricultural labor force ever since the days of World War II. At that time, informal executive agreements between the United States and Mexico allowed the seasonal importation of braceros to help with the harvest. In 1951, Congress passed Public Law 78 which amended an agricultural act of two years earlier and also enacted Public Law 319, which contained the text of the Migrant Labor Agreement between the United States and Mexico. The first statute outlined the bracero program, while the second law spelled out detailed arrangements and established a standard work contract. Under these laws, if domestic labor was not available in sufficient quantity in a given area, braceros might then be brought in from Mexico to harvest the crops. In 1957, the peak year, California brought into its fields 192,000 Mexican workers. After that year, the number of Mexican workers gradually decreased, principally because of mechanization, to about 72,000. Braceros were used primarily to harvest lettuce, sugar beets, lemons, melons, strawberries, tomatoes, asparagus, cotton, grapes and vegetables.

Many critics of the bracero system have complained that it tends to depress wages, to destroy the domestic workers' bargaining power, and to drive American labor out of the agricultural market. Each year, about 8 per cent of the braceros brought into the country desert their families in Mexico and remain in the United States. Their abandoned wives and children have become a great social burden in Mexico. As a result of complaints about the system from both sides of the border, and despite the vociferous protests of the growers' association, Congress rejected a renewal bill and the importation of braceros ended on December 31, 1964. Dire predictions were made that California's agriculture would suffer greatly from a lack of labor at harvest time. It is true that the percentage of foreign workers in California fields fell dramatically with the non-renewal of the bracero agreement from 21 per cent in 1964 to only 2 per cent in 1965. Nevertheless, California agriculture as a whole harvested crops of 37.3 million tons that year—the second highest output in the state's history—using essentially domestic labor. Some 20,000 braceros were admitted under special permit agreements, however.

California's farmers did feel a cost-price squeeze, but by increasing production through new methods, new fertilizers, and improved irrigation, they were able to compete in the national and world markets. In 1966, thousands of special permit braceros were used to harvest various California crops, particularly tomatoes. In that year, crops were successfully harvested with domestic laborers, but farm income suffered. Although gross receipts increased 5 per cent from the previous year, the additional costs of using domestic workers kept net income from rising that much. As a result, many California growers have urged a return to a full-scale bracero program, but the political climate in Washington has made that course unlikely.

There was a trickle of *alambristas* (fence jumpers) from Mexico. However, efficient searches by the U.S. Border Patrol rounded up 15,000 in 1967 of such illegally entered Mexican aliens who tried to work in California's fields.

With the end of the bracero program, efforts to organize California's farm labor have become more active. The agricultural workers of the Great Valley had always been unorganized, despite the unionization of California's principal industries. Then an obscure leader, Cesar Chavez, became the founder and director of the United Farm Workers Organizing Committee. Chavez is an unusually dedicated man who draws a salary of $5 a week and exists on the food and clothing given to him by supporters. He led a strike of field hands on the vineyards around Delano, making the greatest effort to unionize farm workers in California's history. When the strike occurred, it attracted nationwide attention with its picketing, demonstrations and product boycotting. Individuals as disparate as clergymen, entertainers, national union officials, and civil rights leaders lent their support to the strike. Finally, after nearly a year of such activity, the UFWOC won representational elections at three ranches controlled by the DiGiorgio Fruit Corporation. Eventually, in April 1967, a farm labor contract was hammered out as a result of bargaining sessions between teams from the union and management with arbitrators settling disputed issues. This farm labor contract, which could set standards for future settlements in all agricultural states, provided for wage increases, pensions, and vacations, as well as health and welfare benefits. However, Chavez and his lieutenants realized that they had won a battle rather than a war, for they went to Washington shortly after the signing of the DiGiorgio contract to urge that Congress pass a bill placing the previously exempt class of agricultural workers under the jurisdiction of the National Labor Relations Board.

Nevertheless, despite labor troubles, crop reductions ordered by the federal government regulation, insects, and weather problems, in 1966 California's farms produced 37.1 million tons of crops worth $3.95 billion, about 25 per cent of all the food produced in the United States. California's producers did not share equally in this amount, for, as is usual in an agricultural area of such diversity, cash receipt increases were substantial for livestock, poultry, and vegetable crops, moderate for fruit and nut crops, whereas income from field crops declined.

California's agriculture has changed greatly since 1950. There are fewer but larger farms today than at that time. Whereas in the early 1950's there were more than 130,000 farms, by 1964 the total was down to 95,000 farms. By the latter year, 3,000 farms were going out of business annually. Small farms are being amalgamated into larger units; three-fourths of California farms are considered to be "large" holdings. The cost-price squeeze created by higher costs and sluggish farm prices has caused California farmers to become more efficient or to go out of business. More and more investment has gone into land-leveling, wells and complex machinery. As a result, recently the investment in the average four-hundred-acre California farm was just under $200,000, in contrast to a national average of only $48,000 invested in a 333-acre farm.

California not only leads all states in farm production, it outranks Iowa, its nearest competitor, by more than $500 million.

More than 230 crops are grown commercially in California, a greater variety than that grown in any other state. Also, according to the most recent figures, more than one hundred different crops with annual values of more than $1 million each are grown in the state. California produces

43 per cent of the vegetables used in the nation and 42 per cent of the fruits.

California ranks first in the production of forty-four crops, second in nine and third in eight. More than 90 per cent of sixteen crops, including almonds, apricots, artichokes, olives, prunes, lemons, walnuts and plums, are grown in California. Yet California agriculture has faced a variety of other problems. One trouble was the increased competition with its specialty crops from the Mediterranean countries and Mexico. Competition from synthetic products has also proved troublesome. Another problem is the ceaseless struggle against such pests as the pink bollworm, the citrus white fly, and the grape leaf skeletonizer.

Other California resource industries have not fared as well as agriculture. Because of the competitive sales of nonwood building materials and a general slowdown in the building industry, California timber production stood in 1966 at 5.5 billion board feet. This figure was below the record amount of 6 billion in 1959, but somewhat higher than the average of 1950–58.

Commercial fish landings in 1966 were 584 million pounds, a figure which reflects a drop from 1950 when total landings had been 1,366,000,-000. There had been a continuing decline in the weight of the catch during the 1950's and the early 1960's, but the drop has leveled off since 1963.

California's mineral production, including fuels, metals and nonmetals, has increased from a value of just over a billion dollars to an average of about $1.5 billion during the 1950's and 1960's, and reached a value of $1.71 billion in 1966. Petroleum accounted for two-thirds of the state's mineral output in the latter year with a value of $1.1 billion. Petroleum production was running well over 900,000 barrels a day in early 1967.

California is the first state in the Union in foreign trade, since $4 billion annually in imports and exports pass through its ports. It ranks first in exports.

In the category of manufacturing, California in 1963 had reached a total of $17.2 billion, according to the most recent Census of Manufacturers. This figure placed it second only to the state of New York. Moreover, California showed the highest dollar-value increase for any state in the intercensus period of 1958–63—$5.1 billion, or a growth of 42 per cent. By 1965, value added by manufacturing increased to an estimated $18.3 billion. In addition to the aerospace industry, California has many other important types of manufacturing. It leads all the states in food processing, ordnance, and miscellaneous manufacturing. California is also a major producer of transportation equipment, machinery, fabricated metal products, printing and publishing, primary chemicals, and building products.

As early as 1962, California moved ahead of New York in total retail sales to become first in the nation in this category. In 1965, retail sales rose to 29.5 billion dollars, a 5 per cent gain over 1964. By 1966, taxable retail store transactions were up 251.5 per cent from 1950. The Los Angeles–Long Beach metropolitan area ranks second in the nation in retail sales. Ten California metropolitan areas place among the top hundred in retail sales. Californians are known as pacesetters in trying new products, and per capita retail sales in 1965 were 8 per cent above the national average. By 1970, experts estimate that retail sales in California will climb above $40 billion.

California banks in the Federal Reserve System boasted assets of almost $35.8 billion on June 30, 1965. At the same time, this group of banks had deposits of nearly $32 billion. In addition, California could claim the largest network of savings and loan associations in the nation.

With the heavy spending of the federal government in California for war-related industries because of the Vietnam war, California's total employment grew to 1,565,000 for 1966, an increase of 111,000, or 7.6 per cent from 1965. This was the greatest year-to-year growth in manufacturing jobs since the early 1950's. Unemployment in California shrank from an annual average of 422,200 in 1964 to 373,700 in 1966. Although unemployment declined for all age groups, its decline (because of military calls) dropped most greatly for those twenty-five years of age and under.

All these statistics spell a good life for the overwhelming majority of Californians. They earn more and spend more than other Americans. Total personal income rose from $30,378,000,000 in 1955 to $42,980,000 in 1960. By 1965, California had passed New York as the first state in the nation in personal income with $59,958,000,000. Californians' personal income jumped again to $65,330,000,000 in 1966. To put these figures in perspective, in 1965, California, with 9.6 per cent of the nation's population, had 11.3 per cent of the nation's total personal income, and its per capita income was 17 per cent over the national average.

California's population has continued to grow. From 10,643,000 persons in 1950, the population of the state reached 15,863,000 in 1960. By 1964, the number of Californians reached 18,209,000, only to increase to 18,276,-000 in 1965 and to 19,195,000 in 1966. However, in the latter year, this population increase of 469,000 was the smallest annual gain since 1954. The increase of 2.5 per cent was the lowest relative gain since 1948. Still, California's gain was well over twice the national average of 1.1 per cent. Most of the growth was accounted for by net migration, which stood at 270,000 persons. This figure was well below the postwar high of 388,000 persons in 1957. The amount of natural increase in population continued along this downward trend that began in 1961. There was evidence that the new effective contraceptive devices are popular in California and that future birth rates would continue to decrease. This trend was so evident that one of the San Francisco Bay area's leading hospitals (Peralta) announced in the summer of 1967 that it was closing its maternity ward because of a lack of patients!

In terms of geographical gain, the ten southernmost counties of the state have accounted for 62 per cent of the state's growth. According to the best estimates, 11,614,000 people, 61 per cent of the state's total population, live in this area. Los Angeles County alone has just under 7 million inhabitants. According to the best experts, California in 1975 will have a population of 24.5 million persons who will enjoy a personal income of $110 billion (in purchasing power of 1966 dollars) because of a 30 per cent gain in the productivity of labor.

Yet these roseate predictions can only come true if California's economic strength continues unimpaired. While the public sector of the economy—welfare, highways, health, and education—are dependent upon the resources of the private sector of the economy, some Californians have chosen to believe that the reverse is not also true. They may be mistaken, since the private sector is itself dependent upon the effectiveness of the federal, state and local governmental services.

A growing conservative revolt, sparked by the citizens of southern California, shadows the future of the state. Looking only at the rising figures of their tax bills, many citizens of the middle class insist that rigid economy is the most important task of state and local government. This group was the principal force behind the election of Ronald Reagan as governor. Actually, the California taxpayers' revolt can be viewed as part of the rebellion of the well-to-do of the sun states of Arizona, Texas and Florida. These areas are tied together by a social elite which, while enjoying its new-found riches, lacks a social conscience or an attitude of civic responsibility. This *nouveau riche* class does not see that it is to its own best interest to educate other people's children or to take care of the needs of the unemployed in minority groups. Outraged at the events at the University of California's Berkeley campus, they have applauded cuts in California's higher education budgets, despite the fact that by the spring of 1967 Berkeley activists were quiet. At the one-time activist campus, enrollment in the ROTC was up and interest in "causes" was down, and concessions by the administration to the students at the university were minimal. Nonetheless, these conservatives cry that California, the richest state in the nation, cannot afford to educate all its youth through the university level, even though, on a relative basis, Californians were making less of an effort to support higher public education than the citizens of North Dakota or Louisiana.

If it were an independent nation with the same gross product, California would rank with the greatest powers of the earth in wealth. It probably would support its own army, a navy, an air force, and a space program, in addition to the social services it supports as a state and would probably not groan any louder about the taxation needed that it already does. It seems that not the means, but the will, are missing in California to do more in the public sector.

If the thinking of the conservative bloc in California continues to dominate, the state may well enter a period of slackening growth, with all that this would entail for its economy. For if California's higher education program is starved into a gray mediocrity, the sophisticated industries that now seek a haven in the state may stop coming. These industries have been interested in California's ever-widening pool of technicians. If this supply of skilled employees should prove to be inadequate, these industries may choose to locate upon the cheaper land of Arizona or Florida. Any slowdown in economic growth could be serious, since California's economy is geared to a constant climb. Thousands of new jobs must be found every year for its increasing population. California could adjust to a relatively stable population, but it would be painful. There is another facet to the growing economy-minded trend among California voters. If the minority groups of California continue to feel neglected, a period of violence and terror could result within the state. Watts could be multiplied many times in new riots. If the various minorities' rising expectations are checked, it is foolhardy to assume that they will tamely continue to live at a subsistence level in the midst of the greatest widespread opulence the world has ever known.

And yet, when all the unpleasant aspects of California have been paraded—its hedonism, its materialism, its vulgarity, its ostentatious popular culture—there remain many valid reasons why California has been a golden magnet for a population seeking a better way of life. Despite all that men have done to destroy California's climate and natural beauty, something truly beautiful still survives. The California way of life suggests wealth and leisure, not only to Philistines, but to artists and scholars of great merit. California has created a mystique which few regions of the world can match. A visit to San Francisco, and to almost any other place in the state, seems like a pilgrimage to Keokuk. Areas such as Carmel and Big Sur can charm the most jaded world traveler.

And yet California has its problems that must be solved if this opulent way of life is to continue. A fact of California's history as a state is that it has always possessed an ineffective local government. The men who have led it at the state level have generally been ordinary politicians. Yet even without political leaders to match its natural superiority, it has survived, grown, and prospered. California has literally seemed to defy the laws of political gravity. As a result, perhaps even with the lack of political imagination from which its leaders suffer, it can continue to survive. In any event, until the deluge comes, the average Californian will continue to live his informal life, freed from the stuffiness of his birthplace in other areas of the nation.

It has been said, what California is today the nation will be tomorrow, and so perhaps also the entire area of Western civilization. Future generations, within the limits of geography, may all live like Californians. That California is the land of the future is already internationally admitted. In 1966 when the British Broadcasting System showed a television program concerning the world of the future, it decided that the future had already largely arrived in California. Many popular American and foreign magazines have concluded pretty much the same thing—California, for good or ill, is a window on the future.

Bibliographical Note

IN writing this work I have consulted the pertinent federal and California state documents. In addition, as a resident of California for eighteen years I have followed public events closely in the press and the periodical literature while maintaining an extensive file of newspaper clippings, which I have consulted in composing this book.

I have, of course, read the multivolumned works of Hubert Howe Bancroft and Theodore H. Hittell, the great pioneer historians of California. Moreover, I have used as textbooks in teaching classes in California history the works of John W. Caughey, Robert Glass Cleland (as edited by Glenn S. Dumke) and Andrew F. Rolle. Familiarity with these authors has undoubtedly shaped my own thinking on the state's history. I have also utilized many specialized monographs, and have perused with profit the many excellent articles on California history in journals, such as the *Quarterly of the Historical Society of Southern California*, *Pacific Historical Review*, and *California Historical Society Quarterly*.

A Note on Sources and Suggestions for Further Reading on California History

THIS note hopes to provide an impression of the type of historical material available for the further study of California's past. It also aims to serve as a guide for future reading.

Manuscript materials pertaining to California history are widely scattered. Important collections are maintained for the use of historians at the Huntington Library, Bancroft Library and the California State Library. Outside of California, two centers at Washington, D.C., are treasure troves for California historians. The manuscripts division of the Library of Congress has much information upon figures in California's past. In addition, the National Archives contains much detailed data upon California's growth and development. The State Archives at Sacramento hold comparable material. Unfortunately, historians have been less willing to consult the somewhat harder to use archives than the manuscripts in libraries. For the period before 1848, the archives of Spain and Mexico have provided great riches for determined researchers.

General histories of the state, including the multivolume works of Hubert Howe Bancroft, particularly his *History of California* (7 volumes, San Francisco, 1884–90), are Theodore H. Hittell, *History of California* (4 volumes, San Francisco, 1885–97), and Zoeth S. Eldridge, ed., *History of California* (5 volumes, New York, 1915). Excellent one-volume histories of the State are John W. Caughey's *California* (New York, 1953), Robert Glass Cleland, *From Wilderness to Empire*, as edited by Glenn S. Dumke (New York, 1959), and Andrew F. Rolle, *California: A History* (New York, 1963).

CALIFORNIA GEOGRAPHY

R. W. Durrenberger, W. G. Byron, and J. C. Kimura, *Patterns on the Land* (Los Angeles, 1957) is a book of California maps, many of which are unobtainable elsewhere. California's unique geography is discussed in Clifford M. Zierer, ed., *California and the Southwest* (New York, 1956); David W. Lantis, Rodney Steiner, and Arthur E. Karinen, *California: Land of Contrast* (Belmont, California, 1963); and David N. Hartman, *California and Man* (Dubuque, Iowa, 1964).

CALIFORNIA INDIANS

To understand California's aborigines, consult the following: Alfred L. Kroeber, *Handbook of the Indians of California* (Bureau of American Ethnology Bulletin 78, Washington, D.C., 1925); R. F. Heizer and M. A. Whipple, eds., *California Indians: A Source Book* (Berkeley, 1951); C. Hart Merriam, ed., *Studies of California Indians* (Berkeley, 1955); and Theodora Kroeber, *Ishi in Two Worlds: A Biography of the Last Wild Indian in North America* (Berkeley, 1961).

SPANISH BEGINNINGS

For an introduction to Spanish activities in America, see Irving B. Richman, *The Spanish Conquerors* (New Haven, 1919). On the subjection of the Aztecs, consult the classic work by William H. Prescott, *The Conquest of Mexico* (3 vols., New York, 1943). On Cortés himself, see Salvador de Madariaga, *Hernán Cortés, Conquerer of Mexico* (New York, 1941). The advance of the Spanish frontier to the north is covered by Philip W. Powell, *Soldiers, Indians and Silver: The Northward Advance of New Spain, 1500–1600* (Berkeley, 1952).

SPANISH VOYAGES AND OTHER MARITIME EXPLORATIONS

For a number of contemporary accounts, see Herbert E. Bolton, ed., *Spanish Exploration in the Southwest, 1542–1706* (New York, 1959) and Hakluyt's *Principal Navigations*, III (Edinburgh, 1885–90). A more specialized source is Henry R. Wagner, *Spanish Voyages to the Northwest Coast of America in the Sixteenth Century* (San Francisco, 1929).

For a complete discussion of the Mexican-Philippine trade, consult William L. Schurz, *The Manila Galleon* (New York, 1939). For more information on Drake in California, see Henry R. Wagner, *Sir Francis Drake's Voyage Around the World, Its Aims and Achievements* (San Franciso, 1926).

THE JESUIT MISSIONS

Most noteworthy are three works of Peter M. Dunne, *Pioneer Black Robes on the West Coast* (Berkeley, 1940), *Pioneer Jesuits in Northern*

Mexico (Berkeley, 1944), and *Black Robes in Lower California* (Berkeley, 1952). Also see Herbert E. Bolton, *The Rim of Christendom* (New York, 1936).

SPANISH CALIFORNIA

Two older works of enduring value are Irving B. Richman, *California Under Spain and Mexico, 1535–1857* (Boston, 1911) and Charles E. Chapman, *A History of California: The Spanish Period* (New York, 1921). Much invaluable source material can be found in Herbert E. Bolton, ed., *Historical Memoirs of New California* (5 vols., Berkeley, 1926).

On Father Serra, see Omer Englebert, *The Last of the Conquistadores: Junipero Serra, 1712–1784* (New York, 1956) and Maynard J. Geiger, *Life and Times of Fray Junipero Serra* (2 vols., Washington, D.C., 1959). A serious but uncritical work on the missions is Zephyrin Englehardt, *The Missions and Missionaries of California* (4 vols., San Francisco, 1908–15). On the founding of San Francisco, the presidio and mission, see Herbert E. Bolton's *Outpost of Empire* (New York, 1931). The beginnings of Los Angeles are traced in W. W. Robinson's *Los Angeles: From the Day of the Pueblo* (San Francisco, 1959).

EARLY NON-SPANISH VISITORS TO CALIFORNIA

Concerning George Vancouver, consult Marguerite Eyer Wilbur, ed., *Vancouver in California, 1792–1794* (Los Angeles, 1953). On Vancouver the man, see George Goodwin, *Vancouver: A Life, 1757–1798* (London, 1930). For Malaspina's visit, consult Donald C. Cutter, *Malaspina in California* (San Francisco, 1960).

The Russians in California have attracted much writing. See Thomas C. Russell, ed., *The Rezanov Voyage to Nueva California in 1806* (San Francisco, 1926), and the same editor's *Langsdorff's Narrative of Rezanov's Voyage to Nueva California in 1809* (San Francisco, 1927). Rezanov's story is told in Hector Chevigny, *Lost Empire, The Life and Adventures of Nikolai Petrovich Rezanov* (New York, 1937). The Russian and Yankee search for the sea otter is chronicled in Adele Ogden, *The California Sea Otter Trade, 1784–1848* (Berkeley, 1941).

MEXICAN CALIFORNIA

Life in Mexican California is sketched in Richard Henry Dana's classic, *Two Years Before the Mast: A Personal Narrative of Life at Sea* (New York, 1840). An American pioneer in Mexican California, William Heath Davis, has written *Seventy-five Years in California* (San Francisco, 1929). For two leading Californios of this period, see Myrtle Mason McKittrick, *Vallejo, Son of California* (Portland, Oregon, 1944), and George L. Harding, *Don Augustin V. Zamorano, Statesman, Soldier, Craftsman, and*

California's First Printer (Los Angeles, 1934). The story of the end of the missions is traced in Gerald J. Geary, *The Secularization of the California Missions* (Washington, 1934).

AMERICANS OVERLAND TO CALIFORNIA

The coming of the mountain men to California has been well told. Jedidiah Smith has been the subject of Maurice S. Sullivan's *Jedediah Smith, Trader and Trail Breaker* (New York, 1936), and Dale L. Morgan's *Jedidiah Smith and the Opening of the West* (Indianapolis, 1953). James Ohio Pattie spoke for himself in *The Personal Narrative of James O. Pattie* (Philadelphia, 1962). On the fur trade generally, see Bernard De Voto, *Across the Wide Missouri* (Cambridge, Mass., 1947).

The land trails to California are described in Ralph Moody, *The Old Trails West* (New York, 1963). Sutter has finally found a competent biographer in Richard H. Dillon. Dillon's work is entitled *Fool's Gold: The Biography of John Sutter* (New York, 1967). Pioneer doctor John Marsh is recalled in George D. Lyman, *Dr. John Marsh, Pioneer* (New York, 1930).

The ill-fated Donner party is best understood by reading George R. Stewart's *Ordeal by Hunger: The Story of the Donner Party* (New York, 1936, 1960). On the same subject there is the old, but interesting, C. F. McGlashan, *History of the Donner Party: A Tragedy of the Sierra* (San Francisco, 1879).

AMERICAN CONQUEST OF CALIFORNIA

For American expansionist interest in California, see Norman A. Graebner, *Empire on the Pacific* (New York, 1955). Also consult Frederick Merk's book on American annexationist spirit at the time, *Manifest Destiny and Mission in American History* (New York, 1963).

For Larkin's California activities, see John A. Hawgood, ed., *First and Last Consul: Thomas Oliver Larkin and the Americanization of California—A Selection of Letters* (reprinted Palo Alto, 1967). On Frémont, see Allen Nevins, *Frémont: Pathmarker of the West* (New York, 1939). Frémont's reports have been made accessible in Allen Nevins, ed., *Narratives of Exploration and Adventure* (New York, 1956).

On the period of American conquest generally, see the older but still useful Josiah Royce's *California: From the Conquest in 1846 to the Second Vigilance Committee* (Boston, 1886). Military rule is covered in Theodore Grivas, *Military Government in California, 1846–1850* (Glendale, 1963). Controversial General S. W. Kearny has found a competent biographer in Dwight L. Clarke in his *Stephen Watts Kearny, Soldier of the West* (Norman, Oklahoma, 1961). Howard Lamar has edited an interesting personal account of a Navy observer, *The Cruise of the Portsmouth,*

1845–1847: A Sailor's View of the Naval Conquest of California (New Haven, 1958).

THE CALIFORNIA GOLD RUSH

Two modern books which are basic to an understanding of the California gold rush are Rodman W. Paul's *California Gold: The Beginning of Mining in the Far West* (Cambridge, Mass., 1947) and John W. Caughey, *Gold Is the Cornerstone* (Berkeley, 1948).

Contemporary accounts which describe the hurly-burly of the gold rush include Walter Colton, *Three Years in California* (New York, 1854); Bayard Taylor, *Eldorado* (2 vols., New York, 1850, reprinted in one volume, New York, 1949); Louise Clappe [Dame Shirley], *The Shirley Letters from the California Mines* (Notes by Carl Wheat, New York, 1949); and William Perkins, *Three Years in California: Journal of Life at Sonora, 1849–1852* (with an introduction and annotations by Dale L. Morgan and James R. Scobie; Berkeley, 1964). On the social life of gold-rush California, read Elisabeth Margo, *Taming the Forty-niner* (New York, 1955).

CALIFORNIA EARLY STATEHOOD

Basic works for this period are Joseph Ellison, *California and the Nation, 1850–1869* (Berkeley, 1927); William H. Ellison, *A Self-Governing Dominion: California, 1849–1860* (Berkeley, 1950); Cardinal L. Goodwin, *The Establishment of State Government in California, 1846–1850* (New York, 1914).

California's Constitution of 1849, together with the *Journals* of the California Legislature have been reprinted by Robert G. Cleland's *Constitution of the State of California* (San Marino, 1949).

VIGILANTISM AND FILIBUSTERS

Disappointingly popular is Stanton A. Coblentz, *Villains and Vigilantes: The Story of James King of William, and Pioneer Justice in California* (New York, 1936). A leading vigilante's life has been written: James A. B. Scherer's *The Lion of the Vigilantes: William T. Coleman and the Life of Old San Francisco* (Indianapolis, 1939). A general history of San Francisco which is particularly good for the "old" city is Oscar Lewis, *San Francisco: Mission to Metropolis* (Berkeley, 1966). Sources for the vigilantes are Mary Floyd Williams, *Papers of the San Francisco Committee of Vigilance of 1851* (Berkeley, 1919) and William T. Coleman, "San Francisco Vigilance Committee," in *Century Magazine*, XLIII (November, 1891), pp. 133–50.

French filibustering activity is covered by Rufus Kay Wyllys, *The*

French in Sonora, 1850–1854 (Berkeley, 1932). William Walker is thoroughly described in Laurence Green, *The Filibuster* (New York, 1937).

TRANSPORTATION TO AND WITHIN CALIFORNIA

On the maritime routes to California, see John H. Kemble, *The Panama Route, 1828–1869* (Berkeley, 1943); Oscar Lewis, *Sea Routes to the Gold Fields* (New York, 1949); and Octavious T. Howe, *Argonauts of '49* (Cambridge, Mass., 1923).

On the overland trails, consult Ralph P. Bieber, *Southern Trails to California in 1849* (Glendale, 1937), and George R. Stewart, *The California Trail, An Epic with Many Heroes* (New York, 1962), as well as Moody's work already mentioned.

For the story of staging and freighting, read Oscar O. Winther, *Express and Stagecoach Days in California* (Stanford, 1936); Leroy R. Hafen, *The Overland Mail, 1849–1860* (Cleveland, 1926); Roscoe P. and Margaret B. Conkling, *The Butterfield Overland Mail, 1857–1869* (3 vols., Glendale, 1947); Ellis Lucia, *The Saga of Ben Holladay: Giant of the Old West* (New York, 1959); and Edward Hungerford, *Wells Fargo: Advancing the American Frontier* (New York, 1948).

On the Pony Express and its connection with overland freighting, see Raymond W. and Mary L. Settle, *War Drums and Wagon Wheels: The Story of Russell, Majors and Waddell* (Lincoln, 1966); by the same authors, consult "The Pony Express: Heroic Effort—Tragic End" in Waddell F. Smith, *The Pony Express* (San Francisco, 1960); and also by the Settles, *Saddles and Spurs, The Pony Express Saga* (Harrisburg, Pennsylvania, 1955). For a somewhat contrary view of the role of Wells, Fargo & Company in the Pony Express operation, see W. Turrentine Jackson, "A New Look at Wells Fargo, Stagecoaches and the Pony Express," *California Historical Society Quarterly* XLV (December, 1966), pp. 291–324.

On railroads, see George T. Clark's *Leland Stanford* (Palo Alto, 1931), and Oscar Lewis's popular account, *The Big Four: The Story of Huntington, Stanford, Hopkins and Crocker, and of the Building of the Central Pacific* (New York, 1938).

CALIFORNIA'S FINANCIAL AND ECONOMIC DEVELOPMENT

California's financial development in the nineteenth century is traced by two works of George D. Lyman, *The Saga of the Comstock* (New York, 1934) and *Ralston's Ring: California Plunders the Comstock Lode* (New York, 1937). Oscar Lewis's *The Silver Kings* (New York, 1947) tells what became of the Comstock fortunes.

For a look at California's mining frontier in comparison with the remainder of the West, see Rodman W. Paul, *Mining Frontiers of the Far West, 1848–1880* (New York, 1963).

CALIFORNIA'S EARLY POLITICS

For California politics generally, consult the old but useful Winfield J. Davis, *History of Political Conventions, 1849–1892* (Sacramento, 1893). For a workmanlike estimate of the gubernatorial careers of the California governors, consult Howard Brett Melendy and Benjamin F. Gilbert, *The Governors of California: Peter Burnett to Edmond G. Brown* (Georgetown, California, 1965).

CALIFORNIA IN THE CIVIL WAR ERA

California during the Civil War is covered in a variety of works. E. R. Kennedy has chronicled the southerners' attempts to win California for the Confederacy in his *The Contest for California in 1861* (Boston, 1912). Also consult Milton H. Shutes, *Lincoln and California* (Stanford, 1943). For California's contributions to the war, read Aurora Hunt, *The Army of the Pacific* (Glendale, 1951), as well as Jay Monaghan, *Civil War on the Western Border* (Boston, 1955) and Oscar Lewis, *The War in the Far West, 1861–1865* (Garden City, New York, 1961). For personal reminiscences of this period in California, see Francis P. Farquar, ed., *Up and Down California in 1860–1864: The Journal of William H. Brewer* (Berkeley, 1949).

LATE-NINETEENTH-CENTURY CALIFORNIA POLITICS

Later nineteenth-century California politics may be studied in Cornelius Cole, *Memoirs* (New York, 1908) and Lauren E. Crane, ed., *Newton Booth of California* (New York, 1894). On the Constitution of 1879, the classic work is Carl Brent Swisher, *Motivation and Political Technique in the California Constitutional Convention, 1878–79* (Claremont, 1930).

LAND TITLES AND THE DECLINE OF THE CALIFORNIOS

On the clouded California land titles, consult W. W. Robinson, *Land in California: The Story of Mission Lands, Ranchos, Squatters, Mining Claims, Railroad Grants, Land Scrip, Homesteads* (Berkeley, 1948). The plight of the Californios in the years after the American conquest is traced in Leonard Pitt's *The Decline of the Californios: A Social History of the Spanish-Speaking Californians, 1846–1890* (Berkeley, 1966). For life in American southern California, see Robert G. Cleland, *Cattle on a Thousand Hills: Southern California, 1850–1880* (San Marino, 1951).

The southern California land boom of the later nineteenth century is best recaptured in Glenn S. Dumke, *The Boom of the Eighties in Southern California* (San Marino, 1944).

VIOLENCE AND BANDITRY

California outlaws have been described in books such as Walter Noble Burns's, *The Robin Hood of El Dorado: The Saga of Joaquin Murietta* (New York, 1932); Joseph Henry Jackson, *Bad Company: The Story of California's Legendary and Actual Stage-Robbers, Bandits, Highwaymen and Outlaws* (New York, 1949), and the same author's *Tintypes in Gold: Four Studies in Robbery* (New York, 1939).

CALIFORNIA'S ECONOMIC GROWTH
(LATE NINETEENTH AND EARLY TWENTIETH CENTURIES)

California's early agriculture in the American period is described in John S. Hittell, *The Resources of California* (San Francisco, 1863). A small but important part of Paul W. Gates's work, *The Farmer's Age: Agriculture, 1815–1860* (New York, 1960) deals with California agriculture. For the later period, see Claude B. Hutchison, ed., *California Agriculture* (Berkeley, 1946).

On specific agricultural topics, consult Herbert J. Webber and Leon D. Bachelor, eds., *The Citrus Industry: History, Botany, and Breeding* (2 vols., Berkeley, 1943); Robert L. Kelley, *Gold vs. Grain: The Hydraulic Mining Controversy in California's Sacramento Valley* (Glendale, 1960); Vincent P. Carosso, *The California Wine Industry, 1830–1895* (Berkeley, 1951); and E. T. Treadwell, *The Cattle King* [Henry Miller's biography] (New York, 1931).

A general economic history of California is Robert G. Cleland and Osgood Hardy, *March of Industry* (Los Angeles, 1929). California banking is discussed in Ira B. Cross, *Financing an Empire* (4 vols., Chicago, 1927).

THE CHINESE AND CALIFORNIA'S LABOR MOVEMENT

On the Chinese in California as a problem to the white workers, see Mary R. Coolidge, *Chinese Immigration* (New York, 1909); Gunther Barth, *Bitter Strength: A History of the Chinese in the United States, 1850–1870* (Cambridge, Mass., 1964); and Elmer C. Sandmeyer, *The Anti-Chinese Movement in California* (Urbana, 1939).

On the labor movement, consult Ira B. Cross, *A History of the Labor Movement in California* (Berkeley, 1935).

THE CALIFORNIA INDIANS AND THEIR DISPERSAL

Consult Stephen Bonsal, *Edward Fitzgerald Beale: A Pioneer in the Path of Empire, 1822–1893* (New York, 1912); J. Ross Browne, *The Indians of California* (San Francisco, reprinted, 1949). Concerning the Modoc War, see Keith A. Murray, *The Modocs and Their War* (Norman, Oklahoma, 1959) and Max Heyman, *Prudent Soldier* [biography of General E. R. S. Canby] (Glendale, 1960).

LITERARY AND CULTURAL GROWTH

Some representative books on California's literary growth are Franklin D. Walker, *San Francisco's Literary Frontier* (New York, 1939); Pauline Jacobson, *City of the Golden 'Fifties* (Berkeley, 1941); Franklin D. Walker, *A Literary History of Southern California* (Berkeley, 1950); Edward C. Kemble, *A History of California Newspapers* (New York, 1927); and John Bruce, *Gaudy Century: The Story of San Francisco's Hundred Years of Robust Journalism* (New York, 1948).

On the California theater, see G. R. MacMinn, *The Theater of the Golden Era* (Caldwell, Idaho, 1941), and Constance Rourke, *Troupers of the Gold Coast: Or the Rise of Lotta Crabtree* (New York, 1928).

Concerning the subject of education, read William W. Ferrier, *Ninety Years of Education in California* (Berkeley, 1937). On the University of California's early beginnings, see two other works of Ferrier, *Origin and Development of the University of California* (Berkeley, 1930) and *Henry Durant, First President of the University of California* (Berkeley, 1942).

CALIFORNIA POLITICS IN THE PROGRESSIVE ERA

California politics after 1900 can best be studied in George E. Mowry's *The California Progressives* (Berkeley, 1951). San Francisco's municipal political scandals can best be traced in Walton Bean's *Boss Ruef's San Francisco* (Berkeley, 1952), and the more popular Lately Thomas, *A Debonair Scoundrel: An Episode in the Moral History of San Francisco* (New York, 1962).

THE SAN FRANCISCO QUAKE AND FIRE

San Francisco's catastrophe of 1906 is described in Monica Sutherland, *The Damnedest Finest Ruins* (New York, 1959) and John C. Kennedy, *The Great Earthquake and Fire, San Francisco 1906* (New York, 1963).

CALIFORNIA'S JAPANESE IN THE EARLY TWENTIETH CENTURY

The early-twentieth-century troubles are recounted in Thomas A. Bailey's *Theodore Roosevelt and the Japanese-American Crisis* (Stanford, 1934). Supplement this older work with Raymond A. Esthus, *Theodore Roosevelt and Japan* (Seattle, 1967).

GROWING URBAN AND INDUSTRIAL PROBLEMS OF THE TWENTIETH CENTURY

One aspect of urban problems has been covered in Spencer Crump's *Ride the Big Red Cars: How Trolleys Helped Build Southern California*

(Los Angeles, 1962). Los Angeles' growth is told in W. W. Robinson, *Los Angeles from the Days of the Pueblo* (Los Angeles, 1959), and also in Remi Nadeau, *City-Makers* (New York, 1948).

Los Angeles' quest for water has been explored in Remi Nadeau, *The Water Seekers* (New York, 1950). For San Francisco, see Oscar Lewis' general history of San Francisco already cited and Harold Gilliam's *San Francisco Bay* (Garden City, New York, 1957).

On California's labor problems, see the pertinent pages in Foster Rhea Dulles, *Labor in America: A History* (New York, 1955, 1960), and Samuel Yellen, *American Labor Struggles* (New York, 1956). On the difficult times for unions during the prosperity of the twenties, see Irving Bernstein, *The Lean Years: A History of the American Worker, 1920–1933* (Boston, 1960). On the more specialized study of the plight of labor before World War II in southern California, see Louis B. Perry and Richard S. Perry, *A History of the Los Angeles Labor Movement, 1911–1941* (Berkeley, 1963).

On the Mooney-Billings case, see Curt Gentry, *Frame-up: The Incredible Case of Tom Mooney and Warren Billings* (New York, 1967). Gentry's account lacks scholarly detachment and the best-balanced account is an as yet unpublished doctoral dissertation written at the University of California in 1960 by Richard Hindeman Frost.

Californians sought to solve some of their problems by recourse to utopian colonies, and easterners sought out the state to establish their dream settlements. These attempts are chronicled in Robert V. Hine's *Utopian Colonies* (New Haven, 1966).

On the California of the twenties, see Lately Thomas, *The Vanishing Evangelist* [Aimee McPherson] (New York, 1959). For the politics of this period of the twenties, consult Richard B. Harvey, "California Politics: Historical Profile," in Eugene P. Dvorin and Arthur J. Misner, *California Politics and Policies: Original Essays* (Reading, Mass., 1966), pp. 3–26. Also see Robert G. Cleland, *California in Our Time, 1900–1940* (New York, 1947).

CALIFORNIA'S UNIQUE INDUSTRIES

For the motion-picture industry, see Leo C. Rosten, *Hollywood: The Movie Colony, the Movie Makers* (New York, 1941); A. R. Fulton, *Motion Pictures: The Development of an Art, from Silent Films to the Age of Television* (Norman, Oklahoma, 1960). For a more specialized treatment see Edward Wagenknecht, *The Movies in the Age of Innocence* (Norman, Oklahoma, 1962).

A general history of air travel which devotes proper attention to California is Hugh Knowlton, *Air Transportation in the United States: Its Growth as a Business* (Chicago, 1941). A history of a single company is Western Air Lines, *Wings Over the West: The Story of America's Oldest Airline* (n. p. 1951). Lamentably, a detailed account of California's aviation and aerospace industry is yet to be written.

CALIFORNIA AND THE GREAT DEPRESSION

Although Paul N. Woolf's *Economic Trends in California, 1929–1934* (Sacramento, 1935) has all the statistics, the spirit of the depression in California is best captured in John Steinbeck's novel, *The Grapes of Wrath* (New York, 1939).

The California New Deal era has a basic account in Robert E. Burke's *Olson's New Deal for California* (Berkeley, 1952).

William Randolph Hearst, whose career spans the period from the 1880's to his death in the 1950's, has found a competent biographer in W. A. Swanberg, who wrote *Citizen Hearst: A Biography of William Randolph Hearst* (New York, 1961).

CALIFORNIA DURING WORLD WAR II

A comprehensive history of the state during World War II is lacking, but two works of Carey McWilliams pay much attention to this era, *Southern California Country* (New York, 1946), and *California, The Great Exception* (New York, 1949).

There has been much writing on the subject of the relocation of the Japanese during the conflict. Carey McWilliams started the chain with his *Prejudice: Japanese–Americans, Symbol of Racial Intolerance* (Boston, 1944). An internee told her story in *Citizen 13660* (New York, 1946). Morton Grodzins continued the writing in a polemical vein in *Americans Betrayed* (Chicago, 1949). Works such as Dorothy S. Thomas and Richard S. Nishimoto, *The Spoilage* (Berkeley, 1946), Leonard Bloom and Ruth Riemer, *Removal and Return* (Berkeley, 1949), and Dorothy S. Thomas and others, *The Salvage* (Berkeley, 1952), are more clinically sociological in their treatment. A specialized aspect is covered in Leonard Broom and John I. Kitsuse in their *The Managed Casualty: The Japanese-American Family in World War II* (Berkeley, 1956).

POSTWAR CALIFORNIA

For a perceptive overview of the entire Pacific area down into the recent period, see Earl Pomeroy, *The Pacific Slope* (New York, 1964). A journalistic view of the Pacific region is Neil Morgan's *Westward Tilt* (New York, 1963). Also valuable is Remi Nadeau's *California, The New Society* (New York, 1963).

The imbroglio in California over oath-taking as it effected the university is described in David P. Gardner, *The California Oath Controversy* (Berkeley, 1967).

On the recent politics of California, see Richard Nixon's view in *Six Crises* (New York, 1962). To this should be added the latest biography of a towering figure who dominated California politics for over a decade, J. D. Weaver's *Warren: The Man, The Court, The Era* (Boston, 1967).

California—The Dynamic State (Santa Barbara, 1966) is a series of original essays by well-known specialists who looked at Pat Brown's California and found it generally good.

On the bracero problem, see Ernesto Galarza, *Merchants of Labor: The Mexican Bracero Story* (Santa Barbara, 1964).

Concerning the Negro problem in California, consult the Governor's Commission on the Los Angeles Riots, *Violence in the City—An End or a Beginning?* (Los Angeles, 1965). Also read *Burn, Baby, Burn: The Los Angeles Race Riot, August, 1965* (New York, 1966) by Jerry Cohen and William J. Murphy.

For a look at the fine arts in California, consult the California Arts Commission, *The Arts in California: A Report to the Governor and the Legislature on the Cultural and Artistic Resources of the State of California* (Sacramento, 1966).

For a discussion of California's losing fight against the spoliation of its natural resources, see Raymond F. Dasmann, *The Destruction of California* (New York, 1965). Something is being done to try and prevent the complete ruin of the state's natural beauty; see the new quarterly *Cry California*, published in Sacramento.

A penetrating in-depth look at the California of 1967 can be found in a special issue of *Saturday Review* (September 23, 1967).

Index

Aberdeen, Lord, 210
Abortion law, 570
Abrego, Pedro Narváez José, 215
Academy of Asian Studies, 553
Academy of Sciences, 336, 438, 546
Adams, John, 212
Adams, Maude, 442
Adams, Will, 33
Adams and Company Express, 256, 257
Adams No. 28 (oil well), 421
Adams-Onis Treaty, 2
Aerojet General Corporation, 555–556
Aerospace Corporation, 556
Agriculture, 4, 5, 259, 301, 328, 391–412,
    487–490, 579: Burbank's experiments in,
    397; citrus fruit, 397–406, 580: develop-
    ment of, 405, 489; Civil War, 315–316;
    clash with mining industry, 409–412;
    crops: number grown, 579–580, reduc-
    tions, 579, values (1937), 489–490; di-
    versification, 395–396; droughts: 1862–
    1864, 258, 1876–1877, 378; dry farming,
    395–396; effects of Gold Rush on, 257–
    260; employment, 396, 472, 477–478;
    growth, 539; Indian, 12–13, 396; irriga-
    tion and, 407–409, 490–493; Japanese-
    American, 396, 467, 470, 489, 514, 519;
    Korean War, 538; migrant labor and,
    577–579; missions, 67, 113; production
    rate, 579–580; railroads and, 259, 260,
    397; refrigeration and, 420, 488; soil
    variety, 3–4; Spanish colonial, 106;
    truck farming, 259, 488, 514; vegetable
    production, 397, 488; World War I, 485;
    World War II, 524: wage earnings, 525–
    526
Air pollution, 575–576
Alameda County *Gazette*, 304
Alarcón, Hernando de, 38–39
Albatross (ship)
Alberni, Pedro de, 118

Alcatraz Island, 311, 352
Alemany, Archbishop Joseph Sadoc, 332–
    333
Alexander (vessel), 129, 130
Alexander I, Czar, 135
Alien Land Act, 471
Allen, Lawrence, 509
Allen, Willis, 509
Almond crops, 405
Almonte, Juan Nepomuceno, 200
Alta California (newspaper), 336, 416, 433
Altimira, Father José, 153–154
Alvarado, Juan Bautista, 42, 162, 180, 183,
    186–192, 215, 263; background of, 186;
    uprisings against, 187–188
Alvarado, Pedro de, 21, 22, 26, 40–41
Amadís de Gaula (Lobeira), 41
Amador, Rafael, 159
American Bridge Company, 475
American Commonwealths, 428
American Federation of Labor, 470, 476,
    506, 561
American Fur Company, 195–196
American Pacific Squadron, 221–222
American Party, 288
American Railway Journal, 364
American Railway Union, 420
American Revolution, 127, 129
Anaheim, 399
Anderson, Glenn, 572
Anti-Chinese Association, 382
Anti-Debris Association, 411
Anza, Juan Bautista de, 87–94, 96, 99, 100,
    102, 441
Anza Trail, 159
Aoke, Viscount Shuzo, 468
Apache Indians, 12, 74, 89, 175, 176, 293
Apache Pass, 359
Apple industry, 403
Appleton & Company, 166
Apricot orchards, 404

Archy (slave), 277
Argonaut (ship), 122
Argonne, Battle of the, 485
Arguello, Alférez Luís, 140, 141, 146
Arguello, José, 140, 141–142
Arguello, José Darío, 146
Arguello, Luís, 153–155, 163
Arguello, Santiago, 263
Arguello y Maraga, María de la Concepción, 140–141, 142, 146
Armijo, Manuel, 227
Armour, Philip, 247
Arnold, H. H., 556
Arriaga, Julian de, 95
Arrillaga, José Joaquin de, 116, 118, 125–126, 140, 145, 146
Art, 425–427, 439
Ashley, William Henry, 171
Asiatic Exclusion League, 467
Asparagus canning industry, 488
Associated Glider Clubs of Southern California, 553
Astor, John J., 181
Astrolabe (ship), 120
Atala (ship), 151
Atchison, Topeka & Santa Fe Railroad, 372–373, 417, 459
Athabascan Indians, 12
Atherton, Gertrude, 433
Atlantic and Pacific Line, 372
Atondo y Antillón, Isidro, 62–63, 67
Atrevida (ship), 123
Austin, Mary, 431–432
Automobiles: air pollution, 576; industry, 485–486, 487; motor vehicle registration, 557–558
Aviation industry, 529–530, 580: employment, 555; growth of, 523, 538–539; Korean War, 538; World War II, 522–524
Avila, José María, 157
Ayala, Manuel, 89
Aztec Indians, 20–23, 35, 38

B. T. Reed (firm), 166
Bad Water, 3
Gailey, Godard, 346
Bailey, James, 365
Baja California: discovery of, 36; Indians, 12; mission chain, 68–71
Baker, Edward D., 287, 300
Bakersfield, 4, 179
Balboa, Vasco Núñez de, 25, 33–34
Balkwill, John, 327–328
Balneotherapy, 416
Baltimore ships, defined, 146
Bancroft, Hubert Howe, 94, 438, 439–440
Bandini, Arcadia, 164
Bandini, Juan, 156, 187, 263

Bandini family, 185
Bank of America, 494, 530
Bank of California, 379
Banking system, 494, 502
Banning, Phineas, 458
Baptist Church, 332, 436
Baranov, Aleksandr, 131, 134–139, 142–143
Barbour, George W., 344–345
Bard, Thomas R., 448
Barnaby Rudge (Dickens), 378
Barrett, Lawrence, 441
Barron, Eustace, 190, 210
Barrows, David Prescott, 543
Barrymore, John, 441
Bartleson, John, 197–199, 201, 202, 313, 376
Bartlett, Washington A., 247, 248, 262, 446
Baseball teams, 552
Baus and Ross Associates, 536
Bay Area Rapid Transit District (BART), 557
Beale, Edward Fitzgerald, 345–346, 392
Bear Flag revolt, 220–221
Bear River, 410–411
Beat Generation, the, 550, 553
Beaver trade, 179, 180
Becerra, Diego de, 36
Becknell, William, 175
Beerstecher, Charles J., 386
Begg, John, 164
Belasco, David, 441
Bell, Alex, 292–293
Bell, Alexander, 262
Bell, Theodore A., 450, 454–455, 498
Bella Union (gambling saloon), 339
Bellows, Henry W., 312
Benicia, 278, 279, 297, 436
Benjamin, Judah P., 310
Bennett, Charles, 240
Benny, Jack, 569
Benton, Thomas Hart, 217, 219, 321, 329
Bering, Vitus, 74, 133
Berkeley, 279, 335
Berkeley, University of California at, 435, 544–545, 558, 582
Berkeley *Gazette*, 498
Berliner Ensemble (theatre group), 550
Bernhardt, Sarah, 441, 442
Bethlehem Steel Corporation, 521
Betsey (grigantine), 129, 131
Between the Gates (Taylor), 415
Beyond the Hundredth Meridian (Stegner), 550
Bianca (ship), 290
Bidwell, John, 197–199, 375, 382: background of, 197; expedition of 1841, 197–199, 201, 202, 313, 376
Bierce, Ambrose, 429–430, 432
Bierstadt, Albert, 425–426

Bigelow, Harden, 327
Bigler, John, 275, 298, 328, 455
Billings, Warren K., 480–482, 511
Biograph Company, 494
Birch, James, 256, 356–357
Birth of a Nation, The (motion picture), 495
Birth rate, 582, 469
Bishop, W. H., 415
Black, Shirley Temple, 571
Black Ledge Massacre, 353
Black Panthers (organization), 573
Blast (journal), 480
Block, Jeremiah Sullivan, 323
Bocanegra, Juan María de, 214, 216
Bodfish, G. H., 364
Bodega y Cuadro, Juan Francisco de, 125
Boggs, Lilburn W., 263
Bohemian Club, 426, 433
Bolaños, Francisco de, 41, 43
Bolton, Charles E., 379–380
Bolton, Herbert E., 441
Bonneville, Benjamin, 178
Bonney, 204
Boody, E. Manchester, 507
Boone, Daniel, 173
Booth, Edwin, 340, 441
Booth, Newton, 377–378
Borica, Diego de, 111, 116–117, 118, 126–128
Boston ships, 127–133, 163: decline of, 164; meaning of, 127
Botón (Indian), 70
Bouchard, Hippolyte de, 146–151
Boulder Canyon Project Act, 492
Boussole (ship), 120
Bracero system, 577–578
Branciforte, 116–117, 150, 324
Brannan, Sam, 240, 283, 284, 292
Brecht, Bertold, 550
Breckinridge, John C., 304, 305, 317
Bridger, Jim, 204
Bridges, Harry, 505, 506
Bridges, 512
Briggs Commission, 412
Bright, John, 311
British Broadcasting System, 584
British East India Company, 122, 135, 210
Brocks, Samuel H., 308
Broderick, David C., 289, 297–300, 304: duel with Terry, 300, 309; feud with Gwin, 298–300, 302
Bronson v. Rodes, 317
Broughham, William, 125
Brown, 129
Brown, Aaron V., 356, 361
Brown, Edmund G., 482, 545, 562–564, 566–569, 572, 574: background of, 562; governorship, 563–564

Brown, Mrs. Edmund G., 562
Brown, John, 129–130, 225
Bryan, William Jennings, 448, 470
Bryant, William Cullen, 415
Bryant & Sturgis (firm), 165, 166
Bryce, James, 433
Bubonic plague, 449
Bucareli y Ursúa, Antionio María, 86, 89, 95, 96, 98, 118
Buchanan, James, 219, 275, 299, 302, 303, 357, 361
Buckley, Christopher A., 446, 461
Budd, James H., 447–448, 511
Buenaventura mission, 85, 114, 126
Bull Moose Convention, 455
Bunker Hill Mining & Trading Company, 243
Burbank, Luther, 396–397
Burch, John C., 304
Burdick, Eugene, 549–550
Burgess, Gelett, 429
Burnett, Peter H., 261, 273, 275, 276, 347
Burns, Daniel, 461
Burns, Hugh M., 537
Burns, William J., 476
Burns-Porter Act, 563, 574
Bustamente y Guerra, José, 123
Butler, Anthony, 213
Butrón, Manuel, 118
Butte County, 410
Butterfield, John, 357–358
Butterfield Line, 357–359
Butts, Judge, 304
Byron Springs, 416

Cabaret (musical), 550
Cabrillo, Juan Rodríguez, 24, 41–45, 60, 152
Cacafuego (ship), 51
Cain, James M., 549
Calhoun, John C., 274
California: boundaries, 1–2, 535: Constitutional Convention (1849) on, 271–272; civil wars, 186–192, 377; first American in, 123–124; income level, 581, 582; land area, 1–2; Mexican rule, 145–236: attitude toward American immigration, 200–201, beginning of, 145–154, colonization project, 158–159, education, 333, end of, 236, land grants, 160, 167–168, revolt against, 155–156, unemployment, 160; origin of name, 41–42; population growth, 581–582; Russian settlement, 9, 134–144, 175: background of, 128, end of, 184, fur trade, 128, 131, 133–139, furthest penetration of, 184; Spanish rule, 18–144: agriculture, 106, beginning of, 27–28, 62–81, education, 333, end of, 152,

government, 19, 23–24, 29, 95–97, 104–106, Indian policies, 19, Jesuit missionaries and, 64–71, judicial system, 24, land grants, 97, 117–118, missionary disputes, 106, population, 82, 116, 117, social life, 108, 116; state budget, 564, 570; statehood, 261–279: admission to Union, 274–275, Compromise of 1850 on, 274, Constitutional Convention on, 267–272, slavery question and, 261, 265, 267, 273–274; U. S. acquisition: American Pacific Squadron and, 221–222, background of, 193, 208, early sentiment for, 212, 217, Great Britain and, 209–211, overland immigration and, 193–208, Webster's scheme for, 213–214, Washington on, 212
California (Royce), 428
California Battalion (Civil War), 314
California the Cornucopia of the World (Hoag), 415
California Democratic Council (CDC), 561
California driver, defined, 487
California Fruit Growers' Exchange, 400
California for Health, Pleasure, and Residence: A Book for Travellers and Settlers (Nordhoff), 415
California Highway Commission, 487
California: A History of Upper and Lower California (Forbes), 210
California Immigrant Union, 414
California Institute of Technology, 436–437, 523, 555
California—An Intimate History (Atherton), 433
California: It's Attractions for the Invalid, Tourist, Capitalist, and Homeseeker (Madden), 415
California Miners Association, 412
California Polytechnic School, 499
California Stage Company, 256, 356
California Star (newspaper), 240, 336
California Star Oil Company, 422
California Steam Navigation Company, 371
California Winegrowers' Association, 402
California the Wonderful (Markham), 431
Californian (newspaper), 224, 240, 262, 336, 337–338
Calistoga, 416
Call, Daniel, 151
Call of the Wild, The (London), 432
Callis, Eulalia de, 107–108, 115
Cambón, 94
Camp Drum, 458
Camp Pendleton, 525
Camp Roberts, 525
Campbell, Alexander, 289
Campbell, Thompson, 322
Campbell, William Wallace, 543

Canby, Edward Richard Sprigg, 351
Cannibalism, 206, 207, 208
Cantaloupe industry, 488
Captain Jack, Chief, 349–352
Carbajal, Luís de, 27
Carleton, James, H., 314
Carlos, Chief, 91, 93
Carmany, John H., 338–339
Carmel, 85
Carmel mission, 118
Carmen (opera), 442
Carmencita, 180
Caroline (ship), 295
Carpentier v. Atherton, 316–317
Carr, J. B. 408–409
Carranco, Father Lorenzo, 70
Carrillo, Carlos Antonio, 149, 188
Carrillo, José Antonio, 156, 185, 187–188, 226, 268–269: arrested, 188; at Constitutional Convention, 269
Carrillo family, 185
Carson, Christopher "Kit," 175–176, 218, 224, 228, 230–231
Carson City, Nevada, 218
Carter, Artie Mason, 443
Carter, Edward W., 551
Caruso, Enrico, 442
Casey, James P., 287–289
Casserly, Eugene, 377, 378
Castañada, Juan, 188
Castillero, Andrés, 187
Castillo, Domingo, 39
Castro, José, 151, 184–185, 186, 189–190, 191, 218–219, 223
Castro, Manuel, 227
Castro, Martina, 188
Catherine II, Empress, 133–134, 135
Cattle industry, 342, 392–394: development of, 177; in 1826, 165; impact of gold rush on, 257–258; no-fence law, 258; ranchforms, 391–393; rustling, 380
Caucasian Chalk Circle, The (Brecht), 550
Cavalleria Rusticana (opera), 442
Cavallo, Juan, 121
Cavendish, Thomas, 53–55
Cement industry, 487
Census of Manufacturers, 580
Central Intelligence Agency, 547
Central Labor Council, 473
Central Overland California and Pike's Peak Express Company, 362
Central Pacific Railroad, 365–369, 372, 377: beginning of, 365, 366; construction of, 367; monopoly, 382; Silver Palace cars, 369; terminus, 368
Central Valley, 4, 573–574
Centralist Constitution (Mexico), 185, 186
Century of Dishonor, A (Jackson), 353

Cermeño, Sabastián Rodriguez, 54, 55–57, 58,60
Chandler, H., 435, 547
Chandler, Norman, 547
Chandler, Mrs. Norman, 551
Chandler, Otis, 547
Chapman, Caroline, 340
Chapman, Charles Edward, 31, 33, 106
Chapman, Joseph, 148, 151, 162
Chapman, William S., 394
Charles III, King, 71, 75
Charles V, Emperior, 24, 29, 35, 42
Chase, Salmon P., 316
Chatham (tender), 124
Chavez, Cesar, 578–579
Chessman, Caryl, 563
Cheyney, John Vance, 431
Chicago Bridge and Iron Company, 521
Chicago Tribune, 470
Chickamauga, Battle of, 309
Chico, Mariano, 185
Chico, 436
Chicori, 70
Chiles, Joseph B., 201
Chiles expedition party, 201, 218
Chinese-Americans, 375, 396: acts of violence against, 381–383; discrimination against, 246, 381–382, 387, 388, 468, 473; excluded from vigilante committees, 288; immigration, 388, 447; population, 381, 573; race riots, 382; railroad employment, 367, 381; state tax on, 246
Chlapewski, Charles 429
Chorpenning, George, 361
Christian Scientist Church, 452
Christopher, George, 568
Chumash Indians, 14
Civil Fund, 264
Civil War, 258, 275, 278, 282, 296, 302, 303–319, 326, 335, 346, 359, 360, 374, 396, 402, 434, 445, 458: agriculture, 315–316; Alcatraz Island fortifications, 311; California volunteers, 313–315; Confederate sympathizers, 305–312: newspaper, 308; Sanitary Commission, 312–313; stagecoach mail routes, 359, 360; Virginia City stagecoach holdup, 312; western confederacy sentiment, 303–305; 365; whaling industry, 311, 344
Clamor Público, El (newspaper), 337
Clappe, Louise Amelia Knapp Smith, 338
Claremont, 400
Clarion (brig), 147
Clark, George H., 453
Clark, Walter Van Tilburg, 549
Clark, William H., 389
Clark, Tom, 515
Clarke, George Rogers, 212

Clay, Henry, 217, 274
Cleveland, Richard J., 130–131
Climate, 3, 5, 6, 397
Clipper ships: beginning of, 250; California to China route, 250; *See also* Boston ships; names of ships
Clyman, James, 202
Coast Seamen's Journal, 473
Coast Seamen's Union, 473
Cochimí Indians, 69
Cody, William F., 362
Colchero, Sánchez, 52
Cole, Cornelius, 304, 306, 365, 373, 375
Coleman, William Tell, 247, 287, 288, 383, 414
College of the Holy Names, 436
College of San José, 333
Collier, J. C., 266
Collier's (magazine)
Colnett, James, 122
Coloma gold strike, 239, 240
Colorado River: boundary dispute, 2, 574; Indian massacre at, 101–102
Colton, David D., 317
Colton, Walter, 224, 262
Colton, Mrs. Walter, 262
Columbian Exposition of 1893, 421
Columbus, Christopher, 18, 19, 33, 64
Columbus, Diego, 19
Colusa County, 470
Comanche Indians, 173, 359
"Comedy of Errors, A" (Sienkiewicz), 429
Commission of Immigration and Housing, 479
Compromise of 1850, 274, 276
Comstock Lode, 254, 309, 367
Concepción (ship), 36, 37
Condors, 6
Confederate States of America, 305, 307, 309, 310, 314
Congregational Church, 332, 436, 452
Congress (ship), 221–222, 226, 231, 262
Congress of Industrial Organizations (CIO) 506
Conness, John B., 305–306, 374–375, 376
Conservation, 343, 577
Consolidated Aircraft of San Diego, 523
Consolidated Vultee Company, 523
Constant (ship), 54, 55
Constitution of 1824 (Mexico), 185, 186
Constitution of 1837 (Mexico), 263, 267
Constitution of 1849, 2, 267–274, 276, 278, 332–333, 335, 384: in Convention, 267–272; terms of, 270–271
Constitution of 1879, 272, 335, 385–388, 446: in Convention, 384–385; ratification of, 386, 433; terms of, 385–387
Contra Costa County, 380, 404

Cook, Captain James, 121, 124
Coolbrith, Agnes, 431
Coolbrith, Ina Donna, 431, 432
Cooper, James Fenimore, 565
Cooper, John B. E., 163
Cooper ore industry, 315
Cora, Charles, 287–289
Coral Sea, Battle of, 524
Corney, Peter, 147, 148, 150
Coronado, Francisco Vásquez de, 24, 26, 38, 39
Cortés, Hernando, 19–27, 33, 35, 36, 38, 40, 42, 57: background of, 20; Mexico expedition, 19–24
Cosmopolita, El (newspaper), 214
Cota, Leonardo, 229
Cotton industry, 485, 524: beginning of, 396; growth of, 489
Count of Monte Cristo, The (motion picture), 494
Coxey, Jacob, 420
Crabb, Henry A., 276, 294–295
Crabtree, Lotta, 341
Crandall, 256
Cranston, Alan, 564, 565
Crédit Mobilier Company, 366, 368
Creighton, Edward, 363
Creoles, defined, 108
Crescent City, 5, 8
Crespi, Juan, 73, 77, 80, 441
Crocker, Charles, 336, 438
Crocker, Edwin B., 304
Crocker Art Gallery, 426
Croix, Teodoro de, 75, 86, 96, 97, 102
Crow, Walter J., 389
Crum, A. J., 410
Druz, Doña, 185
Cuauhtémoc (commander), 23
Cunningham, W. H., 172
Cupeño Indians, 347
Curtis, Glenn, 522
Cut-Throat Bar (mining camp), 249
Cuyler's Harbor, 44
Cyane (ship), 214, 216, 219, 222–223, 311

Daedalus (supply ship), 124, 125
Daily Morning Chronicle, The, 433
Dairy industry, 406–407, 489
Dana, Richard Henry, 166, 458
Darrow, Clarence, 427, 476–477
Darwin, Charles, 396
Dasmann, Raymond, 577
Davis, Jefferson, 307, 308, 374
Davis, Colonel Jefferson C., 352
Davis, William Heath, 164, 169
Dawes Act, 353
Day, William, 163
De Long, Martin, 403

De Mille, Cecil B., 495
De Smet, Pierre Jean, 198
De Soto, Hernando, 94
De Witt, John L., 514–515
De Young, Charles, 433
De Young, Michael H., 420–421, 433, 448
Death Valley, 3
Death Valley Days (TV program), 567
Debs, Eugene V., 420, 475
Deciduous Fruit Protective League, 451
Defense-space industry, 554–555
Delaware Indians, 195, 218
Delicate Ground (drama), 340
Delmas, 401
Democratic Party: Civil War sentiments, 303–304; factionalism (1851), 297–300
Demokrat (newspaper), 337
Den, Nicholas, 327
Department of Fish and Game, 6
Department of Water Resources, 574
Depression of 1929, 251, 443, 472, 486, 496, 501, 502–512: Dust Bowl migrants, 503–505; placer-mining, 247; technocracy movement, 506–507; unemployment, 502, 503
Descubierta (ship), 123
Desire (ship), 54, 55
Destruction of California, The (Dasmann), 577
Dewey, George, 468
Dewey, Thomas E., 532–533
Dharma Bums, The (Kerouac), 550
Dianetics: The Modern Science of Mental Health (Hubbard), 554
Díaz, Melchoir, 39–40
Dickens, Charles, 378
Dickson, Edward A., 452
Diego, Francisco García, 161, 162
Diego de Alcalá, San, 59, 79
Dies Committee, 536
Digger Indians, 178, 344
DiGiorgio Fruit Corporation, 579
DiMaggio brothers, 552
Dinsmore, William B., 359–360
Diputación (legislature), 186–187
Discovery (sloop), 124
Discrimination, 571 – 573: anti-Chinese, 246, 381–382, 387, 388, 468, 473; anti-Filipino, 471–472; anti-Japanese, 466–471, 513; anti-Korean, 468; anti-Mexican, 472; education, 468–469; Roosevelt (Theodore) on, 468–469
Disney, Walt, 552
Disneyland, 552
Divorce rate, 419
Doak, Thomas W., 151, 162
Dockweiler, John F., 510
Dodge, Asa, 129

Dodge, Grenville M., 366
Dolly Vardens, the, 378, 382
Dominguez, Domingo, 225
Dominguez, Juan José, 118
Dominican missions, 72, 73, 85, 174
Donahoe Act, 542–543, 546
Donner, George, 203, 206, 207, 208
Donner, Mrs. George, 207, 208
Donner, Jacob, 203
Donner expedition party, 203–208: cannibalism, 206, 207, 208; Indian attacks on, 205
Donner Lake, 205, 206, 207
Dorr, Ebenzer, Jr., 128–129
Douglas, Donald, 522–523
Douglas, Helen Gahagan, 535
Douglas, Stephen A., 274, 299, 304, 374
Douglas, Thomas, 333
Douglas, William, 121
Douglas Aircraft Company, 523, 556
Downey, John G., 305, 318
Downey, Sheridan, 511, 535
Dragon's Teeth (Sinclair), 548
Drake, Sir Francis, 49, 50–53, 55, 124
Drake's Bay, 44, 52, 56, 60
Dramatic Chronicle, The (newspaper), 433
Dreiser, Theodore, 548
Dreyfus case, 481
Duarte, 399, 400
Duels, political, 309
Duflot de Mofras, Eugene, 212
Duhault-Cilly, Captain, 211
Dumke, Glenn S., 543
Duncan, Frank, 504
Durán, Narciso, 185
Durant, Henry, 254
Durkee, John L., 290
Durst, Richard, 478
Dust Bowl migrants, 472, 503–505, 548
Dyer, Leroy S., 351

Eagle (vessel), 133, 164
Earthquakes, 6–8, 79, 91: Anchorage, Alaska (1964), 8; number of, 6; Richter scale ratings, 7; 1812, 146; 1906 (San Francisco), 6, 7, 8, 439, 441, 442, 463, 468: casualties, 460, 461, causes of, 460, damage estimates, 461, fires, 460–461, 485–486, insurance claims, 461; 1933 (Long Beach), 7, 505
Eayrs, George Washington, 133
Echeandía, José María, 155–157, 172, 174, 175, 182
Echeveste, Juan José de, 95
Eclipse (ship), 132
Edith (ship), 268
Education, 333–334, 435–438, 540–546, 561, 569, 582, 583: community college,

437–438, 542, 543; development of, 333–336; discrimination, 468–469; first schoolhouse, 262; loyalty oaths, 537; missionary, 333; Monterey Convention on, 270, 276, 333; per capita expenditures, 540–541; public, 334, 335, 540–542; religious, 332, 335, 435; school attendance statute, 334
Edwards, 504
Eine Blume aus dem goldenen Lande: oder, Los Angeles (Salvator), 415
Eisenhower, Dwight D., 515, 533, 535, 536, 567
Eisenhower, Milton, 515
El Dorado County, 312: mining camps, 249; wine industry, 402
Eldefonsa, Doña, 185
Elections: cross-filing system, 456, 498; direct primary, 450; 1844, 217; 1846, 261, 262; 1849, 272–273; 1860, 300, 304; 1864, 318; 1871, 377; 1882, 445–446; 1890, 447; 1894, 444–448; 1932, 507, 509, 536; 1936, 536; 1948, 532–533, 536; 1952, 536, 567; 1956, 536, 567; 1958, 562; 1960, 563; 1964, 565–566; 1966, 567–569; first, 153; Progressive movement, 445–465: machine politics and, 446, 461, 465; publicity organizations, 536; on sectionalism, 302
Eliza (ship), 129
Elizabeth I, Queen, 51, 53, 55
Elliott, W. L., 485
Emancipation Proclamation, 376
Employment, 419, 529, 569, 577–579: agriculture, 396, 472, 477–478; aviation industry, 555; Chinese railroad, 367, 381; migrant-labor, 472, 519–520; World War I, 472; World War II, 522, 525–526
Encomienda system, 23–24
End Poverty in California (EPIC), 508, 510
Engle, Clair, 562, 564
Enterprise (ship), 129, 137
Entertainment industry, 443, 549, 554, 568
Episcopal Church, 332, 553
Estee, Morris M., 445
Estrada, José Mariano, 148, 155
Estrella, La (newspaper), 337
Estudillo, Joaquín, 164
Estudillo, María Jesus, 164
Etches, Richard Cadman, 122
Euphemia (brig), 282
Eureka, 2, 4, 5, 449
Evacuation Repayment Act, 518
Ewer, Ferdinand C., 338
Explorers, 31–61, 143, 144: fur trade, 170–179; *See also* names of explorers

Fages, Pedro, 81, 84–85, 92, 102, 107, 111,

115, 118, 120, 121
Fail-Safe (Burdick), 549
Fair Employment Practices Commission, 564
Fairbanks, Douglas, 495
Fama (ship), 214
Fandango, The (painting), 425
Farley, James, 510
Farragut, David Glasgow, 289
Farwell, S. B., 322
Faults (crustal fractures), 7
Feather River, 410–411, 574
Federal Bankruptcy Act, 518
Federal Bureau of Investigation, 515
Federal Farm Security Agency, 504, 505
Federal Reclamation Service, 491
Federal Reserve System, 581
Federated Trade and Labor Unions of the Pacific Coast, 473
Felch, Alpheus, 322
Felton, John B., 375
Fenelon, François de la, 186
Ferdinand V, King, 19
Ferrelo, Bartolomé, 44, 45
Feud of Oakfield Creek, The (Royce), 390, 428
Fickert, Charles, 480
Field, Stephen J., 316, 325
Fifth California Infantry (Civil War), 314
Figueroa, José, 157–158, 159, 160, 161, 162, 177, 184, 325
Fig industry, 406
Filibusters, 292–296, 310, 347: end of, 296; meaning of, 292
Filipino population: discrimination against, 471–472; employment, 396; immigration, 471–472
Fillmore, Millard, 274, 275, 288, 321, 322, 329, 345
Filthy speech movement, 545
Firebrands for Jesus (religious sect), 496
Fishing industry, 343–344, 580
Fitzgerald, F. Scott, 548–549
Fitzgerald, O. O., 317
Fitzpatrick, Thomas, 198
Flora (ship), 164–165
Flores, José María, 225–229, 232
Flores, Manuel de, 121, 122
"Fool's Prayer, The" (Sill), 431
Foote, Henry S., 301
Forbes, Alexander, 209–210
Forbes, James A., 210
Forbes, John, 210
Ford, H. L., 221
Ford, Richard, 479
Forster (settler), 231
Fort Alexander, 135
Fort Bent, 227
Fort Bridger, 203, 204, 362

Fort Cap au Gris, 173
Fort George, 179
Fort Gunnybags, 290, 291
Fort Hall, 179, 198, 201–204
Fort Kearny, 362
Fort Klamath, 350, 352
Fort Laramie, 203, 204, 362
Fort Leavenworth, 227, 235
Fort Nez Perce, 179
Fort Ord, 525
Fort Ross, 44, 144, 148, 151, 175: abandonment of, 182–184; apple orchards, 403; economy, 180–182; shipbuilding at, 181; Sutter's purchase of, 196
Fort Sumter, 305, 359
Fort Vancouver, 173, 177–178, 179, 180, 196
Fort Yuma, 309, 357
Fortune (magazine), 509
Fosdick, 206
Francis, Saint, 65, 73
Franciscan missionaries, 65, 71–73, 84, 85, 93, 107, 110, 161, 331, 401: apple orchards, 403; mission disputes, 106
Francisco, Chief, 91, 93
Francisco de Borja, mission of, 109
Free speech movement, 544–545
Frémont, John C., 8, 94, 179, 202, 217–220, 228, 239, 263, 297: background of, 217; challenges Mason to duel, 235; court martial trial, 235–236; election of 1849, 274–275; Mexican War, 223–224, 231–233; quarrel with Kearny, 234–235
Frémont, Mrs. John C., 217, 274–275
Frémont (brig), 268
Fresno, 4, 452, 551: education, 436, 438; union movement, 477–478
Fresno County, 381: agriculture, 470; industry, 422
Fresno *Republican*, 452
Friedlander, Isaac, 394
Friendly Persuasion, The (West), 549
Friends of Ronald Reagan, 567
Fruit industry, 397–406, 524, 580: development of, 177; growth of, 405, 489
Fry, Caleb T., 376
Frye, William P., 458
Fugitive-slave law, 276–277
Fullerton, 438
Fur trade, 126: Apache Indian, 176; explorers, 170–179; Fort Ross, 180; Russian, 128, 131: beginning of, 133–134; contact with Americans, 132, 139; Sea otter, 127–128
Fuster, Father Vincente, 93

Gage, Henry T., 448–449, 462
Galaup, Jean François de, 120, 211, 405

Gale, William Alden, 165
Gali, Francisco de, 55
Galileo (Brecht), 550
Gallant (ship), 129
Gálvez, José de, 75–77, 87, 95–98, 134
Gange (whaler), 211
Garcelon, G. W., 400
Gardner, Earle Stanley, 549
Garfías, Manuel, 226
Garland, Hamlin, 427, 548
Garner, William R., 189, 190
Garrá, Antonio, 347
Garrison, 308
Gathering of Zion, The (Stegner), 550
Geary, John White, 273, 281–282
General Electric Theater (TV program), 567
General Land Office, 329
Gentlemen's Agreement, 469, 471
Geography, 1–9
George, Henry, 255, 427, 428, 506, 508
Giannini, Amadeo Peter, 494
Gibson, Hugh, 485
Giddings and Company, 357
Gilbert, Edward, 272, 273
Gilbert, John, 495
Gilbert, Sir William, 387
Gili, Bartolomé, 110
Gillett, James N., 449–450, 452, 464: background of, 449; highway program of, 487
Gilman, Daniel Coit, 335–336, 435
Gilman, R. H., 399
Gillespie Archibald, 219, 223–226, 233: at Battle of San Pasqual, 230, 231; rule of Los Angeles, 224–225
Gilroy, John, 151, 202
Gilroy, California, 94, 151
Ginsberg, Allen, 550
Gladstone, William Ewart, 418
Gladstone, California, 418
Glendora, 172
Glenn County, 409, 470
Gold mining industry, 342: controversy with farmers, 409, 412; decline of, 247; Nevada stocks and, 254–255; techniques: deep-gravel, 253, long toms, 252, vein, 252–253
Gold Rush of 1848–1857, 175, 237–251, 439: amount extracted, 241, 247; beginning of, 237–241; claim jumping, 241; foreign immigration and, 250; '49ers, 243–247, 329; number of, 243, 245; types of, 245–246; impact, 249–251: on agriculture, 257–260, economic, 341–344; largest nugget found, 247; lawlessness and, 280, 281; lode areas, 241–242; transportation during, 255–256; travel routes to, 243–244
Golden Era (newspaper), 337–338, 430

Golden Gate Bridge, 512
Golden Gate International Exposition of 1939–1940, 525
Golden Hind (ship), 51–53
Goldwater, Barry, 565–566, 567
Goldwyn, Samuel, 495
Golf courses, 552
Gómez, Luciano, 148, 149
Gómez, Manuel, 148
Good Government League, 464
Goodbye to Berlin (Isherwood), 550
Gouge Eye (mining camp), 249
Government: first California charter, 95; legislative gerrymandering, 566; military rule (1846–1849), 222–260, 261–267: alcaldes, 262, 263–264, financing, 264, gold rush and, 265, unpopularity of, 266; mining camps, 266; missionaries, 66, 67; Spanish colonial, 19, 23–24, 29, 95–97, 104–106; administrative districts, 104
Goycoechea, Felipé de, 126
Graham, Isaac, 186, 189–190, 191, 192
Graham Affair, 189–190, 210
Grand Army Journal, The, 434
Grand Captain of the South (ship), 51
Grange movement, 378, 384, 470
Grapes of Wrath, The (Steinbeck), 504, 548
Graves, Richard P., 561
Gray, Andrew F. V., 231
Greathouse, Ridgely, 310, 311
Greenback-Labor Party, 388
Greenwood, Brittan, 207
Grey, Zane, 548
Gridley, Reuel C., 313
Griffith, David Wark, 495
Grigsby, John, 203
Grijalba, Juan de, 20, 24
Grimes, Eliab, 263
Grizzly bears, 6
Groeme, John, 123–124
Gross, Robert E., 523
Guadalupe-Hidalgo, Treaty of, 2, 271, 320: ratification of, 261; terms of, 234, 236: land title, 321
Guaicuro Indians, 69
Guaymas, Battle of, 294
Guerra, Ana María, 163
Guerra, José de la, 150, 153, 155, 163, 194
Guerra, María Teresa de la, 163
Guide to California, the Golden State, A (Nordhoff), 415
Gutiérrez, Nicholás, 185–186
Guzmán, Nuño de, 24–26, 35, 36, 40, 42
Gwin, William M., 269–270, 297–300: arrested, 308; at Constitutional Convention, 271; election of 1849, 274–275; feud with Broderick, 298–300, 302; pro-Southern sentiment, 303–304; on Span-

ish-Mexican land titles, 321
Gyselar, Captain, 147

H. H. Bancroft & Company, 439
H.M.S. Pinafore (Gilbert and Sullivan), 387, 442
Hager, John S., 378
Haggin, James B., 408
Haight, Henry H., 376–377: background of, 376; governorship, 366–367
Haight, Raymond L., 508
Hale, Edward Everett, 41
Hall, Hiland, 256, 308, 322
Hall, William Hammond, 408–409
Halleck, Henry W., 248, 264, 269, 306, 321
Ham and Eggs plan, 509, 510–511
Haraszthy, Agoston, 401–402
Harbison and Stewart Company, 422
Harbors, 8, 457–460, 484, 490
Hardy, James H., 308, 309
Hargraves, Edward H., 249–250
Harpending, Asbury, 308, 310–311
Harriman, E. H., 423, 461
Harriman, Job, 448, 476–477
Harrison, William Henry, 213
Harte, Bret, 337–338, 339, 428, 433
Hartnell, William E. P., 162–165, 268, 321, 333
Hartt, Mills P. H., 389
Hastings, Lansford W., 201–204, 269
Hatfield, George J., 510
Hawkins, John, 50
Hayes, Rutherford B., 388
Hazard (ship), 129
Health boom of 1880's, 416–417
Hearst, George, 433, 446
Hearst, Phoebe Apperson, 336
Hearst, William Randolph, 336, 430, 433–434, 448, 454–455, 546–547
Heinzelman, Samuel P., 348
Hell's Angels (motorcycle gang), 559
Heney, Francis J., 453, 456, 463, 464, 498
Henley, Thomas J., 346
Henry E. Huntington Library and Art Gallery, 438–439
Henshaw, George, 197
Herrin, William F., 451, 454, 463
Herron, Walter, 205
Hesperian (magazine), 338
Hetch Hetchy Valley, 493
Hidalgo y Costilla, Miguel de, 152
Hide and tallow trade, 162, 164–167
Higgins, James, 176
Highway system, 538, 557, 582: appropriations, 487; beginning of, 450; road mileage, 538
Híjar, José María, 158, 159
Hill, Thomas, 426

Hippie movement, 558
History of California (Tuthill), 439
Hitch, Charles J., 546
Hittell, John S., 414
Hittell, Theodore H., 328, 440
Hoag, I. N., 415
Hockaday, John M., 361
Hoffer, Eric, 550–551
Holladay, Ben, 360
Hollister, 111
Hollywood, 422, 495–496, 554
Hollywood Bowl, 443
Homberg, Simon, 418
Homes and Happiness in the Golden State of California (Truman), 415
Homesteads, 392, 393
Honda, Harry, 517
Hoopa Indians, 348
Hoover, Herbert, 437, 485, 492, 503
Hoover Library of War, Peace and Revolution, 438
Hopi Indians, 17
Hopkins, Mark, 246, 247, 304, 365–373, 414
Hopkins, Sterling V., 290–291
Hopper, De Wolfe, 441
Horsely brothers, 494
Houston, Sam, 213
Howl and Other Poems (Ginsberg), 550
Hubbard, Lafayette Ronald, 554
Hubbel, Ezekiel, 137
Hudson, Thomas, 122
Hudson Bay Company, 135, 173, 177–183, 196, 210: founded, 179; merger, 179, 180; Sacramento River expedition, 177
Hughes, Charles Evans, 457
Hughes Aircraft Company, 556
Hull, Patrick Purdy, 341
Humboldt, California, 436, 452
Humboldt Bay, 8, 500
Humboldt County, 5, 338: dairy industry, 407; Indian population, 17
Humboldt State Teachers College, 499
Humbug (mining camp), 249
Humphrey, Isaac, 240, 242
Hunsdon, Lord, 53
Hunt, Jefferson, 301
Hunt, Timothy Dwight, 332
Huntington, Collis P., 304, 365–373, 423, 431, 459–560
Huntington, Henry E., 423, 438–439, 460
Hupa Indians, 17
Hurtado de Mendoza, Diego, 36
Hutchings' California Magazine, 338
Huxley, Aldous, 550
Huydobro, Manuel Bernal, 70
Hwui Shan, 31
Hydraulic Miners Association, 411–412

Hydraulic mining, 410–412

I, Governor of California, and How I Ended Poverty. A True Story of the Future (Sinclair), 508
I Am a Camera (motion picture), 550
Ibarra, Diego de, 27
Ibarra, Juan María, 157
Icarus (warship), 296
Ice Age, 10
Ide, William B., 220, 221
Immigration, 414–415, 419: Chinese, 388, 447; Dust Bowl migrant, 472, 503–505; Filipino, 471–472; gold rush and, 250; health boom and (1880's), 416–417; Japanese, 466–471: beginning of, 466–467, Gentlemen's Agreement on, 469, 471; Mexican, 472; in 1947, 529; promotional groups, 415–416; Southern Pacific railroad and, 414–415
Immigration Act of 1907, 469
Immigration Act of 1924, 471
Imperial Valley, 472, 488, 505
Inca Indians, 34, 38
Independence League, 450
Indian agents, 345–346
Indians, 6, 10–17, 20–27, 36, 59, 69, 344–353, 375, 396: agriculture, 12–13, 396; auctioning off of, 347; basket weaving skills, 14; Colorado River massacre, 101–102, 103; dwellings, 14; effects of missions on, 112–115; languages, 11, 12; last major uprising, 349; mortality rate, 160; number of, 11; physical traits, 11; polygamy, 70; population, 11, 16–17; religion, 14–15; reservations, 345–346, 348, 349; Spanish policy toward, 19; stagecoach raids, 359, 360; treaties, 344–345; wars, 15, 16, 26, 27, 39, 41, 43, 70, 344, 347, 349–353: at San Diego, 91–93; *See also* names of tribes
Industrial Workers of the World (I.W.W.), 477–487, 497: decline of, 483; federal prosecution of, 482
Industry: in 1848, 260; growth of, 260, 539; Korean War, 538; loyalty oaths, 537; manufacturing statistics, 580; mission, 111, 113; prosperity, 484–501; Vietnam War, 581; World War I, 484–485; World War II, 520, 524: demobilization and, 528–530; *See also* names of industries
Ingram, R. Henry, 312
Inouye, Daniel K., 517
Inquisition, 27
Inside Daisy Clover (Lambert), 550
Internal Revenue Service, 534
International Association of Bridge and

Structural Steel and Ironworkers, 475–476
International Longshoremen's Association, 505–506
International Longshoremen's Union, 557
International Workingmen's Association, 473
Inyo County, 516
Iphigenia (brig), 121, 122
Iron industry, 260
Irrigation, 406, 407–408: acreage, 409; agriculture and, 407–409, 490–493; Alabama Hills incident, 492; controversies over, 408–409; desalinization of water and, 575; mission, 407
Irwin, William, 382, 384, 386, 445
Isabella I, Queen, 19
Isbell, Olive Mann, 333
Isherwood, Christopher, 550
Islas, Santiago de, 100
Iturbide, Agustín, 152, 154
J. W. Chapman (Schooner), 310–311
Jackson, Andrew, 213, 217, 318
Jackson, David E., 171, 173, 177
Jackson, Helen Hunt, 353, 428
Jackson, James, 350
Jackson, Waldo and Young Company, 177
Jansen, C. J., 284
Japanese-American Citizens League, 517
Japanese-Americans: agriculture, 396, 467, 470, 489, 514, 519; birth rate, 469; discrimination against, 466–471, 513; immigration, 466–471; Issei, 513, 518; Kibei, 513, 515, 516; Nisei, 513, 515–518; picture-bride marriages, 469, 498; population, 573; World War II, 511–519: internment, 515–517; Lippmann on, 514; property losses, 518
Jayme, Luís, 91–92
Jeffers, Robinson, 548
Jefferson, Thomas, 212
Jenkins, John, 284
Jensen, Jackie, 552
Jesuit missionaries, 64–71, 198
Jesús de Noe, José de, 262
Jimenez, Fortún, 36
Joaquin gangs, defined, 286
John Begg (ship), 164
John Begg and Company, 163
John Birch Society, 570
Johnson, Albert M., 453
Johnson, Andrew, 325, 375, 377, 415
Johnson, Grove L., 453
Johnson, Hiram W., 449, 452–457, 464, 470, 492, 497, 499, 531, 535: background of, 452–453; gubernatorial campaign, 453–455
Johnson, Mrs. Hiram W., 453

Johnson, John Neely, 288–291
Johnson, Lyndon B., 565–566, 567
Johnston, Albert Sidney, 307
Jolson, Al, 496
Jones, Thomas Catesby, 214–216, 222
Jones, William Carey, 321
Jones Affair, 214–216
Jordan, David Starr, 437
Jouan, Auguste, 323
Joven Guipuzcoana (ship), 214
Judah, Theodore D., 257, 364–368
Julia (schooner), 290
Jungle, The (Sinclair), 433
Junior colleges, 437–438
Junípero, Father, *see* Serra, Father Junípero
Juno (ship), 139–142, 210

Kahn, Julius, 468
Kaiser, Henry J., 521
Kalem Company, 495
Kamehameha, King, 147
Karok Indians, 17
Kaweah River, 407
Kearney, Denis, 383, 384, 387, 473
Kearny, Stephen Watts, 227–231, 233, 263:
    background of, 227; quarrel with Fré-
    mont, 234–235; wounded, 230
Keating, Edward M., 547
Keene, Laura, 340
Keene Associates, 536
Kefauver, Estes, 534
Keith, William, 426
Kelley, Hall Jackson, 177–178
Kelsey, Andrew, 202
Kelsey, Benjamin, 202
Kemble, E. C., 240
Kennedy, John F., 563, 565
Kennedy, Robert F., 565
Kenny, Robert W., 532
Kern, Edward M., 218
Kern County, 560: industry, 422, 493;
    land titles, 392; population growth, 414;
    water supply, 574
Kern River, 218, 407, 408
Kerouac, Jack, 550
Kerr, Clark, 543–546
Keseberg, Louis, 205, 208
Keyes, James, 411
Keyes, Mrs. Sarah, 203
KFI (radio station), 487, 537
Khrushchev, Nikita, 552
Kibbe, William C., 348
Kilburn, R. L., 403
Kimball, Oliver, 132, 139
King, James, 286–287, 288, 440
King, Martin Luther, Jr., 572
King, Thomas Butler, 267, 269, 272
King, Thomas Starr, 306, 310, 312–313

Kings River, 407
Kings River Canal Company, 409
Kino, Father Eusebio Francisco, 62, 63, 67,
    68, 441
Kipling, Rudyard, 429
Klamath Indians, 349
Klondike Gold Rush, 432, 474
Knight, Goodwin J., 560–563
Knights of the Columbian Star, 306–307
Knights of the Golden Circle, 306–307, 310
Knights of Labor, 473
Knowland, William F., 535, 561–562
Know-Nothing Party, 288, 296, 297, 298,
    300
Korean War, 536, 538, 555
Korean-Americans, 468
Krips, Joseph, 551
Kroeber, A. L., 11
Kruzenstern, Adam, 138
Ku Klux Klan, 507, 533
Kuchel, Thomas H., 542, 561, 568
Kuskov, Ivan, 136, 143

La Argentina (frigate), 147, 148
La Mesa, Battle of, 232
La Paz mission, 70
La Purísima Concepción mission, 100, 101,
    146, 154
La Salle, Robert Cavelier de, 94
Lafitte, Martin, 211
Lake Tahoe, 202, 275, 342, 575
Lambert, Gavin, 550
Land Act of 1851, 321, 322–323, 324
Land Act of 1866, 329–330
Land boom of 1880's, 417–419, 442
Land of Little Rain , The (Austin), 432
Land of Sunshine (publication), 415
Land titles, 320–330: commission investiga-
    tion on, 321–322; federal attitude
    toward, 321; fraud and, 320–330: Li-
    mantour's, 323–324; Guadalupe-Hidalgo
    Treaty on, 321; Mexican, 160, 167–168,
    321, 322; mining claim, 329, 330; rail-
    road, 370–371, 392; Spanish, 320, 322;
    squatters, 320–321, 325–328, 391
Lane, Franklin K., 449
Lane v. Oregon, 317
Langdon, William H., 450, 465
Laplace, Cyrille Pierre, 212
Lark, The (ed. Burgess), 429
Larkin Thomas O., 166, 193, 195, 215, 217,
    222, 263, 269
Larkin, Mrs. Thomas O., 193
Lasky, Jesse, 495
Last Tycoon, The (Fitzgerald), 549
Lasuén, Father Fermín Francisco de, 109–
    112, 116–118, 123
Lassen Peak (volcano), 3

Latham, Milton S., 300, 302, 305
Law and Order Men, 289, 290
Law of the Range, The (motion picture), 494
Lawrence, James, 176
Le Conte, John, 435
Le Heros (ship), 211
League of Lincoln-Roosevelt Republican Clubs, 452, 453, 545
Leahy, Doc., 442
Leakey, Louis B., 10
Leavenworth and Pike's Peak Express, 361
Leese, Jacob, 180
Lelia Byrd (brig), 130–131
Leon (ship), 211
Leonard, Zenas, 178
Leoncavallo, Ruggiero, 443
Levant (sloop), 222
Levering Act, 537
Lewelling, Seth, 403
Lewis, Sinclair, 432
Liars Flat (mining camp), 249
Libraries, 438–440
Lick, James, 438
Lick Observatory, 543
Life in California (Robinson), 163
Limantour, José Yves, 323–324
Lincoln, Abraham, 264, 287, 300, 304, 306, 307, 311, 318, 319, 323, 377: assassination of, 433; railroad bill, 365
Lincoln, Mrs. Abraham, 220
Lindbergh, Charles A., 523
Lippitt, F. J., 272
Lippmann, Walter, 514
Lissner, Meyer, 455
Liszt, Franz, 340
Literary Digest, 492
Literature, 427–433, 547–551
Lives of Celebrated Spaniards, 186
Livestock industry, 166, 177, 257–258, 380, 391–394, 489, 524, 538
Loaysa, Juan Garcia Jofre de, 35, 36, 47
Lobeira, Vasco de, 41
Lockheed Aircraft Corporation, 523–524
London, Jack, 431, 432
London Times, 210
Lone Pine, 7
Long Beach, 452, 581: Cunard liner purchase, 551–552; earthquake of 1933, 7, 505; industry, 487; Negro districts, 572; sagging land surface problem, 576; World War II, 525
Long Beach *Press*, 507
López, Esteban, 60
López, Francisco, 237
López de Legaspi, Miguel, 47
Loreto mission, 68, 69, 70, 74, 75
Los Angeles, California, 99, 100, 166, 180, 185, 186, 200, 241, 242, 262, 503, 504,

581: air pollution, 575–576; area annexations, 422; Chinese race riot, 382; colonial government, 104–106; cultural growth, 441–442; Diputación, 157, 185; during civil wars, 186, 187, 188, 191–192; early theatrical activity, 340; expansion of, 422; first skyscraper, 424; Gillespie's rule of, 224–226; growth of, 422, 486; harbor facilities, 457–460, 484, 490; Indian auctions, 347; industry, 529; land claims, 324; Mexican War, 223–226, 231–233, 358; newspapers, 337; population, 422: 1860, 257, growth, 414, Japanese, 517–518; railroad line to (1864), 257; rainfall, 5; real estate boom (1880's), 417, 418; settlement of, 164; size of, 422; Stockton's capture of, 232; telegraphic service, 363–364; transit system, 557; union movement, 474–477, 483, 506; Vigilance Committee, 285; water supply, 490–492; Watts riot, 549, 571–572: estimated damage, 572; World War II, 520, 521, 525
Los Angeles Chamber of Commerce, 451, 497
Los Angeles Clearing House Association, 492
Los Angeles County, 281, 301, 342, 348, 380, 381, 503, 537, 547: agriculture, 470, 488; Indian population, 17; industry, 421, 422, 487, 493, 496; Ku Klux Klan rally, 573; orange groves, 399; population growth, 414, 582; unemployment, 529; water supply, 574; wine industry, 401
Los Angeles *Daily News*, 507
Los Angeles Dodgers, 552
Los Angeles *Express*, 452
Los Angeles Harbor Commission, 460
Los Angeles International Airport, 539
Los Angeles Museum of History, Science and Art, 426
Los Angeles *News*, 337
Los Angeles Philharmonic Orchestra, 443, 551
Los Angeles & San Bernardino Land Company, 391
Los Angeles-San Pedro Railroad, 371
Los Angeles *Star*, 304, 337
Los Angeles *Times*, 434–435, 447, 480, 491: circulation (1967), 547; on Progressive movement, 454; union opposition, 475, 476
Los Angeles Vineyard Society, 407
Loughead, Allan, 523
Loughead, Malcolm, 523
Louis XIV, King, 63
Love, Harry, 286

Low, Frederick, 318, 374–376
Loyalty oaths, 537–538
Loyola, Ignatius, 64
Loyola University, 436
Lubin, Simon J., 479
Ludwig, King, 340–341
Luís (Indian guide), 205
Lumber industry, 260, 342, 484, 580
Lutuomian language, 12
Lux, Charles, 392–393, 395, 408, 409
Lynch, Attorney General, 559
Lynchings, 284, 285
Lyon, Nathaniel, 347

M. H. de Young Memorial Museum, 426
McAdoo, William Gibbs, 507, 511
MacArthur, Douglas, 516
McCarthy, P. H., 464–465
McClatchy family, 434
McClellan, George B., 318
McCloskey, Paul, 571
McConnell, John R., 305–306
McCullough, Hugh, 164, 165
McCullough, John, 441
McDougal, John, 273, 275, 289
McDuffie, James Y., 346
McKee, Redick, 344–345
McKinley, William, 448, 459
McLain, George, 563
McLoughlin, John, 179–180
McMahon, Green, 202
McManigal, Ortie, 476
McNabb, James, 290
McNamara, Father Eugene, 210–211
McNamara, James B., 476–477, 480
McNamara, John Joseph, 476–477
McNeil Island Federal Penitentiary, 534
McPherson, Aimee Semple, 496–497, 553
McTeague (Norris), 429
McWilliams, Carey, 534
Madden, Jerome, 415
Magellan, Ferdinand, 19, 35
Maguire, James G., 448
Maguire, Thomas, 339–340
Mail routes: Pony Express, 361–363; stage-coach, 356–360: Civil War, 359, 360; steamship, 244, 361, 371
Majors, Alexander, 361–363
Malaspina, Alejandro, 123–124
Maloney, J. P., 290
Man with the Hoe and Other Poems, The (Markham), 430
Manifest Destiny, 213, 217
Manila Galleon trade route, 46–49, 52–56, 60–61
Mann, Thomas, 550
Marcy, William G., 269
Marin County, 512

Mariposa, California, 337
Mariposa War, 348
Markham, Edwin, 430–431, 432
Markham, Henry H., 446–447
Marlow, Julia, 441
Marsh, John, 195, 197
Marshall, James Wilson, 202, 239–240
Marshall gold strike, 16
Marston, William, 333
Martin, Glenn L., 522–523
Martin Eden (London), 432
Martinez, Estevan José, 121–122
Marvin, John Gage, 333–334
Marysville, 305: early theatrical activity, 340; flood of 1875, 411; newspapers, 336; Vigilance Committee, 285
Masamune, Date, 33
Mascagni, Pietro, 442
Mason, Richard Barnes, 235, 240, 263–266
Massett, Stephen C., 339
Matteson, Edward E., 410
Mayan Indians, 20
Meacham, Alfred B., 349, 350–351
Meares, John, 122, 123
Mechanics' Institute Library, 336
Mehta, Zubin, 551
Mendocino County, 380
Mendoza, Antonio de, 24, 26, 37–47
Mental health programs, 569–570
Mercantile Library, 336
Merchants and Manufacturers Association, 475, 476
Mercury (ship), 133
Merriam, Frank Finley, 499, 507–508, 510, 511, 560
Merritt, Ezekiel, 220, 226
Mervine, William, 222–223, 226
Methodist Church, 332
Methodist Episcopal Church, 335
Mexican War, 179, 222–236, 282, 403, 445: beginning of, 222; end of, 233–234, 261
Mexican-Americans, 396, 577–579: discrimination against, 472; education, 542; immigration, 472; population, 573; World War II, 519–520: wage earnings, 525–526
Micheltorena, Manuel, 162, 190–192, 215, 216, 323: appointed governor, 190; attitude toward American immigration, 200
Michigan State University, 544
Midway, Battle of, 524
Migrant Labor Agreement, 577
Mildred Pierce (Cain), 549
Miller, Henry, 392–393, 394, 408, 409
Miller, Henry (author), 549, 550
Miller, Joaquin, 430, 432
Millet, Jean François, 430
Milligan, John, 151

Millikan, Robert A., 436–437
Mills, Cyrus T., 436
Mills, Mrs. Cyrus T., 436
Mills, William H., 400
Mills College, 436, 551
Mining camps: government, 266; religion in, 332; theatrical activity, 340
Mining industry, 341–342, 379, 484–485: claims, 329, 330; clash with farmers, 409–412; decline of, 414; hydraulic, 410–412; Nevada stocks and, 254–255; techniques, 252–253
Minns' Evening Normal School, 335
Mirea, Margarita, 118
Mission system, 16, 98, 112–115, 320: agriculture, 67, 113; decree of 1831 on, 156; development of, 85; expansion of, 109–110; government, 66, 67; industry, 111, 113, 401; irrigation, 407; last founded, 153; number of, 109; Pious Fund, 66–67, 68, 95, 161, 162, 332; results of, 112–115; secularization of, 159, 161, 167, 188, 189, 320; *See also* names of missions
Missionaries, 64–70: Baja California, 68–71; Baptist, 332; Dominican, 72, 73, 85, 174; forbidden free postage, 106; Franciscan, 65, 71–72, 73, 84, 85, 93, 106, 107, 110, 161, 331, 401, 403; fur trade, 176; hide trade, 165, 167; Jesuit, 64–71, 198; Russian Orthodox Church, 134, 137
Mix, Tom, 495
Mixton War, 26, 27, 39, 41, 43
Modjeska, Helena, 429, 441
Modjeska, Ralph, 429
Modoc County, 516
Modoc War, 349–353: cost of, 352–353; peace meetings, 351
Mojave Desert, 3, 176, 458
Mojave Indians, 11, 171, 172, 174
Molina, 149
Montalvo, Ordóñez de, 41
Montemayor, 27
Monterey, Conde de, 57, 59, 60
Monterey, California, 75, 152, 179, 180, 241, 262, 266, 278: Bouchard's capture of, 148–149; civil wars, 187, 190, 191; colonial government, 104–106; Constitutional Convention at, 267–272, 274, 276, 301, 332, 333; fishing industry, 343; garrison revolt (1828), 155; Jones attack on, 214–216; Mexican War, 222–223, 261; naming of, 59; settlement of, 80–81, 82, 85, 96, 164; tourist industry, 416; Vancouver at, 125–126; vigilante committees, 291; World War II, 523
Monterey Bay, 56, 78, 120
Montesclaros, Marqués de, 60–61
Montez, Lola, 340–341

Montezuma, Emperor, 20, 21, 23
Montgomery, John D., 223
Montgomery, Zach, 304
Montoya, 26
Mooney, Thomas J., 480–482, 511
Mooney, Mrs. Thomas J., 480, 481
Moraga, Gabriel, 145–146
Moraga, José, 90, 93, 94
Moran, Thomas, 426
More, Thomas, 328
Morehead, Joseph C., 292, 293, 347
Mormon Battalion, 237, 239
Mormon Church, 237, 271, 431
Morrill Land Grant Act, 335, 394
Morris, Albert, 190
Morrison, Judge, 276
Morse, Samuel F. B., 363
Mosby, John, 315
Motion picure industry, 443, 549, 554, 568: growth of, 494–496; production costs (1939), 496
Motion Picture Patents Company, 494
Motorcycle gangs, 558–559
Moulder, Andrew J., 335
Mount Helena, 184
Mount Whitney, 3
Muir, John, 493
Mulholland, William, 490–491
Murietta, Joaquin, 286, 430
Murphy, Mrs., 208
Murphy, George, 565, 566
Murphy family, 202
Museums, 426, 546, 551
Music, 442–443, 551
Mussel Slough incident, 388–390
Mutiny on the Bounty (Nordhoff and Hall), 415

Naglee, Henry M., 306
Nahl, Charles C., 425
Napa County, 402
Napoleon I, 158, 196
Napoleon III, 305
Narváez, Pánfilo de, 21, 22, 42
Nash, John H., 263
Nash, W. H., 403
Natalia (ship), 158
Nation, The, 534
National Academy of Sciences, 555
National Aeronautics and Space Administration (NASA), 556
National Erectors Association, 475, 476
National Labor Relations Board, 579
National Recovery Act, 505, 506
National Science Foundation, 555
Native Sons of the Golden West, 440, 470
Navajo Indians, 12, 17
Negroes, 69, 147, 375: education, 542;

excluded from vigilante committees, 288; law barring testimony of, 278; Monterey Constitutional Convention on, 270, 276; population, 571; slavery, 266–267, 374, 375; Watts riot, 571–572

Neva (ship), 138

Neve, Felipe de, 96, 102, 104, 106, 116, 263: colonial governership, 107–108, 115; dispute between Serra and, 97–99

New Almaden, 252

New Deal, 505, 507, 511, 532, 536, 547, 561

New York *Evening Post*, 415

New York *Herald*, 242

New York Stock Exchange, 495

Newspapers, 224, 336–338, 433–435: bilingual, 337; Confederate sympathies, 308; first, 262, 337; foreign, 337; labor union, 473

Nielsen, Alice, 442

Nieto, Manuel Pérez, 118

Ninth Wave, The (Burdick), 549

Nixon, Richard M., 535, 561, 563, 564, 567, 570

Nobel, Robert, 509

Nootka Claims Convention, 123

Nootka Sound: Spanish ship seizures at, 121–123; Vancouver at, 126

Nordhoff, Charles, 415

Norris, Frank, 390, 429, 455, 456

North, John Wesley, 398

North American Aircraft Company, 523

North West America (schooner), 121–122

North West Company, 179–180, 181

North Western Company, 243

Northwest Ordinance of 1787, 270

Nothing Impossible (religious sect), 496

Nuesta Señora de Esperanza (galleon), 54

Nye, Michael C., 197

Oakland, 335, 539: Civil War meetings, 305; education, 436; industry, 487; Negro districts, 572; squatter outbreaks, 327

Oakland *Tribune*, 535

O'Cain, Joseph, 129, 131–133, 136–139, 142

O'Cain (ship), 131–132

Occidental and Oriental Steamship Company, 371

Occidental Presbyterian University, 436

O'Connor Act, 384

Octopus, The (Norris), 390, 429

Odd Fellows Library, 336

Ogden, Peter Skene, 178

Ohio State University, 544

Old Mexico and Her Lost Provinces (Bishop), 415

Old Spanish Trail, 176

Old Woman's Gun, Battle of the, 226, 232

Older, Fremont, 462, 463, 464

Olga (sloop), 137

Olive oil industry, 405–406

Olson, Culbert L., 481, 509, 510–512, 531

On the Road (Kerouac), 550

On the Waterfront (motion picture), 549

Oñate, Cristóbal de, 27

Oñate, Juan de, 28

Ontario, California, 399

"Opportunity" (Sill), 431

Orange County, 118, 397, 400, 441, 470, 552

Orange industry, 398–400: beginning of, 398–399; production, 400

Oregon Trail, 198, 354, 356

Ord, E. O. C., 324

Ord, James L., 272

Oroville Dam, 574

"Orso" (Sienkiewicz), 429

Ortega, Ignacio, 151

Ortega, José, 86, 87, 92

Ortega, José Francisco, 262

Ortega family, 149

Otis, Harrison Gray, 434, 435, 447, 454, 475, 476, 477, 547

Otter (ship), 128–129

Outlaws, 379–381

Overland Mail Company, 359–360, 362, 363

Overland Monthly, 338–339, 428

Overland Telegraph Company, 363

Owens, Roy C., 509

Owens Valley, 7, 490–492

Ox-Bow Incident, The (Clark), 549

Oxenham, John, 49–50

Oxman, Frank C., 480

Pachappa Orange Growers' Association, 400

Pacheco, Romauldo, 155, 157, 377, 378, 382

Pacheco, California, 394

Pacific (newspaper), 336

Pacific Coast Oil Company, 422

Pacific Electric Land Company, 423

Pacific Electric Railroad, 423–424

Pacific Fur Company, 181

Pacific Gas and Electric Company, 573

Pacific Mail Steamship Company, 244, 361, 371

Pacific Monthly, 338

Pacific Museum, 341

Pacific Poems (Miller), 430

Pacific Railway Act, 365–366

Pacific Rural Press, 392

Pacific Telegraph Company, 363

Padrés, José María, 158, 159

Pagliacci, I (opera), 443

Pakenham, Richard, 210
Palm Springs, 416
Palma, Chief, 94, 100, 102
Palmerston, Lord, 210
Palóu, Francisco, 73, 85–86, 89, 94, 98, 109, 110, 441
Panic of 1837, 197, 217, 250, 270, 271, 368
Panic of 1873, 379
Panic of 1893, 409, 419–421, 437, 447
Panic of 1907, 450
Pardee, George C., 449
Parrott, 222
Partridge, John S., 463
Pasadena, 232, 443
Pattie, James Ohio, 173–175
Pattie, Sylvester, 173, 174
Pattie family, 173, 176, 177
Paul I, Czar, 135
Paulham, Louis, 522
Pawnee Indians, 344
Payran, Stephan, 284
Peach crops, 403–404
Peacock (ship), 123
Pear crops, 404
Pearl Harbor, bombing of, 471, 513, 514
Peek, Paul, 537
Pellier, Louis, 404
Pellier, Pierre, 404
Pelton, John Colter, 333
Peña, Cosme, 187
People's Independent Party, 382
People's Protective Alliance, 382
Peralta, Luís, 169
Peralta, Pedro de, 28
Pereira, William, 551
Pérez, Juan, 76–77, 78
Perez de la Torre, Diego, 26
Perkins, George C., 387, 445, 451
Perry (taxpayer), 316
Perry, David, 352
Perry, Matthew C., 466
Personal Narrative of James Ohio Pattie, The, 175
Pesquiera, Ignacio, 295
Petit-Thouars, Abel du, 211
Petroleum industry, 4, 247, 342, 485, 580: development of, 421–411; first oil well, 421; growth of, 493–494; Korean War, 538; pipelines, 493; tidelands oil dispute, 534–535; World War II, 522
Phelan, James D., 306, 456, 461–462, 464, 474, 493
Phelps, Timothy G., 382
Philbrick, H. R., 533–534
Philip II, King, 29, 46, 47
Philips, John G., 290
Phoenix (schooner), 136
Phylloxera (plant lice), 402

Pickett, James Chamberlayne, 214
Pickett, William, 431
Pickford, Mary, 495
Pico, Andrés, 232–233, 237, 302, 313
Pico, Francisco, 227
Pico, Jesús, 232–233
Pico, Pío, 156, 157, 192, 210, 211, 223, 228: arrested, 188; land grants of, 321
Picolo, Father Francisco María, 68
Pierce, Franklin, 289, 298, 303, 322
Piercy, Charles W., 304, 308–309
Pike, 205
Pike, Bishop James, 553
Pike, Zebulon, 94
Pike's Peak Express Company, 360
Pilgrim (brig), 166
Pima Indians, 87, 88
Pindray, Charles de, 293
Pioneer (journal), 338
Pioneer Stage Company, 360
Pious Fund, 66–67, 68, 95, 161, 162, 332
Pit, The (Norris), 429
Pitt, Thomas, 127
Pixley, Frank M., 316
Pizarro, Francisco, 33, 34
Placentia, 399
Placer County, 405
Placerville, 305, 312
Plan of Iguala, 152
Pocahontas (vessel), 157
Polk, James K., 216–217, 219, 242: mining property proposal, 329; remits Frémont's court martial, 236
Pomona College, 436
Pond, Edwin B., 447
Pony Express, 361–363
Pool, Thomas B., 312
Poole, Alonzo W., 389
Population: Chinese, 381, 573; distribution, 451; 1860, 249; 1870, 260; 1878, 384; 1880–1890, 413; 1920, 486; Filipino, 471–472; growth of, 395, 413–414, 421, 486–487, 529, 530, 538, 540: World War II, 525; Indian, 11, 16–17; Japanese-American, 573: birth rate, 469; legislative districting by, 500; Mexican-American, 573; Negro, 571; rural, 413; school age, 543, 544: 1858–1890, 334; Spanish colonial, 82, 116, 117, 140; urban, 414, 451
Populists, 448, 451
Port Chicago, 525
Portilla, Pablo, 156
Portolá, Gaspar de, 71, 72, 76–81, 82, 84, 86, 87, 110
Portsmouth (ship), 222, 223, 247
Post Office Appropriations Bill, 356
Postman Always Rings Twice, The (Cain), 549

Poultry industry, 407, 489, 524
Poverty Bar (mining camp), 249
Powell, J. W., 5
Powers, Jack, 327
Preparedness days parades, 479–480, 481
Presbyterian Church, 332, 436
Prices Current (newspaper), 336
Princess Royal (ship), 122
Princeton (ship), 223
Progress and Poverty (George), 427
Progressive movement, 445–465, 497, 498, 499, 533: beginning of, 452; development of, 450; leadership background, 451–452; Roosevelt (Theodore) on, 456
Progressive Party, 455, 456–457
Prohibition, 489, 491, 498, 501
Prohibition Party, 455, 502
Promontory Point, Utah, 368, 369
Prostitution, 240, 249
Prune orchards, 404
Psychosomatic Institute (religious sect), 496
Pueblo settlements, 95, 96–97, 117
Pullman Palace Car Company, 420
Pullman strike of 1894, 420, 474
"Purple Cow" (Burgess), 429

Quakers, 436, 498
Quartz mines, 253, 342, 379, 412
Queen Mary (liner), 551–552
Quicksilver mines, 252
Quo Vadis? (Sienkiewicz), 429

Race riots, 549, 571–572: Chinese, 392; in 1966, 572
Radio industry, 487
Rae, William Glen, 180, 209
Rafferty, Max, 542
Railroad Act of 1866, 370–371
Railroad industry, 9, 250, 255, 257–259, 354–373: agriculture and, 259, 260, 397; Constitution of 1879 on, 385, 386–387; electric interurban lines, 423–424; first transcontinental, 364–373: Chinese labor on, 367, completion of, 368, surveys on, 364; land titles, 370–371, 392; monopoly, 373, 378, 382; Mussel Slough incident, 388–390; Silver Palace cars, 369; taxes, 386–387; tours to Los Angeles, 416; train robberies, 380;
Rainfall, 3, 5
Ramirez, Angel, 187
Ramo, Simon, 556
Ramona (Jackson), 353, 428
Ramparts (magazine), 547
Rand Corporation, 556
Randolph, Edmond, 307
Raousset-Boulbon, Gaston de, 293–294
Reagan, Ronald, 563, 567–570: back-

ground of, 567; popularity of, 570; University of California and, 545–546, 569
Real, Corte, 35
Reapportionment, 566
Reconstruction Finance Corporation, 521
Reconstruction period, 375, 377
Reconstruction and Reemployment Commission, 527
Recreation facilities, 552
Red Dog (mining camp), 249
Redding, Pearson B., 297
Redlands, California, 399
Redlands University, 436
Redondo, California, 458–459
Redondo Railway Company, 459
Redwood trees, 179, 577
Reed, James Frazier, 203, 204, 205, 207
Reformed Drunkard, The (drama), 340
Reglamento Provisional (charter), 95, 97
Religion, 332, 335, 419, 553–554: declining influence of, 553; education, 332, 335, 435; Indians, 14–15; in mining camps, 332; sects, 496–497
Requena, Manuel, 398
Reservations (Indian), 345–346, 348, 349
Resources, 341, 577
Resources of California, The (Hittell), 414
Retirement Life Payments plan, 509
Revilla Gigedo, Conde de, 115
Revolution of 1917, 482
Rex (gambling ship), 531
Rezanov, Nikolai Petrovich, 134–135, 137–142, 143
Rhodes, James A., 569
Rice crops, 488–489
Richardson, Friend W., 498–499, 500, 501
Richardson, William Entonio, 159
Richardson, William H., 287
Riders of the Purple Sage (Grey), 548
Rigoletto (opera), 442
Riley, Bennett, 266, 267, 269, 272, 273
Rivera y Moncada, Fernando, 77, 80, 82, 84, 86–87, 89, 92–95, 99–102, 118, 158
Riverside Banking Company, 419
Riverside County, 574
Roan Stallion (Jeffers), 548
Robbins, Thomas M., 262
Roberts, Samuel, 283
Robidoux, Antoine, 197, 262
Robidoux, Louis, 262
Robinson, Alfred, 163
Robinson, Charles, 326, 327
Robinson, Jackie, 552
Rocha, Corporal, 92
Rodríguez, Manuel, 130, 131
Rogue River War, 348
Rolph, James, 465, 500–501, 503, 507, 569

Roman, Anton, 338
Roman Catholic Church, 187, 203, 332:
    education, 332; excommunications, 186
Roméu, José Antonio de, 115–116
Roney, Frank, 473
Roosevelt, Franklin D., 505, 507, 514–515,
    532, 547
Roosevelt, James, 532
Roosevelt, Theodore, 452, 455–457, 463:
    on anti-Japanese discrimination, 468–
    469; on Progressive movement, 456
Ross, Edward A., 428
Rough and Ready (mining camp), 249
Roughing It (Twain), 313
Rover (ship), 163
Rowan, James, 129
Rowell, Chester H., 452
Rowen, Henry S., 556
Rowland, John, 199–200
Royce, Josiah, 390, 427–428
Rubery, Alfred, 310, 311
Rubi, Mariano, 110
Ruef, Abraham, 453, 462–465
Rumford Fair Housing Act, 564, 565, 571
Russell, Lillian, 441
Russell, William H., 361–363
Russian-American Fur Company, 135, 142,
    181
Russian Orthodox Church, 134, 137
Russo-Japanese War, 468
Ryan, Arabella, 287, 289
Ryan Aeronautical Corporation, 523

Saavedra, Alvara de, 35–36
Sachem (ship), 165
Sacramento (launch), 184
Sacramento, California, 183, 184, 245, 266,
    306, 318, 356, 413: becomes capital, 278,
    279; early theatrical activity, 340; growth
    of, 248; land claims, 324; Pony Express
    route to, 362; squatter outbreaks, 326–
    327; stagecoach line, 256; stock exchange,
    254, 255; Vigilance Committee, 285
Sacramento *Bee*, 434
Sacramento *Standard*, 304
Sacramento Valley: agriculture, 329, 394,
    405; migrant worker camps, 505; pear
    orchards, 404; wine industry, 402
Sacramento Valley Railroad, 370
Sailor's Union of the Pacific, 473
Sainsevain, Louis Jean, 401
St. Mary's College, 436
Saint Simeon (sloop), 136
Sal, Hermanegildo, 125
Salcedo, Felipe de, 47
Salinas, California, 148
Salinas Valley, 78, 127, 202
Salinger, Pierre, 564, 565, 566

Salmon, Norvell, 296
Salvador (Indian guide), 205
Salvator, Ludwig L., 415
Salvatierra, Father Juan Maria, 67–68, 69
Samish, Arthur H., 533–534
San Andreas (crustal fracture), 7
San Andreas, California, 337
San Antonio (ship), 76–80
San Antonio, California, 400
San Antonio de Padua mission, 85, 111,
    112–113
San Antonio and San Diego Mail Route,
    356–357
San Augustin (ship), 55–56
San Bernardino, California, 262, 371, 400,
    423: Confederate sympathies, 305; land
    titles, 392
San Bernardino County, 399
San Bernadino Mountains, 176, 327
San Bruno Indians, 63
San Buenaventura mission, 98, 109, 111,
    149, 188, 398
San Buenaventure (sailboat), 56
San Carlos (ship), 76–77, 79, 89
San Carlos Borroméo de Carmelo mission,
    80, 189
San Diego (flagship), 58, 59–60
San Diego Bay, 8, 59
San Diego, California, 2, 44, 75, 157, 212,
    254, 256, 262, 268, 492, 495: during
    civil wars, 187, 188; colonial government,
    104–106; cultural growth, 441; educa-
    tion, 436; first foreign ship at, 126; In-
    dian War, 91–93; industry, 529; land
    titles, 392; Mexican War, 224, 226, 229,
    230, 231; Portolá expedition to, 79–80;
    rainfall, 5; Spanish settlement, 82–84,
    85, 86: Indian uprising, 91–93; tourist
    industry, 416; union movement, 478;
    World War II, 520, 525
San Diego County: agriculture, 405; citrus
    crops, 401; Indian population, 17; in-
    dustry, 524; population growth, 414
San Diego Land and Town Company, 409
San Fernando College, 97, 106, 161
San Fernando Rey de España mission, 72,
    111, 113, 176, 215
San Fernando Valley, 490–491
San Francisco, California, 7, 78, 79, 96, 125–
    126, 159, 180, 184, 212, 241, 246–248,
    254–256, 266, 278, 281, 284, 336, 358:
    bubonic plague of 1900, 449; Civil War
    meetings, 305; cultural growth, 441–444;
    early theatrical activity, 339–341; earth-
    quake of 1906, 6, 7, 8, 439, 441, 442,
    463, 468: casualties, 460, 461, causes of,
    460, damage estimates, 461, fires, 460–
    461, 485, 486, insurance claims, 461;

earthquake of 1857, 7; education, 436: discrimination, 468–469; government: colonial, 104–106, 1848, 281–282, military, 264; growth of, 247–248, 413; Haight-Ashbury district, 558; harbor facilities, 484; industry, 260; land area of, 484; land claims, 324–326; lawlessness in, 281–291: lynchings, 284–285; murders (1849–1856), 286, vigilante committees and, 284–287, 291; museums, 426, 546; Nevada gold mines and, 254, 255; population, 315: colonial, 140, 1846, 247, growth of, 248, 413–414, Japanese, 518; Progressive movement in, 462–465; race riots, 572; railroad link to (1864), 257; rainfall, 5; revolt (1828), 155; squatters in, 325–326; stagecoach line to, 256; surveyed (1835), 247; Sydney Town, 282, 284; telegraphic service, 363–364; transit system, 557; union movement, 473–474, 483, 505–506; water supply, 492–493; World War II, 521, 525

San Francisco de Asís mission, 94
San Francisco Baptist Association, 332
San Francisco Bay, 8, 52, 56, 79, 124
San Francisco *Bulletin*, 440, 462
San Francisco *Chronicle*, 420–421, 448, 467–468, 520–521
San Francisco *Daily Evening Bulletin*, 287
San Francisco *Daily Herald*, 336
San Francisco *Examiner*, 430, 448
San Francisco Giants, 552
San Francisco *Herald*, 288, 304
San Francisco Institute of Arts, 426
San Francisco International Airport, 539
San Francisco Merchants' Association, 462
San Francisco-Oakland Bay Bridge, 512
San Francisco Opera Association, 443
San Francisco Society of Regulators, 282–283
San Francisco de Solano mission, 153–154, 159
San Francisco Stock Exchange, 254, 379
San Francisco Symphony Orchestra, 443, 551
San Gabriel (ship), 38–39
San Gabriel mission, 85, 88, 91, 99, 109, 111, 172, 176, 226: orange groves, 398; runaway Indians at, 113
San Gabriel Orange Grove Association, 398–399
San Gabriel River, 407
San Gabriel Valley, 399, 445
San Jacinto, battle of, 213
San Joaquin County, 488
San Jóaquin Valley, 179, 211, 454, 493: agriculture, 405, 488; industry, 422; mi-

grant worker camps, 505; peach crops, 404; reclamation, 407, 409; wheat industry, 328, 394
San José (supply ship), 77
San Jose, California, 191, 199, 241, 252, 256, 266, 279, 297: Civil War meetings, 305; education, 335; railroad links to (1864), 257; settlement of, 96, 164; telegraphic service, 363–364; Vigilance Committee, 285
San José del Cabo mission, 70
San José de Guadelupe mission, 111, 113, 176
San Jose *Tribune*, 308
San Juan Bautista mission, 111, 113, 117, 151
San Juan Capistrano mission, 7, 92, 95, 109, 111, 117, 132, 146, 149–150
San Luis Obispo, California, 278: Mexican War, 232–233; rainfall, 5
San Luis Obispo County, 407
San Luis Obispo de Tolosa mission, 85, 111, 117
San Luis Rey, California, 187
San Luís Rey de Francia mission, 111, 231, 347
San Miguel Arcángel mission, 111, 113
San Miguel Island, 44
San Pablo (ship), 47
San Pasqual, Battle of, 229–230
San Pedro (ship), 38–39
San Pedro, California, 76: fishing industry, 343; union movement, 483
San Pedro Bay, 457–460
San Pedro y San Pablo Bicuñer (mission-pueblo), 100, 101
San Rafael Arcángel mission, 151, 153
San Salvador (ship), 43
San Simeon, 546, 547
Sánchez, Father Bernardo, 172
Sanchez, Pedro, 64–65
Sanitary Commission (Civil War), 312–313
Santa Agueda (ship), 37–38
Santa Ana (galleon), 54–55
Santa Ana River, 398, 407
Santa Anna, Antonio López de, 159, 190 213
Santa Barbara, California, 100, 109, 126, 180, 241, 262, 278, 301, 495: colonial government, 104–106; during civil wars, 192; earthquake of 1925, 7; education, 436; garrison revolt (1828), 156; Mexican War, 224, 226, 223; settlement of, 104; tourist industry, 416
Santa Barbara County, 4, 348
Santa Barbara Islands, 59
Santa Barbara mission, 405
Santa Barbara *Press*, 434

Santa Catalina (ship), 38–39
Santa Catalina Island, 59, 327
Santa Catalina mission, 174
Santa Clara de Asís mission, 94, 96
Santa Clara County, 125, 312
Santa Clara University, 335
Santa Clara Valley: agriculture, 404; squatter outbreaks, 328; tomato industry, 488
Santa Cruz, California, 117, 463
Santa Cruz mission, 110, 113, 116–117, 150
Santa Fé Trail, 173, 176, 177, 197, 199, 227
Santa Inés mission, 119
Santa María, Father Vincente, 126
Santa Monica, 459
Santa Paula, 422
Santa Rosa (privateer), 147, 148, 149
Santa Rosa, California, 397
Santa Terésa, Treaty of, 191
Santaella, Father, 68
Santíago mission, 70
Santo Tomás (ship), 37–38, 58, 59
Sargent, Aaron A., 318, 373
Saroyan, William, 548
Sarría, Father Vicente Francisco, 110–111
Sauer, Carl, 13
Savage, James D., 348
Savannah (ship), 221, 226
Sawyer, Lorenzo, 411
Scannell, David, 460
Schenk, Mrs., 338
Schmitz, Eugene E., 462–463, 465, 468
Schmitz, John G., 570
Schofield, John M., 349
Schulberg, Budd, 549
Scientology, cult of, 553–554
Scott, Charles Lewis, 304, 308
Scott, Howard, 506–507
Scott, W. A., 307–308
Scott, Winfield, 234, 236
Screen Actors Guild, 567
Sea otters, 6, 127–128
Sea Wolf, The (London), 432
Seamen's Protective Association, 473
Second Massachusetts Cavalry (Civil War), 314
Sectionalism: attempts, 301–302; election on, 302
Seismic sea waves, 7–8
Selig, William N., 494
Seminole War, 352
Semi-Tropical California (Truman), 415
Semple, Robert, 220–221, 224, 262, 269, 271, 496
Senán, Father José, 153–154
Sequoia University, 554
Sergas de Esplandían, Las, 41
Seris Indians, 87
Serra, Father Junípero, 72–74, 77–81, 84–86, 93, 97–98, 106, 108–109, 111, 118: arguments between Fages and, 84–85; background of, 72–73; dispute between Neve and, 97–99
Sespe Settlers League, 328
Settler's League, 389–390
Seven Cities of Cibola, legend of, 34
Sexton, Joseph, 405
Seymour, Sir George, 222
Shaler, William, 130–131
Shannon, William E., 270
Shakespeare, William, 340
Shark (schooner), 222
Shasta County, 404–405
Shaw, George Bernard, 427
Sheep industry, 258, 260
Shelikhov, Anna, 135, 138
Shelikhov, Grigorii Ivanovich, 134–135, 136, 138
Shell, Joseph C., 564
Shelley, John F., 561
Shenandoah (ship), 311, 344
Sherman, William Tecumseh, 257, 263, 264, 288, 289, 290
Sherwood, William A., 272, 273
Shiloh, Battle of, 307
Shipbuilding industry, 260, 527: at Fort Ross, 181; steamer mail routes, 361; World War II, 521
Shirley Letters (Clappe), 338
Shoshonean Indians, 12, 15
Showalter, Dan, 308–309
Shubrick, William B., 235, 263, 264
Sibley, Henry H., 314
Sienkiewicz, Henryk, 429
Sierra Gordo mission, 73
Sierra Nevada mountain range, 4–5: first men to cross, 172; gold deposits, 242; snowfall, 5, 8, 368; Walker Pass, 179
Sigondis, Lepine de, 293
Silk industry, 396
Sill, Edward Rowland, 431
Silliman, Benjamin, 342
Silva, Captain, 222
Silver mines, 342
Simons, Titus, 170
Simpson, George, 179, 180, 182, 183
Sinclair, Upton, 432, 433, 508, 510, 548
Sioux Indians, 195
Sitka colony, 136–137, 138
Sixty Years in California (Davis), 164
Skinner, Otis, 441
Slacum, William A., 213
Slavery, 25, 26, 27, 269–270, 276, 277, 374: abolished, 375; sectionalism and, 301; statehood and, 261, 265, 267, 273–274: Constitutional Convention, 269–270
Sloat, John D., 222–223, 336

Sloat, Lewis, 336
Slurbs, defined, 576–577
Smith, Don Carlos, 431
Smith, Jedediah Strong, 170–173, 175, 176, 177, 179
Smith, Joseph, 431
Smog, 575–576
Snyder, John, 205
Social Control (Ross), 428
Socialist Labor Party, 448
Socialist Party, 473, 476, 477
Sola, Pablo Vincente de, 146, 147, 149–153, 164, 186
Soledad mission, 110–111, 116
Solís, Joaquín, 155–156, 158
Sonoma, California, 220, 221, 266, 332, 339: founded, 159; wine industry, 402
Sonoma County, 380, 397, 407
Sonoma grapes, 401
Sonoma mission, 117
Sonora, 248–249, 306: land claims, 324; newspapers, 337; Vigilance Committee, 285
Sonora *Democrat*, 304
South Sea Company, 122
Southern California Fruit Growers' Association, 451
Southern California Rapid Transit District, 557
Southern Californian, The (weekly), 337
Southern Pacific Railroad, 257-258, 370–373, 395, 416, 423, 447, 459, 641, 464: criticism of, 450–451; immigration and, 414–415; lobbyists of, 445, 448, 533; monopolistic control, 373; Mussel Slough incident, 388–390; political activities, 451, 452, 454; rate war, 417
Southwest Museum, 426
Space Technology Laboratories, 556
Spanish-American War, 474
Spas, 416
Specific Contract Act, 316–317
Spence, David, 263
Spencer-Roberts and Associates, 567
Spirit of Saint Louis (airplane), 523
Spirit of the Times (newspaper), 415
Sports, 6, 443, 552–553
Spreckels, Rudolph, 463–464
Spring Valley Mining Company, 410
Sproul, Robert Gordon, 543
Squatters, 325–326, 391: in 1920's, 328; political pressure, 328
Squaw Man, The (motion picture), 495
Stagecoach lines, 256: decline of, 360; mail service, 356–357; robberies, 379–380
Standard Oil Company of California, 422
Standish, Philander, 394
Stanford, Leland, 304, 306, 316–318, 336,

414, 437, 438, 445: background of, 306; campaign of 1890, 447; election of 1861, 305, 306; at Promontory Point ceremony, 368; railroad investments, 365–373
Stanford, Mrs. Leland, 437
Stanford family, 437
Stanford University, 428, 443: founded, 437; Hoover Library of War, Peace and Revolution, 438
Stanislaus County, 488
Stanton, Charles T., 205, 206
Stanton, Edwin M., 323–324
State Agricultural Society, 259
State Association of District Attorneys, 530
State Conciliation Service, 532
Steamship Sailors' Union, 473
Stearns, Abel, 156, 163–164, 185, 209, 269, 391
Steel industry, 521–522
Stegner, Wallace, 550
Steinbeck, John, 504, 548
Steinhart, Ignatz, 438
Stephens, William D., 457, 481, 497–499
Sterling, George, 431, 432–433
Steuart, William M., 273
Stevens, Elisha, 202
Stevens-Murphy expedition of 1844, 202
Stevenson, Adlai E., 535, 536
Stevenson, Colonel, 282, 332, 339, 346, 403
Stevenson, Robert Louis, 428–429
Steward, Colonel, 184
Stewart, T. K., 405
Stockton, Robert F., 223–228, 230, 232, 235, 261–263
Stockton, California, 248, 254–255, 278, 335: early theatrical activity, 240; Vigilance Committee, 285
Stockton *Argus*, 308
Stockton *Democrat*, 308
Stokes, Edward, 228
Stoneman, George, 445–446
Stovall, 277
Strauss, Levi, 306
Stravinsky, Igor, 551
Stuart, James, 284–285
Studebaker, John, 247
Suárez del Real, 189
Sublette, William F., 171 173
Sublette family, 203
Submarine warfare, 524
Subterraneans, The (Kerouac), 550
Suburbs, beginning of, 486
Suffrage, 377, 386, 419
Suhr, Herman, 479
Sullivan, Sir Arthur, 387
Sumner, Edwin Vose, 307, 308
Sun Yat-sen, 427
Sunday in the Mines (painting), 425

Sunset (magazine), 415
Supreme Order of Caucasians, 382
Surfing, 552–553
Sutter, John Augustus, 169, 183, 191, 195–196, 218, 272, 326: background of, 195; at Constitutional Convention, 269; election of 1849, 273; gold discovery, 237–240; purchases Fort Ross, 183–184, 196
Sutter County, 410
Sutter's Fort, 200, 201, 202, 205, 220, 232, 239, 248: construction of, 196; Frémont at, 218
Swasey-Todd Company, 202–203
Swett, John, 317, 335
Swift, John F., 446
Swing, Philip D., 492

Taft, William Howard, 452, 457
Tagle (ship), 164–165
Talbot, T., 226
Tameral, Father Nicholas, 70
Taoism, 553
Taos-Santa Fé mountain men, 173
Tápis, Father Estévan, 118
Tarabal, Sebastian, 88, 89
Tarkington, Booth, 377
Taxes: corporation, 387, 446; foreign ship (1849), 262; property, 391, 557; railroads, 386–387; real estate, 275, 434; school, 334
Taylor, Benjamin F., 415
Taylor, William, 149
Taylor, Zachary, 234, 267
Teamsters Union, 474
Technocracy movement, 506–507
Tehama County, 409
Telegraph companies, 363–364, 385
Télémaque (Fenelon), 186
Television industry, 549, 554, 568
Temperance Party, 318
Temple, John, 262
Tenney, Jack B., 536–537
Territorial Enterprise, The (newspaper), 338
Terry, David S., 289–290, 291: Confederate sympathies of, 308–309; duel with Broderick, 300, 309
Tetrazzini, Luisa, 442
Texis, Lloyd, 408
Theory of Business Enterprise, The (Veblen), 428
Theory of the Leisure Class, The (Veblen), 428
Thirty Dollars Every Thursday Plan, The, 509
Thomas, Eleazar, 351–352
Thomas, Judge, 276
Thomas, Robert H., 197
Thomas Edison Company of New Jersey, 494

Thompson, R. A., 322
Thompson, Waddy, 213, 216
Thornton, Harvey I., 304, 322
Thurso's Landing (Jeffers), 548
Tibbets, Luther, 399
Tibbets, Mrs. Luther, 399
Tidelands oil dispute, 534–535
Tilden, Douglas, 426–427
Time of Your Life, The (Saroyan), 548
Times-Mirror Company, 547
Tobacco industry, 396
Todd, Alexander, 256
Todd, William L., 220
Todd & Company Express, 256
Todos Santo mission, 70
Tolosa, Juan de, 26–27
Tolstoy, Leo, 427
Tom the Trapper, 189
Tomato canning industry, 488
Torre, Joaquínd de la, 221
Tourist industry, 416, 419, 424, 502, 503, 552, 558
Townsend, Francis E., 508–509
Townsend Plan, 508–509, 511
Transportation system: appropriations, 512; development of, 512; first freeway, 512; gold rush days, 255, 256; stagecoach, 356–360: fares, 358–359; Indian harassment, 359, 360, robberies, 379–380
Treasure Island, 525
Tres Reyes (frigate), 58, 60
Trevino de Bañuelos, Baltasar, 27
Trinidad (ship), 37–38
Trinity County, 306
Trist, Nicholas P., 236
Tropic of Cancer (Miller), 549
Tropic of Capricorn (Miller), 549
Truck farming, 259, 488, 514
Truckee, 291
True Believer, The (Hoffer), 551
Truman, Benjamin Cummins, 415
Truman, Harry S., 533, 535
Tucker, Racine, 207
Tulare County, 291: agriculture, 470; citrus crops, 401;
Tulare Post, 308
Tule River, 407
Tuthill, Franklin, 439
Twain, Mark, 313, 428
Two Years Before the Mast (Dana), 166
Tyler, John, 193, 213, 216, 217

Ugarte, Juan de, 68, 69–70
Ugly American, The (Burdick), 549
Ulloa, Francisco de, 37–38, 39
Umpqua Brigade (beaver trappers), 180
Unemployment, 382, 419–420, 529: decline, 538, 581; Depression of 1929, 502,

503; during Mexican Rule, 160
Unemployment insurance, 532, 561, 571
Union Grammar School, 334
Union Iron Works, 260
Union Labor Party, 462, 464, 474
Union Oil Company, 422
Union Pacific Railroad, 336, 450: Oregon Short Lines, 371–372; terminus, 368
Union Party, 317–318, 374–376
Unions, 420, 462, 472–483, 505–506, 530, 556–557: closed-shop, 474, 483; Depression of 1929, 505–506; membership growth, 556; newspapers, 473; opposition to, 474–483; World War I, 482; *See also* names of unions
Unitarian Church, 332, 452
United Farm Workers Committee (UFW-OC), 578–579
United States (ship), 214
United States Border Patrol, 578
United States Constitution, 261, 265, 385: Thirteenth Amendment, 270, 375; Fourteenth Amendment, 377; Fifteenth Amendment, 377; Eighteenth Amendment, 489
United States Department of Agriculture, 399, 400. 485
United States Department of Interior, 493
United States Department of Justice, 514
United States Mail Steamship Company, 244
United States Maritme Commission, 521
United States Steel Company, 521
United States Supreme Court, 389, 390, 481, 504, 518, 533, 535, 538, 560, 566, 571, 574
University of California, 254, 335–336, 428, 435–436, 527, 551: Bancroft Library, 438, 439, 441; Berkeley campus, 435, 544–546: impact of hippies on, 558, student revolt, 544–545, 582; Board of Regents, 544, 545–546; California history chair, 440–441; chartered, 335; College of Science, 334; enrollment, 544; expansion of, 543–544; "filthy speech" movement, 545; free speech movement, 544–545; Greek drama theatre, 442; Lick Observatory, 543; loyalty oath dispute, 537; Reagan and, 545–546, 569; sit-ins, 544–545
University of California at Los Angeles (UCLA), 436, 543, 552
University of Michigan, 443
University of the Pacific, 335
University of San Francisco, 436
University of Southern California, 437, 552
Unruh, Jesse M., 564
Urdaneta, Andrés de, 47

Utopian Society, 507

Valdés, Juan Bautista, 87
Van Buren, Martin, 213, 217
Van Noort, Oliver, 58
Vancouver, George, 124–127, 140: background of, 124; California expedition, 124–127
Vandalia (ship), 226
Vanderbilt, Cornelius, 296
Vallejo, Encarnación, 163
Vallejo, Ignacio, 158
Vallejo, José, 148
Vallejo, Mariano G., 148, 158, 163, 183, 186, 188–189, 199, 216, 263, 278, 325, 339: appointed comandante, 186; arrested, 220; at Constitutional Convention, 269
Vallejo family, 186
Vallejo, California, 370
Vasquez, 204
Vásquez, Tiburcia, 380–381
Veblen, Thorstein, 428
Velasco, Luís de, 47, 57
Velásquez, Diego, 19, 20, 21, 25
Velie, Lester, 534
Ventura, California, 305, 342, 492
Ventura County, 421, 493
Venus (frigate), 211
Verdugo, José Maria, 118
Verger, Rafael, 98–99
Victoria, Manuel, 156–157, 158, 163, 182
Victoria (ship), 43
Vienna Ladies' Orchestra, 442
Vietnam War, 545, 567, 571, 581
Vigilanteism, 284–292, 299, 303, 336, 383, 520: anti-union movements, 478; Committee of 1851, 275, 284–287, 291; Committee of 1856, 303; newspaper attack on, 288; opposition to, 288–289
Vignes, Louis, 398, 401
Vila, Vicente, 76, 78, 79, 80
Villalobos, Ruy Gómez de, 43, 46, 47
Visalia *Equal Rights Expositor*, 308
Vizarrón, Juan Antonio, 70
Vizcaíno, Sebastián, 54, 57–61, 75, 76, 78
Vosnesensky, I. C., 184
Voyage autour la Monde (Galaup), 121
Vultee, Gerard, 523

Waddell, James I, 311
Waddell, William B., 361–363
Waldo, William, 275
Waldridge, Dean, 556
Walker, Joel P., 200
Walker, Joseph Reddeford, 178, 200, 201–202, 218
Walker, William, 295–296, 310

Walker Pass, 179, 200
Walker River, 198
Walt Disney Productions, 569
War of 1812, 173, 213, 223, 227, 232
Warehousemen's Union, 557
Warner Brothers, 567
Warren, Earl, 512, 513, 527, 530, 455, 512, 514, 527, 530–533, 561: background of, 530; governorship, 531–532, 533; Supreme Court appointment, 533, 560
Warren, Mrs. Earl, 530–533
Warren (brig), 222, 283
Washington, George, 128, 212
Water pollution, 575
Water supply, 573–576
Waterman, Robert W., 446
Watsonville, 472
Watterson brothers, 492
Watts, Alan, 553
Watts race riot, 549, 571–572
Webb, Charles Henry, 338
Webb, Sidney, 427
Webb, U. W., 470
Webster, Daniel, 213
Welfare and Institutions Code, 504
Weller, John B., 297, 299, 304
Wells, Fargo & Company, 256–257, 312, 359, 360, 379–380
West, Jessamyn, 549
Western Civilian Control Administration, 515
Western Emigration Society, 197
Western Pacific Railroad Company, 370
Whaling industry, 163, 164, 342, 343–344: decline of, 344; during Civil War, 311, 344
What Makes Sammy Run? (Schulberg), 549
Wheat industry, 259, 328, 393–395, 412, 413: acreage, 394, 395; machinery, 394–395
Wheatland riot of 1913, 478–479
Wheeler, Benjamin Ide, 425, 435–436, 543
Wheeler, Osgood C., 332
Whig Party, 217, 272, 288, 296–298, 374
Whitaker and Baxter (firm), 536, 560
Whitney, Asa, 364
Whittier, 436
Who's Who in America, 548
Wildlife, 6
Willey, Samuel H., 332, 333
Williams, Albert, 333
Williams, Isaac, 225
Williams, Ted, 552
Wilmington, 458, 460
Wilson, E. D., 192
Wilson, James, 322
Wilson, Woodrow, 449, 455, 457, 470, 481
Wimmer family, 239

Wine industry, 395, 578, 579: development of, 177, 401–403; first vineyard, 401; mission, 113; Prohibition and, 489
Winning of Barbara Worth, The (Wright), 548
Winship, Charles, 129
Winship, Jonathan, 132
Wolfe, John de, 139
Wolfskill, William, 176, 177, 200, 398
Women at Point Sur, The (Jeffers), 548
Wool, John E., 289, 290
Workingmen's Alliance, 382
Workingmen's Party, 383–384, 386, 387–388, 473
Workman, William, 192, 199–200
World War I, 251, 379, 424, 435, 437, 469, 491, 493, 500: agriculture, 485; employment, 472; industrial output, 484–485; liberty loan drives, 485; Ninety-first Division, 485; preparedness days parades, 479–480; union movements, 482; Victory loan drives, 485
World War II, 471, 512, 513–526: agriculture, 524–526; aviation industry, 522–524; casualties, 513; civil defense, 524–525; demobilization, 528–529; employment, 522, 525–526; end of, 529; enemy aliens, 513–514, 515; 442nd Regimental Combat team, 517; industry, 520–524, 529–530; Japanese-Americans, 511–519: internment, 515–517, Lippmann on, 514; property losses, 518; Port Chicago explosion, 525; submarine warfare, 524; wage earnings, 525–526
Wozencraft, Oliver, 344–345
Wrangell, Baron Ferdinand, 182
Wright, Ben, 349
Wright, George, 273, 308
Wright, Harold Bell, 548
Wright Act of 1887, 409
Wyman, Jane, 567

Yaqui Indians, 70
Yerba Buena: American seizure of, 223; renamed, 240
Yokohama Specie Bank, 518
Yorty, Sam, 561, 568
Yosemite Valley, 179
You Bet (mining camp), 249
Young, Clement C., 499–501
Young, Ewing, 175–176
Young, George, 176–178
Yuba Consolidated Gold Fields Limited, 521
Yuba County, 410, 479
Yuba River, 410–411
Yuki Indians, 11–12
Yukian language, 12

Yuma Indians, 39, 40, 88, 89, 90, 94, 100–
    101, 174: massacres, 203, 347, 348:
    Colorado River, 101–102
Yurok Indians, 17

Zabov, 135

Zacatecas, College of, 161
Zamorano, Augustín Vicente, 157
Zen Buddhism, 553
Zinfandel grapes, 401
Zola, Émile, 429
Zuni Indians, 34, 38, 40